SAMS Teach Yourself

Mac OS® X Digital Media

Robyn Ness

SAMS 201 West 103rd St., Indianapolis, Indiana, 46290 USA

Sams Teach Yourself Mac OS X Digital Media All in One

International Standard Book Number: 0-672-32532-2

Library of Congress Catalog Card Number: 2003102937

Printed in the United States of America

First Printing: May 2003

05 04 03 4 3 2 1

Trademarks

All terms mentioned in this book that are known to be trademarks or service marks have been appropriately capitalized. Sams Publishing cannot attest to the accuracy of this information. Use of a term in this book should not be regarded as affecting the validity of any trademark or service mark.

Warning and Disclaimer

Every effort has been made to make this book as complete and as accurate as possible, but no warranty or fitness is implied. The information provided is on an "as is" basis. The authors and the publisher shall have neither liability nor responsibility to any person or entity with respect to any loss or damages arising from the information contained in this book.

Bulk Sales

Sams Publishing offers excellent discounts on this book when ordered in quantity for bulk purchases or special sales. For more information, please contact

U.S. Corporate and Government Sales
1-800-382-3419
corpsales@pearsontechgroup.com

For sales outside of the U.S., please contact

International Sales
+1-317-581-3793
international@pearsontechgroup.com

Acquisitions Editor
Betsy Brown

Development Editors
Lorna Gentry
Damon Jordan
Scott Meyers

Managing Editor
Charlotte Clapp

Project Editor
Andy Beaster

Indexer
Lisa Wilson

Proofreader
Juli Cook
Tracy Donhardt

Interior Designer
Gary Adair

Cover Designer
Aren Howell

Page Layout
Stacey Richwine-DeRome

Contents at a Glance

Contents

Part II Apple iLife: iTunes, iPhoto, iMovie, and iDVD 207

Lead Author

Robyn Ness holds a master's degree in psychology with a specialization in judgment and decision making. She currently works as a Web developer for the Section of Communications and Technology at The Ohio State University, focusing on issues of usability and content design.

Contributing Authors

Carla Rose has authored or co-authored close to 20 computer books, including *Sams Teach Yourself Adobe Photoshop Elements in 24 Hours*, as well as books on desktop publishing, telecommunications, and more. She is a contributing editor for *Photoshop User* magazine and has written for publications ranging from the *Atlantic Fisherman* to *Adobe Magazine* to *The New Yorker*.

Gene Steinberg first used a Mac in 1984 and never looked back. He writes the popular "Mac Reality Check" column for the Gannett News Service and `USAToday.com`, and is the author of *Sams Teach Yourself the iMac in 24 Hours*. He has also written feature articles and product reviews for such magazines as *MacHome*, *MacAddict*, *MacUser* and *Macworld*, and he presents strange and unusual computing tips on Craig Crossman's "Computer America" radio show.

Todd Kelsey has an extensive background in the independent digital video community. He is the owner of Selendrian Group, Inc., a digital media company that has contracted DVD-related writing projects for high-profile companies such as Adobe. He is also a former performing member and online manager of the major label recording act Sister Soleil, whose last release featured Peter Gabriel. He is the author of *Sams Teach Yourself iMovie and iDVD in 24 Hours*.

John Ray is an award-winning developer and security consultant with more than 16 years of programming and administration experience. He has written or contributed to more than 10 books currently in print, including *Sams Teach Yourself Mac OS X in 24 Hours*. He bought his first Macintosh in 1984, and remains a strong proponent of the computer and operating system that revolutionized the industry.

Dedication

For Johin Iray.

Acknowledgments

I would like to thank Betsy Brown, Damon Jordan, and Lorna Gentry—as well as everyone else at Sams Publishing—who helped bring this book to press. Working with such a capable team made a daunting task do-able.

I would also like to thank the authors of the material from which this book was drawn—Todd Kelsey, John Ray, Carla Rose, and Gene Steinberg. They provided such great information that the hard part of my job was fitting as much of their expertise as possible into this book!

We Want to Hear from You!

As the reader of this book, *you* are our most important critic and commentator. We value your opinion and want to know what we're doing right, what we could do better, what areas you'd like to see us publish in, and any other words of wisdom you're willing to pass our way.

You can email or write me directly to let me know what you did or didn't like about this book—as well as what we can do to make our books stronger.

Please note that I cannot help you with technical problems related to the topic of this book, and that due to the high volume of mail I receive, I might not be able to reply to every message.

When you write, please be sure to include this book's title and author as well as your name and phone or email address. I will carefully review your comments and share them with the author and editors who worked on the book.

Email: consumer@samspublishing.com

Mail: Mark Taber
Associate Publisher
Sams Publishing
201 West 103rd Street
Indianapolis, IN 46290 USA

Reader Services

For more information about this book or others from Sams Publishing, visit our Web site at www.samspublishing.com. Type the ISBN (excluding hyphens) or the title of the book in the Search box to find the book you're looking for.

Introduction

From early on, Apple's Macintosh computer has earned a reputation as *the* multimedia machine. Artists, designers, and digital media professionals use Macs in their work with digital media. And now, recent advancements in computer hardware and software make it possible for you, the home user, to get in on the act.

The purpose of this book is to help you make the most of the Mac's digital media capabilities. We'll begin with the basics you'll need to know in order to use your computer, including information about the Mac OS X operating system and working with files and applications. We'll then go into detail about five specific digital media applications. In the last few chapters, we'll return to a discussion of the operating system as you learn techniques for managing and protecting your computer system and files.

While we've included tips that even seasoned users of Macs and digital media can benefit from, this book is especially written for the following:

- People who have recently switched to the Mac who want to learn the basics, as well as some of the best digital media programs available.
- Long-time Mac users who want to learn the new Mac OS X operating system, as well as work more productively with digital media.
- People who are already familiar with Mac OS X, but want to make the most of iLife—Apple's integrated suite of digital media applications.

Digital Media Applications

Because the Mac is such a fabulous machine for multimedia work, there are a number of computer applications available for it that can be used for various purposes.

In this book, we'll be focusing our attention on four digital media applications created by Apple especially for the Mac. Those applications, available as a collection under the name iLife, are

- **iTunes** stores music as MP3 files and helps you burn custom CDs as well as listen to Internet radio stations.
- **iPhoto** helps you import and organize digital photographs as well as adjust photo quality and share your work.

- **iMovie** enables you to edit digital video. It also includes features that let you add titles and visual effects to your movies.
- **iDVD** enables those with DVD-writing Macs to create their own DVDs containing video, still photos, and music.

We'll also discuss a popular program from the Adobe company called Photoshop Elements, which is used for editing (and creating) digital images.

Necessary Tools

As I mentioned earlier, this book's purpose is to give you the knowledge you need to make the most of the modern Mac's digital media capabilities. Before we begin, we need to make sure you have the right tools for the task ahead.

To start with, you'll need the current versions of the Mac operating system, at least Mac OS X 10.2. Why? All the wonderful digital media software listed above requires (or will work best) under that system.

What do you do if you don't have that version of the Mac OS installed?

You need to determine if your computer can handle it. According to Apple, Mac OS X runs on all original G4 computers, all iBooks and iMacs (including the Bondi 233), all PowerBooks (except the original Powerbook G3), and all beige desktop G3s.

You also need to consider if your computer's processor can handle this operating system. Mac OS X runs on a wide range of processors, but the minimum requirement for decent performance is considered by many to be at least a 350MHz G3.

Finally, you need to make sure you have enough hard drive space and RAM to operate Mac OS X and all the applications you'll want to run. Mac OS X needs 128MB of RAM and 1.5GB of available storage.

If you are serious about working with digital media and your computer doesn't meet these requirements, you'll need to consider upgrading your computer to a newer model. (While this may sound like a drastic measure, it is a necessity. Audio and image files are very resource-intensive.)

Beyond these system requirements, there are also some other hardware needs to consider:

- For making your own CDs (containing data, music, photographs, etc.), your computer must have a drive capable of writing CDs. Alternately, you could use an external CD-burner that is compatible with Mac OS X.
- To get full mileage from iPhoto, you'll need a compatible digital camera.

- If you want to use iMovie, you must have a digital video camera that uses FireWire technology (also known as IEEE 1394 or i.Link) and your computer must have a FireWire connection port. (FireWire allows very large digital video files to be transferred between your camera and your computer. Without it, there is no feasible way to work with video on your computer.)
- To create DVDs with iDVD, your computer must be equipped with Apple's SuperDrive, which can read and write both CDs and DVDs. (Please note, that while external DVD burners are sold, they will not work with iDVD.)

Once you know what your computer needs in order to do its job, we're ready to begin! (If this list of requirements leaves you with unanswered questions, don't worry. We'll be talking about all of these topics in great detail later in the book.)

PART I

Getting Started

Chapter

CHAPTER 1

Setting Up Your Mac

Inside modern Macintosh computers lies the incredible power of one of Apple's G3 or G4 microprocessors, supercharged chips no larger than a postage stamp. These miniature technological wonders have the capability to process millions upon millions of computer instructions every second; in fact, the G4 processes billions of instructions, which puts it in the supercomputer class. In addition, your new computer comes with a sharp, bright color screen; a graphics accelerator; a fast CD drive, or maybe even one that can create DVDs; a built-in modem; and lots and lots of great software.

NEW TERM A *microprocessor* is a little electronic component that crunches numbers and gives your computer its incredible computing power.

NEW TERM A *graphics accelerator* is a chip that makes the images on your computer's screen show up very, very fast.

NEW TERM A *modem* is a clever device that turns the ones and zeros generated by your Mac and other computers into analog signals that can be sent back and forth over telephone lines.

In the first part of this chapter, I'll talk you through installing and setting up your Mac. Then we'll talk about the OS X operating system that you'll use to make full use of your Mac's digital media capabilities.

> Although many of you have worked on other Macs or the computers from that *other* platform (Windows), I realize that some of you are first-time computer buyers. So I'm going to cover a few basics in this first chapter, such as how to figure out what plugs in to where and how to use the mouse. If you've already installed and used computers, you'll be able to advance to Chapter 2, "Exploring the Desktop," in much less time.

Unpacking Your New Mac

Before you unpack your new Mac, find a convenient table or desk for it. It's not too large to fit on a small desk, but many of you will purchase a special table for it. In addition, you might want to buy a mouse pad, although it's not necessary on recent Macs because they use an optical mouse that can work just fine on any smooth surface.

> As with any new purchase, before you attempt to use your new computer give it a once over for visible signs of damage. If something looks broken (or the shipping box is badly damaged), contact your dealer for help. It's a good idea not to try to attempt to use a computer that might be damaged until it has been checked or (if need be) repaired. What's more, most dealers will exchange a computer that's DOA (dead on arrival).

Regardless of where you place it, you'll want to think about the following setup for maximum comfort:

- Make sure your shoulders are in a relaxed position when you set up the keyboard. Apple suggests putting your upper arm and forearm at a right angle, wrist and hand making roughly a straight line. Then again, at my age, I doubt that I'm going to change the positions I've learned over the decades.
- The mouse is best placed at the same height as the keyboard. If you buy a computer table with one of those slide-out trays for a keyboard, make sure it's wide enough to hold the mouse, too.
- Don't forget a comfortable chair that provides good support and a reasonable amount of adjustments so that you can easily tailor it to your needs, and the needs of others who might be using your Mac.

1

Hooking Up Your Mac

I know you're excited to turn on your new computer. I remember when I bought my first new car and just wanted to go out and cruise the highways and try out the engine and handling.

However, you can't just turn on your computer and browse the Internet. You have to hook up a few things first. So let's go through the steps:

▼ To Do

1. Place your Mac on a desk.
2. Follow the suggestions in the previous section, entitled "Unpacking Your New Mac," to position your computer correctly.
3. Plug in the power cord, and take the other end and plug it into a convenient AC jack. *Don't turn it on yet! You need to do a few more things before it will work properly!*
4. How do you plug things into your Mac? Let's take a look at the flat-panel iMac as an example (see Figure 1.1).

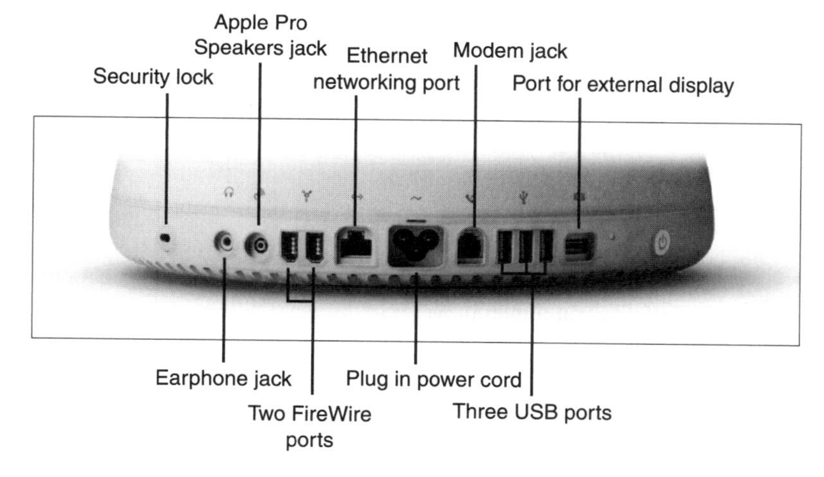

FIGURE 1.1
Plug it in before you try to turn it on.

NEW TERM

- A *Universal Serial Bus*, or USB for short, is a piece of technology that enables you to connect up to 127 different accessories to your Mac. In addition to the keyboard and mouse, you can add extra drives, printers, scanners, digital cameras, joysticks, and more. (We'll discuss USB in greater detail in Chapter 7, "Choosing Peripheral Devices.")

NEW TERM

- *FireWire* is a high-speed peripheral standard that enables you to connect DV camcorders, fast hard drives, and other products to recent Macintosh computers. (We'll discuss FireWire again in Chapter 7.)

▼

NEW TERM
- A *network* is not as complicated as it sounds. Whenever you hook two computers together, or just attach a printer to your Mac, you are on a network—just as in your office, when you try to make new friends or business contacts.

NEW TERM
- *Ethernet* is a popular networking technique that offers high performance and easy setup.

The placement of ports and jacks varies from model to mode, but the jacks and ports are more or less the same.

5. Take the keyboard's cable and connect to one of the Universal Serial Bus jacks (it really makes no difference). Don't force the plug, it only connects in one direction (the side with the special symbol on it is at the top).
6. Plug the mouse into either jack on the keyboard. It really doesn't matter if you use your mouse left-handed or right-handed.

A mouse is the pointing device you use to point to items on your Mac's display and to click them (which is the act of selecting them). Although a mouse or similar device is used on all personal computers, the Mac is unique because only one button is needed. In contrast, computers supporting other computer operating systems, such as Windows, require at least two buttons.

7. If you want to use your computer's built-in modem to connect to a network, connect a modular phone plug into the modem jack (the one labeled with the phone receiver icon). Put the other end in your phone jack, or connect to the second jack (if any) on a telephone.
8. To connect your Mac to a regular Ethernet network, a cable modem or just to a single printer with an Ethernet connection, plug in the network cable to the jack on your Mac.

Although the modem and Ethernet jacks look almost the same, they serve different purposes. The smaller jack, for your modem, is used to dial up the Internet or send faxes. The thicker jack, for Ethernet, is used to connect your computer to a network printer, to another computer to share files, or to access a high-performance Internet connection (we computer geeks call it "broadband").

9. If you have a Mac with a FireWire port, you can hook up a FireWire hard drive, DV camcorder, or other high performance device to either of the two FireWire ports. I'll tell you more about FireWire in Chapter 7.
10. Turn on your Mac. Where's the power switch? That, too, varies from model to model, but it is typically a round button.

Your Mac's Startup Routine

As soon as you start it up, your Mac will make a little sound. For the next minute or two, it will go through a startup process during which several screens will appear. The first is a gray Apple logo on a white screen. You'll then see an introductory screen where the components that are loading will be identified.

NEW TERM The *Operating System* is the fuel that feeds the engine or processor that runs your Mac. It's software that makes all the disparate components of your computer run in harmony and controls how the various programs you run operate. Without an operating system, your computer would be like a car without gas.

Setting Up Your Account

The first time you start a new Mac, you'll have a close encounter with Apple's Setup Assistant.

The Setup Assistant's layout frequently changes, so I'm not going to show what it looks like here. I will, however, give you an idea of the sort of information that's requested, so you can be ready to respond.

If you decide to take the quiz offered by the Setup Assistant, just read the questions you see on the screen before answering. (You can always change the answers later if you come up with a better one.) Click the Continue button to move ahead.

That little pointer you see on your screen when you move the mouse around is the mouse *cursor*. Its shape changes for different functions. For example, it will become a blinking vertical bar if you click an area where you enter text, and it will switch to a little hand if you point the cursor at something that can be activated with a single mouse click. When your computer is thinking over an operation you activated, the cursor changes to a little spinning watch.

I'll list most of the types of questions the Assistant will ask you. Not all the information listed will be covered, so don't be surprised if the precise topic isn't dealt with. Just read the directions carefully and the answers will come easily.

To fill in information, point the mouse cursor in the little text area and click. You'll see a blinking insertion point to signify that you are in the right text area. To move from one text area to another, press the Tab key on your keyboard.

Actually, you don't have to answer any of the Setup Assistant's questions. You can dismiss the Assistant whenever you want and answer the questions later. The Setup routine is needed to prepare your registration information on your new computer, to set up Internet access, and to set the correct time for your computer's clock.

Here's a list of the types of questions you'll be asked as the Mac OS X Setup Assistant progresses (but remember, some of this might change as Apple updates the way it runs):

- **Welcome**—Choose your country from the list.
- **Registration**—At the end of the setup process, your information will be sent on to Apple. Click Continue to progress through the screens. And, yes, you can opt out of receiving email offers from Apple.
- **Create Your Account**—Mac OS X is a multiple-user system, which means that you can set up a separate account for every person who will be using your Mac. But the initial setup is for you, as owner (or administrator) of your Mac. Because there are some specifics here that will matter later on down the road, you may want to skip ahead to the next section for an explanation. Chapter 27, "Sharing (and Securing) Your Computer," will tell you how to set up those other accounts.
- **Get Internet Ready**—Do you have an Internet account. You can take this opportunity to sign up with EarthLink, Apple's default service and get a free trial, or add information from your previous ISP. You'll also have to select the means by which you connect. You can use your computer's built-in modem, a network connection, a cable modem, or DSL. Not sure what to do? Check with the service you're using about what connection method you're using. Or just leave it alone and worry about getting on the Internet later (see Chapter 4, "Using the Internet," for more information).

If you're an AOL member, you can't set up your account here. Just tell the assistant you're not going to connect to the Internet right now.

- **Now You're Ready to Connect**—If you set up your Internet connection, you'll sit back for a moment now, as your registration information is sent to Apple. Just be patient, and you'll be ready to move to the next setup screen.
- **Set Up Mail**—Mac OS X includes a neat little email program, simply called Mail. Here's where you need to set it up to work with your service. If you're not sure what to put here, just bypass the screen for now. You can set it up later.

Not sure what information to enter to access the Internet? You need to use the information given to you by your current service or copied from another computer that uses that service. If you're not sure, call the service and ask what to do next. For now, you can bypass this setting and do it later.

- **Select Time Zone**—Where do you live? Just pick the time zone so that your Mac's click is correct, and your messages and files will have the proper time stamping.
- **Thank You**—You're welcome. This is just the final Setup Assistant screen. There, that wasn't so bad, was it? In just moments, you'll see your Mac's desktop, ready and waiting for you to begin using your computer.

Creating Your Account

As part of the setup process, you must configure your first user account. That account is used to control access to the system and to prevent unauthorized changes from being made to your software. The Create Your Account dialog box is shown in Figure 1.2.

If more than one person uses your computer and you want to keep your work separate, you can create multiple user accounts. Each user has a private password to access the operating system. This provides a measure of security and keeps different programs from interfering with each other. On the other hand, if you're the only user and don't want to log in each time, you can configure your system to start without a login. Both of these issues are covered in Chapter 27.

The account setup fields are explained here:

Name—Enter your full name.

Short Name—The short name is the name of your account. It should be composed of eight or fewer lowercase letters or numbers. Spaces and punctuation aren't allowed.

Password—The Password field is used to enter a secret word or string of characters that Mac OS X uses to verify that you are who you say you are.

Verify—The Verify field requires you to type the same string you entered in the Password field. This step ensures that the password you typed is actually what you intended.

Password Hint—Type a phrase or question that reminds you of your password. If you attempt to log in to your system three times without success, the hint is displayed.

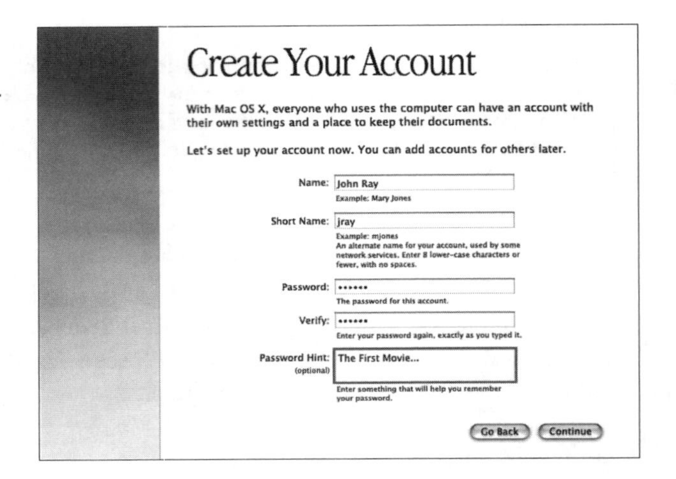

FIGURE 1.2
Create the account you use to access your Mac OS X system.

Turning It All Off

All Macs have to do a little internal housekeeping whenever you shut them down. Here's how to turn off your computer:

- Take your mouse and point to the Apple menu (that thing on the top of the screen with an Apple icon), and then click and hold. Then move the cursor to Shut Down and release the button, to select it. Within a few seconds, the computer will comply and turn itself off.

If you listen carefully after the Shut Down command is engaged, you'll hear the hard drive on your computer churning a little bit. That's normal. The Mac OS is designed to do a few chores with the drive before the computer is ready to turn itself off.

The Sleep function is used to put your computer into a low-power mode. The screen will darken, but the computer will still be on, and a simple press of any key on the keyboard will restore it to life. Anything you worked on before it went to sleep will still be there, ready to be worked on again. If you're planning on using your computer later that day, Sleep is fine and your computer will be up and running a lot faster than shutting it down and turning it on again.

If you accidentally shut off the computer by pulling the power cord, or there's a power failure, in most cases it will work just fine the next time you start it up. If you happened to be working with a file at the time, there's always the possibility the file might have become damaged, or there might be minor damage to the hard drive's catalog directory, so just be careful.

Discovering the Help Menus

Are you new to the Macintosh world or to computers in general? Well, take it from me, the mouse takes a little while to get used to, but after a couple of exercises you'll be working it like a pro.

Apple has a Help menu where you can receive tips and information. To get there, just point the mouse to the Help label and hold the mouse switch. Choose Mac OS from the menu to open a list of help topics.

To get from one to the other, just click the underlined link, known as a *hyperlink*. That click will open an information screen explaining what the function is all about. When you get the basics, choose the section in this book that covers the topic for a complete tutorial.

If you're having a bit of trouble getting to the Help menu, here's a fast tip. Just point the mouse cursor to the item on the menu bar labeled Help and click the mouse button once. The Help menu will sit there until you pick a command (or about 15 seconds if you don't make a selection).

Keyboard Power

Don't feel that using your computer will confine you to the mouse. As you'll see throughout this book, there are many ways to use the keyboard (see Figure 1.3) to help you get around.

If you haven't used a computer before, you'll find a few odd keys surrounding the normal range of letters and numbers.

Here's what they do (from left to right, top to bottom, and so on):

- **Esc**—This is similar to the option on a Windows-based computer. It enables you to stop a function for some programs.
- **F1 through F15**—These are function keys. For some programs, you'll find they activate additional features. The manuals or online help for those programs will explain what they do.

- **Help**—Opens the Help menu for some (but not all) programs.
- **Home**—They say you can't go home again, but the purpose of this is to take you to the top of a document page or directory window.
- **Page Up**—This keystroke takes you up a page or single screen in a program (but not all software supports the feature).
- **Page Down**—The reverse of Page Up. It takes you down a page or single screen in a program that supports the feature.
- **End**—Not available on the compact Mac keyboards, this command moves you right to the end of a document page or window.
- **Numeric keypad**—It's similar to a calculator, and you might find it convenient to enter numbers in a program.
- **Enter**—Used to activate a function. In many programs, the Return key and the Enter keys each trigger the start of a function, but only the Return key is used to end a paragraph when you write text in a program.
- **Control**—This is a modifier key. You press Control along with an alphanumeric character to activate a special function in some programs.

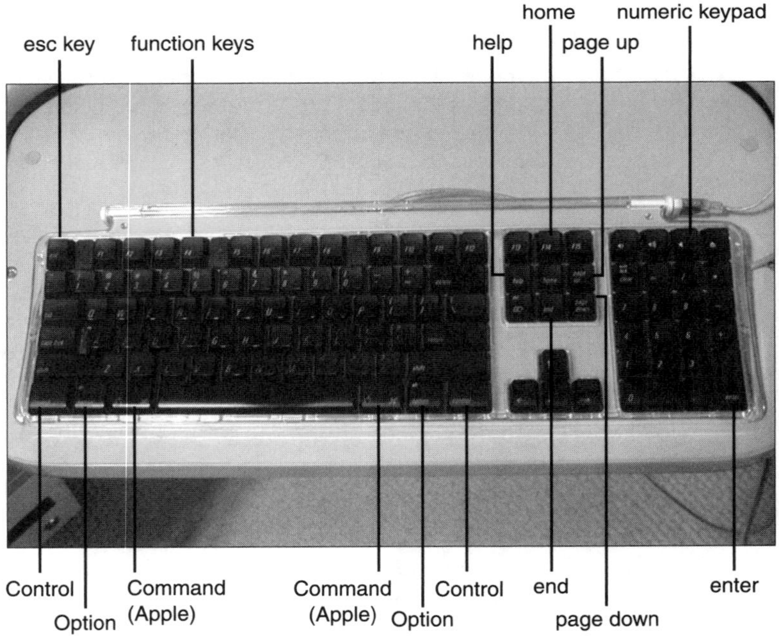

FIGURE 1.3
Here's the Apple Pro keyboard.

You can also use the Control key and a mouse click (pressed at the same time) to activate a special feature called Contextual menus. This feature opens a menu of command functions that apply to the item you're working on. If you've used Windows, the result is much the same as a right click.

- **Option**—Another modifier key. It's often used (along with an alphanumeric key) to get you a special character when you're typing a document (such as a foreign accent or symbol). This key is identical to the Alt key on a Windows keyboard.
- **Command**—It's sometimes called the Apple key because some keyboards show the Apple symbol there instead of the cloverleaf. It's another modifier key, used along with an alphanumeric key, to activate a command.
- **Media Keys**—The four keys at the left control both sound and drive media. The first three do precisely what the icons show, reduce volume, raise volume, or mute your Mac's speakers. The last is used to eject a selected CD or open and close the CD tray on the flat-panel model.

A Tour of Mac OS X Technology

Now that you've set up your Mac and learned the very basic functions, let's take a look at what's "under the hood." I'm referring to the Mac operating system, OS X. The release of OS X in 2001 represented a revolutionary departure from the traditional Mac OS, which offered greater system stability and flexibility wrapped in a luxurious user interface. The current version of Mac OS X is Version 10.2, code named Jaguar presumably because it's powerful, sleek, and fast.

Mac OS X consists of 11 separate pieces that work together and complement each other (as represented in Figure 1.4). Let's take a brief look at the components. As we do so, we'll also examine how they influence its features.

FIGURE 1.4
This layered model represents the complex architecture of Mac OS X.

Aqua			AppleScript
Cocoa	Java 2	Carbon	Classic
Quartz	OpenGL	QuickTime	Audio
Darwin - Open Desktop			

Mac OS X is made up of several components that work together to run applications, generate images, and provide a cutting-edge user experience:

- **Aqua**—Aqua provides a graphical user interface (GUI) that controls the appearance of windows, buttons, and other onscreen controls.

- **AppleScript**—The AppleScript language enables users to write scripts that interact with other software on the computer.
- **Cocoa**—Cocoa is a programming environment that enables applications for Mac OS X to be built from scratch quickly.
- **Java 2**—Mac OS X supports the development and deployment of Java-based programs.
- **Carbon**—Carbon is an interface for developing programs that run on Mac OS 8/9 as well as Mac OS X.
- **Classic**—The Classic environment enables existing Mac OS applications to run under Mac OS X.
- **Quartz**—Quartz is Apple's new 2D imaging framework and window server, which is based on the Portable Document Format (PDF).

> You might recognize PDF as a common file type for forms and documents available on the Internet. PDFs are especially useful for distributing forms because they reproduce the page layout regardless of the type of computer receiving the information. If your Internet browser has called for you to downloaded Adobe's Acrobat Reader, you've already encountered PDFs.

- **OpenGL**—OpenGL is the industry standard for 3D graphics.

> Mac OS X, with the help of OpenGL, performs a variety of eye-catching visual effects, such as seamlessly fading between screensaver images and scaling icons. However, some computers that can handle the other demands of Mac OS X have a graphics card that isn't capable of producing these effects. If you find that transitions between images are jerky, your graphics card might be to blame. However, rest assured that the other less-cosmetic aspects of Mac OS X are unaffected.

- **QuickTime**—Apple's award-winning multimedia technologies are built into the graphics foundation of Mac OS X. Jaguar's QuickTime 6.0 includes the new MPEG-4 standard for Internet viewing.
- **Audio**—Mac OS X continues Apple's tradition of providing world-class audio support for musicians and audiophiles.
- **Darwin**—The Unix-based core operating system.

New Term *Unix* (pronounced *YOU-nix*) is an operating system developed at Bell Labs during the 1970s. Unix was created to be a stable and powerful development platform for programmers. However, it has traditionally been run in the form of text commands, which can be a bit intimidating for casual computer users. Mac OS X preserves the power of Unix while adding the usability of a Mac interface.

Installing Mac OS X

In case you've had your Mac for a while and it didn't come with Mac OS X installed, this section will guide you through the basics of installing it. (If you need a reason to make the change, a lot of the best software for using digital media on the Mac is available only for OS X—including iPhoto and the most recent version of iMovie.)

From the time OS X was released until 2002, Apple shipped computers with software for both OS X and the previous operating system, OS 9. The reason for this is simple. During development of OS X, Apple had the foresight to know that its long-time users couldn't switch to the new operating system, no matter how well it worked, until the applications and hardware they had come to depend on were available for it. By designing OS X and updates to OS 9 in such a way that the two systems could co-exist, users were getting the best of both worlds—their old familiar applications and hardware and a new state-of-the-art operating system that could pave the way for even better hardware and applications later on.

Because a broad range of software and hardware is now available for the new operating system, Apple has stopped offering OS 9 as a separate product, and has even stopped making computers that can boot directly into OS 9. The good news is that OS 9 lives on as the "Classic" environment in OS X, and most older Mac programs can still be used in this mode. We'll talk about using Classic applications in more detail in Chapter 3, "Working with Windows, Folders, Files, and Applications."

The first thing you must do is make sure that your system can handle Mac OS X. The system requirements for Mac OS X are higher than previous versions of the Mac OS. According to Apple, Mac OS X runs on all original G4 computers, all iBooks and iMacs (including the Bondi 233), all PowerBooks (except the original Powerbook G3), and all beige desktop G3s.

Although Mac OS X can run on a wide range of processors, the minimum requirement for decent performance is considered by many to be at least a 350MHz G3. If you're using an older or slower Macintosh, it might exhibit extreme sluggishness with Mac OS X. Users of original iMacs and iBooks might want to consider upgrading their computers, rather than experience the frustrations of overloading their machines' processors.

In addition to the processor requirement, Mac OS X needs 128MB of RAM and 1.5GB of available storage. If you meet these requirements, you're ready to begin!

Preparing Your Hard Drive for Mac OS X

You have 2 choices about how to configure your system. The best configuration depends entirely on your needs.

The simplest path to upgrade from Mac OS 9 to Mac OS X is to upgrade to the most current version of Mac OS 9, and then to install Mac OS X. Apple recommends this approach only if you have existing data and cannot start from scratch. If you choose this path, your system is ready for Mac OS X installation after you install Mac OS 9.

Another configuration option is a *clean install*, which means you want to disable your current system folder and install a new one. Why choose this option? Although installing on top of an existing Mac OS 9 system is acceptable, it might not lead to the best possible performance. You avoid some types of system problems if you clear out your system and start from scratch. However, you must move your system preferences from the folder labeled Previous System to your new system folder so that your application settings aren't lost.

> Even though a clean install won't delete your existing data, backing up your documents is still a recommended practice. System updates often update the drivers for your hard disks, which, although unlikely to cause problems, is a serious enough action to take the cautious route.

Installing Mac OS X

When installing Mac OS X, installation wizards do most of the work. Follow these steps to start installing Mac OS X:

1. If you're currently running Mac OS 9 and have inserted the Mac OS X CD-ROM, double-click the Install Mac OS X icon. Your computer will display a welcome message, restart after a few moments, and begin to boot from the CD-ROM. If you're starting the installation from a power-off state, make sure that the CD-ROM is in your drive, and start the computer while holding down the C key.

   While the installer boots, you'll see a Mac OS X loading screen. It's normal for this screen to stay visible for a few minutes. The installation procedure begins immediately after the operating system is loaded.

2. The next several screens ask you to choose the language in which you'd like the entire operating system to be displayed. You must click Accept for the licensing agreement.

3. Next, you must choose the drive that will contain Mac OS X. Click the icon of the drive that corresponds to the volume you've prepared for Mac OS X. A circle and arrow form over the selected drive. Click Continue to move on to the final step.
4. Click the Install button to copy all the standard Mac OS X components to your computer. If this is the first time you've used Mac OS X, this is the best course of action to take. Advanced users can consider clicking the Customize button to display the individual components that can be added and removed from the system.

Summary

In this chapter, you unpacked your brand new Mac. Then you connected everything together and turned it on for the first time. From here, you ran through Apple's setup assistants to get your computer set up and connected to the Internet. You also got a quick primer on the purpose behind those extra keys on the keyboard. You also learned a bit about the components of the Mac operating system, and how they add up to a machine built for high performance. Finally, in case your computer didn't come with it already in place, you learned how to install the OS X operating system.

CHAPTER 2

Exploring the Desktop

In the very old days of personal computing, the screen displayed just plain text. You had to type the instructions on the keyboard to tell your computer to do something. There wasn't even a mouse to click.

When Apple created the Mac they did it differently (and, no doubt, that's where the idea for the commercial—Think Different—was first spawned, although it came years later).

The Mac was designed to relate to you in a way that was familiar to anyone who works in an office, using a desktop. Common elements on the computer are shown as little pictures (icons) to serve as illustrations of the purpose of a specific item.

> It's true that there are still computers today that are set up to work with a text (command-line) interface. There's of course DOS on the PC side of the personal-computer arena, and Unix, the industrial-strength operating system that forms the foundation of Mac OS X, which can work with either a text or a graphical user interface.

Modern Macintosh computers are the descendants of that original Mac with its picture-based user interface. In this chapter, we'll tour your desktop and learn to use the Finder and the Dock. We'll also find out about customizing your system with System Preferences.

The Finder

The Finder is the application that Mac OS X uses to launch and manipulate files and applications. Unlike other tools and applications, the Finder starts immediately after you log in to the system and is always active. (In addition to helping you locate your files, the Finder handles all common tasks, such as creating, deleting, moving, and copying files and folders. We'll save discussion of those functions for the next chapter.) The items on your desktop are identified by little pictures, or *icons*, that tell you their function. This is one of the great features of a graphical operating system because, as they say, a picture tells a thousand words, or in this case, gives you a fast clue as to what kind of file you're looking at.

Here's a quick look at some of the icons you'll see most often and what they represent:

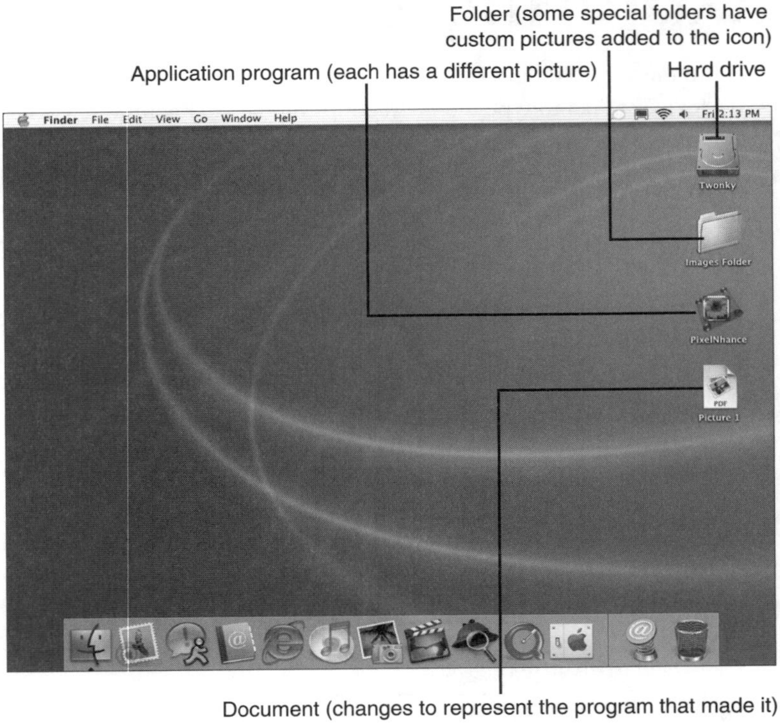

Folder (some special folders have custom pictures added to the icon)
Application program (each has a different picture)
Hard drive
Document (changes to represent the program that made it)

FIGURE 2.1
Each icon accesses a specific item or feature.

You can interact with the Finder in several different ways. There's a menu bar for the Finder, but there's also the Finder window, which has several different modes and view options. We'll take a look at the menu system first, and then the basic view options for Finder windows.

The Finder Menu Bar

Your TV's remote control has buttons that turn on the TV or change channels. On the Mac, there are several ways to give the computer instructions to do something. The first one I'll talk about is the menu bar, that long, gray-shaded strip with thin horizontal lines that lies at the top of your Mac's screen.

> If you've used Windows, you'll see one big difference between the way the menu bar works on the *other* side and on the Mac. With Windows, each program you use has its own menu bar, so you might find several menu bars across your computer's screen. On a Mac, however, there's only one menu bar, at the very top, which changes to reflect the features of the program currently in use. The advantage is that you only have to point your mouse in one specific place for it to work properly.

About the Menu Bar

The Mac's menu bar has a set of labels that you click to open a list of functions (commands). In the next few pages, I'll take you through the Finder's menu bar, where you'll discover what all those commands really accomplish.

> As you explore menu bar commands, you'll see that many of them are common from one program to another. That's a reflection of how consistent the Mac OS interface is. So when you learn what these commands do for the Mac OS X Finder, you'll also see how they work in other programs, such as iTunes, iPhoto, iMovie, iDVD, and Photoshop Elements, which we will explore in depth later in this book. The knowledge you gain here will go a long way towards learning how to use those programs.

Touring the Application Menu

Each application you use for Mac OS X has its own menu to the right of the Apple icon (which refers to another menu I'll tell you about shortly, the Apple menu). The application menu will always have the name of the active application, such as the Finder (see Figure 2.2).

FIGURE 2.2
The application menu has a basic set of commands for a specific program.

Although many of the menus you see will be the same or similar when you use other applications on your Mac, some will be quite different. Each program has a separate set of functions that require different menu bar labels.

To Do

Checking Out the Application Menu

Here's how to see the contents of this menu:

1. Move your mouse cursor to the Application menu.
2. Click the Application menu and hold down the mouse button. A list of the commands that are available from that menu will pop up on your screen.

Actually, the pop-up menu drops down, and if you use Windows you are probably used to calling them drop-down menus. Because this is a Mac, I'll use the word pop-up or pull-down to be consistent with Apple's terms.

3. To activate a command, move the mouse cursor to that item. You'll see a dark rectangle around it to show it has been chosen (or *selected*).
4. Release the mouse button to activate the command.

If holding down the mouse button isn't comfortable for you, just release right after you click a menu bar label. The menu will just stay there so you can easily point to a specific command. After you've done that, click that command. The menu will disappear and the command will be activated.

> You'll notice that some items are gray (or *grayed out*). Those commands are only available under certain conditions (such as Eject, which is used to remove a selected disk's icon, such as that of a CD, from the desktop and eject it), or if you select a specific icon to which the command applies. If the command is grayed out, you won't be able to perform that function.

- **About the Finder**—Select this to learn something about the program you're using. Usually, you'll see the version number and the name of the publisher of the program.
- **Preferences**—This command opens a dialog box where you can make a few settings on Finder functions (see Figure 2.3). Feel free to play with the settings. You can always change them back.

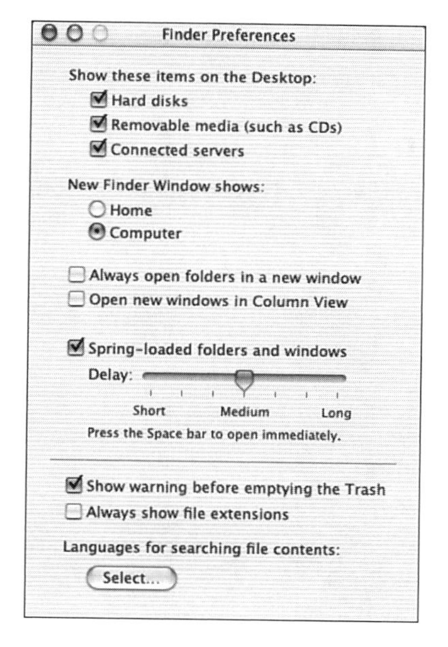

FIGURE 2.3
The Finder's preferences. Click an item to activate that feature or function.

- **Empty Trash**—When you drag an item to the trash can at the bottom of your screen, on the Dock, you can remove the item permanently with this command. We'll talk more about deleting files with Trash later in this chapter.

> Did you put the wrong item in the Trash? Click on the Trash icon in the Dock, and a folder will open showing its contents. Now you can drag the items that you don't want to delete out of the Trash. When you activate the Empty Trash function, however, it's too late. We'll discuss the Trash again shortly.

- **Services**—This is a clever Mac OS X feature that enables one program to call on the features of another to perform a function. A cool example would be to type the address of a Web site, copy it, and then select a browser from the Services window and have it open that site.
- **Hide Finder**—Hides the window of the application, to help reduce the clutter of windows on your desktop.
- **Hide Others**—Hides the windows for all other programs, so you can easily work with the one you're using.
- **Show All**—Reverses the previous two features.

Depending on the program you're using, an application menu might have additional functions. For example, other programs will include a Quit command that closes the program and all its documents in one operation.

Touring the File Menu

Now let's tour the File menu (see Figure 2.4). The following commands are available in the Finder's File menu:

FIGURE 2.4
The File menu controls basic file manipulation features of your computer.

File
New Finder Window ⌘N
New Folder ⇧⌘N
Open ⌘O
Open With ▶
Close Window ⌘W
Get Info ⌘I
Duplicate ⌘D
Make Alias ⌘L
Show Original ⌘R
Add to Favorites ⌘T
Move to Trash ⌘⌫
Eject ⌘E
Burn Disc...
Find... ⌘F

- **New Finder Window**—Creates an Extra Finder window, which can help you work more easily with files from different locations. This way if you want to move files from different locations, you can get an easier handle on their exact positioning and not move the wrong file to the wrong place.
- **New Folder**—Creates a container to store files (or more folders). You can insert folders within folders to your heart's content (but don't overdo it) just by dragging

one over to the folder you want to put it in. Wait for the target folder to highlight before releasing the mouse button. We'll talk more about working with folders in the next chapter, "Working with Windows, Folders, Files, and Applications."

You don't have to use your mouse for all commands. Some functions have keyboard shortcuts, too. You'll see them listed at the right of the command label on a menu. The cloverleaf key stands for the Apple or Command key on your Mac's keyboard. If you hold down that key plus the second key listed, it will activate that function.

- **Open**—Opens a folder, or launches a program and brings a document to your screen.
- **Open With**—Allows you to choose an application to open a selected file. (This option will be grayed out, or unselectable, if you don't have a file selected.)

Some commands in a menu have a right arrow next to them. If you see the right arrow, it means clicking on it will open a second menu (a *submenu*) showing additional functions that apply to that command.

- **Close Window**—Used to close the selected Finder window.
- **Get Info**—Use this command to learn more about a selected icon, apply access privileges to it, and, in the case of a document, even change the application used to open it.
- **Duplicate**—As it says, it will make a copy of the item you've selected.
- **Make Alias**—I'll cover this in more detail in Chapter 3. An Alias in Mac OS parlance is an icon that points to the original. It has lots of cool uses, as you'll see later, the most important of which is to be able to access a file or application that's buried deep into a folder, without having to figure out where it is.
- **Show Original**—When you select the alias, or pointer to the original file, this command opens the original file, wherever it's located on your hard drive.
- **Add to Favorites**—If you want to call up a program or document often, you'll want to make it a Favorite, so you can get to it quickly. The selected item joins the list of Favorites that are accessed when you click the Favorites icon in the Finder's toolbar.
- **Move to Trash**—Puts a selected item in the trash can in your Mac's Dock—that taskbar that sits along the bottom (or side) of the screen.

- **Eject**—This command can be used to eject CDs, floppy disks, and so on.
- **Burn Disk**—If your computer has a built-in CD burner, you can use this command to make a CD.

Mac OS X's disk-burning software can also work with some external CD drives. See Chapter 11, "Using iTunes," for more details about burning CDs.

- **Find**—This command opens your system's search feature to locate files on your hard drive.

If you see three dots (an ellipsis) next to a menu command, you'll see another screen (a dialog box) when you select that function. You will have to make some choices from the dialog box to activate a function (that's why it's a dialog).

NEW TERM A *dialog box* is a screen or window where you can interact with your computer to make choices about a selected function. For example, if you want to print something you'll see a dialog box where you type how many copies you want of each page and what pages you want to print.

NEW TERM A *window* as described here is not that *other* platform, but a rectangular-shaped object that displays such things as a list of files, the contents of a folder, or the contents of a document (such as a letter to your mom). I'll explain more about how this all works in Chapter 3.

Touring the Edit Menu

The next menu is called Edit (see Figure 2.5). It's used to make changes to a selected item.

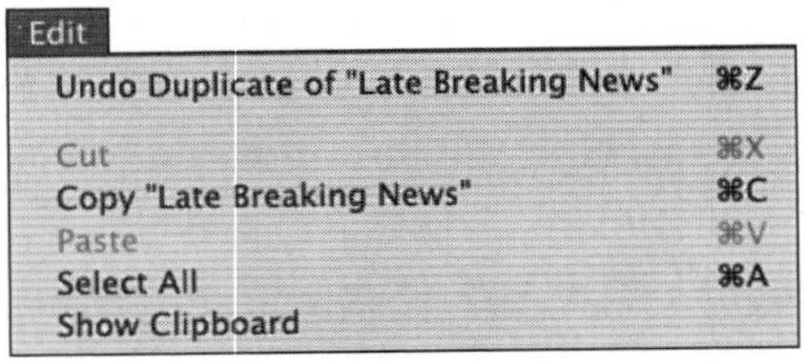

FIGURE 2.5
Use the Edit menu to make changes to a selected item.

```
Edit
Undo Duplicate of "Late Breaking News"   ⌘Z
Cut                                      ⌘X
Copy "Late Breaking News"                ⌘C
Paste                                    ⌘V
Select All                               ⌘A
Show Clipboard
```

Here's the list of commands that are used to edit something. Once again, if something is grayed out, it means that command isn't available to work on the item you've selected.

The Edit menu includes the following items:

- **Undo**—They say there's no going back, but on the Mac this isn't always true. If this command is black, it means that the last action you took to edit something can be rescinded. Except for a very few programs, such as Microsoft Word, you can only do this sort of thing once. If it says Can't Undo, as in the example I'm showing, it simply means that function doesn't work for a particular item you've selected.
- **Cut**—This isn't used for removing files. It's designed to remove a text or picture you've selected and store it in a little invisible place called the Clipboard.

NEW TERM The *Clipboard* is a place in the Mac's memory where the item you copy is held in storage until replaced with another copied item—or until your computer is restarted or shut down. You use the clipboard whenever you copy or cut an item from your documents, such as a word, a phrase, or a picture.

> Be careful what you do after you cut something. If you perform another operation (even typing a single letter), you may not be able to Undo the original function (unless the application supports multiple undo or redo, such as Microsoft Word X).

- **Copy**—This command makes a duplicate of the selected word or picture and stores it in the Clipboard. When an item is selected, the Copy command will include the name of the item (so you have a way to confirm your choice).
- **Paste**—Use this command to insert an item you've copied with the Copy command or removed with the Cut command.

> Under Mac OS X, you can copy files too with these Edit commands. Just select a file, choose Copy, click the folder to which you want to copy the file, and select Paste. The Undo command will reverse the copy operation.

- **Select All**—This command does precisely what the name implies. It highlights all the items in the selected window.
- **Show Clipboard**—This command opens a small document window showing the contents of the Clipboard.

Touring the View Menu

The next stop on our trip around the menu bar is the View menu (shown in Figure 2.6). It's used to control how items on your computer's desktop are displayed. (We'll take a more detailed look at these options in Chapter 3 when we discuss windows.) The first three choices in the menu are either/or propositions with a checkmark to the left of the one you select.

FIGURE 2.6
The View menu shows how items are displayed on the desktop.

Here's a quick look at how the View settings work (adding the word View for clarity because it's not shown in the menu itself):

- **[View] as Icons**—This is the normal setup; everything is displayed as a colorful icon (shown in Figure 2.7).

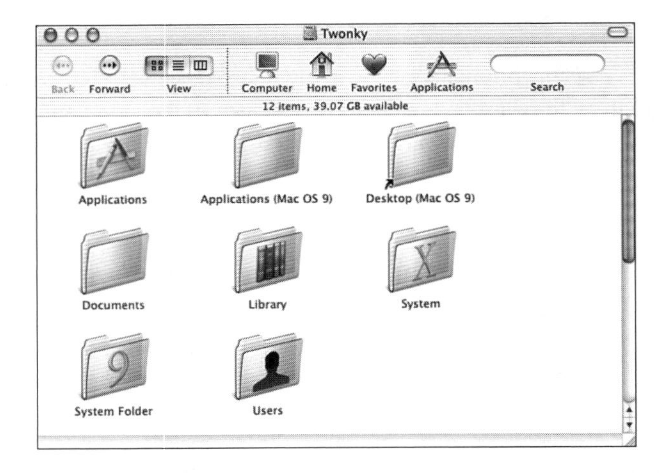

FIGURE 2.7
The normal display scheme for items on the desktop is the Icon view.

- **[View] as List**—Sometimes known as list view. It offers you a simple text listing or directory (see Figure 2.8). If you have a lot of items in a directory, this option makes them all take up a lot less screen space.

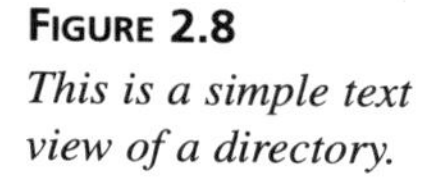

FIGURE 2.8
This is a simple text view of a directory.

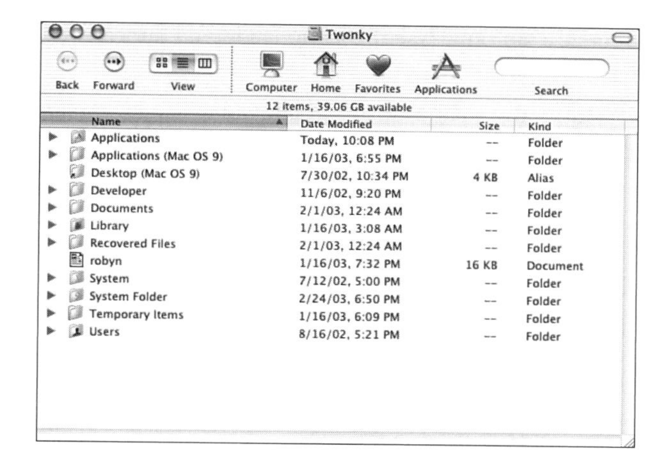

- **[View] as Columns**—This function divides the Finder's listing into neat rows (see Figure 2.9). Click any item in any row, and you'll see the contents (or a preview icon) in the column to its right. When you click a folder in the right column, it will display the contents within that folder. The little resize handle at the bottom right can be used to make the Finder window smaller or larger (or just click the Maximize button to expand to the largest size to accommodate the contents).

FIGURE 2.9
Column view makes it easier to burrow deep down into the files on your Mac.

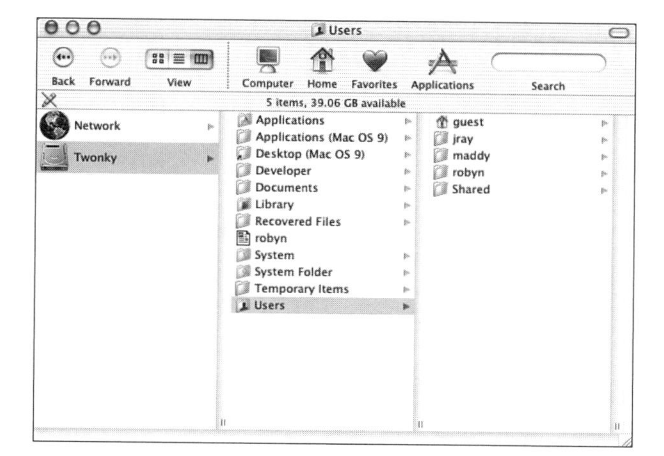

- **Clean Up**—If your icons are spread around, this helps clean them up with a neater arrangement. Now if it would only work that way in my office, I'd be all set.
- **Arrange**—An easy way to sort the contents of a window by Name, Date Modified, Date Created, Size, or Kind.
- **Hide Toolbar**—The little row of icons at the top of a Finder window can be hidden this way (it changes to Show Toolbar after the toolbar is hidden).

- **Customize Toolbar**—Use this command to add or remove icons from the Finder's toolbar.
- **Show Status Bar**—Choose this command to see information about a folder or a drive, including the number of items and the amount of disk space available.
- **Show View Options**—This will open a Setting dialog box (see Figure 2.10) that enables you to make further adjustments on how items on the desktop are set up. (Your options will change depending on whether your are working with windows in icon, list, or column view.)

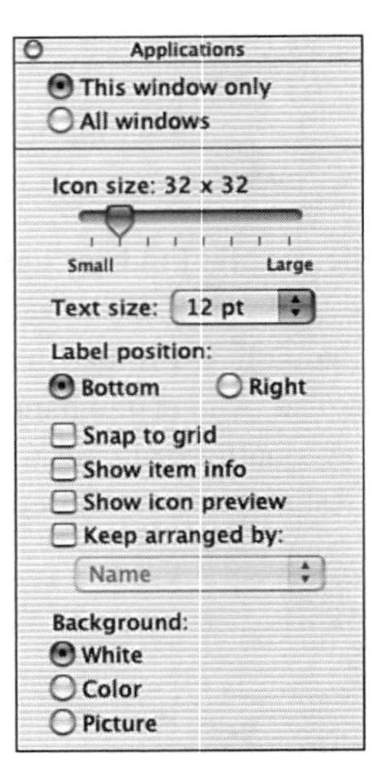

FIGURE 2.10
Pick your View setup choices from this dialog box.

What you see in the View Options window depends on what sort of Finder view you've selected. Some options, for example, don't appear in column or list view.

Touring the Go Menu

This menu (shown in Figure 2.11) is a speedy way to move from one folder or feature to another from the Finder.

Let's take the Go menu items one by one:

- **Back**—Returns to the previous Finder window, if you've viewed one before the one you're currently in.
- **Forward**—This takes you to a Finder window that you've backed out of, if there is one.

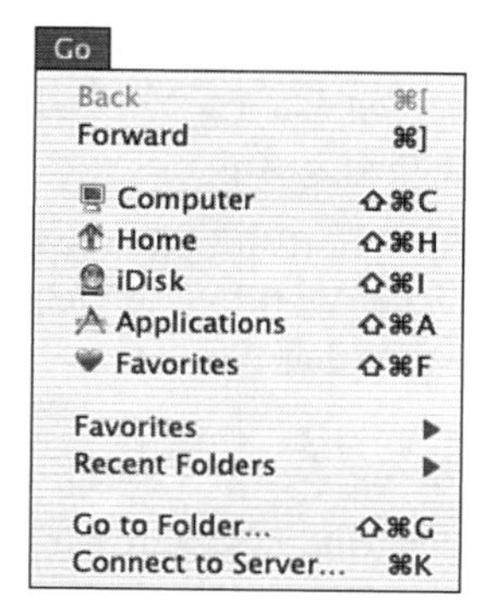

FIGURE 2.11
A fast way to get from here to there, the Finder's Go menu.

2

As you'll see, the bill of fare in the Go menu mirrors some of the standard Finder toolbar icons.

- **Computer**—This takes you to a Finder window that lists all your available drives plus your networking setup.
- **Home**—Under Mac OS X, this takes you to your personal user folder, the one that has your name. It enables you to easily view all your personal folders and files.
- **iDisk**—Use Apple Computer's convenient storage space. You just have to purchase a .Mac membership to get iDisk space.

Not yet a .Mac member? Visit `www.mac.com` to see if an account would be worth it to you.

- **Applications**—The Mac OS X programs that come with your computer are included in this folder, plus the ones you've added.
- **Favorites**—This opens the folder that contains your Favorites list. (The option right below it is a list of the items in your Favorites folder, so you won't even have to open it for access.)
- **Recent Folders**—Shows you a submenu displaying up to ten recently accessed folders. You can also access recent files and folders, but that feature is reserved for the Apple menu (I'll get to that shortly).
- **Go to Folder**—No searching needed. Choose this command and you'll see a little dialog box. Type the name of the folder and click Go, and you'll see that folder open in the selected Finder window. So, if you have selected the Applications folder, and want to go to the Utilities folder, enter Utilities in the Go to Folder window (it works on the top or active folder window).

- **Connect to Server**—This is a very powerful feature. It enables you to easily network your computer with other Macs. You can also network your Mac with computers running server versions of Windows or Unix.

NEW TERM A *server* is a computer that hosts files for distribution to other computers. For example, when you call up a site on the World Wide Web, you're actually connecting with a computer that stores the files for that Web site.

Touring the Window Menu

This is a fast way to manage the open Finder windows. Here's a list of the available commands:

- **Zoom Window**—This command expands a window to the maximum size needed to contain its contents (up to the maximum available space on your screen).
- **Minimize Window**—This command reduces the window and sends it to the Dock, where it shows up as a colorful icon.
- **Bring All to Front**—Brings all open windows in the Finder to the front, for fast access (even if you hid them previously).

We'll discuss Zoom and Minimize and what they do in greater detail in Chapter 3.

Beneath these commands will be a listing of all open windows for fast access.

Touring the Help Menu

When you run into a problem while working on your Mac, or if you just have a question, you'll want to keep this book at hand. But you'll also want to consult Apple's Help menu.

Each program will have its own set of Help choices. At the Finder, you'll see Mac Help, which opens a convenient window (see Figure 2.12) where you can learn more about functions and features of Mac OS X.

I'm not ignoring the right side of the menu bar. It contains your Mac's clock, plus one or more icons for quick access to some system functions, such as the settings for your computer's display, speaker volume, and so on. These icons are called "menu extras" and you can choose which icons appear. You'll learn more later in this chapter when we discuss System Preferences.

FIGURE 2.12
Click an item once to learn more about that feature.

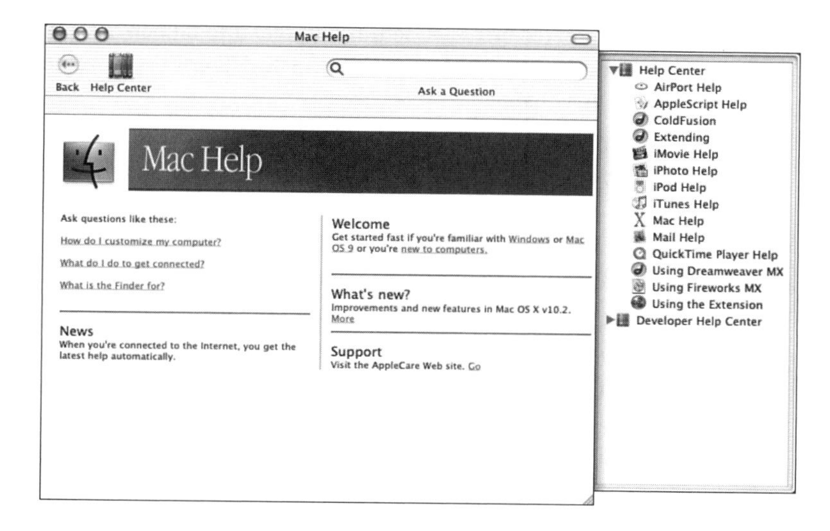

2

Touring the Apple Menu

Our last menu bar option is actually the first on your screen, the Apple menu, which is, of course, identified simply by the symbol of an Apple (see Figure 2.13). The nice thing about the Apple menu is that the very same commands are available in every Mac OS X application you use on your Mac. That's why it has special commands.

FIGURE 2.13
The Apple menu offers quick access to more programs and documents.

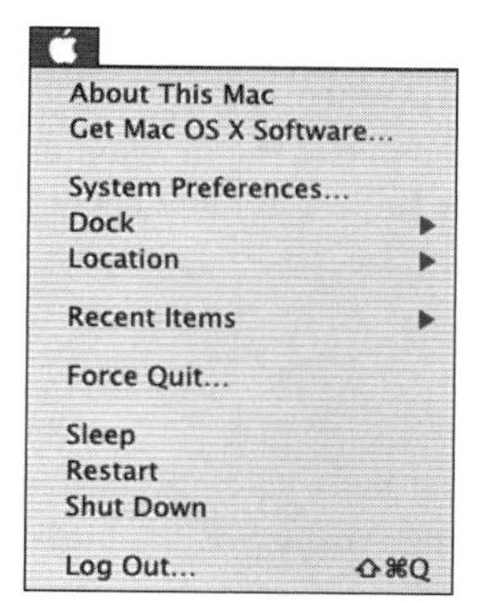

- **About This Mac**—This one opens a screen that gives you some basic information about the Mac OS version you have, and the amount of memory installed.
- **Get Mac OS X Software**—This selection shoots you over to Apple's Web site, where you learn about the latest software that runs under Mac OS X. All right, it's a commercial page, but it's a good way to learn about the latest and greatest Mac software.

- **System Preferences**—Use this command to launch an application to customize the way your Mac works under Mac OS X. I'll cover this subject in more detail at the end of this chapter.
- **Dock**—Use this command to customize the way the Dock, the colorful taskbar along one edge of your Mac's screen, runs. You can, if you want, have it hang at the bottom, left, or right of the screen. I'll cover the Dock in the next section.
- **Location**—This is a feature of Mac OS X that enables you to set your Mac to automatically network with different setups in different places.
- **Recent Items**—Click this submenu to see a list of recent applications and documents for speedy access.
- **Force Quit**—This feature enables you to get out of trouble when a program freezes or stops working properly. I'll cover methods of dealing with such problems in Chapter 29, "Recovering from Crashes and Other Problems."
- **Sleep**—This command puts your system into an idle or low-power mode. The screen will turn off, but the computer will remain on with anything you're working on still intact. Just press any key to awaken your sleeping computer. And it doesn't even snore.
- **Restart**—After installing a new program (or in case a program crashes or stops running for some reason), you should always use the Restart command. It causes the computer to go through its normal shutting down routine, but then it starts up normally.
- **Shut Down**—Turns off your computer.
- **Logout**—Mac OS X is a multiple-user operating system, which means everyone who has access to your computer can be set up with their own user account and have their own private space for files. When you Logout, you'll be returned to a prompt where you can select a user name to log in again or choose the Restart or Shut Down functions. I'll cover this subject in more detail in Chapter 27, "Sharing (and Securing) Your Computer."

The Finder Window

To help users manage their files, the Finder includes a specialized window, which is accessed by double-clicking the icon for the Mac OS X hard drive on the desktop.

Mac OS X introduces two modes of operation in the Finder window. The first of the two, single-window mode, is the toolbar version of the Finder. When the toolbar is present, double-clicking a folder opens the item you just clicked in the current window, replacing the previous contents.

The second mode, a toolbar-less version of the Finder window, can be entered by clicking the clear, oval-shaped toolbar button in the upper-right corner of the Finder window. In this mode, you can double-click folders to open additional windows. (We'll talk more about working with windows in the next chapter.)

The File System

Now that we've examined the Finder menus and learned a bit about Finder windows, let's explore the Finder's file system.

After you double-click the icon for your Mac OS X drive from the desktop, you will see a collection of permanent folders, as shown in Figure 2.14. These folders contain preinstalled applications, utilities, and configuration files for your system, known collectively as *system folders*. You cannot modify these system-level directories or move them from their default locations. Don't worry too much about that because you can create folders and files *within* these locations, if necessary.

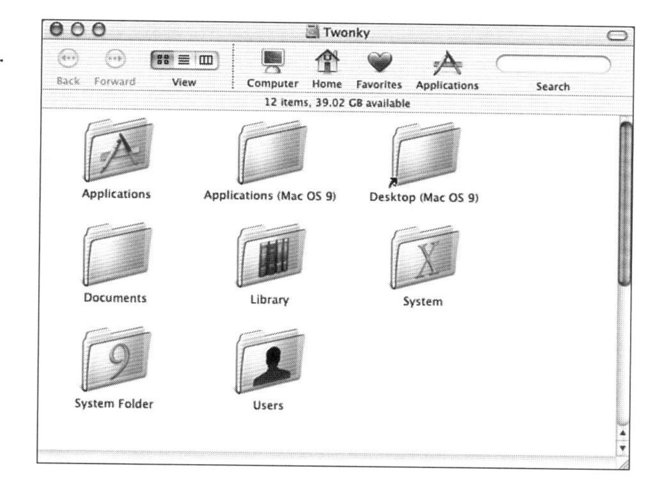

FIGURE 2.14
At the top level of your hard drive are several folders, each with a specific purpose.

The following list describes the folders at this level, which are the starting point for accessing most of your system's functions:

- **Applications**—The Applications folder contains all the preinstalled Mac OS X applications, such as Mail, QuickTime Player, and many others. Within the Applications folder is the Utilities folder, which contains the tools necessary to set up your printers, calibrate your display, and other important tasks.

Unlike most other system-critical folders, the Utilities folder *can* be modified by a Mac OS X user. You can move, rename, or delete the folder if you'd like, but such changes should be made only with great caution because the performance of some applications could be disrupted.

- **Library**—Although it doesn't have a strict definition, Library serves as a storage location for application preferences, application libraries, and information that should be accessible to anyone using the computer. Some of the folders in Library are used by applications to store data such as preferences, whereas others hold printer drivers or other system additions made by the user.
- **System**—Next on the list is the Mac OS X System folder. These files and folders shouldn't be changed because they are necessary for your computer to operate.
- **Users**—As mentioned earlier, Mac OS X is a true multiuser operating system in which each user has a private account in which to store their files. The Users folder contains the home folders, or *home directories*, of all the users on the machine.

  Figure 2.15 shows the Users folder in List view for a system with three users: robyn, jray, and guest. Your home folder can be considered your workplace. It's yours alone because most of the files and folders stored there are protected from other users. Even though you can see the folders for every user, you can access only the Public and Sites folders in another user's home folder. Other folders are displayed with a red minus symbol in their lower-right corner to indicate that no access is available to that location. Chapter 27 discusses setting up additional user accounts.

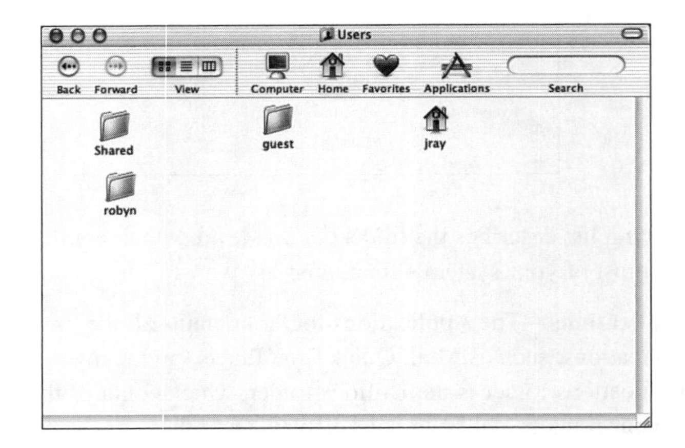

FIGURE 2.15
All users have their own home folder, but they cannot access the contents of each other's home folder.

- **System Folder (Mac OS 9), Applications (Mac OS 9), Desktop (Mac OS 9), and Documents**—If you have a version of Mac OS 9 installed along with Mac OS X, you might see folders for Classic system files and applications as well as documents created under Classic mode.

Now that you've seen the basic file structure of your hard drive, let's look at some other aspects of the file system: Computer, Home, Favorites, and Applications.

The "Computer Level" of the File System

Although you can see your computer's hard drives on the desktop, they are also visible in the Computer view of your Finder window. This is one of several default shortcuts available in the Finder toolbar. To see the Computer view, double-click the icon for your hard drive and then click the Computer icon. (You can also access this window when you don't have the Finder window open by choosing Computer from the Go menu in the Finder menu bar.)

> Any additional FireWire or USB drives (and other types of removable media) that are plugged into the system appear as icons in the Computer view of the Finder window in addition to being displayed on the desktop. We'll discuss Firewire and USB in our discussion of peripheral devices in Chapter 7.

The Home Directory

Another default shortcut is to the home directory. As you learned earlier, your home directory is the start of your personal area on Mac OS X. There, you can save your own files and no one can alter or read them.

Your home directory is named with the short name you chose when you created your Mac OS X user account. Several default folders are created inside your home directory. Those folders and their purposes are as follows:

- **Desktop**—The Desktop folder contains everything that shows up on your desktop.
- **Documents, Movies, Music, and Pictures**—These four folders are generic store-all locations for files of these kinds. You don't have to use these folders; they're merely recommended storage locations to help you organize your files.
- **Library**—The Library folder is the same as the top-level Library folder in the System folder. Within the subfolders in this folder, you can store fonts, screensavers, and many other extensions to the operating system.
- **Public**—The Public folder provides a way for you to share files with other users on your computer without granting total access. Also, if you plan to share your files over a network, you can do so by placing them in the Public folder and activating file sharing in the Sharing System Preferences panel. This is discussed in Chapter 27.
- **Sites**—If you want to run your own personal Web site, it must be stored in the Sites folder. To share your site with the outside world, you also have to enable Personal Web Sharing, which we will delve into in Chapter 27.

Although folders for different file types exist by default, you can do nearly anything you like with your home folder. The only folders that should not be modified are the Desktop and Library folders. They are critical to system operation and must remain as they are.

Favorites and Applications

In addition to Computer and Home, there are two remaining aspects of the file system that can be accessed from the toolbar of Finder windows—Favorites and Applications. These shortcuts to programs and files make those programs and files accessible from anywhere in the Finder.

You determine the contents of Favorites. Favorites enable you specify the folders that you want to access quickly. To add an item, simply select the folder you want to be a favorite and drag it to the Favorites icon on the Finder window toolbar, or choose Add to Favorites from the File menu (Command-T).

Clicking the Applications icon jumps you to the system Applications folder.

Performing File and Content Searches

In addition to organizing your files, the Finder enables you to find applications by filename, and documents by filename or by content. But the best part is that the search results are interactive. You can launch located programs and applications by double-clicking their icons in the results window. Also, dragging a file or folder to the desktop or a Finder window moves that object to a new location. This is a quick way to clean up when you accidentally save a file to the wrong folder.

People who've been using Macs for a while may be surprised that the Finder performs the function of finding files, rather than an application called Sherlock. Sherlock is still a part of the Mac software package, but rather than performing local file searches, it now searches only Internet content. In case you're wondering, we'll take a look at Sherlock in Chapter 5, "Using Other Basic Applications."

An easy way to search for a file by name only is through the Finder window. To do this, open a Finder window by double-clicking the folder or drive containing the file you want to find. Then type your search term in the Search box in the toolbar. Remember, if the toolbar isn't visible, you can show it by clicking the oblong button at the upper right of the window's title bar. If the search box isn't visible, you might have to enlarge your window by dragging from the diagonal lines in the bottom-right corner.

If you'd like to do a search of file contents or search more than a defined folder, choose Find (Command-F) from the File menu. The File dialog box is shown in Figure 2.16.

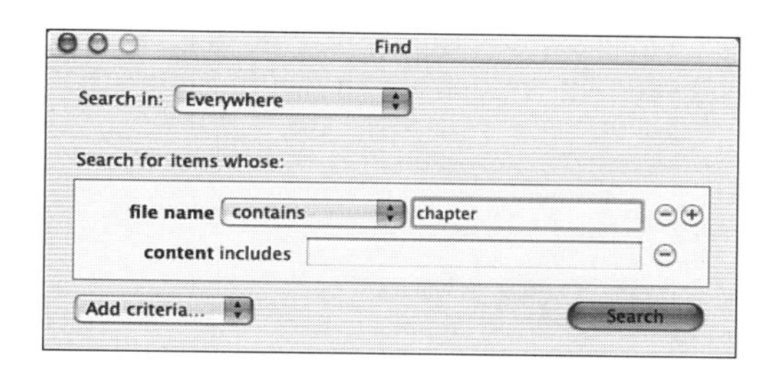

FIGURE 2.16
Use the File dialog box to locate files by name or content.

When the screen in Figure 2.16 appears, follow these steps:

1. Choose what to search. Your options are
   - **Everywhere**—Examines all drives and user accounts.
   - **Local Disks**—Examines only the current drive, but all user accounts.
   - **Home**—Examines only the home directory of the person currently logged in.
   - **Specific Places**—Displays a list of available drives for you to choose from. You can also click the Add/Remove button to insert or remove specific folders.
2. Pick whether to search for filenames, contents, or both. Enter your search text into the appropriate field(s). If you want to add additional search terms in these categories, click the + button for each option.
3. If you want to refine your search further, click the Add Criteria pop-up menu for setting options, including Date Modified, Date Created, Kind, and Extension. The additional search parameters appear below the filename and content search boxes followed by - and + buttons to remove them or add additional variations.
4. Click the Search button to start the search.

In a few moments, the search results are displayed. For each result, Find lists the filename, the date it was modified, its size, and the kind of file it is. After an item is highlighted, its path is shown in the details pane at the bottom of the window. Double-clicking the path opens the file, folder, or application.

Searching for file contents requires that the directory containing the file be indexed or cataloged. You can index a folder, or check for the last date of last indexing, using the Get Info command, which is discussed shortly.

Finder Preferences

The Finder Preferences can be used to adjust settings that control how you interact with your desktop and icons. Open these settings by choosing Preferences from the Finder application menu. The available options are shown in Figure 2.17.

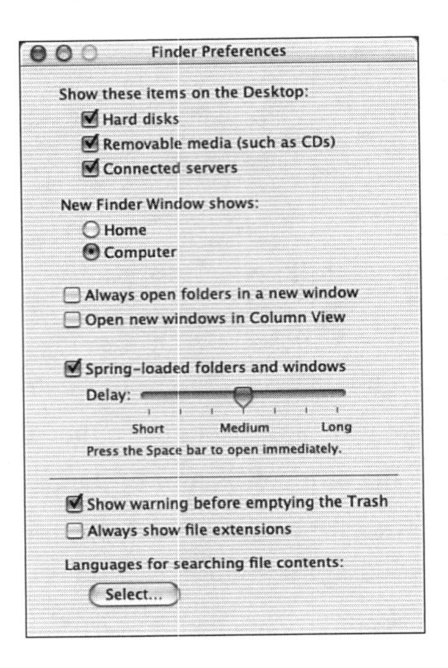

FIGURE 2.17 *Finder Preferences control file extensions, Trash warnings, and more.*

Among the preference settings are whether to display icons for the hard drive, removable media, or connected servers on the desktop and the default content displayed by new Finder windows. You can also adjust the delay for spring-loaded folders. *Spring-loading* is the desktop behavior that occurs when you drag a file or folder on top of another folder, and it springs open to move inside.

Close the Finder Preferences pane when you're satisfied with your settings

The Dock

Along one edge of your screen (either the bottom, left, or right) is a colorful banner of icons known as the Dock. The Dock is used as a taskbar, to show which applications you're running, minimized or reduced versions of a document window, and programs you want to use frequently.

The Dock, shown in its default state in Figure 2.18, has several functions, including displaying icons for open applications, storing minimized (but still open) documents, and providing a resting place for the Trash.

Figure 2.18
The Dock is a useful tool for organizing your desktop.

Whenever you launch an application, its icon will appear in the Dock (if it's not already there), and the icon will bounce as it's opening. When opened, a small triangle will show that it is open. When you quit or close the application, the triangle disappears. (For applications that haven't been set to remain in the dock, the icon may also disappear from the Dock.)

To launch an item that is in the Dock, just click the icon once and the Dock will take it from there. As the application launches, you'll see the icon bounce. When the Dock expands to the full width of the screen, it'll automatically get smaller as you add more icons to it.

Here's a fast overview of how the Dock works and how it's used:

- **Left (or Top) Portion**—There's a separator bar on the Dock. At its left (or top) are icons for applications. The ones you've opened have a triangle next to them.
- **Right (or Bottom) Portion**—At the right (or bottom) of the vertical bar are document icons representing the documents you've reduced or minimized.
- **Trash**—At the extreme right (or bottom) is the Trash, the place to drag files that you want to throw away.

You can also drag URLs into the document side of the Dock. A single click launches your default Web browser and opens it to the saved address.

- **Separator Bar**—The separator bar splits the Dock into the application and file/folder areas. To make the Dock larger or smaller, click the separator bar and then move the mouse up to increase the size or down to reduce it if positioned horizontally, or move it left and right if your Dock is positioned vertically. If you hold down the Option key on your keyboard when you do this, the Dock stops at fixed sizes (in 64-pixel increments, to be technical about it).

Moving an icon to the Dock doesn't change the location of the original file or folder. The Dock icon is merely a shortcut to the real file. Unfortunately, if a docked application has been moved, the Dock can no longer launch that application.

Why is a Dock icon suddenly bouncing up and down without letup? It means the program the icon represents is trying to tell you something with an onscreen message. Just click the icon to move to the application and find out what it wants.

Docked Applications

The left (or top) portion of the Dock contains all docked and currently running applications. You can add applications to this side of the Dock to create a quick launching point, no matter where the software is located on your hard drive. Dragging an application icon to the Dock adds it to that location in the Dock.

To make an active application a permanent member of the Dock, simply do the following:

1. Make sure that the application is running and that its icon appears in the Dock.
2. Click and hold on the icon to pop up a menu.
3. Choose the option Keep in Dock. (If the application already has a place in the Dock, you won't be given this option.)

After you've placed an application on the Dock, you can launch it by single-clicking the icon. To switch between active applications, just click the icon in the Dock that you want to become the active application.

You can also switch between open applications by holding down Command-Tab. This moves you through active applications in the Dock in the order in which they appear. When you reach the item you want to bring to the front, release the keys to select it.

Dropping is a shortcut for opening documents. To open a document in a specific application, you can drag and drop the document icon on top of the application icon. In Mac OS X, you can use the application's Dock icon instead of having to locate the real application file on your hard drive.

Also, to force a docked application to accept a dropped document that it doesn't recognize, hold down Command-Option when holding the document over the application icon. The application icon is immediately highlighted, enabling you to perform your drag-and-drop action. (Keep in mind, however, that many applications can only work with files in certain formats—forcing an application to open something it doesn't have the capacity to read won't get you very far!)

To remove an item from the Dock, make sure that the item isn't in use and drag it out of the Dock. It disappears in a puff of smoke (literally—try it and see).

In addition to providing easy access to commonly used applications, the Dock icons also give you feedback about the functions of their applications. While an application is loading, its icon begins to bounce (unless configured not to) and continues bouncing until the software is ready. Also, if an open application needs to get your attention, its icon bounces intermittently until you interact with it. The Dock also signals which applications are running by displaying a small triangle in those application icons. Some applications even customize the Dock's icons to display useful information, such as Mail's ability to show the number of new messages in its Dock icon.

Docked Windows, Files, and Folders

Let's talk about the left, or bottom, portion of the Dock. You can drag commonly used documents to this part of the Dock, and a link to them is stored for later use. You can also drag commonly used folders to this area of the Dock for easy access. Click-holding (or right-clicking) a docked folder displays a list of its contents and the contents of the subfolders in that folder.

Minimized windows labeled by the icon for their associated application are also placed in this portion of the Dock. In addition to easy window recognition, these window miniatures can serve another useful purpose. Depending on the application, minimized windows might continue to update as their associated applications attempt to display new information. QuickTime Player, for example, continues to play movies.

Trash Can

The next feature I'll discuss is the Trash (see Figure 2.19). That's the place you send your files and folders when you decide you no longer need them. The first figure shows the Trash is empty. The second, shown in Figure 2.20, shows the Trash filled with one or more files.

FIGURE 2.19
This trash can is empty.

FIGURE 2.20
The trash is full, and the files are ready to be zapped.

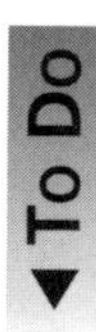

The Trash is also used for ejecting disks and CDs. To avoid user fears that this might hurt the contents of the disk, Mac OS X now conveniently changes the Trash icon into the Eject symbol when you drag a disk icon to it.

You don't have to use the Trash when ejecting disks. Ctrl-clicking a mounted volume opens a contextual menu with an Eject option. Alternatively, you can highlight the disk to remove and choose Eject (Command-E) from the Finder's File menu or press the Eject key on some models of the Apple USB keyboard.

Removing Trashed Files

To get rid of your files, simply follow these steps:

1. Click and drag a program's icon onto the trash can icon, which will be highlighted as soon as the icon is brought atop it. See Figure 2.21 for the effect.

FIGURE 2.21
When you release the mouse, the file is placed inside the trash can.

2. Choose Empty Trash from the Finder's application menu, which opens the request for confirmation, as shown in Figure 2.22.

When you click and hold the trash icon, you'll see an Empty Trash command, which is a fast way to delete its contents. But be forewarned: There is no second chance, no warning. When you choose this command, the contents of the trash are gone.

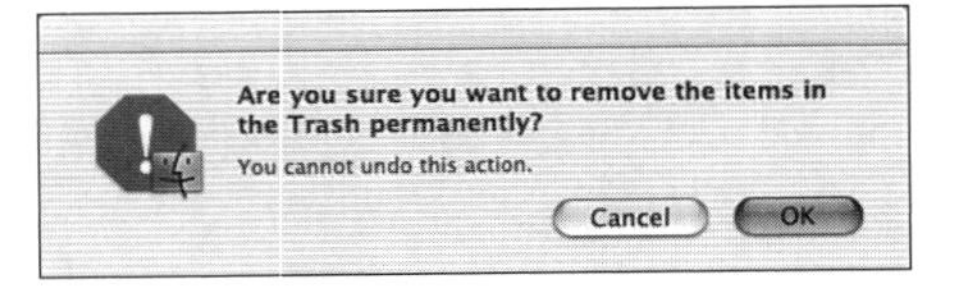

FIGURE 2.22
Do you really want to zap that file?

When you OK the message, the file will be history.

Before you empty the trash, be sure you really want to get rid of those files. If you're not certain, click Cancel. When you dump those files, they are gone, probably for good (although there are a few programs that might recover them if you make a mistake).

The Trash works like a folder. If you're not sure what's inside, just double-click it to open the directory list. If you decide not to trash something, click and drag that icon from it.

Customizing the Dock

After you get used to the idea of the Dock, you probably want to customize it to better suit your needs.

If you have a small monitor, you might want to resize the Dock icons to cover less area. The easiest and fastest way to resize the Dock is to click and hold on the separator bar that divides the Dock areas. As you click and hold on the separator bar, drag up and down or left and right (if your Dock is placed vertically). The Dock dynamically resizes as you move your mouse. Let go of the mouse button when the Dock has reached the size you want.

After playing with different Dock sizes, you might notice that some sizes look better than others. That's because Mac OS X icons come in several native icon sizes, and points between those sizes are scaled images. To choose only native icon sizes, hold down the Option key while using the separator bar to resize.

For more fine-tuning of the Dock, turn to the System Preferences panel. The Dock has a settings panel in System Preferences for adjusting its size and icon magnification and for making it disappear when not in use.

When you've made your selections, choose Quit (Command-Q) from the System Preferences application menu.

System Preferences

Mac OS X enables you to control many aspects of your system, from desktop appearance to user access. Conveniently, you can tailor these settings to your own needs from one centralized place, System Preferences, as shown in Figure 2.23.

To access System Preferences, simply click the Dock icon that resembles a light switch; it should be located in the row of icons at the bottom of your screen—or choose System Preferences from the Apple menu. As you can see in Figure 2.23, the elements of System Preferences are organized by function. We'll take a quick inventory of the preferences here, but you'll learn more details about System Preferences throughout this book as we discuss different topics.

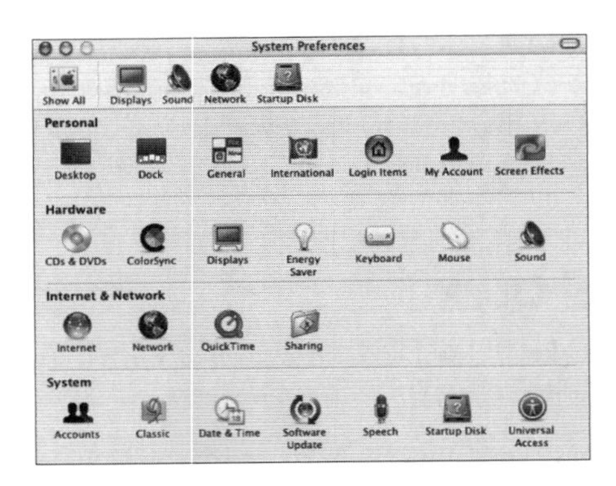

FIGURE 2.23
Mac OS X gives you a lot of ways to tailor Mac OS X to your needs.

When you've launched System Preferences, all you need to do is click an icon to open a specific settings panel. When you want to move to the next setting, you can either click an icon on the top of the System Preferences application, or click Show All to display all the icons in one place. For faster access, the preferences are all grouped into categories, and that's the way I'll cover them here.

Many of the settings made via the System Preferences application apply strictly to the user who is logged in when those settings are made. If other users are set up in the Users preference panel to work on your computer, they can set their own user settings, none of which will interfere with your own. The exceptions are those preference panels (such as Network and Sharing) that have a lock on the lower-left corner; these are settings that apply system wide and can only be accessed via someone with owner (administrator) access.

Setting Personal Preferences

From Desktop to Mac OS X's screensaver, these are the individual options that cover the way your computer interacts with you.

- **Desktop**—What sort of desktop pattern would you prefer? When you open the Desktop preference panel (shown in Figure 2.24), all you have to do is click a picture, drag it into the little well, and your computer's desktop background changes within a few seconds. Click the Collection pop-up menu to see more selections, or to locate one of your own folders for background use. If you don't like the one you pick, just choose another one, drop it into the well and the pattern will change.
- **Dock**—The colorful taskbar at the bottom of your Mac's screen doesn't have to stay in one place. Click the preference panel, shown in Figure 2.25, and choose whether it should sit on the bottom, left, or right side of the screen. You can also

select whether to use a Genie or Scale effect when a Finder window is minimized to the Dock. You can also set the size of the Dock, and whether it'll magnify when the mouse moves over it. The most visually arresting icon is the effect you see when you minimize a window. By default, it's the Genie effect, where it seems to shrink an animated effect. The option Scale effect reduces the window just by making it smaller as it drops to the Dock; less visual but faster.

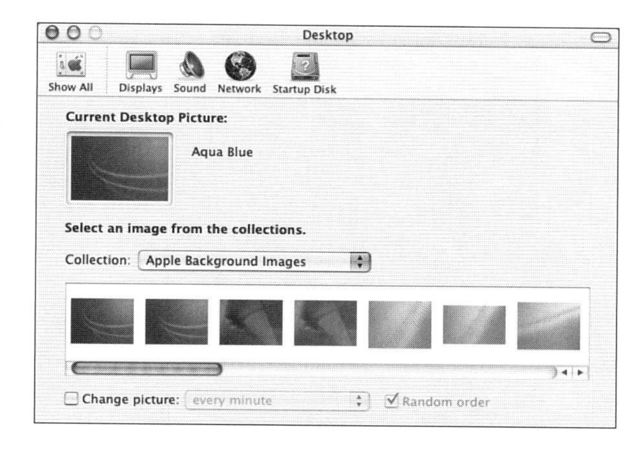

FIGURE 2.24
Drop the picture into the well to change Mac OS X's desktop pattern.

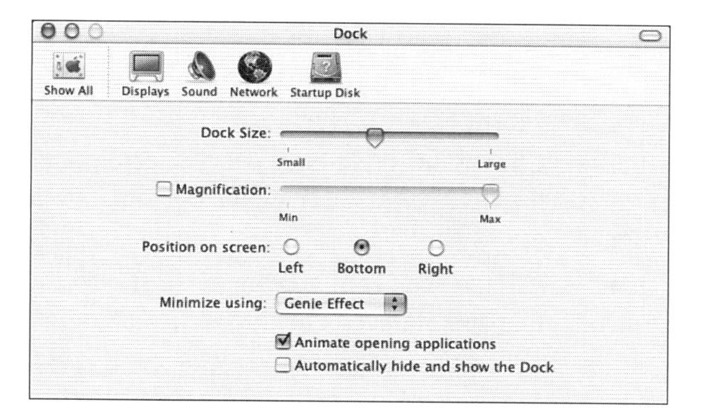

FIGURE 2.25
Use this preference panel to choose how the Dock works.

Would you like to impress your friends? When you minimize something to the Dock, or restore (maximize) a reduced window, hold down the Shift key. This will slow the Genie or Scale effect to a crawl. It's exactly what Apple CEO Steve Jobs does when he demonstrates Mac OS X during his famous keynote addresses at the Macworld Expo trade shows. After a while, you or your friends might tire of the effect, but it's fine to show it off on occasion.

- **General**—This preference panel, shown in Figure 2.26, covers several settings. First, there's the background theme (choose Aqua or Graphite and the highlight color). You can also choose how scroll arrows at the right side of the window appear, and how many recent items (applications and documents) are displayed in the Apple menu. The final setting covers the starting point for Mac OS X's font smoothing, which makes text appear less jagged on the screen. Feel free to experiment with any of these settings. They won't harm anything, and you can always put things back if you don't like the results.

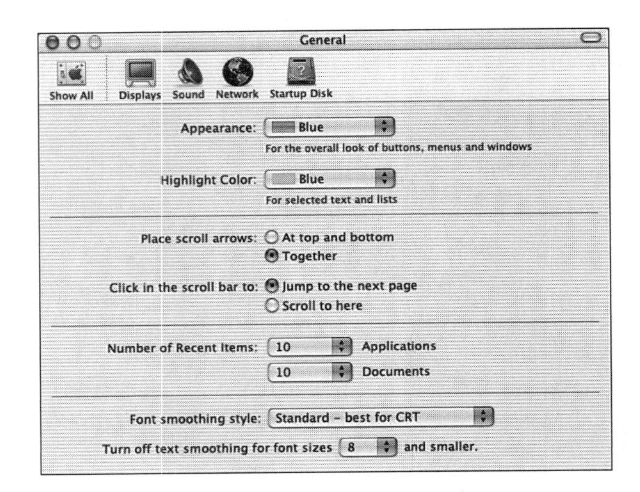

FIGURE 2.26
This setting controls basic appearance of your Mac OS X user environment.

- **International**—Choose this preference panel to determine which languages are preferred first. Mac OS X is an international operating system that works with many languages.
- **Login Items**—Here, you can configure an application to launch automatically whenever your computer starts by clicking the Add button to select the program.
- **My Account**—The settings under My Account enable users to change their own passwords, picture icons, and cards in the Address Book application. (We'll talk more about the Address Book in Chapter 4, "Using the Internet.") Some of the options in the My Account pane are repeated in the Users pane, which we will discuss a bit later.
- **Screen Effects**—Mac OS X gives you a neat screensaver (shown in Figure 2.27) that puts a fancy pattern on your Mac's screen when it's idle for a few minutes. Click the mouse, or any key on the keyboard, to dismiss it. After you select a pattern, click the Activation tab to specify how long your computer sits doing nothing before the screensaver is activated. You can click the Hot Corners tab to specify a location on your screen where you can activate the screensaver.

FIGURE 2.27
Use Mac OS X's screensaver to make your screen look pretty when it's idle.

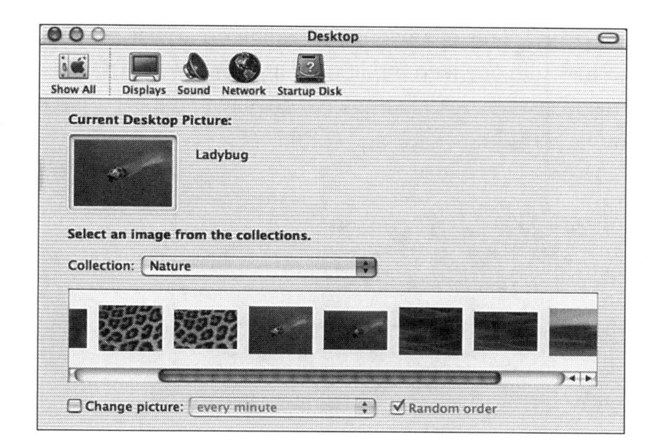

2

Setting Hardware Preferences

The next set of Mac OS X preference panels control how you interact with your hardware from mouse to monitor. I'll cover the essentials next.

- **CDs & DVDs**—This panel allows you to choose what your computer will do when a CD or DVD is inserted into your drive. The default settings, shown in Figure 2.28, launch the appropriate application when you insert a music CD, photo CD, or DVD. When you insert blank media, the Finder will prompt you to choose an application to suite your purpose.

FIGURE 2.28
Choose which application is activated when you insert a CD or DVD.

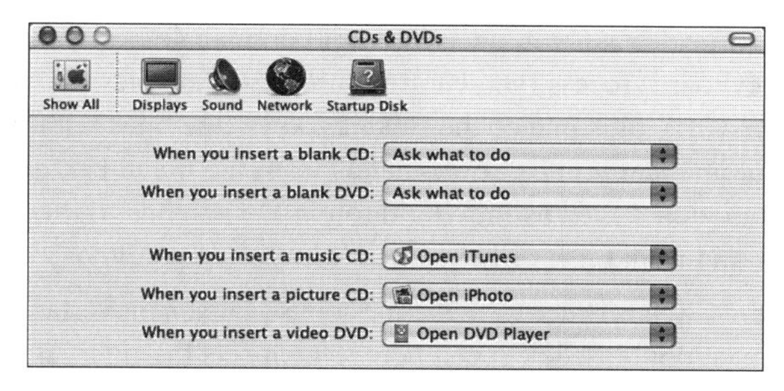

- **ColorSync**—This is a native Mac technology that enables you to match color from scanner to computer to printer. We'll talk about this further in Chapter 8, "Monitors and Colorsync."
- **Displays**—This preference panel is used to set color depth (the number of colors displayed) and the resolution of your desktop display. The Show Displays in the Menu Bar option enables you to change display settings from the menu bar without having to open System Preferences.

- **Energy Saver**—This is a way to cut down on power usage and also let your computer go into idle or Sleep mode after a given period of time, as shown in Figure 2.29. You can specify separate settings for display and hard drive by clicking the check box and moving the sliders back and forth.

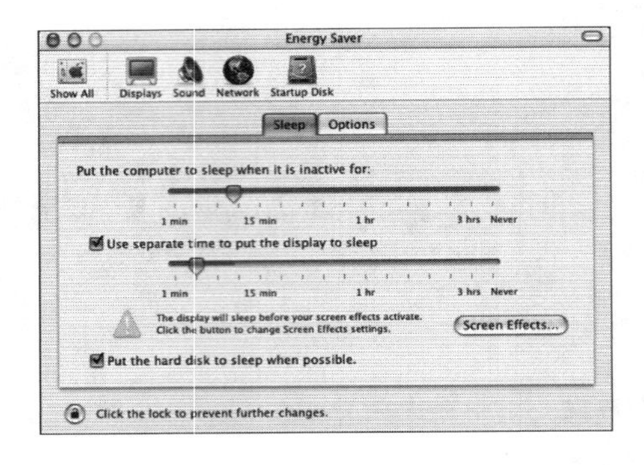

FIGURE 2.29
Specify the Sleep or rest interval from here.

Does your Mac's screen suddenly blank out? One possible reason is that it's been idle for a while and the Energy Saver preference settings have become active. To awaken your computer, just press any key on the keyboard and it'll come to life in seconds.

- **Keyboard**—There are two levels of settings here. One controls how fast keystrokes repeat when you press and hold down a key on the keyboard. The other, Full Keyboard Access (shown in Figure 2.30), enables you to press a modifier key (such as Ctrl), plus one of the function keys (the ones with the F1 to F15 on them). This automatically pulls down menus from the menu bar, and directly accesses other functions, such as moving through Dock icons, right from the keyboard. Try it! You might like it (I do!).
- **Mouse**—Click a slider to make the mouse cursor move faster or slower. You can also adjust double-click speed here, which sets the interval between the two clicks. Try a few settings and see which are most comfortable for you. If you're using an iBook, this panel controls the trackpad settings, too.

Do you access a particular preference very often? Some, such as Displays and Sound, have an option to put up a settings icon in the menu bar of the System Preferences window. You can also drag the item's icon to the top of the System Preferences window, just as Displays, Sound, Network, and Startup Disk appear now. By doing that, you save a step to access those features.

FIGURE 2.30

This range of settings enables your computer's keyboard to access menus, the Dock, active windows, and so on.

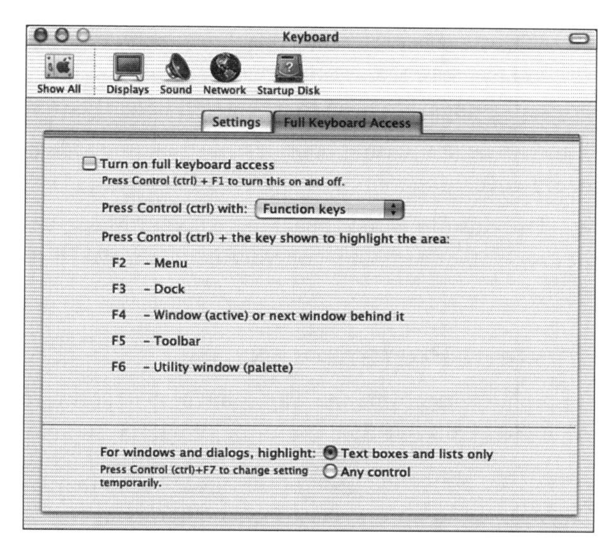

- **Sound**—Pick the sound levels for both system sounds and overall volume. If your Mac has a special set of speakers attached, such as the iSub or Harmon-Kardon SoundSticks, you might see additional options to adjust settings for these products. Choose the option to put the sound settings in the menu bar for fast access.

The standard Apple Pro keyboard also has three media keys (in the upper-right row) that set volume. One to reduce the level, the second to increase the level, and the third to mute (turn off) the sound.

Setting Internet and Network Preferences

The settings you choose in these preference panels control your Internet and network access, including file sharing, which is the capability to share your files with other computers. The QuickTime settings are used to make your computer work best with multimedia files. Let's go through the list:

- **Internet**—There are four settings offered in this preference panel that cover the way your computer works while online (except for some services provided such as AOL and CompuServe 2000, which don't use these settings). Click the .Mac tab to set up or configure your account with Apple's handy set of Web-based features. The iDisk tab shows you how much space you're using in your .Mac server space. The email tab is used to control the settings used to send and receive email. The Web tab enables you to select a home page (the page your browser calls on when you launch it), a default search site, and where downloaded files go (the default is on your Mac OS X desktop).

- **Network**—Choose this preference panel to specify how your computer interacts with a local network or your Internet connection. You'll need to contact your ISP for other user settings that need to be entered here. (See Chapter 4 for specifics.)
- **QuickTime**—The key setting optimizes a streaming video to your Internet-connection speed. I covered that in more detail in Chapter 5.
- **Sharing**—Use this preference panel to give your Mac a unique name and also to share files with other computers on your network. (We'll return to this panel in Chapter 27.)

Setting System Preferences

The final set of preferences covers the way some system software elements interact with you on your Mac. So here's our final run-through with System Preferences settings.

- **Accounts**—This preference panel is used for Mac OS X's multiple-users feature, which enables you to set up your Mac so other users can run it and have their own personal sets of documents, fonts, and preference settings. (We'll give this section special attention in Chapter 27.)
- **Classic**—Under Mac OS X, whenever you launch an old or Classic Mac OS application, the Classic environment is in use. This preference panel controls how Classic runs on your computer. The most useful option is to have it start whenever you start your Mac, so you don't have to wait an extra minute or so for it to get rolling when you run a Classic application.
- **Date & Time**—To keep your system's clock ticking accurately, this preference panel (shown in Figure 2.31) is called into play. The first setting, under the Date & Time tab, is used to change date and time (it doesn't work if automatic network time synchronization is chosen). The second, Time Zone, is used to specify your location so that your email and message board posts have the right date and time. The Network Time option is the most useful. You can click a time server from the NTP Server pop-up menu, and then have the time automatically adjusted whenever you are online and the time is found to be off or when your computer starts up. The final setting, Menu Bar Clock, is used to choose whether your clock is displayed as text or an icon, and whether such things as seconds and the day of the week are included in the display.
- **Software Update**—This is a clever feature of Mac OS X (shown in Figure 2.32) that will search out Apple's Web site for needed updates. When you click Automatically and specify an interval from the pop-up menu (Daily, Weekly, or Monthly), Software Update will go into action as soon as you make an Internet connection on the appointed day. Click Update Now to connect to your Internet account and see if any updates are available. If they are, a separate Software

Update application will open in the Dock. When you click that application, you'll see the list of updates along with some information on what they do. From here you can download the updates and they'll be installed after retrieved. (We'll revisit this option in Chapter 28, "Managing Your System.")

FIGURE 2.31
Click a tab to set Date & Time preferences.

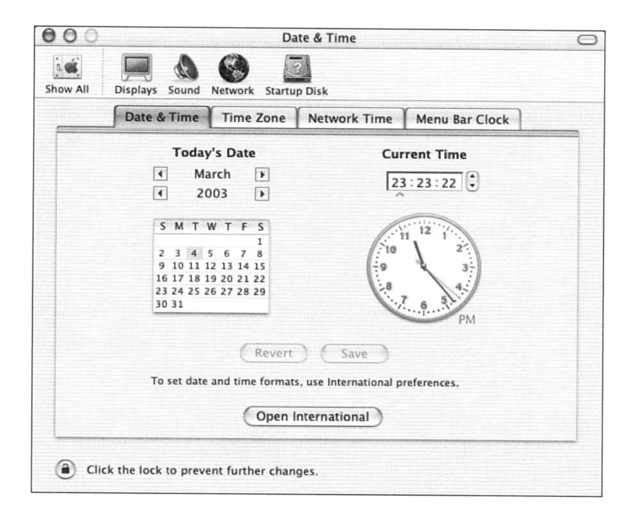

FIGURE 2.32
Like magic, Software Update figures out if Mac OS X needs an update and will give you the chance to receive those updates.

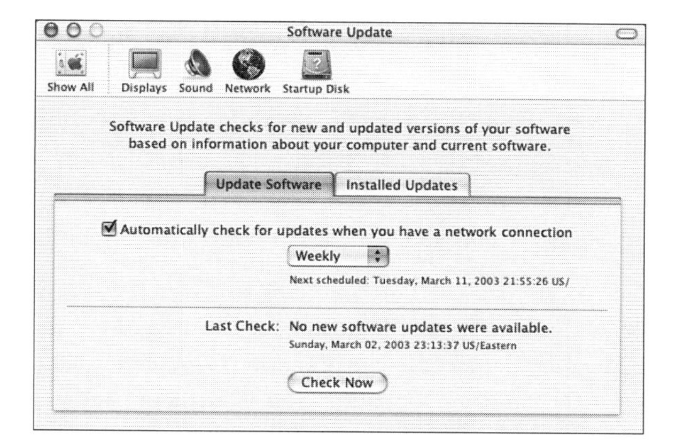

- **Speech**—Some day, you will be able to have a conversation with your computer (Computer, wash the dishes; Computer, take out the trash!), but right now Apple's Speech preference settings are pretty limited. You can have text read back to you in several preset voices (more or less, but not always perfectly), or use the Listening feature to hear simple commands in the spirit of Computer, Restart! Give it a try, but don't expect miracles.

- **Startup Disk**—This is the preference panel that enables you to restart your computer using a different hard drive partition, if one is set up. This is most commonly used by people who are able to start their computers directly in Mac OS 9.x, which may be necessary in order to run older Mac software that isn't compatible with OS X's Classic mode. (You'll learn more about running applications in Classic mode in Chapter 3.)
- **Universal Access**—These preferences allow users with disabilities to tailor their system to their abilities. Because there are several important features available here, we'll take an in-depth look at them in the next section.

Universal Access

The Universal Access Preferences enable you to interact with your computer in alternative ways to provide greater accessibility for those with disabilities. The Seeing and Hearing tabs contain special settings for users with low vision or poor hearing. If you have difficulty using the keyboard and the mouse, Universal Access also enables you to customize their sensitivity.

While you're in the Universal Access panel of System Preferences, your computer reads you the items under your cursor as if you've enabled the Text Under the Mouse option of the Spoken User Interface tab of the Speech panel.

Seeing

The options under the Seeing tab, shown in Figure 2.33, affect the size or contrast of the elements on screen.

Turn Zoom On activates a feature that enlarges the area of the display near the mouse cursor. Using key commands, you can zoom in (Command+Option++) several levels to examine text or detail in any application, and then zoom back out (Command+Option+-). In Zoom Options, features such as degree of magnification can be configured.

Switch to White on Black displays white detail on a dark background. You can also toggle the display between color and grayscale, which shows only white, black, and shades of gray.

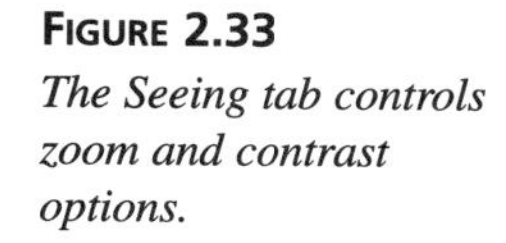

FIGURE 2.33
The Seeing tab controls zoom and contrast options.

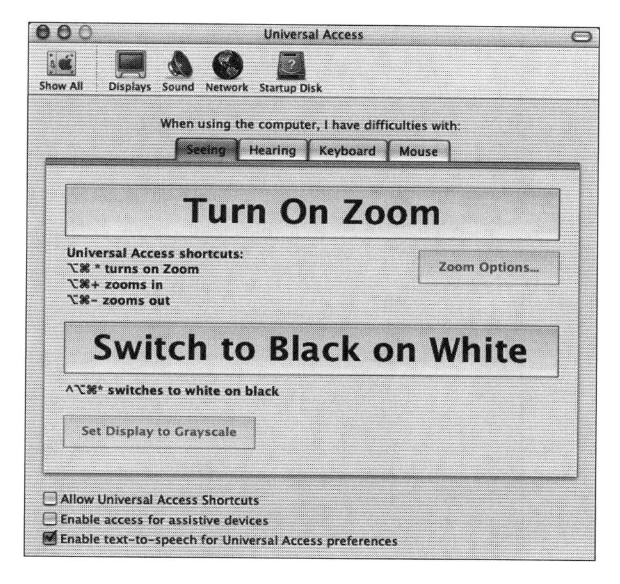

Hearing

The Hearing tab enables you to have your computer notify you of alert sounds by flashing the screen. You can also open the Sounds Preferences panel to adjust volume.

Keyboard and Mouse

The Keyboard tab is shown in Figure 2.34. The Sticky Keys option helps with typing key combinations, such as Command+C, so you can press only one key at a time. After Sticky Keys is set, you can turn the feature on or off by pressing the Shift key five times in succession. You can also use the Set Key Repeat button to open the Keyboard pane settings to minimize accidental multiple key presses.

For those who would rather use the numeric keypad than the mouse to direct the cursor, you can turn on Mouse Keys under the Mouse tab. Like Sticky Keys, Mouse Keys can be turned on or off by pressing the Option key (instead of Sticky Keys' Shift key) five times. The Mouse tab also contains settings to control mouse movement.

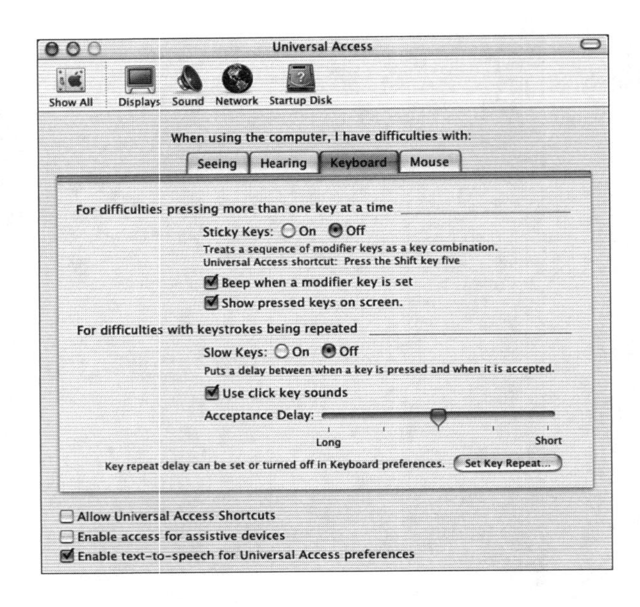

FIGURE 2.34
Change keyboard and mouse sensitivity in Universal Access.

Menu Extras

As we mentioned in a note earlier in this chapter, Mac OS X offers a feature that gives users quick access to common system settings: Menu Extras. They appear as icons at the upper right of the menu bar. A number of Menu Extras are shown in Figure 2.35.

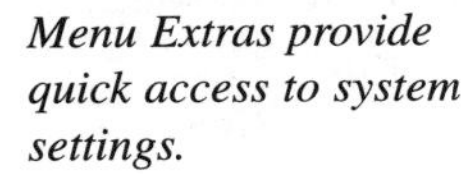

FIGURE 2.35
Menu Extras provide quick access to system settings.

Each Extra is added to the menu bar through individual Preferences panels that correspond to an item's function. You can activate or deactivate an Extra by clicking the Show *<option>* in Menu Bar check box for the corresponding option. For example, under Displays in the Hardware group, you can turn on the Displays Menu Extra.

A few of the Menu Extras available under Mac OS X include

- **Date & Time**—Displays the time and date graphically as a miniature clock or by using the standard text format.
- **Displays**—Adjusts the resolution and color depth of the display from the menu bar.
- **Volume**—Changes the sound volume.
- **Battery**—For PowerBook and iBook users, this option tracks battery usage and recharge time.

- **AirPort**—Monitors AirPort signal strength and quickly adjusts network settings. (The AirPort is a device that enables computers to be connected to the Internet without wires. It's discussed further in Chapter 7, "Choosing Peripheral Devices.")

Clicking a Menu Extra opens a pop-up menu that displays additional information and settings. Items such as Battery and Date & Time can be modified to show textual information rather than a simple icon status representation, as shown in Figure 2.36.

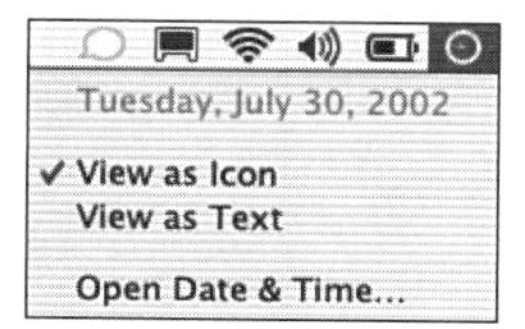

FIGURE 2.36
Set the time or switch between icon view and text view.

Users can alter the order of Menu Extras by holding down the Command key and dragging an icon to a different position.

Summary

In this lesson, you learned how to use the elements on your computer desktop, including Finder menus and windows and the Dock. You also discovered how your computer's Trash feature enables you to remove unwanted items. Finally, we talked about System Preferences, which allow you to customize your computer so that it looks and runs better.

CHAPTER 3

Working with Windows, Folders, Files, and Applications

Have you kept up with me so far? In the first two chapters, you've set your computer and operating system and discovered the neat, orderly Mac desktop, which is designed to mimic a typical office desk in terms of layout.

On your computer screen, you see a visual representation of what you want (an icon), and you use your mouse or keyboard to select and work with that item. In this chapter you will learn how to interact with windows, folders, files, and applications.

Windows

While Finder windows were introduced in the last chapter during our discussion of the file system, here we are going to take an up-close look at windows and their use. Basically, windows are holders that appear on your desktop to display whatever you are working on. Finder windows contain listings of folder, files and applications, while application windows provide a workspace where you can write a document, view an image, or do whatever it is the application was designed for.

To make an open window active, you click it (it makes the title black and brings it to the front). Every time you open a folder or drive of any kind (including your hard drive as we discussed in the last chapter) by double-clicking it, it opens a Finder display window (see Figure 3.1). The one I'm showing here is the icon view.

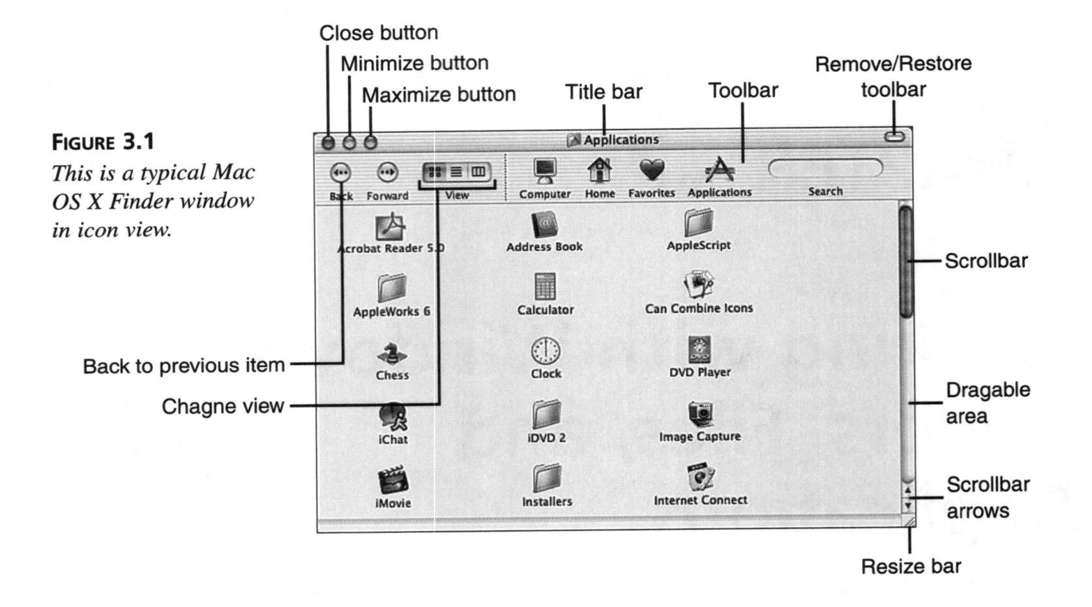

FIGURE 3.1
This is a typical Mac OS X Finder window in icon view.

Close/Minimize/Zoom

In the upper-left corner of each window are the Close (red ×), Minimize (yellow –), and Zoom (green +) buttons. Differentiated only by color and position, the corresponding symbol appears in each button when the mouse cursor nears.

If you choose the Graphite appearance option in the General panel in the System Preferences icon, you won't see the colors. Regardless of the appearance choice you make, when you move your mouse over a button, you'll see an "×" appear in the Close button, a "-" in the Minimize button and a "+" in the Maximize button to remind you of what it does.

Clicking the Close button closes the open window. The Mac OS X Minimize button shrinks the window into an icon view and places it in the Dock. This icon is a miniature of the original window—down to the items it contains. In some cases, the icon even updates its appearance when the parent application generates new output. Clicking the icon in the Dock restores the window to its original position and size on the screen.

When you close a document window, you aren't closing the program. The program remains active until you choose Quit from the application menu—or the File menu in a Classic Mac OS application—or press Command-Q.

Double-clicking the title bar of a window has the same effect as clicking the Minimize button. The window shrinks to fit in the Dock.

The keyboard shortcut Command-M also minimizes the current window and reduces it to an icon on the right side of the Dock (M = minimize). To make a minimized icon larger again, just click once on that icon in the Dock.

The Zoom button (usually) opens the window to the size necessary to display the available information. Most Windows PC users expect the maximized window to fill the entire screen. However, if there are only three icons to be shown, Mac OS X doesn't waste space by filling up your window with blank space.

Holding down Option while clicking the Minimize or Close button results in all the windows in the current application being minimized or closed.

Hide/Show Toolbar

In the upper-right corner of some windows (including the windows for the Finder and applications such as Mail and Preview, which we'll look at in some later chapters) is an elongated button, called Hide/Show Toolbar, that can be used to quickly show or hide special toolbars in the top of the application window. The result of hiding the toolbar in the Mail application is shown in Figure 3.2.

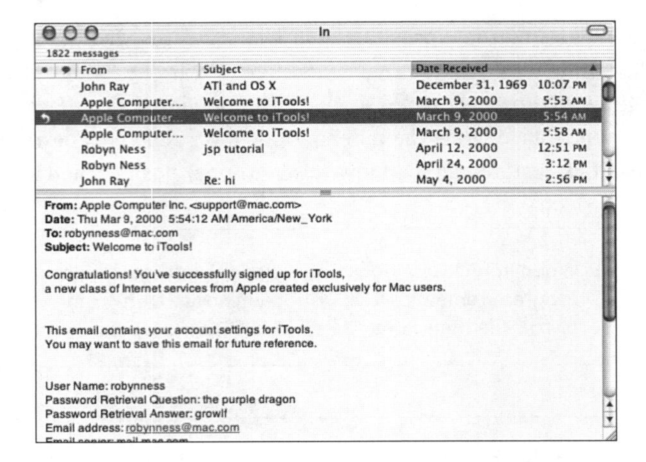

FIGURE 3.2
With the task toolbar hidden, the window occupies less screen space.

Apple advocates toolbars in applications to increase usability and efficiency. However, because individual developers must write their programs to support the toolbar button, you shouldn't expect all applications with toolbars to have the Hide/Show Toolbar button.

The toolbar version of the Finder window provides several useful controls for viewing and navigating your files.

In the upper-left corner of the toolbar are the Back and Forward arrows—click it to return to the previous folder. Using this technique, you can dig many levels deep into the file system, and then quickly back out by using the Back button. The Forward arrow enables you to follow the same path back to inner levels.

By default, there are several other elements in the toolbar, as shown in Figure 3.1. From left to right, you see the View selector, buttons to Computer, Home, Favorites, and Applications, and the Search text entry field.

Separate from the Finder toolbar is the status bar, which shows the number of items in a folder and the amount of space available on the drive. The status bar can be toggled on and off by using the Show/Hide Status Bar command in the Finder's View menu. The status bar can also contain one of two icons in the left corner of the bar: a grid pattern that indicates use of the snap-to-grid function, and a pencil with a slash through it that indicates a folder is read-only.

Finder Window View Options

Let's take a look at the view options for Finder windows. Three buttons in the View selector enable you to control the way information is displayed in the Finder window.

Icon View

The first time you log in, the Finder is in toolbar mode and using Icon view. If you've already been using the Finder and are no longer in Icon view, you can quickly switch to Icon view by choosing As Icons from the View menu or by clicking the first button in the View selector of the toolbar. Figure 3.1 shows the Finder window in Icon view. In Icon view mode, you can navigate through the folders on your drive by double-clicking them.

List View

The next view to explore is the Finder's List view. You can switch to List view by clicking the middle button in the Finder's View selector or, if the toolbar isn't present, by choosing As List from the Finder's View menu. Demonstrated in Figure 3.3, the List view is a straightforward means of displaying all available information about a file or folder in tabular form.

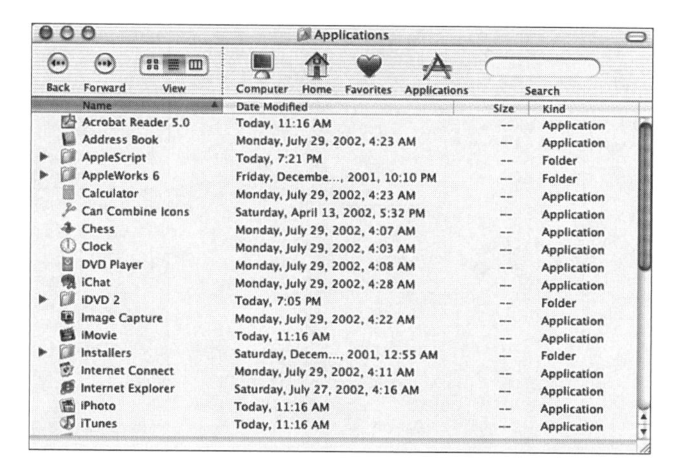

FIGURE 3.3
List view packs a lot of information into a small amount of space.

The columns in the List view represent the attributes for each file. Clicking a column highlights it and sorts the file listing based on that column's values. For example, if you want to locate the most recent files in a folder, you can view the folder contents in List view and click the Date Modified header. By default, the column values are listed in descending order. Clicking a column header again reverses the sorting order. An arrow pointing up or down at the right of each column indicates the current sort order.

You can change the width of the columns by placing the mouse cursor at the edge of the column and click-dragging to the left or right. You can reposition the columns by clicking and dragging them into the order you want. However, the first column, Name, cannot be repositioned.

When a folder appears in the file listing, a small disclosure triangle precedes its name. Clicking the triangle reveals the file hierarchy within that folder. As with Icon view, double-clicking a folder anywhere in this view either opens a new window (if you're in toolbar-less mode) or refreshes the contents of the existing window with the new location.

Column View

Unlike other views, which can either overwhelm you with information or require multiple windows to move easily from point to point, the Column view is designed with one thing in mind: ease of navigation.

The concept is very simple: Click an item in the first column and its contents are shown in the next column. Click a folder in this new column and its contents are shown in the next column, and so on. Figure 3.4 shows a multicolumn display that reaches down two levels.

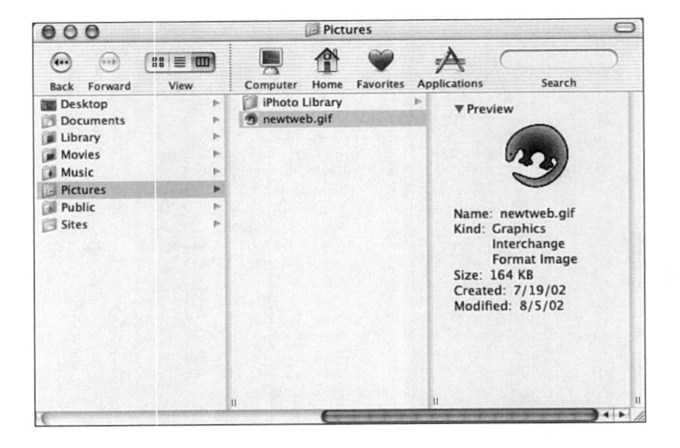

FIGURE 3.4
Using the Column view, you can easily navigate through the folders on your hard drive.

If you use the horizontal scrollbar to move back along a path, the folders you've chosen remain highlighted in the columns. You can, at any time, choose a different folder from any of the columns. This refreshes the column to the right of your choice. There's no need to start from the beginning every time you want to change your location.

One *big* bonus of using Column view is the ability to instantly see the contents of a file without opening it. If you choose a file or application, a preview or description of the selected item appears in the column to the right. For an example, take a look at the far right column in Figure 3.4, where a representation of an image file is displayed. When you choose an application or a file that cannot be previewed, only information about the file is displayed, such as the creation/modification dates, size, and version.

Show View Options

For each of the three Finder window views, there are additional settings that you can customize by choosing Show View Options from the View menu. You can also choose whether your changes apply to the current window only or to all Finder windows.

For Icon view, you can scale icons from the smallest to largest size by dragging the Icon Size slider from the left to the right. You can choose how the icon is labeled, including the font size and label placement. You can set how the icons are arranged and what color the window background is.

List view enables you to choose small or larger icons, text size, and which columns of information to display with the filenames.

Column view gives you options for text size and whether to include icons in the preview column. There are no global settings for this view.

Customizing Toolbar Shortcuts

You can customize your Finder toolbar by adding other predefined Mac OS X shortcuts or by removing the default items in this way:

1. Choose Customize Toolbar from the View menu.
2. From the window containing all the available shortcuts (shown in Figure 3.5), locate the item you want to add.

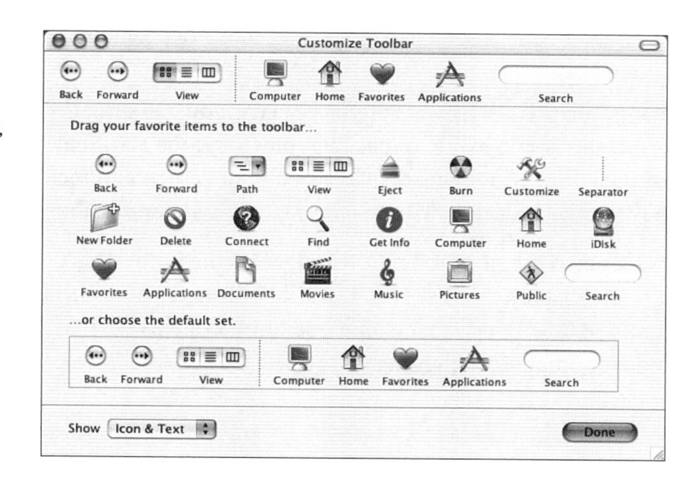

FIGURE 3.5
Finder shortcuts give you single-click access to applications, folders, and special features.

3. Add a shortcut by dragging it from the window to wherever you want it to appear on the toolbar.

In addition to these predefined options, users can define their own shortcuts. To do this, simply drag common applications, documents, and folders to any place on the toolbar.

When you modify your toolbar, it's modified for all Finder windows in your workspace, not just the currently open folder. However, the changes that you make to your toolbar don't affect other user accounts on the same computer.

When folders and applications are added to the toolbar, a single click on the icon opens or launches the selected item. Users can also drag documents onto an application icon or folder icon in the toolbar to open the file by using the application or to move the file into a folder.

Window Scrolling, Moving, and Resizing

Because windows can't always to be large enough to show everything inside them at once, they support a feature called scrolling. Scrolling allows you move the viewable area of a window's contents by moving up and down (or left and right). The tools that allow scrolling appear on the left for vertically scrolling and on the bottom for horizontal scrolling. Here is a description of each:

- **Scroll arrow**—Click it to move up or down slightly through a directory or document window. Hold down the mouse when clicking an arrow to get a continuous motion.
- **Scrollbar**—Click and drag on this bar to move back and forth through your folder list or document. The distance you can move depends on how big the listing or document is.
- **Draggable area**—This is the place where you can drag the scrollbar (see following). If the area is white rather than blue (and the scrollbar isn't there), it means that the entire window is displayed on your screen and there's nothing to scroll to. You'll notice that there's both a horizontal and vertical draggable area.

Another characteristic of Mac OS X windows is the borderless content area. As shown in Figure 3.6, the display in most Mac OS X application windows stretches to the edge of the content window. In contrast, some operating systems such as Mac OS 9 and Windows offer window borders for dragging.

FIGURE 3.6
The content in a window goes right to the edge.

To drag a window, you must grab it by its title bar.

Just hold down the Command key and click a title and you'll see a little pop-up menu that shows you a list of all the folders where the item is located (sometimes called a folder hierarchy).

To resize a window, click and drag the resize icon in the lower-right corner of each window. Many applications in Mac OS X take advantage of live resizing; that is, as you resize the window, its contents adjust in real-time (such as Web pages in Internet Explorer). However, unless you have a fast computer, live resizing can be slow.

There are a few new tricks you can use when working with Mac OS X windows. If you hold down the Command key, you can drag inactive windows located behind other windows. If fact, holding down Command enables you to click buttons and move scrollbars in many background applications.

Another fun trick is holding down the Option key while clicking on an inactive application's window. This hides the frontmost application and brings the clicked application to the front.

Finally, rather than switching to another window to close, minimize, or maximize it, positioning your cursor over the appropriate window controls highlights them—enabling you to get rid of obtrusive windows without leaving your current workspace.

Window Widgets

In addition to scrollbars and resize boxes, there are several other interface controls you need to know about. We'll call them *window widgets*. Samples of many of the Mac OS X Aqua window widgets are shown in Figure 3.7.

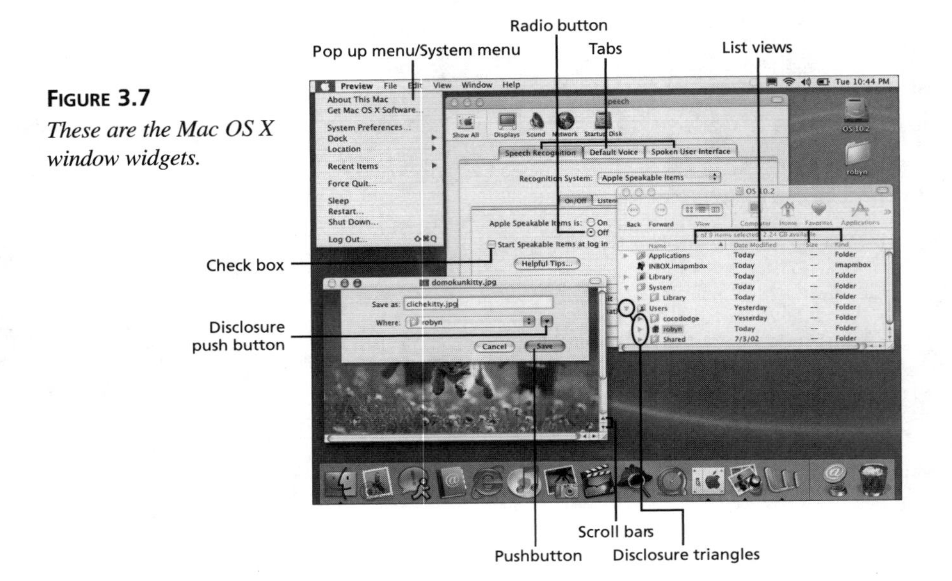

FIGURE 3.7
These are the Mac OS X window widgets.

Aqua interface elements include the following:

- **Pushbuttons**—Pushbuttons are rendered as translucent white or aqua ovals with appropriate label text. They're typically used to activate a choice or to respond to a question posed by the operating system or application. The default choice, which is activated by pressing the Enter key, pulses for easy visual confirmation.
- **Check boxes/radio buttons**—Check boxes are used to choose multiple attributes (AND), whereas radio buttons are used to choose between attributes (OR).
- **List views**—Clicking a category, such as the Date Modified heading shown in Figure 3.7, sorts by that selection. Clicking the category again reverses the direction of the sort (ascending to descending or vice versa). To resize category headings, click the edge of the heading and drag in the direction you want to shrink or expand the column.
- **Pop-up menus/system menus**—Single-clicking a menu drops down the menu until you make a selection. The menu can stay down indefinitely. With Mac OS X's multitasking system, other applications can continue to work in the background while the menu is down.

- **Disclosure triangles**—Disclosure triangles continue to work as they always have. Click the triangle to reveal additional information about an object.
- **Disclosure pushbuttons**—Like disclosure triangles, these pushbuttons are used to reveal all possible options (a full, complex view) or to reduce a window to a simplified representation. They are used in the new File Save sheets.
- **Scrollbars**—Scrollbars visually represent the amount of data in the current document by changing the size of the scrollbar slider in relation to the data to display. The larger the slider, the less data there is to scroll through. The smaller the slider, the more information there is to display.
- **Tabs**—Tabs separate settings within a single window into categories by their functions, and you can see different options in each tab. By breaking up long lists in this way, windows with many options are less overwhelming, but you might have to click between tabs to find the control options you're looking for.

Sheet Windows and Window Trays

Two unique interface elements are sheets and window trays. Normally, when a computer wants to get your attention, it displays a dialog box containing a question such as, "Do you want to save this document?". If you have 10 open documents on your system, how do you know which one needs to be saved?

Sheet windows are used in place of such traditional dialog boxes. Sheets connect directly to the title bar of an open window. As shown in Figure 3.8, these messages appear inside the window they're associated with, so you'll be able to tell what the question you're answering will affect.

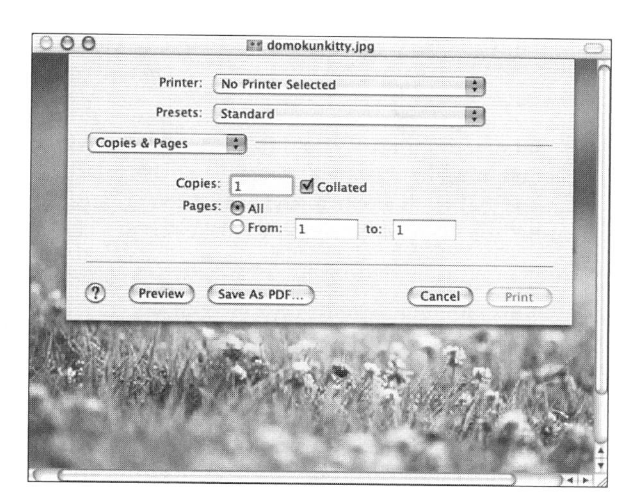

FIGURE 3.8
The sheet appears to drop from an open window's title bar.

Sheets are used just like regular dialog boxes, except that they're attached to a document. Unlike many dialog boxes, which keep you from interacting with the rest of the system until you attend to them, sheets limit access only to the window in which they appear.

A window tray is an interface element that can be used by software programmers. A tray is used to store commonly used settings and options that might need to be accessed while a program is running. Figure 3.9 shows the Mail application's window tray holding a list of active mailboxes.

FIGURE 3.9
Window trays hold options that are needed often during a program's execution.

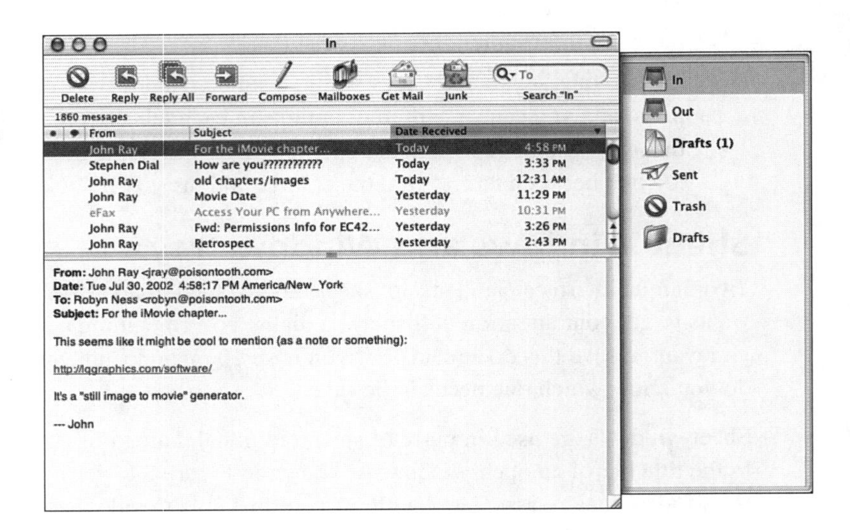

To use active trays in applications that support their use, you typically click a button in the toolbar. After a tray is open, you can drag its edge to change the tray's size.

By default, the tray slides out from the right of the main window after you click a button to activate it. If the window is too close to the side of the screen, the tray is either forced out on the other side of the window or pushes the main window over to make room.

Now that we're comfortable with what windows can do, let's take a look at folders.

Folders

In computer terminology, a folder is the computer equivalent to your file folder in your office, and it has a similar look, as shown in Figure 3.10.

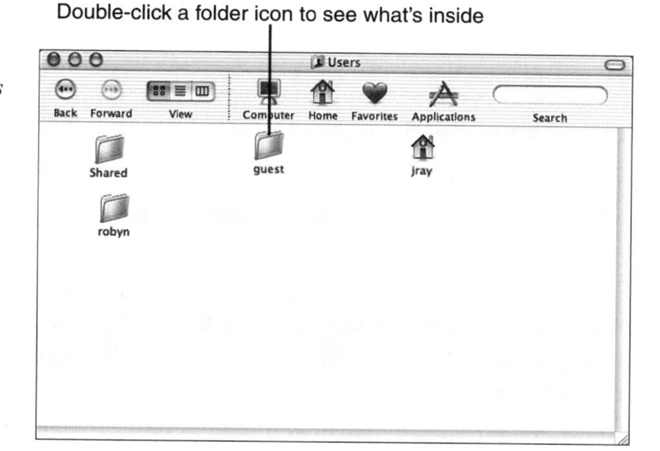

FIGURE 3.10
A folder on your Mac's desktop can hold a file or simply another folder (or many of each).

3

A fast way to find the folder you want among those listed is to type the first letter of the icon's name on your keyboard. The first folder with that letter in it will be selected (highlighted) and will appear bright as day. Who said you always need a mouse?

You can easily reorganize your desktop simply by clicking and dragging on a folder and putting it inside another folder (or pulling it out of one).

It's so easy to move folder and file icons around that you can easily move things that shouldn't be moved. Don't move the files that are within an application's folder because the program might not run if all its files aren't in place. Don't touch any of the files in the Mac OS X Library folder or System folder unless you understand the consequences. Moving the wrong file to the wrong place might prevent your computer from running or starting properly. Fortunately, you cannot move files from the Mac OS X System folder (they are copied instead). If you accidentally move a file, the only solution is to put it back where you found it (otherwise, you might have to undergo a reinstallation of the application or the Mac OS itself—a fix we will discuss further in Chapter 29, "Recovering from Crashes and Other Problems").

Working with folders is simple. You click it once, and then drag the icon to move it somewhere. You double-click it to view its contents.

In addition, there are some neat ways to move things around using the keyboard.

Here are some of the things you can do without ever touching a mouse. The techniques work for both folder and file icons (way cool):

- Use the arrow keys on the keyboard to move from icon to icon. Movement is in the direction the arrow points (up, down, left, right).
- Use the Tab key to move from one icon to the next in alphabetical order.
- Hold down the Shift key if you want to select more than one consecutive folder at a time.
- Hold down the Option key when you double-click a folder icon to open that icon, *and also* close the parent folder the icon is in. So, if you double-click an icon inside the Applications folder, while holding down the Option key, the Applications folder is itself closed.
- Hold down the Option key when you drag a file or folder icon to another folder's icon, and you'll make a copy of the original. The original will just stay where it is.
- Hold down the Cmd key when you want to separately select two or more folders that aren't next to each other.

Files

Compared to a folder, the file icon actually does something other than just function as a container. If you double-click a program's icon, you open the program itself. When you open a file, it does two things: launches the program that made the file, and then opens the folder and brings it onto your screen. I'll cover the elements of a directory and document window a bit later in this lesson.

The great thing about the Mac Operating System is that many of the skills you use to handle folder icons work in the very same way as file icons. So, you don't have to learn anything new to work with them. This is one of the wonderful features that makes the system so easy to master.

Applications

As you may have gathered from the discussion of the Applications folder in the previous chapter, applications are computer programs designed for various purposes. Applications appear as icons on the desktop just like folder and files, and can be worked with in the same way.

Be careful about renaming application icons. The Mac OS Finder keeps a directory of document and program links that enable you to double-click a file to open the program. If you rename the program's icon, however, (such as calling your AppleWorks software "The Great Starship"), it might upset those links. There's nothing to prevent you from changing a document file's name, though.

To launch an application, locate its icon in the Applications folder (or wherever it may have been saved), and double-click it. (Note that some applications' icons appear in the Dock as well as in a folder on your desktop. You can launch them by clicking on their docked icons.) While an application is opening, its icon will appear to bounce in the Dock until it is ready for use. (At the end of this chapter we will talk about how to use a special kind of application that was written to operate in an older Mac operating system.)

There is another way to launch applications—by simply double-clicking a file that was created by an application. This makes sense, because in order for the file to open, its parent application will also need to be running.

In cases where you want to open a file in an application other than its parent application, you can use a technique called *dropping*. To open a document in a specific application, you can drag and drop the document icon on top of the application icon, either in a folder window or the Dock. Also, to force a docked application to accept a dropped document that it doesn't recognize, hold down Command-Option when holding the document over the application icon. The icon is immediately highlighted, enabling you to perform your drag-and-drop action.

Opening Unrecognized Files

If you attempt to double-click a document that the system does not recognize, Mac OS X warns you that there is "no application available to open the document." If you're sure that a program on your system is capable of viewing the file, select the Choose Application option. You are prompted to choose the application that can open the file.

By default, the system tries to guess the best application for the job—but sometimes it fails. If the system doesn't allow you to pick the appropriate application, change the selection in the Show pop-up menu to read All Applications rather than Recommended Applications.

Force-Quitting Applications with the Process Manager

A feature that's sometimes necessary when using applications is Force Quit, which exits a program that has stopped responding. In Mac OS X, the Option-Command-Esc keystroke brings up a process manager that contains a list of running applications. Applications that the system deems to have stopped responding are marked in red. To force an application to close, choose it in the list and click the Force Quit button.

Forcing an application to quit does not save any open documents. Be sure that the application is truly stalled, not just busy, before you use this feature.

You can also access the Force Quit feature from the Apple menu, or by opening the pop-up Dock menu for a running application and pressing the Option key to toggle the standard Quit selection to Force Quit. If the system deems that an application has stopped responding, a Force Quit option appears in the Dock pop-up menu.

If the Finder seems to be misbehaving, you can choose it from the application list. The Force Quit button becomes the Relaunch button, enabling you to quit and restart the Finder without logging out.

Creating Aliases

Now that you know about folders, files and Applications, let's take a look at aliases that can help you manage them. Aliases are shortcuts or points that represent a folder, file, or application. They let you have access to anything you need from anywhere you need it—without making redundant copies or moving the original from its current location.

If you move the alias of a file to the trash, the original is not deleted, just the alias. If you really want to delete the original, too, you need to drag both icons to the trash. If you trash the original and not the alias, the latter becomes nonfunctional, although the Finder will usually give you the chance to pick another file for it to point to when it's double-clicked.

Figure 3.11 shows an alias icon. The little arrow at the lower left indicates that this is not the actual folder or file, but a pointer to it (hence the arrow). Double-click this alias icon for a folder, and you'll see the contents of the original folder.

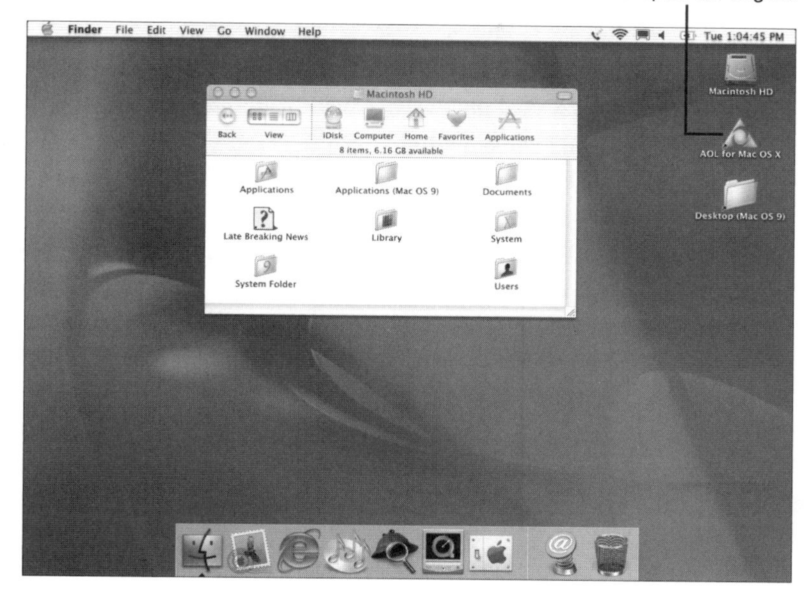

FIGURE 3.11
Not live, but Memorex, or rather an alias or pointer to the original icon.

To create an alias for an original file, folder, or application, press Command-L when you select an icon. You can also click the File menu and choose the Make Alias command, or hold down Command-Option while dragging a folder, to accomplish the same thing.

> A fast way to know if an icon is an alias is the icon itself. If it's an alias, it'll always have a little upward-pointing arrow at the lower left. Another way to see whether it's an alias is to select the icon and choose Get Info from the Finder's File menu. Under Kind, it'll say it's an Alias.

Renaming, Copying, and Deleting

To rename a file or folder in the Finder, click once to select the file, and click a second time on the file's name. The filename will become editable in a few seconds. Alternatively, you can use the Get Info option in the Finder File menu (Command-I) to edit the name in a larger field. (We'll be looking at the Get Info option in depth in just a moment.)

Copying

Copying a file or folder creates an exact duplicate of an original. (Note that this is different from creating an alias to a file, which is just a pointer and not a separate object.) The new file contents and creation/modification dates are identical to those of the original. There are a number of ways to create a copy in Mac OS X:

- **Drag a file to a different disk**—Dragging a file to a disk other than the one it is currently stored on creates a copy with the same name as the original.
- **Drag a file while holding down the Option key**—If you drag a file to a folder on the same disk it is currently located in while holding down the Option key, a duplicate of that file is created in the new location. The copy has the same name as the original.
- **Choose Duplicate from the contextual or Finder menu**—If you want to create an exact duplicate of a file within the same folder, highlight the file to copy, and then choose Duplicate from the Finder's File menu (Command-D), or Ctrl-click the icon and choose Duplicate from the pop-up contextual menu. A new file is created with the word *copy* appended to the name.

As the file is copied, the Finder displays an alert box in which you can see the progress of the copy operation. If multiple copies are taking place at the same time, the statuses of the operations are shown stacked on one another in the Copy alert box.

If you attempt to copy over existing files, the Finder prompts you and asks whether you want to replace the files. Also, if you attempt to replace existing files to which you don't have access, the copy operation fails.

Deleting

As you may recall from the previous chapter, your Mac allows you to delete items from the desktop, and consequently from your hard drive. It is very important to remember that deleting files and folders permanently removes them from your system.

Like copying a file, there are a number of ways to delete one:

- **Drag to Dock Trash**—Dragging an icon from a Finder window into the Dock's Trash is one of the most obvious and easy ways to get rid of a file.
- **Finder toolbar**—A Delete shortcut can be added to the Finder's toolbar (refer to the section above on customizing Finder window toolbars for details). Any items selected can be quickly moved to the Trash by clicking the Delete shortcut. Delete is *not* one of the default toolbar icons.

Moving an item on your desktop to the Trash does not delete it permanently. Instead, it places the item inside the trash folder. The Trash icon in the Dock fills with crumpled paper when it contains items waiting to be deleted. To completely remove a file from your system, choose Empty Trash from the Finder's Application menu or press Shift-Command-Delete.

If you want to rescue a file you've accidentally sent to the Trash, you can click the Trash icon and drag the file's icon out of the window.

Getting File Information

The Info window can display detailed information, such as graphical previews and user permissions, about your files and folders. The default view of the Info window can be displayed by selecting the file you want to examine in the Finder, and then choosing Get Info (Command-I) from the File menu. As shown in Figure 3.12, the General section supplies basic facts about the selected resource.

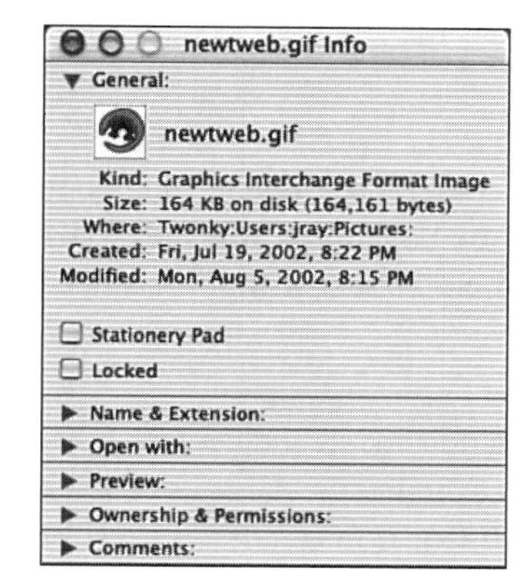

FIGURE 3.12
General information includes basic size, location, and type information about a file.

If the file you're viewing is an alias file (remember, an *alias* is a shortcut to the place where the real file is stored), the General section shows the location of the original file along with a Select New Original button that enables you to pick a new file to which the alias should be attached.

Name & Extension

When you name your documents, you may include a *file extension*—a period followed by several letters at the end of a name that indicates what kind of file it is. Common examples of file extensions are `.doc` for Microsoft Word documents and `.html` for Web pages. The Name & Extension section enables you to choose whether to view the filename with or without its extension. For folders and applications, the Name & Extension section simply shows the name of the item. Many other operating systems rely on file extensions to identify file types. If you plan to exchange files with other systems (Windows), you might want to verify that your files include them before sending them through e-mail and so on.

Open with Application

If you select a document icon (not an application or a folder), you should be able to access the Open With section in the Info window. If you download a file from a non–Mac OS X system, your computer might not realize what it needs to do to open the file. The Open With section enables you to configure how the system reacts.

To use this feature, click the disclosure triangle next to Open With. The default application name is shown as the current choice in a pop-up menu containing alternative application choices. Use the pop-up menu to display options and make a selection. If the application you want to use isn't shown, choose Other, and then use the standard Mac OS X File dialog box to browse to the application you want to use.

If you have a group of files that you want to open with a given application, you can select the entire group and follow the same procedure, or use the Change All button at the bottom of the window to update all files on your system simultaneously.

Content Index

When you view the Info panel for a folder, the Content Index option enables you to index the folder's contents or check the last time it was indexed. Indexing allows searches on a folder to be performed on the text within files, not just on the filenames.

Preview

If you select a QuickTime-recognized document, another Get Info option is available: Preview. Preview enables you to quickly examine the contents of a wide variety of media files, including MP3s, CD audio tracks (AIFFs), JPEGs, GIFs, TIFFs, PDFs, and many more.

If you're previewing a video or audio track, the QuickTime Player control appears and enables you to play the file's contents. Figure 3.13 shows a movie trailer being played within the Preview section.

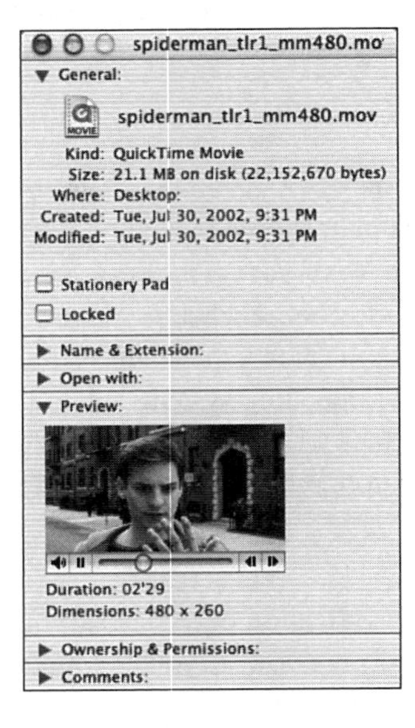

FIGURE 3.13
Play movie files using the Finder's Get Info Preview feature.

If you select a folder or an application, the Preview section displays its icon.

Languages

For an application, the Info panel includes a section called Languages that enables you to see which languages the application recognizes. If you uncheck the currently active language, the application's menus are presented in another available language the next time you open it.

Ownership & Permissions

Mac OS X is a multiuser system, and by default all the files and folders on your system identify themselves with the user who created them. That means only the owner can move or modify them. Applications have different permissions depending whether they are shared or stored in a personal account. The Ownership & Permissions section enables you to change who owns a file, what other groups of users can access it, and what actions can be performed on it. You learn more about working with multiple user accounts and administrative access in Chapter 27, "Sharing (and Securing) Your Computer."

Comments

The Comments section enables you to create notes attached to specific files, folders, and applications.

Running Classic Applications

As briefly discussed in Chapter 1, "Setting Up Your Mac," the Classic environment is a way for you to operate some older Mac software while still using the newer Mac OS X operating system. Using Classic, almost any application that was functional in Mac OS 9 can run inside Mac OS X.

You *must* have at least 128MB of memory to use Classic. Also, a 400MHz G3 (or faster) computer is recommended. *Why?* Classic is a process running *under* Mac OS X. When it's in use, your computer is really supporting two operating systems simultaneously. As you can imagine, this is quite resource intensive.

Launching Classic

The Classic environment needs to be launched only once during a Mac OS X login session, and it can be launched manually or automatically. After it's running, Classic remains active (but mostly unnoticeable) until you log out or manually force it to shut down.

How can you find out whether a piece of software on your hard drive is indeed a Classic application? You can always ask the Finder. Simply select the icon for the program in question and choose Get Info (or press Command-I) from the Finder's File menu. A Kind of Classic Application indicates that the software requires Classic to operate.

There are two ways to launch the Classic environment: through the Classic panel in System Preferences, as mentioned in the last chapter, or by double-clicking a Classic application.

First, let's start Classic from the System Preferences panel. Here's what to do:

1. Locate the System Preferences icon in the Dock and double-click it (the icon looks like a wall-mounted light switch) or choose System Preferences from the Apple menu.
2. In System Preferences, click the Classic icon to open its Preferences panel.
3. Click the Start/Stop tab of the Classic Preferences panel. Here you see several options, including a Stop or Start button for manually turning Classic off or on, Restart for when you want to reboot Classic, and Force Quit for when the Classic system is unresponsive after a crash.
4. In the Start/Stop tab, click the Start button to launch Classic. Mac OS 9 takes a few minutes to boot, and then you're ready to run your older applications.

Let's try the second way to launch Classic:

1. Locate an older, non–Mac OS X application in your Mac OS 9 Applications folder, and double-click it.

Yes, there's only one step. If Classic isn't already running, it boots automatically before the application you've chosen is launched. It may take a little while for both Classic and the application you've launched to open and be ready for use. Remember that, after it's started, Classic remains in the background until you log out of Mac OS X or manually stop Classic. Even when you log out of all Classic applications, Classic itself is still running.

The Classic System Preferences panel shows the status of the Classic environment—that is, whether or not it's running. Because Classic does not appear as an active task in the Dock, this is one way to check its status.

Although it's true that in most cases Classic will run until you log out or manually stop the process, it's still (like Mac OS 9 itself) susceptible to crashes. If Classic crashes, so do any applications running within it. You must restart the Classic process to continue working.

Using Classic Applications

The first time you open a Classic application, you'll notice that several interesting things happen.

Be careful not to alter settings in a Mac OS 9 control panel! When running Classic, the Mac OS X menu bar is replaced by the Mac OS 9 menu bar with a rainbow apple at the upper left in place of the solid-color one you usually see. Using the Mac OS 9 Apple menu, you can access all the earlier system's control panels and associated functionality. Settings in control panels such as Appearance and Sound are harmless enough, but it's possible to accidentally disrupt your network connections by working with the TCP/IP and AppleTalk control panels. It's best to avoid the Mac OS 9 control panels altogether.

Visually, Classic applications look different from applications that run under OS X. These older applications appear just as they would under Mac OS 8 and 9. The Aqua appearance does not carry over to the windows, buttons, and other interface elements, but the Mac OS X Dock and Process Manager do recognize Classic applications.

After it starts, Classic is easy to use without extra detail about how it interacts with Mac OS X. You simply operate programs as you normally would. However, there are a few exceptions that might be confusing for you:

- **Copy and paste/drag and drop**—Two of the most common means of moving data in the Mac OS suffer when working between native and Classic applications. It can take several seconds before data copied from one environment is available for pasting into another. Dragging and dropping text and images between native and Classic applications fails altogether.
- **Favorites**—Although Favorites are available in the Mac OS 9 environment, they do not transfer between Classic and Mac OS X.
- **Open and Save dialog boxes**—Mac OS X applications are aware of the special folders and files used by the system and take care to hide them. The same cannot be said for Classic applications. The Open and Save dialog boxes clearly show the invisible items. Although normal, these invisible files could be alarming to users not accustomed to seeing them.

> Note that when using the Classic environment, applications still need to access all hardware through Mac OS X, so software trying to access hardware directly will fail for devices not compatible with Mac OS X. (See Chapter 7, "Choosing Peripheral Devices," for more information about devices compatible with your Mac.)

Users expecting a completely seamless work environment might be disappointed by these shortcomings, but they're relatively minor quirks in a very convenient arrangement.

Summary

In this chapter, we've covered many of the basics of interacting with the Mac desktop with a focus on windows, folders, files, and applications. We looked at various view options for the Finder window, as well as some more general window features including scrolling, moving, and resizing. You also learned about folder, files, and applications and how to make aliases for them. You also learned how to rename, copy, and delete them. Finally, we discussed running older Mac applications in Classic mode.

CHAPTER 4

Using the Internet

Mac OS X is extremely easy to configure for dial-in, ethernet, AirPort, cable modem, and DSL service. If you have a connection to the Internet, this section will help you set up your Mac to access it. Then, you'll learn how to use Internet Explorer as your Web browser for surfing the World Wide Web and find out about some of the services that you can access online by purchasing a .Mac membership from Apple. We will also look at Mail, iChat, and Address Book, three applications from Apple to make emailing and instant messaging your family and friends easy. Let's get started with connecting to the Internet.

Creating an Internet Connection

The first step in connecting to any network (including the Internet) is determining what, exactly, is being connected. Mac OS X supports a number of technologies out of the box, such as standard wired (ethernet) networks, wireless AirPort networks, and, of course, broadband and dial-in ISPs. For each different type of network, you must collect connection information before continuing. Your network administrator or ISP should be able to provide you with the details of your network access, including

- **IP address**—An Internet Protocol address that's used to uniquely identify your computer on the Internet.
- **Subnet mask**—A filter that helps your computer differentiate between which machines are on the local network and which are on the Internet.
- **Router**—A device address used to send and receive information to and from the Internet.
- **Domain name server**—A computer that translates the name you see in your Web browser, such as `www.apple.com`, into the corresponding IP address.
- **ISP phone number**—A number used when creating a dial-in connection.
- **Account name**—A username for your ISP Internet account.
- **Password**—A password for your ISP Internet account.
- **Proxy**—A computer that your Macintosh must interact with to reach the Internet.

If you're using a dial-in connection, chances are good that all you need are a phone number, an account name, and a password. You should be absolutely positive that you have all the necessary information before you continue; otherwise, your computer could behave strangely when attempting to connect with incomplete or inaccurate information.

> Under no circumstances should you *ever* attempt to guess an IP address for your computer. Entering invalid information could potentially disrupt your entire network or cause intermittent (and difficult to diagnose) problems for other users.

With connection information in hand, open System Preferences, and click the Network button in the Internet & Network section. You should now be looking at the control center for all your network connections. Near the top of the panel is a Show pop-up menu. Use this menu to choose between the different types of connections that your computer uses, such as Internal Modem, Built-in Ethernet, AirPort, and Internet Sharing (Ethernet). Let's look at each one and how it can be set up for your ISP.

> If you use different types of connections (for example, a modem at home and AirPort at work), don't worry. A bit later, you'll see how several different connection types can get along without any conflicts.

Internal Modem

If you use a modem to connect to the Internet, choose the appropriate Modem option in the Show pop-up menu. The lower portion of your screen changes slightly to reflect the type of connection you're configuring. You see four tabs that lead to four individual setting panes:

- **TCP/IP**—TCP/IP settings are rarely needed for dial-in connections. Unless you know otherwise, I recommend not touching anything found here.
- **PPP**—The most important pane, shown in Figure 4.1, the PPP settings enable you to set your username, password, and ISP phone number.

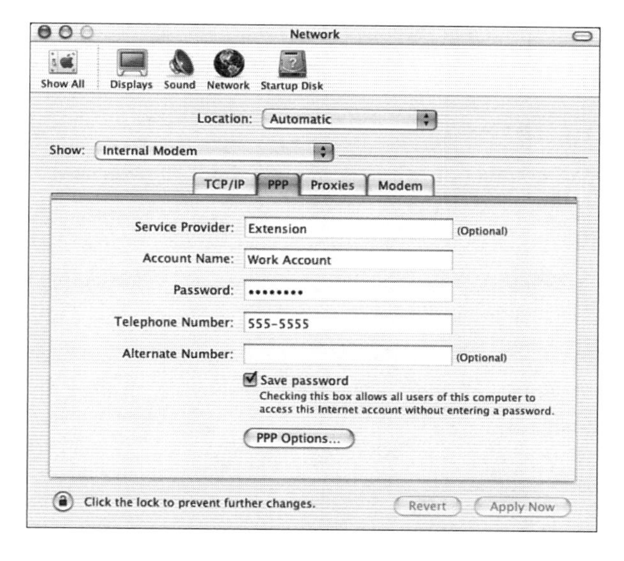

FIGURE 4.1
The PPP options are usually the only thing you need to make a connection.

- **Proxies**—If your ISP has provided proxy servers for your use, you might want to enter them here. A *proxy* manages requests to Internet resources on behalf of your computer to either increase speed or security.
- **Modem**—Settings specific to your computer's modem. If you don't like hearing the annoying connection sound, you can shut off the speaker here. Most important, you can activate the option to Show Modem Status in Menu Bar, which provides a Menu Extra that enables you to easily connect and disconnect from the Internet.

In the PPP tab, enter the username and password you were given for your ISP, along with the phone number for the ISP's servers. If you'd like to keep your password stored with the machine, click the Save Password check box.

There are a number of settings you might want to look at by clicking the PPP Options button. You can configure settings in a sheet to give you the ability to redial a busy connection, automatically connect when starting TCP/IP applications, and automatically disconnect if you choose Log Out from the Apple menu.

Click Apply Now to save the settings. If you chose the PPP option to connect automatically when needed, you should be able to start Internet Explorer and begin surfing the Web.

If you didn't choose to connect automatically, you can use the modem Menu Extra (go to the Modem tab to activate it) to add a quick-control icon to your menu bar. Alternatively, the Internet Connect application can start and stop a dial-in setting. We talk more about that later.

Built-in Ethernet

The next type of connection we look at is the built-in ethernet connection. If you have a wired 10BASE-T LAN or a DSL/cable modem hookup, this is where you'll need to focus your attention. Choose Built-in Ethernet in the pop-up menu. Again, the onscreen tabs change to enable you to fine-tune several related areas. The tabs for the Ethernet settings are

- **TCP/IP**—Unlike the modem TCP/IP settings you saw earlier, the Ethernet TCP/IP pane, displayed in Figure 4.2, offers more configuration options than are typical of a wired network.

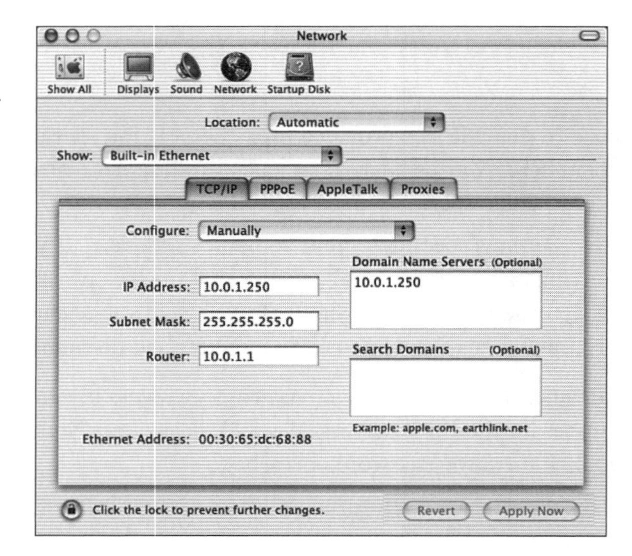

FIGURE 4.2
TCP/IP settings are important for Ethernet-based connections.

- **PPPoE**—PPP over ethernet is a common way for DSL-based services to connect. They generally require a username and password as a modem-based PPP connection does, but operate over a much faster ethernet wire.
- **AppleTalk**—The AppleTalk tab is used to control whether you become part of a local AppleTalk network. AppleTalk is Apple's traditional file-sharing protocol and is discussed further in Chapter 27, "Sharing (and Securing) Your System."
- **Proxies**—If your ISP has provided proxy servers for your use, you might want to enter them here.

As you can see in Figure 4.2, you definitely need a few items before you can successfully operate an ethernet connection. Fill in the information that you collected from your network administrator or ISP now. If you're lucky, at least a portion of these settings can be configured automatically by a BOOTP (boot protocol) or DHCP Dynamic Host Configuration Protocol) server on your network.

BOOTP and DHCP often provide automatic network setup on corporate and cable modem networks. If your network supports one of these services, you can use the Configure pop-up menu in the TCP/IP tab to select the appropriate protocol for your connection. Again, it's important that you do not *guess* what you need to connect—using invalid settings could disrupt your entire network.

If you're required to use PPPoE, click the PPPoE tab. In this pane, you can supply a username and password for your connection and enter optional identifying data for the ISP.

Near the bottom of the pane is a check box that enables you to view your PPPoE status in the menu bar. Clicking this check box adds a new Menu Extra that displays activity on your connection and gives you quick control over your settings.

Click the Apply Now button when you're satisfied with your ethernet setup. You should be able to immediately use the network software on your computer, such as Mail and Internet Explorer.

AirPort

The next connection method, AirPort, is available only if you've added an AirPort card to your system and are within range of a wireless base station. AirPort is Apple's 802.11b-based wireless networking device that enables you to connect to the Internet without the burden of running network wires or phone lines.

To configure your AirPort connection, choose AirPort in the Show pop-up menu. AirPort setup, surprisingly, is identical to ethernet. The same TCP/IP, AppleTalk, and Proxies tabs apply. There is, however, one additional tab that's essential to configure properly: the AirPort tab, shown in Figure 4.3.

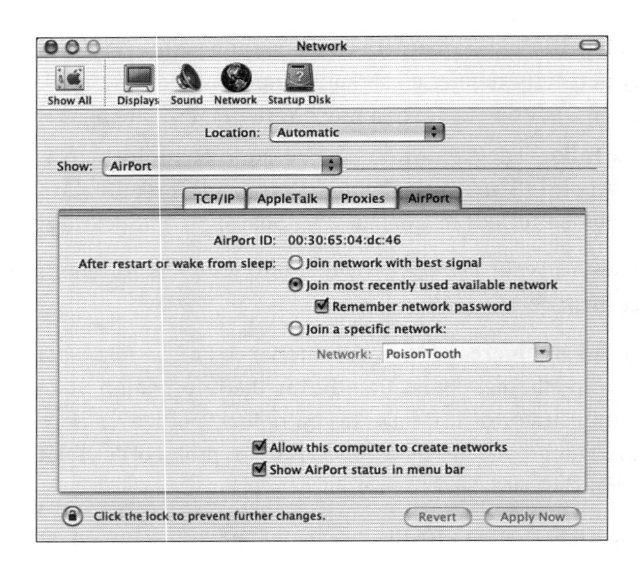

FIGURE 4.3
Choose the AirPort network you want to connect to or set criteria so that your system can choose.

In the AirPort tab, you can direct your computer to Join the Network with Best Signal, Join the Most Recently Used Available Network, or Join a Specific Network.

AirPort networks are identified by a network name. When the Join a Specific Network radio button is selected, you can use the Network pop-up menu to choose one of the detected AirPort (or AirPort-compatible) networks, or manually type the name into the Preferred Network text field.

Finally, as with the modem and PPPoE settings, you can activate yet another Menu Extra—the AirPort signal strength—by clicking Show AirPort Status in Menu Bar. This Menu Extra also gives you the ability to instantly switch between the different available wireless networks and even shut down AirPort service if you like.

Click Apply Now to start using your wireless network.

Internet Sharing (Ethernet)

The final Networking option is a bit different from the ones previously discussed. Internet Sharing allows computers with multiple network cards to be connected to the Internet in a traditional way (using modem, ethernet, or AirPort) and to share their connection with another computer using either ethernet or AirPort. Although it's an interesting feature, it should be used with great care because this configuration can interfere with established networks.

Click the Start button to start sharing your active Internet connection.

Other computers should be configured to obtain their settings automatically (DHCP) and should be connected to the same network interface that's being shared.

For example, let's imagine that you have a computer connected via Ethernet and you want to share the connection via its AirPort card. First, start Internet Sharing, and then configure your other AirPort-capable computers to connect to the wireless network you just created. The client computers that have their AirPort TCP/IP settings configured to DHCP are immediately able to connect to the Internet.

Internet Sharing uses your computer to create a miniature local TCP/IP network that it manages. It controls all the settings on the client computers and ensures that requests to (and from) the Internet move back and forth as they should.

Setting Multiple Connection Options and Locations

That wasn't so bad, was it? Everything that you need to get yourself connected to the Internet is all located in one System Preferences panel. Unfortunately, not all users' network setups are so easy. Many of us use our PowerBooks at home to dial in to the network, and then go to work and connect via ethernet, and, finally, stop by a coffee shop on the way home to relax and browse the Web via AirPort.

In Mac OS X, all your different network connections can be active simultaneously! This means that if it is possible for your computer to find a way to connect to a network, it will! Obviously, you don't want it trying to dial the phone if it has already found a connection, and, true to form, Mac OS X is smart enough to understand that if it *is* connected, it doesn't need to try any of the other connection methods. In fact, you can alter the order in which it tries to connect to the network by choosing Network Port Configurations in the Network Preferences panel's Show pop-up menu. This configuration pane is shown in Figure 4.4.

Here you can see that there are four port configurations: one modem, two ethernet, and one AirPort. I can drag these different configuration settings up and down in the list to determine the order in which Mac OS X attempts to use them. If you prefer that the computer *doesn't* attempt to connect using one of these configurations, deselect the check box in front of that item.

Using the New, Duplicate, and Delete buttons on the right side of the pane, you can create alternative configurations for each of your built-in connection methods. These new configurations appear in the Show pop-up menu and are set up just as you set up the modem, ethernet, and AirPort connections earlier.

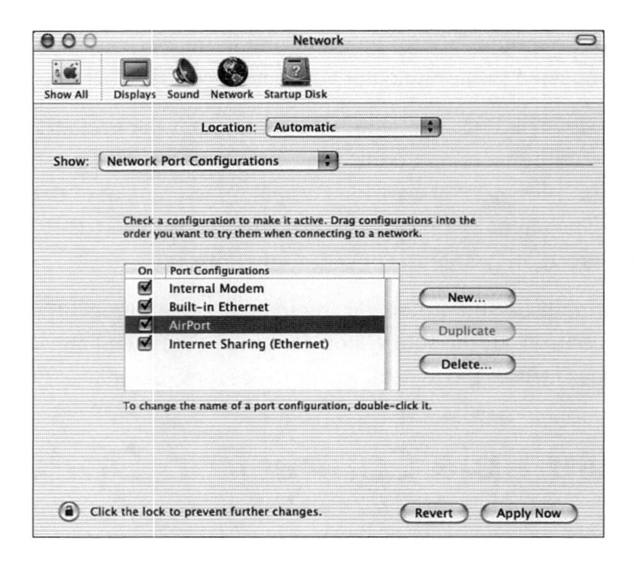

FIGURE 4.4
Adjust which connection settings take precedence over the others.

Locations

Mac OS X creates collections of port settings called *locations* that you can easily switch between. So far you've been dealing with a location called Automatic, shown in the Location pop-up menu of the Network Preferences panel.

To create a new location, choose New Location from the Location pop-up menu. After you create a new location, you can edit the port configurations and priorities just as you have under the default Automatic location. To manage the locations that you've set up, choose Edit Locations in the Location pop-up menu.

Switching from one location to another is simply a matter of choosing its name in the Location pop-up menu or the Location submenu under the systemwide Apple menu.

Choosing a new location immediately makes the new network settings available and could disrupt any connections currently taking place.

Using Internet Connect

The Internet Connect application is the final stop in your tour of Mac OS X network utilities (/Applications/Internet Connect). This is a rather strange application that offers a shortcut to the same features found in the Network Preferences panel. It can be used for both modem and AirPort connections to quickly log in to different configurations in your current location.

The Modem side of the Internet Connect application is displayed in Figure 4.5.

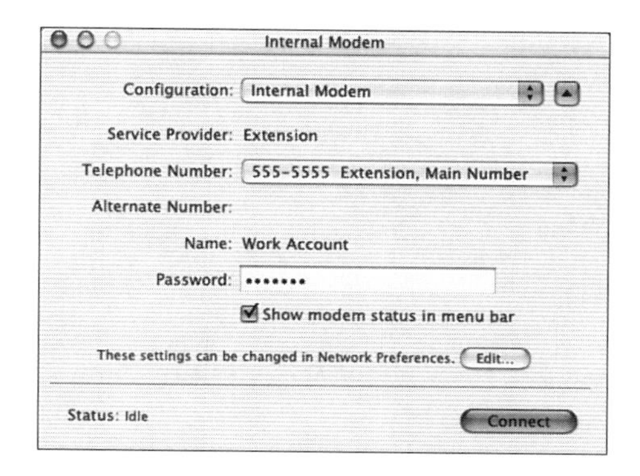

FIGURE 4.5
The Internet Connect application enables you to easily log in to your ISP.

If your window appears much smaller than this, you might need to click the disclosure pushbutton at the far right of the window.

To log in to your ISP via modem, follow these steps:

1. Choose the modem configuration you created earlier in the Configuration pop-up menu at the top of the window.
2. Enter the phone number for your ISP or choose one from the pop-up menu.
3. The login name should already be set as configured in the Network Preferences panel. If you didn't save your password in the panel, you must enter it here.
4. Click the Show Modem Status in Menu Bar check box to add the modem Menu Extra to your screen.
5. Click Connect to start using your dial-in connection.

After you've connected to your ISP, the Connect button changes to Disconnect, giving you a quick way to break the modem connection.

AirPort users also stand to benefit from the Internet Connect application. Along with modem configurations, AirPort settings are also shown in the Configuration pop-up menu. Choosing an AirPort-based configuration displays the status of the connection and signal strength, as shown in Figure 4.6.

Use the Turn AirPort Off (and subsequent Turn AirPort On) button to disable or enable the AirPort card in your computer. To switch to another wireless network, use the Network pop-up menu.

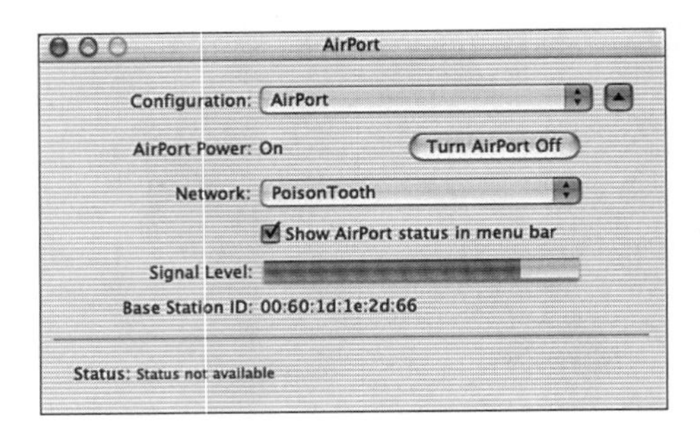

FIGURE 4.6
Internet Connect can also control your AirPort settings.

Finally, to see a readout of the signal strength at all times, check the Show AirPort Status in Menu Bar check box.

As you can see, many of the features of the Internet Connect application are already accessible through the Network Preferences panel. Regardless, the Internet Connect application offers a quick means of viewing your connection status and changing common settings.

Web-Browsing Basics

Now that you know how to connect to the Internet, let's look at browsing the web.

The first time you open a Web browser, such as Internet Explorer, on your computer it goes to a special location called a home page.

A *home page* is similar to the cover of a book. It's the introductory page of a Web site. A typical home page will tell you about the site and offer fast access to other parts of the site (or to other sites with similar content).

Using Internet Explorer

1. Click the Internet Explorer icon on the Dock to launch Apple's default browser (if it's not there, check the Applications folder). This will launch the Microsoft browser and create an Internet connection if one hasn't already been created. When connected, the home page set as your browser default will appear (see Figure 4.7).
2. Click any title or button where the mouse cursor changes to a hand to see another page.
3. To return to the previous page (whatever it is), click the Back arrow on the toolbar. The Forward arrow takes you back to the page you visited before clicking Back (if there is one). Click the Home icon to go back to the home page set for our browser.

FIGURE 4.7
The default home page for your browser will appear when you launch your browser while connected to the Internet.

Feel free to spend a little time clicking here and there to see whatever information suits your fancy. A quick click of the Home icon on the toolbar gets you back where you started. Your browser will track your visits via a history file, which we will cover in more detail in just a little while.

> If you've visited a lot of sites during your session, you can access any one of them quickly by clicking the Go menu and selecting that site from the list.

Making Sense of URLs

The clever people who designed the World Wide Web devised a way to summon a site quickly without knowing the exact route. Unfortunately, it's not in plain English, so it might seem a little confusing. You call up a Web site by its URL.

URL is short for Uniform Resource Locator, and it's the syntax used to identify a Web site so that it can be accessed. I'll dissect a URL in the upcoming pages, so you can see the stuff from which they're made.

Let's see what all those little letters and numbers mean by calling up a common, garden-variety Web site—Apple's. You can access it this way:

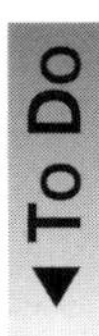

Accessing a Web Site

1. Click the Address field below your browser's toolbar.
2. Enter the following: `http://www.apple.com` (do it exactly as I have written it).
3. Press the Return or Enter key on your Mac's keyboard. Your Web browser will send the request for the site across the Internet, and then retrieve the information to display in your computer. In a few seconds, you'll see Apple Computer's home page, just as you see in Figure 4.8.

FIGURE 4.8
Welcome to the home of the "Think Different" folks, Apple Computer, Inc.

When you open your Internet Explorer browser, you'll find there's already an icon for Apple Computer and other Apple Web pages right below the Address field. To add a site to the toolbar just access the site, click the icon next to its address, and drag it to the toolbar. You can also drag URLs right to the Dock and have them a click away from access. If you want to remove an item from the toolbar, Command-click the item and choose Delete from the pop-up (Contextual) menu. You can also drag the URL to the trash to accomplish the same result.

4. To see more information at Apple's site just click any of the colorful pictures.

Not all pictures you see at a Web site can be clicked to take you to another destination. You'll know you can access such a destination (or link) with a picture when your mouse cursor changes to a hand whenever you point it over the picture.

Let's dissect Apple's URL to see what the information means:

- **http://**—This prefix, short for hypertext transfer protocol, tells the browser that you're asking for a Web site. If it has an ftp:// prefix, it means you're accessing a file transfer site instead (it stands for file transfer protocol, and we'll talk more about it in Chapter 27.
- **www**—This information tells the browser this is the URL for a Web site, though a number of URLs don't include it. Rather than guess, just use whatever address is given for the site to be sure you get the right one.

If a site's URL has the telltale www letters in it (and not all do), you can skip the http:// prefix and just enter the rest of the address. The Web browser is clever enough to know what you want.

- **apple**—This is the first part of the site's domain name.

  A *domain* is the online equivalent of the Web site's street address. It tells the browser where to go to get what you want.

Each part of a URL, except for the prefix, is separated by a period (referred to as a "dot" in the computer universe) or a slash. Don't forget to enter the correct character where needed to get to the right place.

- **com**—This identifies the site as commercial. The suffix **edu** means the site is an educational institution, **org** represents an organization of some sort (usually a charitable organization or club), and **gov** represents a U.S. government agency. If you see **be** as the suffix the site is located in Belgium. When the suffix is **ca** the site is located in Canada, whereas **uk** represents the United Kingdom (and **co** identifies a commercial site from that country). Additional suffixes are found in other parts of the world, and others are added from time to time.

If you've visited a site before, you'll notice your Web browser will try to fill (or autofill) the missing information when you begin to enter the URL, by putting up a pop-up menu. Just move the mouse to select the site you want, if you see the correct one, and press Return or Enter to get to where you want. Otherwise, continue to enter the proper address.

URLs are usually not case sensitive, so it really shouldn't matter whether you enter the address with uppercase or lowercase letters. But if a site has a password as part of a URL, you'll need to type that perfectly (uppercase and lowercase, as required).

Making Your Own List of Web Favorites

Over time, you'll visit Web sites you want to return to again and again, but the Go menu's history file is only good for a few dozen sites. The older sites are automatically removed from the list.

What to do?

Fortunately, your browser has a way to store the URLs of sites for quick retrieval. You can take advantage of this feature by using the Favorites menu. It's the best trick this side of *Star Trek's* "beam me up Scotty" routine to quickly get where you want to go.

Storing URLs

1. Access the site you want to revisit regularly.
2. Click the Favorites menu (see Figure 4.9) and choose the first option, Add Page to Favorites. The site you've opened will immediately become a part of this menu. Real neat!

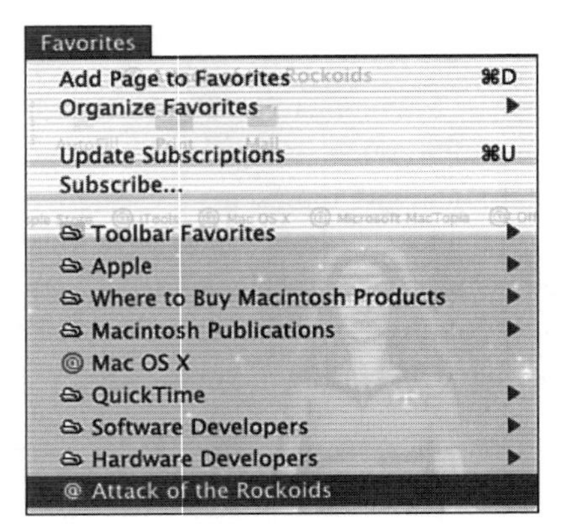

FIGURE 4.9
Your Favorites menu can be quickly customized to your taste.

You can save a trip to the Favorites menu by typing Command-D to add the page to the list.

3. If you want to check the sites you've added to change or remove them, choose the second command in the Favorites menu, Open Favorites, instead. Or choose the Favorite button on the toolbar.
4. To remove a site, simply select it from your Favorites directory and press the Delete key. Acknowledge your decision to delete on the next screen and zap—it's gone. Once again, you can also access your Favorites by clicking on the tab at the left of the browser window.

Take That Cache and Zap It

The word cache has several meanings, but for our purposes it's a secret place where you store things. I suppose a Web browser's cache is secret because it's not visible unless you look for it. But, it's a place where recent artwork you've accessed from a Web site is stored, so you can revisit the place and not have to wait as long for the page to appear.

Normally, your Web browser is designed to empty older cached artwork, so it doesn't get too large and slow down performance. At times, though, things still bog down anyway.

What to do? The easiest step to take is simply to empty the cache, which means your browser will have to build it again. But, more often than not, it makes your computer seem faster when accessing the Internet.

Here's how it's done with Internet Explorer (just check the preferences of other browsers to look for delete cache options):

1. With Internet Explorer running, choose Preferences from the application menu.
2. Click the arrow next to Web Browser to make sure it points down.
3. Now click Advanced and look for the Cache category and click the Empty Now button (see Figure 4.10).
4. To finish up, click the OK button. This action will clear the contents of the cache file used by Internet Explorer.

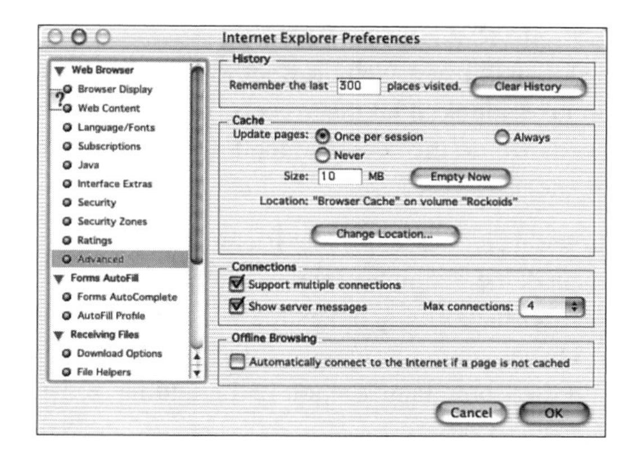

FIGURE 4.10
Tell that cache to take a ride.

Downloading

To update your software or get new software, you might need to download a file from the Internet as discussed in Chapter 6, "Installing Additional Software." IE makes this task easy with the Download Manager (shown in Figure 4.11), which opens when you're downloading a file to show you the file's status (such as how far it has progressed) and to enable you to stop the download if you change your mind. The Download Manager also shows you the last 10 files you downloaded—a handy feature when you can't remember what you have done and what you haven't.

When you're downloading files, you should be aware that you're transferring someone else's files to your hard drive and those files could carry a virus. A *virus* is a malicious program meant to harm your hard drive or network. When downloading, use a reputable site and never download a file if you don't know what that file does. You might also want to have antivirus software on your computer to scan for viruses. See Chapter 29, "Recovering from Crashes and Other Problems."

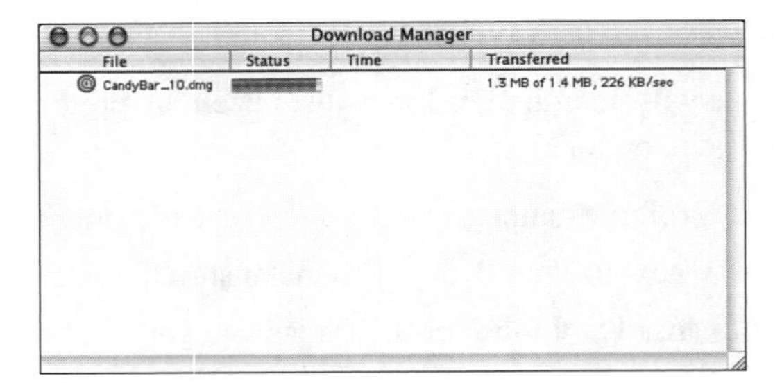

FIGURE 4.11
The Download Manager is a separate window in Internet Explorer.

Refer to Chapter 6 for examples of downloading and installing programs.

Setting Preferences

So far you've learned how to use a Web browser to visit different sites on the Internet. You're now going to take a look at all the aspects of IE that can be customized and altered to fit your needs. To do this, you use the Preferences dialog box found in the Explorer application menu.

Click on Explorer in the menu bar and select Preferences, or simply press Command-;. The first time it's opened, the dialog box shows preferences from the Browser Display category on the left. After that, it remembers the last thing you chose. If it isn't already open, click Browser Display in the Preferences dialog box. Here you can change your default home page. In the Home Page section in the middle of the Browser Display panel, select the URL (Web address) in the Address field, and type `http://www.google.com`. This makes the Google search engine page your home page, so it appears whenever you open Internet Explorer. Click OK. Close IE by choosing File, Quit from the menu bar, or by using Command-Q. Open IE again by clicking the icon in the Dock or in your Applications folder. Notice that the page that opens first is Google. You can set any page on the Web or on your hard drive to be your home page.

Whenever you want to view this home page, click the Home button in the button bar.

Although there are far too many categories of preferences to cover here, there are a few you should be aware of. One is the Toolbar Settings in the Browser Display category. By default, the toolbar displays both icons and text. If you're running low on screen space, you might want to have these buttons display only icons or text to reduce the height of the toolbar.

If you select the Web Content category in the list in Internet Explorer Preferences, you can choose several options that speed up the time it takes to load a page in your browser. The most useful thing you can do if you're using a slow connection is to uncheck the Show Pictures check box. If this box isn't checked, the large picture files that slow down many pages aren't displayed.

Many sites today rely heavily on pictures to create their menu structure and convey the general message of the Web site. Although a good Web designer should have alternative tags that display text instead of the picture, many designers don't take the time to code them into their pages, rendering the text tags useless if you don't display the pictures.

In the Advanced panel of the Preferences dialog box, as shown in Figure 4.12, you find some of the settings referred to earlier in this section. One setting is the number of pages you visited that your browser stores in its history. The history stores 300 pages by default, but this number can vary from 0 to 1,000. Another thing to notice in the History section is the big button labeled Clear History. Regardless of how many places you've told the browser to remember, when you click Clear History, all those places are no longer part of the browser's history. You might say they're history! Doing so prevents anyone who is using your account from discovering where you've been.

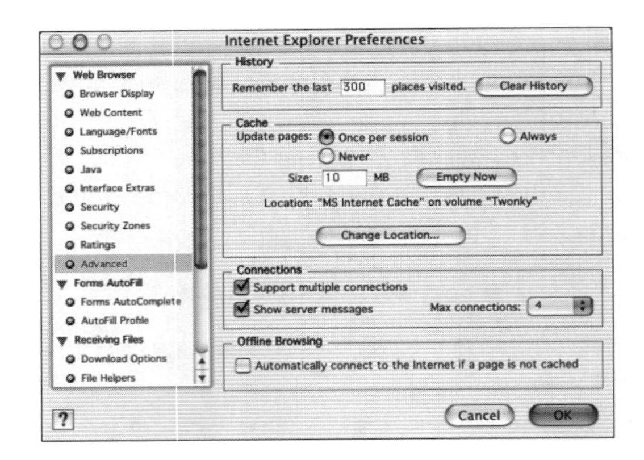

FIGURE 4.12
The Advanced panel in the Preferences dialog box is where you can go to clear the history.

.Mac Membership

Now that you've mastered the basics of Web browser use, let's look at *.Mac*—a Web-based set of applications and services designed by Apple for Mac users (although some services are also available to PC users). You can purchase a year-long membership at `www.mac.com` to receive the following:

.Mac replaces a now-defunct free service from Apple called iTools.

- **Email**—Accessible from anywhere you have a Web browser, mac.com email accounts include 15MB of storage space.
- **iDisk**—100MB of storage space, accessible from both Macs and PCs, for backing up or sharing your files across the Internet. You can connect to the iDisk from the Go menu of the Finder and choosing iDisk (Shift-Command-I).
- **HomePage**—Apple's HomePage application can generate a basic Web page and transfer it to the Apple server. You can further edit the created pages or substitute pages of your own design.
- **Backup**—Created by Apple, Backup helps transfer your files to iDisk or burn to CD or DVD using an internal CD-RW or SuperDrive. It also helps you schedule regular backups and, if the time comes, restore your files.

Full access to .Mac benefits requires a paid subscription, but you can sample some .Mac features for free. A 60-day free trial of .Mac includes an email address and 5MB of space, 20MB of iDisk space, Backup software to help you store files in your iDisk, and use of HomePage to create and share your Web page.

Without either a full or trial membership to .Mac, you can send iCards and access the public folders of .Mac members.

- **iCards**—Send iCards via email to your friends and family. Members of .Mac have the added ability to use photos of their own.

Another small application available through .Mac is the .Mac Slide Publisher, which enables you to upload a set of images to your iDisk for use as a screen saver by others running Mac OS X. Even though you can only have one slide show operational at a time, this is a fun way to share pictures with friends and family.

To set a .Mac slide show as your screen saver, go to the Screen Effects panel of System Preferences and choose .Mac in the Screen Effects list. Then click the Configure button to enter the .Mac membership name of the person whose slides you want to view—you're welcome to subscribe to my .Mac slide show by entering `robynness` in the text entry field. Click OK to set your selection. It takes a moment for the images to be downloaded from the Internet to your computer. You can test the slide show by clicking the Test button in the Screen Effects tab.

- **Anti-Virus**—Download McAfee's Virex software to protect yourself from harmful computer viruses.

Additional software for download appears on the .Mac page from time to time, so the list above is not comprehensive. I recommend you check it out to see if purchasing a membership would be worth the cost.

Setting .Mac Preferences in Mac OS X

The applications that make up .Mac are easily and seamlessly integrated into Mac OS X. If you sign up for a .Mac account, you'll find that the easiest way to make sure that your .Mac account works with your operating system is to set up your account in System Preferences for Mac OS X.

Click the System Preferences icon in the Dock or choose System Preferences from the Apple menu. In the System Preferences panel, click the Internet button under the Internet & Network category. Click the .Mac tab at the top of the panel, as shown in Figure 4.13. Enter your information in the .Mac Member Name and Password fields. By entering the .Mac member information, you're giving Mac OS X access to the information so that you don't have to enter it in multiple applications that interact with .Mac.

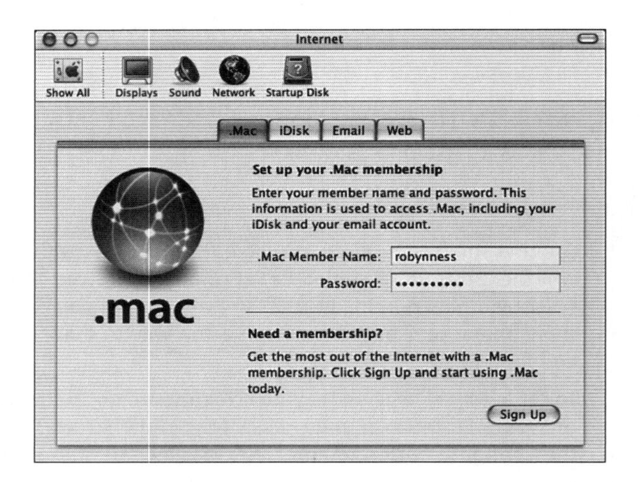

FIGURE 4.13
The Internet Preferences panel opened from System Preferences.

The iDisk tab of the Internet preference panel helps you monitor the amount of space your files use. Under the Public Folder Access section of this tab, you can set read/write permissions and even password protect your public folder.

Mail

The Mail application is Apple's own email program for the Macintosh. Mail offers a cutting-edge interface, junk-mail detection heuristics, and searching mechanisms that can make managing hordes (or even a trickle) of email messages fast and painless.

If you have a third-party email application that you want to use instead of Mail, you can set it as your default email program in the Internet panel of System Preferences under the Email tab. This enables Mac OS X to launch your mail program automatically when you click a mailing address link in a document or your web browser.

If you've used an email program before, you'll be completely comfortable with Mail's interface. The toolbar at the top of the window holds commonly used functions for creating, responding to, and searching messages.

In the center of the window is a list of the active messages in each mailbox. The list columns (from left to right) display read/unread status, online buddy status for iChat, sender, subject, and day/time sent by the sender. As with most list views, the columns can be sorted by clicking their headings or reordered by dragging the heading to the desired position.

Figure 4.14 shows the Mail application, ready for action.

FIGURE 4.14
Use Mail to send and receive email.

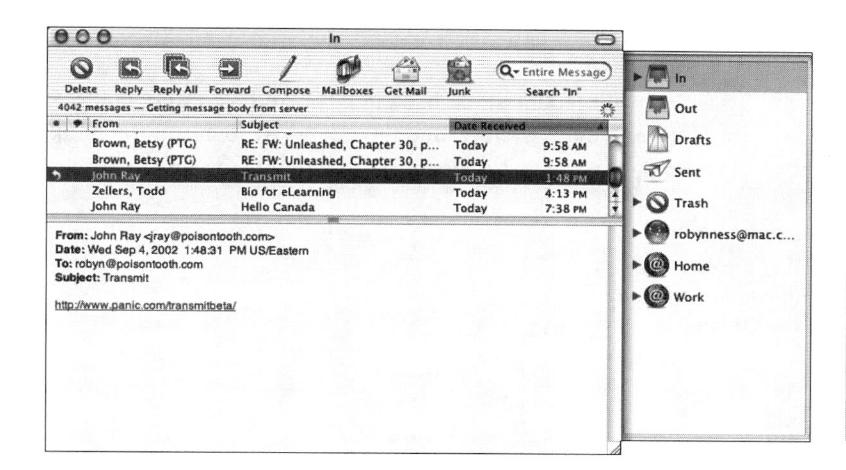

To display the accounts and mail folders that have been added to the system, click the Mailboxes toolbar button or choose Show Drawer (Shift-Command-M) from the View menu. The mailbox drawer slides out from the side of the Mail window. You can use the disclosure triangles to collapse and expand the hierarchy of mail folders that you create. The number of unread messages is displayed in parentheses to the right of each mailbox.

When Mail is open, its icon in the Dock displays the total number of unread messages in all Inbox folders.

Adding or Editing an Account

When you install and set up your computer's operating system, the Installer prompts you to create a default email account, which creates a single account for a single person. If you choose to skip that step or want to add another account, you can add or edit email accounts in the Accounts pane of the Mail Preferences dialog box.

To open this dialog box, start Mail by clicking the stamp-like icon in the Dock or launch the program from the Applications folder. Then choose Preferences from the application menu and click the Accounts icon. Existing email accounts are listed on the left. The options available include

- **Add Account**—Add a new email account
- **Edit**—Edit the selected account
- **Remove**—Delete the selected account
- **Check for new mail**—Change how often *all* the email accounts are polled
- **New mail sound**—Select the sound that's played when a new message arrives on the server

To add a new account to the list, click the Add Account button. An account information sheet appears that's divided into three tabs: Account Information, Special Mailboxes, and Advanced. The general Account Information tab is shown in Figure 4.15.

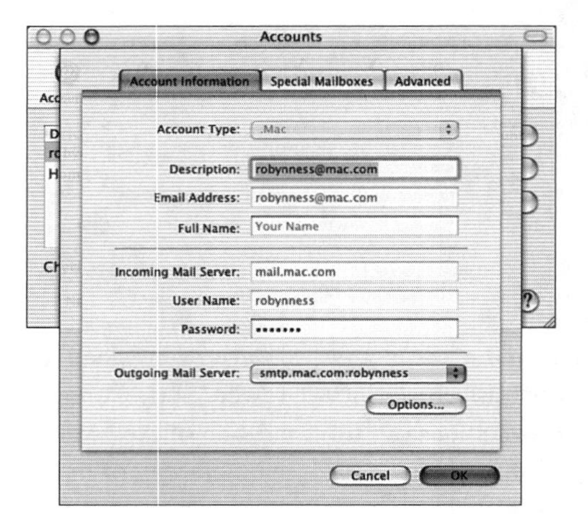

FIGURE 4.15
Enter the new email account information into this tab.

Use the Account Type pop-up menu to set the account type. Instead of just IMAP or POP accounts, there are three options:

- **.Mac**—Configures a .Mac IMAP account with the appropriate Apple defaults. (We'll talk more about .Mac membership later in this chapter.)
- **POP**—Creates a basic POP3 account.
- **IMAP**—Creates a basic IMAP account.

POP3 Versus IMAP

If your email provider supports both POP3 and IMAP, you're in luck!

POP3, although extremely popular, is not practical for people with multiple computers. POP3 works much the way it sounds: Email is "popped" from a remote server. Incoming messages are stored on the remote server, which in turn waits for a connection from a POP3 client. The client connects only long enough to download all the messages and save them to the local hard drive.

In this process, the server stores email temporarily and handles short-lived connections, so the burden of long-term storage and filing rests squarely on the shoulders of the user. Unfortunately, after a message transfers from the server, it's gone. If you go to another computer to check your mail, it won't be there.

The more computers you use, the more fragmented your messages become. Some provisions exist for keeping messages on the server, but in reality it's a hassle and rarely works as planned. Although the same message can be downloaded to multiple machines, deleting it from one machine won't delete it from the others. The end result is, quite frankly, a mess!

IMAP takes a different approach. Instead of relying on the client for message storage, IMAP servers keep everything on the server. Messages and mail folders remain on the server unless the client explicitly deletes them. When new messages arrive, the IMAP client application downloads either the message body or header from the server, but the server contents remain the same. If multiple computers are configured to access the same email account, the email appears identical on all the machines—the same folders, messages, and message flags are maintained. In addition, IMAP supports shared folders among different user accounts and server-based content searches.

The drawback to IMAP lies mostly in the email provider—supporting IMAP's additional features and the added storage costs often aren't economical on a large scale. If your ISP doesn't support IMAP and you want to take advantage of it, sign up for a .Mac account. Apple's POP and IMAP services are fast, reliable, and—for what you get—economical.

After choosing your account type, you must fill in several other fields:

- **Description**—The description is a name you give the email account. It's for your use only and can be something simple, such as Work or Cable Modem.
- **Email Address**—Enter the full email address for the account you're adding.
- **Full Name**—This is the name that's transmitted with your email address. For example, I would fill it in with Anne Groves. You'll see the full name in the header of an email like this: "`Robyn Ness`" `<robynness@mac.com>`.

- **Incoming Mail Server**—This could be something such as `mail.mac.com`.
- **User Name**—This is the name you use to log on to the server, such as `robynness`.
- **Password**—This is the password you need to log on to the server.
- **Outgoing Mail Server**—This is the server you use when sending mail.

Near the bottom of the Account Information tab is the Options button, which launches the SMTP Server Options window. *Authenticated SMTP* is used when the server you're sending mail through checks to make sure that you're authorized to send mail through it by requesting a username and password. To connect using authenticated SMTP, click the Use Authentication When Sending Mail check box, and then fill out the SMTP user and password fields. Consult your network administrator or ISP for this information.

> If you have multiple email accounts and want to be able to choose which address shows up in the From field of your outgoing messages, simply add your various accounts to Mail. The next time you send a message, a pop-up menu appears in the message composition window. From that menu, you can choose which account is listed as the sender. The default email address is the first one placed in the list of accounts. If you want to change this, drag the accounts listed in the Accounts pane of the Mail Preferences pane to the order you want.

After you've created an account, you can change additional settings in the Special Mailboxes and Advanced tabs.

Special Mailboxes Settings

By default, Mail includes special mailboxes for storing various kinds of messages, including drafts, sent messages, junk mail, and trash. The Special Mailboxes tab of the Accounts sheet enables you to activate features for these mailboxes.

The available options differ depending on whether the selected account is IMAP/.Mac or POP. For IMAP/.Mac accounts, you can configure the following settings:

- **Store Draft Messages on the Server**—Messages that you've started, but not sent, are called *draft messages*. Checking this option enables you to store a message on the server until you're ready to send it.
- **Store Sent Messages on the Server**—Opt to save sent messages on the server to be accessed from different computers. You can also choose intervals at which sent messages are deleted from the server.

- **Store Junk Messages on the Server**—Mail comes with a built-in junk mail filter. Choose to store messages deemed to be junk on the server to be accessed from different computers or to delete them quickly.
- **Move Deleted Messages to the Trash Mailbox**—Check this box if you want deleted messages to be stored in the Trash folder. Enable this setting if you want to be sure not to permanently delete messages you might need.
- **Store Deleted Messages on the Server**—Store deleted messages on the server to be accessed from different computers in case you still want to view them, even from other computers. You can also choose how long to wait before deleting them permanently.

For POP accounts, you can activate the following features:

- **Erase Copies of Sent Messages When**—Choose how long to store copies of the messages you send before they're erased.
- **Erase Messages in the Junk Mailbox When**—Choose how long to store messages deemed junk mail before they're erased.
- **Move Deleted Messages to a Separate Folder**—Check this box if you want deleted messages to be stored in a special folder. Enable this setting if you want to be sure not to permanently delete messages you might need. You can also choose how long the deleted messages remain in the folder before they're permanently erased.

Advanced Settings

Click the Advanced tab to further fine-tune your account settings. The available options change depending on the account type you've chosen. Figure 4.16 displays the Account Options tab for IMAP (or .Mac) accounts.

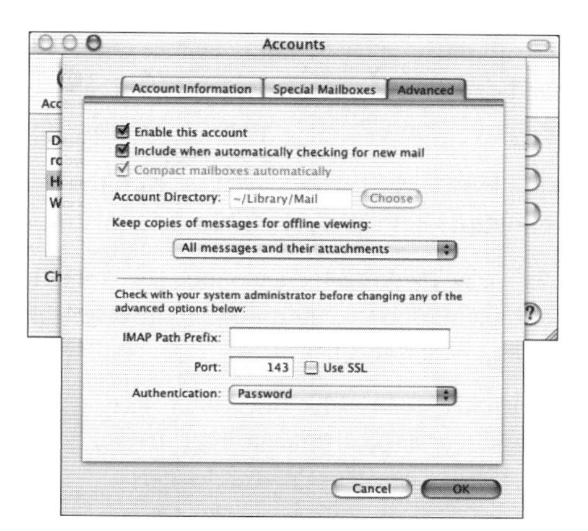

FIGURE 4.16
Each type of email account has different available options.

Choices available from the Advanced tab include

- **Enable This Account**—Includes the account in the listing under the Get New Mail In Account selection of the Mailbox menu. If not enabled, this account is ignored until you change the setting.
- **Include When Automatically Checking for New Mail**—If this option is selected, the account is polled for new messages at the interval set in the Preferences Account panel. If this option isn't selected, the account is polled only when the user manually checks the account.
- **Compact Mailboxes Automatically**—For IMAP/.Mac accounts, this option cleans up the local mailbox files when exiting Mail. The benefit of using this option is slight, and it can slow down the system when dealing with large mailbox files.
- **Remove Copy from Server after Retrieving a Message**—When this option is checked for POP accounts, messages are removed from the server at the interval selected in the pop-up window. Deselect this option to leave email on the server. The Remove Now button enables you to clean up your POP account on the server by deleting all messages that have already been downloaded to your local machine.
- **Prompt Me to Skip Messages over # KB**—For POP accounts, this option enables you to automatically skip messages larger than a set number of kilobytes. This is useful for keeping large attachments from downloading and bogging down your connection.
- **Account Directory**—The local directory where the Mail application stores your messages. It's best to leave this setting at its default of Library/Mail.
- **Keep copies of messages for offline viewing**—With IMAP/.Mac accounts, the local machine has the option of storing the text of all messages along with their attachments (All Messages and Their Attachments), storing only the text of all messages on the local machine (All Messages, but Omit Attachments), storing messages that have been read (Only Messages I've Read), or never storing messages on the local drive (Don't Keep Copies of Any Messages).

The remaining options are a bit more sensitive with regard to operating your mail. You shouldn't alter them without the help of your system administrator.

- **IMAP Path Prefix**—For IMAP/.Mac accounts, this specifies the IMAP prefix required to access your mailbox. Usually this field is left blank unless your mail server administrator specifies a value.
- **Port**—The default IMAP port is 143; the default POP server port is 110. If your server uses a different access port, enter it here. If you don't know what port you should use, contact your system administrator.

- **Authentication**—Some SMTP servers use authentication to prevent spamming and other unauthorized use. If your server requires authentication to *send* mail, use the authentication options to specify a username and password.

Composing Messages

To start a new email message, click the Compose button in the toolbar or choose New Message (Command-N) from the File menu. To reply to an existing message, select that message in the list view, and then click Reply in the toolbar to start a new message or choose Reply to Sender (Command-R) from the Message menu. If you want to reply to all recipients of the message, use the Reply All button.

The composition window appears, as shown in Figure 4.17.

FIGURE 4.17
Mail supports styled messages and drag-and-drop attachments.

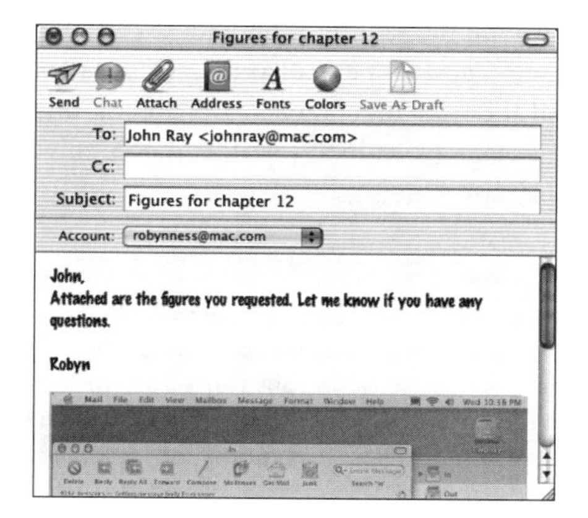

By default, three fields are provided for addressing the message. Fill in the To line with the address of the primary recipient. If you're sending the message to more than one person, separate multiple addresses with a comma. Use the Cc: line to add other recipients who aren't part of the main list. The primary recipients can see these addresses. The Subject line is used to show the subject, or title, of the email.

Mail has an automatic complete feature similar to the one available in Microsoft Internet Explorer. When you begin to type someone's email address, the program will offer options to complete the address. It stores not just the contacts in your Address Book, but the recent names you've used.

Additional fields are accessible from the Edit menu. Choose Add Bcc Header (Shift-Command-B) to add a Bcc: header, or Add Reply-To Header (Option-Command-R) to add an alternative reply address. A Bcc (blind carbon copy) header works like a normal carbon copy, but does not allow the recipients to view each other's email addresses or names. A Reply-To header is used to provide an alternative address for replying. For example, if I'm sending email from my `robyn@shadesofinsanity.com` account but want replies to go to `robynness@mac.com` instead, I would enter the `mac.com` address in the Reply To field.

> If you would rather use your long-term memory for something other than email addresses, you can use the Address Book application to store your addresses. We discuss this later in the chapter.

To create the message itself, type the text into the window's content area. You can use the toolbar to pick fonts and colors, and you can also drag images and files directly into the body of the message to send them as attachments. Depending on the type of file, images and files are added to the message as an icon (application, archive, and so on) or shown within the message body (picture, movie).

> Be aware that to view email with special rich text formatting, the recipient must have a modern email program such as Outlook Express (or, better yet, Mail!). Rich text is the use of various fonts and formatting other than just plain old text. To create a message that anyone can view as you intend it, compose the content in Plain Text mode, which is selected in the Format menu.

To send the message, click Send in the toolbar or choose Send Message (Shift-Command-D) from the Message menu.

A Fast Guide to Internet Addresses

As you saw earlier, Internet addresses have to follow a strict format to work. The same is true with email addresses. Here's how to address your email so that it gets to the right place without any problem.

For this example, I'll dissect an email address for an AOL account, `gene@aol.com`:

- **gene**—This is the user name, or screen name.
- **@aol.com**—This is the domain name, the location where the email account is located.

Here are a couple other email addressing tips:

- **Don't use the spacebar!** The Internet doesn't recognize an empty space and will ignore everything before it, so be careful not to insert spaces inside email addresses.
- **Caps don't matter!** Uppercase, lowercase, makes no difference.

Receiving Mail

To read a message, click the message entry in the listing in the main Mail window. The message contents will appear in the bottom window pane along with an abbreviated header containing information about the message such as who sent it and when.

You can also double-click a message to open it in its own message window. When you're finished reading the message you opened, click the Close button in the upper-left corner of the window or press Command-W.

The simplest way to delete a message is to use the Delete button in the toolbar. Pressing the Delete key or choosing Delete from the Message menu also removes the active message or selected group of messages from the listing. Deleted messages aren't immediately removed from the system; they're transferred to a Trash folder. What happens from there can be configured in the Special Mailboxes tab of the Accounts Preference pane, which was discussed earlier.

Additional Mail Preferences

We already looked at the Accounts portion of Mail Preferences, but the Mail Preferences dialog box also contains many of the program's hidden features—including signatures and mailbox filters. Open the Mail Preferences dialog box by choosing Preferences from the application menu.

Fonts & Colors

The Fonts & Colors pane controls the default fonts used in the message list and message bodies. Options in the Font & Colors pane include font and text color settings.

> Using a fixed-width font (such as Courier or Monaco) is recommended for plain-text messages. Many plain-text messages are formatted using spaces for positioning elements, so using a proportional (non-fixed width) font results in a skewed or sometimes unreadable display.

Viewing

The Viewing Preferences pane controls the amount of header detail that should be displayed as well as several features related to the appearance of messages, including highlighting of message threads and display of HTML-rendered messages.

Composing

Choose formatting options for your message. The Composing pane includes a variety of settings, including Rich/Plain Text options, automatic spell checking, addressing options, and reply format.

Signatures

A *signature* is a block of text added to the end of an email to tell others who you are or how to contact you. I use mine to add my job title and address. Others use signatures to insert a favorite quote. The Mail application handles multiple different signatures with ease in the Signatures pane of Mail Preferences, shown in Figure 4.18. Signatures added by the account owner are listed on the left side of the pane.

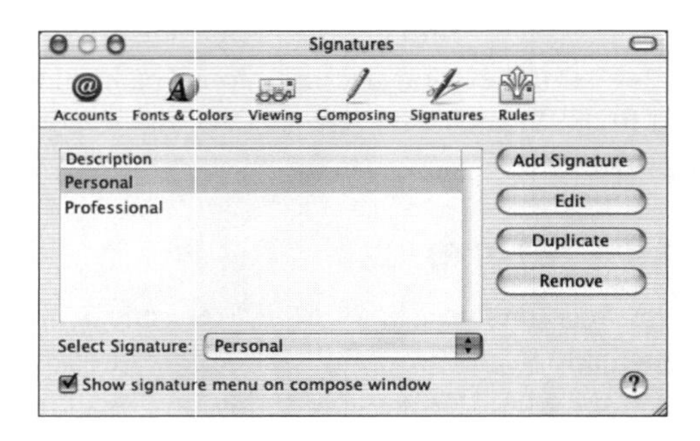

FIGURE 4.18
Create multiple signatures in the Mail application.

Options in the Signatures pane enable you to add, edit, duplicate, remove, and select signatures.

Rules

Using rules is like having your own personal assistant to tell you what messages are important and which ones are junk. Rules (also called *filters*) can perform actions on incoming messages, such as highlighting them in the message list, moving them to other folders, or playing special sounds.

Each rule in the list is evaluated once per incoming message (unless the Active box is unchecked). In fact, multiple rules can act on a single message. To change the order in which the rules are applied, drag rule entries in the list to the order you want.

Managing Junk Mail

With the increasing popularity of email has come an increase in annoying junk email. Mail attempts to help you avoid wading through unwanted mail with built-in junk mail filtering.

By default, the junk mail filter starts in training mode. When a message comes to you that Mail feels might be junk mail, the message is highlighted in brown. A button appears at the top of the message so that you can correct Mail if it has incorrectly identified the message as junk. If a junk mail message slips past Mail, you can select the message and choose Mark as Junk Mail from the Message menu or click the Junk icon in Mail's toolbar. Over time, Mail learns from your input.

When you feel that Mail is no longer misidentifying messages, you can switch to automatic mode. In automatic mode, Mail creates a Junk mailbox in which it automatically places suspected junk mail so you don't have to see it at all. However, it's suggested that you periodically review the contents of the Junk mailbox to make sure that nothing important was delivered there.

Remember, you can set the length of time mail stays in the Junk mailbox before it's deleted in the Special Mailboxes tab of the Accounts panel that appears when you create or edit an account.

There are four self-explanatory options for manipulating the rule list: Add Rule, Edit, Duplicate, and Remove.

Adding a rule is simple. Each rule is a single step that looks at portions of the incoming message to determine how to react. Figure 4.19 demonstrates the rule creation process.

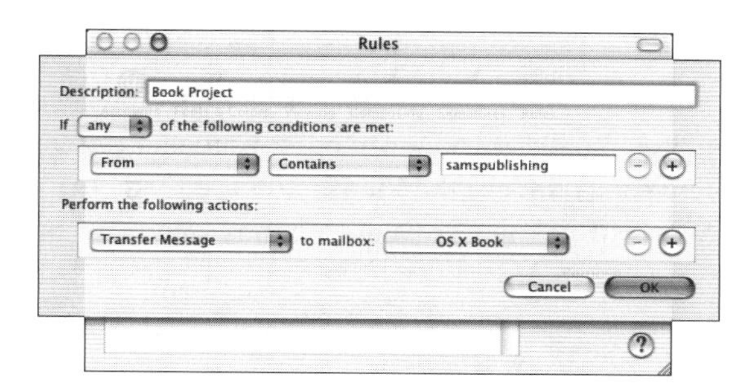

FIGURE 4.19
Mail's rules are simple to create.

1. Click on the Add Rule button to make a new rule. The sheet shown in Figure 4.19 appears.
2. Enter a description; it's used to identify the rule in the listing.

3. Decide on the criteria that must match the incoming message. The search criteria are the header field to use in the comparison, what comparison to use (Contains, Begins With, and so on), and the text to look for. For example, to match a message from my editors' accounts, I'd use From, contains, and `samspuplishing`. Clicking the + or - button adds or removes additional search criteria.
4. To finish the rule, set the action(s) that should run if the criteria match:
   - **Transfer Message**—Transfers the message into one of your system mailboxes.
   - **Set Color of Message to**—Sets the highlight color for the message.
   - **Play Sound**—Plays a system (or custom AIFF) beep sound.
   - **Reply To/Forward/Redirect Message**—Sends the message to another email address. Click the Set Message button to enter text that will be included with the message being sent.
   - **Delete Message**—Deletes the message. Useful for automatically getting rid of common spam messages.
   - **Mark as Read**—Keeps the message, but doesn't display it as a new message.
   - **Mark as Flagged**—Marks the message with a flag in the status column of the message listing.

   Use the + and - buttons to apply and remove additional actions.

Click OK to set and activate the rule.

Address Book

Address Book is a contact information manager that integrates with Mail. The main window, shown in Figure 4.20, has two view modes: Card and Columns view and Card Only view. To toggle between them, use the View buttons at the upper left. You'll do most of your work with Address Book in Card and Columns view.

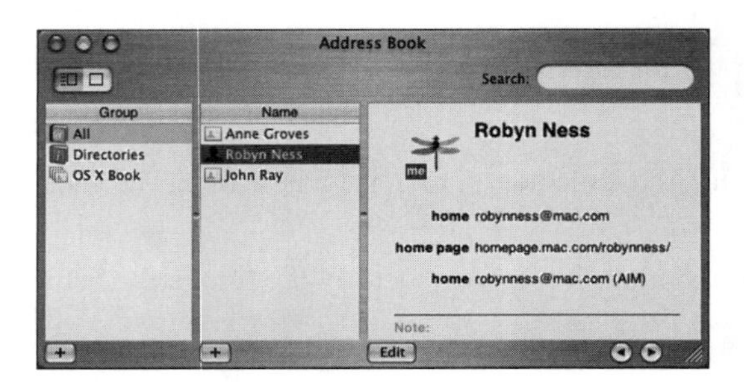

FIGURE 4.20
Address Book, shown here in Card and Columns view, keeps track of your contact information with a simple uncluttered interface.

Adding and Editing Cards

To add a card, select All from the Group column and then click the + button below the Name column. This opens a blank card in the far-right column where you can type what information you want to save.

There are fields for name, work and mobile phone, email address, homepage, AIM name, and address, as well as a space at the bottom for notes. You can tab between fields or click into the ones you want to insert. You can add as much or as little information as you like, but an email address is required if you plan to use the card with Mail.

If the label to the left of the field doesn't match the information you want to add, you can adjust it by clicking the up/down arrow icon. This opens a pop-up menu with several common labels, as well as an option to customize.

In the upper-right corner of the card column is the default card icon. If you want to add a custom picture, clicking the default icon opens a sheet from which you can navigate to any image stored on your computer or attached drive. A simple way to add icons for each of your contacts is to select an image from those stored in /Library/User Pictures or drag an image from the Finder into the image well.

When you're finished adding information, click outside the card pane.

To edit a card you've already created, select the name of the individual from the Name column and click the Edit button below the card column.

To delete a card, select it and press the Delete key on your keyboard. You are asked to confirm the action before it's carried out.

Adding Groups

You can organize your cards into your own custom groups, which can be used to send email to a common collection of people.

If you have a large number of cards to work with but have no need for mailing to custom groups, you can enter keywords in the Notes section of the cards. You can then use the Search field, located at the upper right of the Card and Columns view, to see only those cards that contain your chosen keyword.

To create a group, click the + button under the Group column and type a name for it. Then select the All option in the Group column and drag contacts from the Name column to the group's name to populate your new group. You can hold down the Command key to select more than one addressee at a time.

You might be wondering about the Directories item in the Group column. It represents a special feature of Address Book that connects to remote servers capable of sharing contact information using a technology called LDAP (Lightweight Directory Access Protocol). LDAP servers are commonly used to hold personnel account data for large companies. You can add an LDAP server to Address Book by selecting Directories and clicking the + button below the Group column, as long as you know the name or IP address of the server and the correct search base setting. If you don't know this information, it's best not to try to add a directory without help from your network administrator.

Using Address Book with Mail

Address Book integrates neatly into Mail. When you open a compose window, an Address icon appears in the toolbar. Clicking it opens a window, shown in Figure 4.21, that contains all the contacts and groups you've stored in Address Book. Simply double-click the names of everyone you want to send the message to, or select a previously created group, and the addresses appear in the To field. If you want to send a carbon copy, select the names and click the CC: button.

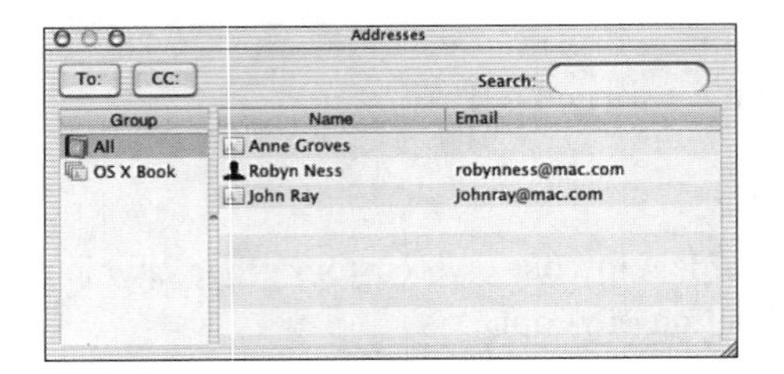

FIGURE 4.21
Mail's Addresses window displays information stored in Address Book.

If you receive email and want to save the sender's address, you can add people to the Address Book from within Mail. Select the message and choose Add Sender To Address Book from the Message menu, or use the keyboard shortcut Command-Y. You must edit the card to add information in addition to the name and email address, but it's a start!

Address Book uses the common vCard format (saved as a `.vcf` file) to store information. When using Mail, you can attach your own vCard to an email by dragging your listing from Address Book into the compose window. To add a vCard someone else has sent you to Address Book, simply drag the vCard attachment from the message window into Address Book.

You can open an Address Book window at any time by choosing Address Book from the Window menu.

iChat

Apple's iChat (path: /Applications/iChat) is a program that enables you to send instant messages to other people while they're at their computers. These messages appear on the recipients' screens so that they can reply to you immediately. An example of a chat session in progress is shown in Figure 4.22.

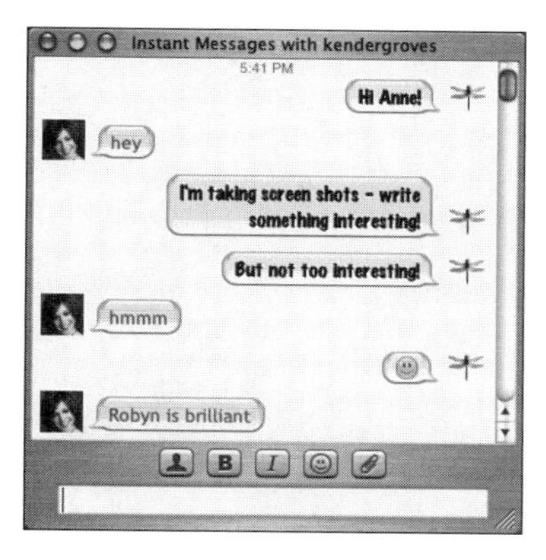

FIGURE 4.22
Chatting with iChat is simple and fun.

4

iChat enables you to communicate in real-time with people who use Mac.com or have an AOL Instant Messenger (AIM) account. You also need one of those types of accounts yourself. If you want to purchase a Mac.com membership or sign up for a trial account (as we will discuss in just a moment), visit `www.mac.com`. Alternatively, you can sign up for a free AOL Instant Messenger account at `www.aim.com`.

If there are other users on your local network using iChat, you don't need to use an AIM or Mac.com account to chat with them. Apple has integrated a technology called Rendezvous into iChat that allows it to scan for other nearby users and add them to a special list for you to see and chat with. Also, if two or more people with AirPort wireless-capable computers are near each other, their computers can use Rendezvous to communicate without any Internet connection at all.

To set up iChat, choose Preferences from the iChat menu and click the Accounts button. Check the Enable AIM option, and then enter your AIM screen name or your full Mac.com email address, and then enter your password. You also have the option of activating or deactivating Rendezvous and adjusting how iChat is activated.

Adding Buddies

When you log in to AIM through iChat, a Buddy List window appears onscreen to show whether your friends are online and available to chat, as shown in Figure 4.23. If you're logged into Rendezvous as well, another window shows people on your local network.

FIGURE 4.23
You can easily see who's available to chat with using the buddy list; the listings for people who aren't connected to the AIM server are dimmed.

Your buddy list is stored on the AOL Instant Message server, so you can log in to your account from any computer and see whether your buddies are online.

Let's see how to add buddies to the Buddy List:

1. If the Buddy List window is open, click the + button at the bottom of the iChat Buddy List window. (If the Buddy List window isn't open, make sure that you're logged in to AIM under the iChat menu, and then open the buddy list from the Window menu.)
2. A sheet containing your Address Book entries appears, as shown in Figure 4.24. If the person you want to add to your buddy list has an AIM or Mac.com listing, select the person and click Select Buddy.

   If the person doesn't show AIM or Mac.com information, click the Select Buddy button to add that information. If the person isn't currently in your Address Book, click the New Person button to create a new entry. Enter your friend's AIM or Mac.com screen name, as well as his real name and email address, in the window that appears. Click the Add button to save your new buddy.

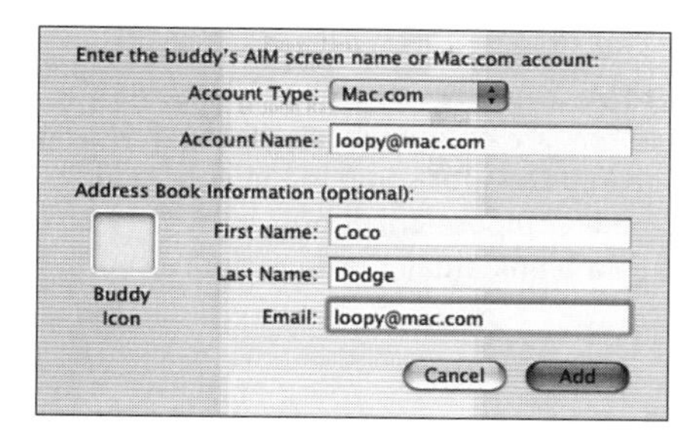

FIGURE 4.24
Choose a chat buddy from the list in your Address Book or add someone new.

Address Book and iChat are integrated such that adding a new buddy to iChat automatically adds a new card in Address Book. However, because your buddy list is stored on the instant messenger server, you can't remove a buddy simply by deleting an Address Book card. Instead, you must select the buddy in the buddy list, and choose Delete from the Edit menu.

Also, keep in mind also that deleting a buddy from your buddy list does not remove that person's card from your Address Book.

Sending and Receiving Instant Messages

As you've learned, your buddy list shows who's available to chat at the very instant you're logged in. To start a chat session with someone who's online, just double-click that person's name in the buddy list, or select a person and click the Send Instant Message button at the bottom of the Buddy List window. This opens a chat window similar to the one shown in Figure 4.22. Type your message in the message area at the bottom of the window and press Return on your keyboard. In the upper portion of the window, you'll see your own message and whatever reply the other person sends.

In addition to sending ordinary text messages, iChat enables you to send any kind of file. To send a file, drag its icon into the message area of a chat window and press Return on your keyboard. The recipient can then drag the file onto her desktop. If you send image files, they appear inside the chat window as part of the conversation. (For maximum compatibility with people using AIM programs other than iChat, it's recommended that you stick with JPEG and GIF image formats.)

You can also send graphical emoticons to other users of iChat. The smiley button near the bottom of the chat window shows you what's available.

If you receive a message, your computer makes a sound and a message window pops up. When you click on the chat window, it expands to show the message area where you can type a response.

Mail is linked to your buddy list, which shows whether the senders of messages in your In box are online when you check your mail. Also, if you've entered an email address for someone in your buddy list, you can select the entry and click the Compose Email button at the bottom of the Buddy List window to open a blank email message addressed to that person.

Group Chat Sessions

You can participate in chats with different people simultaneously, each contained in a separate window. You can also start a chat session with more than one other person in which all participants can see the messages from everyone else.

To start a group chat, perform the following steps:

1. Choose New Chat from the File menu.
2. Click the Add (+) button at the bottom of the participants list to choose the people you want to invite.
3. Type a message inviting the participants. When the invited buddies receive the chat request, they can choose to accept or decline. If they accept, they can send and receive messages as part of the group.

Additional Preferences and Application Settings

There are many ways to customize iChat, both in appearance and operation.

You can change the appearance of the chat windows under the Messages section of the iChat Preferences (shown in Figure 4.25), including changing your font, font color, and balloon color.

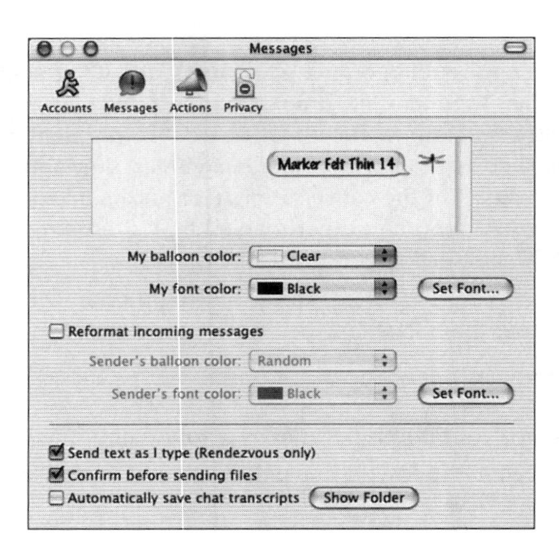

FIGURE 4.25
Change your Messages preferences to reflect your mood.

In addition to changing your font and balloon attributes, you can express your personality by replacing your buddy icon with an image of your choosing. Simply drag a new image into the image well at the top of the Buddy List window. A special editing window opens to enable you to position the image.

You can also replace the icons of people in your buddy list who haven't set their own. (Or, if someone has set an icon that you don't like, you can choose to display something you like better.) Open the Info window by clicking the Show Buddy Info button at the bottom of the Buddy List window, select a new image, and check the box for Only Use This Picture.

Under the Actions preferences, choose what iChat does when you or your buddies log in or out.

The Privacy preferences enable you to choose who in the AIM/Mac.com community can send you messages. Choose categories of users, such as those in your buddy list, or name individual users who can or cannot contact you.

If you're logged into iChat but don't want to be disturbed by requests to chat, you can change your status in the buddy list from Available to anything you choose. Simply choose Custom, and type a new message. It appears beneath your name in other people's buddy and Rendezvous lists.

Summary

In this chapter, you learned how to setup your Internet connection. Then, we covered several applications that use the Internet. You learned about browsing the web and how to use Internet Explorer, a web browser that comes bundled with your Mac software. You learned how to set up accounts in Mail and iChat as well as how to receive and send messages in each. You also saw how Address Book is integrated to store information about your contacts.

CHAPTER 5

Using Other Basic Applications

Your computer operating system includes a number of utilities and applications that enable you to start working (and playing) as soon as your Mac is up and running. The included software ranges from simple desk accessories, such as Calculator and Stickies, to media players, such as QuickTime and DVD player. This chapter looks at those basic applications as well as several others.

Calculator

The Mac's system Calculator, shown in Figure 5.1, is located in the Applications folder. You can toggle between basic mode and advanced mode, which supports trigonometry functions and exponents.

You can operate the Calculator by clicking the buttons in the window or by using your numeric keypad. The number keys on your keypad map directly to their Calculator counterparts, and the Enter key is equivalent to clicking the equal button. The Paper Tape button opens and closes a tray to display inputs. You can print the tape by choosing Print Tape from the File menu.

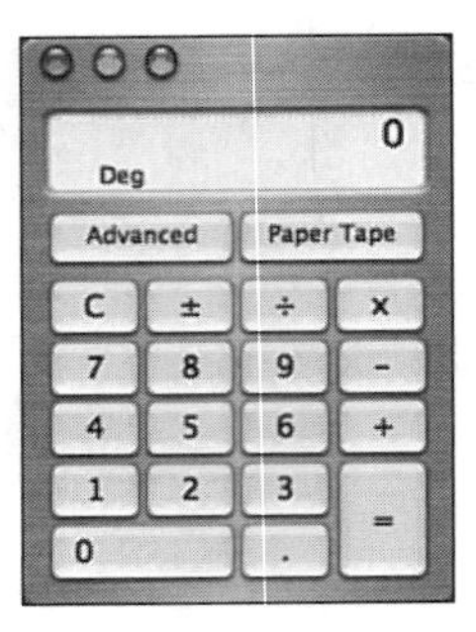

FIGURE 5.1
The Calculator in default mode offers basic arithmetic functions.

Another useful, if unexpected, feature is the Calculator's Conversion function. It enables you to easily perform conversions of currency, temperature, weight, and a variety of other measurement units. Simply enter a value in the Calculator, and then choose the desired conversion type from the Convert menu. In the sheet that appears from the top of the Calculator, choose the units to convert from and those to convert to and click OK. A currency conversion is depicted in Figure 5.2.

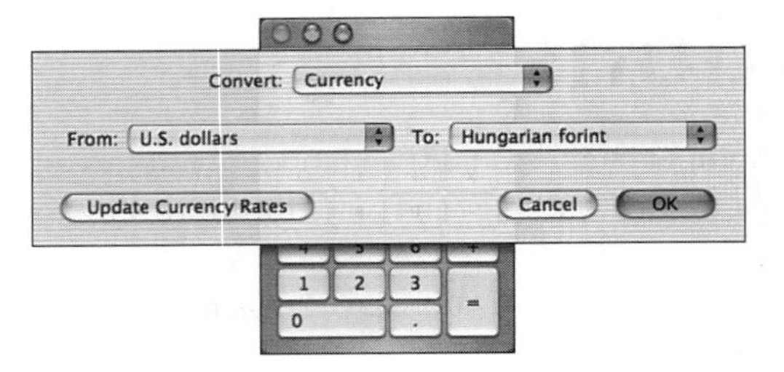

FIGURE 5.2
You can update currency rates when choosing monetary units in the currency conversion sheet.

Clock

The Clock, found in the Applications folder, is a digital/analog timepiece designed to fit into the Mac OS X Dock or float on the desktop as a *windoid* (a floating, non-editable window). By default, starting the Clock application places a clock face in the Dock.

To configure the Clock application's time display, choose Preferences from the application menu. The Clock Preferences dialog box is displayed in Figure 5.3.

FIGURE 5.3
Configure the Clock application's display.

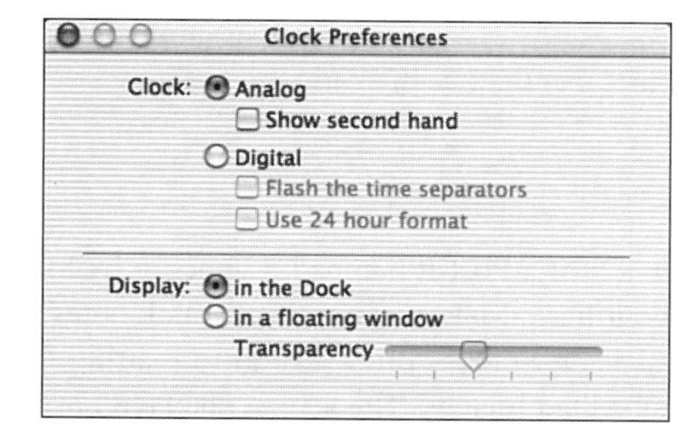

Choose your Clock settings based on a combination of analog, digital, and window types:

- **Analog**—The default view of the Clock is the analog wall-clock style. If you like, click the Show Second Hand check box to display the Clock's second hand in addition to the minute and hour hands.
- **Digital**—The digital Clock display resembles a tear-off calendar page. Both the date and time can be seen in this view. The digital display offers the options of flashing the time separators (:) each second and displaying the time in 24-hour mode.
- **Display**—Finally, the Clock can be shown as an icon contained in the Dock (its default mode) or in a windoid with variable transparency, as shown in Figure 5.4. If you choose the floating window option, drag the transparency slider from left to right to change the window's transparency.

FIGURE 5.4
When on the desktop, the Clock floats on top of everything else.

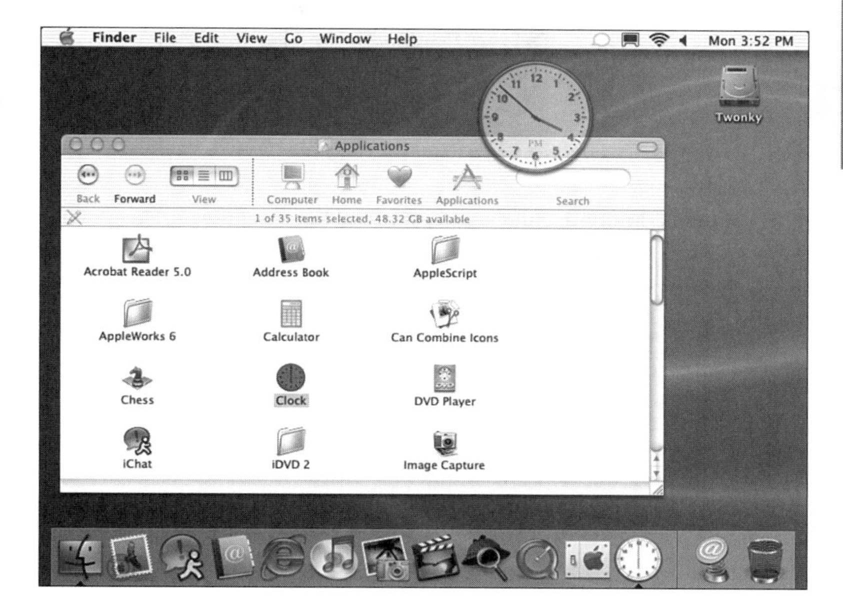

After you make your choices, the changes take effect immediately. To automatically launch the Clock at startup, use the Login Preferences dialog.

Stickies

Stickies are a digital version of a Post-it notepad. Launch it by locating its icon in the Applications folder of your hard drive. You can store quick notes, graphics, or anything you might want to access later. Stickies offer several formatting features, such as multiple fonts, colors, and embedded images. The screen displayed in Figure 5.5 is covered with sticky notes.

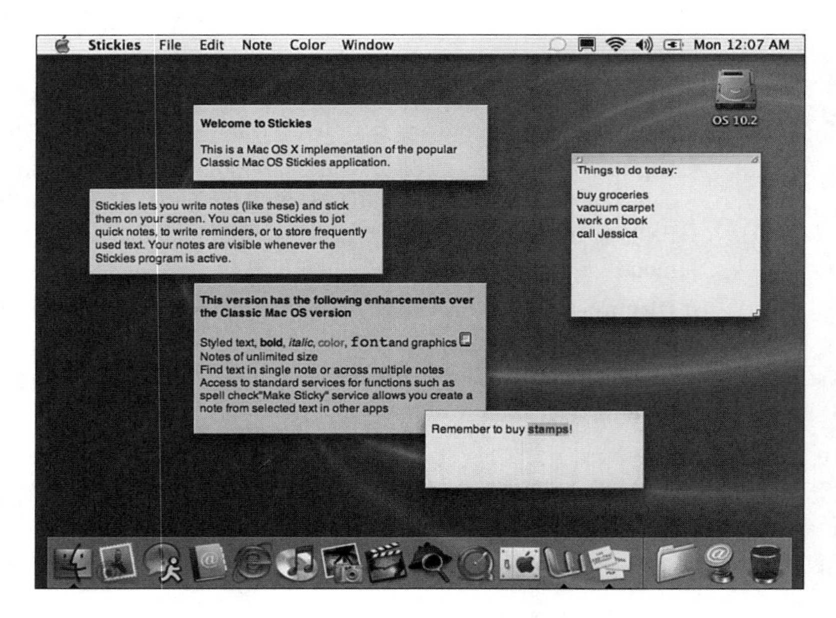

FIGURE 5.5
Sticky notes can contain any information you want.

Stickies do not use the standard Mac OS X window. Instead, each window appears as a colored, borderless rectangle when it isn't selected. When a window is active, three controls appear:

- **Close box**—The close box in the upper-left corner of the sticky note closes the active note. Closing a note erases it.
- **Maximize/Minimize**—In the upper-right corner is a second box that changes the shape of the current note to best fit the text. Clicking the box toggles between two sizes for the current note.
- **Grow box**—Dragging the grow box, located in the lower-right corner, dynamically shrinks or expands the window.

In addition to the three visible controls, Mac OS X Stickies also support a feature called "windowshading." Double-clicking the title bar of an active window shrinks it to the size of the title bar. Double-clicking the title bar a second time returns the window to its previous size. When in windowshaded mode, the sticky note displays the top line of text from its contents in the title bar of the collapsed window.

Strangely enough, you cannot minimize Stickies into the Dock. Choosing Miniaturize Window from the Window menu will windowshade the active note.

The Stickies application has very few configuration options—using the Preferences located under the application menu, you can enable or disable confirmation of the window closing. The rest of the menus enable you to customize the sticky notes that you currently have open.

Sticky notes are not, as you might think, individual documents. All the notes are contained in a single file that's written to your Library folder. The File menu in Stickies enables you to create new notes, export individual notes to text files, and print the contents of notes:

- **New Note** (Command-N)—Creates a new blank note.
- **Close** (Command-W)—Closes the active sticky note.
- **Save All** (Command-S)—Saves changes to all notes.
- **Import Classic Stickies**—Imports note files from Mac OS 8/9.
- **Import Text**—Imports a text file into a new note. Text can be in plain text or rich text format (RTF). Font style information is retained if you use rich text format.
- **Export Text**—Exports the active note to a text file.
- **Page Setup**—Configures printer page setup.
- **Print Active Note** (Command-P)—Prints the active note.
- **Print All Notes**—Prints all notes.

In addition to the normal Edit menu items are two components you might not expect in a simple Post-it application: Find and Spell Checking.

Stickies also installs a service that's accessible from the Stickies application menu's Services item (Shift-Command-Y). Using the Stickies service, you can quickly store selected text from any application in a sticky note.

The Note menu offers control over the text formatting in each note, including font and text formatting and colors. Copy Font is an unusual selection that copies the font style from the current text selection (size, font face, color, and so on) so that you can easily apply it elsewhere by using the Paste Font command. Floating Window enables you to set the chosen note to float in front of all other windows, even when other applications are active. Translucent Window makes the selected note transparent so that whatever is behind it will show through. The Use as Default option enables you to apply the current color, location, and font setting as the default for new notes. Use the Note Info option to display the creation and modification dates for the active note.

What would a sticky note be without a bright-colored background? The Color menu contains the common Post-it colors for your enjoyment (yellow, blue, green, pink, purple, and gray).

TextEdit

A text editor called TextEdit can also be found in the Applications folder. TextEdit can save files in plain text or the RTF format and gives you advanced control over text and fonts. Its RTF files can be opened in popular word processing programs, such as Microsoft Word, and display all formatting attributes.

When you start it, TextEdit opens a new `Untitled.rtf` document for you to begin working with. If you want to open an existing document, choose Open (Command-O) from the File menu.

TextEdit's Open dialog box enables you to select any type of file, including binary files such as images. To read a file, however, it must be a supported document type, such as plain text, Hypertext Markup Language (HTML), or RTF. By default, TextEdit opens HTML documents and displays the styled information similar to the way a Web browser would display it. Figure 5.6 demonstrates TextEdit's rich text editing capabilities. To open an HTML file and edit the source code, you must adjust the preferences—the rendered view of a Web page cannot be edited.

For the most part, you should be able to open TextEdit and start creating and editing text documents. However, you can use a number of preferences and features to customize its appearance and functionality.

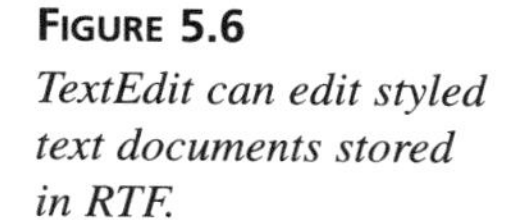

FIGURE 5.6
TextEdit can edit styled text documents stored in RTF.

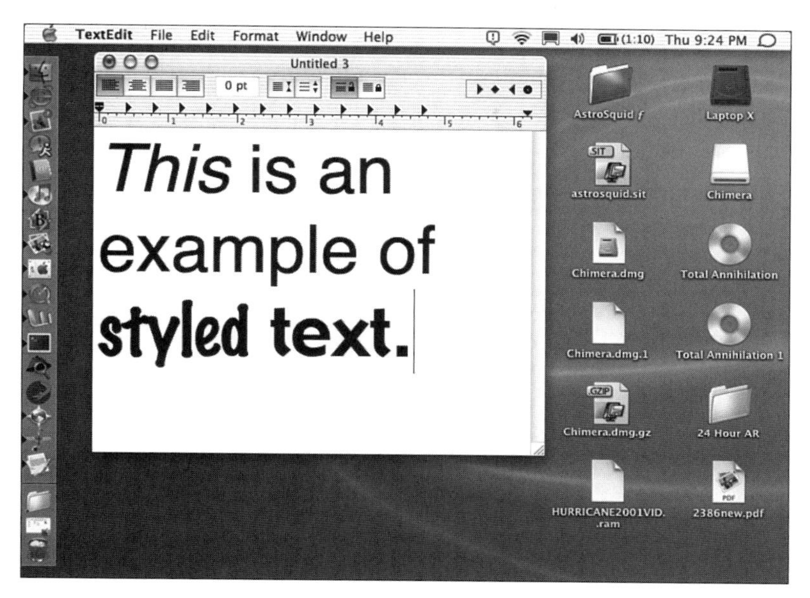

Preferences

The TextEdit Preferences dialog, shown in Figure 5.7, controls the default application preferences. Most of these options can be chosen from the menu bar and stored on a per-document basis as well as for the entire application.

FIGURE 5.7
The TextEdit Preferences dialog enables you to control a range of features.

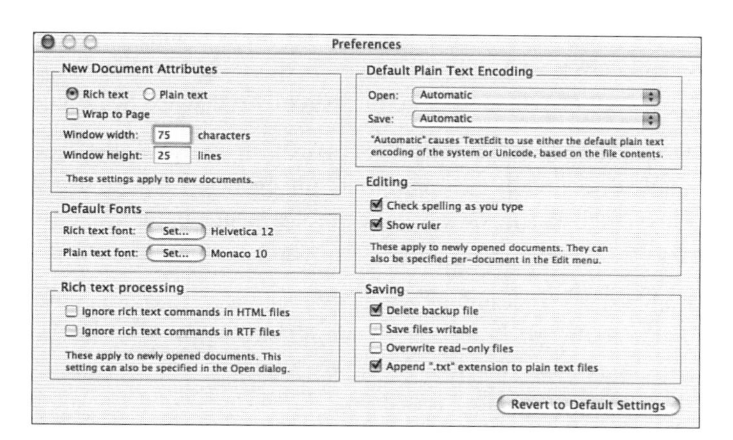

Use the Set buttons in the Default Fonts section to choose new default fonts for rich text and plain text documents. The default fonts are Helvetica 12 and Monaco 10, respectively.

The New Document Attributes section of the dialog includes an option for Rich Text or Plain Text. It enables you to select the Wrap to Page check box so that lines will fit the page width.

The Window Width setting lets you specify the width of new windows in characters. Similarly, the Window Height setting enables you to set the height of new windows in lines.

To have TextEdit automatically check your spelling as you type, select the Check Spelling as You Type check box in the Editing section. Misspelled words will be underlined in red. Ctrl-click the misspelled word to open a contextual menu that enables you to choose from a list of corrections, ignore the word, or add it (the Learn option) to the Mac OS X dictionary.

The options in the Saving section include

- **Delete Backup File**—Removes the TextEdit backup file after a document is successfully saved.
- **Save Files Writable**—Saves files with write permissions turned on; that is, they can be edited later.
- **Overwrite Read-only Files**—Overwrites files, even if their permissions are set to read-only.
- **Append ".txt" Extension to Plain Text Files**—Adds a `.txt` extension to the end of plain text files for cross-platform compatibility and ease of recognition.

By default, TextEdit attempts to read style information in whatever file it opens. Allowing automatic detection enables TextEdit to open files created on other operating systems, such as Windows, and transparently translate end-of-line characters.

When opening or saving a document, TextEdit gives you the opportunity to override automatic detection of the appropriate file encoding type to use. To choose an alternative encoding, such as Unicode, use the pop-up menus in the Default Plain Text Encoding section.

To disable rich text commands in HTML and RTF files, click the corresponding check box in the Rich Text Processing section. Ignoring the style information opens the document as a plain text file, showing all the control codes and tags used to embed the original styles. This is required for editing HTML tags within a Web page.

To save your settings, close the TextEdit Preferences panel. To revert to the original configuration, click the Revert to Default Settings button.

Menus

The TextEdit menus provide control over fonts and other document-specific information. Most of the application preferences can be overridden on a per-document basis from the main menus.

You can open, save, and print documents by using the File menu.

The Edit menu contains the basic copy and paste functions, along with the find, replace, and spell-checking features introduced in Stickies.

The Format menu enables you to control your font settings and text alignment. In addition, you can toggle wrapping modes, rich text and plain text, and hyphenation.

Rulers

During the discussion of Stickies, you learned that find/replace and spell checking are common features in Mac OS X applications. The Ruler, accessed from the Text option of the Format menu in TextEdit, is another common component. Using the Ruler, you can visually adjust tabs and other layout features of the active document. You can also use it to easily and visually change formatting and placement of text.

Chess

The only game bundled with Mac OS X is Chess, also located in the Applications folder. Chess is a full-featured chess game that includes support for speech recognition. The Chess interface, shown in Figure 5.8, is simply beautiful.

FIGURE 5.8
Chess is a GUI front end to GNUChess.

When Chess starts, it displays a new board ready for play. Move a piece by dragging it from its original position to the location you want. If a move is invalid, Mac OS X plays the system beep, refuses the move, and displays a message in the window's title bar.

Preferences

To control the game's difficulty or to change to a computer-computer or human-human game, open the Chess Preferences dialog box. Use Chess's preferences to control how difficult the game will be, who is playing, and whether speech recognition should be used.

If you're using speech recognition, be aware that Chess recognizes only a few patterns to control your pieces:

```
<Piece> <Square> to/takes <Square>
Castle kingside
Castle queenside
Take back move
```

For example, `pawn b2 to b4` is a valid opening move.

Finally, if you've selected the Computer vs. Computer option in the Chess Preferences dialog box, the game won't start until you click the Start Computer Vs. Computer Game button in the Controls dialog box, which is accessed via the Game menu.

Menus

You can access a few additional preferences by choosing the Controls option from the Game menu. In the Controls dialog box, each player is represented by a chess piece, as shown in Figure 5.9. Beneath each player's settings is a white progress bar. When the computer is thinking about a move, the bar fills in from left to right to indicate how close the computer is to making a move. To force the computer to move before it has finished thinking, click the Force Computer To Move button.

Clicking the color well to the right of the player name launches the system Colors panel where you can choose a new color for each player's pieces. The color is not applied until you click the Set Piece Colors button. Keep in mind, however, that the game still makes references to the pieces using their original colors.

The Move menu is used to ask for a hint and to replay or take back the last move. In a sense, the Move menu lets you cheat.

Use the View menu to toggle between a grayscale two-dimensional representation of the board (Shift-Command-A) and the default 3D board (Shift-Command-B).

FIGURE 5.9
Use the Controls dialog box to set some additional game preferences.

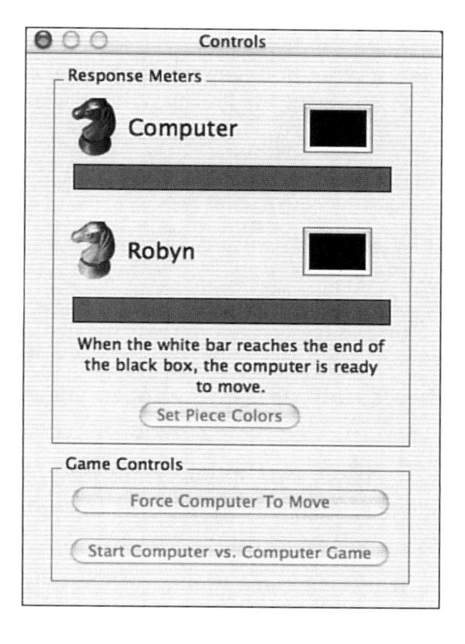

Preview

For viewing PDF files and images of all sorts, use the Preview application in your system Applications folder.

> The standard graphic file format in Mac OS X 10.2 is PDF. One nifty result is that you can make a PDF of nearly any document on your system. Simply choose Print from the File menu and click the Save As PDF button, or use the Print Preview command to open your file in the Preview application and save from there.

Preview can be launched in a number of ways. First, you can double-click the application file. Doing so starts Preview, but doesn't open any windows. You must then choose Open from the File menu to select a file to view.

Second, you can open Preview by dragging the image or PDF files onto the Preview icon in the Finder or Dock.

Third, Preview is integrated into the Mac OS X printing system, so clicking Preview in any Print dialog box starts it.

If you want to view a series of images in one Preview window, select them all and drag the set on top of the Preview icon in the Applications folder or in the Dock.

When you open an image or PDF document in Preview, it shows up in a window with a toolbar across the top, as shown in Figure 5.10. The following options are located in the toolbar:

- **Thumbnails**—Opens and closes a tray window, shown in Figure 5.10, which displays small representations of the pages or files open in the current Preview window. Clicking a thumbnail will show the main viewing area.
- **Zoom In and Zoom Out**—These two options enable you to view a larger or smaller version of the selected image or PDF. If the image is larger than the Preview window, scrollbars will appear.
- **Rotate Left and Rotate Right**—Enable you to turn the viewed file counter-clockwise or clockwise by 90 degrees at a time.
- **Backward and Forward**—If you have more than one image open in the current Preview window, you can move through the set using the Backward and Forward arrows.
- **Page Number**—When you're viewing a multipage TIFF or PDF file, Page Number enables you to enter a page number to jump directly to that page.

FIGURE 5.10
The Preview window includes a toolbar where you can easily alter the viewing style of your files or move between pages.

Just as you can for Finder windows, you can hide the Preview toolbar by using the oblong button at the upper right of the window's title bar.

In addition to viewing files, you can use Preview to convert a file to one of several common file types and export it to a new location. To do this, choose Export from the File menu and enter a filename. Then choose a location to save in and a file format. The Options button reveals additional settings for color depth and filter options.

Overall, Preview is a fine tool for viewing PDFs and images of different formats. However, if you have a file that won't open in Preview or needs additional editing, download and register GraphicConverter from `http://www.lemkesoft.com/us_index.html`. GraphicConverter handles dozens of image formats and provides basic editing utilities.

QuickTime

You may recall from Chapter 1 that QuickTime is one of Mac OS X's imaging components. By using its technology, system applications can support reading or writing many different image formats. You might also know that QuickTime can be used to play digital media, both from within a Web browser and as an application on your desktop. Let's take a closer look at the QuickTime 6 media player.

QuickTime supports most common digital media formats, including those for movies, MP3 files, WAV files, images, and interactive applications. QuickTime 6 also supports MPEG-4, the global standard for multimedia, which is designed to deliver high-quality video using smaller file sizes.

You can learn more about the supported formats by visiting Apple's QuickTime specification page at `http://www.apple.com/quicktime/products/qt/specifications.html`.

Watching QuickTime movies play in your Web browser window is probably the most likely place you will experience QuickTime, so let's take a look at the controls of the QuickTime browser plug-in. Figure 5.11 shows a QuickTime movie playing in the Internet Explorer browser.

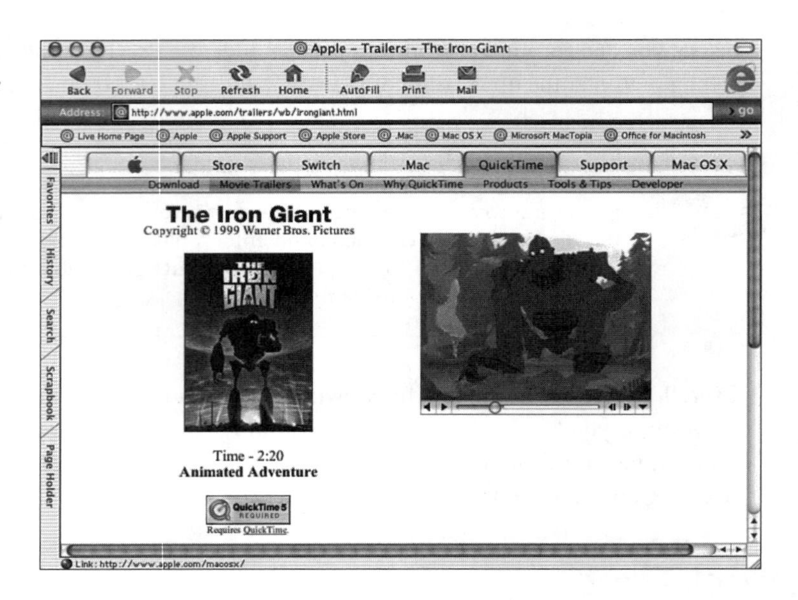

FIGURE 5.11
Many users experience QuickTime through their browsers.

The movie controls are located across the bottom of the video. If you've used a VCR or other media player, you've certainly seen these before. However, there are a few shortcuts you might want to know.

For example, clicking the speaker icon on the far left can instantly mute the volume. You can also control the volume level using the up-arrow and down-arrow keys on the keyboard.

To increase the volume beyond its normal limit, hold down the Shift key while dragging the volume control.

Playback controls also can be activated from the keyboard, saving the need to mouse around on your screen. To toggle between playing and pausing, press the Spacebar. To rewind or fast forward, use the left-arrow and right-arrow keys, respectively.

At the far right of the control bar is the QuickTime menu (indicated by the down arrow), which gives you easy access to QuickTime settings.

If the movie being played is streaming from a remote server, some of these controls might not be available. For example, on-demand streaming video can't be fast-forwarded or rewound, but static files can be. The available controls depend entirely on the movie you're viewing.

The QuickTime Player

The QuickTime Player application provides another means of viewing movies and streams. In fact, many users might be surprised to find that they can use the QuickTime Player application to tune in to a variety of interesting streams—ranging from news to entertainment—without the need for a separate Web browser. Apple has been working with entertainment and news outlets for the past few years to develop QuickTime TV. The stations available in QuickTime TV provide streaming media 24 hours a day. Don't have a good source for National Public Radio (NPR) in your neighborhood? Use QuickTime TV to play a high-quality NPR stream anytime, anywhere.

> Minimizing a QuickTime Player movie *while* it is playing adds a live icon to the Dock. The movie (with sound) continues to play in the minimized Dock icon. Even if you don't have a use for this feature, give it a try—it's extremely cool!

To use QuickTime Player, open it from its default home in the Dock or from the Applications folder. After the default QuickTime window opens, click the QuickTime icon button at the lower right to launch the Apple QuickTime view, as shown in Figure 5.12.

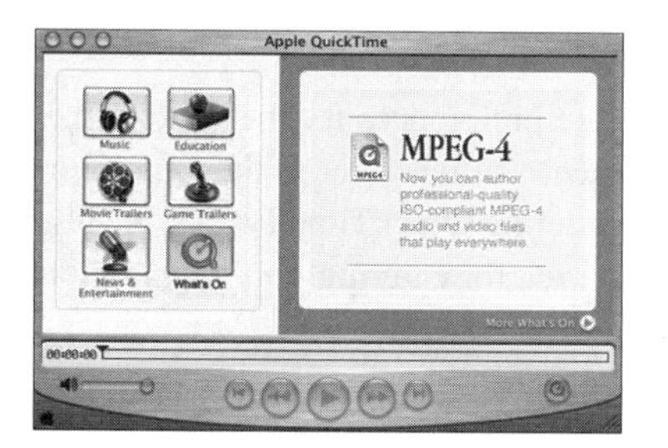

FIGURE 5.12
The Apple QuickTime view enables you to choose from several categories of content.

The left side of this view lists several categories from which you can choose what to view or listen to. Clicking a category launches your default Web browser and brings up a page listing the available content. Selecting a listed item launches a new Apple QuickTime window in your desktop to play the item.

When QuickTime starts to load a streaming video clip, it goes through four steps before displaying the video:

- **Connecting**—Makes a connection to the streaming server.
- **Requested Data**—Waits for acknowledgement from the remote server.
- **Getting Info**—Retrieves information about the QuickTime movie.

- **Buffering**—QuickTime buffers several seconds of video to eliminate stuttering from the playback.

If the player stalls during any of these steps, there might be a problem with the remote server or your transport setting (how your computer talks on the Internet). Try another streaming source, and if it still fails, use the QuickTime System Preferences panel to select an alternative transport.

You can use QuickTime Player to play information from other sources in addition to QuickTime TV. QuickTime refers to every media type as a movie. For example, you can open and play CD audio tracks and MP3s by selecting the Open Movie command from the File menu. Even though there aren't any visuals, these media types are referred to as *movies* in QuickTime's vocabulary.

You can open local movie files by choosing Open Movie from the File menu (Command-O) or by dragging a movie file onto the QuickTime Dock icon. If you have a streaming server URL, you can select Open URL (Command-U) from the File menu to directly open the stream.

QuickTime Preferences

The Preferences submenu, found in the QuickTime Player application menu in your menu bar contains three different choices: Player Preferences, QuickTime Preferences, and Registration.

The Player Preferences settings are preferences for the QuickTime Player application itself, whereas the QuickTime Preferences settings refer to the QuickTime System Preferences panel. If you're interested in registering QuickTime (which we highly suggest), the Registration option provides an input area for entering your registration code.

The Player Preferences dialog box is shown in Figure 5.13.

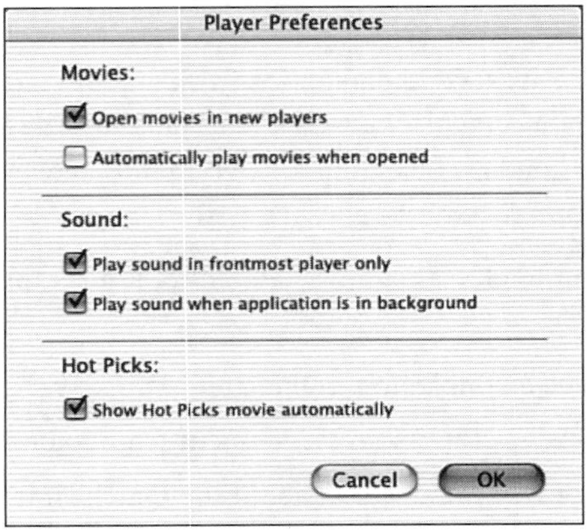

FIGURE 5.13
Choose how QuickTime Player reacts to opening and playing movies.

Use the following options in the Player Preferences dialog box to control how the application handles multiple movies and playback:

- **Open Movies in New Players**—By default, QuickTime Player reuses existing windows when opening new movies. To open new movies in new windows, select this check box.
- **Automatically Play Movies When Opened**—Does what it says! When checked, QuickTime Player starts playing a movie immediately after it's opened.
- **Play Sound in Frontmost Player Only**—By default, sound is played only in the active player window. To hear sound from all playing movies simultaneously, uncheck this option.
- **Play Sound When Application Is in Background**—If this option is checked, sound continues to play even when QuickTime Player isn't the active application.
- **Show Hot Picks Movie Automatically**—Automatically fetches and plays Apple's Hot Pick movie when QuickTime Player is started.

Click OK to save the application preferences.

The QuickTime System Preferences panel (located in the Internet & Network section of System Preferences) enables you to change QuickTime's settings for better quality playback and to make other modifications. Let's discuss some of the more useful settings.

The first tab controls QuickTime's plug-ins, shown in Figure 5.14. Plug-ins are used when movies are viewed in a Web browser.

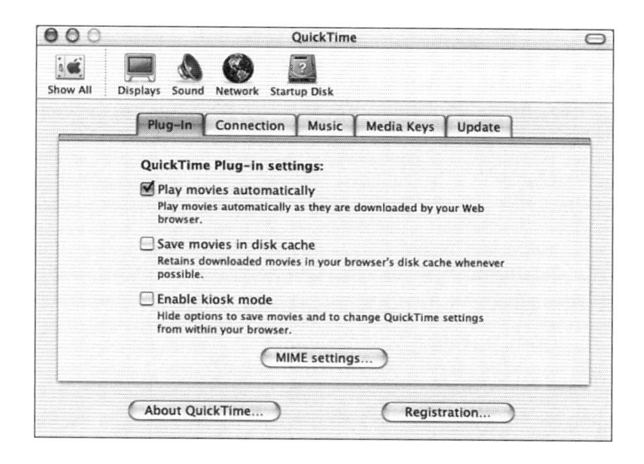

FIGURE 5.14
Use QuickTime's System Preferences to optimize display for your system.

The Play Movies Automatically option directs QuickTime to start playing a movie after enough of it has been buffered. This option applies to movies that aren't streamed. Select the Save Movies in Disk Cache option to temporarily store a clip to speed up repeated viewings. The Enable Kiosk Mode option makes it possible for movies to run continuously unattended for demonstrations and presentations.

Click the MIME Settings button to open a list of all the MIME types that QuickTime can handle and everything it's currently configured to display. MIME stands for Multipurpose Internet Mail Extension and defines a set of document types, such as text, HTML, and so on.

Some items (such as Flash) are intentionally disabled because they're better handled by other browser plug-ins.

The Connection tab, shown in Figure 5.15, configures the type of network access QuickTime can expect your computer to have. This information helps QuickTime choose the appropriate type of media to display, depending on how fast it can be received.

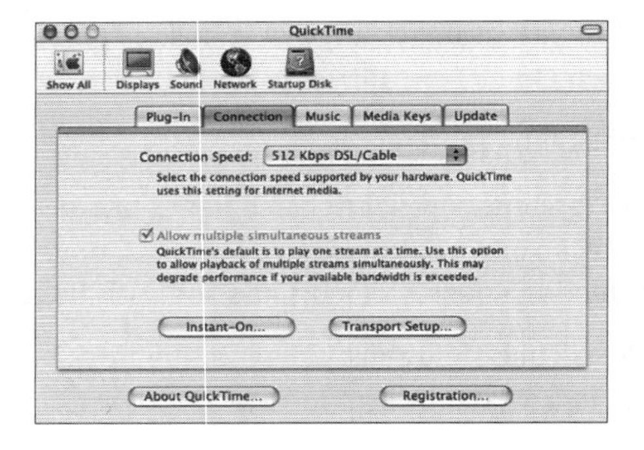

FIGURE 5.15
Choose your connection speed and transport type for the best movie quality.

The Transport Setup button is used to choose the protocol for streaming. By default, QuickTime attempts to choose the best transport based on your network type. It's best not to change these settings unless you're having difficulty viewing media.

By default, QuickTime allows only a single media stream. If your bandwidth enables you to do so, click the Allow Multiple Simultaneous Streams option to stream many sources at once. This option is automatically selected when you specify a high-speed connection method.

The Music and Media Keys panes enable you to change QuickTime's default MIDI music synthesizer and to enter access keys for secured media files, respectively. Most users won't need to use these panes. The final tab, Update, contains settings for updating your version of QuickTime, either manually or automatically.

As you work with QuickTime, you quickly discover the thousands of high-quality video streams available on the Internet. For starters, be sure to check out Apple's `http://www.apple.com/quicktime/` site for the best movie-trailers anywhere. To sample some real-time streaming video of a nature site, point your browser to `http://www.racerocks.com/`—an interactive and very live nature preserve.

DVD Player

If your computer came equipped with an internal DVD drive, you'll want to make use of DVD Player, an application for displaying DVD content on your computer screen. To start DVD Player, simply insert a video DVD into your system, or double-click the DVD Player icon in the Applications folder. By default, Mac OS X launches DVD Player automatically when it detects a DVD in the drive. At startup, a video window and playback controller appear onscreen. The playback controller is shown in Figure 5.16.

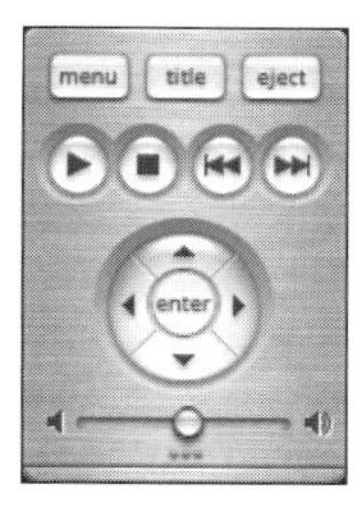

FIGURE 5.16
DVD Player's controller window keeps all the needed controls in one convenient place.

Use the controller window as you would a standard DVD remote. Basic playback buttons are provided, along with a selection control and a volume slider directly under the primary playback controls.

Six additional advanced controls are accessible by clicking the three dots right of the controller window. This opens a window tray containing Slow, Step, Return, Subtitle, Audio, and Angle buttons. In Figure 5.16, the controller window is shown with the window tray extended. If you prefer a horizontally oriented player control, choose Controller Type, Horizontal (Shift-Command-H) from the Controls menu. You can switch back to the vertical layout at any time by choosing the Vertical (Shift-Command-V) option from the same menu.

To navigate onscreen selections without the use of the controller, you can simply point-and-click at a DVD menu item to select it. To navigate with the keyboard, use the arrow keys and press Return.

Although the onscreen controller can be used for most everything, DVD Player also provides keyboard commands for controlling playback. The following options are available under the Controls menu:

- **Controller Type**—Choose Horizontal (Shift-Command-H) or Vertical (Shift-Command-V) orientation
- **Play/Pause**—(Spacebar) Play or pause the video
- **Stop**—(Command-.) Stop the current video from playing
- **Fast Forward**—(Command-right arrow) Speed through the video playback
- **Rewind**—(Command-left arrow) Move backward through the video playback
- **Previous Chapter**—(right arrow) Skip to the previous chapter on the DVD
- **Next Chapter**—(left arrow) Skip to the next chapter on the DVD
- **DVD Menu**—(Command-`) Stop playback and load the menu for the active DVD
- **Volume Up**—(Command-up arrow) Increase the volume
- **Volume Down**—(Command-down arrow) Decrease the volume
- **Mute**—(Command-K) Mute the sound
- **Eject**—(Command-E) Eject the current DVD

When fast-forwarding or rewinding, the view is displayed at an accelerated rate. Use the Scan Rate option under the Controls menu to set the speed to two, four, or eight times faster than normal.

DVD Player Preferences

The preferences for DVD Player are split across three tabs. The Player tab, shown in Figure 5.17, enables you to set how DVD Player reacts upon system startup and insertion of a DVD. You can also choose the viewer size.

The Disc tab contains settings for default language and the option to enable DVD@ccess, which allows DVD Player to recognize and react to embedded hot spots that link to Internet Web sites.

The Windows tab turns on and off controller help tags and window status messages, which appear while a movie is playing.

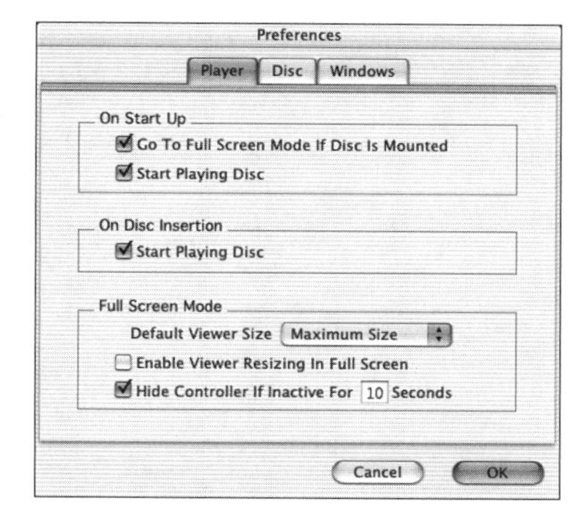

FIGURE 5.17
Change how DVD Player is activated and the size of the viewing window.

Sherlock

As its name implies, the Sherlock application is something of a detective, tracking down information on the Internet from the clues you provide. Some people might find it hard to get excited about a search tool, but Sherlock is far from ordinary. With specialized search categories, including yellow pages and a dictionary, Sherlock will quickly become your one-stop reference tool.

Sherlock is basically a collection of Internet search functions, each packaged as its own channel. The default channels are listed in the Channels panel, as shown in Figure 5.18. They're also listed in the toolbar at the top of the window, along with any additional channels to which you subscribe.

Long-time Mac users might be confused by the recent incarnation of Sherlock, which doesn't include the option to search the local machine's files. That feature is now available directly from the Finder by selecting Find from the Finder's File menu or with the keyboard shortcut Command-F. Refer to Chapter 2, "Exploring the Desktop," for further information.

Each channel provides a specific kind of information, gathered from another source and displayed within the Sherlock interface. You'll notice that on the Channels page is a button labeled Terms of Use, which opens a sheet explaining that Apple doesn't produce most of the content displayed in Sherlock.

Let's take a look at each default channel's use and special features.

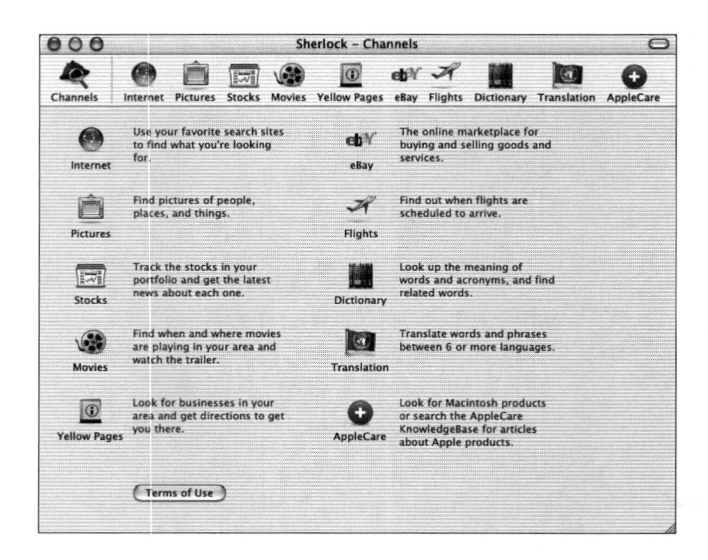

FIGURE 5.18
The Channels area of Sherlock displays the available search functions and brief descriptions of each.

The Internet Channel

The Internet channel compiles search results from popular Internet search sites, such as Ask Jeeves and Lycos. As shown in Figure 5.19, each search result lists the title and address of a Web page, a relevance rating, and the search site or sites that provided the entry.

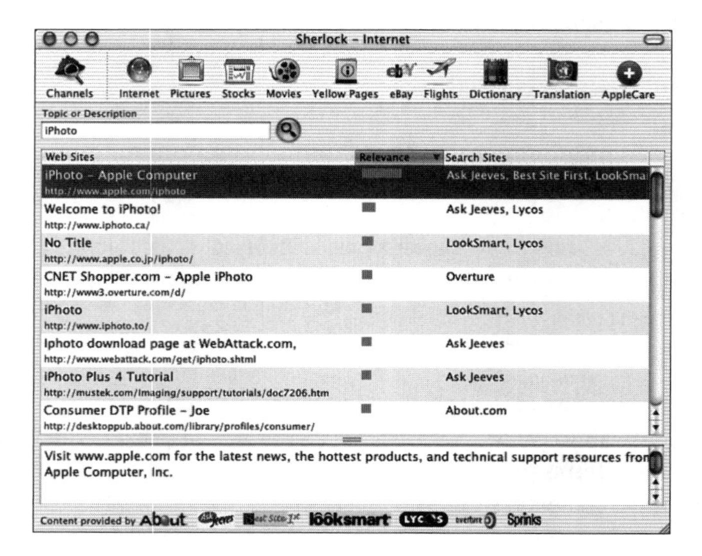

FIGURE 5.19
Searching the Internet from a variety of search engines is simplified by Sherlock.

To perform an Internet search, simply type your search terms into the text entry field at the top of the Internet channel panel and click the green Search button or press Return.

When the results listing appears, you can select an entry with a single click to see a site description if one is available. Double-clicking launches your default Web browser and opens the page you requested.

The Pictures Channel

Similar to searches using the Internet channel, the Pictures channel queries photo databases for digital images based on your search terms. Thumbnail images of the results are displayed in the results pane, as shown in Figure 5.20. Double-click a thumbnail image in the results to open a Web page displaying the full-sized picture.

FIGURE 5.20
Results appear as thumbnail images—double-click one to see the original.

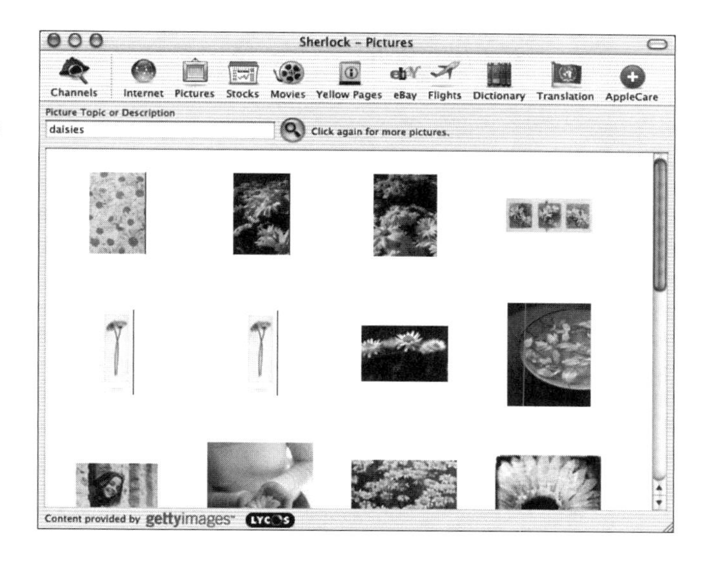

The photos displayed in the Pictures channel searches might not be free for commercial use. Read the terms of service from the originating site if you have any questions about what's allowed.

The Stocks Channel

The Stocks channel, shown in Figure 5.21, provides details about the market performance of publicly traded companies. The information shown includes the stock price at last trade, price change, price range over the course of the day, and the volume of shares traded. You can also view charts of a company's performance over the past year or week or for the current day.

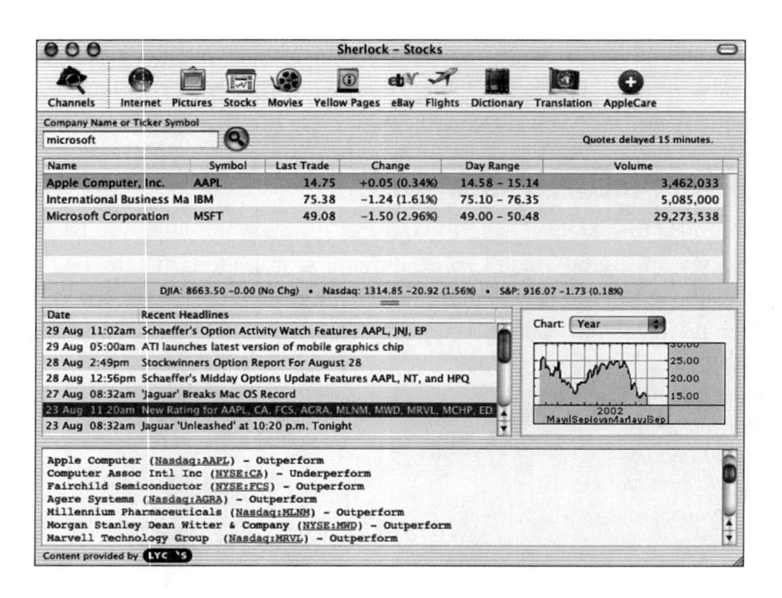

FIGURE 5.21
Enter a company's name or market symbol to see information about it, including recent news stories.

To find information about a company, enter its name or market symbol. Market symbols are unique identifiers, but many companies have similar names or several separate divisions. If you enter a name, you might see a sheet asking you to choose the company you're interested in. When the correct name or symbol appears in the text entry field, click the green Search button or press the Return key.

Market symbols and companies with similar names can make it difficult to ask for the listing you really want. If you don't enter the exact market symbol, some guesswork might be involved for Sherlock to return any results. Always check to make sure that the displayed information is for the company you thought you requested!

In addition to providing stock quotes, Sherlock also displays recent news articles pertaining to the selected company. To read a story, select its headline from the left of the chart and the bottom pane displays the full text.

The Movies Channel

Sherlock's Movies channel, shown in Figure 5.22, pulls together all the information you need to choose a movie and a theater in which to view it.

FIGURE 5.22
The Movies channel displays a QuickTime preview of the selected movie as well as theater addresses.

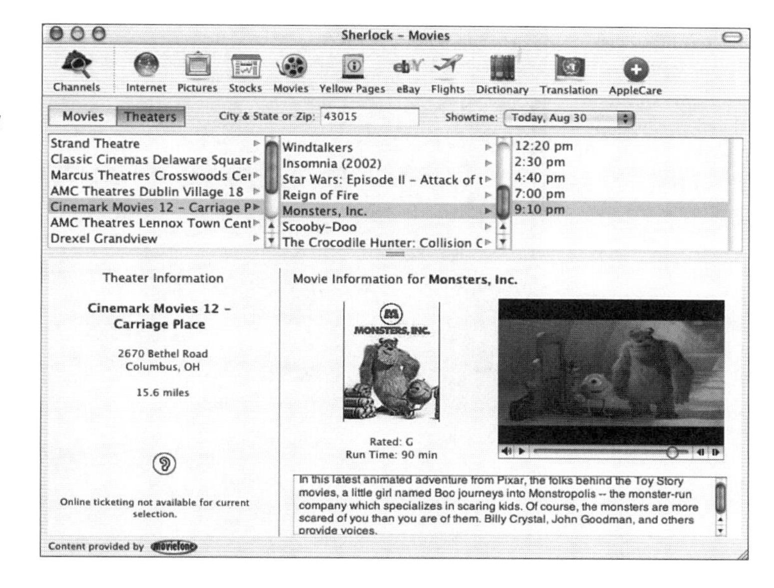

To use the Movies channel, you must enter either your city and state or your ZIP Code. Then you can choose to search either Movies or Theaters in your area. The Showtime pop-up menu enables you to choose the date of interest to you.

Choose one of the movie and theater listings at the top of the panel that's of interest to you, and the bottom panes of the window fill with theater and movie information. In addition to a text summary of the movie, you can watch a preview for the selected option in QuickTime.

> To play the QuickTime preview, you might be prompted to set your network connection information in QuickTime Preferences if you haven't already done so. Refer to the section on Quicktime above for more details.

The Yellow Pages Channel

Use the Yellow Pages channel, shown in Figure 5.23, to obtain the phone number and address for a business and to view a map of its location. Simply enter the business name and either the city and state or the ZIP Code of the area to search, and click the green button. In the middle pane, choose from among the list of potential matches to see detailed information.

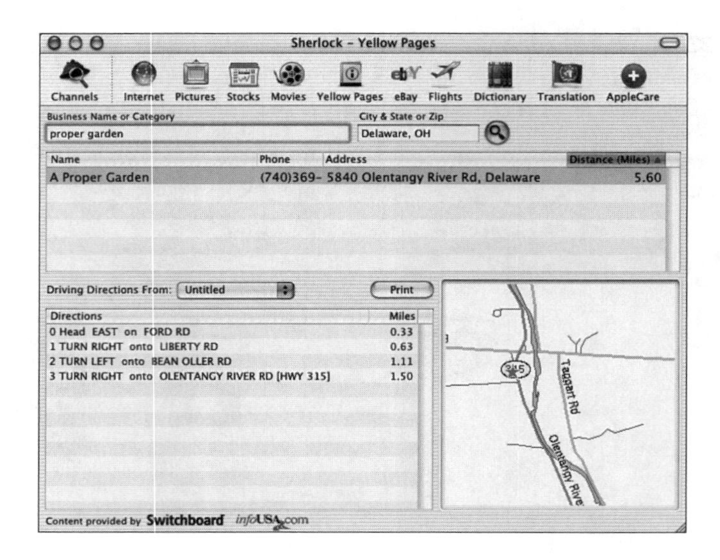

FIGURE 5.23
Obtain contact information and personalized driving directions to businesses.

To receive driving directions, you must first enter an address in the Locations tab of the Sherlock Preferences. To do so, follow these steps:

1. Choose Preferences, shown in Figure 5.24, from the Sherlock menu.

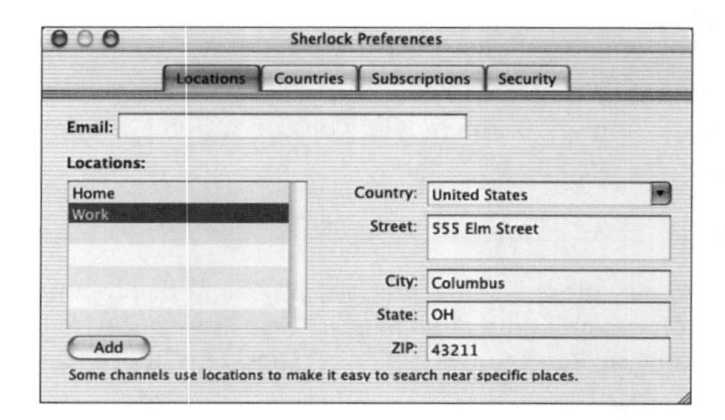

FIGURE 5.24
You can enter multiple addresses in the Locations tab.

2. Click the Add button to create an untitled entry under Locations.
3. To change the label of your new location, double-click on the word Untitled until only that word is highlighted and then type a new label. Keep in mind that you can have more than one location entered, so change it to something meaningful.
4. Fill in the information on the right side of the window.
5. Close the Preferences window. Your entry is saved as you type. To delete an entry, simply select it from the Locations listing and press the Delete key on your keyboard.

When you return to the Yellow Pages channel, you can select the location you added in the Driving Directions From pop-up menu. The Directions pane fills with step-by-step instructions.

The eBay Channel

From the eBay channel, you can search active eBay auctions and track those of interest to you. To search, enter keywords in the Item Title text entry field and set your other parameters, such as product category, region, and price range, and then click the search button. When you choose a result from the search, its details fill the bottom panes of the screen, as shown in Figure 5.25.

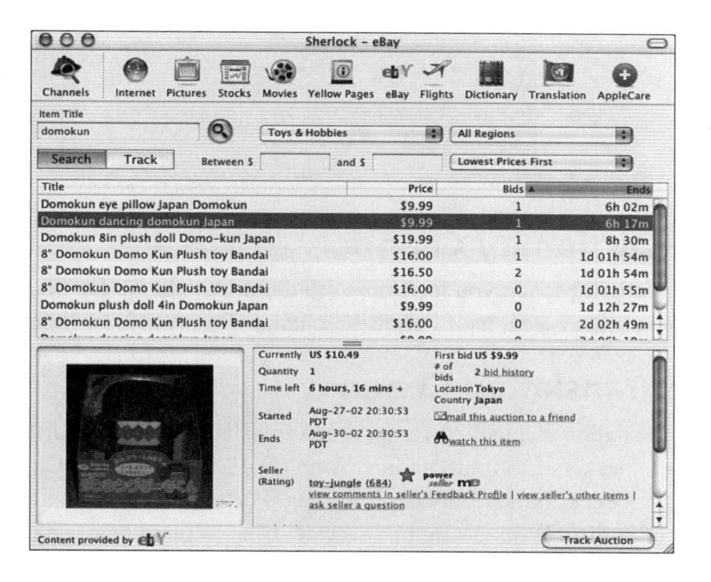

FIGURE 5.25
If you enjoy online auctions, the eBay channel will delight you.

To track an item, highlight it in the results listing and click the Track Auction button at lower right. Changing to Track mode using the button just below the search field reveals a list of only those items you're tracking. To remove an item, select it and press the Delete key on your keyboard.

The Flights Channel

For information on current flights, go to the Flights channel. Here you can view flight status by route or by airline and flight number. Select a specific flight for details about the aircraft and flight. For some entries, you can also view a chart depicting the plane's position en route, as shown in the lower-right corner of Figure 5.26.

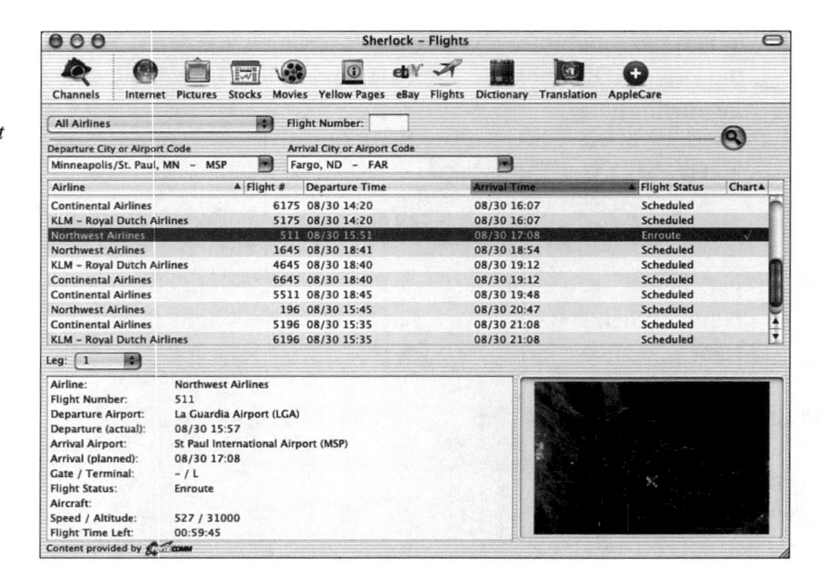

FIGURE 5.26
View the status of specific flights, including a chart of the flight path.

The Dictionary Channel

As you might expect, you look up word definitions in the Dictionary channel. For some words, you also see a list of phrases containing that word from *Roget's II Thesaurus*.

The Translation Channel

The Translation channel performs rough translations between different languages. English speakers can translate into Simplified and Traditional Chinese, Dutch, French, German, Greek, Italian, Japanese, Korean, Portuguese, Russian, and Spanish, and then back to English. When using this service, keep in mind that computer-generated translations do not match the output of a skilled human translator.

The AppleCare Channel

If you have a specific technical question that Help Viewer can't resolve, the AppleCare channel enables you to search the AppleCare Knowledge Base for reports about Apple products and issues.

Now that we explored the channels, let's examine the features accessible in Sherlock's preferences.

Sherlock Preferences

Sherlock's preference dialog box, shown earlier in Figure 5.24, contains four tabs—Locations, Countries, Subscriptions, and Security—in which you can adjust Sherlock's settings. We discussed the Locations configurations earlier during our look at the Yellow Pages channel.

The Countries tab enables you to specify which countries' channels you want to receive. By default, only the country you selected during set up is turned on, but other countries in which the same language is spoken also appear. To see a list of all countries, check the Show All Countries box.

The Subscriptions tab enables you to add additional channels to Sherlock. Although the current version of Sherlock—version 3.5—is somewhat new, in the past it was common for Web site owners to write plug-ins for Sherlock that allowed it to include those sites in its searches. In the Subscriptions tab, you can add channels created by people outside of Apple.

The Security tab contains settings to enable channels from non-Apple sources. If you don't enable the Web sites of channels you've added in the Subscriptions tab, you are asked to approve each channel that's not part of Apple's basic set. The Security tab also contains settings to manage cookies that might be encountered by Sherlock as it searches the Internet on your behalf.

Cookies are small files sent to your computer from Web sites. Sites use cookies to keep track of you as you interact with the site. (This is because the computer running the Web site doesn't have another way to recognize that you're the same person who looked at the preceding page.) Even though cookies are mostly harmless, some people don't like the idea of having others track their movements on the Internet, even if the information is most likely never seen by human eyes.

Summary

Your computer comes equipped with a wealth of helpful and fun applications, ranging from the simple (but not so simple!) Stickies to Sherlock, a convenient search tool. In this chapter, we looked at the use of some basic productivity applications, including Calculator, Clock, and TextEdit. You then learned about some more entertaining options, such as Chess, QuickTime, and DVD Player. We wrapped up the chapter with a tour of Sherlock 3, your system's built-in Internet search tool.

CHAPTER 6

Installing Additional Software

Although Mac OS X comes with many programs and tools offering a wide range of features, at some point you'll probably want to add additional software to your system. In this chapter, we will talk about how to install software. Even though software installation is not difficult, Mac OS X supports several different methods of doing so. Following that, we'll discuss several hardware topics related to installing and running applications, including checking the amount of RAM and the amount of free space on your hard drive.

Installing Software

When it comes to expanding your collection of software, your first question might be "What are my options?" You'll be pleased to hear that, despite being a relatively new operating system, Mac OS X already has many available applications. The only tricky part is knowing where to find them.

Fortunately, a number of good online libraries feature Mac OS X software. (If you need to learn more about how to get online or how use a Web browser, those topics are discussed in Chapter 4, "Using the Internet.")

The following sites present the latest and greatest Mac OS X programs that are available for download or on CD-ROM (by purchase):

- **VersionTracker**—`www.versiontracker.com/vt_mac_osx.shtml`—Updated continually, VersionTracker's Web site is often the first to carry new Mac OS X software. As a nearly comprehensive catalog, it also works as a handy reference guide. To find what you need, just type the name or a keyword for a product into the search field.
- **Mac OS X Apps**—`www.macosxapps.com/`—This site features in-depth discussions about new software and uses.
- **Apple's Mac OS X Downloads**—`www.apple.com/downloads/macosx/`—Although smaller than the previous two sites, Apple's software compendium is well documented and easily navigated.

Later in this hour, we recommend several interesting applications on these sites that you might want to try.

Task: Downloading and Installing Software

Although there's no single installation technique for all software that's available for the Mac OS X, you'll see in this hour that there are two common methods. Obviously, you should read the documentation that comes with your software if you want to be certain of the results, but for those who are anxious to double-click, this section offers a basic description of what to expect.

> If you would rather purchase your software from a mail-order or in-store vendor, just make sure to read the product information to ensure compatibility with Mac OS X, or with Mac OS 9 if you need to run the application in Classic mode, as discussed in Chapter 3, "Working with Windows, Folders, Files, and Applications." The installation process for disc images (explained later in the hour) still applies.

Begin by choosing a piece of software you'd like to try that is available online. The sites listed previously offer free software for all purposes (for some suggestions, look ahead a couple pages), and sometimes limited-time trials of commercial software can be downloaded. After you locate where to download the software, you're ready to begin:

1. On the software download page, determine which version your system requires and click that link. Be sure to choose a version that's made for Mac OS X.

2. If you're using Internet Explorer, your system begins downloading your selection, and a Download Manager window, similar to that shown in Figure 6.1, appears on your screen.

FIGURE 6.1
You can monitor the status of an item as it downloads.

Download Manager

File	Status	Time	Transferred
Virex_7.1.dmg	Complete	About one minute	3.5 MB
V7020718.dmg	Complete	< 1 minute	2.9 MB
RealOnePlayerOSX...	Complete	< 1 minute	4.7 MB
neko_saver.0_91a...	Complete	< 1 minute	33 KB
PixelNhance.dmg		< 1 minute	1.1 MB of 3.9 MB, 159 KB/sec

3. When the download is finished, several icons appear on your desktop, similar to Figure 6.2. The icon with the extension `.gz` represents a special file that has been encoded for easy storage and download. We'll talk more about this in the "Opening Compressed Files with StuffIt Expander" section later in this chapter. Another common type of download file ends with a `.sit` extension and contains the same files, but in an unencoded and compressed form.

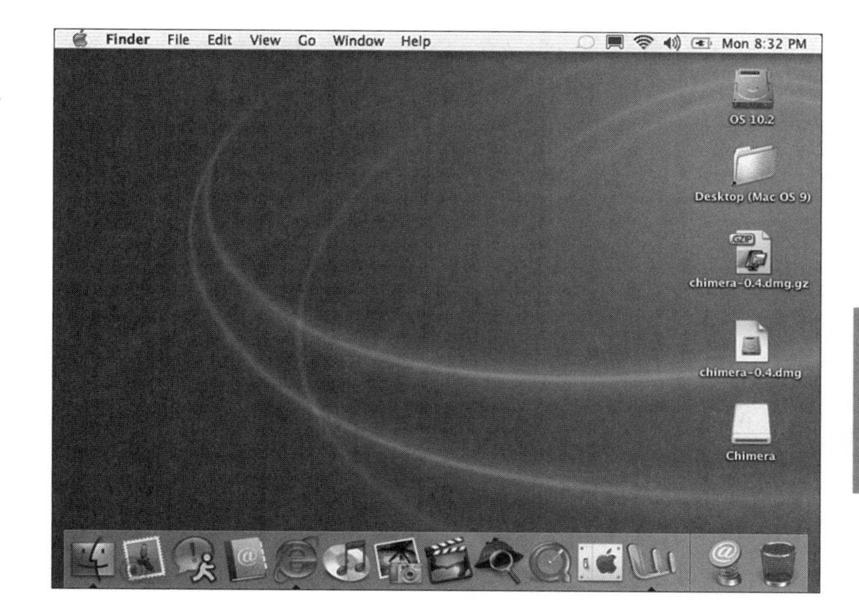

FIGURE 6.2
When you download software, several new icons appear on the desktop.

4. The final installation step could differ, depending on the application you're working with. Here are the three major variations:

   If a folder icon appears on your desktop, you must open it to reach the application file. The folder also usually contains a ReadMe file that explains what to do next. This kind of install exists only for very small programs.

   If a file icon with the extension `.pkg` or `.mpkg` appears, double-clicking will start the Apple Installer, which provides a simple step-by-step guide to installation. (The Apple Installer, by the way, is also used by most commercial software distributed on CD.)

   Finally, if a disk image icon appears, as with the Chimeradisk icon shown second from the bottom in Figure 6.2, double-clicking it mounts the disk, which you can then double click to open a Finder window containing the installation instructions. (By the way, you can recognize disk images because they have the `.dmg` file extension.)

   For example, when installing the Chimera Web browser, opening the disk icon results in the screen shown in Figure 6.3, which contains an icon for you to drag to the Applications folder on your hard drive.

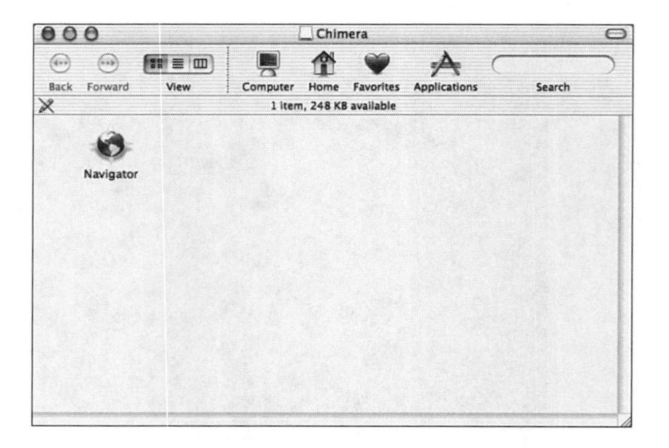

FIGURE 6.3
To install Chimera, simply drag the image to a folder in a Finder window.

When you've placed the file or folder where you want it, usually in the Applications folder, your application is ready for use. You can also place applications in other folders, if you have good reason. (We'll discuss this further in a little while.)

> To uninstall most software, simply locate the application file or folder and drag it to the Trash. Under Mac OS X, you should find most application folders in the systemwide Applications folder.

You can drag all the files that appeared on your desktop during download and installation to the Trash.

To eject a disk image from your computer, you can't be running the software contained on that disk.

If you try to move a disk image to the trash and get an error message that the item is in use, you probably didn't copy the contents of the disk image to your hard drive and are instead working off the disk image. To fix the problem, close the file, and then copy the disk image to the Mac OS X drive. Now the disk image should eject.

Opening Compressed Files with StuffIt Expander

You might have noticed that the downloaded files launch another application whose icon appears briefly in the Dock, as shown in Figure 6.4. That application is StuffIt Expander.

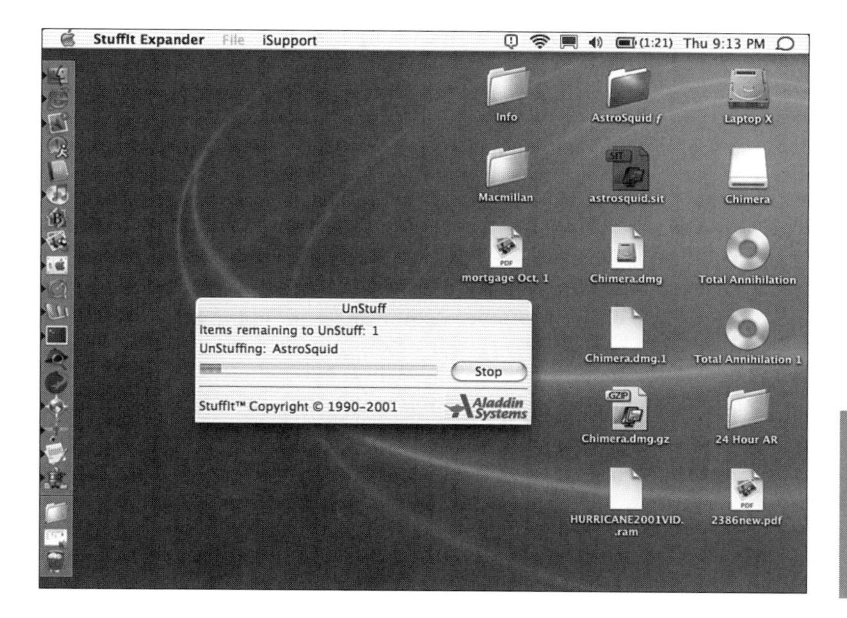

FIGURE 6.4
When the download is finished, StuffIt Expander goes to work.

You need StuffIt for use with compressed files. Because applications tend to be very large files, they come in a compressed form that takes up less space and makes downloading them faster and easier. These compressed files are also referred to as *archive files* because they're compact and easily stored.

Compression can be done in several different ways. Mac OS X supports several methods, including `.sit` (StuffIt) files and `.tar` and `.gz` files.

To install applications that come as archive files, you must return them to their original state. Recovering a full-sized file from its archive file is known as *extraction*. That's where StuffIt Expander, a tool included with Mac OS X, comes into play.

StuffIt Expander uncompresses most common archive types, and makes it simple for anyone to start downloading software. Most of the time, StuffIt Expander opens automatically when it's needed and leaves uncompressed folders on the desktop along with the original archive file. An example of this was shown in Figure 6.2 (the icon with the `.gz` text below it).

StuffIt Expander is located on your system at `Applications/Utilities/StuffIt Expander`. You might never need to start it manually, but you can use a number of settings in its Preferences dialog box to control actions, such as how StuffIt deals with files after extraction.

Choosing an Applications Folder

Mac OS X is a multiuser system, something that will be fully explained in Chapter 27, "Sharing (and Securing) Your Computer." For now though, we will talk about the implications of a multiuser system and where to place software you install on you system. When it comes to installing software, this seemingly small detail really matters.

When you install applications, keep in mind that other users don't necessarily have access to your home folder. If you install a large application in your home folder, you might be the only person who can use it, which could lead to other users installing copies of this same application on the same machine. To best utilize disk space and resource sharing, major applications should be installed in the system's Applications folder or in a subdirectory of Applications, rather than inside your home folder, so that everyone can use it.

One other issue: Be sure to read your software license agreements regarding operation by multiple users. If an application is licensed for only a single user (rather than a single computer), it should not be placed in the Applications folder where any other person can have access.

Some Software Suggestions

Let's look at some applications currently available for your Mac. These programs have been selected based on their unique features and immediate availability (either in full or demo form) over the Internet.

Although we recommend the following software, keep in mind that many other fine programs are available and that number grows daily. The following should serve only as a starting point for exploring the possibilities.

Useful Applications

Even before Mac OS X was released, developers were looking forward to exploiting its advanced networking, multitasking, and graphics capabilities. The following sections describe a few interesting applications. Some you might have heard of, whereas others are entirely new to the Mac platform.

- **Mozilla** (`www.mozilla.org`) is a Web browser related to Netscape Communicator—in fact, it's the open source project from which recent versions of Netscape were developed. The Mozilla software developers emphasize standards compliance and stability, and their product includes many new features before they appear in Netscape. (Camino, a version of Mozilla built especially for Mac OS X, is also available.)
- **OmniWeb, by the Omni Group** (`www.omnigroup.com/`), is an alternative Web browser with some amazing features. For example, if you've been annoyed by Web sites that spontaneously open lots of new browser windows that fill your screen, you can limit JavaScript's capability to open new windows. In addition, OmniWeb has a top-notch rendering engine that produces crisp pages and is an excellent choice for online presentations.

Games

If you're looking for computer games, try one of these:

- **Burning Monkey Solitaire** (`www.freeverse.com/flash/bms.mgi`) offers several versions of the Solitaire card game, including Klondike, Freecell, and 52 Card Pickup, delivered in an interface filled with taunting monkeys, as shown in Figure 6.5.

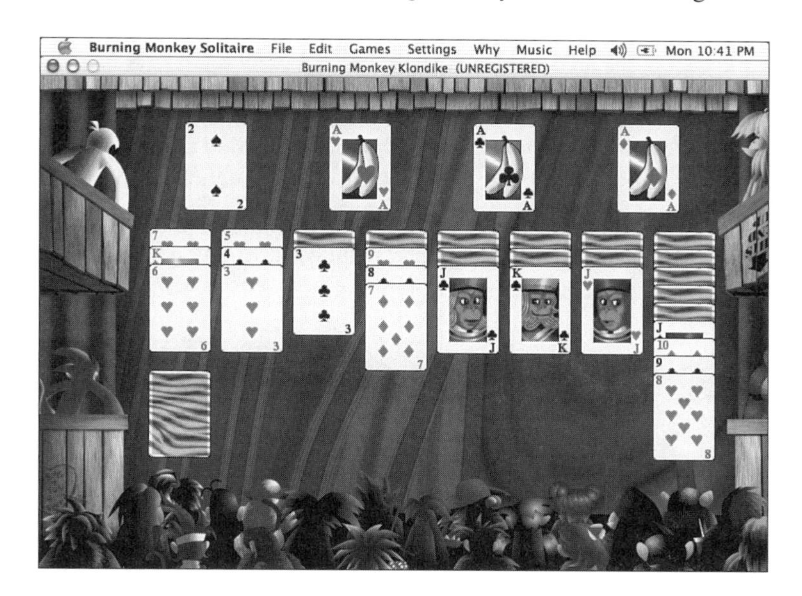

FIGURE 6.5
Burning Monkey Solitaire offers traditional Solitaire in an untraditional setting.

- **Battle Cocoa** (eng.osxdev.org/battlecocoa/), which was written especially for Mac OS X using Cocoa, is a smooth-playing Tetris clone with network play capacity.

Screensavers

Mac OS X comes with several attractive screensavers, but many people delight in finding new and interesting ones. Spice up your system by downloading one of these excellent replacements:

- **Mac OS X Screensavers 3.0** (www.epicware.com/macosxsavers.html) is a collection of popular screensavers that have been transplanted from another platform. Although several years old, this set is still pleasing to the eye.
- **Neko.saver** (homepage.mac.com/takashi_hamada/Acti/MacOSX/Neko/index.html) turns one or more animated cats loose on your desktop to play, sleep, and scamper across your screen.

To install a screensaver, simply place its application file in the system folder Library/Screen Savers or in your own ~/Library/Screen Savers folder, depending on whether you want public or private access. Remember that after you've installed a new screensaver, you still must choose it in the your Screen Effects Preferences to activate it.

Task: Checking Free Hard Drive Space

One consideration when installing software is how much hard drive space you have. Unlike RAM which we will discuss in a moment, memory on your hard drive is long-term storage. That is, when your Mac turns off, information such as the programs you've installed, and the files created with them, stay there.

To check your available hard drive space in Mac OS X, follow these steps:

1. Go to the main hard drive icon on your Mac in the upper-right corner of your screen, hold down the Ctrl key on your keyboard, and single-click the icon.
2. Select the Get Info option as shown in Figure 6.6. The Hard Disk Info window (see Figure 6.7) will appear and display information about your hard drive, including the amount of free space you have.

A hard drive icon might not necessarily be named *hard drive* because you can change the name of your hard drive. To do so, click once on the letters beneath the icon; let go of the mouse button but hold the mouse pointer in position. When the text becomes selected, you can just type in the new name.

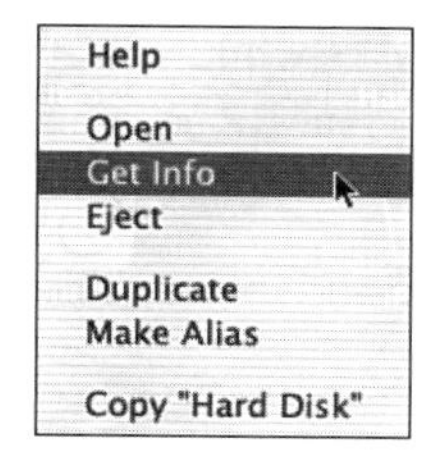

FIGURE 6.6
The Get Info option gives you the low-down.

FIGURE 6.7
The Info window.

Besides the room taken up by applications, digital media (such as music, photographs, and video) take up a lot of space. If you find yourself running low on storage, you can invest in an external drive. We'll discuss the options further in Chapter 7, "Choosing Peripheral Devices."

Task: Verifying Available Memory

Do you have enough memory (RAM)? Mac OS X itself uses a lot of memory, and the more you have the better performance will be. While Mac OS X includes a highly advanced virtual memory feature to get the most out of existing memory, if there isn't enough memory to run all your programs your system can bog down noticeably.

Mac OS X requires a minimum of 128MB of RAM, but the sweet spot, where performance takes the greatest boost, is roughly twice that. This makes a RAM upgrade not just a luxury, but an essential need for optimal performance.

RAM is different from hard drive space: RAM is the chip memory that your Mac can use while it's turned on. Think of it as being the conscious memory of your computer—when you turn off your Mac, the contents of the RAM goes away. But just as your own short-term memory helps you to perform daily tasks while you're awake, the RAM in your Mac helps it to perform its own tasks. Sufficient RAM is necessary for you to effectively run some complex applications, such as iMovie, or to run a combination of less-taxing applications all at once.

RAM, which is measured in megabytes, is getting cheaper all the time, and you might want to add some memory to your Mac. To expand this short-term memory in your computer, you buy and install extra chips. While the computer is turned on, the RAM helps it to process information more efficiently. Then, when the computer is turned off, the RAM is empty again.

Hard drive space, usually measured in gigabytes, is the long-term memory on your computer. You can always erase something you've stored in your hard drive when you're done; but unlike RAM, unless you delete something, the file will stay there even when the computer is turned off.

To check how much RAM you have, first make sure that you're in the Finder. The Finder on your Mac is like the main hotel lobby; so, if you have several programs running, the Finder is the central place in your Mac.

To switch to the Finder:

In Mac OS X:

1. Click on the Apple menu in the upper-left corner of the screen (see Figure 6.8).

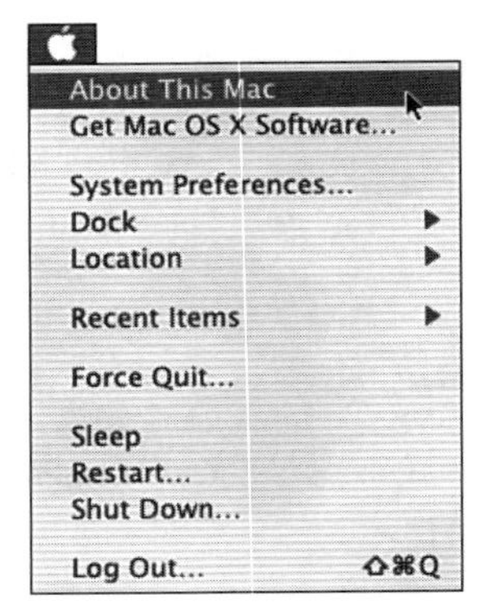

FIGURE 6.8
The Apple menu.

2. Choose About This Computer (see Figure 6.9).

FIGURE 6.9
The About This Computer window, displaying memory information.

If you find that what you have isn't quite enough, you'll want to consider a RAM upgrade. After the upgrade, you'll be able to run more programs at the same time. By having more memory available the operating system doesn't have to use as much of your computer's hard drive to store program code. That way, things run noticeably faster, and you'll see fewer delays as you launch or switch applications.

> In case you're wondering, you don't have to do anything special to allocate memory to your applications; Mac OS X will automatically allocate the amount of memory a program needs to run efficiently. However, if your system has a very small amount of RAM, don't expect Mac OS X to work miracles.

Summary

In this chapter, we discussed the basics of adding new software—from finding what you need to downloading and installing it. Although we focused on easy-to-obtain, downloadable software, the issues we discussed also apply to purchased software discs. (Remember that, in Mac OS X, it matters where you place new applications on your system—try to use the Applications folder for its intended purpose.) We ended the chapter with a look at hard drive and RAM space and how to determine how much of each is available.

CHAPTER 7

Choosing Peripheral Devices

While your Mac is a marvelous tool in and of itself, there are times when you may want to supplement its capabilities with peripheral hardware, such as printers, scanners, digital cameras, and even additional hard drives. Fortunately, recent Macs come equipped with USB and FireWire ports, which make connecting to such things easy. USB and FireWire are two different standards used to convey data between computers and various devices.

> If you have an older peripheral device that connects via SCSI instead of USB or FireWire, you can check with your local Apple computer vendor for a SCSI-to-USB adapter or a SCSI-to-FireWire adapter. Such adapters enable you to use older scanners, hard drives, and other devices on your computer. The only downside is with hard drives; they'll run slower on a USB port (the SCSI-to-FireWire adapter is better if your computer has FireWire).

USB Basics

Your computer comes with a flexible connection port called USB (short for *Universal Serial Bus*). Bearing a flat, rectangle shape, it enables you to attach up to 127 separate and distinct items that will expand its capabilities.

> USB cables have two types of plugs, so that you can connect the correct end to the correct end. The part that plugs into your computer (or a hub) is small and rectangular. The side that goes into the device itself is square. Some USB devices support a different style of connection, but it is always obvious which end goes where.

Here are some advantages of USB:

- **Speed**—The USB port is capable of up to 12 megabits per second transfer speed. This is perfect for scanners and input devices such as keyboards and mice.
- **Easy Hookup**—As you'll see shortly from the seven steps for hooking up a FireWire or USB device, it's about as easy as it can get. So, if you are anxious to try out your new peripheral, you'll be glad to know that it will be up and running in minutes.

> USB is *hot-pluggable*, which means you can attach and detach the item (with a few cautions) without having to turn off your computer.

- **Growing Selection**—In this cross-platform world, the manufacturer of a USB product for the PC can easily make it work on a Mac, simply by writing a new software driver (and with some mice and keyboards, new software might not even be needed).

Before you buy a USB peripheral, you'll want to check the requirements to see if you need anything extra. Don't forget the cable. For some reason, not all manufacturers supply them. If in doubt, ask your dealer.

If you have used up all your USB ports, you may need to purchase an expansion hub. It's a small box with a half dozen or so extra USB outlets. The hub shown in Figure 7.1 is typical. Plug it into one of the computer's USB ports and fill up the ports with as many USB devices as you have. When you hook up a large chain of USB devices, you might need a hub, which is a central connecting device. Some items work as hubs (such as an iMac's keyboard), and some don't.

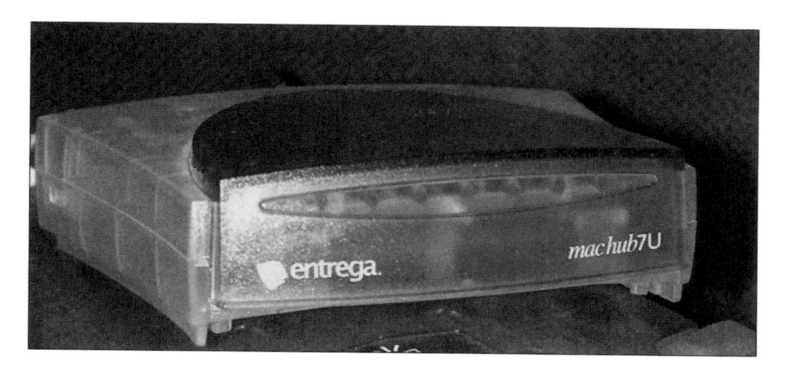

FIGURE 7.1
This is 7-port Entrega Mac hub.

FireWire Basics

Developed by Apple, FireWire is much faster than the other popular standard, USB. For that reason, FireWire is ideal for working with information-rich content, such as audio and video. In fact, it works so well that Apple won a Primetime Emmy Award in 2001 for its contributions to the television industry.

FireWire and USB are totally separate technologies. You cannot hook up a USB device to a FireWire port, or vice versa (the plug layouts don't even match).

FireWire enables you to hook up all sorts of high-speed devices to your Mac. Most digital camcorders, for example, have FireWire connections, and if you plan to use iMovie, which we will introduce later in this book, you absolutely must have a computer and a camera that are FireWire-ready.

You can also use your Mac's FireWire capability to hook up FireWire-based hard drives, removable drives, CD drives, tape backup drives, and scanners. FireWire features a plug-and-play capability similar to USB. You install the software, and then plug in the device and it's recognized, just like that.

Not all FireWire-compatible devices refer to this technology as FireWire. Depending on the manufacturer, it might also be known as IEEE 1394 or i.LINK, but they work just the same.

FireWire really comes into its own when you need the highest possible performance on your Mac. As of this book's writing, dozens and dozens of FireWire products are available, and more are coming to market. You'll want to check with your dealer to see what's available.

Printers

An entire book could be written about all the varieties of printers. In this section, we'll make do with a snapshot of what's available: inkjet printers, laser printers, dye-sublimation printers, thermal wax printers, and imagesetters.

Inkjet Printers

At the inexpensive end of the spectrum are home and office inkjet printers, almost all of which can deliver acceptable quality color printing. Examples of inkjets include HP's Deskjet series, Canon's Bubble Jets, and Epson's Stylus printers.

Not all inkjet printers support PostScript, the page description language that enables images to be printable at any resolution or color setting. Only certain models are capable of interpreting this language and reproducing images saved with this language.

Inkjet printers work by spraying microscopically small dots of colored ink onto a sheet of paper. The most common four-color inkjet models utilize a time-proven process of blending cyan, magenta, yellow, and black inks to reproduce most colors in the spectrum—in other words, they use the CMYK model. Higher-end printers refine this model by adding light cyan and light magenta, for a better, smoother rendition of sky, skin, and other pale and pastel tones. With the standard four-color process, large patches of a bright pastel hue—for instance, the sky—might not appear solid. Instead, the dots of cyan and magenta that compose such patches are visible. In other words, when limited to just four colors of ink, bright pastel colors may not reproduce well. The addition of the two lighter shades of ink (light cyan and light magenta) refines the appearance of brighter, blended tones, making the sky look like the sky, for example, and not a dotted mess.

Kodak and Epson have introduced printers that use the Hexachrome system. The ENCAD division of Kodak has also introduced its own eight-color process, Octachrome, that couples Hexachrome's additions of orange and green with the pastel inks (light cyan and light magenta) of the older six-color process. These newer processes aren't common yet, but in the computer world, everything gets smaller, faster, smarter, and less expensive practically overnight. Naturally, a six- or eight-color printer will give you a better print than a four-color printer, all other things being equal. But all things are *never* equal, and you can get surprisingly good results from even the less expensive printers if you're careful about preparing the picture for printing. Figure 7.2 shows the inner workings of a typical inkjet printer.

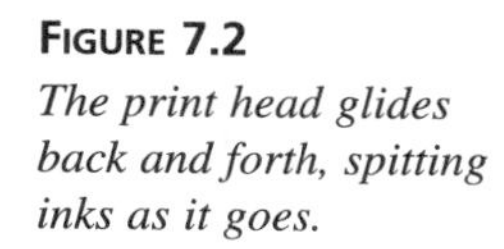

FIGURE 7.2
The print head glides back and forth, spitting inks as it goes.

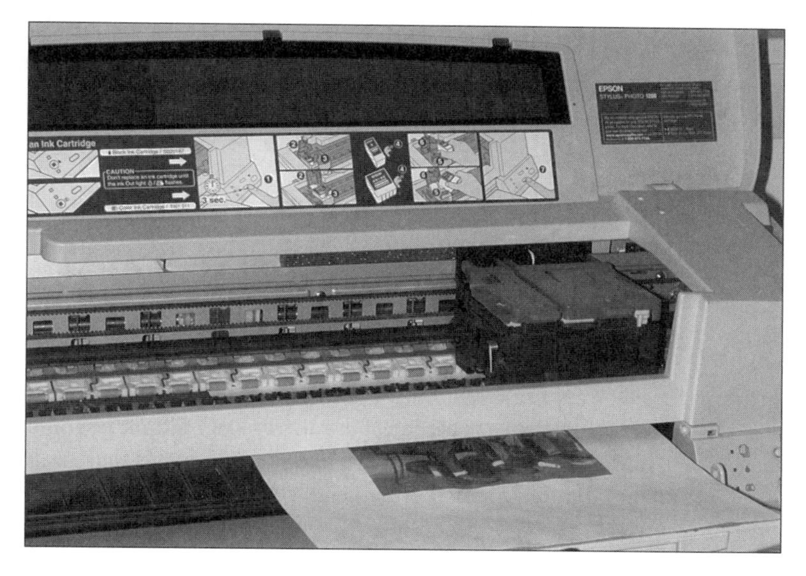

For your very best work, consider looking for a service bureau with an Iris printer. In the art world, Iris prints are very highly prized. (Art dealers may also call them giclée prints—*giclée* is French for "squirted.") High-end inkjets, such as the Iris, can cost tens of thousands of dollars but are perfect for graphics professionals. Iris and similar art-quality printers are sometimes found at service bureaus or art studios. They can produce very large prints, up to 33"×46", with remarkable detail and quality. You can have an Iris print made of your work, but prints tend to be expensive. Prices average around $150 for a single 16×20 print, but this is money well spent if the picture deserves the extra expense and effort. Some do.

Laser Printers

The laser printer is the professional standard and a good balance of price, quality, and speed. Laser printers abound from well-known companies such as Hewlett-Packard and Xerox.

Most laser printers produced today output 600 to 1200 dpi, and are particularly good with halftone and grayscale images. Some can subtly alter the size of the printed dots, thus improving quality. Laser printers are generally faster than inkjet printers, but they tend to be more expensive.

Laser printers work by heat-fusing powdered toner to the paper. Color lasers use a four-color toner cartridge. Color laser prints can be very good if you like bright colors and don't mind the shiny surface that you're likely to get in areas where the toner is quite dense.

Dye-Sublimation Printers

Dye-sublimation printers are expensive photographic-quality printers. You get what you pay for; image quality is superb. These printers use special ribbons and paper. You can't use ordinary paper with them, and the specially coated paper is expensive. You can often find these printers at a service bureau, where you can get a single dye-sub print for a modest fee. If you're satisfied with small but perfect prints, look into the new desktop dye-sublimation printers. Several companies make them at reasonable prices. The drawback is that they only make 4×6 prints.

Imagesetters

Imagesetters are printers used for medium- or large-scale commercial printing jobs. These large, expensive machines burn the image onto photographic film or paper. That film is then developed and used to make printing plates that are used for the actual printing. We're talking high resolution here: 1,200–2,400 dpi, or even better.

Imagesetters don't print in color, per se. Instead, you have to create a separate image for each color you want printed. These are called *separations*.

Choosing a Paper Type

What you print on makes almost as much difference as how you do the printing. You can get various types and weights of paper for all kinds of printers. There are special papers for inkjet and laser printers. If you want your picture to resemble a photograph, consider investing in a pack of photo-weight glossy paper. It's a thick paper with a glossy surface that really does help make your inkjet- or laser-printed picture look like something that came out of a real darkroom rather than a computer.

You can get coated papers for printing color on inkjet printers. These give you photo-quality prints with a matte surface, rather than a glossy one. Transparency paper is clear acetate film, specially treated to accept the inks. Use it to make overhead projection slides and overlays.

You can also get art papers for some kinds of inkjet printers. These are heavy rag papers, much like artists watercolor paper. One place to find these is `http://www.inkjetmall.com/store`. I've had very good luck printing on Somerset Smooth and Somerset Velvet with the Epson Photo 750 and 1200 printers. These fine art papers are ideally suited to printing pictures that you've converted to imitation watercolors, pastel drawings, and so on because they are the same papers generally used for those techniques. If you use a heavy art paper, feed in one sheet at a time and set the printer for thicker paper (if it has such an option). Inexpensive drawing papers from the art supply store can also work quite well. I bought a pad with 24 sheets of Academie drawing paper for less than $2, and am quite happy with the prints it makes.

Scanners

A basic desktop scanner is a device that looks and works something like a photocopier. It contains a lens and a glass platform that holds the original while you scan it. The lens is attached to a moving bar that slides up and down beneath the glass platform, "reading" the image one line at a time, and saving the data in a form the computer can reproduce on its screen. The scanner also has a built-in light that is color balanced to give you its best approximation of daylight. This helps assure that the color you see in the scanned image is accurate compared to the original. Some scanners have an additional carrier, drawer, or backlight on the cover so they can scan negatives and slides as well as prints. Most current scanners connect to the computer via a USB port. At the time of this writing, only a few can use FireWire. Figure 7.3 shows a typical scanner.

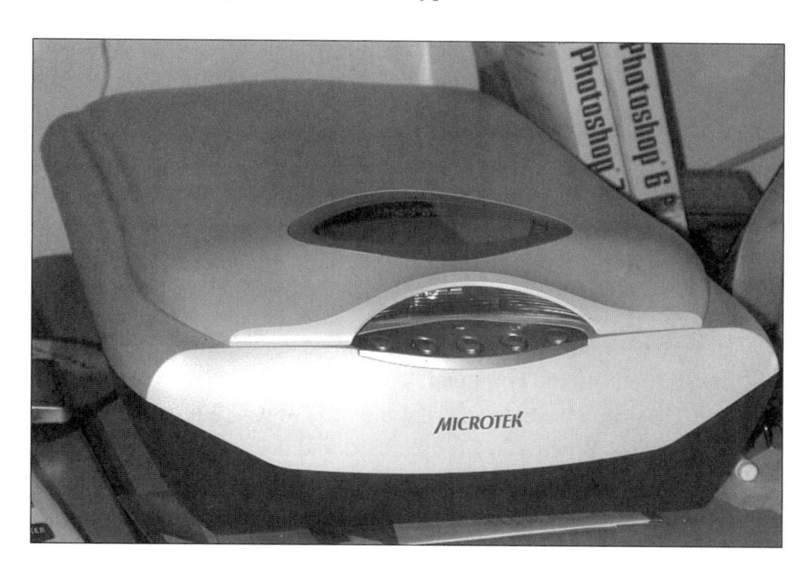

FIGURE 7.3
This is a Microtek ScanMaker 5700.

There are also high quality drum scanners. They have very high resolution, and consequently large price tags. You can have your photos scanned on one of these at a service bureau or print shop like Kinko's for a reasonable fee. Whether you only need an occasional scan, this may turn out to be more cost effective than purchasing a less expensive (but less capable) unit for home use. There are multipurpose combination scanner/fax/printer/copiers that will handle all your office chores. "Jack of all trades, master of none" certainly applies here. They do everything more or less okay, but nothing well.

Scanners typically come with several different pieces of software included. The first thing you need to install is a driver. This enables you to "drive" the scanner using the computer to control it. The makers of the scanner supply drivers for both Mac and Windows platforms. Even if your scanner is a couple of years old, you will be able to find updated versions of the driver that will work with recent software on the manufacturer's Web site (provided that the company is still in business).

Most scanners also come with a simple graphics program, such as Photoshop Elements (which we will discuss in detail later in this book), and with *Optical Character Recognition (OCR)* software. OCR is an exceptionally clever and useful application that scans pages of text and identifies each character, punctuation mark, and space. After identifying them, it puts the text into an open word processing document so you can edit and patch as needed, and then save the scanned page as a text document.

Digital Cameras

Yes, you can still take pictures with film, but a new generation—a digital camera—is available that can record pictures that you store on your computer. Best of all you don't have to take the film to the photo finishing store and wait for the prints to return. Digital cameras open new possibilities for photography. What's more, Apple's iPhoto software, which we will look at in Chapter 12, "Using iPhoto," makes the process of organizing your pictures and getting prints as easy as pie.

Digital cameras and scanners have a lot more in common than digital cameras and film cameras. Film cameras rely on light and chemistry to produce an image. Digital cameras use a device that collects image data much like the scanner does.

However, digital scanners differ from scanners in one important way. Scanners send the data directly to the computer. They don't have any storage media. Cameras have memory. They may have an internal memory and/or a removable memory card, stick, or floppy disk. When you fill up a card and need more memory, you remove the full card and pop in an empty one. Memory cards are intended to be reused. They're not for long-term data storage. So, at some point, you need to get the data off the card or out of the camera and into the computer. There are several ways to do this, depending on the make and model of camera you use, but typically this involves attaching the camera to your computer via a USB connection.

Digital video cameras also require storage media, usually in the form of tapes. However, because of the size of video files, most modern cameras connect via FireWire.

You can also purchase inexpensive video cameras (such as the iREZ Kritter USB and QuickCam), which enable you to record video directly into your computer. They won't replace your camcorder, but they are nice for simple images. And you can use them with a special type of software, videoconferencing, which enables you to send videos via the Internet.

The USB and FireWire connectors on digital cameras and video cameras are very delicate. Be sure you are inserting them right side up, and don't use force. You can replace a damaged cable, but getting either the camera's or computer's USB port replaced is expensive and time-consuming.

Additional Peripheral Devices

Besides the extras talked about so far, you can supplement or replace some of the essential components of your computer system. Here are several options that you can connect using your computer's USB or FireWire ports:

- **CD Burner**—If you don't have an Mac with a built-in CD burner, you can buy a standalone product with much of the functionality. Separates, however, might not be able to take advantage of Apple's ultra-slick, Finder-level CD writing feature.
- **Hard Drives**—You can add extra hard drives to your computer for additional storage, which comes in handy especially if you plan to work with space-hogging digital media. The only consideration is that the USB port doesn't really exercise the maximum speed of a large hard drive, so you might prefer FireWire, if your computer has that feature. USB drives are fine, though, for occasional use or just to back up your precious files. You'll learn more about backup possibilities in Chapter 28, "Managing Your System."
- **Input Devices**—You're not limited to your iMac's keyboard and mouse, although they are suitable for most folks. But it's nice to know there are alternatives. If you've migrated from the Windows platform, for example, you'll be able to take advantage of a mouse with extra buttons (the second being used for the context menus you otherwise invoke when you Option-Click on something). In addition, you can purchase joysticks for computer games, keyboards for special needs (or just in the form of those offered on regular Macs), and even trackballs (sort of an upside-down mouse), which some prefer to a regular mouse.

Connecting FireWire and USB Devices

If you've connected peripheral devices to computers from that *other* platform (called Windows), no doubt you've become used to playing with special interrupt settings. With FireWire or USB, you don't have to worry about dealing with those arcane setups. Instead, you can easily add such devices as you need them and remove them just as quickly.

If you have an older Mac with a SCSI peripheral port, hot swapping is a no-no (except if you have one of those special terminator devices designed for that purpose). If you try a hot swap, you might cause your computer to crash, or risk damage to the electronics of the device itself or the Mac's SCSI chip (requiring a motherboard replacement). On these other Macs, shut down before you try to change anything.

Here's a tried-and-true FireWire and USB installation method (some changes might apply to specific products, and they'll tell you that in the documentation):

▼ To Do

Connecting a Peripheral to Your Computer

1. Unpack the device and check for an installation CD.
2. If there's an installation CD, it means that special software (a driver) is needed to make the device work. Just place the installation CD in your computer's drive.

Mac OS X has built-in support for many of the things you connect via FireWire or USB. But some printers, scanners, and CD or DVD burners will most likely need special software. Before you try to use any of these products, check the documentation or the publisher's Web site to confirm that the product works with Mac OS X. Or pay a visit to VersionTracker.com (`http://www.versiontracker.com`) for the latest updates.

3. Double-click the Installer icon and follow the instructions to install the new software.

Under Mac OS X, you might see a prompt where you have to authenticate yourself as administrator of your computer before a software installation can begin. This is, as the TV cops say, just routine. Mac OS X is a multiple-user operating system (as we'll explain in Chapter 27, "Sharing (and Securing) Your Computer," and it just wants to know that you are authorized as chief cook and bottle washer of the system. Just use the same password you gave yourself when you first set up Mac OS X and you'll be ready to go.

4. After installation, you should be able to connect and use your device right away. In a rare situation, you might see a Restart button (although Mac OS X shouldn't need it). If you see such a button, click it and sit back and wait for your Mac to restart itself.

5. Connect one end of the device's cable to the free plug on your iMac's connection panel or the free plug on your keyboard.

If you cannot find a place to plug in a USB device, you'll probably need a hub, which extends the number of ports available for USB connections. You can buy a hub at your dealer. Before you purchase a USB device, you'll want to check the available connections so that you don't have to make a return trip for another item. Bear in mind, however, that some USB devices need to be hooked up directly to the Mac, rather than to a hub. So if it still won't work, try a direct connection as an alternative.

6. Connect the other end of the cable to your peripheral.
7. Turn on the device. You'll then want to check your instructions about using the device. Some products, such as scanners, require that you run special software to operate them.

Some scanners also have special hardware locks to protect the delicate circuitry. Before you turn on a new scanner, check the documentation and see if such a thing exists. Usually, it'll be a switch or a button with a lock icon on it. If you fail to unlock the mechanism you might damage the unit when you try to use it.

I don't want to mislead you about a USB device being hot-pluggable. There are times when you shouldn't unplug the device. For example, if you have a disk in a SuperDisk drive, Zip drive, or similar product, eject the disk first, before removing the drive. If you are working in a document that is using the device, make sure that you quit the program before removing the device. Otherwise, you'll risk a crash or possibly a damaged file or a damaged disk directory (the table of contents used to locate files on the disk).

AirPort

Now let's consider another peripheral option to supplement your existing system—one that doesn't use USB or Firewire: Apple's Airport.

In the past, when you wanted to network a computer, you had to run a wire from one to the other or to a hub (a central connecting point). If you've ever tried to do this in a home or office environment, though, you have the problem of wrapping messy wires around walls, furniture, under carpets, and so on. No doubt you have almost tripped over a stray networking cable.

Apple's AirPort wireless-network system is designed to get around that limitation. You don't have to fiddle with cables or complex setups. And you can (depending on your surroundings) be up to 150 feet from another AirPort-equipped computer or the AirPort Base Station and still get undiminished performance.

Here's an overview of AirPort products and features:

- **AirPort Interface**—If you have a Mac that includes AirPort capability, you just need to install a little credit card–sized module, an AirPort card, and then set up the software to make it run. AirPort software is already installed with your operating system.

  Just launch the AirPort Setup Assistant and choose your wireless networking options. You can even set up the Network panel of Mac OS X's System Preferences application to put a little status icon in the menu bar, so you can turn AirPort on and off and log into a network. After you're hooked up, you can connect to any other Mac OS computer that has AirPort installed (up to 10 computers without degrading performance). Or you can connect directly to the next product I'll tell you about, the AirPort Base Station.
- **AirPort Base Station**—This product, which looks like something out of a science fiction movie (see Figure 7.4) forms the hub or central point of an AirPort wireless network. It has a built-in 56K modem and two 10BASE-T Ethernet ports. You can use it to share an Internet connection across an AirPort network, a regular Ethernet network (using cables), cable modems, or DSL modems.

FIGURE 7.4
This is version 2.0 of the AirPort Base Station, used as the central connection point of your wireless network.

When hooked up, your AirPort wireless network can be used to connect computers within your home or office or in a classroom. Because it's wireless, you don't even have to be inside a building to connect. As long as you're in range of another AirPort-equipped computer or the AirPort Base Station, you can connect as efficiently as if you were connected with old-fashioned cables.

- **Cross-Platform Standard**—The AirPort wireless networking system uses an international standard, 802.11b, also known as Wi-Fi, which is supported by Mac and Windows computers. What that means is that you can connect to a wireless network powered by products from other companies, such as Asante, Proxim, and even the PC maker, Compaq, and those other computers with 802.11b capability can connect to an AirPort Base Station.

You aren't even limited to an Apple AirPort Base Station as the central connection point. The makers of network equipment all have variations on the Wi-Fi theme, some with four or eight plugs, so you can use them for a larger wired network. Just check out the possibilities with your favorite Mac dealer.

Summary

In this chapter, we talked about USB and FireWire options for connecting additional devices to your computer. Depending on your needs, a great number of peripherals are available for easy hookup. You'll soon be printing, shooting pictures, scanning artwork, and even, perhaps, using a designer keyboard and mouse. If you have a computer that comes with Apple's handy AirPort card (or if you can install one later), you'll also be able to network without the need for a messy cable.

CHAPTER 8

Monitors and ColorSync

Your Macintosh is a fantastic tool for communicating visually. However, there are some tricks for keeping what you create on your screen looking the same no matter where it's viewed. Images look different when viewed on different monitors or when printed. To solve the problem of "what you see isn't quite what you get," Apple created ColorSync—a means of ensuring consistent color reproduction on different output devices. This chapter introduces ColorSync and walks you through the process of calibrating your system's monitor. You learn everything you need to know about color calibration and how to work with Mac OS X's monitor settings.

Configuring Displays

To change settings for your monitor, there's only one place to do it: the Displays System Preferences panel in the Hardware category. This panel is a bit unusual in that it can change drastically depending on what type of monitor is connected to your system. Users of Apple's CRTs see geometry information for adjusting image tilt, size, and so forth. The exact panel display depends on the monitor type. Those who have more than one monitor can arrange the monitors' location on the desktop and choose where the menu bar appears.

Resolution and Colors

To access your Display tab settings, open the Displays panel of System Preferences. Here you can see the basic settings for your monitor—color depth and resolution—as shown in Figure 8.1. What you see might vary slightly depending on the type of monitor you're using.

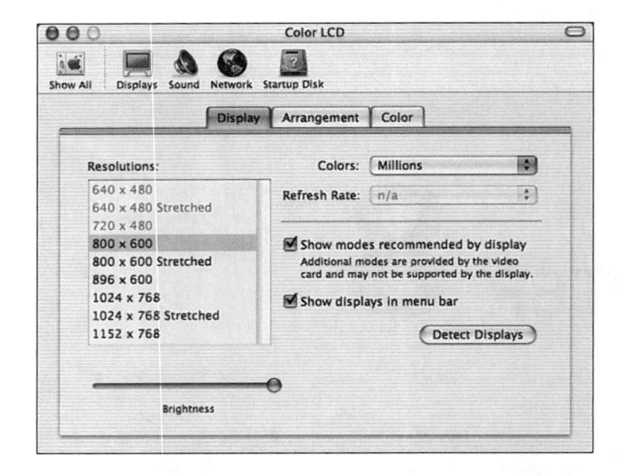

FIGURE 8.1
The Display tab of the Displays System Preferences panel controls monitor colors and resolution.

Available resolutions for your display are listed in the left column. Choosing a new resolution immediately updates your machine's display. At times, the panel might not show all the possible resolutions that your computer supports. In that case, you can uncheck the Show Modes Recommended by Display check box to see all the possible resolutions.

If you set the resolution or color depth on your monitor, it changes the system setting for everyone who uses that computer. The settings are not specific to your account.

Displays Menu Extra

If you find yourself switching colors or resolutions often, click the Show Displays in Menu Bar check box. This activates a Menu Extra, shown in Figure 8.2, that makes it simple to switch between different settings.

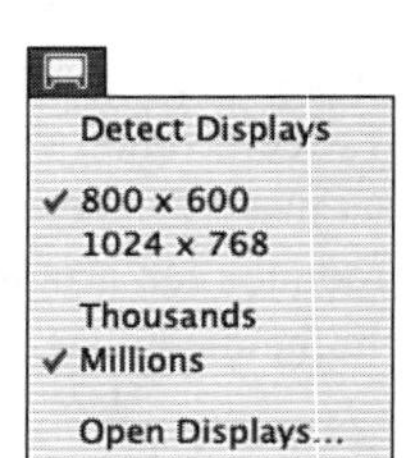

FIGURE 8.2
The Displays Menu Extra provides instant access to color and resolution settings.

Multiple Monitors

If you're lucky enough to have multiple monitors to connect to your system, Mac OS X enables you to use all of them simultaneously as a single large display. Note that you still need a video card for each monitor you're connecting or dual display support from a single video card. Users of iBooks and iMacs see a mirroring of their desktop on any added monitors rather than an addition of new desktop area.

Mac OS X automatically recognizes when multiple monitors are connected to the system and adjusts the Displays Preferences panel accordingly by adding an Arrangement tab. For example, Figure 8.3 shows the settings for a PowerBook G4 with an external VGA monitor connected.

There's no need to reboot to connect an external display. Just plug it in and start mousing!

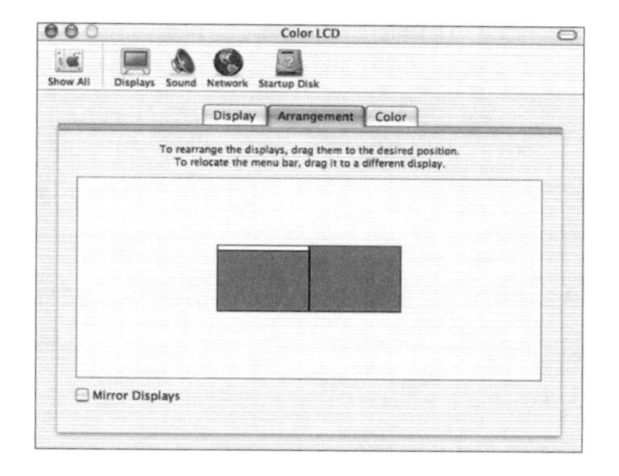

FIGURE 8.3
The Displays System Preferences pane changes to handle multiple monitors.

In the Arrangement tab, you can control how the two monitors interact by dragging the corresponding rectangle. To move a monitor so that its portion of the desktop falls on the left or right of another monitor, just drag it to the left or right in the Arrangement tab. The menu bar can also be moved by clicking its representation in the Arrangement tab and dragging it to the monitor you want it displayed on. The changes you make to the arrangement take effect immediately; no need to reboot!

If you have multiple monitors connected, you'll also notice that each monitor has its own copy of the Displays System Preferences pane displayed in the center of the screen. By using these separate panes, you can change the color and resolution for each display independently.

Geometry

If you're using an Apple CRT display or a third-party CRT display that supports geometry settings through software, you might see an additional Geometry tab in the Displays Preferences panel. This tab is used to fine-tune the image on your display through actions such as rotating or resizing so that it has no obvious distortions. Read the operator manual that came with your monitor for more information.

Using these controls actually creates minuscule adjustments to the voltages that produce images on your screen. LCD displays generate their pictures in an entirely different manner and don't require separate geometry settings.

Color

The final tab in the Displays System Preferences panel, Color, is where you can create the ColorSync profile for your monitor or choose from one of the preset profiles that come with the system. A Colorsync profile is a collection of parameters that define how your device (in this case, your monitor) outputs color. Figure 8.4 shows the available color settings.

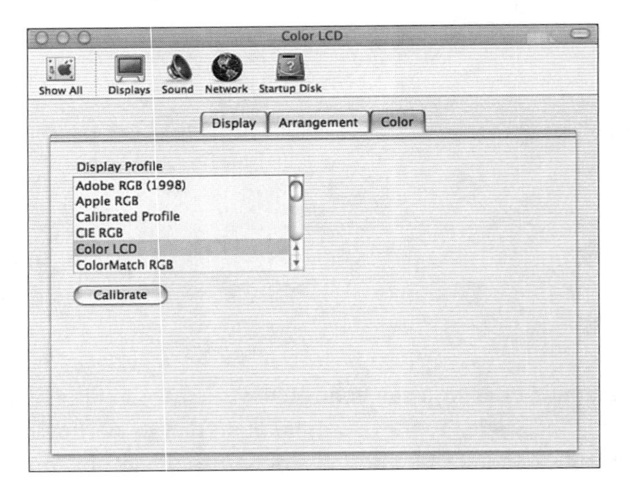

FIGURE 8.4
The Color settings are used to choose a ColorSync monitor profile or launch the calibration utility to make a new profile.

By default, Mac OS X tries to pick the profile it thinks is best for your system, but that doesn't mean it is necessarily in "sync" with your monitor. The color quality of both CRTs and flat panels varies over time, so you still might want to run a calibration even if there's already a setting for your monitor. To start the color calibration process, click the Calibrate button.

Even if you're not at all interested in graphics output and are absolutely convinced that there's no need to calibrate your system, you might still want to run the calibration utility. It gives you the ability to change how your screen looks in ways that the built-in brightness controls cannot.

For example, with a few clicks, you can create deeper, richer colors, or make whites warmer and more appealing. In short, you might have to be a graphics professional to understand the technical details of the calibration process, but the results speak for themselves.

Using the Display Calibrator Assistant

The Display Calibrator application is a simple assistant that walks you through the process of creating a profile for the monitors connected to your computer. If you didn't launch the calibrator through the Displays System Preferences panel, you can run it directly from /Applications/Utilities/Display Calibrator.

The steps in the calibration process differ depending on the type of monitor you're using. Adjustments to CRT (cathode ray tube) monitors, such as those in the eMac, follow these steps: set up, native gamma, target gamma, tristimuli values, target white point, and conclusion. For LCD monitors in flat panel displays and laptops, the calibration process skips over several of the steps that aren't applicable.

Task: Calibrate your Display

TASK

1. When the Display Calibrator Assistant starts, it provides a brief explanation of what it's about to do and gives you the option of turning on expert mode, as shown in Figure 8.5. Click the right arrow at the bottom of the window to begin. You can use the right and left arrows at any time to move forward and backward between the different steps.

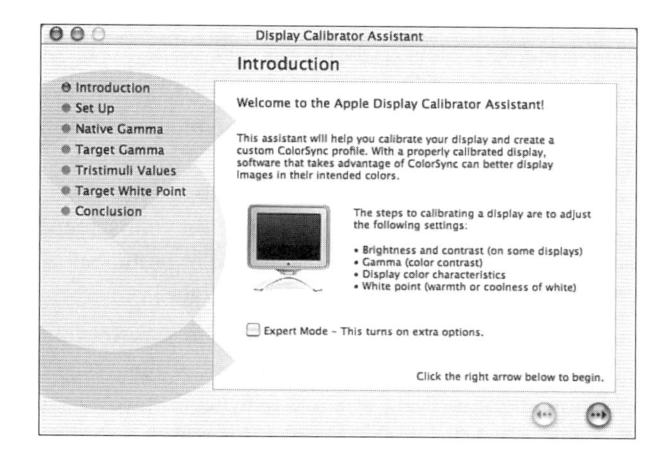

FIGURE 8.5
Turning on expert mode enables more precise adjustment; sticking with the normal mode limits your options to predefined settings.

2. The first step, Set Up: Display Adjustments, matters for CRT monitors only. It helps you adjust the brightness on your display to achieve the right black levels. To

begin, turn the contrast control on your monitor up as high as it goes. Next, take a close look at the block in the middle right of the window. At first glance, the block, shown in Figure 8.6, might look completely black. In reality, the dark block is composed of two rectangles with an oval superimposed on them.

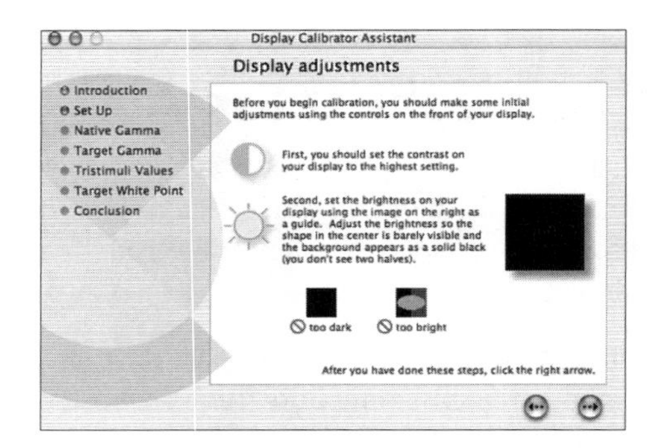

FIGURE 8.6
Adjust the brightness level on your display until the block blends together.

Using your monitor's brightness control, adjust the image so that the two rectangles blend together and the oval is barely visible. It's best to sit back a little, away from your screen, to gauge the effect.

3. The next step, Determine Your Display's Current Gamma, also applies only to CRT monitors. Brightness does not increase linearly on computer displays. As the display increases a color's brightness on the screen, it isn't necessarily the same size step each time. To correct this, a *gamma* value is applied to linearize increases in brightness. In the second step of the calibration process, you adjust the gamma settings for the different colors your computer can display. For more information about Gamma, visit `http://www.bberger.net/gamma.html`.

   As shown in Figure 8.7, the current gamma calibration shows a block containing the Apple logo. Using the sliders below the block, adjust the logo's brightness so that it matches the background color as closely as possible. It's impossible to get a perfect match, so don't worry if you can still see the apple. It's best just to squint your eyes until you can't make out the text on your screen, and then perform the adjustments. (If you're in expert mode, you're prompted to adjust lightness and darkness for each of the primary colors of light [red, green, and blue].)

4. The next step, for both CRT and LCD monitors, is Select a Target Gamma. The target gamma for your display is useful for deciding what images on your monitor look like on other displays. PCs and televisions have varying gamma settings that don't match your Macintosh defaults. This makes it difficult to create graphics on your Mac that look right on a PC monitor. Using the target gamma settings shown in Figure 8.8, you can make your Mac's display look very much like that of a standard PC.

To adjust the gamma setting, select the radio button corresponding to your viewing needs. The picture in the upper-right corner of the window gives you an idea of what your choice does to your monitor's output. Choosing Uncorrected Gamma usually results in a very bright and washed-out image. (Those in expert mode use a slider to set the gamma, which offers more precise control.)

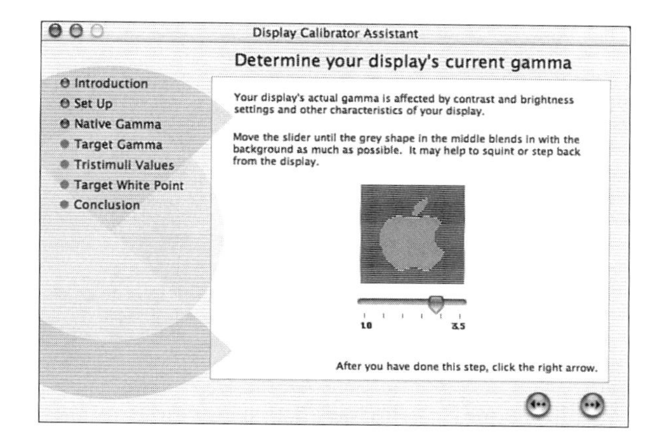

FIGURE 8.7
Match the apple color to the block background.

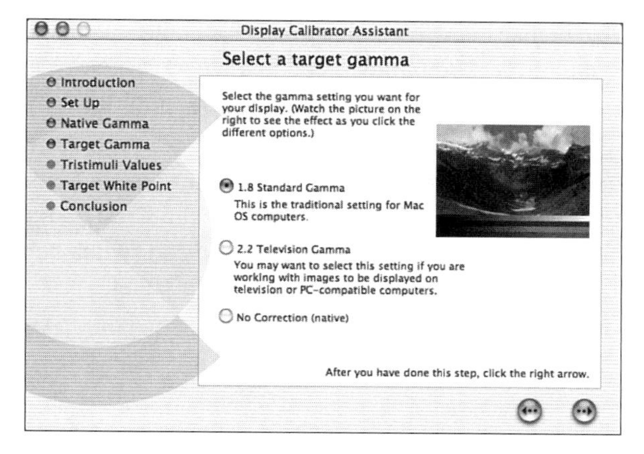

FIGURE 8.8
Choose the gamma setting to use on your monitor.

If you have noticed that some video or computer games appear too dark on your screen, you can compensate for this by decreasing your monitor's gamma settings.

5. For those with CRT monitors, the next step is Tristimuli Values, which relates to the variation in chemical phosphors used in tube monitors. Here, the goal is to select the menu item that most closely matches your monitor.

6. The final calibration step for both CRT and LCD displays is Select a Target White Point. As you know, the *color* white is not a color, and is hardly ever truly *white*. When your computer displays a white image, it probably has tinges of blue, yellow, or even red. This variation is known as the *white point*. The white point settings are displayed in Figure 8.9.

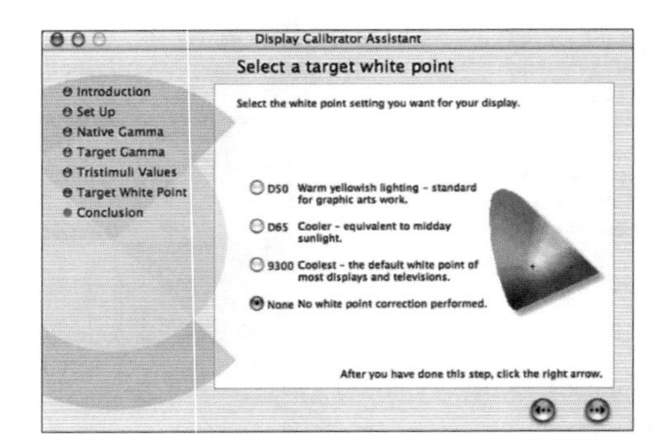

FIGURE 8.9
Choose the target white point setting to use on your monitor.

To set a white point, choose from the listed options by selecting the appropriate radio button. (Once again, those in expert mode have a slider to set a more precise level. The higher the white point value, the cooler the display; the lower it is, the warmer the display. You might need to uncheck the No White Point Correction [Native] check box before you can make any modifications while in expert mode.)

7. At the conclusion of the calibration process (see Figure 8.10), you're prompted to name your profile. Entering descriptive names for your creations makes it simple to tell them apart. Save the profile by clicking the Create button. The new profile goes into effect immediately. Remember that you can switch between profiles in the Color tab of the Displays System Preferences panel.

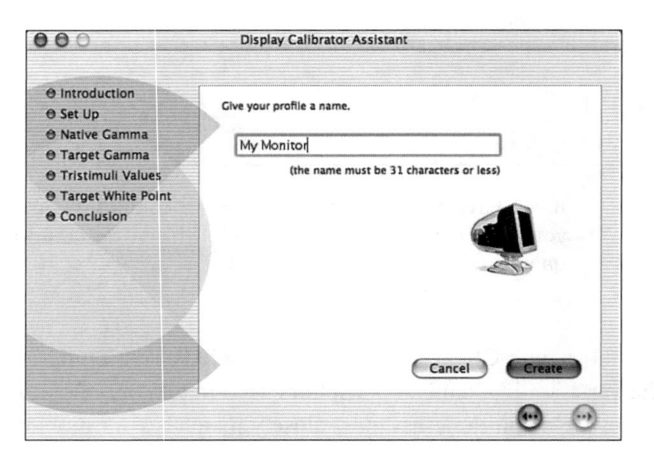

FIGURE 8.10
Enter a name for your calibrated profile.

Introduction to ColorSync

As you work with color images and color output devices, you soon realize that there is no standard color monitor, printer, or scanner. A *color space* is a method for representing the possible output colors for a device by using a hypothetical one- to four-dimensional space. Each dimension in the space represents different intensities of the components that define a color. For example, a common space is RGB (red, green, blue). This three-dimensional color space is defined by using the three primary colors of light. Many other spaces exist that address other specific needs, such as printed color.

Although every monitor you buy is undoubtedly an RGB monitor, the RGB color space it supports varies depending on the quality of the monitor's components. Different phosphors produce slightly different shades of red, green, and blue. Cheap monitors might have a slight yellow or green tint to them, whereas LCD panels have vibrant hues but less consistency in gradations than professional CRT displays.

The same goes for printers and scanners. A scanner that costs more is likely to have a far broader and more consistent color space than its cheaper cousins. If you've ever seen a scan that looks dull and muddy, you're seeing a limitation of the scanner's supported color space.

ColorSync's challenge is to make sure that the colors you intend to print or display are what you end up getting. To do this, ColorSync uses a CMM, or color matching module, to translate between different color spaces. In addition, different devices (including your monitor) can have ColorSync profiles that describe the range of color they can reproduce. Using Display Calibrator Assistant, as discussed in the previous section, you can create a profile for your system's monitor. You'll find other profiles on the disks that come with your peripheral devices. You can install profiles by dragging them to the /Library/ColorSync/Profiles folder at the system level or in your home directory.

ColorSync System Preferences Panel

To make it simple for graphics professionals to switch between different groups of ColorSync settings, or *workflows*, Apple included a ColorSync Preferences panel in Mac OS X. Using this panel, you can set up a workflow for your input devices, display, output devices, and proofing.

In addition, the ColorSync Preferences panel enables you to set default profiles for each of the ColorSync-supported color spaces (RGB, CMYK, and Gray) and choose a default color-matching technology that maps from one Colorsync profile to another. Many of these features aren't active unless you've installed additional software on your computer, however.

Figure 8.11 shows the main tab of the ColorSync Preferences panel: Default Profiles.

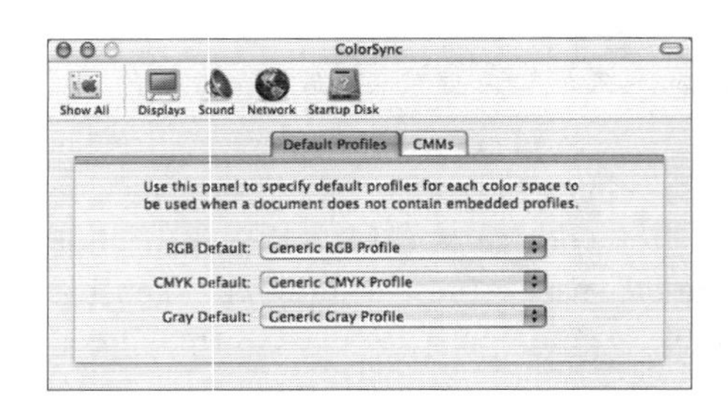

FIGURE 8.11
The ColorSync Preferences panel enables you to set up default collections of profiles.

Use the pop-up menus to choose from the installed Input, Display, Output, and Proof profiles. This chooses the default profile to be used with a document when a document doesn't specify a profile of its own. Don't be surprised if you don't see many options under these menus. You might want to check the disks that came with your digital camera or scanner to see whether they include color profiles.

The other tab, CMMs, functions similarly. The CMMs tab offers the option of selecting alternative color matching modules. The default Mac OS X installation includes only one CMM, so there's very little to see here.

ColorSync Utility

The final component of the ColorSync system is the ColorSync utility, located at /Applications/Utilities/ColorSync Utility. This program has a number of different functions, such as verifying and repairing ColorSync profiles, viewing the installed profiles, and listing ColorSync-compatible devices that are registered on your system.

When first launched, the ColorSync Utility defaults to the Profile First Aid function shown in Figure 8.12. Click the Verify or Repair button to check the installed profiles on the system.

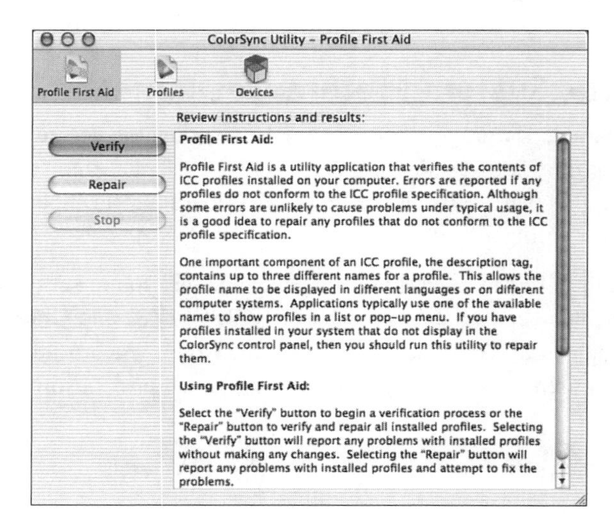

FIGURE 8.12
Verify and repair installed profiles.

To switch between the utility's different functions, click the icons at the top of the window. The second feature is the profile viewer, which is viewed by clicking the Profiles icon.

In this window, you can navigate through the installed ColorSync profiles on the system and display details for each one by selecting it from the list at the left of the display. Figure 8.13 shows the details for one of my profiles.

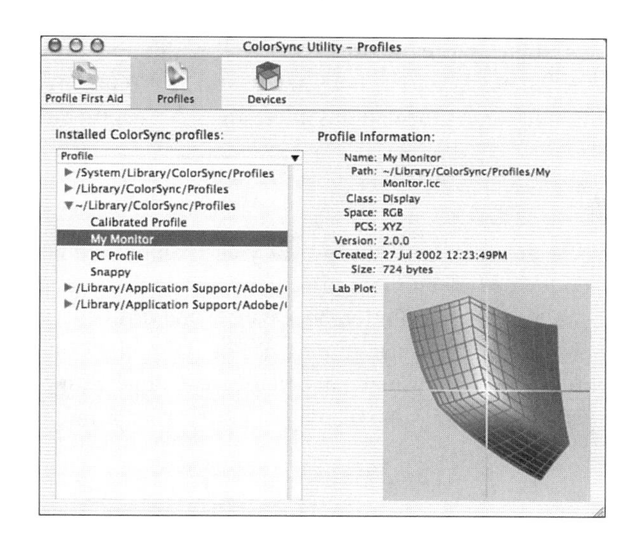

FIGURE 8.13
Easily navigate through all the installed profiles and display their details.

Click the Devices icon at the top of the window to view the utility's final feature. Each type of device is displayed as a category at the left of the window. Expanding a category shows the supported devices in that classification. For example, the Displays category features Color LCD and VGA Display devices, as shown in Figure 8.14.

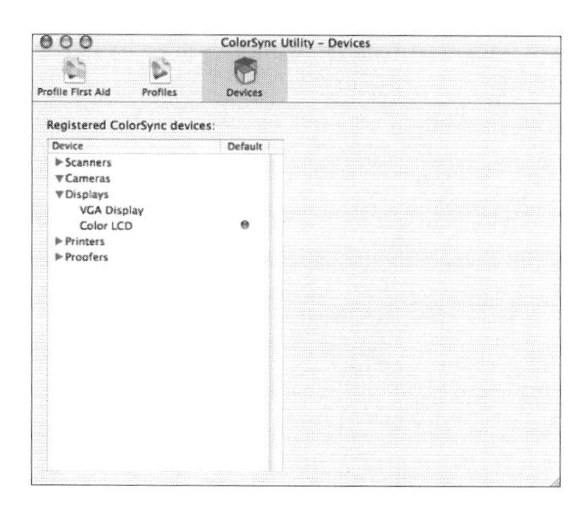

FIGURE 8.14
View the available ColorSync devices on your system.

When you find the device you want to configure, select it from the list. The right side of the window is updated to show information about the device, including its factory profile and any custom calibration profile you've created. Use the pop-up menu to choose a new profile for a given device, and click the Make Default Display button to set a device as the default to be used in a given ColorSync category.

Whew! I know this all sounds complicated, and, frankly, it is! Color calibration is an important part of the Macintosh operating system and part of what makes it widely revered among graphics professionals. If you fall within that group, it's good to know that these features are available. If not, they're still fun to play with because they can breathe new life into a monitor that has a less-than-perfect picture.

Summary

Apple gives you a great deal of control over your monitor and how it displays images. In this chapter, you learned about monitor settings and calibration as well as the ColorSync system and the related System Preferences panels and utilities. Even if you don't use your Mac for precise, professional graphic design, you might find that creating custom ColorSync profiles for your system can benefit work done with photographs and video, and anything else that involves the display of color on your monitor!

CHAPTER 9

Setting Up Printers and Fonts

The Macintosh has always been good at creating works of art, but to share your creations, you might want to print them. This chapter looks at the basic steps for setting up a printer and printing your documents, as well as at font and printer management—two important factors in producing quality output from your system.

Setting Up a New Printer

Regardless of the kind of printer you buy, the basic hookup steps are similar. The process usually takes just a few minutes from the time you crack open the box until the printer is up and running.

▼ To Do

The setup steps for inkjets and laser printers are similar, so I'll describe them together here, with a few notes to show where things might diverge:

1. Unpack your printer and check the device for little bits of tape and cardboard that are left from shipping.

> I cannot overemphasize the need to remove packing materials before you try to use a printer. Some of those little bits of tape and cardboard can literally lock up the printer (maybe damage the delicate plastic parts inside) if you try to use it without removing this material. If in doubt, check the printer's setup manual for information.

2. Plug it in to the power source (AC line or power strip) and install the ink cartridges or toner assembly (whichever applies) as instructed by the manufacturer.

> Inkjet printers are usually set up so you actually have to turn them on and push a button to move the inkwells into the proper place for installation of the cartridge or cartridges (some models do it automatically when you open the cover). In addition to documentation, such printers might also have a chart inside to show you how to install cartridges.

3. Use the appropriate connection cable to attach the printer to your computer. Some makers include the cable, other printers come without, so you have to buy it separately (like the battery for your child's brand new toy). Depending on the kind of printer or connection setup you have, you will be using either the Ethernet port or a USB port (you can use the empty jack on your keyboard for the latter connection).

> If you're using an Ethernet printer, you will either need to install a hub (a special connection interface) or use a crossover cable (which is designed for a direct connection between your computer and another Ethernet device) for the hookup to work. Check with your dealer for the requirements.

4. Get out the manufacturer's software CD, insert it into your computer's drive, and install the printing software.

> If you bought a new printer, check the manufacturer's Web site or `www.versiontracker.com` for the latest printer software. Most new printers ship ready to roll with Mac OS X, but sometimes updates online are newer (and better) than the ones shipped with the product.
>
> If you purchased a new printer that doesn't work with Mac OS X, and OS X support was promised (this is important!), take the printer back to the

dealer and ask to exchange it for a compatible model. You shouldn't have to contend with a problem here, because most dealers will give you a money-back guarantee on new merchandise.

After the software installation is done, you are ready to add the printer so your computer will recognize it.

Adding Printers with Print Center

In Mac OS X, the Print Center application (located in the Utilities folder of the Applications folder on your hard drive) maintains and manages everything printer related.

When you start the Print Center application, it opens a small window listing all the available printers that have been configured on your system. For example, in Figure 9.1, one printer is configured for my computer.

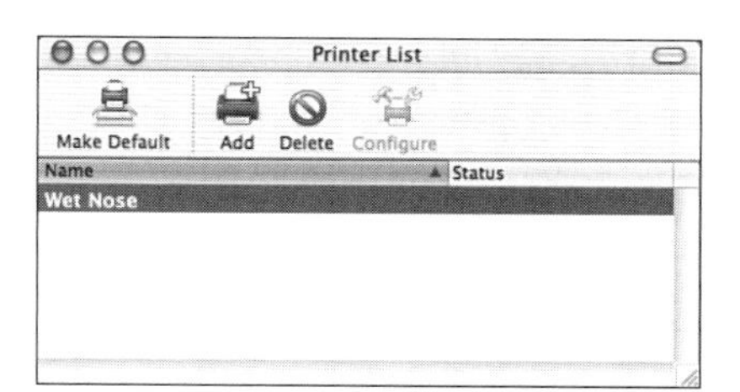

FIGURE 9.1
Print Center shows a list of the printers configured on your system.

If a printer is set as the default printer, its name appears in bold type. You can make a different printer the default by choosing its name in the list, and then selecting Make Default (Command+D) from the Printers menu.

Obviously, switching between printers isn't of much use until you set up a printer or two on your system. To do this, first click the Add button at the top of the Printer List window. A printer selection sheet appears, similar to the one in Figure 9.2.

At the top of the dialog box is a pop-up menu that offers several different ways in which you can find and connect to your printer:

- **AppleTalk**—Shown in Figure 9.2, AppleTalk is the choice to make if you're connecting to a local network Mac printer.
- **Directory Services**—If you're connected to a Mac OS X server computer or another directory service, there's a chance it's sharing printer information with your system. Choosing Directory Services displays the printers available to your computer through a network directory server.

- **IP Printing**—LPR is used for many types of printers that allow access over TCP/IP. If you need to access a printer that isn't on your local network, this is probably the choice you want to make.
- **USB**—USB printers are the personal printers that plug into the USB ports on your computer. Canon, Epson, and HP printers typically connect via USB.

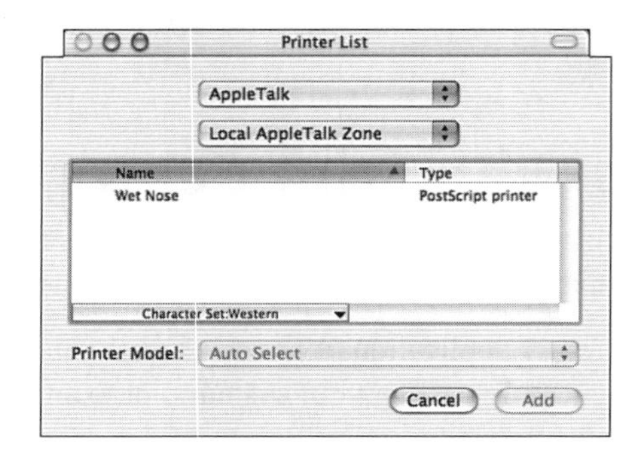

FIGURE 9.2
Use the Add Printer sheet to configure any connected printing devices.

Below are the four main ways of connecting any manufacturer-specific drivers that have been installed on the system, such as Epson and Lexmark. If you're using one of these printers, you should select the corresponding option here.

If you choose AppleTalk or USB, Print Center attempts to locate potential printers that your machine can access and automatically displays them. To finish adding a printer, select it from the list of detected devices. Mac OS X then attempts to automatically detect the type of printer you've chosen and select the appropriate driver. Sometimes, however, you must use the Printer Model pop-up menu at the bottom of the dialog box to manually pick a printer type. Finally, click Add to add the selected printer to the Print Center listing.

IP printers are configured a bit differently. If you choose IP printers in the pop-up menu, you're asked for information on where the printer is located and how to connect, as shown in Figure 9.3.

Talk to the printer's administrator to determine the IP address and queue name for the remote device. Many times you can choose to use the default queue and simply enter an IP address. Because of the nature of IP connections, you *must* manually choose a printer model. Click Add to finish adding the printer.

For any of the printer connection types, if Mac OS X can't automatically find your printer model, you might need to contact the manufacturer and download additional drivers for the system.

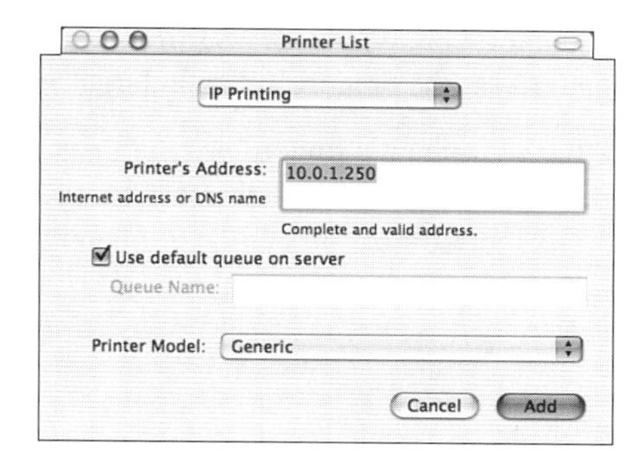

FIGURE 9.3
IP printers require additional configuration.

9

Now that you've learned to set up printers, let's look at how to print a document.

Printing Your Document

There are two menu commands shared by most applications that you use when printing:

- **Print** (Command-P)—Print the active document and configure settings for your chosen printer
- **Page Setup** (Shift-Command-P)—Choose how the document is laid out when printing

Let's start with the standard Page Setup dialog box, shown in Figure 9.4.

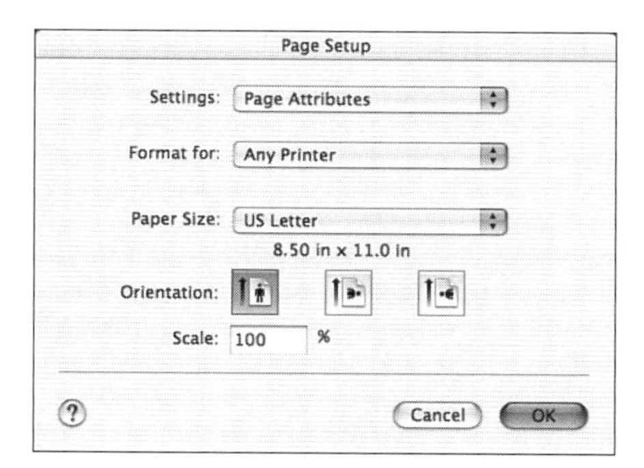

FIGURE 9.4
Choose the basic layout settings for your print job.

In the Page Setup dialog box, you can use the Settings pop-up menu to choose Page Attributes, Custom Paper Size, or Summary to see a description of how the page will be printed, including margin and size information.

The Format For pop-up menu enables you to choose which printer the page is being laid out for. Because different printers support different page sizes and margins, it's important to format a document for the appropriate printer before starting the print process. Use the Paper Size settings to select from standard paper sizes that your device supports.

Finally, you can use the Orientation buttons to choose from normal, landscape, and reverse landscape layouts and to set the Scale value to enlarge or shrink the output.

After making your Page Setup settings, it's time to use the Print dialog box shown in Figure 9.5 to finish configuring your printer and start the print job. Choose Print from the File menu or use the keyboard shortcut (Command-P) to open the Print dialog box.

FIGURE 9.5
The Print settings are used to configure the printer and start the print job.

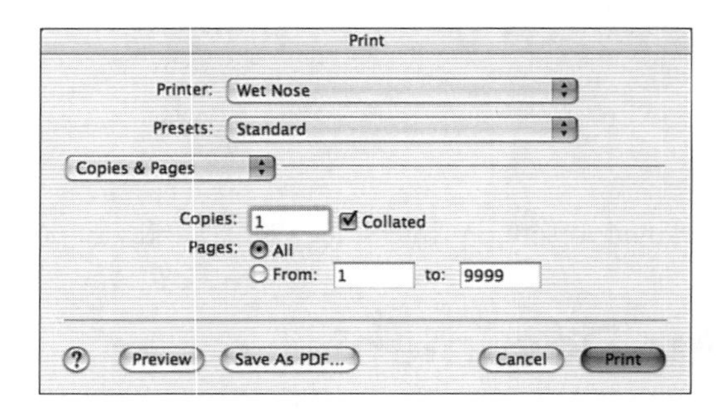

If you've used a printer before, you probably recognize most of these settings. You can enter your page print range, the number of copies, and so on, and then click Print to start printing the document.

One interesting feature of Mac OS X is the Preview function, which displays content from another program in a PDF format. If a Mac OS X application can print, it can also generate a PDF.

If you want to send your document to someone who might not have the same software you have, you can use Preview's Save As dialog box to make a copy in PDF format. A PDF document can be read and printed with full accuracy by any computer user who has Adobe's Acrobat software installed (Mac or Windows). Apple's Preview application, discussed in Chapter 5, "Using Other Basic Applications," also reads such files.

The default information displayed when you open the Print dialog box is the Copies & Pages settings. Using the pop-up menu near the top of the dialog box, you can select other common setting panes for your printer. These are a few that you may see:

- **Layout**—Have your printer print multiple document pages per printer page. This setting is useful if you want to print a long document for review.
- **Duplex**—Toggles printing to both sides of a piece of paper, if available.
- **Output Options**—If you want to output directly to a PDF file, you can set this option in the Output Options pane.

- **Error Handling**—You can choose how the system responds to errors that occur during printing. The options are No Special Reporting and Print Detailed Report.
- **Paper Feed**—Many printers have multiple paper trays. The Paper Feed settings enable you to choose which feed is active for a given print job.
- **Printer Features**—The Printer Features pane contains any special features offered by the connected printer.
- **Summary**—The Summary settings displays the status of all the preceding settings in one convenient location.

If you change several settings and want to save them for use from time to time, choose Save As under the Presets pop-up menu. Your custom settings will show up under Presets at the top of the Print dialog box for any later work.

A nifty extra of the Mac OS X printing system is the Print Center icon. When printing, it displays an animation of pages going through your printer and a count of the remaining pages to print. If there is an error, it displays a red page containing an exclamation mark to get your attention.

The Page Setup dialog box will change from printer to printer, when you switch from one program to another and, most important, when you switch from a Classic to Mac OS X application. So I'm just covering the basic features here. Your printer's documentation will offer extra setup instructions.

Checking the Progress of Your Print Job

As soon as the initial processing of a document is done, the Print Center icon will appear in the Dock when you're printing from a Mac OS X application. To see how the job is doing, click the icon, which opens the print queue window (see Figure 9.6).

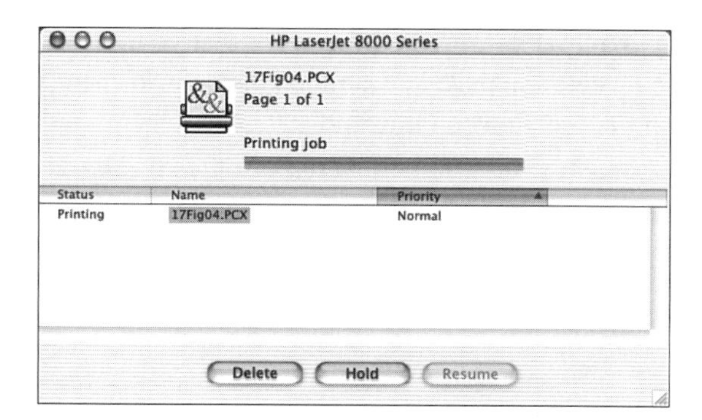

FIGURE 9.6
See which document is being printed, and which are left.

With the print queue displayed, you're able to check the progress of a print job and also manage the queue, to a limited degree.

Here are the options, identified by the buttons at the bottom of the screen:

- **Delete**—Removes the selected job from the queue.

It's usually not a good idea to stop a print job that's already begun because you risk a possible paper jam if the paper is already feeding through the printer (this applies strictly to inkjet printers, not laser printers, which print the page in a single, uninterrupted process). Some printers have a reset button that will move the page through the paper trays, but the best way to avoid a possible problem is not stopping an active print job.

- **Hold**—Keeps the selected job in the list, but won't print until you choose otherwise.
- **Resume**—Resumes printing of the selected document.

In addition to being able to stop and resume existing jobs, you can also halt the entire print queue, which is done by choosing Stop Queue from Print Center's Queue menu. After you make this selection, printing will stop after a few seconds to finish the existing page. The next time you look for the command it will change to Start Queue, so you can resume outputting your documents.

Solving Printing Problems

Sometimes, instead of getting a perfectly printed document, you get only an error message on your screen. What should you do?

First, see if the message tells you what's wrong. It's not always easy to solve printing problems because even a small error in the Page Setup box (for example, the wrong paper size), or a lack of paper, might cause the problem.

Here are some things to check:

- **Out of paper/paper jammed**—Make sure that your printer has enough paper, and check to see whether a page has jammed inside it. If there's a paper jam, check the manufacturer's directions on how to fix it.
- **Make sure that it is on and connected**—It's very easy to disconnect something (maybe during redecorating or to use the outlet for another item). Double-check your connections and make sure that the printer's on light is illuminated. Also check your printer's documentation on error lights and what they mean.

- **Look at the Page Setup box**—If you choose the wrong paper size, or the wrong paper orientation, the printer might just give up the ghost. You'll want to double-check those settings.
- **For laser printers**—Choose the right PPD file: So-called PostScript laser printers use special files called *PPDs* that tell the printer driver about the printer and its special features (such as extra trays, larger paper sizes, and so on). You might need to make sure that your PPD file is installed. PPD files, under Mac OS X, go inside a folder called Library, under the following path (or folder hierarchy): Library/Printers/PPDs/Contents/Resources/English.lproj (or whatever language you're using). You should also make sure that you choose the proper printer in the Page Setup box because that setting delivers the proper paper choices. If the PPD file isn't there, check your printer's software disks or contact the dealer or manufacturer to get one.

Adding Fonts

To create effective output, you need professional images and text. Mac OS X comes with a larger collection of fonts than any other version of the Mac operating system and supports more font formats than ever before including

- `.dfont` suitcases
- `.ttf` TrueType fonts
- `.ttc` TrueType font collections
- `.otf` OpenType fonts
- PostScript Type 1 fonts
- All previous Macintosh font suitcases

In short, if you have a font, chances are that you can install it on Mac OS X and it will work.

Font files are stored in the system /Library/Fonts folder or in the Library/Fonts folder inside your home directory. If you have a font you want to install, just copy it to one of these locations and it becomes available immediately. You must restart any running applications that need access to the fonts, but you don't need to restart your computer.

Using the Fonts Panel

Applications that enable you to choose fonts often use the built-in font picker shown in Figure 9.7. This element of the Macintosh operating system is designed to make finding fonts easier among different pieces of software. To see the Fonts panel, open the TextEdit application in the Application folder, and then choose Format, Font, Show Fonts from the menu.

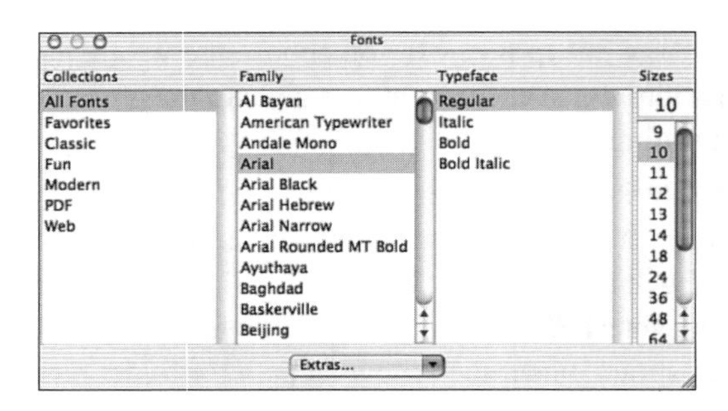

FIGURE 9.7
The Fonts panel is a system wide object for choosing fonts.

In its expanded form (as shown in Figure 16.7), the Fonts panel lists four columns: Collections, Family, Typeface, and Sizes. Use these columns much as you use the Column view of the Finder—working from left to right. Click a collection name (or All Fonts to see everything), and then click the font family, typeface, and, finally, the size.

If you prefer a more simplified view of the panel, use the window resize control in the lower-right corner of the panel to shrink the Fonts panel to a few simple pop-up menus.

Near the bottom of the expanded Fonts panel is the Extras pop-up menu, from which you can select several special features of the new font system:

- **Add to Favorites**—Adds the current font choice to the Favorites font collection.
- **Edit Collections**—Creates and edits new collections of fonts.
- **Edit Sizes**—Chooses the list of sizes that appear as choices in the Fonts panel, or use a slider to control the size.
- **Show Preview**—Shows a preview of the selected font.
- **Show Characters**—Shows the Character palette displaying each of the characters for a selected font.

Instant access to the Character palette from any application can be added in the Input Menu tab of the International System Preferences panel. Simply check the box in front of Character Palette and an icon appears in the menu bar of any active application. To remove the icon, simply return to the Input Menu tab and uncheck the box.

- **Color**—Picks a color for the font.
- **Get Fonts**—This selection launches your Web browser and takes you to a special Apple page from which you can buy fonts. This service is not yet in operation, but it appears to be coming soon.

One final note about fonts: Not all applications use the system Fonts panel. When it's not supported, you're likely to see pull-down menus listing every installed font.

Summary

In this chapter, we put all our attention on printers, printing, and fonts. We covered the basic steps involved in setting up a printer. We then discussed using the Print Center application to make your computer recognize the available printers and to manage print jobs. You also learned how easy it is to use the font system. The addition of a system wide Fonts panel makes it simple to build font collections and find your way through hundreds of available typefaces.

PART II

Apple iLife: iTunes, iPhoto, iMovie, and iDVD

Chapter

Chapter 10

Introducing iLife

The CEO of Apple, Steve Jobs, has spent a lot of time in the past few years talking publicly about making the Mac the center of your digital lifestyle. The introduction of iLife carries this vision forward by bringing together updated versions of the four easy-to-use digital media applications already available from Apple—iTunes, iPhoto, iMovie, and iDVD.

The updates made to these applications include added features that allow you to conveniently cross over from one to another. For instance, you can build a slide show of your digital photographs in iPhoto with accompanying music from your iTunes music library and then, with the click of a button, transfer that slide show to iDVD for finishing touches and writing to disc.

Avid Mac fans know that Steve Jobs makes several public addresses each year to announce new products and computer advancements available from Apple. These events are known as "keynotes," and you can watch them as they happen on the Apple Web site via a streaming QuickTime video feed.

Incidentally, Apple recently released a presentation-building application called "Keynote," which is a competitor for Microsoft's PowerPoint application. In announcing it at a keynote, Steve Jobs said it was originally written just for him to use during his keynote presentations. Isn't that cool?

Now let's take a brief look at the four applications that make up iLife.

Introducing iTunes

If you like music, iTunes (shown in Figure 10.1) can serve as your CD player, MP3 ripper, song organizer, jukebox, and CD burner. Amazingly, iTunes is simple enough to use that even if you've never burned a CD, ripped an MP3, or listened to Internet radio, you can be doing all three within five minutes—tops.

NEW TERM *MP3* is a compression system that reduces the size of a music file by a factor of 10 to 15, or more. How's this magic accomplished? By removing data that the human ear either cannot, or doesn't hear as well. Audio quality can be almost indistinguishable from a CD, or, if you opt for more compression, audibly different.

FIGURE 10.1
Here's a glimpse of iTunes.

As you will learn in the next chapter, *ripping* and *burning* are creative, not destructive, acts when it comes to digital music. *Ripping* is basically encoding a song for storage on your computer, and *burning* is writing information, including music, to a CD!

iTunes is also perfectly suited for handling streaming MP3s. If you've never listened to Internet radio before, you'll appreciate how quickly and easily iTunes enables you to find the type of music you want to hear and start listening.

iTunes also interacts with the Internet to look up information about your CDs, such as the artist and song title.

You'll learn how to use iTunes in the next chapter.

Introducing iPhoto

Have a digital camera? If so, you may have struggled to keep track of image files with arcane names such as 200214057. With Apple's iPhoto, there's an easy way to store, organize, edit, and even share your photographs. iPhoto even connects directly to many digital cameras, so you can skip loading special software.

Some people feel that film cameras might be replaced by digital cameras altogether. As these clever devices get cheaper, and both image and home-printing quality goes up, it becomes harder and harder to justify the trip to the supermarket to get that roll developed.

Perhaps iPhoto's greatest strength is that it allows you to visually search your entire photo collection without opening and closing folders so you don't have to remember film rolls or dates while looking for the ones you want. Viewing tiny thumbnail images of hundreds of your pictures at a time, demonstrated in Figure 10.2, allows you to scan for the one you want. (If you need to see each image in greater detail, you can also increase the size of this preview.)

FIGURE 10.2
iPhoto makes it easy to manage a lot of images.

We'll cover iPhoto in detail in Chapter 12, "Using iPhoto."

Introducing iMovie

At one time, editing a home video was a chore. You had to sit and copy each section separately from your camcorder to your VCR in the order that it was to be viewed. Pros call this *linear* editing because everything is put in place in the exact sequence.

iMovie, an easy-to-use digital video editor, makes all that unnecessary. Being able to edit a digital video using a computer is a revelation because you can copy the clips or segments in any order you want. Then, during the editing process, you put things in order. This process is called *nonlinear,* and it's a lot more flexible.

iMovie is a ground-breaking application. Traditionally, non-linear digital video editing was only available to professionals willing to spend thousands of dollars. iMovie brings these capabilities to hobbyists.

Although iMovie, seen in Figure 10.3, is astoundingly simple to learn, it includes advanced features that you can use to make the most of your video footage. You can combine separate video clips using transitions, add sound effects and voiceovers, create title text, and export your final work into formats others can view.

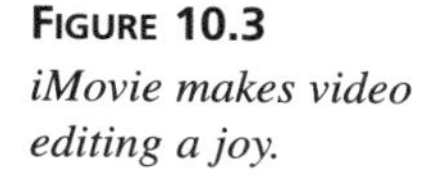

FIGURE 10.3
iMovie makes video editing a joy.

A large part of what makes iMovie work so well is FireWire, the connection standard we discussed in Chapter 7, "Choosing Peripheral Devices." In fact, to work with digital video from your camcorder using iMovie, you must have a computer *and* a camera with FireWire ports. That's because digital video files can be very, very large, and getting them onto your computer would be impossibly slow without FireWire.

How can you tell if your Mac came with FireWire ports? Check the connection panel and see if you have any FireWire connectors. You can identify them by their peculiar shape. Thin, oval at one end, squared off at the other.

Digital video cameras usually have a slightly different style Firewire connector (small, like a slightly misshapen rectangle) that may be labeled "IEEE 1394" or "iLink" in the camera documentation.

If you don't have a FireWire connection, you can still use iMovie for making slide shows from still photos.

Chapters 13 through 17 cover most of the things you can do with iMovie, including adding effects and exporting.

Introducing iDVD

Are you still buying movies on videotape? Well, that's a technology that might eventually go the way of 8-track tape. The fastest growing consumer electronics product is the DVD player. A DVD puts the contents of an entire movie on a disc the same size as a CD.

Using Apple's iDVD, you can now create your own DVDs, complete with navigation menus and motion (moving) menus.

iDVD, shown in Figure 10.4, allows you to share your home movies and still images, and integrates with both iPhoto and iMovie.

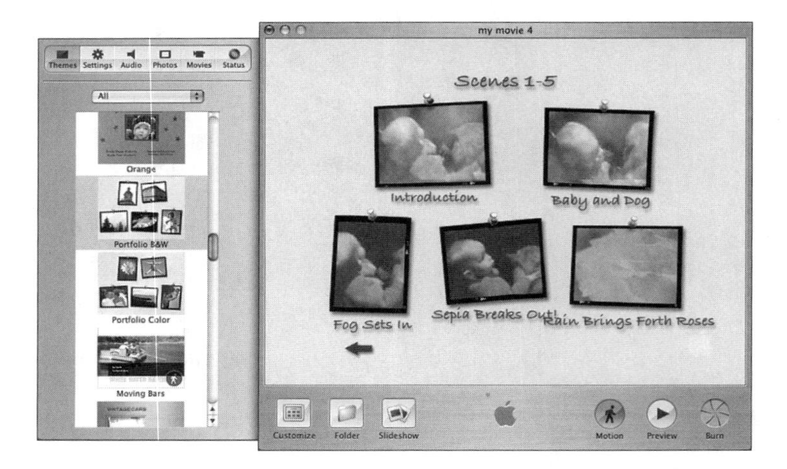

FIGURE 10.4
iDVD lets you share your digital video and digital images using professional-quality features.

To run iDVD, your computer must be equipped with a special optical drive that Apple dubs the "SuperDrive." This drive, manufactured by Pioneer or Sony, the large Japanese consumer electronics companies, can play CDs and DVDs, and burn both.

To burn your own DVDs, you will need DVD-R discs. While they may look like CDs, their capacity is much greater—4.7GB, which is large enough to hold at least an hour of average video and many, many image files.

The DVDs you write will play on most DVD players and the DVD drives on a personal computer. However, some of the oldest DVD players, made during the first year the format was introduced, cannot play them. Check Apple's Web site, at `http://www.apple.com/dvd/compatibility/`, to see a list of the players that have been tested and found compatible. Newer players, even if not listed at the site, will likely work without any problem.

Like the other applications included in iLife, iDVD was designed to offer a wide range of features that are easy to use. We'll talk more about iDVD's features in Chapters 18 through 20.

Installing the iLife Applications

Now that you've heard about the delights that await you when you use iTunes, iPhoto, iMovie, and iDVD, how do you get them? Well, there are several options available.

First, you should check your Applications folder to see if they are already installed. If you find them, you'll want to check their version numbers to ensure that you have the latest software. You need to have at least version 3 of iTunes, iMovie, and iDVD and version 2 of iPhoto to get the most from them. (Earlier versions were not designed to integrate with each other.)

Apple often makes minor updates to their applications that make them run better, so even if you have the versions mentioned above, you'll want to visit the Apple Web site to see if there are newer versions, or version updates, listed for download. For instance, there was an update for iMovie 3.0.2 listed at the time of this writing.

If you don't find these applications on your hard drive, you have two options. The first, if you want iTunes, iPhoto, and iMovie, is to download them from Apple's Web site.

If you have a slower Internet connection, or if you want to use iDVD, you'll need to purchase the iLife software package. (This package includes all four applications, even though the other three are free in download.)

iTunes, iPhoto, and iMovie are available for free via download—why isn't iDVD? The answer to that lies in the size of the iDVD application and files. Basically, it's HUGE and trying to download it would tie up a lot of your computer's resources for a very long time. Trust me, if you want iDVD it's worth the money to pay for the installation discs.

To install, double click the installer icon or disc icon that appears on your desktop and follow the prompts. You will be asked to authenticate yourself first, which means you enter the password for the administrator (or owner) of the computer. When you do that, just OK the license agreement, click the various Continue and Install buttons and the software will be set up on your computer in short order.

Apple recently released iTunes 4, which adds access to the iTunes Music Store to iTunes' previously existing features. (The music store allows you to purchase and download song files from participating recording companies.)

If you purchase iLife, you'll actually receive two installation discs. One is a CD containing iTunes, iPhoto, and iMovie; the other is a DVD containing all four applications. (I said previously that iDVD is HUGE—in fact, it's so large that it has to be offered on a DVD rather than a CD.) Having two separate discs helps ensure that those without the Apple SuperDrive can still reap the benefits of iLife without having to spend hours downloading the components. Make sure you use the right disc for your system.

Summary

This chapter introduced you to iLife and the applications it encompasses. iTunes can be used to turn your Macintosh into the centerpiece of your entertainment system. iTunes gives you access to audio media in a straightforward and entertaining manner, and its special features make organization a snap. iPhoto helps you manage and share your digital photographs. With features for editing and sharing your work, you can easily spend hours perfecting your images and preparing them for display. iMovie, a digital video editing application, allows you to turn your home movies into finished products with titles, music, and transitions. It also lets you share your movies in several popular formats. Finally, iDVD lets you share your video or still photos in the popular DVD format, with features that rival those of professionally made DVDs. If you're a music enthusiast, digital photographer, or budding film-maker, iLife is for you.

CHAPTER 11

Using iTunes

If you like music, iTunes can serve as your CD player, MP3 ripper, song organizer, jukebox, eye candy, and CD burner. Amazingly, iTunes is simple enough to use that even if you've never burned a CD, ripped an MP3, or listened to Internet radio, you can be doing all three within five minutes—tops.

> No, rip and burn have nothing to do with discarding secret documents in a fireplace. It's really all about music.
>
> In the 21st century, ripping is the process of copying music tracks from an audio CD to a computer. Burning is the process of making a CD. Both pastimes are as popular today as making tape cassette copies of recorded music was a few years ago.

Setting Up iTunes

The first time you launch iTunes, it runs through a setup assistant to locate MP3s and configure Internet playback. At any time during the setup procedure, click Next to go to the next step, or click Previous to return to the preceding step. Clicking Cancel exits the setup utility and starts iTunes.

The first step of the setup process, displayed in Figure 11.1, enables you to set Internet access options.

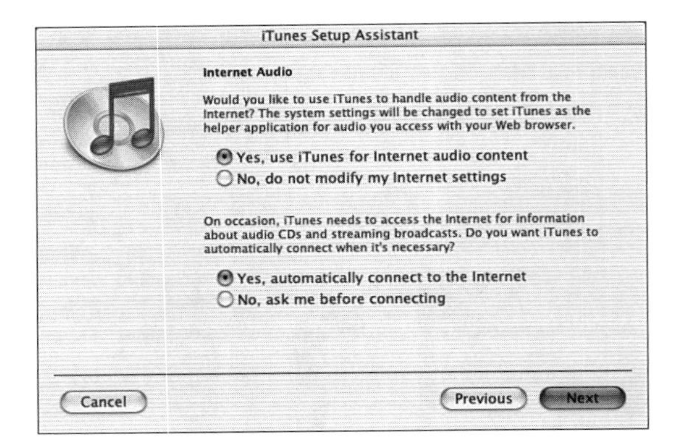

FIGURE 11.1
Choose how iTunes works with your Internet applications.

iTunes is perfectly suited for handling streaming MP3s. If you've never listened to Internet radio before, you'll appreciate how quickly and easily iTunes enables you to find the type of music you want to hear and start listening. If you already have a streaming music player, tell iTunes not to modify your Internet settings.

iTunes also interacts with the Internet to look up information about your CDs, such as the artist and song title. The Yes, Automatically Connect to the Internet radio button, selected by default, enables this feature. To force iTunes to prompt you before connecting to the Internet, click No, Ask Me Before Connecting. Click Next when you're satisfied with your responses.

During the final step of the configuration, you're prompted to decide how iTunes will find MP3s. By default, iTunes locates all the MP3 files on your drive. To disable this feature, click No, I'll Add Them Myself Later. The process of searching the drive for MP3 files can take a while, so I prefer to add MP3s when I want to.

Click Done to begin using iTunes.

The iTunes Interface

Everything you need to do anything in iTunes is found in the main window, pictured in Figure 11.2. The main control areas are listed here.

Player Controls—The player controls move between different songs, play, pause, and adjust the output volume of the currently playing track. Clicking directly on the sound slider moves the volume adjustment immediately to that level.

Status Information—Displays information about the currently playing song. The top line displays the artist, the name of the song, and the name of the album. Clicking each of the status lines toggles between different types of information. Likewise, the Elapsed Time line can be toggled to display remaining time and total time.

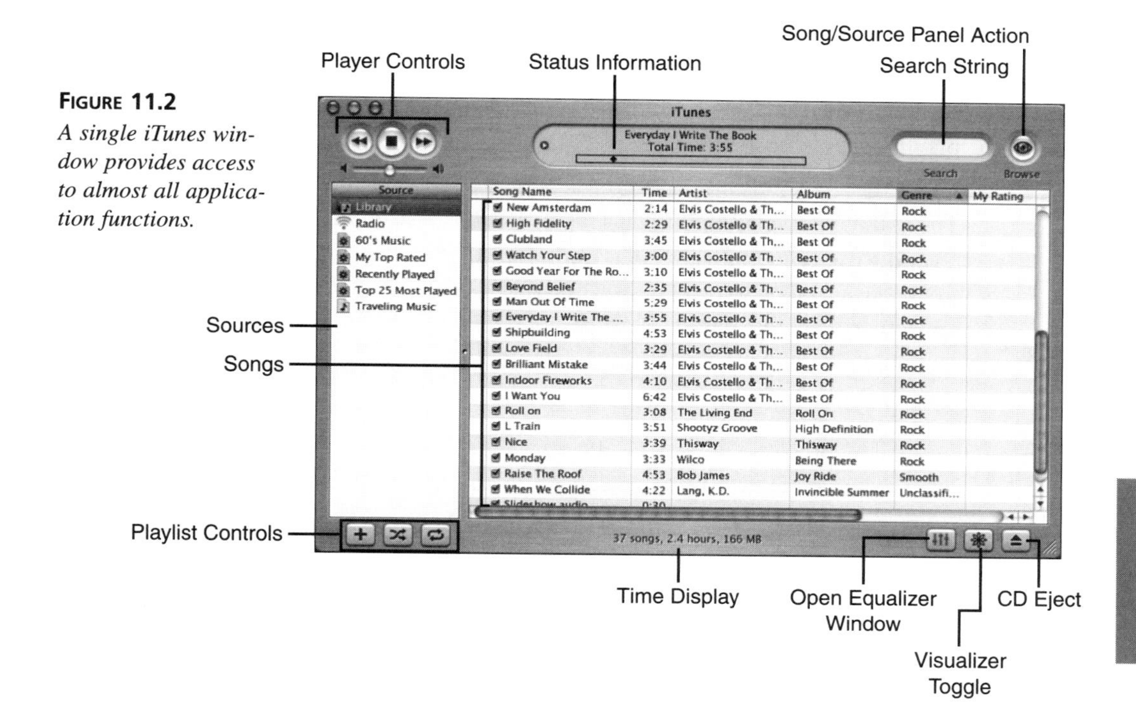

FIGURE 11.2
A single iTunes window provides access to almost all application functions.

The progress bar shows how far the playback of the current song has progressed. Dragging the progress bar handle moves the playback back or forward in the audio track.

Finally, a stereo frequency monitor can be displayed by clicking the arrow on the right of the status display.

Search String—Typing a few letters into the iTunes Search field immediately displays all audio tracks in the current playlist or library that match the string in any way (artist, song, album).

Song/Source Panel Action—The action button performs a different function depending on what source is currently being viewed. As you work in different areas of the program, this button changes to an appropriate action for that area:

- **Library**—When viewing the main song library, the action button toggles between two different browse modes. The first mode, shown in Figure 11.2, is similar to the Finder's List view. Each audio track is listed on its own line. The second mode uses a layout similar to the Column Finder view: The first column lists the artist and the second column shows the albums for that artist. Finally, a lower pane shows a list of the song tracks for that artist and album.

- **Radio Tuner**—The Radio Tuner's action button is Refresh, which reloads all available stations from the iTunes Internet radio station browser.
- **Playlist**—A *playlist* is your own personal list of music that you've compiled from the main library. Playlists are the starting point for creating a CD. When viewing a playlist, the action button is Burn CD.
- **CD**—When a CD is inserted, iTunes prepares to import the tracks to MP3 files. The action button is Import when a CD is selected as the source.
- **Visual Effects**—No matter what source is selected, iTunes can always be toggled to Visualizer mode to display dazzling onscreen graphics. When the visual effects are active, the action button becomes Options for controlling the visual effects.
- **Source**—The Source pane lists the available MP3 sources. Attached MP3 players, CDs, playlists, the central music Library, and Radio Tuner make up the available sources.

Double-clicking a source icon opens a new window with only the contents of that source. This is a nice way to create a cleaner view of your audio files.

Songs—A list of the songs in the currently selected source. When in the main Library view, you can click the action button to toggle between a simple list and a column-based browser. Double-clicking a song in the list starts playback of the selected list beginning at that song. To change the visible fields in the list, choose View Options from the Edit menu. Among the available pieces of information for each song are Name, Time, Artist, Album, Genre, Play Count, and the time it was Last Played.

Playlist Controls—Three playlist controls are available: Create Playlist, Shuffle Order, and Loop. As their names suggest, these buttons can be used to create new playlists and control the order in which the audio tracks are played back.

Time Display—At the bottom of the iTunes window is information about the contents, playing time, and total file size of the currently selected source. The default mode displays approximate time—clicking the text toggles to precise playing time.

Open Equalizer Window—The Equalizer, shown in Figure 11.3, enables you to choose preset frequency levels by musical genre or to set them manually by dragging the sliders. The mode defaults to Flat, which means all the controls are set in the middle of their range.

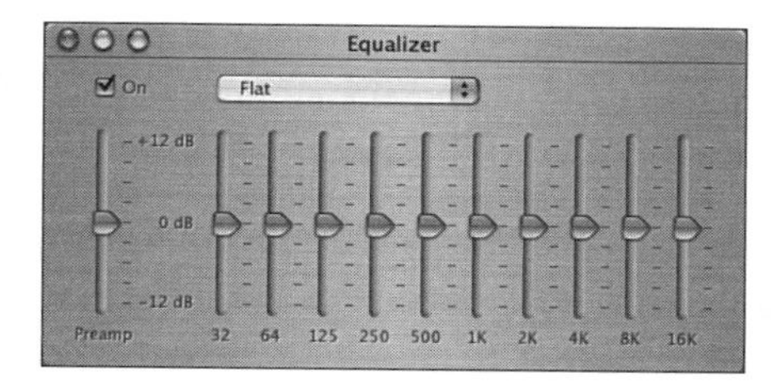

Figure 11.3
Choose how iTunes plays your music using iTunes' built-in equalizer.

Visualizer Toggle—Turns the visualization effects ("music for the eyes") on and off.

CD Eject—Ejects the currently inserted CD.

So, now that you know what the controls are for, let's take a look at putting iTunes through its paces.

Adding MP3s

Encoding, or ripping, CDs enables you to take the tracks from a CD and save them in the MP3 (MPEG Layer 3) format. MP3 is a highly compressed audio format that has become very popular in recent years—much to the dismay of the recording industry.

> In cooperation with the five major recording labels, Apple launched the iTunes Music Store—which integrates with version 4 of iTunes to allow you to search a music library and purchase individual song files for $0.99 each. The iTunes Music Store is a great way to expand your music collection with high-quality recordings. Visit www.apple.com/music/ for more details.

To encode your own MP3 files from a CD, find the CD you want to use and then follow these steps:

1. Insert the CD into your Macintosh.
2. iTunes queries an Internet CD database to get the names of all the tracks on your disk. During iTunes setup, if you chose to not have this happen automatically, select Get CD Track Names from the Advanced menu and press the Stop button.
3. Click the CD name in the Source pane to display all the available tracks.
4. Select the tracks you want to encode. If no tracks are selected, the entire CD is imported.
5. Click the Import action button to encode the selected tracks. As the tracks are importing, the CD plays and a small graphic appears to show whether it has been imported or is currently being imported.

The CDDB Internet database contains information on hundreds of thousands of CDs. In the unlikely event that your CD isn't located, it is listed as Untitled.

If iTunes couldn't find your song information, or you aren't connected to the Internet, you can edit each MP3 file's stored artist/title information by hand by selecting the file and choosing Get Info (Command-I) from the File menu.

You can even submit your updated information back to the Internet CD database by choosing Submit CD Track Names from the Advanced menu.

After you add songs to your Music Library, iTunes enables you to easily assign ratings to them. Simply locate the My Rating column in the song listings and click on the placeholder dots to add from 1 to 5 stars for each song. To sort by rating, simply click the My Rating header.

By default, the encoded MP3s are stored in Music/iTunes/iTunes Music found in your home directory. An entire CD can take from 5–74 minutes to process, depending on the speed of your CD-ROM drive. To pass the time, you can continue to use iTunes while the tracks are imported. When the import finishes, your computer chimes and the MP3s are available under the Library source listing.

If you're working with an existing library of MP3s rather than a CD, you can easily add them to your MP3 Library. Use the Add To Library option from the File menu to choose a folder that contains MP3s. Alternatively, you can simply drag a folder of MP3s from the Finder into the Library song list.

The process of importing MP3s takes time. Each MP3 is examined for ID3 tags (which identify information such as artist and title of a song) and is cataloged in the iTunes database. If you're adding MP3s to iTunes from a network drive, be prepared to take a quick lunch break.

◀ TASK

Task: Creating and Working with Playlists

The key to many of the remaining iTunes features lies in creating a playlist. As we mentioned earlier, a playlist is nothing more than a list of songs from your Library.

1. To create a new playlist, click the Create Playlist button in the lower-left corner of the iTunes window, or choose New Playlist (Command-N) from the File menu.

2. The new playlist ("untitled playlist") is added to the Source pane. Select the playlist, and then press the Enter key to rename it. The next step is to add songs to the playlist.
3. Select Library in the Source pane.
4. Verify that the song you want is in the main MP3 Library. If it isn't, you must first add the song to the Library.
5. Select one or more songs in the Songs pane.
6. Drag your selection to the playlist in the Source pane.

Using the Smart Playlist option, you can automatically create playlists based on criteria such as genre or your personal song ratings. Simply choose New Smart Playlist from the File menu, set your criteria, and name your playlist. As an added bonus, Smart Playlists can also be set to update themselves with the Live Updating option as new material is added to your Music Library.

The selected songs are added to your playlist. Click the playlist to display the songs. You can drag the tracks within the song pane to choose their order.

Burning CDs and Exporting to MP3 Players

After a playlist has been built, you can drag its name from the Source pane to any listed MP3 player source. The files are automatically copied to the connected player. If the player does not have enough available space, you must remove files from your playlist or select the external player and remove tracks from its memory. (We'll give special attention to using iTunes with Apple's iPod MP3 player at the end of this chapter.)

Not all Macs have a built-in CD burner. If yours doesn't, you can add an external CD-burning drive. iTunes works with a number of makes and models from such companies as LaCie, Plextor, Que, Sony, VST, and other popular brands. You'll want to check with your dealer or Apple's iTunes Web site (`http://www.apple.com/itunes`) for the list of supported devices. Even if you can't burn a CD, you can still rip tracks from an audio CD using your computer's CD drive.

If you have a Mac with a supported CD burner, you can use a playlist to burn an audio CD laid out exactly like the playlist.

When burning CDs, you have a choice between a couple types of CD media. The first type, CD-R, is what's called a write-once CD. That means you can write your files to it just once and that's it. If you make a mistake, you have to use another CD. The CD-RW media can be erased and used over and over again, up to a thousand times. In that way, it's like a regular drive except that CD drives run slower.

If you plan on using the files only temporarily and replacing them over and over again, the extra cost of the CD-RW is worth it. Otherwise, stick with the CD-R.

Regarding the price of blank CDs, well, the best thing to do is try a brand and see if it works. If you get lots of disk errors, try a different brand. The big names, such as Fuji, Imation, Maxtor, and Verbatum, should work with any CD burner. You should try a few of the private store labels before buying a large bundle.

To make a CD, just insert a blank CD into your computer's CD drive (if it came with a CD burner) or into a connected CD burner. Your MP3 music player's instructions will tell you how to copy music to one of these devices.

If you have an older CD player, CDs you create yourself might not work. Unless you've spent a bundle on that CD player, it might be worth purchasing a new CD player to have the flexibility of making your own CDs.

With the CD in place, double-check your play list, and then click Burn CD to make your custom disc. Depending on the speed of your CD burner, making a CD can take up to half an hour. When you're done, you can eject the CD (pressing the Eject button at the lower right of the iTunes window). Repeat the previous steps to make more play lists and more CDs.

Listening to Internet Radio

Depending on your connection speed, Internet radio could be your ticket to high-quality commercial-free music. Unfortunately, most dial-in modems have poor sound quality, but DSL and cable modem users can listen to much higher quality streams. To see what's available and start listening requires only a few clicks:

1. To display a list of available streaming stations, click Radio in the Source pane. After a few seconds of querying a station server, a list of available music genres is displayed.

2. Each genre can be expanded to show the stations in that group by clicking its disclosure triangle. Stations are listed with a Stream (station) name, Bit Rate, and Comment (description). The bit rate determines the quality of the streamed audio—the higher the bit rate, the higher the quality—*and* the higher the bandwidth requirements.
3. Double-click a station to begin playing, or select the station and then click the Play button. iTunes buffers a few seconds of audio, and then starts playing the streaming audio. If iTunes stutters while playing, look for a similar station that uses a lower bit rate.

> Conversely to what seems logical, you can drag stations from the Radio Tuner source and play them in a playlist. The playlist plays as it normally would, but starts playing streaming audio when it gets to the added Internet radio station.
>
> You cannot burn a radio station to a CD or store it on an external MP3 device.

Playing Audio

As I'm sure you've discovered by now, the iTunes player controls work on whatever source you currently have selected. After a song plays, iTunes moves to the next song. You can also control the playing via keyboard or from the Controls menu:

- **Play/Stop**—Spacebar
- **Next Song**—Command+right-arrow key
- **Previous Song**—Command+left-arrow key
- **Volume Up**—Command+up-arrow key
- **Volume Down**—Command+down-arrow key
- **Mute**—Option+Command+down-arrow key

> Some of these functions are also available from the iTunes Dock icon. Click and hold the Dock icon to display a pop-up menu for moving between the tracks in the current audio source.

To randomize the play order for the selected source, click the Shuffle button (second from the left) in the lower left of the iTunes window. If you want to repeat the tracks, use the Loop button (third from the left) in the lower-left corner to toggle between Repeat Off, Repeat Once, and Repeat All.

The iTunes window is a bit large to conveniently leave onscreen during playback. Luckily, there are two other window modes that take up far less space. Quite illogically, you access these smaller modes by clicking the window's Maximize button.

After clicking Maximize, the window is reduced to the player controls and status window. Even this window is a bit large for some monitors, though. To collapse it even more, use the resize handle in the lower-right corner of the window.

To restore iTunes to its original state, click the Maximize button again.

Visualizer

The iTunes Visualizer creates a graphical visualization of your music as it plays. While playing a song, click the Visualizer button (second from the right) in the lower-right corner of the iTunes window, or select the Turn Visualizer On (Command-T) option from the Visuals menu to activate the display. Figure 11.4 shows the Visualizer in action.

FIGURE 11.4
The Visualizer displays images to match your music.

The Visuals menu can control the size of the generated graphics as well as toggle between full-screen (Command-F) and window modes. To exit full-screen mode, press Esc or click the mouse button.

While the windowed Visualizer display is active, the Options action button in the upper-right corner of the window is active. Click this button to fine-tune your Visualizer settings.

Reviewing iTunes Options

As you can see, building play lists in iTunes and making CD copies can be done in just a few minutes. Easy as pie! If you want to look at the power of the program, however, there are some useful options to get you better quality CDs and fine-tune the program.

You'll find them under Preferences in the iTunes application menu (it's in the Edit menu with the Mac OS 9.x version).

Here's a brief look at the three preference dialog boxes available with iTunes:

- **General**—When you click the General tab (see Figure 11.5), you have three categories of preferences you can set. Under Display, you can pick a text size from the two pop-up menus and whether the musical genre (such as Country or Rock) should be displayed in your play list. The Internet option simply enables you to select the same choices you made when the original iTunes Setup Assistant appeared. Under CD Insert, you indicate with the pop-up menu what to do when you insert a music CD. The default is Show Songs, but you can also decide to both play and import the contents of a CD automatically.

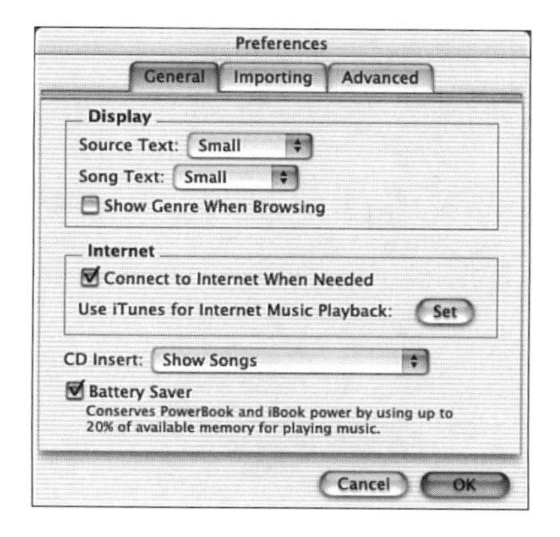

FIGURE 11.5
Choose various display options for iTunes here.

- **Importing**—Now click the Importing tab (shown in Figure 11.6) to decide how imported music is handled. The key setting here, the Configuration pop-up menu, enables you to choose the data rate in kilobits per second. The higher the data rate, the better the quality of the encoded music. Anything lower than 128 kbps is quite different (and inferior) to the quality of a regular audio CD. Above that figure it gets mighty close and sometimes almost impossible to tell the difference. Remember also that the higher the data rate, the more disk space a music file occupies on your hard drive.

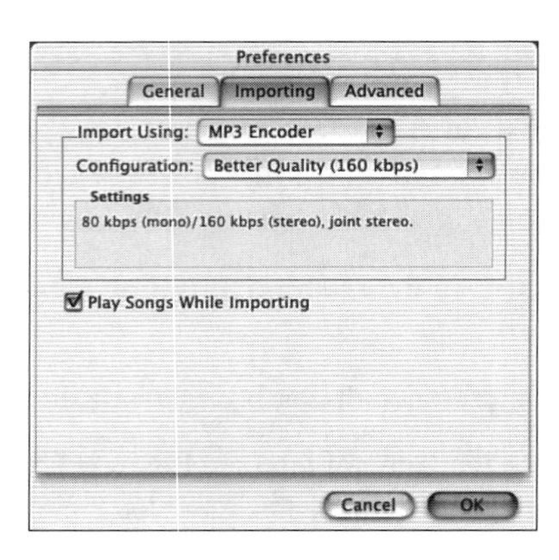

FIGURE 11.6
Pick the CD encoding rate here for best quality.

- **Advanced**—The final option isn't one that you'd see very often (shown in Figure 11.7). The first setting is where to place your play list, and the rest are specific to the kind of CD burner you are using and how you want the gap between musical tracks handled.

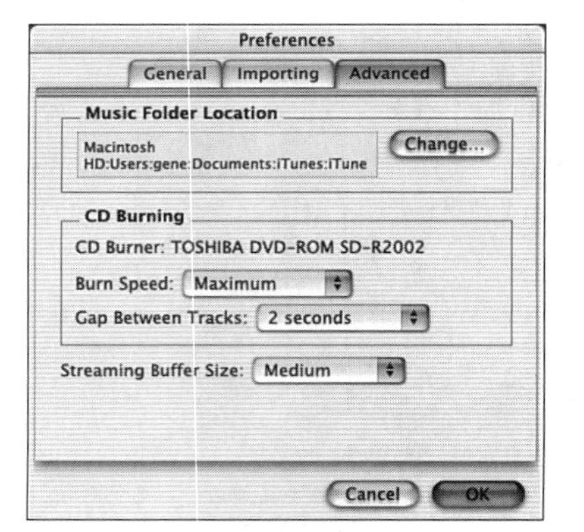

FIGURE 11.7
The location of your play lists and settings for your CD burner are shown here.

Using Your iPod with iTunes

Apple's tiny digital music player, the iPod (see Figure 11.8) can serve double-duty. You can use it as an extra FireWire hard drive for your computer as mentioned in Chapter 7, "Choosing Peripheral Devices," or you can just stick with its core function, which is a hand-held (or pocket-held) music device.

Making your iPod work with your Mac is an almost automatic process, so I'll be brief about it (aren't you glad?).

FIGURE 11.8
The iPod delivers digital music with style.

11

▼ To Do

Updating Your iPod's Music Library

1. To dock your iPod to your Mac, first make sure your Mac is running.
2. Take the FireWire cable that comes with your iPod (or any regular FireWire cable for that matter) and plug it into your iPod and your computer's FireWire port. When connected, you'll see a FireWire icon on your iPod's display. When set up, iTunes will open automatically and your iPod will automatically synchronize its music library with the one on your computer.

Some FireWire cables, especially those designed for DV camcorders, have a 4-pin cable at one end. These won't work with your iPod, which requires a 6-pin cable to enable it to draw current from your computer, used for recharging its battery.

3. If you prefer to transfer music manually, connect your iPod as described previously and allow iTunes to launch.
4. Select your iPod in the iTunes source list (the list of music libraries), and click the iPod icon at the bottom right of the iTunes window, which opens the program's preferences box.

▼

5. With preferences displayed on your computer's screen, check the item labeled Manually Manage Songs and Play Lists.

> You won't be able to use your iPod with other computers without it replacing your music library if you use the standard option to automatically update your play list when your iPod is attached to your computer. That's because it'll base its play list strictly on the Mac to which it's connected. If you feel you want to use the iPod on different Macs, use the manual song management option described previously.

Summary

In iTunes, Apple has latched on to a craze, especially among younger people. The iTunes software can quickly convert your CDs into a library of MP3s or vice versa, and give you access to thousands of radio stations that play the kind of music you want to hear, 24 hours a day. It'll even sync with your iPod to make your music portable. But that's only part of the picture. If you have a computer with a built-in CD burner (or a separate CD burner), you can make a music CD with your favorite tunes. If you're a music enthusiast, Mac OS X is the operating system for you.

CHAPTER 12

Using iPhoto

Apple's iPhoto brings all the functions you need for working with digital photographs together in one interface, shown in Figure 12.1, with different modes for Import, Organize, Edit, and Book. You move between modes by clicking the row of buttons under the viewing area.

> You may see the option "Share" in the row of buttons under the viewing area. This means you haven't updated to the most current version of iPhoto, which is the one we'll be discussing here. I recommend that you download the new version from the Apple website before continuing.

> Many recent digital cameras with USB connections are compatible with iPhoto. You can find out whether yours is one of them at `http://www.apple.com/iphoto/compatibility/`.
>
> If your digital camera isn't compatible with iPhoto, Apple recommends using a peripheral device to read the camera's memory card directly. The type of storage media used by your camera dictates whether you need a PCMCIA Flash Card reader or some other kind.

Those without digital cameras can still use iPhoto to organize digital images sent from other people and to store scanned images. We talk more about importing files into iPhoto from your hard drive later in this chapter.

The iPhoto interface contains several distinct areas, some of which change depending on the current mode. The bottom pane contains mode-specific functions, and the upper-right viewing area takes on different appearances to support the mode you're in. You can resize the contents of the viewing area using the slider to the right of the mode buttons.

To jump between the smallest and the largest possible display sizes, click on the small and large image icons at either end of the resize slider.

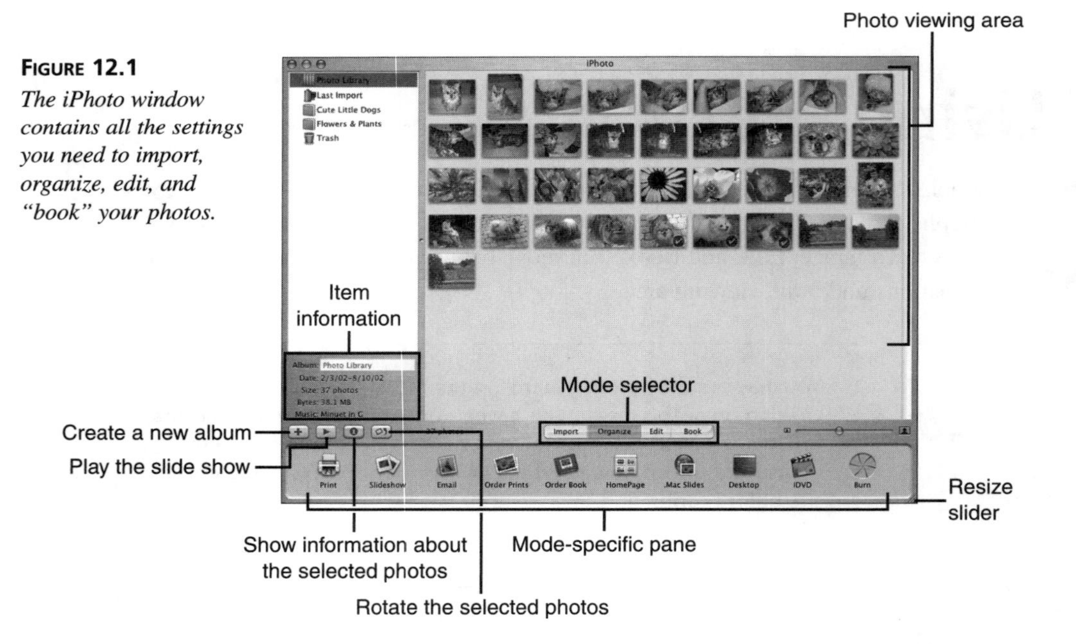

FIGURE 12.1
The iPhoto window contains all the settings you need to import, organize, edit, and "book" your photos.

The elements along the left side are available regardless of iPhoto's mode. Let's take a look at them now.

The Photo Library contains all the images imported by iPhoto. Last Import is a special unit containing the most recent pictures. Below Last Import are albums, the special sets of pictures you put together. Selecting one of these items fills the viewing area with thumbnail images of its contents.

Below the Photo Library and albums is a section containing information about the selected item. For example, in Figure 12.1, Photo Library is selected, so the information section displays the name of the selection, the range of dates for the images it contains, the number of images it contains, and the total file size of its contents. It also displays the music currently selected to accompany slideshows, which we will discuss shortly. If a specific thumbnail image were selected, the given information would be the image title, date imported, size of image in pixels, file size, and current slide show music. You can change the title or the date by typing in those fields.

Additional details about a selected image can be accessed from the Show Photo Info command in the File menu. This launches a window containing information about the image, file, and originating camera. If your camera supports it, the window also contains technical details such as shutter speed, aperture, and use of a flash for the photograph.

There are also four buttons just above the mode-specific pane:

- **Create a new album**—Enables you to create a special group of chosen photos that you can arrange in any way or export as a unit. We'll talk more about albums later.
- **Play the slideshow**—Plays a full-screen slide show, complete with music, of all the photos currently displayed in the viewing area. You can alter the slide show settings under the Slideshow option of the Organize mode, including the length of time each slide plays and the song to accompany the slide show—you can even choose a song from your iTunes folder.
- **Show information about the selected photos**—Toggles the information area through its different configurations, including one containing a field to add comments about the selected photo. (In another configuration, the info section is hidden entirely.) We'll talk about how you can perform searches on this Comments field in a little while.
- **Rotate the selected photos**—Rotates the selected items. You can set the rotation direction to clockwise or counterclockwise in the iPhoto application preference dialog.

Importing Image Files

The first time you connect a supported camera to your computer and set the camera to its playback or transfer mode, iPhoto will open automatically. If it doesn't, you can manually launch iPhoto either from the Dock or the Applications folder. The iPhoto window will be in Import mode.

Mac OS X includes in its Application folder the Image Capture program that downloads images and media files from supported cameras and card readers. It also works with TWAIN-compliant flatbed scanners (given an appropriate driver) to scan images.

The Import pane, shown in Figure 12.2, displays the camera status, Import button, and an option to delete images from the camera after they're stored in iPhoto.

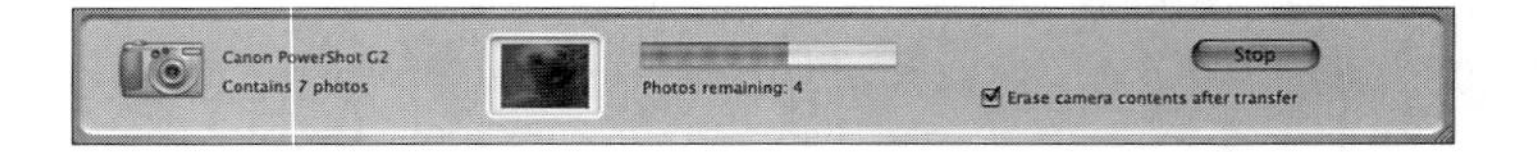

FIGURE 12.2
The Import mode enables you to follow the progress of your files as they're transferred from the camera to your computer.

To import the photos on your camera, click the Import button in the lower-right corner of the window. If the box for Erase Camera Contents After Transfer is checked, the Confirm Move sheet appears and asks you to approve deletion of the original photo files from the camera. Thumbnails of the transferring images appear in the image well of the Import pane along with the number of photos remaining to be transferred. When the import is complete, the new images will appear in the photo viewing area along with any other images you've imported.

By default, new *rolls* (groups of pictures imported at one time) are added to the bottom of the viewing area, but you can change that to order with the most recent at the top inside the application preference panel.

To import images already stored on your hard drive or other media, simply select them and drag them onto the Photo Library. Thumbnails appear as if the images were another "roll" of film.

Organizing Images

After you've imported some image files into iPhoto, switch to the Organize mode to work with your images. The iPhoto window in Organize mode, shown in Figure 12.1, looks very similar to the Import mode except for the controls in the bottom pane. Here you can choose ways to share your images. We'll talk about those options later in this chapter.

While in the Organize mode, you can choose whether to display the images in your viewing area with additional information, including their titles, keywords, and film rolls, by selecting those options from the View menu.

Selecting Titles displays the title of each image beneath its thumbnail image. The default titles of images imported by iPhoto aren't very helpful. You can give them more meaningful titles as explained earlier.

The Keywords option shows any keywords you've attached to an image file to the right of its thumbnail image. We'll look further at applying keywords in just a moment.

Displaying by Film Rolls divides the photos in the viewing area into sections labeled with roll number, date of import, and number of photos imported.

You can choose to view your images with any, all, or none of those pieces of information.

You can tell iPhoto to order the images in your Photo Library by film roll, date, or title by selecting the appropriate option in the Arrange Photos submenu of the View menu.

You can select an image in the viewing area by single-clicking it. You can select a group of consecutive pictures by clicking just outside the edge of the first photo and dragging to create a box connecting all the photos that you want to select, or select a group of nonconsecutive pictures by holding down the Command key as you click the desired images.

If you want to delete a photo or several photos that are visible in the viewing area, highlight the photos you don't want to keep and then press the Delete key on your keyboard. In the original version of iPhoto, when you deleted a photo it was truly gone forever. In more recent versions, deleted photos are stored in a special Trash area, much like the one for your entire system.

You can view the contents of the Trash by selecting its icon on the left side of the iPhoto window. If you decide to save a photo that you sent to the Trash, you can drag it back to your Photo Library. When you are positive that you don't want to see any of the items in the Trash again, choose Empty Trash from the File menu.

You can also drag selected photos to your desktop, which will make additional copies of them, or into a new album, which we'll discuss later in this chapter.

Applying Keywords

A good way to organize your photo collection is with keywords. When applied, keywords appear next to the image thumbnails in the viewing area whenever you check the box for Keywords.

To open the Keywords/Search window, choose Keywords from the Edit menu.

You can use iPhoto's default keywords or create your own custom keywords. To write your own, choose New from the Keywords pop-up menu at the top of the Keywords/Search window. Then, in the line that appears, type your new keyword.

To change an existing keyword, choose Rename from the Keywords pop-up menu. Keep in mind that the change is passed along to any photos that were assigned the previous keyword.

To delete a keyword, click to highlight it in the keyword list, and choose Delete from the Keywords pop-up menu.

To apply keywords to a photo, select the image thumbnail in the viewing area and highlight the keyword you want to apply by clicking it. Then, click the Assign button below the keyword list. To remove a keyword, select the image and click back into the Keywords/Search menu. All the keywords you've added to the selected photo will be highlighted in the list so you can remove them all, or click on only the one you wish to remove.

Included in the keyword list is a check mark symbol, which acts somewhat differently than the other keywords. Whereas other keywords are visible only when you've chosen to display them in the View menu, the check mark is visible in Organize mode at all times, superimposed in the lower-right corner of the thumbnails it has been applied to. Also, the check box cannot be renamed or deleted as the other keywords can.

After you've applied keywords, you can search your image collection for photos labeled with a given keyword or combination of keywords. Simply open the Keywords/Search window, select the keyword you want to target, and click the Search button near the middle of the window. Only those pictures that match your search appear in the viewing area. Click the Show All button to return to the full photo listing.

In addition to searching by assigned keywords, you can also search for words in your image titles or comments. Just type the word in the Search field at the bottom of the Keywords/Search window. You don't need to click the search button, or even finish typing the word, before iPhoto attempts to match your search criteria. Delete the search term or click Show All to return to the full photo listing.

▼ TASK

Task: Creating an Album

You can't arrange the individual images in your Photo Library just any old way. To choose the sequence of a set of images, you must create an album and add the photos you want to work with. (Keep in mind, that every photo imported into iPhoto will appear in your Photo Library; adding photos to albums doesn't move them out of the Photo Library.)

> You can choose whether to arrange the photos in an album by film roll, date, or title using the Arrange Photos option in the View menu, just as you can for your Photo Library. However, for albums there's a fourth option that lets you arrange your images manually, which gives you the power to arrange them in any order you see fit.

Albums are an especially useful way to organize your photographs into collections, especially if you have a large number of photos. Albums are also a basic unit in iPhoto that's used when creating books, slide shows, and Web pages, which we'll discuss later.

The option to make a new album is available from any mode in iPhoto. To create a new album, perform the following steps:

1. Click the button showing a + sign near the left edge of the iPhoto window, or choose New Album from the File menu.
2. A dialog box appears, into which you can type a name for your album. (If you change your mind later, you can double-click the name of the album in the album list to change it.)
3. When you've named your album, click OK.

The album you created appears at the bottom of the album list at the upper left of the iPhoto interface. If you want to change the order of your albums, select the one you want to move and drag it to a new position. A black bar indicates where the album will be inserted. If you want to remove an album, select it and press the Delete key on your keyboard. Unless the album is empty, you will see an alert asking you to confirm deletion.

To add images to your album, make sure that you're in Organize mode and select the images you want from the viewing area. You can select them one at a time or in groups. Drag your selection to your album name until a black border appears around it. As you drag, a faded version of one of the selected images appears behind your cursor, along with a red seal showing how many items you're dragging.

> The images within albums are something like aliases on your desktop—you can delete a photo from an album without affecting the original file. However, when you delete an image from the Photo Library, it also disappears from any albums to which it has been added.

After you've created an album and added images, you can open the album and drag the contents into any order you want, as long as the Arrange Photos setting under the View menu hasn't been changed from Manually. You can also remove images from the album by selecting them and pressing the Delete key on your keyboard. Because the photos in your albums are always a part of the Photo Library, only the album copy will be removed. (If you want to delete a photo altogether, you'll need to delete it from the Photo Library as you learned earlier.)

Editing Photos

iPhoto's Edit mode enables you to improve your existing photos by resizing them, adjusting their coloration, and performing simple retouching. To edit a photo, select it in Organize mode and click the Edit button. You'll see a screen similar to that shown in Figure 12.3. While in Edit mode, you can use the Previous and Next buttons at bottom right to move through a group of images without going back into Organize mode.

While iPhoto is a fantastic tool for organizing photos and performing simple cropping, you may want to perform your serious editing in a separate program, such as Photoshop Elements.

To open an iPhoto image file in another image editing program, click and drag an image thumbnail from the Organize view onto the icon for the photo-editing program. If you plan to edit with an outside program frequently, you can go into the iPhoto Preferences and set images to open automatically in the outside program when double-clicked.

If you do choose to edit your photos in a program other than iPhoto, keep in mind that changes saved to an original image from an outside program replace the original file in iPhoto's folders, so you cannot revert to the original image as you normally would. It might be best to make a duplicate before you begin editing.

If you choose to further edit an image that has already been altered from within iPhoto, the image is already a copy, so you can revert to the original version. To check whether a file is an original or a copy before you begin editing, look at the File menu to see whether Revert to Original is an available option or it is grayed out. If it is grayed out, the photo you're working with is the original.

When editing a photo that's been added to an album, bear in mind that any changes appear in both the Photo Library and the album.

A major function available in Edit mode is *cropping* or trimming away the unimportant edges around a subject. iPhoto enables you to constrain the size of your cropped images to fit the common photos sizes 4×6, 5×7, and 8×10, as well as ratios such as square, 4×3, and a size to fit the resolution of your monitor.

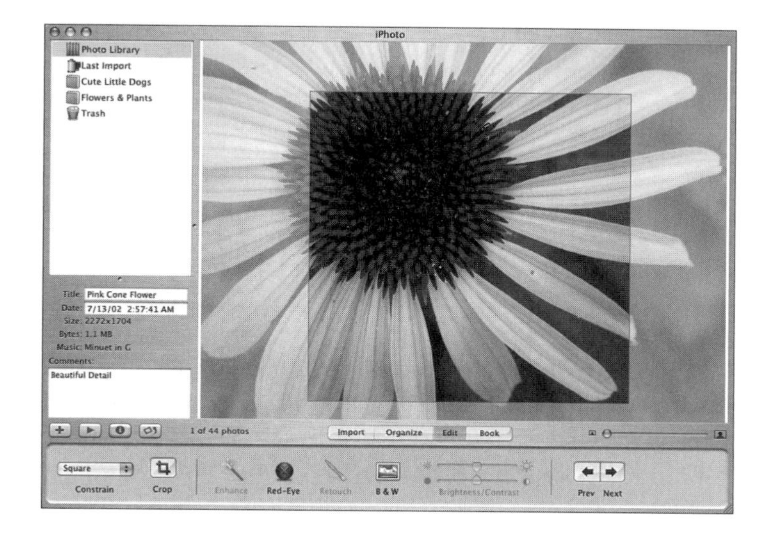

FIGURE 12.3
In Edit mode, you can crop your images or change their color properties.

Depending on the resolution of the images produced by your digital camera, you might not be able to crop to a small section of a photo without the resulting image becoming grainy or fuzzy. This is especially a problem if you plan to order prints from your photos because the images might look okay onscreen, but could be unsuitable for printing. When ordering prints or books, watch out for the low-resolution warning symbol, which looks like a yellow traffic sign. It will appear when creating a book or ordering prints if iPhoto determines that an image's resolution is not sufficient for the requested size of the finished image.

To crop an image, open it in Edit mode and follow these steps:

1. Set a Constrain option if you want to maintain a specific image ratio.
2. In the viewing area, place your mouse pointer at one corner of the object or scene you want to select. Click and drag to form a selection box around it, as shown earlier in Figure 12.3. To reposition the selection box, move your mouse pointer to the center of the selected area until it changes to a hand and then drag the box where you want it.
3. Click the Crop button to apply your change and see the result in the viewing area.

If you find that you don't like the look of the cropped image as well as you liked the original, you can undo your most recent edit by choosing Undo from the Edit menu.

After you make changes to images in iPhoto, you can always revert to the image as it was first imported by choosing Revert to Original from the File menu. This enables you to make changes freely without fear of losing your original. However, if you achieve an effect you like, you might want to duplicate the photo in that state before trying additional edits. To do so, select the desired photo and choose Duplicate from the File menu. That way, choosing Revert to Original after further editing returns you to that state instead of the original form of the image.

In addition to cropping, you can edit your images with the Brightness and Contrast sliders. Brightness makes a photo brighter or darker overall—it can fix minor problems from under- or overexposure. Contrast increases the difference between light and dark elements by making lighter areas lighter and darker areas darker. Contrast also increases the saturation of colors. Although these settings are good for small corrections, keep in mind that they can't save a photograph shot in really poor light conditions.

The Red-Eye and Black & White features enable you to change the coloration of entire photos or the area within a selection box. The Red-Eye option is most useful for reducing red tint from the eyes of people and pets, but it also removes the red tones from any selected area. To correct red eye, mark a crop selection box as tightly around the red eyes as possible and then click the Red-Eye button. Use the Black & White option to convert an entire image to black-and-white or create interesting effects by selecting portions to convert.

iPhoto's red-eye tool leaves a lot to be desired. For one thing, most red-eye regions are round but iPhoto's cropping tool can only make rectangular selections. If you happen to select a portion of anything with red tones in it that lies outside the red-eye region you want to correct, you will also remove the red for that area. One solution is using other photo editing software, such as Photoshop Elements, which we'll discuss starting in Chapter 21.

The Enhance feature also changes the coloration of the selected image. Specifically, it adjusts the colors in the photo for maximum contrast. To use it, simply click the Enhance button. If you find you don't like the results, you can always choose Undo from the Edit menu.

The Retouch option allows you to blend specks and imperfections in your photos into the areas surrounding them. This tool is different from the options we've already discussed, all of which either work on the entire image or a pre-selected area. When using Enhance, your mouse cursor appears as a set of cross-hairs, which you can use to target image flaws. When you have this cursor positioned near a discolored spot, click your mouse button and watch the color in the region around your cursor even out.

When using the Retouch tool, it is useful to enlarge the area you are working with using the resize slider. This helps you see exactly where to place the cursor to blend in a spot.

Designing a Photo Book

Book mode, shown in Figure 12.4, is a specialized option that's used to arrange an album's photos into a book format, including any supporting text. You can then order copies of your book in the Organize mode, as we'll discuss later.

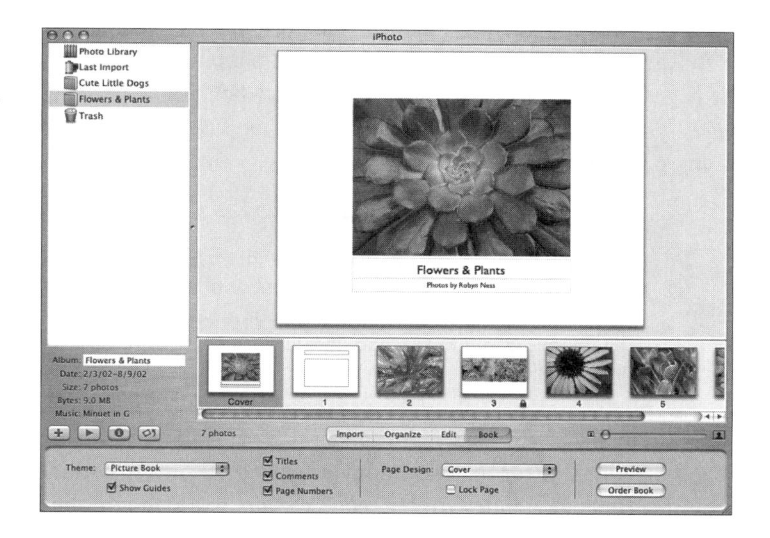

FIGURE 12.4
Book mode enables you to lay out the photos in an album as a book.

In the Book options pane, the Theme pop-up menu enables you to choose a basic style, including Story Book, Picture Book, and Catalog. The options differ in their picture layouts and built-in text areas, and how the photos are arranged on the page. When you choose a theme, the photos in the selected album are placed in a basic template in the order they appear in the album. The individual pages appear in a row at the bottom of the photo viewing area.

It's best to choose the look you want for your book carefully before you start customizing it. If you change from one theme to another, you lose any text (except photo titles and comments) or special page formatting you've made.

Check boxes in the Book options pane also enable you to choose whether to show image Titles, Comments, and book Page Numbers on the pages, if the theme you've chosen includes space for them.

You can also choose whether to show guides for the text boxes. You should check the Show Guides box if you want to edit the text. To edit text within a text area, select a page and type inside the space. If you want to check your spelling for a given page, you can do so by choosing Check Spelling from the Spelling submenu of the Edit menu. You can also change the font of an entire book in the Font submenu of the Edit menu.

When you choose a theme, an album's photos are inserted into the page template in the order in which they appear in your album. For example, the first image in the album is the default cover shot. The Page Design pop-up menu enables you to adjust the templates to show more or fewer images on a selected page. If you like the composition of some of the pages and don't want them to be shifted when you apply new templates to other pages, you must select the pages and check the Lock Page box. You can alter the layout of any page except the cover.

> You can change the order of whole pages by dragging them to a new position. However, to change the cover photo, you must go into Organize mode and rearrange the images in your album to place another photo first. Any changes made to page order in your book are reflected in the order of images in the album.

To get a better feel for the chosen layout, use the Preview button to page through your book in a separate window. When you are satisfied with your book, click the Order Book button to open a window with purchasing details.

Sharing Your Photos

iPhoto offers a variety of ways for you to share your photos with others, both in print and on screen. They are located along the bottom of the iPhoto window when it is in Organize mode.

Sharing Printed Photos

For those who want to share their photos the traditional way, on some sort of paper, iPhoto offers three button choices at the bottom of the window: Print, Order Prints, or Order Book.

Clicking the Print button enables you make print settings for the selected item, including page size, margin width, and number of copies. If you select the Photo Library but not a specific photo, you can print the entire group.

> As with other programs on your Mac, you can also choose to save your images in PDF format from the Print window. PDF documents can be opened by Adobe Acrobat, which is widely available and free, by people who don't have other types of image-viewing software.

The Order Prints and Order Book buttons connect you to remote Web sites where you can choose what to order and supply your billing information. You can order prints of your pictures just as you would with pictures captured on film, or you can order a bound book of an album as you designed it using the Book mode. If you order a book, keep in mind that the base size is 10 pages. If your book has fewer than 10 pages, several pages at the end are left blank. Also, additional charges are made on a page-by-page basis for books of more than 10 pages.

Sharing Photos Digitally

To share your photos digitally with others, you can use the Email option. The Email option enables you to easily email a photo stored in iPhoto. Clicking the Email button brings up a dialog box in which you can choose the size of the image and whether to include the image title and comments. Click the Compose button to open a mail window containing the selected photograph, and then add the email address of the recipient.

If you are a .Mac member, as discussed in Chapter 4, "Using the Internet," you can also make use of the HomePage and .Mac Slides options. Clicking the HomePage button enables you to select up to 48 images from your Photo Library or a specific album to insert into a basic Web page layout that will be stored in your .Mac account. You can view a sample page at `homepage.mac.com/robynness/PhotoAlbum2.html`.

Choosing the .Mac Slides options lets you upload a set of images to your .Mac server space, or iDisk, that can be used as a screen saver by others running Mac OS X. You can only offer one slide show at a time, but this is a fun way to share pictures with friends and family. When you update the slides, their screen savers will also be updated.

> After you upload a .Mac slide show, how can you share it with your family and friends? Tell them to go to the Screen Effects panel of System Preferences and choose .Mac in the Screen Effects list. Then, they must click the Configure button and, in the window that opens, they need to type your .Mac membership name and click OK. It will take a few moments for the images to be downloaded from the Internet to their computers.
>
> If you want to test drive a .Mac slideshow, you're welcome to subscribe to mine, which features my own photographs of flowers and leaves. Simply enter `robynness` as the .Mac membership name in the Configuration window.

If your Mac has a CD burner or a DVD burner, you have two additional options for sharing your images digitally. The Burn option allows you to burn an album, or your entire library, to a CD or DVD. Simply click the Burn button and insert a blank disc when prompted. Then, click the Burn button again to write to the disc.

The iDVD option, available to those with computers equipped with Apple's SuperDrive and with iDVD installed, magically exports your iPhoto slide shows—including music choice and slide timing—into iDVD. All that's left for you to do is choose a background image for the main title page, using iDVD, and burn your DVD. (We'll talk more about iDVD beginning in Chapter 18, "Getting Started with iDVD."

Viewing Your Own Digital Photos

In addition to sharing your photos with others, you can also enjoy them at your own computer with the iPhoto Slide Show and the Desktop options.

The Slide Show option brings up a dialog box in which you can set the duration each image stays onscreen, whether the slides are displayed randomly and whether they repeat, and which music accompanies the show. When you've made your settings, clicking OK starts the iPhoto slide show.

The Desktop option enables you to choose a single photo from your collection for use as a desktop background. To set a desktop, simply select the image you want and click Desktop. Your desktop background is immediately replaced with the selected image. To change your background back to a non-iPhoto background, open the Desktop panel of System Preferences and choose a new image.

Summary

This chapter covered the different modes of iPhoto: Import, Organize, Edit, and Book. You learned how to make albums and lay out your own photo book. You also looked at the various ways in which iPhoto helps you share your images both in print and onscreen.

CHAPTER 13

Getting Started with iMovie

The goal of this first hour is to equip you with the basics you need to understand key concepts and issues in digital video, which will be helpful to keep in mind as you're working on projects.

The iMovie Workspace

iMovie is a simple yet powerful video editor that enables you to develop your video project with three main tools: the Monitor, where you look at the video clip; a shelf, which gives you the ability to look at all the clips you have to work with at a glance; and a special area at the bottom of the screen known as the Timeline Viewer, where you can put together your clips, and make decisions about when you want them to start and end.

iMovie Monitor

You'll find that the iMovie workspace is easy and fun to work with, like a well-planned playroom (see Figure 13.1) and the iMovie monitor will end up being the center of activity. After you've created a new project, the action happens in the Monitor window, which is used both to capture and preview video in iMovie. The deceptively simple Monitor window is a powerful tool that enables you to switch between looking at video that's coming from your camcorder and the clips that you already have on your Mac by toggling the import/edit control, labeled with camera and scissors icons, below the window.

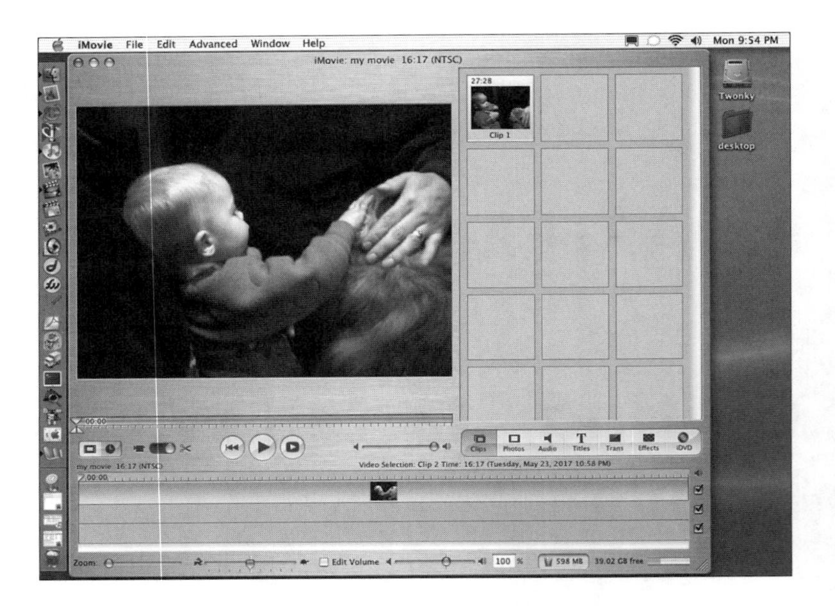

FIGURE 13.1 *The overall iMovie workspace: The Video Monitor, Shelf, and Timeline Viewer.*

The controls for the Monitor window are much like you use on a DVD player and VCR, enabling you to quickly move through your video or jump to a specific location.

Shelf

The value of the shelf, visible to the right of the Monitor window in Figure 13.1, quickly becomes apparent when you connect your camcorder to the Mac for the first time and start capturing clips. It almost seems like alien technology at work as you watch the video clips from your tape start to appear in the shelf. The shelf is like a pantry for video—when you capture video, you load up the shelf with clips and you can take a quick glance to see what you have to work with.

As you'll see in later hours, the shelf gives you several additional tools to enhance your video productions, including transitions, titles, and effects, as well as a place to put audio if you've recorded it separately from your video.

Timeline Viewer

The Timeline Viewer, visible along the bottom of the iMovie interface in Figure 13.1, enables you to make adjustments to your video clips, such as adjusting the start and end times of each clip, as well as adjusting effects and other things that you might add to a clip.

The Timeline Viewer also enables you to see things (clips, transitions, sound effects) as they progress over time.

The Timeline Viewer makes it easy to make more specific adjustments to your project based on situations in which you might want to go to a specific location in a clip. It also enables you to work easily with multiple audio clips, so if you want to add different sounds that you've recorded, it's as easy as clicking and dragging.

Clip Viewer

The Clip Viewer (see Figure 13.2) is an alternative to the Timeline Viewer, representing another way of looking at video clips that some people might prefer. In the Clip Viewer, video clips are treated more like icons. You can easily click and drag an individual clip to position it differently and thus have a different order for your video production. We'll take a closer look at the clip viewer in just a few minutes.

> If you're new to digital video, try imagining iMovie as your "word processor for video." You can re-arrange, delete and add material, but instead of working with paragraphs, you're working with video clips!

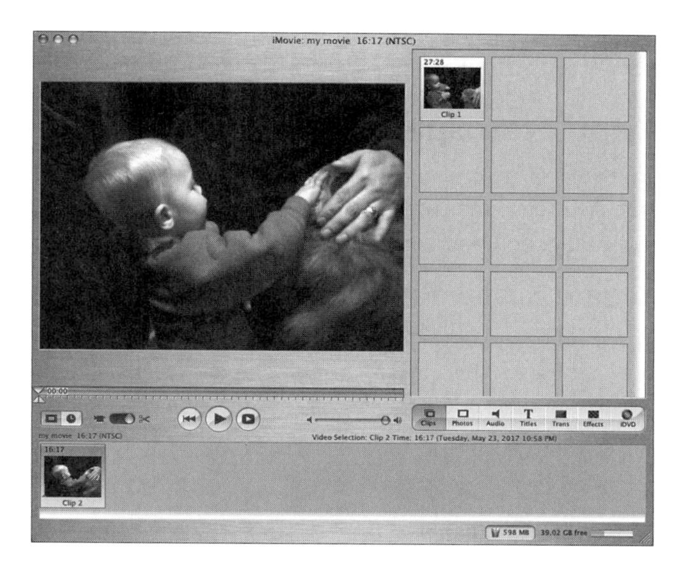

FIGURE 13.2
The Clip Viewer offers an alternative way to look at your clips.

13

Other Important Controls for the Timeline

At the very bottom of the iMovie window in Timeline view is a row of controls (refer to Figure 13.1).

The first control is a slider labeled Zoom that allows you to zoom in on the Timeline to see more detail. As you add more and more scenes to the Timeline, the proportion of the whole that each takes up shrinks—and so do the rectangles representing those clips. Use the Zoom slider to focus in one part of the Timeline by selecting a clip and dragging the Zoom controller to the right.

Next is the Speed slider, labeled with icons of a rabbit (or hare) and a turtle (or tortoise), which may call to mind Aesop's fable about the fast hare and the slow tortoise. (To refresh your memory, the slow-but-steady tortoise wins the race.) This slider controls the speed of the selected clip. If you want a clip (or other element in the Timeline) to be sped up or slowed down, drag the slider toward the appropriate side.

If a slider control button moves sluggishly when you try to drag it, you could instead click on the spot along the slider path where you want to set it. The button will jump precisely to that spot with ease.

Near the middle of the bottom row are controls for audio. Checking the box for Edit Volume will produce a volume level in each of the elements in your Timeline. You can then adjust the volume of each clip or sound file so there aren't unpleasant volume changes. The slider next to the check box controls the overall volume of the movie. There are some additional features of the Edit Volume checkbox, that we will discuss in Chapter 16, "Using Still Photos, Music, and Sound Effects in iMovie."

Trash and Free Space

The bottom controls row also includes a couple of helpful things to manage your iMovie project: the free space indicator and a miniature trash can so that you can easily get rid of video clips that you don't need any more.

Task: Create a New Project

▼ TASK

Before you can begin working on making iMovies, you must know how to create a new project. iMovie makes this easy by bringing up a special screen (shown in Figure 13.3) if you don't already have a project started.

FIGURE 13.3
A startup screen appears if you haven't already started a project.

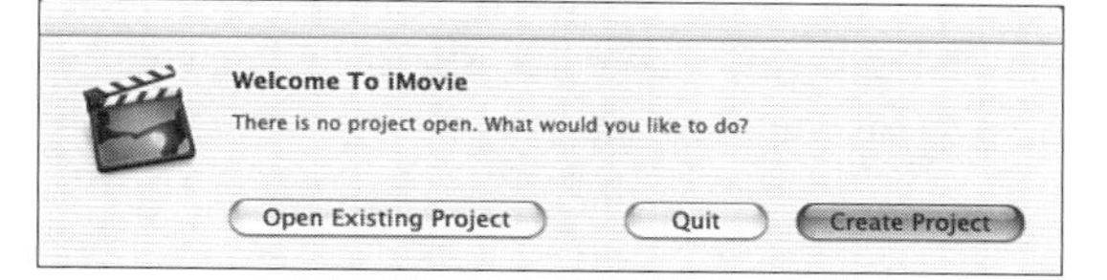

To create a new project:

1. Start iMovie. If you get the window shown in Figure 13.3, click the Create Project button.

   If you don't get this window when you start iMovie, you can choose File, New Project from the menu bar to get the same thing.

2. When you create a new project, iMovie brings up the Create New Project dialog sheet, to ask you where you want to put the project on your hard drive (see Figure 13.4). Type in a name for your movie and click Save if you want iMovie to simply save the file directly to the hard drive.

FIGURE 13.4
The Create New Project dialog.

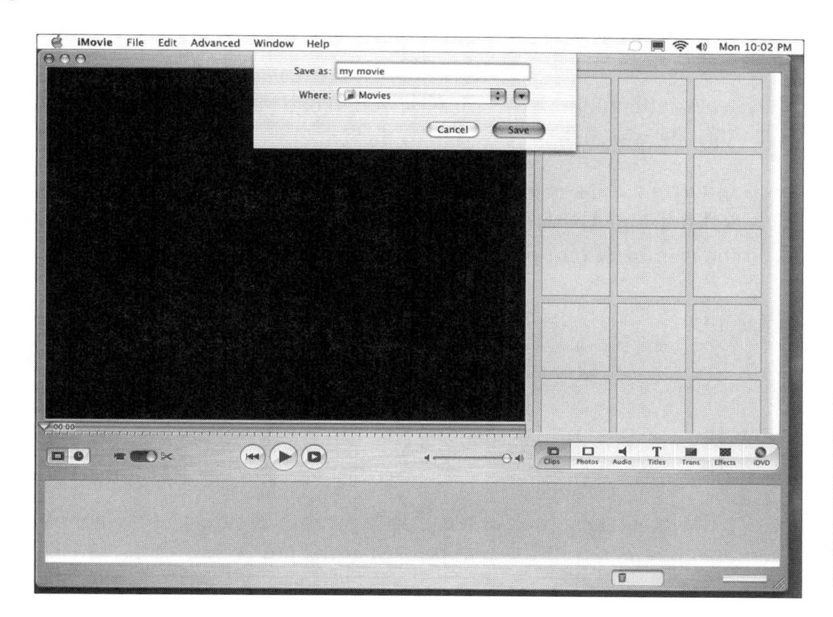

When iMovie creates a project, it puts all of your video material in one location on the hard drive, sort of like a suitcase, making it easy to store everything for your iMovie in one place. When you capture video, all of the clips end up in the project; and even though there are separate files, everything stays together.

13

3. You might want to switch to a more convenient location than the one iMovie suggests (such as the desktop), by clicking the pop-up menu at the top of the Create New Project dialog sheet. This will open a view of your hard drive so you can choose where to save the project.

The Clip Viewer

As you learned earlier, the Clip Viewer is an alternative to the Timeline and might be preferable for some as a way to work with clips. In some ways, the Clip Viewer is the "lite" version of iMovie, so we'll use it to learn about the iMovie interface.

Although the Timeline view provides an excellent way to work with clips and is easy to use, the Clip Viewer is even easier to use, and it might be a good starting place for some people. If you want to have a simplified introduction to working with iMovies, you might want to start in the Clip Viewer and then move on to the Timeline. Also, children might find it easier to play with iMovie in the Clip Viewer because there are fewer skills to master—just clicking, dragging, and dropping.

In the Clip Viewer, you can do just about everything you can in the Timeline, including adding transitions, effects, and titles. One of the only major differences is that you can't work with audio in the Clip Viewer. When you try to drag a sound effect into the Clip Viewer, it switches you back to the Timeline.

Figure 13.5 shows the Timeline with three successive video clips that are arranged from left to right. The leftmost part of the Timeline represents the beginning of the movie, and the rightmost part of the Timeline represents the end of the movie.

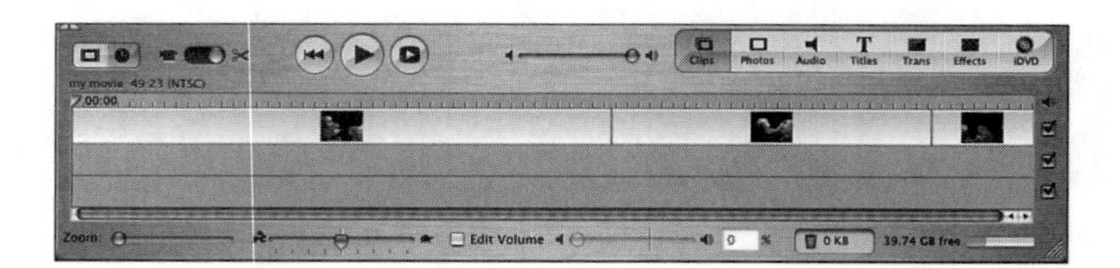

FIGURE 13.5
Three clips in the Timeline view.

Now let's take a look at the Clip Viewer in Figure 13.6, which is accessed simply by clicking on the film frame symbol at the left corner of the screen.

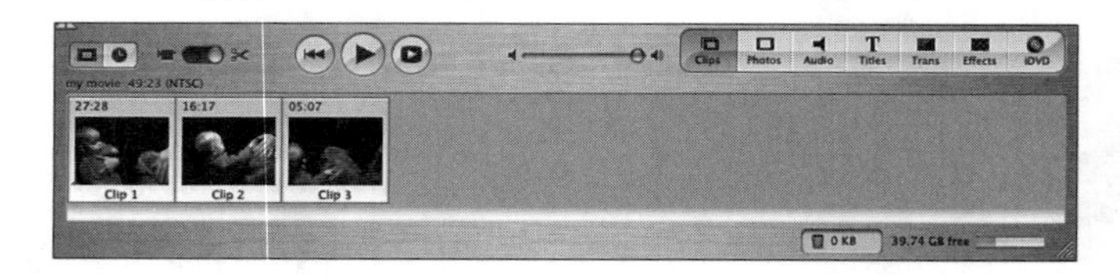

FIGURE 13.6
The same three clips in the Clip Viewer.

The video clips represented in Figure 13.6 are the same video clips that you saw in Figure 13.5. If you have iMovie open, take a moment to click back and forth between the Timeline and the Clip Viewer to investigate the differences.

Some people might prefer to think of the Clip Viewer as being like a *slide sorter* (a device that enables you to easily sort slides that have been developed from a traditional camera). If you've ever seen slides that were developed from traditional film, you'll notice that the icons that represent the Clip Viewer and clip shelf look a lot like slides.

▼ TASK

Task: Adding Clips

Adding clips is very simple in the Clip Viewer. You can basically handle things the same way that you will learn to do in the Timeline: by dragging clips into the Clip Viewer from the Shelf.

1. Open an iMovie project that has several clips in it. If you don't have any clips to work with yet, you might want to search your hard drive for any movie file ending with the extension .mov.

A tutorial folder is not included with iMovie when the software is installed as part of an operating system upgrade or as a separate download. But if you originally had iMovie with your Mac (that is, if you have a FireWire connection), you'll most likely have the folder, unless someone deleted it.

2. To access the Clip Viewer if it's not already open, click on the film frame icon in the lower-left corner of the screen.
3. Choose a clip for your iMovie by single-clicking on one of the clips in the Shelf, holding the mouse button down, and dragging it down toward the Clip Viewer area as shown in Figure 13.7. When you have the mouse arrow over the Clip Viewer area, you can let go of the mouse button and drop the clip there.

▼

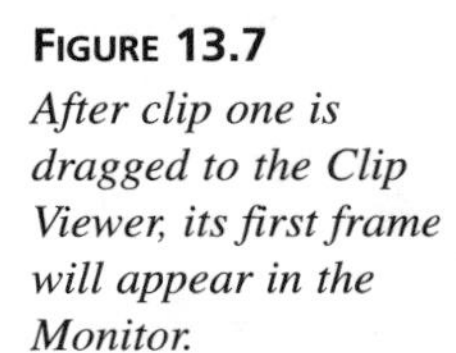

FIGURE 13.7
After clip one is dragged to the Clip Viewer, its first frame will appear in the Monitor.

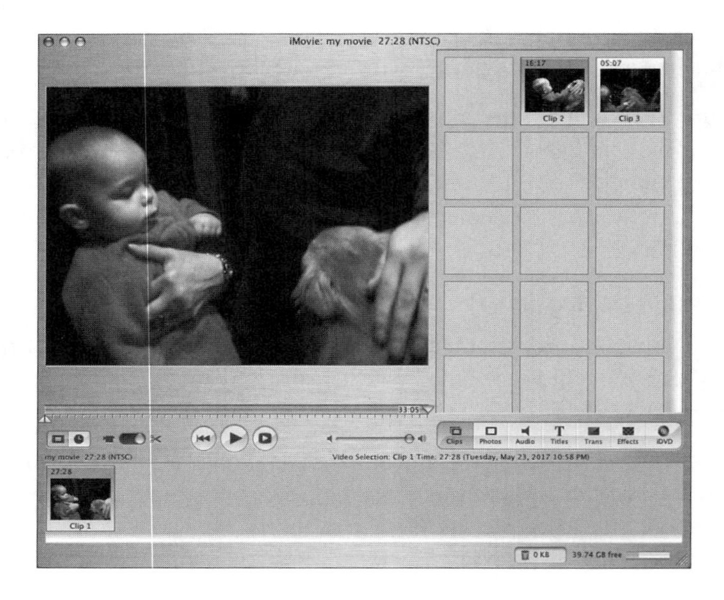

4. To add an additional clip, repeat steps 2 and 3 to drag the additional clip down and drop it to the right of the first clip.

When you've finished dragging clips into the Clip Viewer, they'll be lined up in a row. If one of the clips is a blue color, that simply means it's selected. If you want to deselect it, you can click somewhere other than on the clip in the Clip Viewer.

Previewing Clips

When you want to watch one of the clips you're using in your iMovie, you simply select it by clicking the clip, and then click the Play button. And when you want to preview the entire movie, you click the Play button without any clip selected, and iMovie will play all the clips in succession.

Task: Previewing a Single Clip

It's easy to take a look at a single clip in iMovie when you want to see what it contains.

1. Open an iMovie project with clips that have been dragged into either the Timeline view or the Clip Viewer.
2. Click the film frame icon to display the Clip Viewer.
3. Click once on a video clip to select it in the Clip Viewer.

4. Click the Play button under the Monitor to watch the clip, or click the playhead and drag it to the left and right to rapidly review what's going on in the clip (see Figure 13.8).

FIGURE 13.8
The playhead is at the end of the clip after it plays.

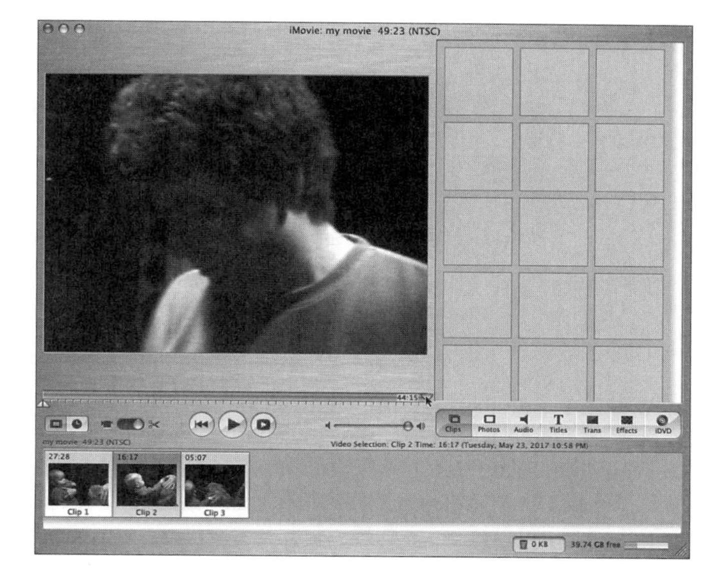

Notice how, in Figure 13.8, iMovie displays how much time each video clip takes up at the upper-left corner of each clip icon. By the time you reach the end of the clip, the playhead is to the far right of the blue bar, telling you how many seconds have elapsed. In video, there are 30 frames per second, so the farthest number on the right reflects the frame, and the number to the left of the colon represents the number of seconds.

Task: Previewing an Entire Movie

Previewing an entire movie is as simple as previewing a single clip; you just have to remember not to have any one clip selected when you click the Play button.

1. Open an iMovie project with clips that have been dragged into either the Timeline or the Clip Viewer.
2. Click the film frame icon to select the Clip Viewer.
3. Click somewhere other than on a clip to make sure that you don't have any clip selected—they should all be a white color.
4. Click the Play button below the iMovie Monitor, and iMovie plays through all the clips, giving you a preview of your entire iMovie.

13

Notice how, in Figure 13.9, iMovie draws a small red marker that moves slowly to the right in the Clip Viewer area as you watch your movie. The position of the red marker corresponds to where the playhead is positioned in the Monitor window as well. Both the playhead and the red marker are essentially ways of keeping track of where you are in your movie project.

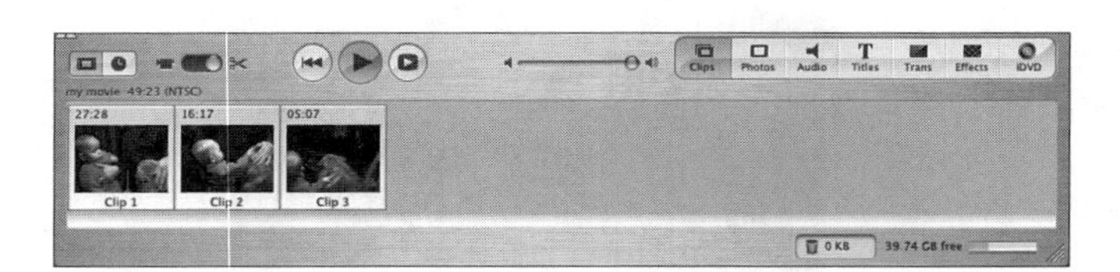

FIGURE 13.9
The Clip Viewer has a red marker (visible here as a thin white line in Clip 1) that goes through the clips when previewing, to indicate where you are in the iMovie.

The folks at Apple, in their typical subtle elegance and imaginativeness, have built a helpful way of seeing where one clip starts and one clip ends directly into the Monitor window. Small vertical lines in the scrubber bar below the Monitor correspond to where one clip ends and another begins. This feature is sort of like having a timeline even when you're in the Clip Viewer.

Enhancing Clips

Adding transitions, or effects, is as simple as it is in the Timeline. In many cases, you simply click a button to display the right palette, drag your enhancement onto the Clip Viewer, and you're there!

Task: Adding a Transition

It's easy to add a transition in the Clip Viewer:

1. Open an iMovie project with clips that have been dragged into either the Timeline or the Clip Viewer.
2. Click the film frame icon to select the Clip Viewer.
3. Click the Trans button in the main iMovie window to display the Transitions palette.
4. Click a transition and drag it to a spot in the Clip Viewer. (Try clicking Fade Out and dragging it into position after the last clip in your iMovie.)

After you drag the transition into place, iMovie attaches a small indicator to show you how the processing is going, with a small red line that moves to the right (see Figure 13.10). When it gets all the way to the right, the transition is officially processed and you can preview the clip.

FIGURE 13.10
The new Fade Out transition is processing, making a preview of what the fade out will look like.

TASK

Task: Adding an Effect

Effects have a few more options, as you'll learn in Chapter 15, "Adding Transitions, Effects, and Titles in iMovie," but adding them to a clip is as easy as any other enhancement.

Let's say we shoot some video in a dimly lit location, and then came home and decide that we want to brighten things up a bit. No problem!

1. Open an iMovie project and click the film frame icon to look at the Clip Viewer.
2. Click the Effects button to display the Effects palette.
3. Choose a clip and click it to select it.
4. With the clip selected, go into the Effects palette and click the Brightness & Contrast Effect to select it.
5. Drag the Brightness slider, shown in Figure 13.11, a bit to the right. Then play with the Contrast setting until the subject is easier to see.
6. You will see the changes, a little bit rough, in the preview window at the top of the Effects palette. (You could also click the Preview button in the Effects palette to view your settings in the Monitor window before applying them, but in some versions of iMovie this feature is disabled.)
7. If you liked what you saw in the preview window, click the Apply button in the Effects palette to tell iMovie that you've decided you want to use this effect. (iMovie will then process the effect, and mark the clip with a checkerboard icon to show that an effect has been applied.)

FIGURE 13.11
The controls in the Effects palette change with the effect you have selected.

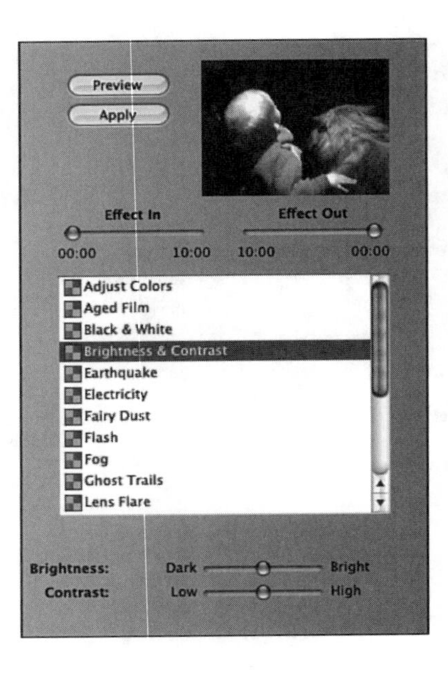

> If you don't like your settings, you can choose Edit, Undo (or hold down the Command key on your keyboard and then press the Z key—another handy way to undo).

Task: Rearranging Clips

One thing that the Clip Viewer comes in particularly handy for is rearranging clips if you want to reposition one clip after another or easily try different combinations of scenes. Open an iMovie project with a few clips in it, and before looking at the Clip Viewer, try the Timeline view (click the clock icon). Notice how things look. For comparison, you might want to try clicking on a clip to try moving it around, as shown in Figure 13.12.

FIGURE 13.12
You can't rearrange clips in the Timeline view—they stretch, but won't move!

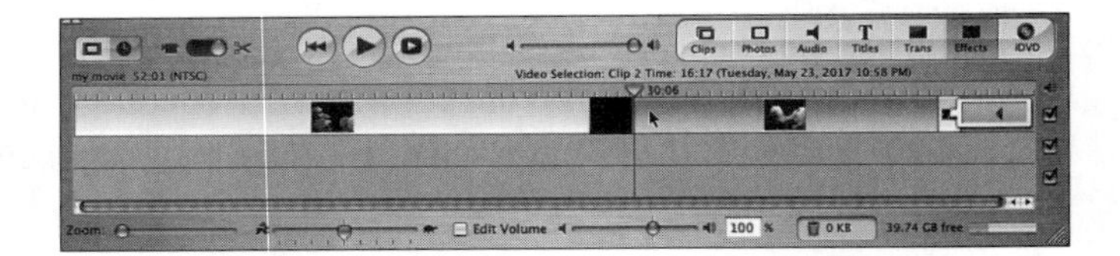

▼ Now you're ready to reposition:

1. Open an iMovie project with at least three clips in it, and click on the film frame icon at the lower left to see the Clip Viewer.
2. Click the first clip, and holding the mouse button down, drag the clip to the right, until a space opens up between the second and third clips (see Figure 13.13).

FIGURE 13.13
The Clip Viewer is a bit more convenient; rearranging is as easy as dragging back and forth.

3. Let go of the mouse button to drop the clip in place.

> Besides repositioning clips, the Clip Viewer is also good for putting clips back on the shelf if you've decided not to use them for the time being. Simply click on the clip to select it, and drag it back into an empty square in the Clips palette.

Digital Video Concepts

iMovie makes it so easy to work with digital video that you don't really have to understand all the nuts and bolts. But getting a better sense of how things work will help you to have more confidence, and will most likely result in better-looking productions. Let's take a look as some of the basic terms and concepts related to digital images and digital video.

Pixels

One of the fundamental concepts in working with digital video is the system that a computer uses to draw images on the screen. Your Mac divides the screen up into a grid of individual pieces called *pixels*, which are essentially individual dots that make up a picture.

It's possible for a computer to talk to a camcorder in such a way that you never have to deal with the measurement of pixels. When you capture video, iMovie automatically chooses the right settings, and you end up exporting to your camera again. When you're working with iMovie, you might never need to consider pixels, but it can be helpful to understand them, especially if you ever need to export an iMovie at a different size than the original. For example, you might want to save a special version of your iMovie to burn on a CD or put on a Web site, and when you do so, you end up saving it at a smaller size, which involves fewer pixels. Later in the lesson, we take a look at how this is done.

One typical way that you might need to work with pixels on your computer is when you adjust the *resolution* of your screen.

Resolution is a term that describes how much detail there is in a computer-generated image. A high-resolution image has more detail, and is considered to be a higher-quality image. Conversely, a low-resolution has less detail, and thus is of lower quality. For example, when you choose a different screen size on your Mac, such as 800×600 pixels, or 1024×768, you're changing the resolution of the screen—and you can see that with higher resolution, more can fit on the screen.

On a Mac, you can adjust the resolution setting in the System Preferences area of your computer. If you aren't familiar with pixels already, you might want to try this to get better acquainted.

Another way to think of pixels is in terms of individual graphics that you see on the screen, such as when you are looking at a Web page. People who work with digital images make adjustments to pixel sizes all the time, such as when they take a large digital picture and make it smaller so that they can put it on a Web page. (You'll learn about this very thing when we talk about saving images files in Photoshop Elements in Chapter 21, "Introducing Photoshop Elements.")

Your Mac draws images in such a way that you don't normally notice that an image is comprised of individual dots, but to get a clearer sense of what pixels actually are, let's take a closer look. In Figure 13.14, you see an image enlarged to 1200% so you can clearly see how the computer is using individual square-shaped blocks to draw the image.

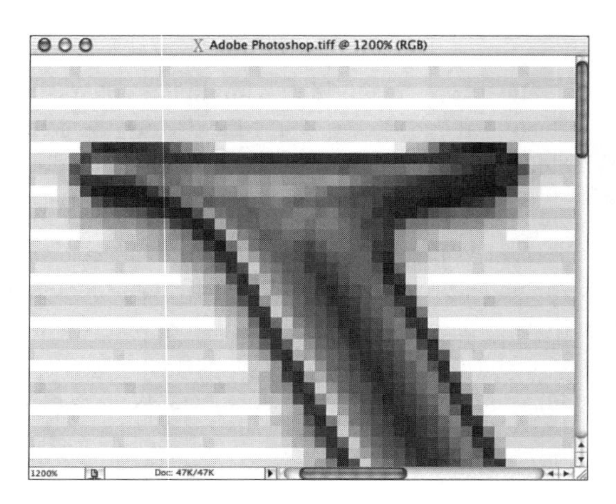

FIGURE 13.14
A close-up view of an image, showing the individual pixels.

Screen Size

The concept of screen size is related to pixels, because a computer screen or video image is made up of rows of pixels. There are differences between the ways that a computer and a television draws images, but to keep things fairly simple, it's generally okay to think of working with video in terms of pixels.

In the United States, televisions use a system called NTSC (National Television Standards Committee). When you design video on your computer for NTSC televisions, it is 720 pixels wide by 480 pixels high when it's displayed at full size.

When you work with video in iMovie, you can see a reduced-size version of the iMovie in the Monitor window.

If you live in Europe, you probably use the PAL system for working with video, which has a screen size of 768×576. The PAL system also uses a different frame rate, a concept that we talk about later in the hour.

As with pixels, the screen size isn't necessarily something that you need to be concerned about. In fact, you could make hundreds of iMovies and deliver them on VHS tape or through iDVD and never even consider the screen size.

One of the great things about iMovie is that it gives you the flexibility of working with video how you want. You can either let your Mac make educated guesses about how to adjust the settings, or you can go in (if you learn a bit about the kind of concepts that we talk about in this hour) and adjust things yourself. iMovie does have its limits, but as you'll see, it has a lot of flexibility as well.

Frame Rate

The *frame rate* of digital video is the number of images that are displayed in a second as they flash by, like frames in a traditional movie. Before television or video existed, moving pictures achieved the simulation of motion by projecting images on movie screens. This effect was achieved by rapidly projecting a succession of images on a screen, and the rate that the images are displayed was called the *frame rate*.

In traditional movies, the individual images and frames are contained in large reels, and they go by at a rate of 24 frames per second. The frames per second measurement has been adopted by digital video, but the measurement depends on a variety of factors, including the country you live in and the way you want to deliver your digital video. For example, if you use the NTSC digital video system, the measurement is most often 29.97 frames per second (fps).

So, as with other settings, you can let iMovie decide what frame rate setting to use. But if you want to, you can tweak your iMovie and change the frames per second manually.

Compression

Compression is another aspect of video that affects the quality of the image and the amount of space that digital video takes up on a hard drive or a disc such as a CD or DVD. Most digital video has some kind of compression already applied. For example, when you simply capture video from your camcorder into iMovie, iMovie compresses the video slightly so that it can display your video on the screen and store it on your hard drive without taking up too much space.

Compression is similar to what people do when they stuff or zip a file to make it smaller so that they can email it. Compression is a kind of digital squeezing.

As with some of the other concepts in digital video, you might not need to think much about compression unless you want to start experimenting with sharing your iMovies in different formats such as email, CD-ROM (if you have a CD burner), and DVD (if you have a DVD burner).

Timecode

Timecode is simply a fancy term for keeping track of where you are in your iMovie. At first glance it doesn't seem like a big deal, but it can come in very handy if you watch your video ahead of time and mark points where you want to edit it.

In iMovie, the timecode is displayed directly to the right of the playhead, and reflects the number of minutes and seconds of video. (A digital video timecode is often displayed with seconds and frames, rather than minutes and seconds, but iMovie makes it easier by displaying minutes and seconds.)

Summary

In this chapter, you were introduced to some basics of digital video editing as well as to the iMovie interface. You took a closer look at the shelf (where video clips are stored), the Monitor (which lets you see the clips), and the Timeline Viewer (which gives you another way to interact with clips). You also learned about the Clip Viewer, the "lite" version of iMovie, an alternative to the Timeline, and a good starting place for people who want to jump right in to digital video editing.

CHAPTER 14

Working with Video in iMovie

The focus of this chapter is working with video, from importing video clips to moving them around within iMovie. You'll learn the way that a camcorder can be connected to your Mac and the process of capturing video through that connection. (Capturing video, simply put, is the process of importing digital video footage from a camcorder into a computer.) You'll also learn some of the basics of video editing and working with film clips.

Importing Video from a File

In a few minutes, we'll get into the process of actually capturing video from your camcorder into your Mac using iMovie. But for now, let's import a file that has already been captured into iMovie. Doing so gives us a file to play with for now.

iMovie is designed primarily to work with video that is captured directly from a camcorder on a Mac, but it is possible to take video from a PC and use it in iMovie. One way to do this is simply to ask whoever is giving the video to you from a PC to save it in DV format (NTSC or PAL or SECAM, depending on what country you live in), to a portable FireWire hard drive, and to import it from there.

To get to the sample file, you must find a movie file on your hard drive. (Some versions of iMovie come with tutorial files containing video, but you may have to search your drive for any file ending in .mov to find something to work with for practice. I'm going to demonstrate with the iTunes 2 splash screen located in the iTunes folder in the Applications Support folder of the Library on my hard drive.)

To search your hard drive, make sure you are in the Finder. (You'll know because the menu next to the Apple menu will say Finder.) Then, open the File menu and choose Find. You'll need to click the Add Criteria pop-up menu and choose Kind in order to search only for movies.

1. Open iMovie and choose File, Import from the menu bar. The Import File sheet will appear from the top of the iMovie window.
2. Click the pop-up menu at the top of the dialog box and navigate to the movie file you located earlier.
3. Select the movie file and click Open (see Figure 14.1). iMovie opens the clip and when it is done, you'll see it in both the Monitor and the shelf, as shown in Figure 14.2.

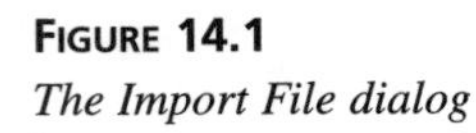

FIGURE 14.1
The Import File dialog box.

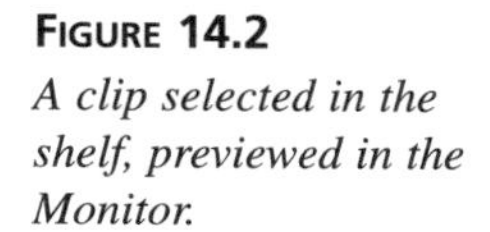

FIGURE 14.2
A clip selected in the shelf, previewed in the Monitor.

Connecting Camcorders

Nowadays, virtually every video camera that you can purchase in a store includes a FireWire connection, which you may remember from Chapter 7, "Choosing Peripheral Devices." FireWire is the magic behind being able to make your own digital movie and DVD projects.

Understanding the FireWire Cable

When you want to connect your digital camcorder to your Mac, you must use a FireWire cable. A camcorder often comes with such a cable, but you can also purchase it separately.

The cable that you need to use has two different kinds of connectors: a smaller end that's known as a 4-pin connector and a larger one on the other side that's known as a 6-pin connector. The smaller, 4-pin connector is the kind most often found on camcorders, and the larger 6-pin connector is most often found on computers.

After you connect the FireWire cable to your computer, you can connect the other, smaller end into the camcorder. The location of the FireWire port on a camcorder varies, but it's usually located behind some kind of protective cover. Figure 14.3 shows the smaller 4-pin end of a FireWire cable and the corresponding port on a digital camcorder.

FIGURE 14.3
Getting ready to plug the smaller end of the FireWire cable into a camcorder.

TASK

Task: Connecting Your Camcorder

In this section we are going to go through the process of how you set up iMovie and connect a camcorder so that you can capture video.

1. Turn on the camera, and insert the smaller (4-pin) end into the FireWire connector on the camcorder. (Insert a tape that you've recorded video on into the camcorder if you haven't already.)
2. Insert the larger (6-pin) end into the FireWire connection on your Mac.
3. Open iMovie and choose File, New Project to create a new project.
4. Click the Camera/Edit Mode switch in iMovie to switch to the camera (DV) mode (see Figure 14.4).

When you plug in most cameras on your Mac, iMovie will automatically switch to Camera Mode, but you can always use the switch mentioned previously if it doesn't happen.

FIGURE 14.4
Switching to Camera (DV) Mode.

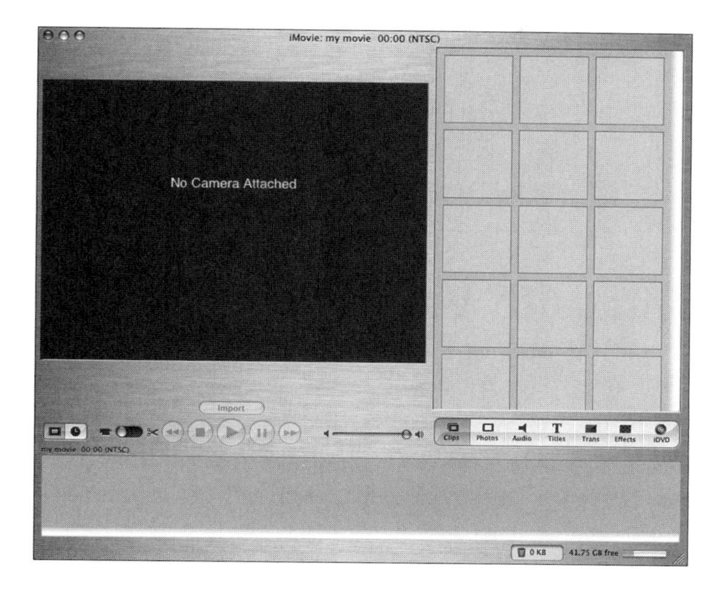

After you've connected your camera, iMovie displays a message confirming that your camera is connected, as shown in Figure 14.5.

FIGURE 14.5
iMovie confirms when a camcorder is turned on and plugged in.

It's easy to record video to a tape and then forget to rewind it—so you might put the tape in your camcorder and press Play to preview it, but not see anything or see a blank blue screen! The material is still there, earlier on your videotape; you just have to rewind to get to it. The only ways you can actually erase video from a digital videotape are to record over it or subject the tape to strong magnetic fields. For the latter, consult "Task: Subjecting Your Tape to Strong Magnetic Fields." Just kidding.

Working with Video

If you're new to working with digital video on your Mac, all you really need to keep in mind is that you're using your camera and your computer like they were a TV and a VCR.

In essence, iMovie becomes your computer VCR, but instead of recording a program from the television, iMovie records video from your camcorder, and that's what capturing video is all about.

Understanding Cueing: Play, Stop, Fast Forward, Rewind

When working with video on your Mac, you use familiar controls to capture and access your video, such as play, stop, fast forward, and rewind.

When you want to capture video, one of the things that you need to do is find a spot in your video where you want to start capturing, and that's where cueing comes into play. Depending on where you left off in the tape, when you use your camcorder to record your video, you might need to play, rewind, and so on to position and review your footage.

This positioning can be done with the camera itself, by looking at its miniature screen. But one of the most enjoyable things about working with digital video through FireWire is that you can control your camera using buttons in the iMovie screen. So, when you connect your camera, you don't necessarily have to use the buttons on the camera itself. When connected through FireWire, iMovie can actually control the camera, so you can use the Play/Fast Forward/Rewind buttons (see Figure 14.6) right in iMovie to go through your tape.

FIGURE 14.6
The play controls in iMovie.

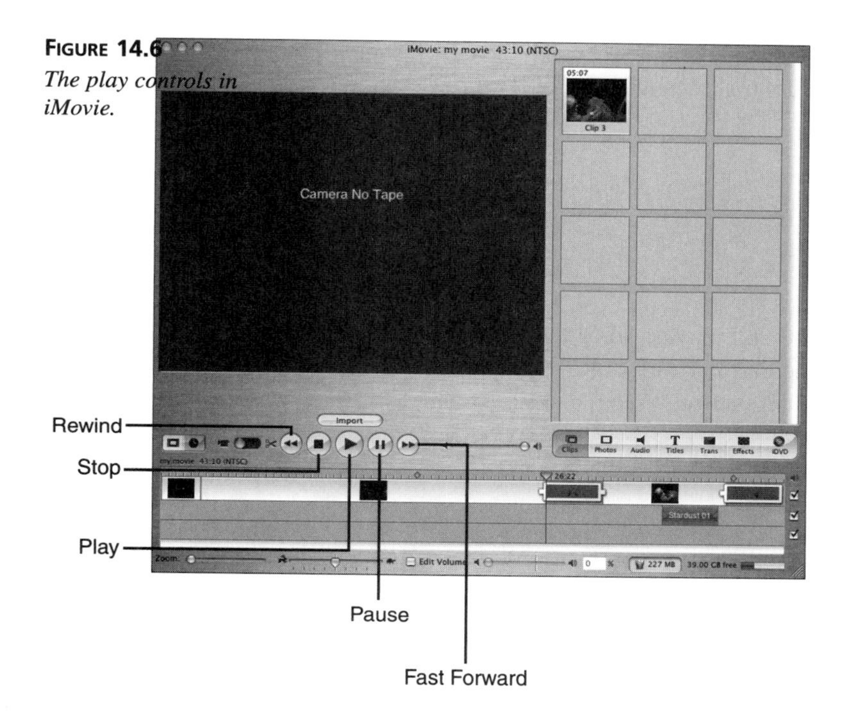

Task: Finding a Spot on Your Videotape Using iMovie

Assuming that you performed the task “Connecting Your Camcorder” earlier, follow these steps:

1. Click the Rewind button to rewind the tape (see Figure 14.7).

FIGURE 14.7
The Rewind button.

2. Click the Play button (see Figure 14.8) to begin playing your video.

FIGURE 14.8
The Play button.

You might need to adjust the sound on your computer.

▼ 3. While the video is playing, try clicking the Fast Forward button (see Figure 14.9) to fast forward through the video while you're watching it. Click again to stop the tape.

FIGURE 14.9
The Fast Forward button.

4. If your video is still playing, click the Stop button (see Figure 14.10), and then click either the Fast Forward or Rewind button. This method of moving through a tape is faster, but you can't see the video moving by.

FIGURE 14.10
The Stop button.

5. Using the play controls, find a spot in your videotape that you want to start capturing at. ▲

There's no official term for fast-forwarding or rewinding from a complete stop. But if you're new to video, you could think of it as *step starting*, where the tape isn't moving and you have to take a step in a particular direction (backward or forward) to get things going. Step starting is the fastest way to get to a certain point on your tape. In contrast, watching footage going by when you're fast-forwarding or rewinding could be thought of as *play previewing*. In other words, you press the Play button, and then press Fast Forward or Rewind. The disadvantage is that things go slower, but you can see exactly what's going on.

It can sometimes be helpful to start just a little before where you want to start capturing video so that you can make a fine adjustment to the starting point of your video clip in iMovie. For example, if you have footage of a short clip and you want to capture the entire thing, you can start a little bit before the action in your short scene begins. Perhaps the footage includes someone jumping off a diving board—you could position the tape a second or two before the jump so that when you capture the video, you can fine-tune exactly when the clip starts so that you don't miss anything.

Capturing Video

When you capture video, one of the nice things that iMovie can do is separate your clips for you. After you shoot video with your camcorder, wherever you pressed Stop and then started shooting a new clip, iMovie is able to separate the clips automatically.

Task: Capturing Video from Your Camcorder

After you've completed the two previous tasks (connecting your camcorder and finding a spot in your tape to start recording), follow these steps:

1. Open iMovie and start a new project.
2. Switch the Camera/Edit Mode switch to the Camera position (DV) (see Figure 14.11).

FIGURE 14.11
Switching to Camera mode to connect with the camera.

3. Click the Import button to start importing footage (refer to Figure 14.5).
4. When you've captured your video, click the Stop button.
5. Now click the Camera/Edit Mode switch (see Figure 14.12) and drag it to the right to switch back to Movie mode so that you can begin to work with your clips.

FIGURE 14.12
The Camera/Edit mode button back in Edit Mode position.

One thing to keep in mind when capturing video is that you must keep an eye on the amount of space available on your hard drive. A common technique is to capture more footage than you think you'll use, and then as you're editing your iMovies, you can delete clips you don't need, which frees up space. Another thing to consider if you're planning to export your iMovies to use in an iDVD project (see Chapter 17, "Exporting iMovies") is that when you export the file, you need just as much space as your project is taking up—in other words, when you export for iDVD, you need more space.

So, when you get hooked on iMovie (not *if*, but *when*—it's inevitable), you'll probably need to start thinking about ways of backing up your projects or expanding the amount of hard drive space you have available. One option is to obtain an external FireWire hard drive. Another option is to store projects on individual DVD discs as data. In other words, instead of burning an iDVD project, you burn all your files to a blank DVD disc so that you can free up hard drive space (see official Web site).

Moving Around in a Clip

One of the most enjoyable parts about playing with footage in iMovie is the way that you can easily move around in a clip in the same way that you might use the remote control on your VCR or DVD player to find a spot in a movie. In iMovie, as you're editing your creation, you'll often want to move through various parts of individual clips or the overall movie as it takes shape. Instead of playing through the entire movie, you can quickly get to the spot that you want, with a control called the *playhead*, which is located at the bottom of the Monitor window (see Figure 14.13).

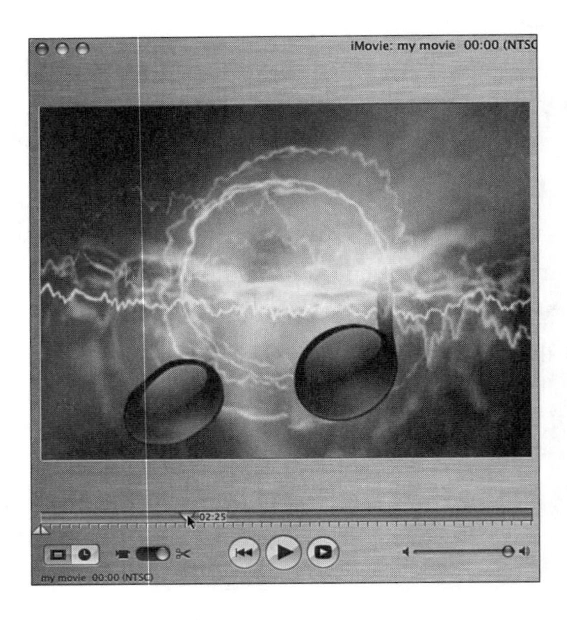

FIGURE 14.13
A close-up view of the playhead along with the timestamp for that spot in your video clip.

Task: Go to a Specific Spot in a Clip

▼ TASK

To prepare for this task, if you don't already have the clip from the previous task open, open it so that you can have something to work with.

To go to a specific spot in a clip:

1. Click on the playhead, and hold down the mouse button.
2. Drag the playhead horizontally to the left or right to find the spot that you want. Notice how the number of minutes and seconds are displayed next to the playhead as you drag it, indicating how far into the clip you are. Try dragging the playhead to a precise time, such as 5:00 (5 seconds).

▲

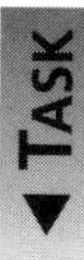

Task: Adjusting a Clip in the Shelf

After you've captured video, the first thing that you must do is to acquaint yourself with the clips you've captured to get an idea of what you have to work with. Playing with clips in the Shelf is a good way to accomplish this.

1. Select a clip in the Shelf by clicking it; the selected clip turns blue.
2. Move the mouse over the text in the clip and click. The area behind the text turns white and you can type a new name in for the clip (see Figure 14.14).

> Another way to see the clip name is to double-click a clip in the Shelf, which brings up the Clip Info dialog box.

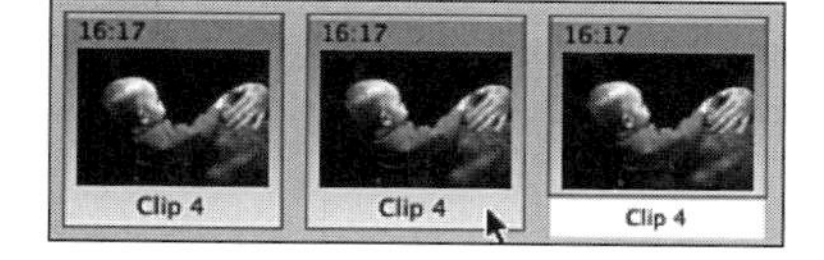

FIGURE 14.14
Renaming a clip: 1) select a clip; 2) click on its name; 3) replace the sample text with new text.

Making Basic Edits

To get a better taste of how the iMovie interface gives you the power of video editing, we'll take a look at how to make a very basic edit using a combination of the Shelf, the Monitor, and the Timeline Viewer.

Preparing a Clip

In this section, we go through the process of making an adjustment to a clip, but first we need to drag the clip into the Timeline Viewer. To prepare the clip, click on it in the Shelf and drag it down and to the uppermost row of Timeline Viewer, which is where you put video clips. When your mouse cursor—which is normally an arrow—changes to an arrow with a "+" next to it, release your mouse button (see Figure 14.15).

After you drag the clip, the Video Monitor looks the same, but the clip now appears on the Timeline Viewer instead of the Shelf, as illustrated in Figure 14.16.

FIGURE 14.15
Before: dragging a clip into the Timeline Viewer.

FIGURE 14.16
After: the clip as it appears in the Timeline Viewer.

Task: Deleting Extra Footage

Now that we have a clip ready to go, we can make an adjustment to it. In our scenario, the adjustment we want to make is to delete some extra footage at the end of the clip.

To delete extra footage:

1. Drag the playhead in the Monitor to somewhere close to the end of the clip—to the point just before the clip switches to another scene.
2. Choose Edit, Split Video Clip at Playhead to mark the spot so that iMovie knows where one clip ends and the next begins. In essence, you've just created two separate clips from one original clip (see Figure 14.17).

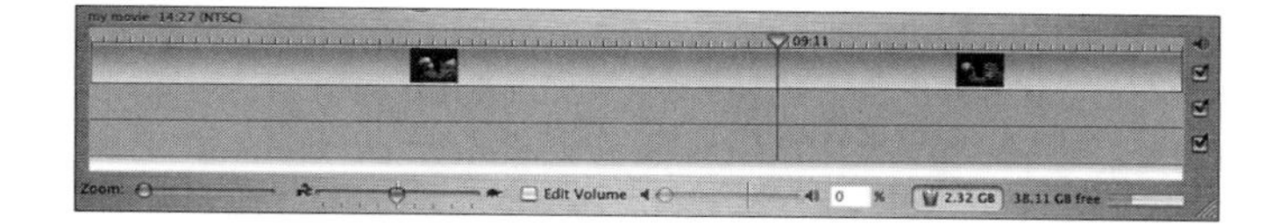

FIGURE 14.17
The newly split clip.

3. In the Timeline Viewer, click the unwanted clip and choose Clear from the Edit menu. The extra footage will be removed.

> You don't have to move clips to the Timeline to split them—you can choose a clip in the Shelf and preview it in the Monitor window, then place the playhead, and split the clip as described in Step 3.

FIGURE 14.18
The remaining clip now expands to fill the entire width of the Timeline.

Task: Deleting a Clip from the Shelf

One of the more common tasks in basic video editing is deleting unwanted video footage. Doing so is very easy in iMovie:

1. Click on a clip in the Shelf to select it.

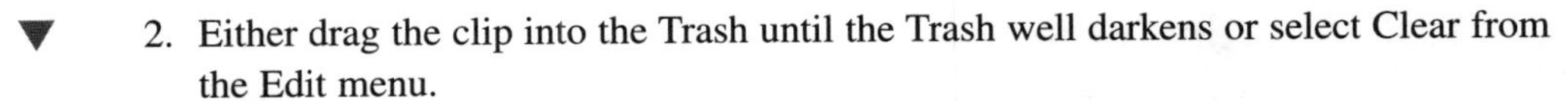

2. Either drag the clip into the Trash until the Trash well darkens or select Clear from the Edit menu.

   You'll probably want to get into the habit of emptying the Trash after you've deleted a clip, or at regular intervals, so that you can keep the maximum amount of hard drive space available to work on your movie.
3. Choose File, Empty Trash to empty the Trash.
4. Click OK in the Confirm dialog box that comes up. Then see how much space you have freed up by checking the free space indicator at bottom-right of the iMovie window.

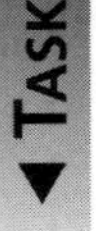

Task: Restoring Clip Media

No video editor is perfect, and sooner or later you'll decide that you want to start over again when adjusting clips. One way to back up is to go through a repeated series of undo steps by pressing Ctrl-Z on your keyboard or choosing Edit, Undo.

Another way is to use the Restore Clip option, which enables you to start over again by bringing clips back to their original state.

If you edit clips, you can only restore clips to the condition they were in up until the last time you emptied the trash, so be careful to clean up only after you're happy with your edits.

For example, you might have recorded a friend talking at great length about an important topic, and toward the end of her monologue, she realizes that another friend has been standing behind her doing a strikingly realistic impression. So, you capture the video clip and make a few adjustments, but accidentally trim the clip too close to the humorous scene at the end. You want to start over again, but aren't sure how. iMovie to the rescue!

1. Click one of the clips in the Timeline that you made by splitting the original clip.
2. Choose Advanced, Restore Clip as shown in Figure 14.19.
3. Click OK in the dialog box that appears to restore the original clip (see Figure 14.20).

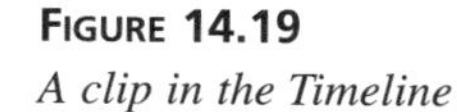

FIGURE 14.19
A clip in the Timeline view.

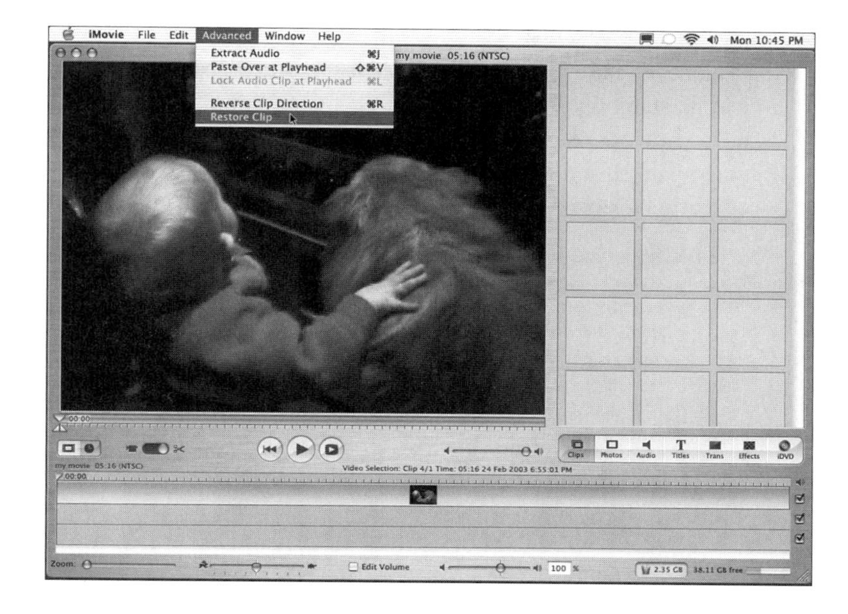

FIGURE 14.20
iMovie asks whether you want to restore the modified clip to its original state.

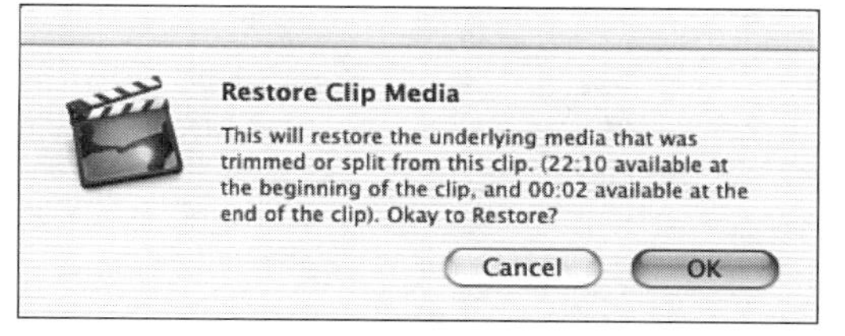

Restoring a clip doesn't merge pieces of the original clip back together. If you split a clip and then restore one of the pieces, the restored clip will contain some of the same footage as the unrestored clip.

TASK

Task: Checking the Size of an iMovie Project

Just about the time you start getting hooked on iMovie, you might realize that your Mac doesn't have an endless amount of storage space on the hard drive, and you need to think a bit more about how much space your projects are taking up.

Chances are that you'll have enough space on your hard drive to work on a few projects at the same time, unless you're working on full-length movies from day one. When

14

you're done and have exported your iMovies to tape or iDVD, you can burn the raw files in your iDVD project folder to CD or DVD or move them to an external hard drive.

Whichever way you go, it can be helpful to learn how to see how much space your project is taking up. It's good to keep an eye on things so that you can decide when you have to delete your collection of accumulated media files (the video clips, animations, video games, and MP3 audio files that you've downloaded from the Internet for purely educational reasons as a part of your ongoing studies in sociology).

1. Locate the folder with your iMovies—when you created a new iMovie project, you named it something.
2. Select the folder and choose Get Info from the File menu. A window will appear, as shown in Figure 14.21.

> In Mac OS X this folder is probably in the Movies folder within your home folder.

FIGURE 14.21
Showing information about your movie.

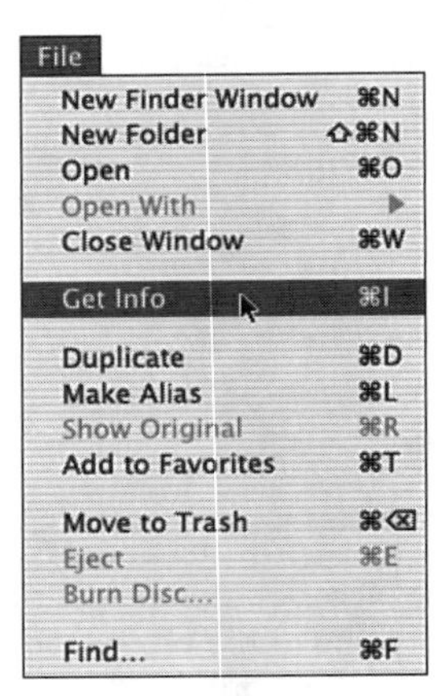

The Get info window will give you a variety of information, including the size of your folder.

Summary

In this chapter, you learned how to get video into your Mac through the process of capturing it using the FireWire interface. You also learned about some introductory, basic video editing tasks, such as adding clips to the Timeline, making adjustments, and deciding to do it all over again to make it perfect.

CHAPTER 15

Adding Transitions, Effects, and Titles in iMovie

In this chapter, we'll look at some enhancements you can make to your movies and clips. First, we'll look at titles, which allow you to add text portions to your movies (or even write a text-only movie). Then, we consider transitions, which enable you to enhance your iMovies with between-clip features, such as fade in, fade out, cross dissolve, and others. Finally, we'll talk about visual effects that can be applied to the clips themselves to change color or add special effects, such as lighting, sparkles, or fog.

Titles

When you're ready to try adding a title to your iMovie, you'll be working in a new area of iMovie: the Titles palette. Until now, you probably spent most of your time simply capturing video and working with clips in the Shelf, the Monitor, and the Timeline. But now you'll start switching back and forth between various windows in the Shelf. If you haven't already tried it, the way you get to the Titles palette if you're looking at clips in the Shelf is simply to click the Titles button.

When the Titles palette comes up, you'll see a number of options, including ways to adjust the size and color of the letters in your title, as well as a list from which you can select different titles (see Figure 15.1).

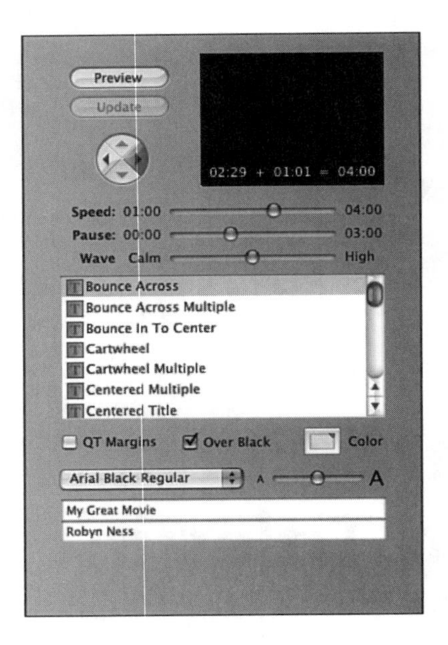

FIGURE 15.1
The Titles palette.

But if you're new to digital video, don't worry about all the options. You can add a title to your iMovie simply by choosing one (such as Bounce In To Center) from the list, clicking on it, and dragging it into the Timeline.

Sooner or later, you'll want to take advantage of all the things you can do to spruce up and modify titles to give your productions a customized touch. To get our feet wet, let's take a look at a couple of the basic titles that are included with iMovie. Later on, we'll dive into adjusting and customizing titles.

Sample Title—Bounce In To Center

Near the top of iMovie's title list is Bounce In To Center, and it's a great starting place to play around with titles. Looking at Figure 15.2, you can get a sense of how the text moves in from the top and bottom of the screen.

FIGURE 15.2
A sample title.

Sample Title—Centered Multiple

At first glance, Centered Multiple might sound like an abstract algebraic principle, but after you start playing with it, its value becomes apparent.

Centered Multiple is an example of a title to which you can add multiple lines of text. In essence, iMovie makes it easy to create multiple "screens" by enabling you to add additional lines of text to some titles.

On the left in Figure 15.3, we see the first screen (imagine the text fading in, pausing, and then fading out), and on the right we see the next screen, where the same thing happens again.

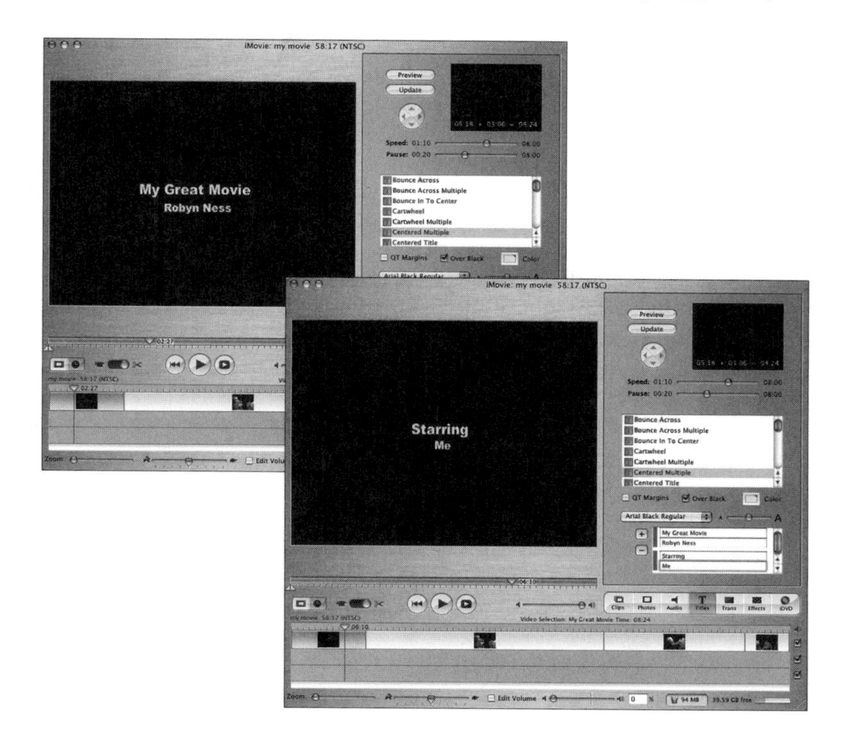

FIGURE 15.3
A fade from left to right.

If you're having difficulty picturing what's going on, don't be concerned. When you start playing in the program, it'll become clear, and you'll see the nice effect that this kind of title has.

iMovie makes it easy to enter text in titles like this one. As with the previous title we examined, the text you enter in the bottom of the Titles palette is what appears in the title (see Figure 15.4).

FIGURE 15.4
The text input area in the Titles palette.

With a multiple line title, you can click-and-drag the blue scrollbar down (the blue scrollbar to the right of the text) to reveal more lines of text.

If you haven't tried them (although we aren't officially in the middle of a task), the + and - buttons to the right of the title text enable you to add and remove lines of text, which generates more screens. This particular title is a nice way to have introductory screens fade in and out before a movie starts.

Now that you've gotten a taste of our two basic titles, take a moment to consider all the titles you have available (see Table 15.1).

15

TABLE 15.1 Titles in iMovie

Title Type	*Description*
Bounce Across	Two lines of text appear from either the left or right and move like a wiggling worm towards the center of the screen.
Bounce Across Multiple	Like Bounce Across, but with multiple screens of text.
Bounce In To Center	Two lines of text appear and move towards the center of the screen.
Cartwheel	Two lines of text, each letter rotating, move diagonally toward the center of the screen.
Cartwheel Multiple	Like Cartwheel, but with multiple screens of text.
Centered Multiple	Multiple titles fade in and out in sequence, one after another. It's a nice movie-style effect.
Centered Title	A single title fades in and out.
Converge	Two lines of text with broadly spaced letters gradually move to the left to form words.
Converge Multiple	Like Converge, but with multiple screens of text.
Converge to Center	Two lines of text with broadly spaced letters gradually move to the center to form words.
Converge to Center Multiple	Like Converge to Center, but with multiple screens of text.
Cross Through Center	Two lines of text start out with letters and lines reversed and rotate until correctly positioned.
Cross Through Center Multiple	Like Cross Through Center, but with multiple screens of text.
Drifting	Multiple lines fade in from different directions.
Flying Letters	Letters of title fade into the screen to form words of title.
Flying Words	Entire lines of title fly in at one time. Nice effect.
Gravity	Two lines of text fall into place from one edge of the screen.
Gravity Multiple	Like Gravity, but with multiple screens of text.
Music Video	Enables you to put a music video–style paragraph of text that can appear in the corner of the screen. Useful.
Rolling Centered Credits	Enter multiple lines of text to get the effect you see at the end of movies. Very nice.
Rolling Credits	Similar to centered credits; different formatting.

continues

TABLE 15.1 continued

Title Type	*Description*
Scroll with Pause	Titles roll on to screen, pause, roll off; helps with being able to read individual credits.
Scrolling Block	Will scroll an entire paragraph of text by; something like the original *Star Wars* credits.
Spread from Center	Two lines of text appear from a pile of letters at the center of the screen.
Spread from Center Multiple	Like Spread from Center, but with multiple screens of text.
Stripe Subtitle	A nice title to put in the corner of a screen to introduce a new section of a video.
Subtitle	Gives you the ability to add text to the screen to simulate the subtitle effect of a DVD.
Subtitle Multiple	Multiple subtitles.
Twirl	Two lines of text appear at the center of the screen with each letter rotating.
Typewriter	Creates the effect of words being typed on the screen.
Unscramble	A jumble of letters separates into two lines of text.
Unscramble Multiple	Like Unscramble, but with multiple screens of text.
Zoom	Creates a zoom effect, moving close in on video.
Zoom Multiple	Multiple zooms.

Using Titles over Black

One simple way to have titles appear is against a black background so that your attention is focused on the title itself. To accomplish this, you simply click on the Over Black option in the Titles palette (refer to Figure 15.4).

Overlay (over Video) Titles

Another method you might want to try is to uncheck the Over Black option so that your title appears over a video clip, as shown in Figure 15.5. The only requirement is that you have a video clip in the project!

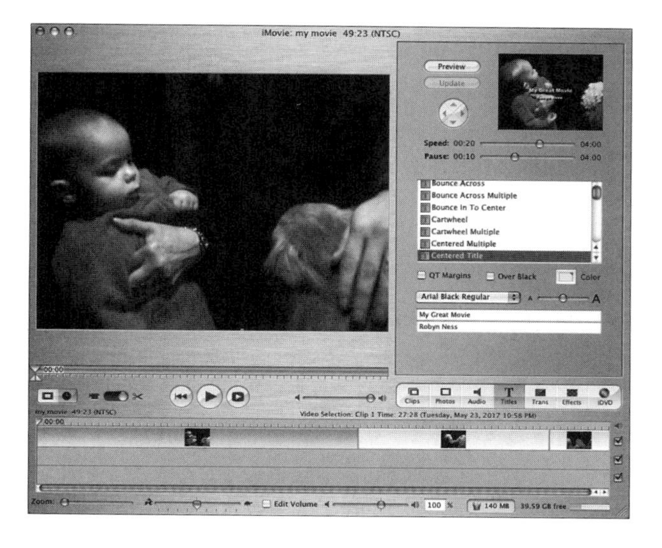

FIGURE 15.5
Clicking on a title with Over Black unchecked to see a mini-preview with the title displayed over a video clip.

Task: Selecting a Title

To begin working with titles, you'll want to know how to find a particular title that was listed in Table 15.1.

1. Click on the Titles button in the main iMovie window to display the Titles palette.
2. Click the blue scrollbar for the list of titles, and drag it down so that the title you're looking for is revealed.
3. When you find the title you want to try, click to select it, as I've done with the Typewriter title near the end of the list (see Figure 15.6).

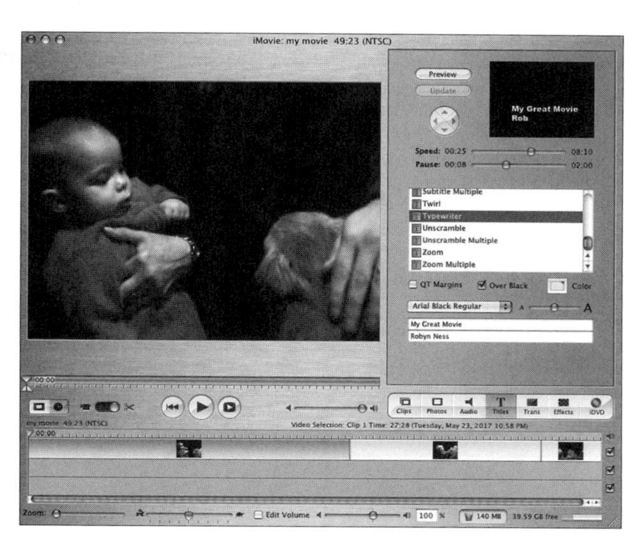

FIGURE 15.6
The selected title will be previewed in the mini-preview window in the Title palette.

Adding Titles

The ultimate goal of making titles is to introduce or otherwise enhance your movie. You could have a title at the beginning, a rolling credit at the end, and any number of titles in between to introduce different scenes (reminiscent of silent movies?) or sections (such as a training video).

If you think back, earlier in this chapter we talked about the two different ways that titles can work: either displayed against a black screen (Over Black), or as an overlay displaying directly over video. Either approach can be fun and work in different situations, but you might want to start out with a standard Over Black title (by clicking the Over Black check box).

Task: Adding a Title to a Movie

Adding a title to a movie is as easy as adding a clip to a movie; it's a very similar, almost identical process. In fact…it is identical. As Austin Powers might say, drag and drop, baby!

1. Open an iMovie project and drag a clip into the Timeline. If the Clip Viewer tab is visible, just click the Clock icon in the lower-left corner of the screen to display the Timeline tab.
2. Click on a title of choice in the Titles palette, and drag it down into the Timeline until your video clip moves aside to make room for the title (see Figure 15.7). Drop the title into the open space.

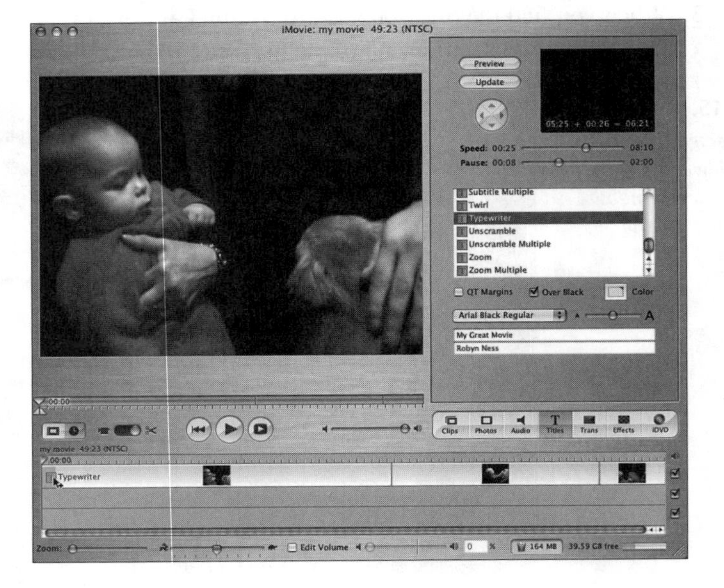

FIGURE 15.7
Dragging a title from the Titles palette down to the Timeline in front of the video clip.

15

3. Notice in Figure 15.8 how the small red bar travels from left to right underneath your title to indicate that the title is being processed.

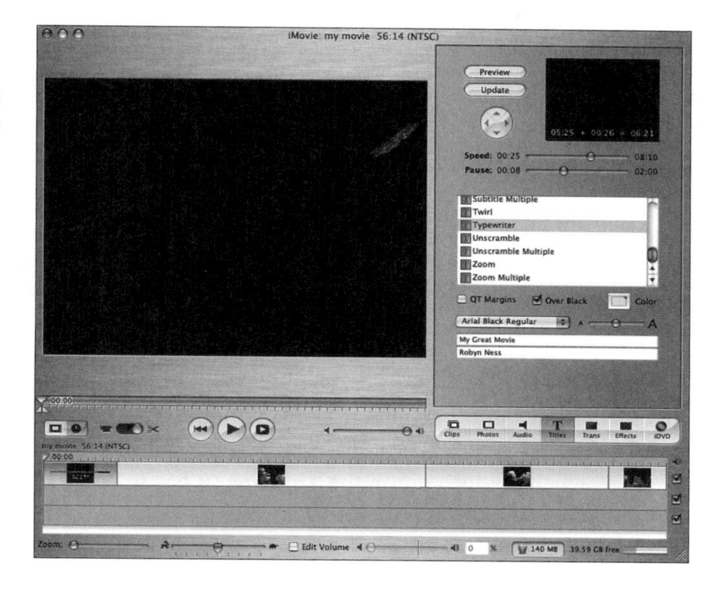

FIGURE 15.8
A little red bar going to the right underneath the title in the Timeline indicates that your Mac is processing your title.

4. Now that your title is in the Timeline, try clicking on the playhead and dragging it through your title to get a quick glance at how the title animates (see Figure 15.9).

FIGURE 15.9
Dragging the playhead to check out the title, just as you would check out a video clip. In essence, iMovie uses the settings in the Titles palette to generate video clips for you.

To experiment with a title that you have created, try changing a setting in the Titles palette, and then clicking the Update button in the Titles palette.

When you've dragged a title into the Timeline, you can click in the Timeline to select it (it'll change to blue) and make adjustments to it. Then you need to click Update for iMovie to process it and give you a preview.

You can actually layer different titles in iMovie. For instance, you can add one long-duration title that is set over black, and have other titles that aren't set over black cross over top of it.

iMovie can quickly build a miniature preview in the Titles palette when you make changes. But digital video takes a lot of processing power. So, in order for it to catch up with changes when you place it in the Timeline, it has to be processed before you can get the final preview of how it'll look on a television.

Adjusting Titles

As soon as you start trying out the different titles, you'll want to know how you can adjust them, and Apple has done an excellent job yet again of making things easy and intuitive, yet flexible. Essentially, you can do no tweaking at all or as much as you want.

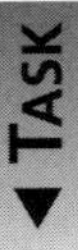

Task: Adjusting a Title

In this task, we look at how to make adjustments to a title. iMovie makes it easy to try things out with titles and then go back and expand or change them, all without having to type in the text over again.

1. Follow the steps in the previous task to select a title. In this example, we're using Drifting.
2. Try clicking the Text Size slider, marked with a small and a large capital A, and dragging it to the left or right to change the size of your title text.
3. To choose a different color for the text, click once on the Color button. A pop-up menu of colors will appear (see Figure 15.10).
4. Click on a color that you want to use for your text, and then click somewhere outside the pop-up menu to deselect it.

15

FIGURE 15.10
Use the color picker to choose a color for your text.

5. Try clicking and dragging the blue Speed slider to the left or to the right to see how it affects the behavior of the title text.
6. To see the miniature preview of a title again, just click on the title, and it will appear again in the preview area.

Task: Typing In a New Title

TASK

It's very simple to change the text for a title; just click and type away.

1. Locate the text input field for the title you're using.
2. Move the mouse arrow and click once on the line you want to change.

   After you single-click it (as opposed to a double-click), a blue outline will appear around the line of text to indicate that it's selected. You'll also see a flashing text insertion cursor, just as you'd have in a word processing program.
3. With the text selected, you can just type in new text to replace the old.
4. Repeat steps 2 and 3 to change an additional line of text.
5. Click the Apply button when you are finished.

Transitions

Transitions could be thought of as the bread and butter of video editing. Or, perhaps, as the peanut butter that makes scenes stick together.

When you deal with clips, if you choose wisely, one clip can in many cases cut to another without anything between the clips. To get a better understanding of the concept of a *cut*, just try watching any few minutes of television or a movie and looking for the spots where the camera switches from one view to another—this usually happens most rapidly in music videos. Some people prefer cutting from one scene to another without any blending.

But there are times when you want to find a way for one clip to lead smoothly to another, and a transition is a perfect way to accomplish this. The following is a list of iMovie's transitions:

- **Circle Closing**—The first clip appears in a gradually shrinking circle, behind which the next clip is revealed.
- **Circle Opening**—The first clip disappears behind a gradually increasing circle containing the next clip.
- **Cross Dissolve**—Blends one video clip into another.
- **Fade In**—Brings the desired video clip slowly into view from nothing.
- **Fade Out**—Fades the video clip slowly out of view to nothing.
- **Overlap**—One clip slides over the other until it completely replaces it onscreen.
- **Push**—One clip "pushes" another off of the screen in the direction chosen, (left/right/up/down).
- **Radial**—One clip "sweeps" another away in a motion like the second-hand on a clock.
- **Scale Down**—Reduces the size of the first clip, while revealing the next clip.
- **Warp Out**—The first clip is split at the center by the next clip in a gradually increasing circle.
- **Wash In**—Brings the desired video clip slowly into view from bright white.
- **Wash Out**—Lightens the video clip slowly out of view to bright white.

Figure 15.11 shows the Transitions palette in iMovie, which can be easily accessed simply by clicking the Trans button. The Transition palette enables you to choose a transition to use in your iMovie, as well as make some simple adjustments to the way the transition appears.

FIGURE 15.11
The Transitions palette.

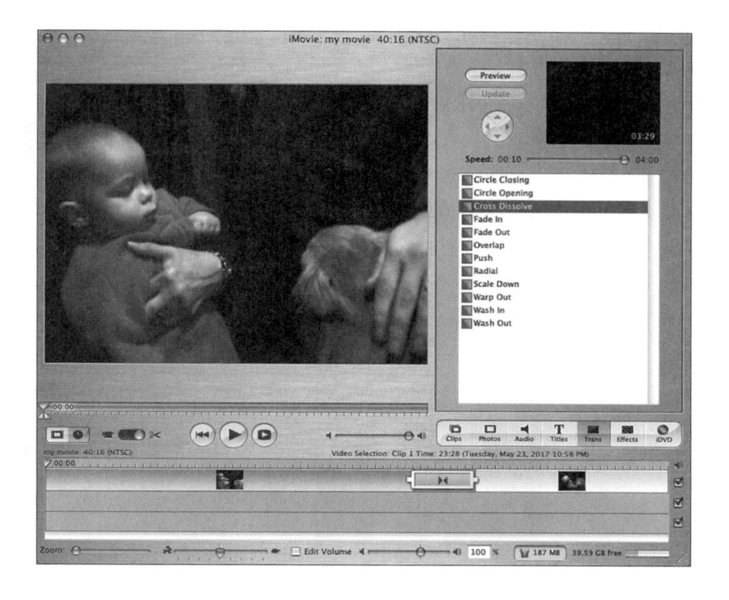

Sample Transition—Cross Dissolve

To get a better understanding of transitions, let's take a look at the Cross Dissolve transition. Simply put, a cross dissolve is a standard tool that's used all the time in television and films to blend one scene into another. You probably see hundreds of cross dissolves every week without even realizing it.

We'll start with a movie containing two clips. If we watched the movie as is, when one video clip ends, it would simply cut from one video clip to another. But a cross dissolve could help the scenes blend.

iMovie gives you the ability to drag-and-drop a transition in between the two clips, and Figure 15.12 shows the transition. The transition appears between the clips.

Essentially what happens over the course of a cross dissolve transition is that you see less of the first clip and more of the second. Figure 15.13 represents the blending of two video clips.

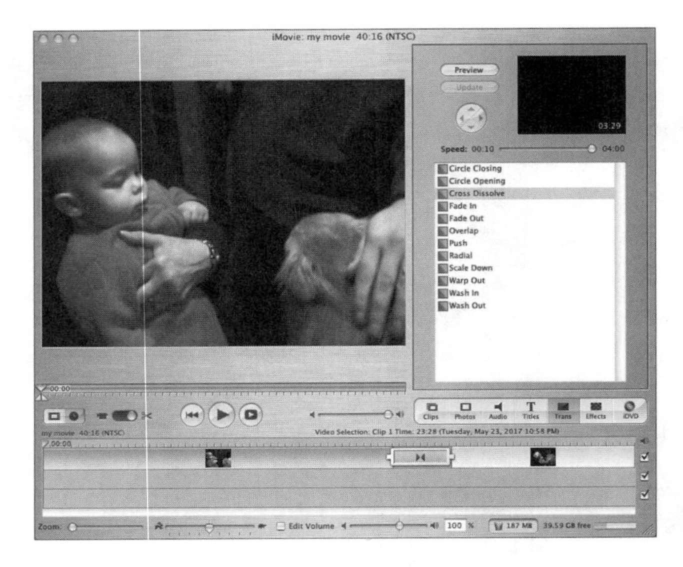

Figure 15.12
Two clips "sandwich" the Cross Dissolve transition.

Figure 15.13
Cross Dissolve—At the beginning, you see the first clip. Toward the middle, you still see the original clip, but you also see a fair amount of the second clip, "merged in" with the original clip. At this stage, both clips are semi-transparent. At the end, you see the second clip.

Working with Transitions

Transitions are very easy to work with. Just as with other enhancements that you can add to an iMovie, a transition takes a few moments to process, and if you add a lot of transitions to your iMovie, you might have to wait a few minutes. But when the processing is done, you have a nice way to spice up your iMovie. It's worth experimenting to find and develop your own style.

In general, there are three ways of working with transitions: adding, adjusting, and removing.

▼ TASK

Task: Adding a Fade In

Adding a transition is as simple as clicking to select it, dragging it into the Timeline, waiting for a moment while it processes, and then watching it to see how you like it.

Keep in mind that to try a transition, you must have at least one video clip in the Timeline. Some transitions are better suited to be before or after a clip (rather than in between), such as the fade in transition, which is a good way to start off your iMovie.

1. Open an iMovie project and drag a video clip from the Shelf into the Timeline.
2. Click the Trans button in the main iMovie window to access the Transitions palette.
3. Click the Fade In transition. After a transition is selected, a mini-preview of it will play in the window at the upper right.
4. If you are satisfied with the selected transition, drag it to a point in the Timeline window to the left of the current clip's centered icon. When you are in the right region, the current clip will move aside to make room for the transition, indicating that you can let go of the mouse button to drop the transition in place.

Which side of a clip you drag a clip to depends on the transition being added. Fade In must come before a clip, so you drag it to the left side of the affected clip. Fade Out must follow the clip, so you would drag it to the right side. If you try to place a transition on the wrong side of a clip, an error message will tell you whether the transition you have chosen must be placed before or after a clip.

Transitions that require two clips to work—such as Cross Dissolve, Overlap, and Push—will give you an error if they aren't sandwiched between two clips. (Somewhat confusingly, this error message is the same one that appears when you place a transition on the wrong side of a single clip—the one that tells you to place the transition on the opposite side of where you've placed it. If you follow that advice with only one clip in the Timeline, another error will tell you to place the transition on the opposite side.)

5. The red processing indicator will show you how long it will be before your transition is processed and you can see the preview of your movie. You can click on the Zoom slider at the bottom of your iMovie window to switch to a larger view of the transition so that you can see the thin red indicator line travel to the right underneath the transition until it's done (see Figure 15.14).

▼

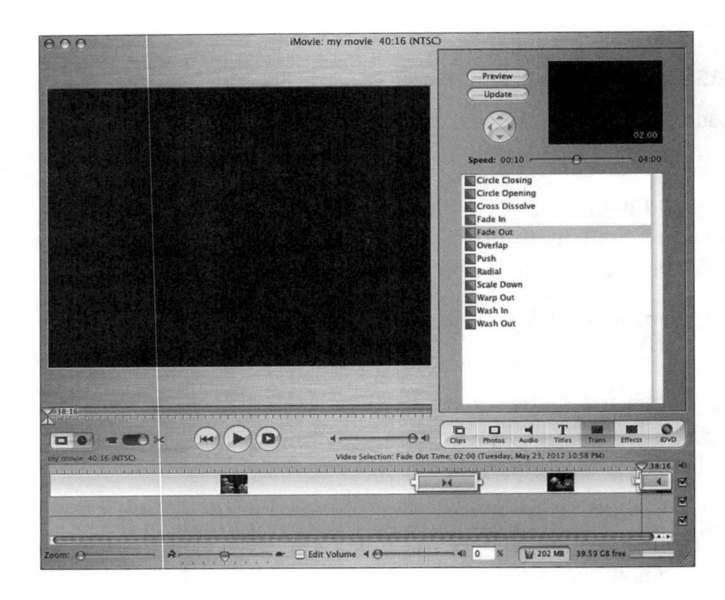

FIGURE 15.14
After a transition is dragged into place, your Mac must think about it for a few moments to make sense of it and deliver the video you're asking for.

6. When the processing is done, try dragging the playhead through the transition to see how your iMovie now starts black and the video clip slowly fades in (see Figure 15.15).

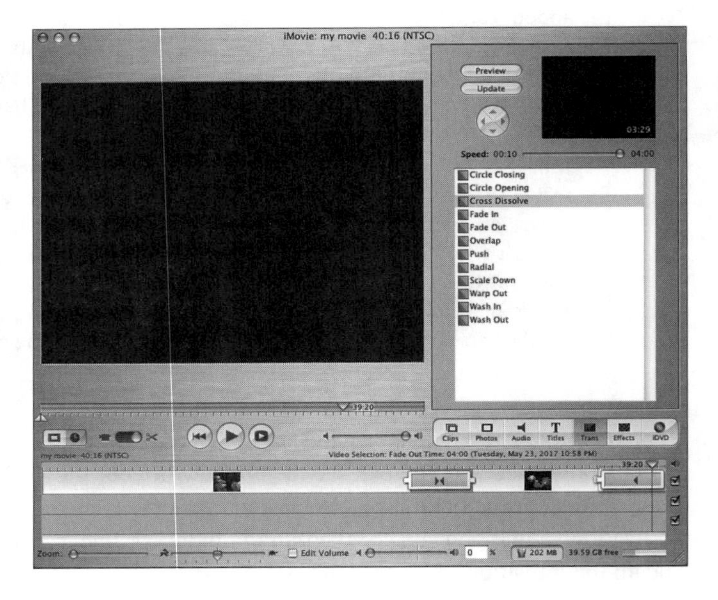

FIGURE 15.15
After the processing is done, you can drag the playhead back and forth to get a quick preview of the transition.

A fade out is like a fade in, but is used mostly at the end of an iMovie or at the end of a clip. You would add it in a similar way, except you would place it at the end of the clip you want to fade away to black.

Task: Changing and Replacing a Transition

At some point, you might want to change a transition that's already been added, and doing so is easy to accomplish:

1. Open your iMovie project in which you have a clip (and a transition) that you want to replace. In Figure 15.16, we see our trusty sample project. In this scenario, we've decided that we want the fade out to be longer; that is, we want the fade to start earlier in the clip.
2. Click on the transition to select it; a translucent box will appear around it.

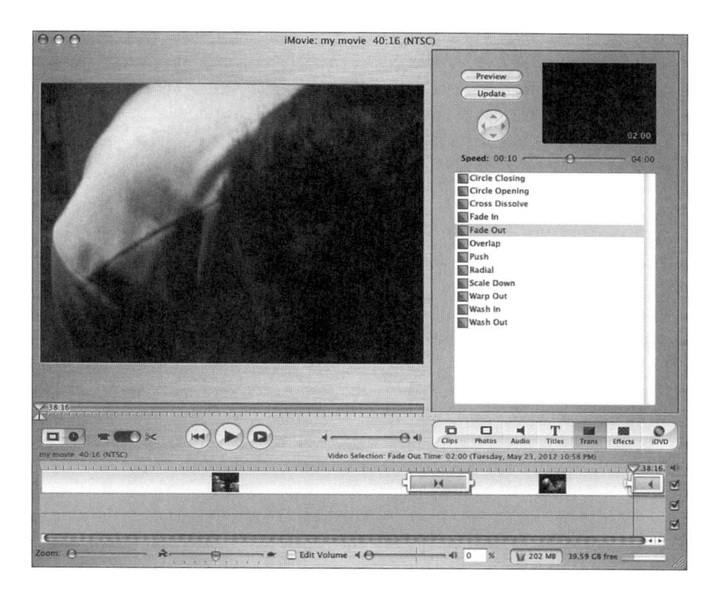

FIGURE 15.16
Selecting the transition.

3. Click on the blue Speed slider in the Transition window to adjust the Speed setting, and change it to four seconds (4:00).

The higher the Speed setting, the more seconds of space the transition will take up. So, if you want a longer transition, you want a higher Speed setting—toward 04:00. For a shorter transition, you want a lower setting—toward 00:10.

4. Click the Update button in the Transition window. When the processing is done, drag the playhead back and forth on the Timeline to see the effect of the adjusted transition, or position the playhead to the left of the transition and click the Play button below the Monitor window.

FIGURE 15.17
Viewing the results of the adjusted transition, which has to process first.

Compare the relative lengths of the transition and video clip in Figures 15.16 and 15.17. Notice how the transition in Figure 15.17, which has been adjusted to 4:00, is longer and therefore takes up more space in the Timeline than the original transition shown in Figure 15.16. The transition starts earlier in the video clip.

Replacing a transition works the same way, except you can choose a different transition than the one that was originally in place. The old one will be removed to make room for your new choice.

Task: Removing a Transition

Removing a transition is simple:

1. Open your iMovie project in which you have a clip (and a transition) that you want to remove.
2. Click on the transition to select it; a translucent box will appear around it.
3. From the Edit menu, select Clear, and the transition will be removed.

Effects

Effects represent another way that you can enhance your iMovies by adding something to them. You take plain video and make it stand out or spice it up to create your own movie-making style.

For example, if you want to give a historic feel to a portion of your iMovie, you could use an effect to make the movie either black-and-white or a sepia tone to give it the feel of an early moving picture.

Sometimes the video you use might give you ideas. For example, there might be a scene in a movie that's supposed to represent a person's dreams, and you could use the Fog effect to give that scene a surreal feeling. Maybe you could even combine it with another effect to change the colors around, and when the person in your iMovie wakes up, everything returns to normal and you don't see the effects anymore.

In essence, to add an effect, you simply choose a clip in the Timeline and then choose and apply an effect—you can make your adjustments anytime you want. If you want to add an effect to only a portion of your iMovie, you use the Split Video Clip at Playhead command (for a refresher, see the section Deleting Extra Footage in Chapter 14, "Working with Video in iMovie") to separate a portion of your video, and then apply the effect to it.

Effects are similar to transitions and titles in that the magic happens in the relevant palette in iMovie (see Figure 15.18); the Effects palette gives you a convenient place to try out different things.

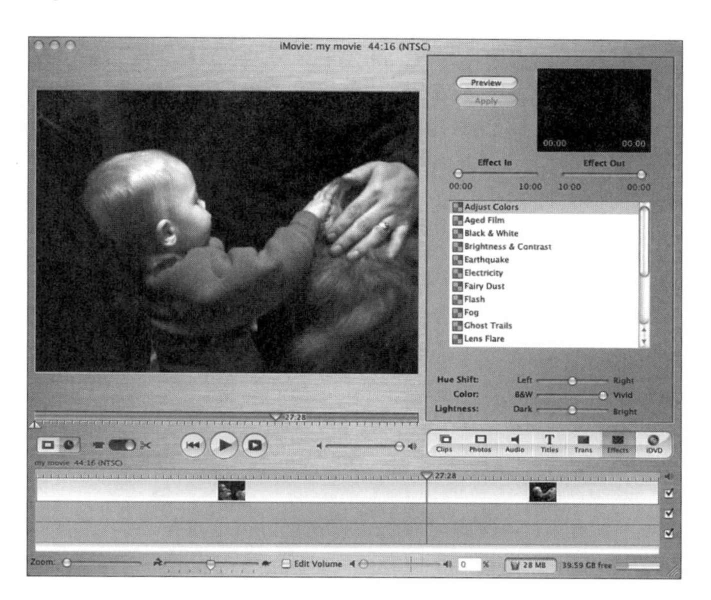

FIGURE 15.18
The Effects palette in iMovie.

If you like to keep things as simple as possible, you can simply choose an effect; but iMovie also enables you to completely customize each effect if you choose to. You might find that you start by simply adding effects with their default settings, and then end up coming back to the Effects palette to try different options when you get ideas for how some adjustment could work better for a particular clip. Table 15.2 lists the effects available in iMovie.

TABLE 15.2 List of Effects in iMovie

Effect Name	*Description*
Adjust Colors	Enables you to adjust various aspects of color, as if you were shining different colored light on your video
Aged Film	Adds dust and scratches to a clip, as if it were from an old news reel
Black and White	Enables you to take a step backward in time before color television or movies
Brightness & Contrast	Very helpful for adjusting video when you want to make it look better, such as video that was shot in low light situations
Earthquake	Makes the image shake and blur is if the video were shot during an earthquake
Electricity	Adds a blue zap of electricity, which you can rotate for better placement
Fairy Dust	Adds a trail of sparkles to the clip
Flash	Adds an instant of bright white to the clip
Fog	Adds an overlay of moving fog to the clip
Ghost Trails	Faint impressions of the clip echo the motion in the real clip
Lens Flare	Gives the feel of an old photograph
Letterbox	Display the clip in letter-box format, with black space in the open area at the top and bottom of the screen
Mirror	Mirrors half of the clip on the other side of the screen
N-Square	Splits the screen in N equal squares containing the selected clip
Rain	Adds an overlay of moving rain to the clip
Sepia Tone	Gives the feel of an old photograph
Sharpen	Can enhance video that's slightly out of focus
Soft Focus	Adds a soft feel to video

Sample Effect—Brightness/Contrast

When you use an effect in iMovie, you choose a clip, such as the one in Figure 15.19, and decide you want to do something to it. In this case, we have a video clip in which we can see that the picture came out a bit dark.

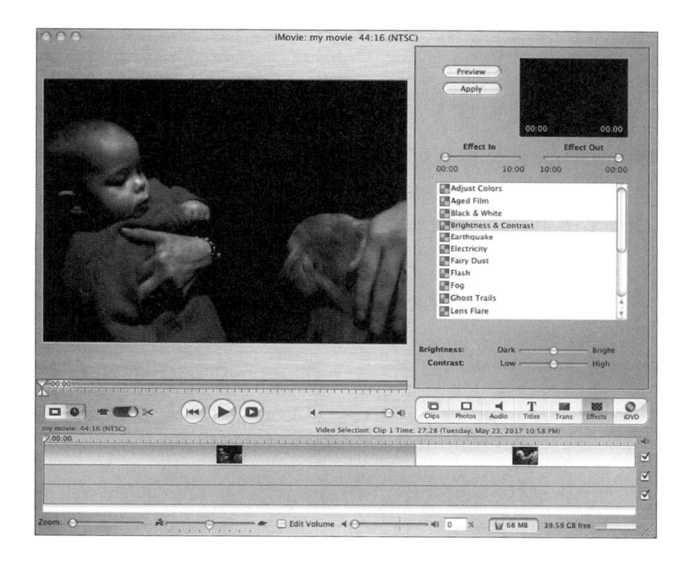

FIGURE 15.19
A dark clip before the Brightness/Contrast effect is applied.

But with a bit of tweaking, using the Brightness/Contrast controls, we can improve the clip so that you can see the subject a bit better (see Figure 15.20).

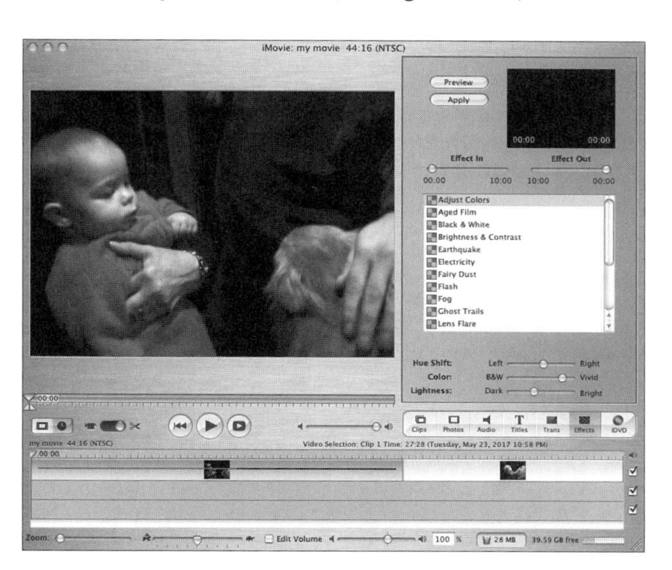

FIGURE 15.20
The clip after the Brightness/Contrast effect is applied.

Because they can be so simple to add, it can be very easy to overdo effects, making things so "affected" that they look worse than when you began. So, if you want to preserve the quality of the video, you have to keep things somewhat balanced by not going overboard and using the most extreme settings in each effect.

Working with Effects

When you try effects out, you can experiment without waiting for iMovie to process, or render, an effect, which can take several minutes. Then when you've made a decision, you can apply the effect and allow iMovie to render it, and you can continue to add other effects to that clip if you want.

In general, the options when working with effects are Preview, Apply, and Restore Clip.

Previewing

The Preview button enables you to see an effect on the main Monitor area in iMovie. It becomes active when you select an effect in the Effects palette.

When you first click on an effect in the Effects palette in iMovie, there will appear a small preview window that contains a miniature version of your iMovie, and it's helpful to get a general sense of what the effect does. But ultimately it's nicer to see how the effect looks at normal size, in the main iMovie Monitor area, as shown in Figure 15.20.

In some versions of iMovie, the Preview function does not work. To see an approximation of the chosen effect with the changes you've made to settings, watch the mini-preview space at the upper right closely as you click on the control settings.

Applying

Applying an effect is simply the process of going beyond the preview stage and actually having iMovie change your video clip by employing the effect on the clip you have currently selected. At this point, iMovie will process (or *render*) the effect, which may take several minutes. The status of the processing will appear as a red bar at the top of the affected clip in the Timeline (see Figure 15.21).

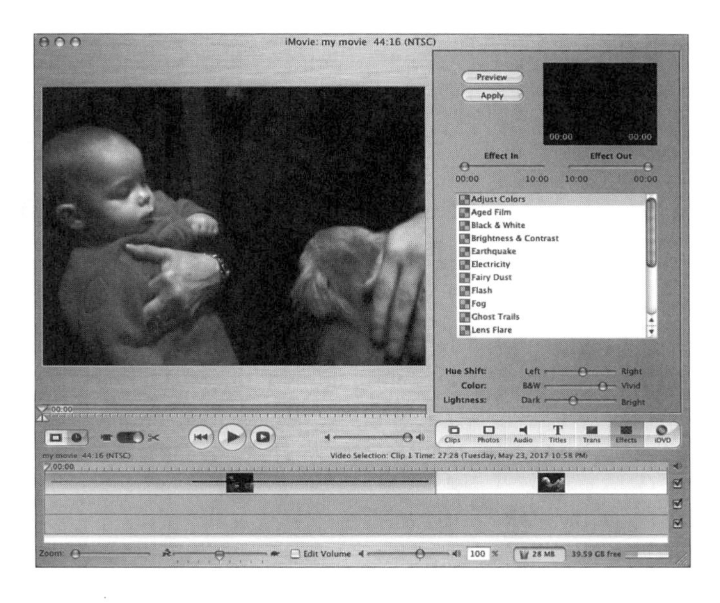

FIGURE 15.21
If you're happy with the preview, you can click Apply.

Restoring Clips

After you apply an effect, if you want to go back to how the clip originally was, you can use the Restore Clip function available under the Advanced menu (see Figure 15.22).

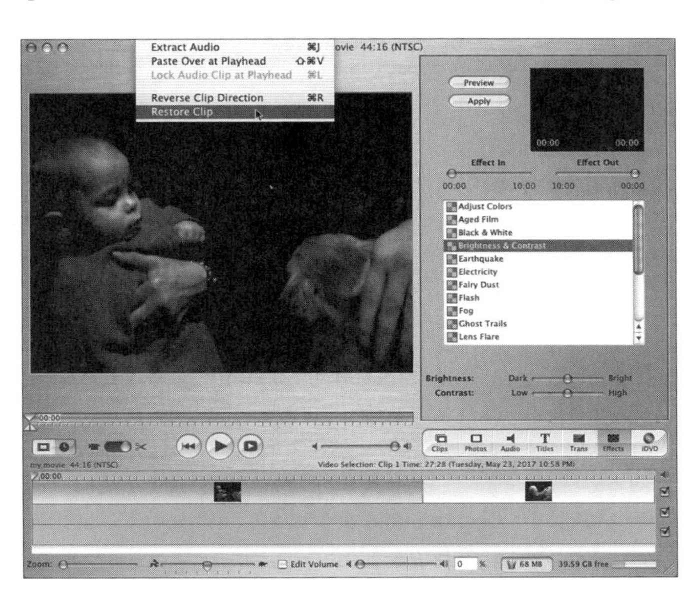

FIGURE 15.22
An effect has been applied and now the same clip can be restored to its original state.

Undo/Redo

The Undo/Redo option in iMovie is a handy thing to keep in mind when working with effects. The top portion of the Edit menu changes to display the standard editing functions that are currently available.

Task: Enhancing a Clip with Brightness/Contrast

In this example, we take a video clip that came out dark and use the Brightness/Contrast effect to tweak the video so that we can see the people in the video better.

1. Open an iMovie project, and if you haven't already, drag a clip into the Timeline.
2. Click once on the clip you want to use in the Timeline in order to select it.
3. Click the Effects button in the main iMovie window to display the Effects palette. Then click the Brightness/Contrast effect as shown in Figure 15.23.

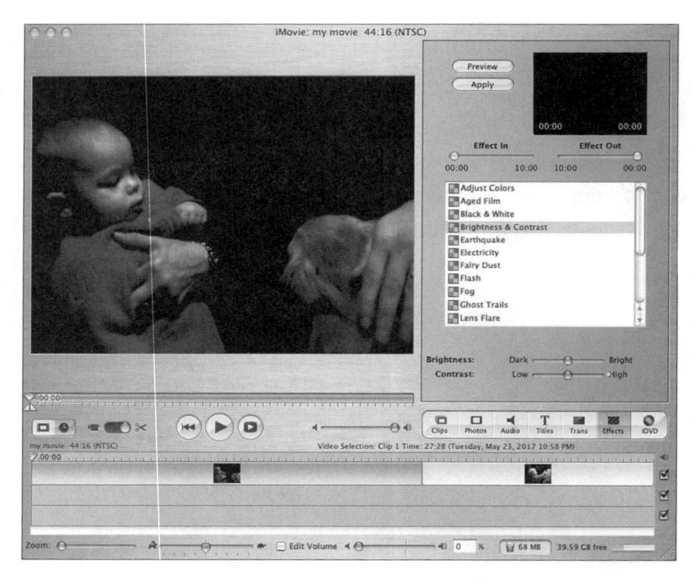

FIGURE 15.23
The Brightness/Contrast effect with the Brightness setting adjusted to be midway between Dark and Bright, and the Contrast setting adjusted to midway between Low and High.

4. Start adjusting the clip through increasing the contrast by clicking the blue slider button, holding the mouse button down, and dragging a small bit to the right to bring out the brighter colors and distinguish the darker colors from them (see Figure 15.24).
5. Now click the Brightness slider button and slowly drag it to the right, keeping an eye on the video clip (see Figure 15.25). At any time, you can click the Preview button in the Effects palette to see how things look in iMovie's Monitor area, or watch the mini-preview window as you adjust the settings.

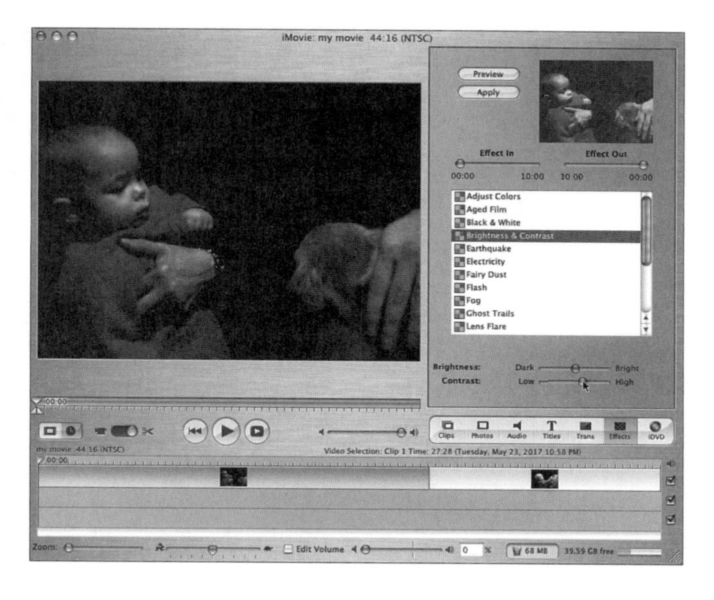

FIGURE 15.24
Moving the Contrast slider toward the higher setting helps to give you a brighter clip.

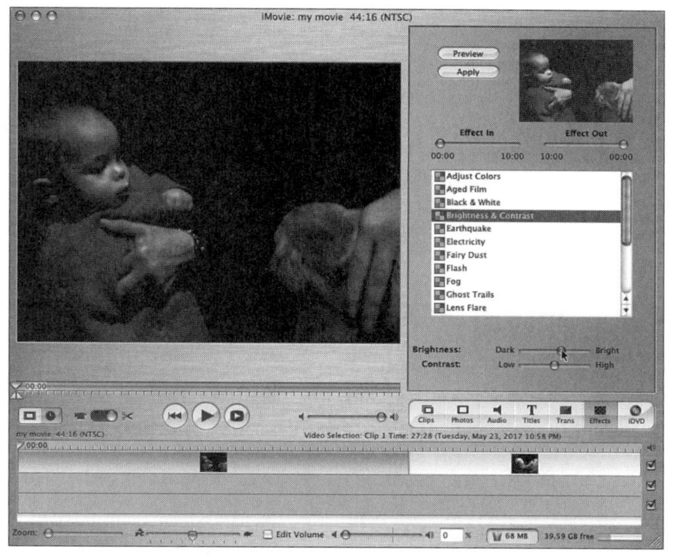

FIGURE 15.25
Moving the Brightness slider from Dark to Bright also enhances the brightness of the clip.

6. When you like how the previews look, click Apply and iMovie will begin to process the video (see Figure 15.26).

▲

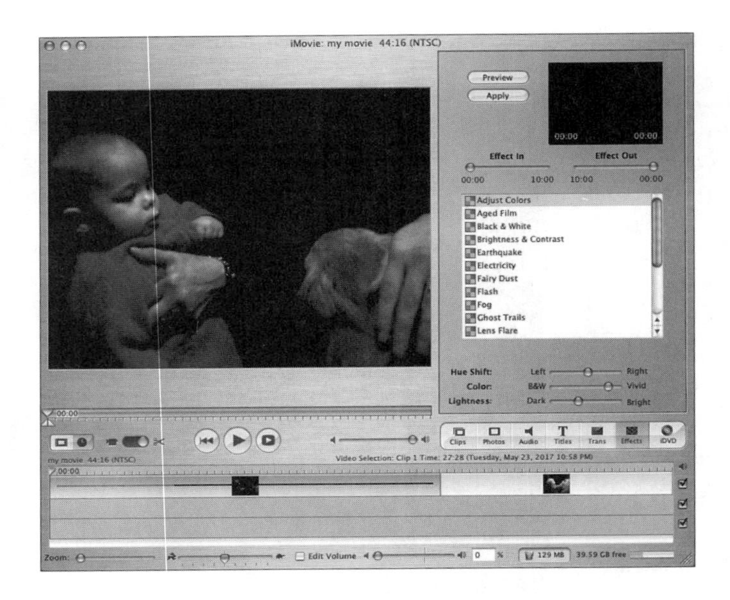

FIGURE 15.26
The clip with the Brightness/Contrast effect renders in the Timeline.

When iMovie is done processing your clip, you can play the movie to see how the effect looks.

> Sometimes, after you apply an effect and iMovie begins to render it, you change your mind. What do you do to stop iMovie from rendering the rest of the clip? If you press the Command key and the period on your keyboard at the same time while iMovie is rendering any element, that process will be cancelled and the clip will remain as it was before you started.

Task: Enhancing a Clip with Adjust Colors

The Adjust Colors effect can come in handy when you want to make certain colors stand out, or want to give the clip a distinct imaginary feel of some kind. It gives you three subsettings that you can play with: Hue Shift, Color, and Lightness.

- **Hue Shift**—Shifts the entire video clip to a different color
- **Color**—Changes the amount and vividness of color, from no color (black-and-white) to Vivid (as much color as possible, which is how the effect starts out with no changes made)
- **Lightness**—Similar to the Brightness/Contrast effect

▼ In this example, we want to give the video a washed-out feeling by taking out the color (also known as *desaturating*) and increasing the brightness/lightness.

1. Open an iMovie project, and with a clip selected in the Timeline, choose the Adjust Colors effect in the Effects palette (refer back to Figure 15.18).
2. Click the Color slider and drag it to the left to make the video black and white (B&W).
3. Click the Lightness slider and drag it to the right to make the video brighter.
4. Click the Apply button in the iMovie window to set iMovie going on processing your video. ▲

The Hue Shift option changes the overall tone of the clip. Dragging the slider from one end to the other should give you nearly the full range of the spectrum, from warm reds to cool blues.

Keep in mind that the colors available in the Hue Shift option depend somewhat on the colors, brightness, and other features of your original video.

Making Changes to Effects

After you've tried effects by simply applying them to successive clips, you'll probably discover that you want to make things more interesting or customized.

You can drag and drop transitions, but the drag-and-drop feature doesn't work with effects.

Because you've already applied an effect to a clip, you will need to reapply the changed effect. To do this, select the clip you want to change the effect for, choose the effect you wish to change, make the changes, and then click Apply. A dialog message sheet window will appear in some cases to let you know that the new effect invalidates the previous one. You must choose OK for your new effect to be processed.

Task: Changing and Updating an Effect

▼ TASK

This example picks up where we left off with the last task. We've decided that we want to try the mysterious Effect In and Effect Out features in the Effects palette. We want to slowly increase the impression that the effect has on our clip over the space of a few seconds by bringing in the effect to give the clip a unique feel and then fading out the effect.

▼ 1. Select a clip in the Timeline that has an effect applied to it.

2. Click the blue slider in the Effect In area of the Effects palette, and drag it a bit to the right to choose the length of time that it takes for the effect to develop to full strength (see Figure 15.27).

FIGURE 15.27
Instead of simply turning on, the effect now fades in over the course of a few seconds.

3. Now click the Effect Out slider and drag it to the left to choose how long it takes for the video to return to normal.
4. Click the Apply button to re-apply the effect with these new settings.

When you click the Apply button, iMovie starts to process the video. In a short while, you can preview it to see the final version of the video. Of course, if the effect doesn't measure up to your expectations, you can continue steps 1–4, trying out different adjustments until you're happy with the effect.

Summary

In this chapter, you found out how you can bring your iMovies one step closer to their Hollywood (or living room) debut by learning about titles, transitions, and effects. You learned how easy it is to make and adjust titles in iMovie. You also learned how iMovie enables you to add professional-looking transitions to a project, which can help digital video to look and feel more like a real movie. Finally, you saw how, in certain situations, an effect such as Brightness/Contrast can actually help you to see your video better if it was shot in a setting where there wasn't much light, also known as a *low-light situation*.

CHAPTER 16

Using Still Photos, Music, and Sound Effects in iMovie

iMovie isn't only useful for people with video cameras. Still images with accompanying sound can be used to create high-impact presentations or documentaries, and can be used to spice up live-action films with professional title and credit backgrounds. Even if you're a digital photographer who is completely satisfied with iPhoto, you'll find that iMovie can create new and exciting ways to display your masterpieces.

If you've added view clips to your project from your camera or from other sources, they've almost certainly had sound accompanying them. What if you decide that you don't like the sound that goes along with your movie clip? Do you have to reshoot the video just for a new audio track? No, not at all. iMovie provides you the ability to use dozens of canned sound effects, record audio from your computer's microphone (if available), use music from your iTunes library, or even take the sound from other video clips and use them with different video sequences.

Photos and iMovie

iMovie is known for the ease of use with which it allows you to import and manipulate digital video with special effects and transitions. iMovie 3 integrates completely with iPhoto 2, providing instant access to your photograph library.

Photographs can be worked with very much like video clips—you can apply the same effects and transitions, as well as using a very special effect designed specifically for digital photograph--an effect dubbed the "Ken Burns Effect." This effect, which we'll discuss later, can add motion and depth to otherwise still images. Figure 16.1 shows a still image within the Timeline—it appears identical to a video clip.

FIGURE 16.1
Still images work virtually identically to video clips within iMovie.

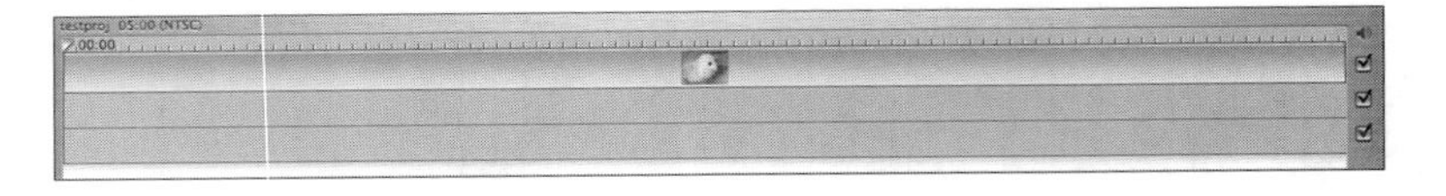

iMovie supports a number of native image formats through QuickTime's media framework. TIFFs, JPEGS, and even PDF files can be dragged into an iMovie project as a source of still images.

Importing into iPhoto

The best and cleanest way to handle importing images into iMovie is to first import them into iPhoto. iMovie automatically connects to your iPhoto library and provides access to all of your digital images the same way it does with digital music and iTunes. The drawback to this is that even if you only want to insert an image or two into iMovie, it's best if they are added to your iPhoto library. Let's review some of the basics of working with iPhoto that were first explained in Chapter 12, "Using iPhoto."

> You should start iPhoto at least once before using iMovie, otherwise the iPhoto/iMovie integration will not be complete, and iMovie may behave strangely when attempting to access photo features.

There are two straightforward methods for getting images into iPhoto. The first is to connect a supported camera to your computer, and then follow your camera's instructions to place it in playback or transfer mode. Your computer will sense the connected camera, launch iPhoto, and present you with the Import pane, shown in Figure 16.2.

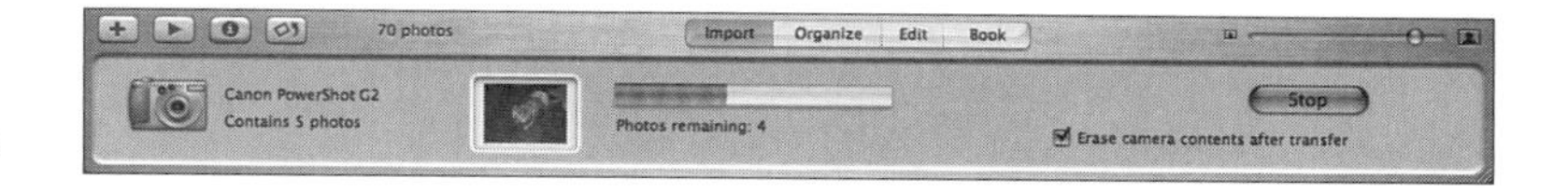

FIGURE 16.2
Images in iPhoto are imported directly from the digital camera.

Clicking the Import button will transfer files from your camera. Thumbnails of the transferring images appear in the image well of the Import pane along with the number of photos remaining to be transferred. When the import is complete, the new images will appear in the photo viewing area along with any other images you've imported. If the box for Erase Camera Contents After Transfer is checked, you will be asked to approve deletion of the original photo files from the camera.

Imported images are stored in groupings called "Rolls" in the Photo library. Any image, in any roll, can be added to an arbitrary "album" by first creating the album (choose New Album from the File menu), then by dragging from the Photo Library into the Album name displayed along the left side of the iPhoto window. This helps you keep track of your images, and provides a convenient means of accessing them in iMovie.

The second method of importing images assumes you already have a group of image files on your computer but not in iPhoto. In this case, you can select them in the Finder and drag them into the iPhoto library. This, once again, will create a new roll in the Photo Library, and give you access to the pictures from within iMovie—no camera required.

Adding Photos to iMovie

As mentioned previously, there are two ways to add photos to iMovie, either from files on your desktop, or via iPhoto integration. Since iPhoto is the preferred method, we'll start there.

iPhoto Integration

To add a photograph that you've previously stored within your iPhoto library, click the "Photos" button in the icon bar in the lower right portion of the iMovie window. The Photo palette should appear, as seen in Figure 16.3.

At the top of the pane are the controls for the Ken Burns effect, followed by the library of iPhoto images that are available. The popup menu at the top of the image catalog can be used to limit the images being displayed to any of the iPhoto albums you've created, or two special categories:

- **iPhoto Library**—All images in the iPhoto library.
- **Last Import**—The last group of images you imported into iPhoto.

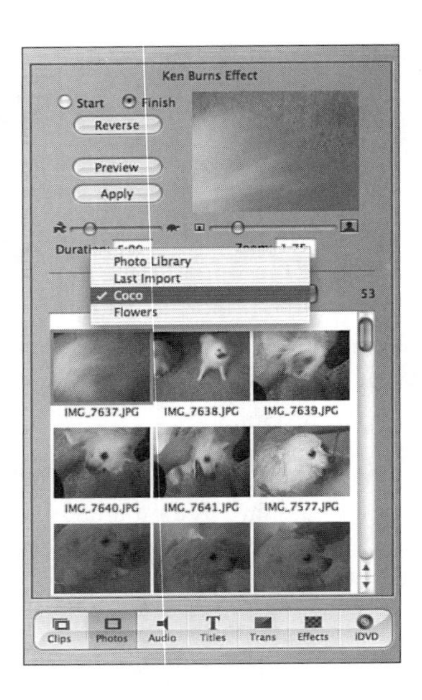

FIGURE 16.3
The "Photos" pane provides direct access to iPhoto images.

Choose the album or category that contains the image you wish to use, then scroll through the image catalog to find the exact picture you want to add.

Finally, drag the image to the Timeline or Clip View at the bottom of the iMovie window. iMovie will behave *exactly* as if you are adding a video clip with a five second duration. Figure 16.4 shows a collection of three images that have been added to the Clip View in iMovie.

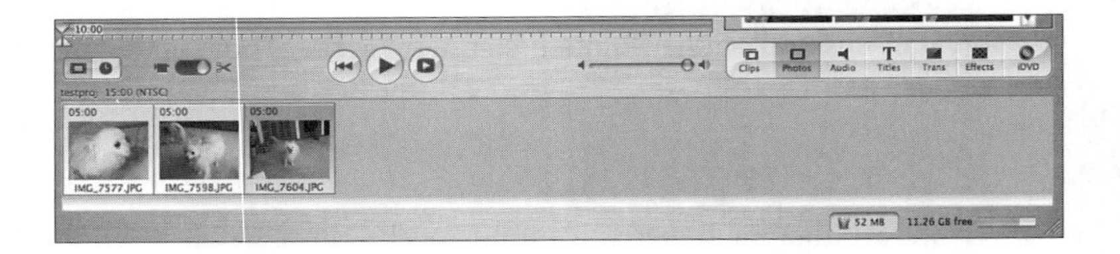

FIGURE 16.4
Just think of still images as video clips without much video.

Unfortunately, this is the point where some of Apple's user friendliness gets in the way. The software will immediately try to render the "Ken Burns" effect within your image. Since we don't even know what the Ken Burns effect *is* yet, we probably aren't that anxious to use it! To cancel the rendering simply add the image to the Timeline, select it within either the Timeline or the Clip View and press the escape (Esc) key. iMovie will stop trying to add the special effect and we'll get exactly what we want—a five second still clip of the photograph.

If you're an adventurous sort and want to disable the automatic application of the Ken Burns effect completely, open the file `~/Library/Preferences/com.apple.iMovie3.plist` in a text editor such as text editor, then look for the line that contains the text `autoApplyPanZoomToImportedStills`. Shortly after that line you'll see the word "`true`". Change the word "`true`" to "`false`", leaving everything else the same. Restart iMovie, and suddenly the program import "still" stills without any extra effort on your part!

The Ken Burns Effect

So, what is the Ken Burns effect that Apple so desperately seems to want us to use? It is a method of bringing life to still images that was pioneered by the filmmaker Ken Burns, who has created many award winning documentaries, and whose work has even been nominated for an academy award.

For a complete background on Ken Burns and his work, visit `http://www.pbs.org/kenburns/`.

The effect is really quite simple—rather than just putting a photograph onscreen while someone narrates, a virtual "camera" pans over the image, zooming in or out as it goes. A photograph of a bouquet of flowers, for example, could start zoomed in on one particular flower, then zoom out, centering the bouquet on the screen as it goes. When the effect is used properly, the end result is stunning and can make the viewer forget that he or she is not watching live video.

To use the Ken Burns effect in iMovie, first make sure that you are in the Photo pane—then select the image that you wish to apply the effect to. At the top of the photo pane are the controls that you will use to determine the path that the virtual camera will take, how long the resulting video clip will be, and how far in or out the virtual camera is zoomed.

For example, I've chosen a picture of an orchid that I wish to apply the effect to. I've decided that I want to start out zoomed in on one of the flowers, then zoom out to show several. To do this, I click the "start" button, then click and drag the image within the Ken Burns effect image well. This will allow me to center where the camera will be starting when the effect is applied. Next, I adjust the Zoom level either using the slider control or by directly typing in the Zoom field. The start settings of my Ken Burns effect are shown in Figure 16.5.

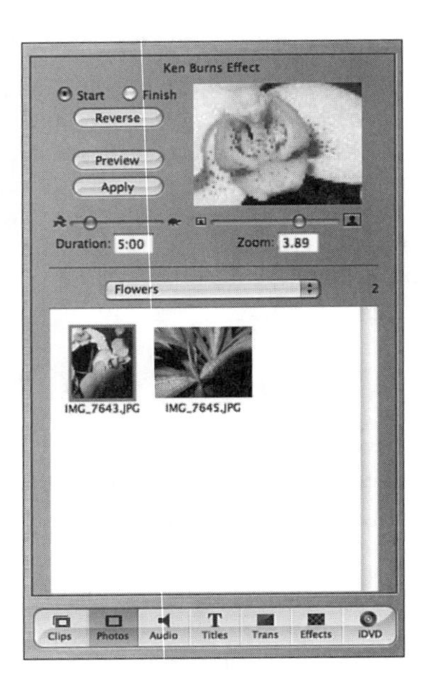

FIGURE 16.5
Choose the starting location and zoom for the image.

To complete the effect, I need to repeat the same process for the "Finish" point of the effect. This time, I click the "Finish" button, click and drag the image so that it appears as I want it in the image well, then adjust the zoom so that I can see several of the orchid's flowers, as seen in Figure 16.6.

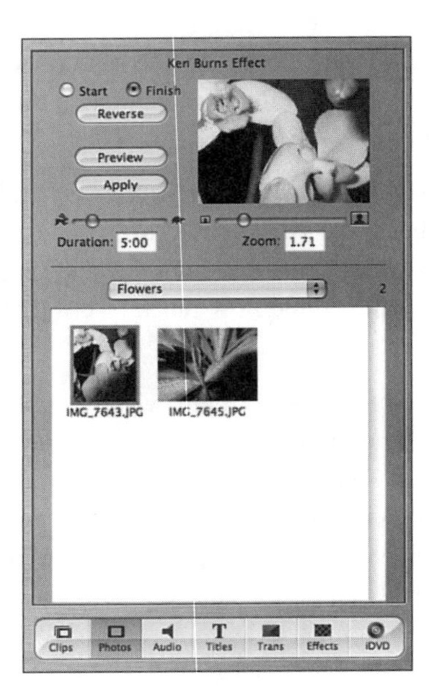

FIGURE 16.6
Set the finish point and zoom level to complete the transition.

To preview the Ken Burns effect before you actually apply it to an image, click the "Preview" button. To reverse the path that the virtual camera takes (effectively switching the Start and Finish points), click the Reverse button. If you want the total time the transition takes to last longer (or shorter) than five seconds, adjust the duration slider, or type directly into the Duration time field. Finally, to add the image with the Ken Burns effect to the timeline or clip view, click the Apply button. The effect make take several minutes to apply (watch the little progress bar that appears above the image in the Clip View or Timeline).

The settings you choose when adding the Ken Burns effect to a photograph are used as the default for subsequent images you add. Since iMovie attempts to apply the Ken Burns effect to *everything*, make sure that what it's doing is really what you want.

Adding Photos Directly

You can easily add photos directly to iMovie by dragging the image files from your desktop into either the Clip Shelf, the Clip View, or the Timeline. In all of these cases, iMovie will add the image, just like a video clip, but, again, will automatically try to apply the Ken Burns effect using the current settings within the Photo pane. As mentioned previously, you can cancel the Ken Burns effect and just use the image as a still by pressing Escape (Esc) or Command-. immediately after adding it to iMovie.

Using Command-. to cancel rendering of the Ken Burns effect will also cancel all active rendering, so be careful not to use it before your titles, transitions, or effects are processed.

So, what if you want to add photos directly, AND use the Ken Burns effect? If the settings for the Ken Burns effect are already configured the way you want before you add your picture, then you literally don't have to do *anything*. Just add your image and allow the Ken Burns effect to automatically be applied. If, however, you'd like to customize the effect for the image you're adding, you must follow these steps:

1. Add the image by dragging it into iMovie.
2. Cancel the automatic application of the Ken Burns effect by pressing Escape (Esc) or Command-..
3. Click on the image in the Clip Viewer or the Timeline to select it.

4. Switch to the Photo pane by clicking the Photos icon in the icon bar in the lower right portion of the iMovie window.
5. The selected image will appear in the Ken Burns Effect pane.
6. Choose the effect settings you want, then click Apply.
7. The Ken Burns effect with your custom settings will be applied to the image you've added to iMovie directly.

As you can see, working with the iPhoto integration is a much more straightforward means to managing images and applying the Ken Burns effect. Hopefully Apple will clean this process up in the future, and add a preference for the automatic application of the Ken Burns effect. For now, however, you've got to make sure that iMovie doesn't start adding effects where you don't want them.

Still Images from Video

One final source for still images is a video clip itself. iMovie makes it easy to create a still image from any frame in a video file. To do this, switch to the Timeline viewer and drag the Playhead until the image that you want to use as a still appears within the main viewer. Next, choose Create Still Frame from the Edit menu. iMovie will add a still image with a five second duration to the available iMovie Clips.

Surprisingly, when you create a still image from a video clip, iMovie will *not* attempt to apply the Ken Burns effect!

Still Images and Duration

A point of confusion when working with still images is the duration, and how duration can be changed. A still image that does not have the Ken Burns effect applied is, by default, treated as a five second video clip. To change the length of time that it will be displayed onscreen, simply double click it within the Timeline or Clip View. A window, as seen in Figure 16.7 will appear, where you can manually enter how long the clip should last.

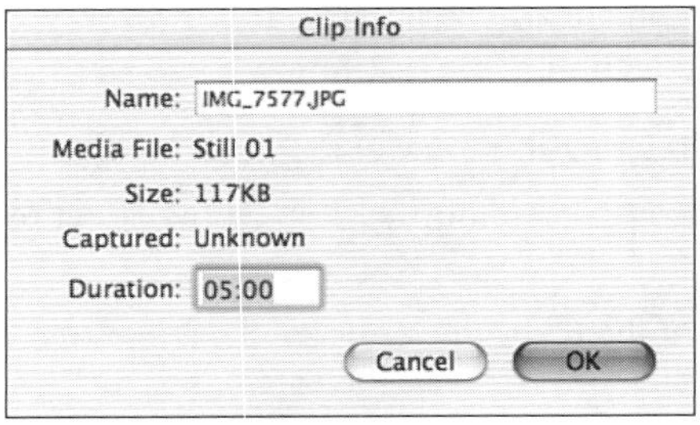

FIGURE 16.7
Change how long a still image will be displayed.

Clip Info

Name: IMG_7577.JPG

Media File: Still 01

Size: 117KB

Captured: Unknown

Duration: 05:00

Cancel OK

The same, however, cannot be said for an image that has had the Ken Burns effect applied. Double-clicking a Ken Burns image will show a non-editable duration, as seen in Figure 16.8.

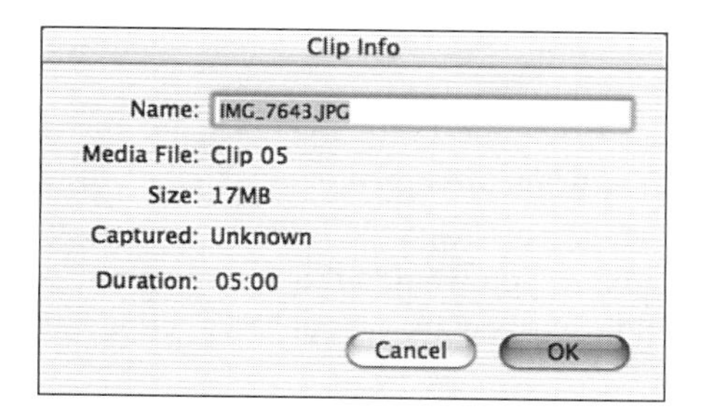

FIGURE 16.8
You cannot alter the duration of a Ken Burns effect image without re-applying the effect.

The reason for this difference is that an image that has had the Ken Burns effect applied to it is effectively a piece of video. It has different frames that iMovie calculated based on the settings you gave it. A "real" still image is just a single frame that iMovie understands it should display for a set length of time.

To change the duration of a Ken Burns effect image, select the image within the Timeline or Clip View, then click the Photos button to switch to the Photos pane. The selected image will be shown in the Ken Burns preview and the settings used to create the image will be loaded. Adjust the duration using the duration slider, then click the Apply button to re-render the effect with the new duration.

Still Images, Effects, and Transitions

iMovie makes it simple to apply effects and transitions to images that you've added to your project. In fact, there is virtually no difference between working with still or Ken Burns effect image clips and video clips. There are two specific situations, however, when you may be prompted to do something that isn't quite clear:

- **Increase Clip Duration**—Sometimes the length of a still image clip isn't long enough for a given transition (a wipe/fade/etc.) to be applied. In this case, iMovie will tell you that the clip must be longer. All you need to do is adjust the duration (as discussed previously).
- **Convert Still Clip to Regular Clips**—Sometimes, when you apply an effect that changes over time—like "Earthquake" that makes each frame shift slightly to create a "shaking" appearance—iMovie will state "This effect generates different results for each frame, which will not show up on Still Clips", as seen in Figure 16.9.

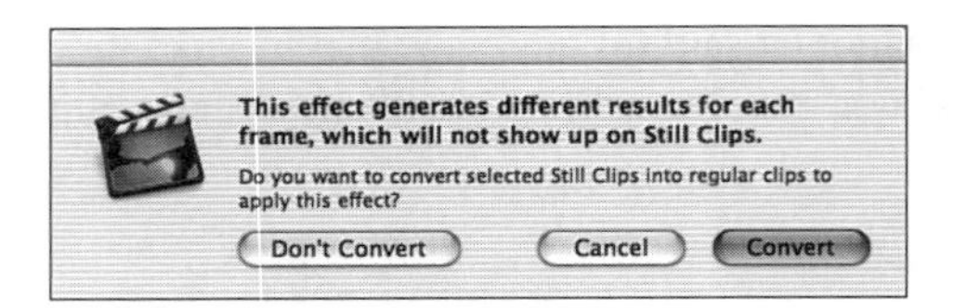

FIGURE 16.9
Some effects require that still clips be converted into regular clips.

In order to apply the effect, iMovie must effectively change the still image into a video clip. Click the Convert button when prompted, and iMovie will render the effect. The only drawback to this is that, like an image with the Ken Burns effect added, you won't be able to change the duration as you would with a normal still image. In order to revert to a normal still clip, you'll need to delete the converted clip, and re-add the original image.

Sound in iMovie

In an iMovie project, sound often plays almost as important a part as video. Sound and music can set the stage for a romance, suspense, comedy, or thriller. It can help create pacing for the movie and smooth through otherwise troublesome video transitions. If you've been using iMovie to import and arrange movies from your camera, you've already got audio in your projects. Movie clips themselves can contain embedded sounds, and these are usually transferred and saved along with the movie files. While this is convenient if you only want to use the sounds you've recorded with your camera, it doesn't give you the flexibility to mix sounds or add additional sounds to your movie.

Audio Tracks

To accommodate additional sound effects, iMovie includes two sound tracks that can hold any sound, music, or audio that you'd like. Figure 16.10 shows the three available iMovie tracks—Video/Audio, Audio Track 1, and Audio Track 2.

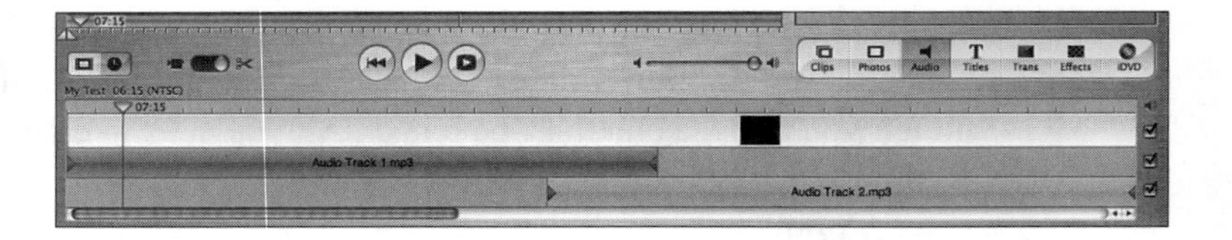

FIGURE 16.10
Audio can be part of a video track, or can be added to either of the two audio tracks.

There is no difference in functionality between the audio 1 and 2 tracks. You can use one track to hold sound effects, the other for background music, or mix and match them as you choose. In addition, each track can overlap audio clips—allowing you almost limitless layers of audio. You could, for example, have a base piece of background music in audio track 1, then, perhaps an environment sound track layered on top of it, and, finally, sound effects layered on top of that in audio track 2. Figure 16.11 shows a layering possibility much like this scenario.

FIGURE 16.11
Audio can be layered via the different audio tracks, or within a single audio track.

You've probably figured this out, but you must be in the Timeline view rather than the Clip View to see the available audio tracks.

Sounds that are added to either of the audio tracks can be moved to the other track by clicking and dragging between the tracks in the timeline. No matter what type of sound you're adding, it is referred to within iMovie as an "Audio Clip."

Audio Playback

However you've decided to layer your audio, iMovie will automatically composite it correctly when you play back your movie project. If you've included audio clips in all of the tracks, they'll automatically all play back when you play the movie.

Sometimes this can get to be a bit of a pain as you try to fine-tune your special effect sounds and don't want to hear the dialog from your video tracks, or the background music you've added. To enable you to focus on a single set of audio, Apple has provided the ability to control audio playback using the three checkboxes to the right of the video and audio tracks, shown in Figure 16.12.

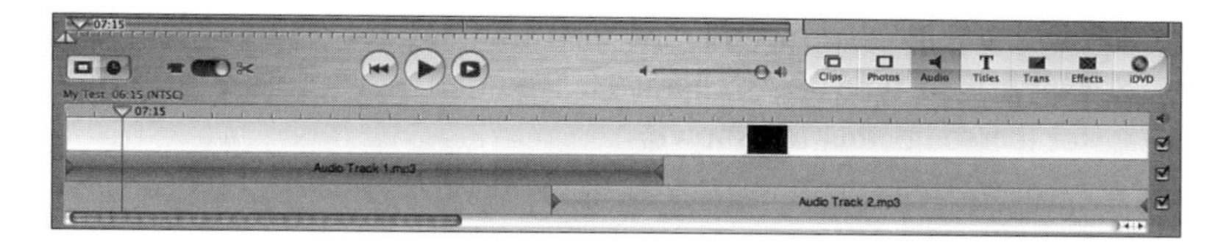

FIGURE 16.12
Turn on and off audio tracks to focus on a particular part of your sound editing.

You can also control the overall volume of the movie using the volume control slider to the right of the main playback controls.

Working with Audio

There are a number of different ways to add audio to a project, so we'll start with one of the most common (and useful), then discuss how to work with audio clips that have been added to a timeline, and, finally, examine other means of importing audio.

Accessing the iTunes Music Library

Adding audio to an iMovie project takes place through the Audio pane, accessed by clicking the Audio button in the icon bar on the lower right half of the screen. Figure 16.13 shows the iMovie window with the Audio pane active.

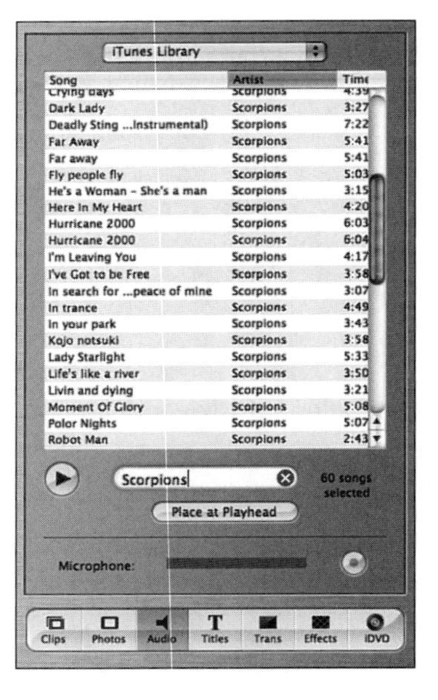

FIGURE 16.13
Access Audio import features by clicking the Audio (speaker) icon in the lower-right portion of the iMovie window.

Your iTunes library is the default source for audio that is added to the project. You can use the pulldown menu at the top of the iTunes listing to choose between your iTunes playlists or type a few characters into the search field at the bottom of the song list to filter the songs that are shown.

> When using the search field to find your iTunes music, you'll notice that an "X" appears at the end of the field after you've typed in a few characters. Clicking the "X" will clear out the search results and return to the full list.

If you have a library of thousands of songs and can't remember which one you're looking for, you can choose a song from the list, then click the Play button underneath the list to listen to the song.

You must remember that using copyrighted material is *against the law*. Be sure that any songs you're using on a movie are public domain or properly licensed. If you're making the movie just for yourself, you can use music you own—but if the final product may be seen by others, you cannot distribute the copyrighted material.

Adding iTunes Audio to the Project

After you've located the song file that you want to add to the iMovie project, position the Playhead where you would like the sound to be inserted, click within the audio track that should receive the sound file, then click the "Place at Playhead" button in the Audio pane. iMovie will take a few seconds (or minutes, depending on the length of the file), then the corresponding audio clip will appear in the selected audio track as a colored bar labeled with the name of the audio file, as shown in Figure 16.14.

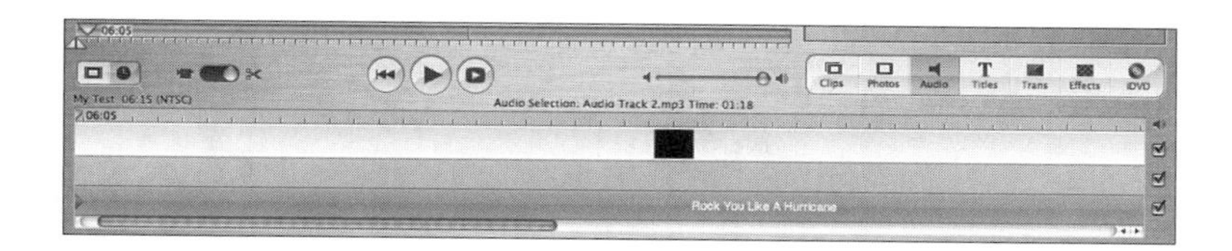

FIGURE 16.14
iMovie has just finished adding the chosen song to the selected audio track.

In the shipping version of iMovie, there is no obvious means of telling which audio track is currently selected. The last track you clicked on is the one used for inserting audio.

If you happen to end up with audio inserted in the wrong track, simply click and drag the audio from one track to another.

Another, perhaps more elegant, way to add audio clips to the project is to drag a name from the list in the Audio pane to the audio track where it should be inserted. As you drag the name into the timeline, a yellow "insert" bar will appear to show you where the audio will be inserted when you stop dragging.

You can even extend this technique to the Finder by dragging audio files directly from your desktop into the Timeline.

Manipulating Audio within the iMovie

Once a piece of audio has been added to an audio track, it can easily be manipulated to match up with your video tracks or the volume can be changed to better mix with the video or other audio files.

Repositioning Audio

Sometimes you place a sound in a movie and it "just doesn't fit," or doesn't sync up with the video. To move an audio clip, click and drag it horizontally within the Timeline. The audio segment will move to any position you'd like within the project. While you are dragging, the playhead will automatically track the start position of the audio, enabling you to position it perfectly within the project, as seen in Figure 16.15.

FIGURE 16.15
Drag the audio clip to reposition it.

> For extremely fine control of audio positioning, click to select the audio clip in the Timeline (it will darken in color to show it is selected), then use the left and right arrow keys to move it frame by frame along the Timeline. Holding down the shift key will increase the movement to ten frames at a time.

If you decide that you want to remove an audio clip from the project, simply click on it, then press Delete or choose Clear from the Edit menu.

Locking Audio to a Video Clip

Often the act of moving audio around is an attempt to synchronize it with a piece of video. iMovie's ability to position on a frame-by-frame basis makes this simple, but what if you decide later that you want to reposition the video clip? If you drag the video, all of your hard work synching the audio will be lost.

To "lock" a piece of audio to the video track, select the audio that you've positioned where you want it, then choose Lock Audio Clip at Playhead from the Advanced menu. The audio track will then be "attached" to the video that occurs at the same place as the audio. Moving the video track within the timeline will move the audio as well, keeping your synchronization intact. You can tell a lock is in place by graphical "pushpins" that appear on the audio and video tracks, as seen in Figure 16.16.

FIGURE 16.16
Pushpins denote an audio track that is locked to a video track.

To unlock an audio clip, select it within the audio track, then choose "Unlock Audio Clip" from the Advanced menu.

> Locking audio to a video clip works *one way*. It does *not* lock the video to audio. If you drag the video clip, the audio will move with it, but not vice versa. Dragging the audio will simply reposition the lock to the video, potentially losing any synching work you've done.

By default, all locked audio clips are displayed with the pushpins all the time. To change the display so that the pushpins are only shown when the audio clip is selected, be sure to check the Show Locked Audio Only When Selected option within the iMovie preferences.

Using Crop Markers

Like video, audio clips also have crop markers that can be used to choose how much, or how little of a clip is played. These two arrows appear at the ends of an audio clip and can be dragged with the mouse to limit audio playback to a certain part of a sound, as demonstrated in Figure 16.17.

FIGURE 16.17
Drag the crop markers to limit what parts of the song are played.

To completely crop (remove) the portions of the audio clip that aren't being played, mark off the appropriate portions with the crop markers, then choose "Crop" from the Edit menu.

Adjusting Volume

Suppose you want soft background music in one portion of your movie, but want it to slowly build to a blaring orchestra in another? Before iMovie 3, the only way to do this was to edit the sound files in another audio program. Now, adjusting the volume is as simple as clicking and dragging.

To edit the volume editing mode, click the Edit Volume checkbox at the bottom of the iMovie window. Within a few seconds, all the audio clips (and the video clips that contain audio) will display little lines through them. These lines represent the volume level of the clips.

To change the volume level of a clip, highlight the clip within any of the tracks (remember, even the video track's audio can be adjusted here), then click and drag the volume adjustment at the very bottom of the iTunes window, or type a new volume level (100% being the "default" volume) into the field beside the volume slider. As you change the volume level, the line will raise or lower within the clip. Multiple clips can even be selected at once (shift-click) and simultaneously be adjusted with this control.

You're thinking, "Okay, that's nice," but it still doesn't get me the fine-tuned control I need to really mix different audio clips together. Don't worry, volume adjustment can be as simple (as we've seen) or as complex (as we're about to see) as you want.

To alter the volume level within a specific part of an audio or video clip, click and drag the volume line within the clip. As you drag, an adjustment "handle" (a big yellow dot) will appear. Dragging this dot up or down raises or lowers the volume at that point. To carry the volume change through to a different part of the clip, simply click wherever you want another volume adjustment handle to be added, and the level changes will be carried through to that point.

Each handle that is added also carries with it a transition point that determines how the audio clip will transition to the new volume level (will it happen abruptly? smoothly?). The transition point is displayed as a small red/orange square to the right of the adjustment handle. The point can be dragged so that it is right above or below an adjustment handle, making for an immediate transition in volume, as seen in Figure 16.18.

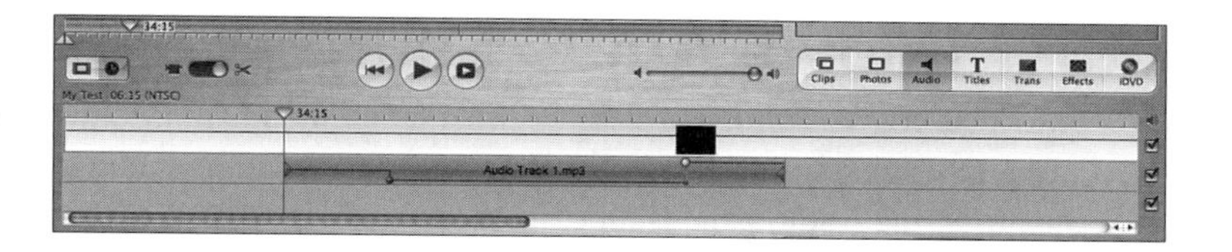

FIGURE 16.18
Moving the transition point directly above or below the adjustment handle will cause an immediate volume transition.

To smooth things out a bit, the transition point can be dragged all the way along the volume line up to another adjustment point. The transition then occurs all the way between these two points. For example, Figure 16.19 shows the same volume adjustment being made as in 16.18, but the transition place over a much larger span of the audio clip.

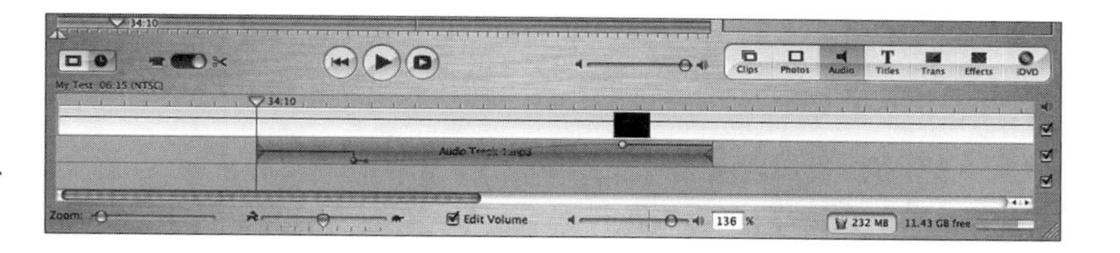

FIGURE 16.19
The transition point can be used to spread the volume transition out over a long span of the audio clip.

Volume adjustment can be used to ramp down an audio clip while ramping up another (similar to video transitions that blend the end of one clip with the beginning of another, this is called a cross-fade), or to create any number of other effects within your project.

Splitting Audio

If you have a sound or song that you want to play part of at one time, and another part at another time, you have two choices—you can import the audio clip twice, or you can simply "split" the existing clip into different pieces and use them wherever you'd like. To split an audio clip, position the Playhead where you'd like the clip to break, then choose Split Audio Clip at Playhead from the Edit menu.

New crop marks will appear at the location of the split within the audio clip. You can use these markers to fine tune the split location, as seen in Figure 16.20.

FIGURE 16.20
Using the split feature will add crop markers at the location of the Playhead.

To "finish" the split, you must choose Crop from the Edit menu, otherwise the split audio segments will still be attached to one another and won't be able to be moved separately.

Other iMovie Audio Sources

Now that you've learned how to work with audio clips in iMovie, let's take a quick look at the other sources of audio that are available for adding audio clips to your project. At the top of the Audio pane is a popup menu with additional choices for importing audio clips. As you've already seen, the iTunes Library and playlists are available.

iMovie Sound Effects

A great source for canned sound effects is the included iMovie sound effects library, accessed by choosing iMovie Sound Effects from the top of the Audio pane in iMovie. The iMovie sound effects, shown in Figure 16.21, encompass a wide range of environmental and special effect sounds. The "Skywalker Sound Effects" (from George Lucas' Skywalker ranch) are extremely high quality effects that can be used to create a very impressive soundtrack.

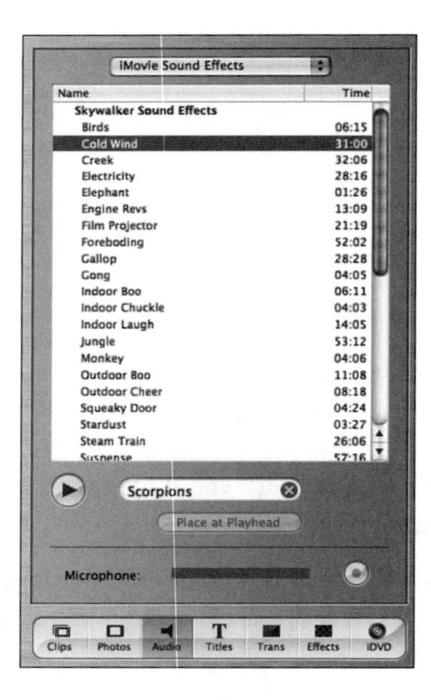

FIGURE 16.21
Choose from dozens of built-in sound effects.

Unlike iMovie music, you cannot click the Place at Playhead button to insert a selected sound effect (I can't imagine why not, but it doesn't work!). Instead, you must click and drag the name of an effect into your audio track. Once it is added, it will behave like any other audio clip.

Audio CDs

To add a sound track from an audio CD, put the CD in your computer's CD-ROM drive, then wait a few seconds. iMovie should automatically switch to Audio CD mode, query the Internet CD database to get a list of track names, and then display the contents of the CD in the Audio palette, as seen in Figure 16.22.

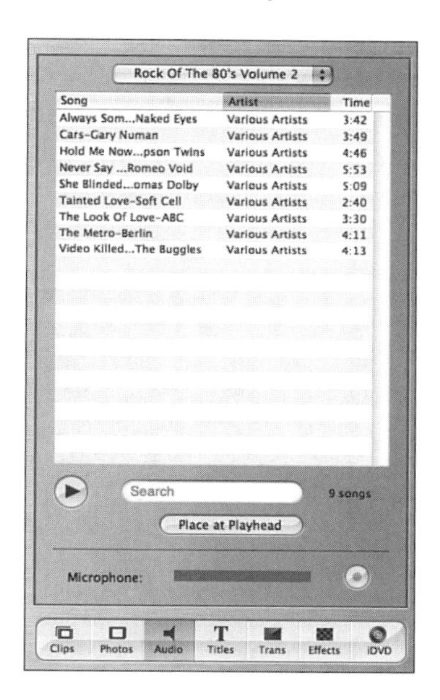

FIGURE 16.22
The contents of the audio CD will be displayed in the Audio palette.

Choose the song you want to add to one of your iMovie audio tracks, then either use the Place at Playhead button or drag the song to the Timeline to add it to the project.

Recording a Voice Track

If you'd like to narrate a portion of the video, position the playhead where you'd like to start recording from your computer's microphone, then click in the audio track that should receive the audio. Finally click the red "Record" button to the right of the Microphone label at the bottom of the Audio pane. A graph of the level of sound input is shown beside the label as it records. To stop recording live audio, click the record button again.

The new audio clips will be added to your project with the sequential labels "Voice 1", "Voice 2", and so on.

Extracting Audio from Video Clips

As we've already mentioned, the video track often also contains audio that accompanies a video clip. When adjusting volume, you can adjust the volume of a video clip just as you would an audio clip in an audio track.

Having video so closely tied to audio, however, has its disadvantages—you cannot manipulate the audio and video independently of one another. Thankfully, iMovie allows you to "decouple" the audio and video from one another. To do this, select a video clip with audio, then choose "Extract Audio" from the Advanced menu. After a few seconds, the audio from the video clip will appear in audio track below the video clip. Figure 16.23 shows a video clip in the timeline before audio extraction, and Figure 16.24 shows the same clip after extraction.

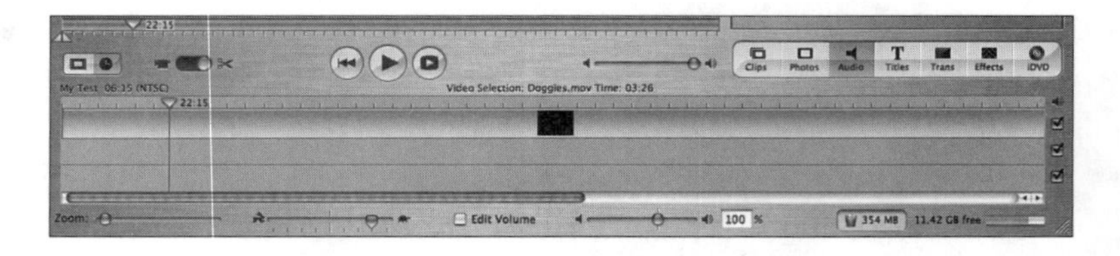

FIGURE 16.23
Normally, audio is embedded in the video clip...

FIGURE 16.24
...but it can easily be extracted.

After audio is extracted from a video file, it can be manipulated like any other audio clip.

In some cases, audio extraction happens automatically. If, for example, you cut and paste a video clip using the Paste Over at Playhead option of the Advanced menu, iMovie will automatically extract the audio of the original clip and move it to an audio track so it is not replaced by the paste over. The video clip that is pasted over will be lost, but the audio will remain.

This feature can be disabled by deselecting Extract Audio in Paste Over within the iMovie preferences.

iMovie has the ability to speed up or slow down video clips, as well as reverse their playback. These features do *not* work on audio clips. You can, however, apply the transformations to a video clip, then extract the audio, and the changes will carry with it.

Summary

In this chapter you learned how to use photographs and audio in iMovie. You learned how still images can be added to iMovie presentations and how they can be made "dynamic" through the use of the Ken Burns effect. In iMovie, a still image behaves almost exactly like a standard video clip, and can have all of the same transitions and effects applied. While simple to use, iMovie's audio features can allow novice editors to create layered audio tracks with ease. You learned how to work with a variety of audio sources available for adding sound to you video project.

CHAPTER 17

Exporting iMovies

In this chapter, you take a look at what you can do with your movies after you complete them—prepare them for email, Web, and disc delivery. You look behind the scenes at how you can export in different directions, and take a brief look at how an iMovie can be delivered with programs such as Mail (for emailing), Roxio's Toast (for CD-ROM and Video CD), and PlayStream's Content Manager (for putting iMovies on the Web). We'll also look at exporting your iMovies to iDVD for delivery via DVD.

When your iMovie is edited and ready to share, there are two ways that you can deliver it. Each method can be easily accessed from iMovie. You can deliver your iMovie using either tape (using a camera) or a file (when you'll be delivering by email, the Web, or disc such as CD or DVD).

When you're going back out to tape, some of the main considerations are how much time you have left on the tape and how long your iMovie is. But you'll generally want to put your iMovie at the beginning of the videotape so that it's easy to get to.

When you want to share an iMovie as a file, the file size could be more of a consideration. When you share an iMovie through email, the Web, or on disc

(CD/DVD), each method of delivery results in a file that has a particular amount of compression. To get an appropriate file size that fits the delivery method, iMovie has to squeeze the file. So, you might notice a considerable difference in the image quality between what you see in iMovie and what you see when you send the file.

As with some other aspects of iMovie, you can take its advice, and when you choose a way to share your iMovie, you can accept the suggested compression settings that Apple engineers have calculated as the appropriate settings for typical situations. Doing so makes it easy to take your iMovie in a number of different directions. (You can also use the Expert settings that were mentioned in Chapter 13, "Getting Started with iMovie" to accomplish advanced adjustment of your iMovie.)

Choosing a Way to Share Your iMovie

When you're ready to export your iMovie, simply choose File, Export from iMovie's menu bar. Then choose one of three options in the Export Movie dialog box: To Camera, To QuickTime, or To iDVD.

Exporting to Camera

When you export to camera, you're connecting the same camcorder that you used to capture your video and sending the finished iMovie back out to Mini-DV or Digital-8 tape. From there, you can watch the finished product by connecting the camera to the television, recording from the camera to your VCR, or sending the tape off to have a number of copies duplicated.

Exporting to QuickTime

When you export to QuickTime, the method you choose to share your iMovie results in a particular kind of file, based on the settings that are chosen and iMovie uses to conform the file to a particular format. For example, when you export an iMovie that you want to email to someone, it creates a relatively small file because it has to travel over the Internet and you don't want the person on the other end to have to wait too long to download the attachment. Or, when you want to burn a CD with iMovie, the CD can hold a much larger file than an email could handle, so the movie quality is much better, but still not as good as the original iMovie.

Exporting to iDVD

When you export to iDVD, the option is basically a preset that generates a high-quality video file that iDVD then converts for use on a DVD disc. It takes up the largest amount of hard-drive space of any of the export options.

Besides exporting to iDVD from the Export dialog box, there's an iDVD palette that lets you add "chapters" to your movie in iMovie and then launch it as an iDVD project. We'll talk about how later on in the chapter.

Making Videotapes from iMovie

To view an iMovie on television from a tape, the first step is to export the movie to your camcorder. Then you can either connect your camcorder to your television, or make a VHS tape from your digital tape (Mini-DV or Digital-8).

▼ TASK

Task: Exporting to Camera

When you've finished your iMovie and are ready to take it to the next level, exporting to a camcorder will allow you to display it on the television. With a few simple steps, you can make the video ready to share in a one-time event, where you play the video only from the camera. Or, after you have exported the video from iMovie to your camcorder, you can then go on to make a tape from there.

1. Load a blank tape into your camcorder and turn it on. (Make sure that you aren't about to record over something you want. Keep a pen around just for labeling tapes—and label those tapes!)
2. Connect your digital camcorder to your computer with a FireWire cable.
3. In iMovie, choose File, Export Movie, and choose Export to Camera from the Export pop-up menu (see Figure 17.1).

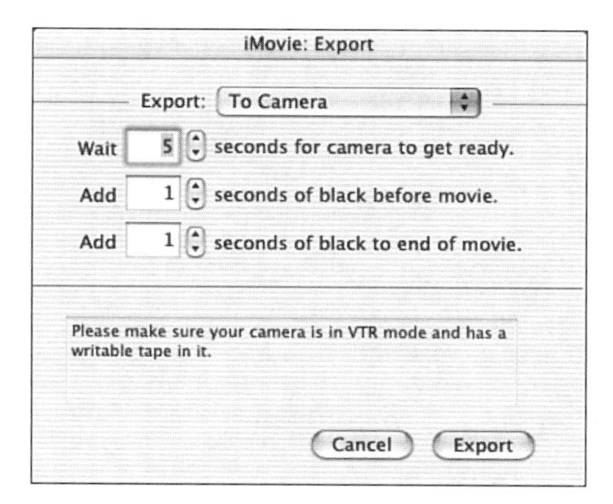

FIGURE 17.1
Exporting an iMovie to a camera.

▲ 4. Click Export.

If you want to make VHS copies of the digital tape that you just made, you can connect your camcorder to your VCR using standard RCA cabling, where you connect a series of cables to the Video Out and Audio Out jacks of your camera. The video connector is usually indicated by a yellow color. Two cables carry the audio, where each cable carries half of a stereo signal (the left audio channel is the white connector; the right audio channel is the red connector) (see Figure 17.2).

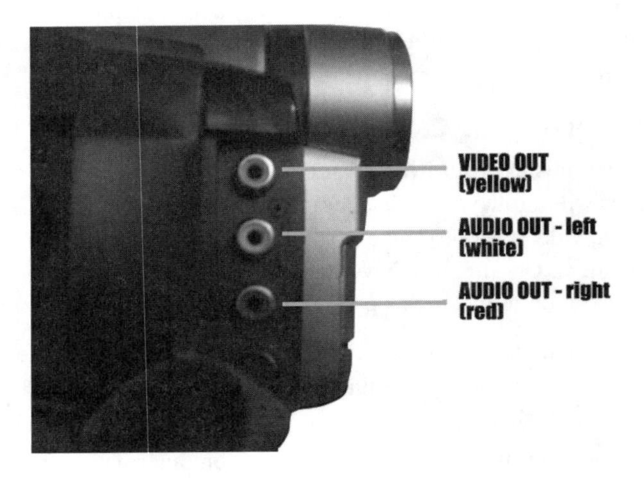

FIGURE 17.2
The Video/Audio Out connectors on a typical camcorder.

Then you connect the cables to the Video In and Audio In jacks of your VCR (see Figure 7.3).

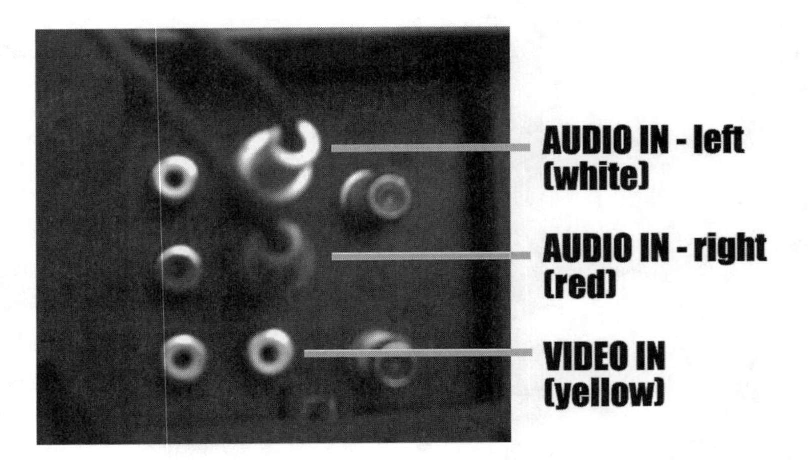

FIGURE 17.3
The Video/Audio In connectors on the back of a typical VCR.

Emailing iMovies

When you want to email an iMovie, you export it from iMovie and save it to your hard drive. Then you connect to the Internet and use your email program to attach the iMovie file to an email. If you've never emailed an attachment before, keep in mind that it can take a few minutes for the attachment to upload, depending on whether you are using a 56K modem or a higher-speed DSL or cable modem connection.

Another thing to keep in mind is that it will probably help you to choose a special name for the email version of your iMovie, such as `my movie-email`. Save it in a place that you can easily find on your hard drive, so that when it comes time to send it via email, you know which file to send and right where it is. (What you *don't* want to do is try to send your original iMovie via email. It'll be several hundred megabytes large, and would probably take a few weeks to send via modem.)

▼ TASK

Task: Exporting to Email

You don't have to do any special preparation of your iMovie to send it via email—that's what the Export function is for: to save it in a format that can be emailed.

1. Choose File, Export, and then choose To QuickTime from the Export pop-up menu.
2. Choose Email in the Formats pop-up menu (see Figure 17.4).

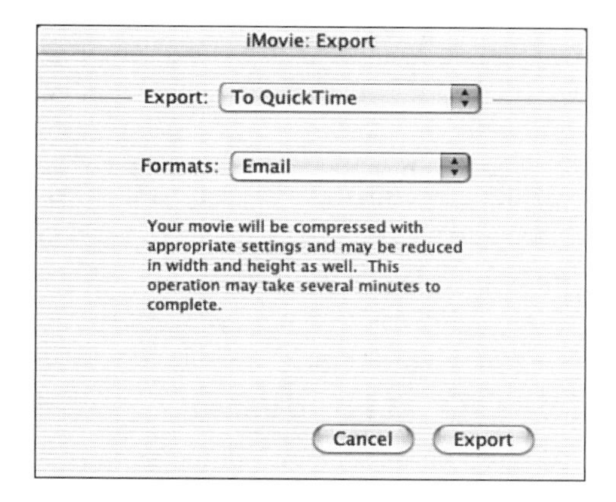

FIGURE 17.4
Exporting an iMovie for email.

3. Click Export and save your iMovie to a spot on your hard drive.
4. Open the program that you use to send email (such as Mail, which we talked about in Chapter 4, "Using the Internet").
5. Compose a new email and click the appropriate button to add an attachment to the email. (In Mail for OS X, you choose Add Attachment from the Edit menu—or simply drag the file into the compose window and skip the next step.)

▼

6. Locate the iMovie that you want to send by email and attach it to your email. Figure 17.5 shows the iMovie attached to the email.

FIGURE 17.5
Looking at an email that has an iMovie attached.

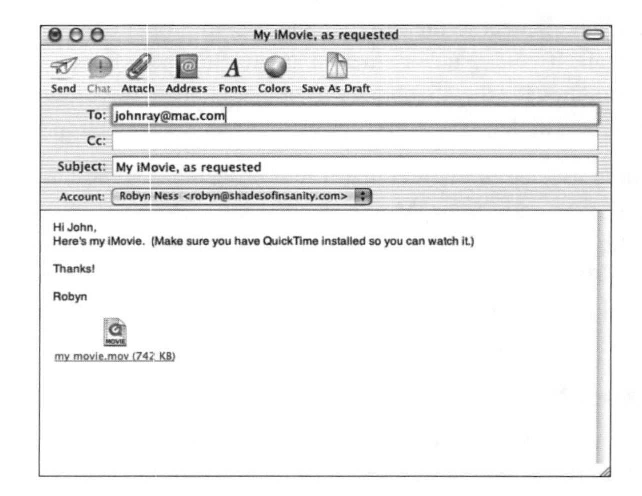

7. Connect to the Internet and send the email (see Figure 17.5). You don't necessarily have to connect to the Internet *before* you attach the email. You can compose an email and attach a file before connecting with many email clients, and then you send the email when you do connect.

Some email programs have file size limitations. For example, at the time of writing, you probably can't send a file larger than 10 megabytes through AOL. (And it would take quite a long time to upload or download that large a file anyway if you're using a 56K modem.)

Putting iMovies on the Web

Putting iMovies on the Web is a bit more involved than putting them on tape or sending them via email, but taking the time to figure out how to do it can make for an ideal way of sharing your iMovies with people who are far away.

There are two ways that iMovie can save your movie for delivery on the Web: as a Web movie or a streaming Web movie. A Web movie is uploaded to a standard Web server and a streaming Web movie is uploaded to a streaming Web server.

Here are some terms and concepts that are helpful to consider; there are entire books and series of books that have been written about each item, but just starting to take a look at each can be helpful down the road when you start to put more things of your own up on the Internet.

- **Server**—A *server* is the name for the computer that's used as the central storage location for Web pages. When you create a Web page on your computer, you have to upload the files to a server. Then, when people view your Web page, the Internet basically functions as a network connection to the server computer. When people hit your Web page, all they're really doing is downloading a series of files (text, graphics, HTML, and so on) from this Web server (the same place that you uploaded the files) to their computer.
- **Standard server (for Web movies)**—This is the most common type of server. When you put your Web page file on the server and a person clicks on the file, it's downloaded like any other file, and then the person double-clicks the file to view it. A standard server is basically any server that doesn't have QuickTime streaming capability. So, if you're not sure what kind of server you have and you don't know that it's specifically capable of streaming QuickTime, chances are that it's a standard server.
- **Streaming server (for streaming Web movies)**—True streaming video is when you're able to watch a video without downloading the entire file. Streaming video enables you to watch video in *real time*, meaning that you establish a connection with a streaming server and watch the video as if it were a miniature television show. True streaming video basically means that you have a smoother, higher-quality experience. Streaming video is usually more expensive and more complicated to set up, but many companies and individuals find that the effort and expense is worth it. In addition to QuickTime, other forms of streaming video that you might recognize include RealMedia and Windows Media. All forms of streaming video require some kind of player application, such as QuickTime, to be present on a person's computer.

Keep in mind that even true streaming video is still dependent on how fast your connection is—video can be streamed on typical 56K modems for example, and the streaming version is smoother than a non-streaming version, but the quality is not as good as you would have on a higher-speed connection such as DSL.

Task: Exporting a Web Movie for Use on a Standard Web Server

You'll probably want to save your iMovies using the Web Movie option, unless you specifically know you'll be using the file on an official QuickTime streaming server. In the next section, we'll take a look at the streaming server as well as investigate an easy-to-use method of streaming video provided by PlayStream.

1. Choose File, Export, and then choose To QuickTime from the Export pop-up menu.
2. Choose the Web option in the Formats pop-up menu (see Figure 17.6).

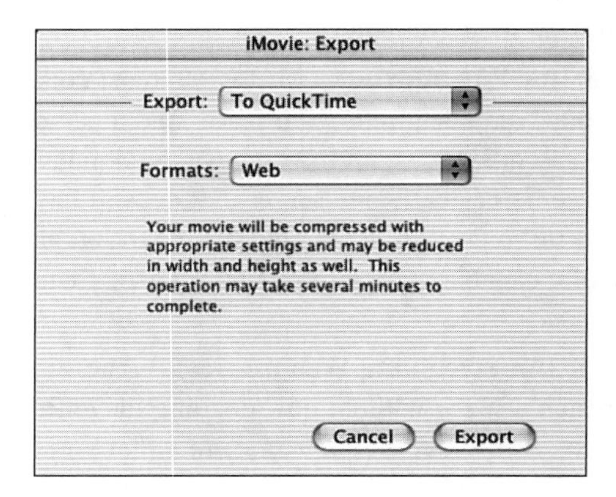

FIGURE 17.6
Exporting an iMovie as a Web movie, for a standard Web server.

3. Click Export and save your iMovie to a location on your hard drive from which you can then upload it to a Web server.
4. Using an FTP application or a Web page creation program such as Dreamweaver, upload your file to your Web site.
5. Using a Web page creation tool, make a link to your iMovie, as shown in Figure 17.7. Here's some sample HTML link code:

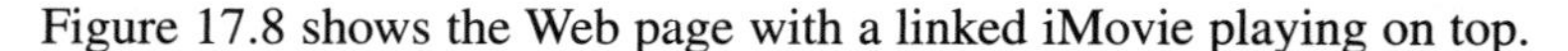

```
Click<A HREF=http://www.psrecords.net/stdwebmovies/fantasia.mov>here</a>
to see Fantasia,<p>a cat who thinks she's a kitten
```

Figure 17.8 shows the Web page with a linked iMovie playing on top.

Even though this isn't a true streaming server, QuickTime has the capability to play as much of the movie as you've downloaded. If you have a very fast connection, it can be almost as if it were a streaming clip.

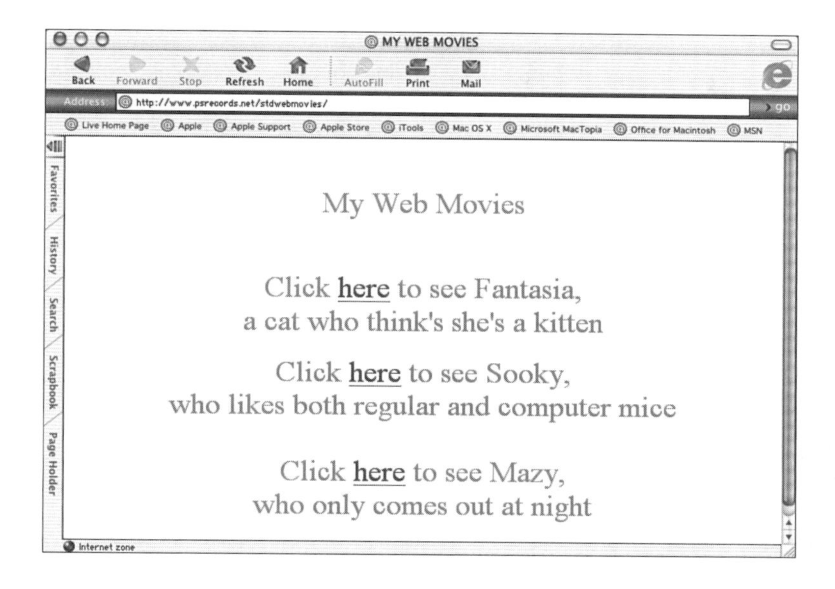

FIGURE 17.7
A sample Web page with simple links to the iMovies that we uploaded.

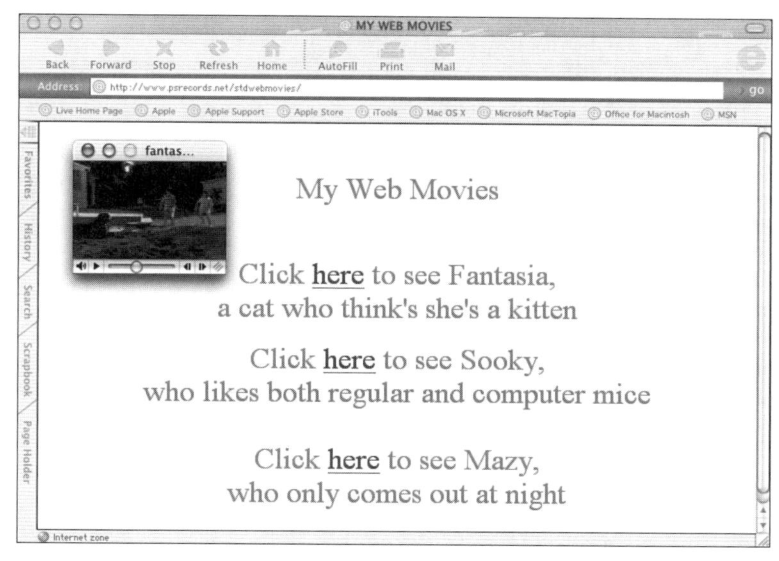

FIGURE 17.8
The iMovie plays when you click on the link.

When you are sharing your iMovies with people on a Web site, you might want to include instructions for people visiting your Web page to describe how they can actually download the file to their hard drive instead of watching it on the Web page. Instruct Mac users to hold the Ctrl key down on their keyboard, click the movie link, and choose Save Link As or Download Link to Disk option (see Figure 17.9).

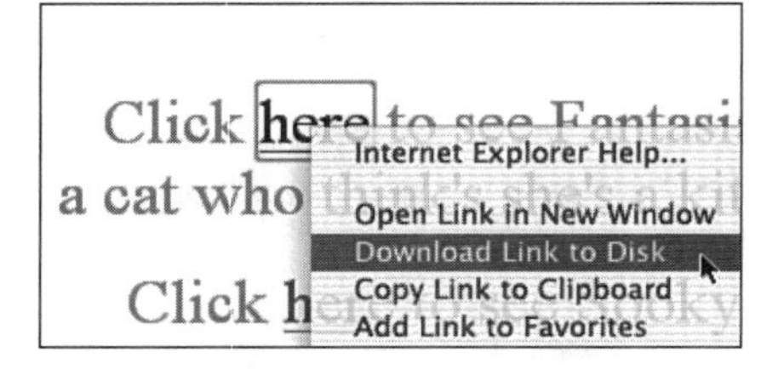

FIGURE 17.9
Holding the Ctrl key down on a Mac while clicking on a link for an iMovie in Internet Explorer.

Instruct Windows users to right-click the link and choose the Save Target As option to save the file to disk.

You might also want to instruct people that, in order to view your iMovie, they might need to download and install the latest version of QuickTime, which is a free download available from `www.apple.com/quicktime/download`.

Task: Exporting for Streaming Server

TASK

Exporting your iMovie as a streaming Web movie for use on a streaming server is similar to exporting your iMovie as a Web movie for use on a standard server.

1. Choose File, Export, and then choose To QuickTime from the Export pop-up menu.
2. Choose the Web Streaming option in the Formats pop-up menu (see Figure 17.10).
3. Click the Export button and save your file on your hard drive in a location you can find later to upload to the streaming server. You might want to name the file so that you can easily distinguish it later as a streaming file, something like `my movie-streaming.mov`.
4. Use your FTP program or Web page creation and upload tool to upload the iMovie to the streaming server.

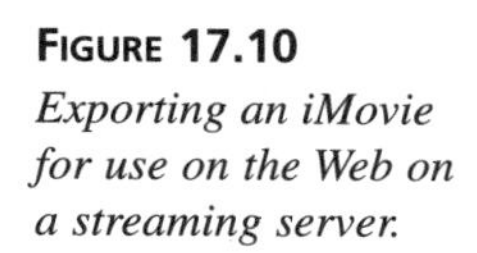

FIGURE 17.10
Exporting an iMovie for use on the Web on a streaming server.

As mentioned earlier, setting up a QuickTime file for a streaming server can be more complex and might require some experimentation and research. At the minimum, you must set up a Web page account and address (`www.websitename.com`) with a host company that's capable of QuickTime streaming. (example: `www.metric-hosting.com`).

But you might also want to investigate a company such as PlayStream, whose mission is to make the process of streaming video as easy as possible. PlayStream has special accounts that exist only to host streaming video. So, if you already have a Web page, you can put your video on a PlayStream account and link to it from your current Web page. Or you may simply want the increased quality of streaming video without the typical hassles, so a service like PlayStream might be a worthy option.

One reason PlayStream is nice is that it offers a free 15-day trial, and its accounts enable you to host the major three forms of streaming video—QuickTime video, Real Media, and Windows Media—so that you can reach the maximum audience. Preparing your video for the different formats can require downloading or purchasing additional software, but it might be worth it because most people usually either have the ability to view video encoded for the Real Player or Windows Media Player.

For some people, it might actually be easier to try a service such as PlayStream and use full streaming video, rather than getting Web creation software. PlayStream enables you to simply use your browser to upload files, and you don't even need your own Web page—when you upload files, you're given a link that you can email to people to get them directly to your video.

Task: Uploading a Streaming Web Movie iMovie for PlayStream

If you want to try the PlayStream option, you can sign up for a free 15-day trial at `www.playstream.com`. It's a way of getting right into putting your iMovie on the Web without spending any money.

1. Go to `www.playstream.com` and log in, and then click on the Content Manager link.
2. Click the Browse button (as shown in Figure 17.11) to locate the streaming Web movie file you saved earlier to your hard drive.

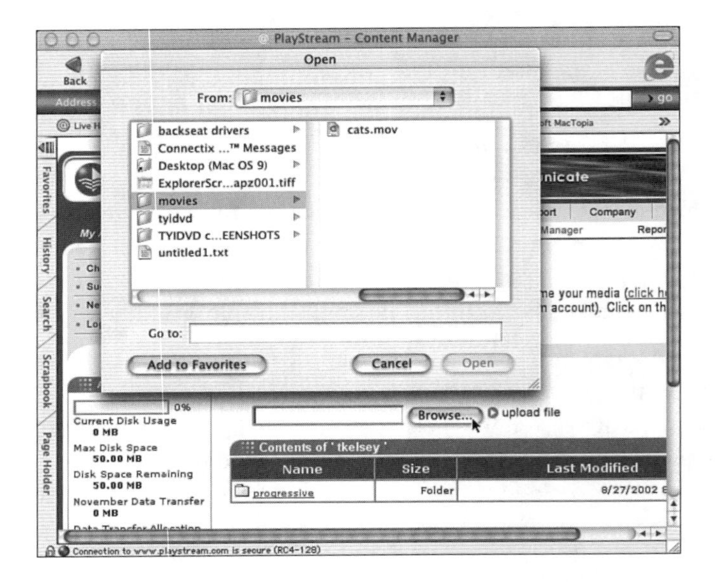

FIGURE 17.11
Using the Browse button right in the Web page to upload your video file—no special software required.

3. Click the Upload File button in the Content Manager on the PlayStream Web page to upload the file to your space on PlayStream. A window pops up (see Figure 17.12) that gives you a progress indicator of the upload.

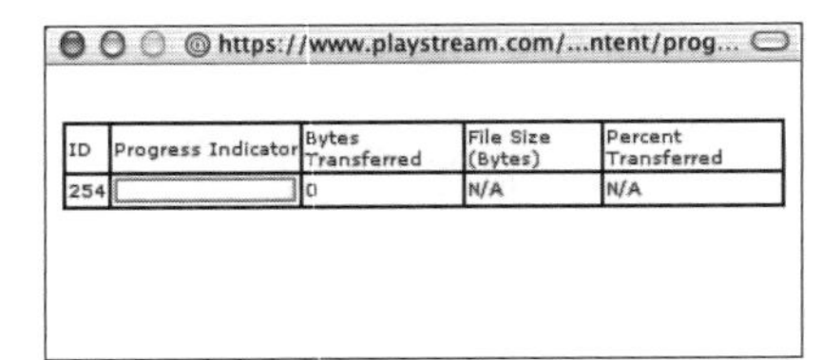

FIGURE 17.12
The Progress Indicator window showing the file being uploaded.

4. After the file is uploaded, select the text in the Stream Link field (see Figure 17.13) and copy the link into memory by going to the Edit menu at the top of the screen and choosing Copy.

▼

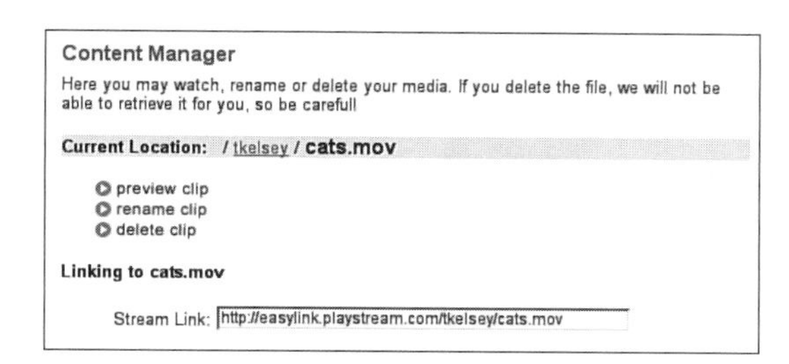

FIGURE 17.13
An automatic link is generated that you can either email to someone, put in a Web page to link to your streaming Web movie, or simply save for later use and paste directly into a Web browser window to see the movie play.

17

5. Paste the link text somewhere you can get it later, such as in an email to yourself or in a text document.
6. To allow access to the movie, insert the Stream Link text in an email, use it as a link on a Web page, or just paste it right in your Web browser. ▲

> You might want to include in your instructions that in order to see your iMovie, some people might have to download and install the free QuickTime software from `www.apple.com/quicktime/download`. Doing so installs a special plug-in file for the person's Web browser (Internet Explorer/Netscape/AOL) that enables them to view the streaming video file.

Burning iMovies to CD

If you have a CD burner and want to share your iMovies via CD, you can simply save as a CD-ROM movie, which generates a QuickTime movie file that you can then burn to CD. If a person is on a Mac, she can see the movie without installing special software. Many Windows PCs have QuickTime software installed, but if it's not on your recipient's computer, she can download it free from `www.apple.com/quicktime/download`.

Another fun option for burning iMovies to CD is called Video CD, where you can actually put the resulting disc in most DVD players. The quality is only a little better than VHS, but you can fit about an hour's worth of video on the disc and it's cheaper than burning DVDs.

Task: Exporting iMovie for CD-ROM

▼ TASK

If you want to share the CD-ROM iMovie, you must investigate how to burn a CD that's compatible with the computer owned by the person you're sharing the iMovie with. If you burn your CD on a Mac, it's compatible with other Macs. But if you want to share it with someone on a Windows PC, you must learn how to burn a PC-compatible CD-ROM or a hybrid CD-ROM that works on both Macs and PCs. We'll take a look at burning with Roxio's Toast (`www.roxio.com`), a popular program that enables you to burn in just about any format you want.

To export an iMovie for CD-ROM:

1. Choose File, Export, and then choose To QuickTime from the Export pop-up menu.
2. Choose the CD-ROM option in the Formats pop-up menu (see Figure 17.14).

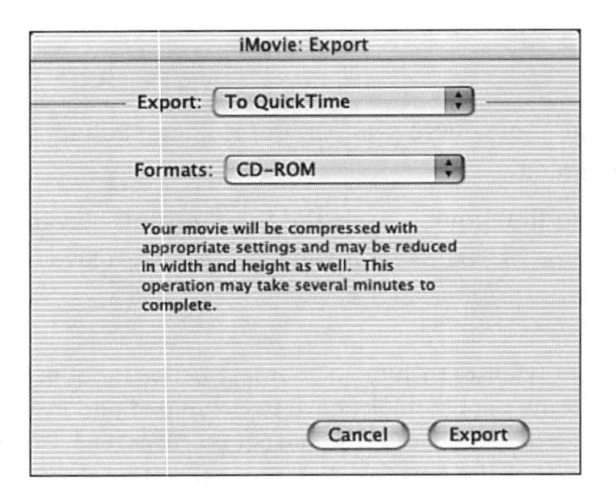

FIGURE 17.14
Exporting an iMovie for delivery on CD-ROM.

3. Click Export and save your file in a location on your hard drive where you can find it later.
4. Using your CD-burning software (such as Toast), drag your CD-ROM movie file into the program and burn a data CD (as opposed to an audio/music CD). Choose a format that's compatible with the computer of the person you're burning it for, such as the Mac OS/PC Hybrid CD option in Toast, which makes the CD-ROM compatible with either Mac or PC.

Exporting iMovies to iDVD

Distributing your iMovies on DVD is the ultimate in digital video. You start by recording your footage digitally, editing in iMovie, and retaining the digital quality by going directly to DVD. iMovie makes creating DVDs simple by linking up with iDVD.

Be aware that you can't use iDVD unless you have a Mac with Apple's SuperDrive, which can read and write both CDs and DVDs.

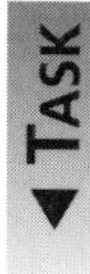

Task: Exporting to iDVD

While there is an Export To iDVD option in the Export dialog box, the message, shown in Figure 17.15, tells you that it is no longer necessary to export to iDVD because iMovie prepares projects for iDVD every time they are saved. You can still choose to "export" your project this way.

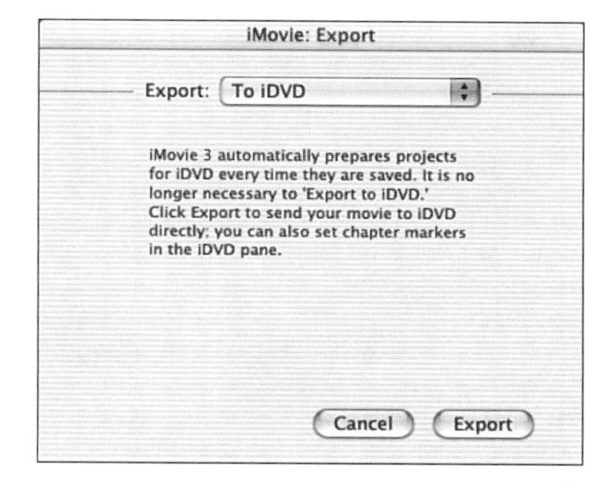

FIGURE 17.15
Exporting an iMovie for iDVD.

Alternatively, you could open the iDVD palette on the right side of the iMovie interface and click the button for Create iDVD Project. It will take a moment for your movie to open in iDVD where you can customize the menus and add additional movies.

Task: Adding Chapters to Your Movie

Besides maintaining video quality, DVDs offer another benefit to your iMovies: chapters. Adding chapters allow you to segment your video project so that people viewing the completed DVD can skip straight to the part they want to see, just like on a commercial DVD.

Follow these steps to add chapters to an existing iMovie.

1. Open a finished iMovie project and make sure you are in Timeline view.
2. Click on the iDVD button in the main iMovie window to display the iDVD palette.
3. In the Timeline viewer, move the playhead to the point in your movie at which you want to start a new chapter.
4. In the iDVD palette, click the Add Chapter button.
5. A row for the newly created chapter will appear in the iDVD palette, where you can type in a Chapter Title, as shown in Figure 17.16.
6. A small yellow diamond will appear in the Timeline viewer to mark the location of chapters, as shown in Figure 17.17.

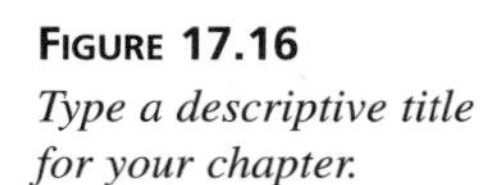

FIGURE 17.16
Type a descriptive title for your chapter.

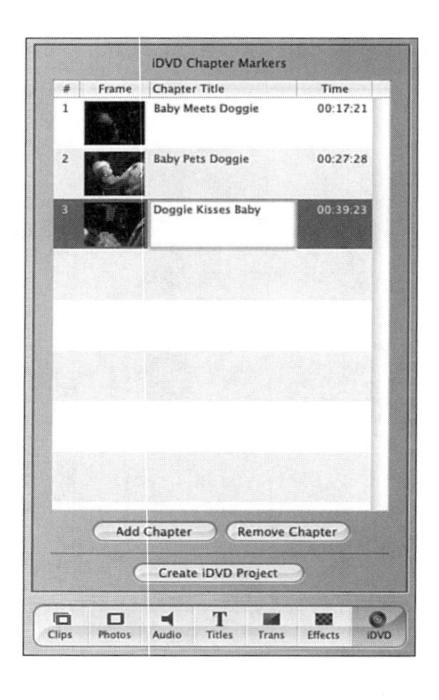

FIGURE 17.17
Chapter markers will appear as yellow diamonds at the top of the Timeline.

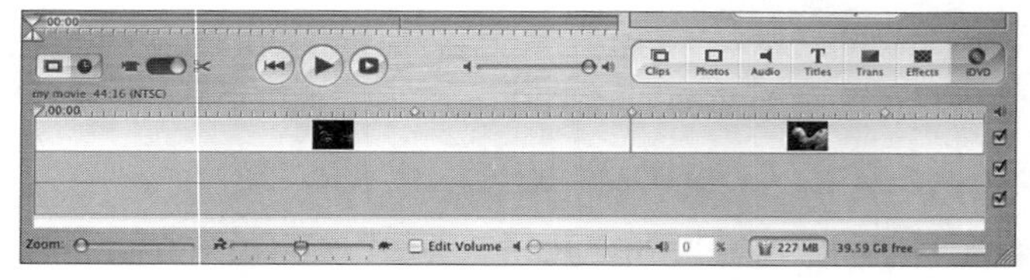

7. You can repeat steps 4 through 6 until you've added up to 36 chapters to your iMovie.
8. When you are finished adding chapters, click the Create iDVD Project button to open your iMovie in iDVD, as shown in Figure 17.18, where you can choose themes to customize the menu that displays your chapters. Before iDVD can be launched, you will be asked to save your project.

   By default, iDVD saves your project in the Documents folder of your user account with the file extension .dvdproj. (We talk about customizing your presentation in iDVD in Chapters 18 through 20.)

FIGURE 17.18
This is an iMovie with chapters after export to iDVD.

Summary

In this chapter, you learned how to take your iMovies and share them in a number of different ways. Some methods, such as streaming Web video, might require more effort than others, but learning how to put an iMovie on the Web can open up new audiences for your creative works. You literally gain the ability to go worldwide with your iMovies!

CHAPTER 18

Getting Started with iDVD

Anyone who has a Mac with a SuperDrive can now make DVD productions using inexpensive hardware and software that only used to be within the reach of Hollywood studios. In this lesson, we begin with a look at DVD basics by investigating the way that DVD video works as well as how iDVD works with video. We then take a look at iDVD, Apple's revolutionary, easy-to-use DVD-authoring software. Finally, we take a closer look at DVD discs themselves and various types of DVD discs, including the kind that you use with iDVD and the built-in SuperDrive.

DVD Players

DVD players make the whole DVD experience possible. In the early days, as in the early days of CD players, prices were high and the availability of DVDs to rent or purchase was limited.

But more recently, sales of DVD players have exceeded sales of VCRs for the first time, even though the vast majority of them won't *record* DVD discs. It's just now that you can find DVD recorders that function like a DVD equivalent of VCRs (see Figure 18.1).

FIGURE 18.1
A typical DVD player from Pioneer.

In the present generation of DVD players and recorders, they all offer the same compatibility with DVD features. DVD manufacturers got together and agreed on what the players would support so that you could take any DVD and play it on any brand of DVD player in your region. (The world is divided into regions, so a DVD from one region will not play in another.)

The DVD Creation Revolution

iDVD is a part of history because before Apple introduced it in early 2001, the only tools available for people who wanted to make their own DVDs were prohibitively expensive.

Not only was the software complex and pricey, but the DVD burners themselves cost more than many computer systems. For example, before iDVD came out, the only available DVD burner cost about 4,000 U.S. dollars, the Pioneer DVR-S201, shown in Figure 18.2.

FIGURE 18.2
Pioneer DVR-S201 DVD burner.

Basically, Apple got together with a few different companies including Pioneer, and made some deals that benefited the digital video–making public. The result was that Apple was able to introduce a desktop G4 Power Mac model that included a DVD burner, as well as iDVD software, for the same price that just a DVD burner alone cost at the time. This DVD burner, known as the SuperDrive, brought the power of DVD authoring to the masses, giving them the ability to take digital video and make it into *DVD video* (see Figure 18.3).

FIGURE 18.3
The revolutionary SuperDrive, on countless desktops around the world, with a blank DVD disc. Thanks, Apple.

Apple issued an important update for some SuperDrive-equipped computers. This update prevents permanent drive damage when some models of SuperDrive manufactured by Pioneer are used with newer high speed media. To see if you need to install this update, follow these steps:

1. Open the Apple System Profiler application, which can be found in the Utilities folder in the Applications folder.
2. Open the Devices and Volumes tab.
3. Expand the CD-RW/DVD-R item by clicking the disclosure triangle.
4. Examine the information given. If Pioneer is the vendor, you may need the update. To find out for sure, look at the Product Identification code. For drives with the Product Identification DVR-104, no update is required if the Device Revision number is A227 or higher. For drives with the Product Identification DVR-103, no update is required if the Device Revision number is 1.90 or higher.

If your drive comes from Pioneer and doesn't have the upgrade in place, go to the Apple Web site (`www.apple.com`), search for "SuperDrive update," and then download and install it before attempting to write a DVD.

How DVD Video Works

DVD video is a form of *digital* video, and much like the way that digital video is stored on a computer hard drive, digital video is stored as data files on the DVD disc. When you insert a DVD disc in a player that's connected to a television, a small computer in the DVD player looks for the DVD video files and displays them on the TV screen.

When you watch or make a DVD, there are two types of video that you can experience: regular video such as a movie (as seen in Figure 18.4), and video that's contained in a motion menu.

FIGURE 18.4
Watching regular video in a DVD.

A *motion menu* is simply any screen on a DVD from which you're making menu choices and something is moving in the background behind the DVD menu. iDVD refers to the video used in motion menus as *background video* (see Figure 18.5).

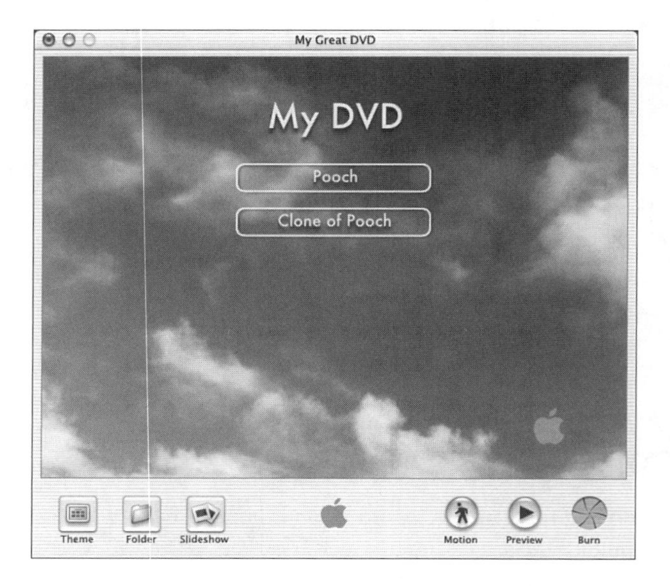

FIGURE 18.5
A DVD motion menu with background video of clouds slowly passing by, which adds an interesting touch to an otherwise motionless DVD menu.

One of the advantages of iDVD is that it enables you to incorporate motion menus in your DVDs by allowing you to choose from various customizable motion menu backgrounds. The creation of motion menus normally can be a complex process, but iDVD gives you the advantage of motion menus without all the hassle.

Working with DVD Video

There are four stages of working with DVD video: preparing, importing, encoding, and burning.

- **Preparing**—In this stage, you edit your video in iMovie and export it in an appropriate format for iDVD. Using a program like iDVD is also known as *DVD authoring*. You'll find that you spend more time preparing the files for your DVD than you spend on any other task. After the files are ready, it's easy to put the DVD together.
- **Importing**—To use your video in iDVD, you must import it into the project you're working on.
- **Encoding**—Digital video must be encoded into the MPEG-2 format for it to work with DVD. In the field of DVD authoring, there are a number of different techniques and tools for encoding video for use in DVD.

For example, DVD Studio Pro is a professional DVD-authoring program—iDVD's "older cousin"—and it uses a separate program for encoding with a number of adjustable settings. There are people in Hollywood known as *compressionists* whose primary task is to use advanced programs to encode video into MPEG-2 format; they attempt to squeeze the highest amount of quality out of the video that will fit on the DVD. iMovie will do your encoding for you.

- **Burning**—When you're done creating your DVD project, you're ready to burn a DVD disc. With iDVD, you insert a blank disc and burn it using the built-in SuperDrive that came with your Mac.

What Is Multiplexing?

When you burn a DVD disc, iDVD has to prepare the files in a process known as *multiplexing*. Multiplexing allows the files to be understood by a DVD player. Multiplexing basically means that iDVD is translating the files into a proper DVD format, which you'll see in the following task.

▼ TASK

Task: Examining a DVD

To get a better sense of what's going on under the hood of a DVD, try taking a closer look at a DVD movie that you own or have rented using your Mac as a "DVD microscope."

18

If you recall from Chapter 5, "Using Other Basic Applications," DVD Player is a program that plays DVDs on your computer desktop.

1. Insert the DVD in the DVD drive on your Mac.
2. Wait a few moments. If your Mac automatically launches the DVD player software, either quit out of the software entirely by pressing Command-Q or choose Quit from the DVD Player menu. If the DVD is taking up the entire screen, you can move the mouse up to the top of the screen to reveal the menu.

The first time you insert a DVD into your drive, you will be asked to set a drive region. Once set, your DVD drive will automatically read disks encoded for that region. If you should need to play a disc from another region, insert it and DVD Player will ask if it should change your region code. Keep in mind, however, that your drive region can only be changed 5 times following the initial setting. After that, it will keep whichever region settings were made last.

▼

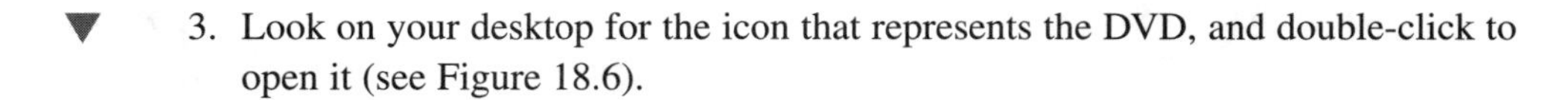

3. Look on your desktop for the icon that represents the DVD, and double-click to open it (see Figure 18.6).

FIGURE 18.6
The DVD icon that appears on the Mac desktop when a DVD is inserted.

4. When the window that represents the DVD opens up, you'll see a `VIDEO_TS` folder. This same folder is on *every* DVD that you can watch in a DVD player. If the `VIDEO_TS` folder isn't there, the DVD player won't understand the disc. Double-click the `VIDEO_TS` folder (see Figure 18.7) to open it.

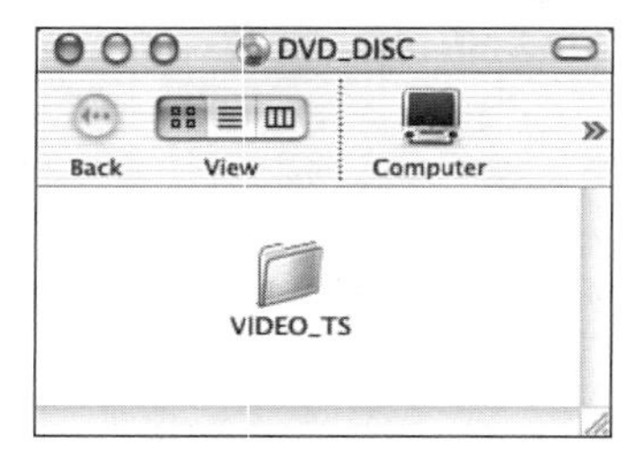

FIGURE 18.7
The infamous `VIDEO_TS` *folder is present on every DVD.*

5. When the `VIDEO_TS` folder opens, you might want to choose View, As List to see the files better (see Figure 18.8).

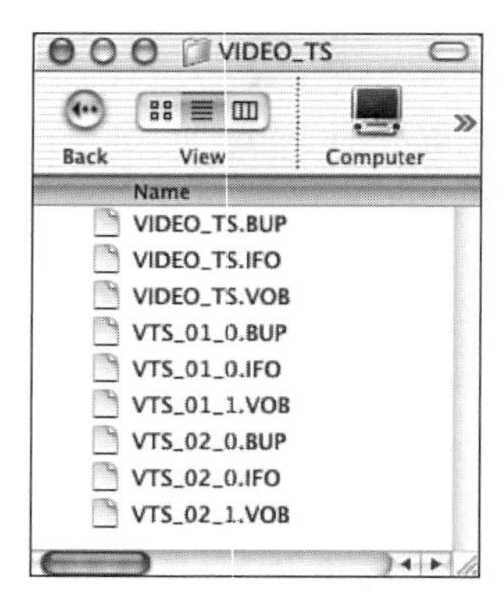

FIGURE 18.8
The files within the `VIDEO_TS` *folder, which contain everything a DVD player needs to create the interactive experience.*

It isn't particularly important to understand what the individual files in a `VIDEO_TS` folder do, but it can be interesting to look at things from the perspective of what a DVD player does. At this point, the digital video files within a `VIDEO_TS` folder have been encoded into MPEG-2 and multiplexed into their final DVD-ready form.

The following list explains what the file extensions (the last three letters of the file) mean for files on a DVD:

- **IFO** (stands for *information*)—These files contain the information about the DVD menu screens that a DVD player uses to construct the interactive experience.
- **BUP** (stands for *backup*)—These files are simply copies of the IFO files.
- **VOB** (stands for *video objects*)—These files are the actual video on the DVD.

Basic iDVD Features

It used to be that putting together a DVD project was a very complex process, requiring the DVD author to perform a great number of steps and have a significant amount of knowledge about the underlying technology. iDVD simplifies the process of DVD authoring—it's as easy as dragging and dropping files into the iDVD window.

The other great thing about iDVD is that it's not only a DVD-authoring program, but it also includes built-in DVD menu design, which basically means that you can make your DVD screens inside the program. This is another area in which DVD authors used to have to spend a lot of time outside the DVD-authoring program creating graphics and designing backgrounds. iDVD includes a number of customizable designs, called themes, that are ready to go.

Themes

The defining characteristic of a DVD is that it gives you the ability to watch digital video interactively on your television. It's possible to make a DVD disc that goes directly to the video when you put it into a DVD player, but most DVDs have some kind of menu. A DVD *menu* is simply a screen that gives you several choices, with selectable buttons of some kind that lead directly to video or to other menus (see Figure 18.9).

Apple, with its consistently good taste, has put together a number of built-in, customizable themes and styles in iDVD, which give you the ability to make DVDs professional-looking menus. Themes are like costumes for a DVD screen. They include different background and button designs that enable you to express yourself and create a unique space to drop your iMovies into.

By default, the Apple logo is shown in the lower right hand corner of all the themes. To remove it, open the iDVD preferences and uncheck the box for Show Apple Logo Watermark.

FIGURE 18.9
A simple DVD menu with a number of choices with the currently selected choice highlighted.

iDVD includes a central window, as shown in Figure 18.10, where you can easily try out different themes, some of which allow you to add your own photos as background.

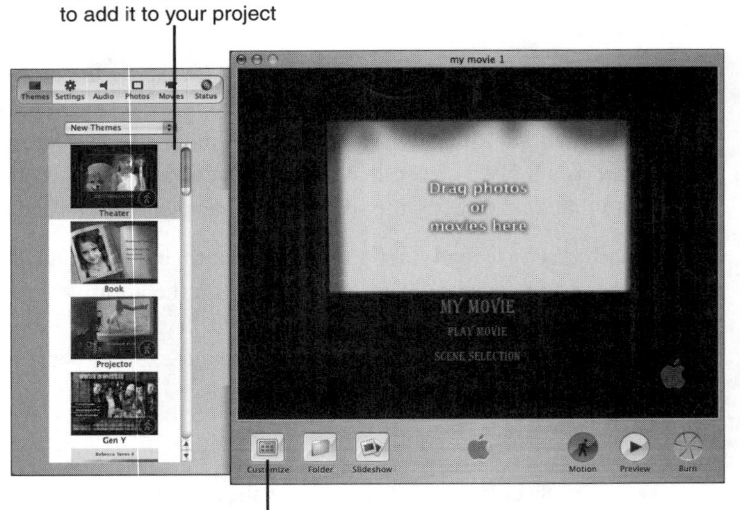

FIGURE 18.10
Choosing a theme in iDVD.

Some of the available themes actually have video clips as backgrounds, and some also include sound. These themes enable you to include what's known as a *motion menu* on your DVD. You can even set your own motion backgrounds in some themes by dragging a movie into the drop zone. You might discover (if you haven't already) that sometimes when you're working on a DVD project, you want to turn off the motion. This is accomplished simply by clicking the Motion button, as shown in Figure 18.11.

FIGURE 18.11
The Motion button to turn on or off motion menus.

You can use the Motion button to turn a motion menu on to see how it looks and then turn the video or sound off while you continue working on your project.

When you want to go beyond the automatic colors that are chosen for text, you can open the Settings panel to select custom colors for text (see Figure 18.12).

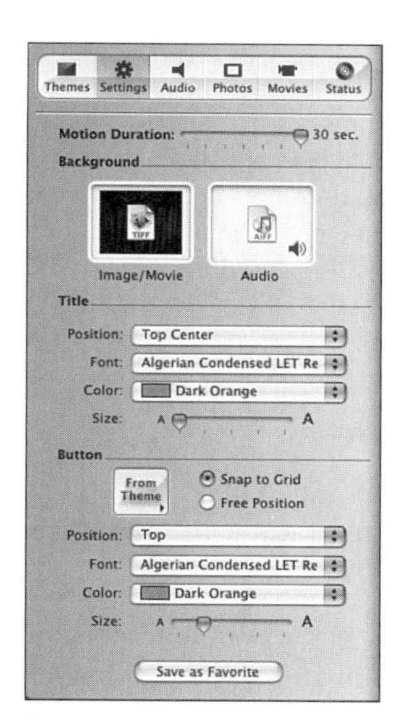

FIGURE 18.12
iDVD gives you the ability to choose your own color and font for text.

Another great feature of iDVD is that it enables you to choose different styles of button shapes for your DVD screens. (These options are also available from the Settings panel shown in Figure 18.12.) In essence, you don't have to be a graphic designer to have good-looking DVD screens, but iDVD makes it easy to experiment and play with different options if you want to.

When you choose to customize your DVD, and if you like what you've done, you can save the settings for later use in a Favorites list. A customized theme can be saved so that you can access it later for other projects, as shown in Figure 18.13.

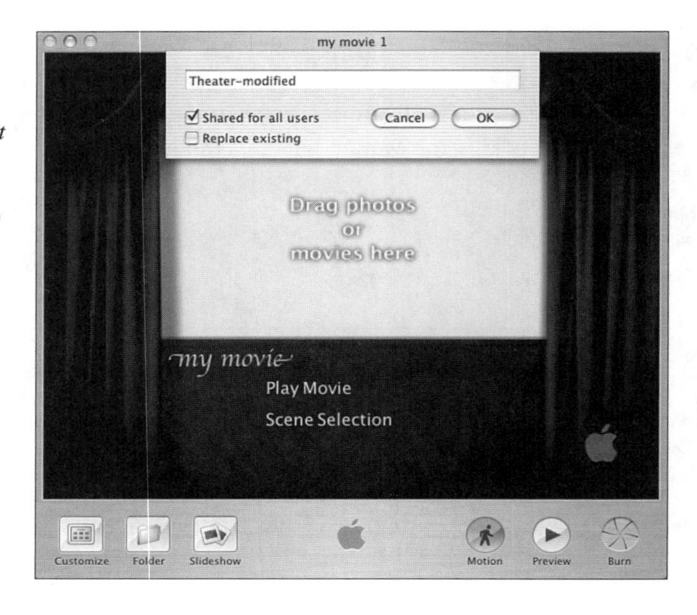

FIGURE 18.13
Saving a customized theme in the Favorites list. (Notice how the text on this screen differs from the original theme shown in Figure 18.10.)

While you can add individual elements (such as movies and slide shows) to your DVD, you can also create folders in the menu and add a secondary menu in which to add even more elements. Simply click the Folder button at the bottom of the iDVD window. Double-clicking a folder will open it, so you can add content and even apply a completely different theme!

Audio, Photos, and Movies

You can insert a variety of DVD content, including music, still photos, and movies. The Audio palette, shown in Figure 18.14, integrates with your iTunes library to allow you to add background music to your chosen DVD theme.

Besides integrating with your iTunes library, iDVD connects directly to your iPhoto library. From the Photos palette, shown in 18.15, you can drag-and-drop photos to create Slideshows, which we'll look at shortly, or to customize themes that contain drop zones. (Refer to Figure 18.9 for an example of a theme containing a drop zone.)

Be sure you've upgraded your version of iPhoto to at least version 2 and launched iPhoto at least once (so it can perform file system changes) before trying to integrate with iDVD.

FIGURE 18.14
Select songs from your iTunes library.

FIGURE 18.15
Drag and drop photos from your iPhoto library.

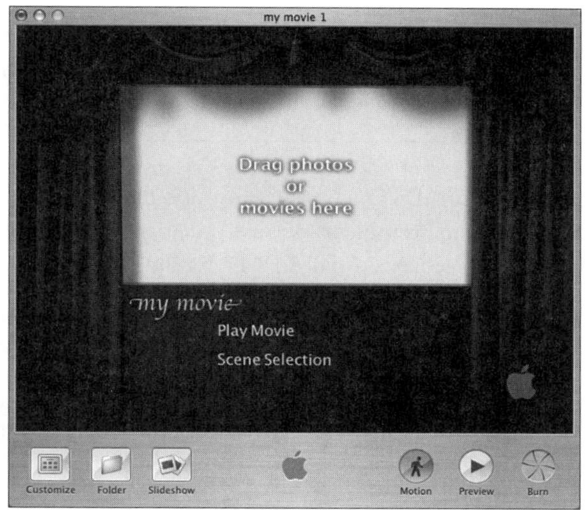

The Movies palette lists all the movies stored in the current user's Movies folder, which is the default location for iMovie to store your projects.

Slideshows

DVD slideshows can be a nice way to share digital pictures, so that people who watch your DVD can see the pictures on their televisions. Just as when you're working with video clips in iDVD, a slideshow is as easy as dragging and dropping digital pictures into the iDVD window (see Figure 18.16).

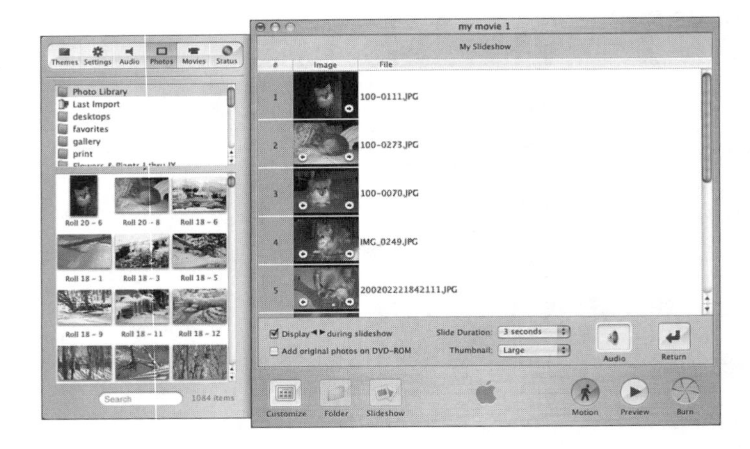

FIGURE 18.16
Slideshow editing window with individual images.

When you drag digital pictures into the editing window, you can easily rearrange them and preview the show, just as you might have done with a traditional slide projector and the infamous slide sorter.

> You may recall from Chapter 12, "Using iPhoto," that you can easily export a slideshow created in iPhoto to iDVD.

There's also an option for iDVD to draw arrows on the screen so when a person views your DVD, there's a visual reminder to press the arrow keys on the remote to select which slide he wants to see. See Figure 18.17 for an example.

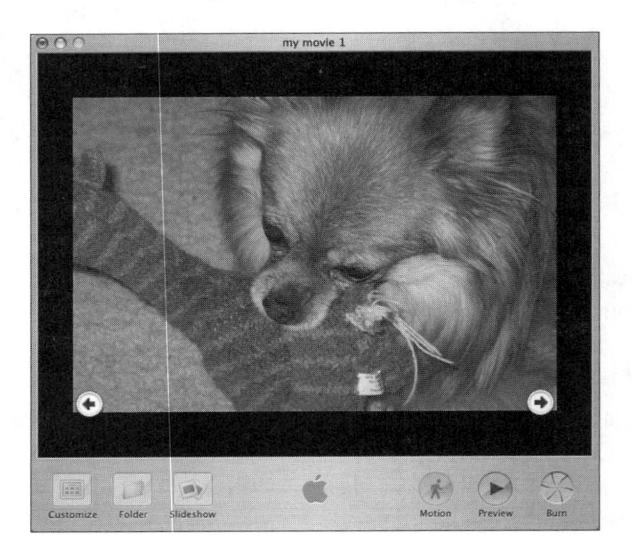

FIGURE 18.17
Slideshow preview showing arrows that indicate there are additional slides to view.

Status

When you make your own DVDs, at some point in the process the computer system has to *encode* the video into a special format (MPEG-2) so that a DVD player can play it properly.

It used to be that you had to use a separate program and adjust a variety of advanced settings to prepare video for DVD. In iDVD, you simply drag your iMovie into the program, and—if iMovie hasn't already encoded it—iDVD automatically encodes the video for you as you work on your project. And if you want to check in on how things are going, iDVD can give you an update on how the encoding is coming along, when you open the Customize tray window and click on the Status tab, as shown in Figure 18.18.

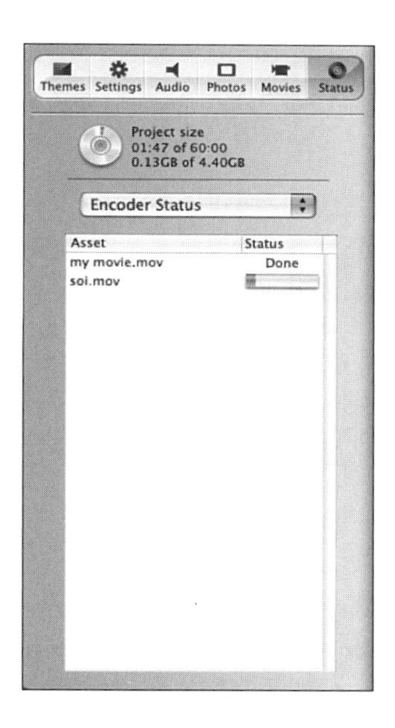

FIGURE 18.18
Taking a look at how encoding is going.

You can also use the Status palette to add DVD-ROM content to your DVD and to organize that "bonus" material into folders.

Disc Burning

When you've finished your DVD project, you probably want to preview it first by clicking the Preview button, and then you're ready to burn a DVD disc. You simply click the Burn button to activate it (see Figure 18.19), and then click it again.

FIGURE 18.19
Clicking the Burn button.

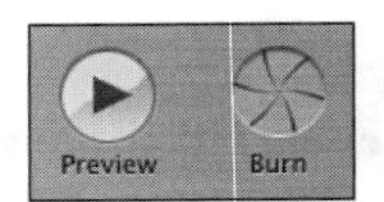

Before

After

When you click the Burn button a second time, the SuperDrive opens. You can insert your DVD disc (see Figure 18.20), and you're off!

FIGURE 18.20
Clicking Burn causes the SuperDrive to open, and you can insert a blank DVD.

DVD Discs

There are many DVD formats and options out there, and the new variety of recordable disc formats could lead to some confusion when you're at a store trying to figure out which kind of blank disc to purchase. This potentially frustrating situation with DVD formats has been brought about by competition among the makers of DVD players who are pitting DVD-R against DVD+RW and so on. But a simple review of what DVD discs are, and what kind are compatible with your Mac, will prepare you to avoid the confusion and get on with having fun.

Recordable DVDs

Recordable DVDs (DVD-R) enable you to write data a single time to a disc. They're much like the CD-R discs that are so popular these days. Much like the phenomena of dropping prices with CD burners and recordable CDs, the price of making your own DVDs will continue to drop.

The kind of recordable DVDs that you can use with the built-in SuperDrive on your Mac are known as DVD-R media, which technically speaking, is called DVD-R General media. In most cases, when people refer to recordable discs, they don't specify DVD-R General media—they drop the word *general* (see Figure 18.21).

DVD-R compatibility is an important factor to take into account when you're considering distribution of a DVD project on DVD-R media. Theoretically, if you make a DVD project and burn a DVD-R disc, that DVD-R disc should play in the majority of DVD players. The newer the player is, the more likely it is to be compatible with DVD-R media. And, vice versa, the older a player is, the less likely it is to accept DVD-R media.

FIGURE 18.21
Apple's DVD-R media, blank and ready to go.

There are compatibility lists online at a variety of sources, including `www.apple.com/dvd/compatibility/`, where companies and individuals have tested DVD-R media with a wide range of players. The questions to ask are what kind of project are you going to share? and what kind of audience is it?

Manufactured DVDs

The only way to guarantee 100% compatibility with all DVD players is to manufacture a DVD. This means sending the project off to be manufactured by automated machinery. There are companies like EMVUSA (`www.emvusa.com`) who are aggressively going after the do-it-yourself DVD market by offering attractive pricing and accepting DVD-R media as a master disc. Accepting DVD-R media as a master disc is a break from the tradition of requiring a DVD project to be submitted on a special format known as *DLT*, or digital linear tape.

In addition to compatibility, other things you gain are the ability to have more professional packaging and a better-looking disc. When a DVD is manufactured, a design is imprinted directly on the DVD itself, rather than a label being applied.

Some advanced DVD formats, designed primarily to allow longer movies or additional footage, have more than one side or more than one layer within the DVD, as seen in Table 18.1.

TABLE 18.1 Capacities of Various Manufactured DVD Formats

Format	*Approximate Capacity*	*Number of Sides*	*Number of Layers*
DVD-5	4.4 gigabytes (4.7 billion bytes)	1	1
DVD-9	7.95 gigabytes (8.5 billion bytes)	1	2
DVD-10	8.75 gigabytes (9.4 billion bytes)	2	1
DVD-18	17.5 gigabytes (18.8 billion bytes)	2	2

Rewritable DVDs

The development of the SuperDrive was a joint effort between Apple and Pioneer, and in addition to recording to CD-Rs, CD-RWs and DVD-Rs, the mechanism that's used in the SuperDrive has the capability to record to DVD-RW discs (see Figure 18.22).

FIGURE 18.22
Pioneer's DVD-RW discs, compatible with the SuperDrive.

You can record to a DVD-R disc only once. At the time of writing, the best price you can get for DVD-R media is $3.00 (U.S.) each, so blank DVDs are still fairly pricey. So, if you're just testing your project, and essentially use the DVD-R disc only once, you're out a few bucks.

> At the time of writing, $3.00 U.S. is a common price that can be found when doing a price search on a Web site such as `cnet.com`.

This makes the idea of using a DVD-RW disc even more appealing. It's a great way to back up video files and to move DVD-related files from one place to another. DVD-RW discs are twice as expensive, but you can use them over and over again.

> Apple doesn't emphasize the fact that the SuperDrive can burn DVD-RW discs, and perhaps for good reason. DVD-RW discs are compatible with only about 70% of DVD players out there, compared with DVD-R discs, which are compatible with closer to 90%.

DVD Storage Capacity

Unless you plan to include computer files on your DVD, as we'll discuss in Chapter 20, "Creating DVDs with iDVD," the best way to think of DVD storage capacity with iDVD is in terms of how many minutes of video you can fit on the disc. The amount of video you can fit on a disc is determined by how much the video is compressed. Because iDVD does the encoding automatically, the limit is about 90 minutes of video on the disc.

If you're talking about the disc in terms of bytes and megabytes, however, you might be familiar with the often-quoted measurement of 4.7 gigabytes (GB)—that is, the claim that you can store up to 4.7 gigabytes of data on a single-layer DVD disc.

This is only partially true. If you were putting data files on a DVD and had 4.7 gigabytes' worth of files on your computer, you'd find that you can fit only about 4.37GB on the DVD—this has to do with the difference between the way data is stored on a computer hard drive and the way it's stored on a DVD. Essentially, you can store 4.7 billion bytes of data on a DVD, but only about 4.37GB.

But regardless of how you look at it, DVD is an incredible medium. The CD format typically allows only 650MB of data on a disc, whereas the DVD format enables you to put up to 4,370MB on a disc! To put this in perspective, consider that many computers you see on the shelves in stores are likely to have 3.5" floppy disk drives. Each of these plastic floppies holds about 1MB of data, so a DVD disc holds the equivalent of about 4,370 floppy disks! (See Figure 18.23.)

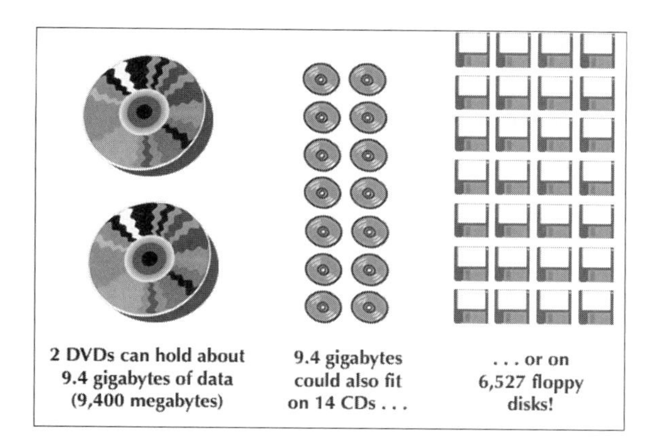

FIGURE 18.23
The relative capacities of different storage methods.

Purchasing the Right Blank DVD Discs

The easiest thing to do when you need to purchase blank discs is to get them directly from Apple, which ensures compatibility and has always had good pricing.

But if you want to get blank DVDS on your own, make sure that you're purchasing DVD-R General media. If the product packaging or salesperson says that the disc is DVD-R but there's no indication of whether or not it's General, chances are that you're fine. You'll occasionally come across DVD-R Authoring media, which won't work in the SuperDrive.

Another thing to look out for if you're shopping for blank discs is that you're purchasing DVD-R (minus R) media and not DVD+R (plus R) or DVD+RW (plus RW) discs. The plus discs are designed for other kinds of DVD burners.

To get a better sense of things, glance through Table 18.2, which gives a good indication of the situation consumers face as a result of the Format Wars. (It's sort of like the VHS versus Betamax competition when VCRs first came out. But, in a nutshell, DVD-R is better and more compatible with DVD players, and that's what you have in the Mac, so get DVD-R media.)

TABLE 18.2 DVD Recordable Media

Format	*Features*	*Compatibility with SuperDrive*
DVD-R (General)	Can be recorded to once	Yes
DVD-R (Authoring)	Designed for older DVD burners; easy to confuse with DVD-R General media	No
DVD-RW	Can be recorded to many times (up to 1,000 times)	Yes (Note: Projects burned to DVD-RW discs are compatible with only about 70% of DVD players)
DVD+R (plus R)	Similar to DVD-R	No
DVD+RW (plus RW)	Similar to DVD-RW	No

Summary

In this chapter, you learned the basics of iDVD as well as some background about DVDs in general. You became acquainted with iDVD and the various options it provides for making a variety of DVD projects that can include a combination of movies and digital pictures. You also learned all about DVD discs—the final goal of every iDVD project.

Chapter 19

Designing DVDs in iDVD

In this chapter, we'll delve into constructing a DVD—from adding content to customizing the look of the menus. We'll also learn some tips and tricks for getting started with a project. Let's start there—at the beginning!

Preparing the DVD Project

To begin, we start a new project in iDVD, adjust a few settings, and generally get things off the ground. There are no particular rules about what you have to do first, but in general it's a good idea to get in the habit of saving your project frequently. As you work on your project, you can get in the habit of choosing File, Save at regular intervals so that you don't lose your work if lightning happens to strike or your Mac freezes up for some reason.

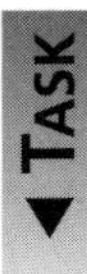

Task: Preparing the DVD Project

To prepare for this project, we get a few things in order to set the stage for importing video into the DVD project:

1. Launch iDVD and create a new project. You will be prompted to name and save your project automatically.

> The name you give your project is the name that will be automatically applied to the DVD disc when you burn your completed project. However, you can change the original project name to a different one by choosing Project > Project Info from the menu at the top of your screen. Then, in the window that opens, simply type a new Disc Name and click OK.

2. Choose iDVD, Preferences to bring up the Preferences dialog box (see Figure 19.1).

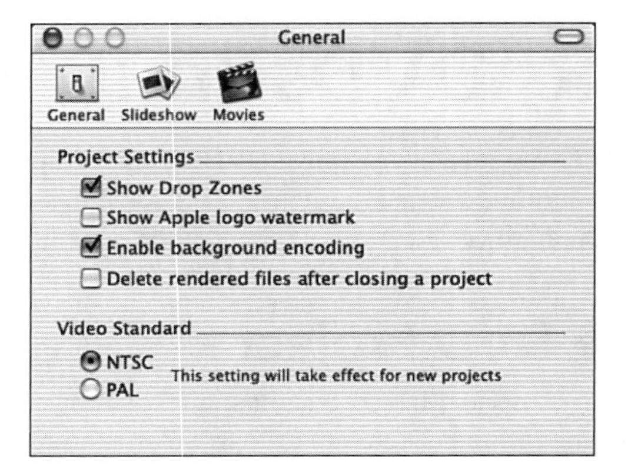

FIGURE 19.1
The iDVD Preferences dialog box.

3. In the Preferences dialog box, click to uncheck the Show Apple Logo Watermark option. This removes the Apple logo from the lower-right corner of the DVD production. Of course, you can leave it in if you want.
4. In the main iDVD window, click the Customize button in the lower-left corner, click the Themes tab if necessary, and click to select a theme (see Figure 19.2). (Using the popup menu in the Themes tab, you can choose to view Old Themes, New Themes, or All. You can also view a subset of Themes you've customized and saved as Favorites.)
5. To customize the title in your theme, click the text so that it's selected (as shown in Figure 19.3) and you can start typing.

FIGURE 19.2
You can use the iDVD Themes menu to select a background for your iDVD project. In our example, we use the Theater theme.

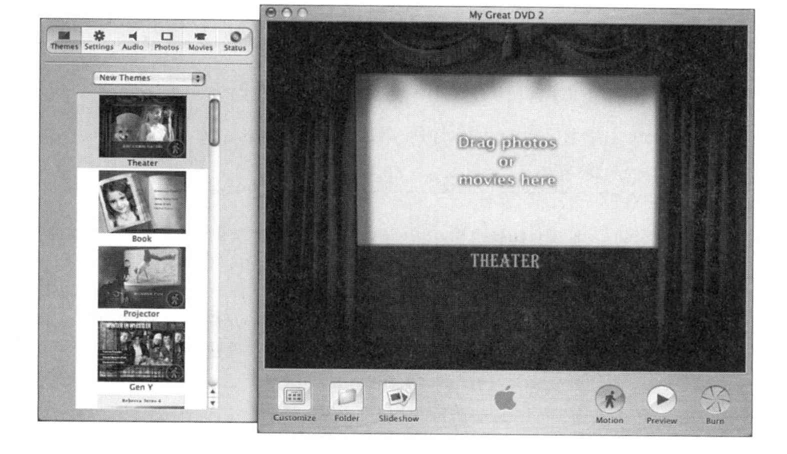

FIGURE 19.3
The placeholder text "Theater" can be replaced with your own text.

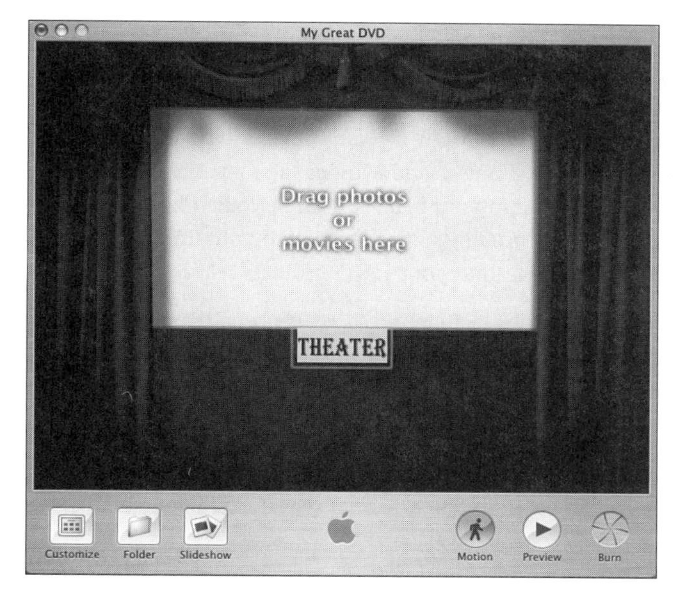

19

Importing Files

You learned in Chapter 17, "Exporting iMovies," that you can create an iDVD project directly from iMovie if you'd like. That would open your iMovie directly into iDVD, including any chapter markers you've added to make it easier for viewers to skip to specific scenes.

If you wanted to add clips rather than your entire iMovie, there are three methods for importing video:

1. Select File, Import, Video.
2. Open the Movies tab in the Customize tray window.
3. Drag the file directly into the DVD from a Finder window.

Remember that video clips imported with iMovie have automatically been encoded in the appropriate format for them to be compatible with iDVD. iDVD supports only QuickTime movies with linear video tracks. Other formats, such as QuickTime VR, MPEG, Flash, streaming or encrypted movies, or QuickTime spanned movies, cannot be added to your iDVD project.

If you try to import a file that is not compatible with iDVD, a message saying "Unsupported File Type" will appear.

Using the iMedia Browsers

The integration between the applications that make up iLife (iTunes, iPhoto, iMovie, and iDVD) is apparent in iDVD's iMedia browser tabs. "iMedia browsers" is the collective term for the Audio, Photos, and Movies tabs—which link directly to the folders on your hard drive that contain your iTunes library, your iPhoto library, and the default location for storing iMovie projects. These tabs give you direct access to these elements so you can incorporate them into your DVD projects.

In order for these tabs to function, however, you need to make sure you are using compatible versions of each of the i-applications. Please see Chapter 10, "Introducing iLife," for more information.

To use the Audio and Photos browser tabs, you will also need to have opened iTunes and iPhoto at least once after they've been updated to compatible versions so your media libraries can be cataloged in a format that iDVD understands.

While iPhoto and iTunes make it more difficult to move the location of your media, iMovie lets you store your movie files anywhere you'd like. To solve the problem of the Movies browser not knowing where to locate your movies files, you can add paths to them in the Movies section of the iDVD preferences.

TASK

Task: Importing Video Files

When you choose a theme for your DVD in iDVD, the DVD buttons consist of either small images or text buttons that represent the video you've imported.

1. Open the folder containing your video clips and drag one directly from the Finder into the iDVD window (see Figure 19.4).

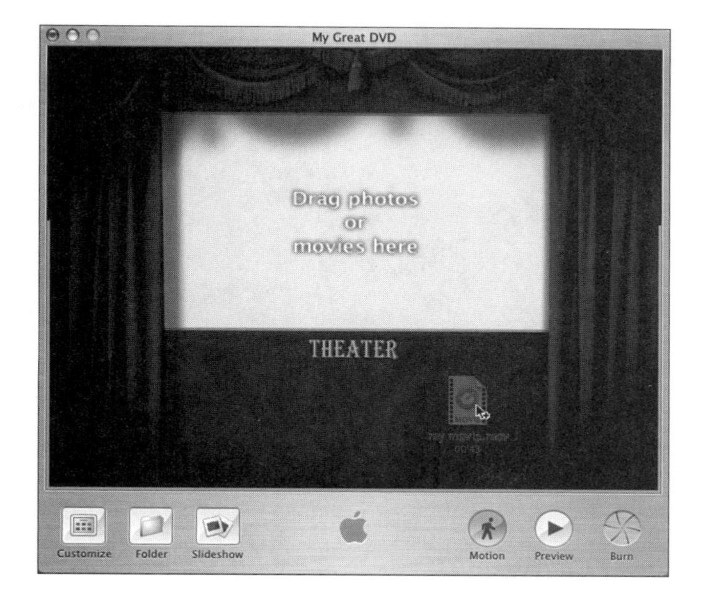

FIGURE 19.4
You can drag QuickTime movies (at the left) directly into the iDVD window, and the filename becomes the DVD button name.

2. Continue dragging the clips into the project, until you end up with something like Figure 19.5.
3. At this point, you could click the Preview button in the main iDVD window to preview the project, which is always a good way of seeing whether things turned out the way you wanted them to.

As you add files to your project, it's wise to keep an eye on the size of your files. (DVDs hold a lot of information, but video takes up a lot of space!) You can monitor the size of your project in the Status tab, as seen in Figure 19.6.

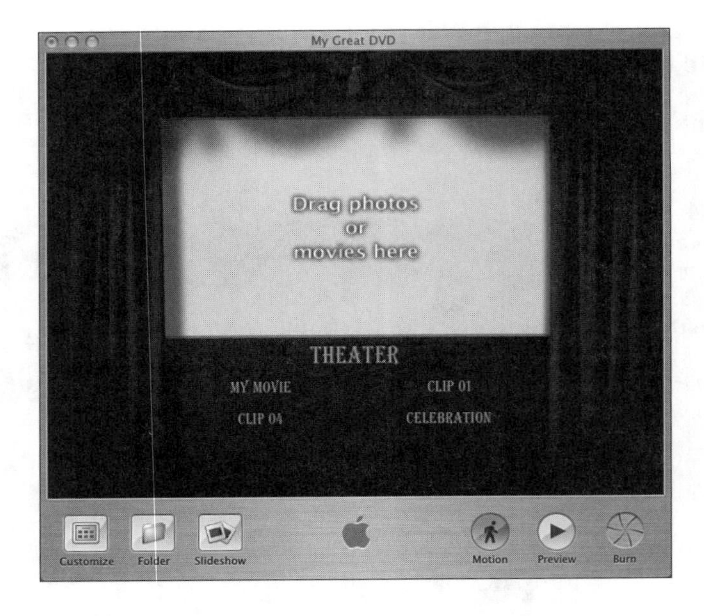

FIGURE 19.5
iDVD automatically creates titles from the filenames of the imported QuickTime movies.

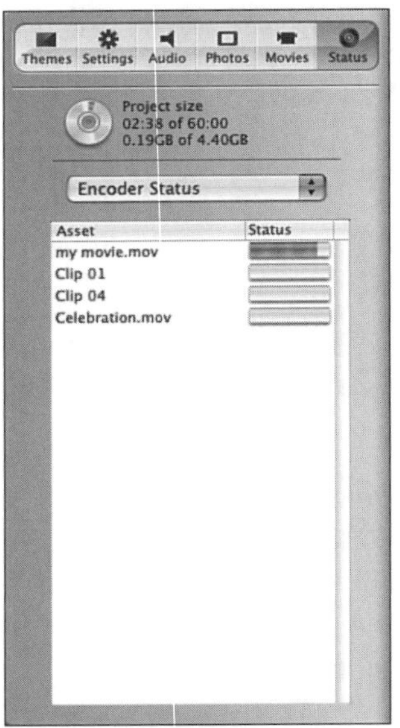

FIGURE 19.6
Encoder status: iDVD encodes your video clips while you work on your project.

▲ Remember, you may need to click the Customize button to get to the Status tab.

iDVD Capabilities

When you're just starting out with a few video clips and DVD screens, you might not need to think much about exceeding iDVD's capabilities. But at some point you'll probably be curious about how many minutes of video you can fit on a DVD, how many menu screens you can have, and so on.

- **Items on a menu = 6**—When you create a DVD, the buttons on the menu screen can lead to movies, slideshows, or other menus. iDVD enables you to have up to six buttons on each screen.
- **Images in a slideshow = 99**—You can add up to 99 digital pictures to each slideshow that you have on your DVD.
- **Movies/slideshows on a DVD = 99**—You can add a total of 99 movies and or slideshows to a DVD project, assuming that the total amount of video used in the movie portion of your DVD does not exceed 90 minutes. Because digital pictures take up a relatively small amount of space, you don't have to be concerned about how many pictures you add.
- **Motion menus in a DVD = 30**—Because motion menus use short video clips, you're limited to using 30 of them on a DVD project, whether you are using a motion menu from a built-in theme or importing your own.
- **Minutes of video in a DVD = 90**—The total number of minutes of video you can fit on a DVD is 90 minutes, or one and a half hours.
- **Encoding for 60 minutes or less = high quality**—If you use less than an hour of video, iDVD encodes your movies at the highest quality setting.

  Technically speaking, iDVD automatically encodes your video at a particular *bit rate*, a setting that essentially determines the quality of your video.

  When computers encode video, the higher the bit rate that's used, the higher quality video you get. And when you have a higher bit rate, the video takes up more space on the disc.

  So, when you have less than one hour of video in a DVD project, iDVD encodes the video at a bit rate of 8 megabits per second (8 Mbps).
- **Encoding for 90 minutes or less = good quality**—When you have between 60 and 90 minutes of video, iDVD uses a lower bit rate so that it can fit more video on the disc. In this situation, iDVD encodes video at 5 megabits per second (5 Mbps).

Creating DVD Menus

In general, DVD menus consist of a background and a series of buttons that lead to other parts of the DVD—such as video clips, which you just learned to add. In iDVD, the first thing you do is choose your background from the list of available themes.

As you learned earlier from importing video, every element you import will appear on the menu as either a button or text label. How they appear depends on the theme you've selected.

Throughout this section, we take a look at some individual tasks that you end up doing as you work on your DVD menus.

Themes

iDVD makes it easy to choose a background theme for your DVD project. You could simply scroll through the list of options in the Themes tab.

There are three basic categories of themes:

- Static background themes display a regular, non-video image. An example is Chalkboard.
- "Motion" themes display short video repeats. An example is Global.
- "Drop Zone" themes include areas where you can add your own slideshows, movies, or still images. An example of a Drop Zone theme is Theater, which you saw earlier, where the stage curtain opens and closes over a space in which you can add your own scene.

Different types of themes suit different purposes, but switching between them isn't difficult. You can always click on a different theme when you're working on your project—iDVD enables you to play and experiment as much as you want. All of the elements in your DVD and the titles you've given them will carry over between themes.

You will notice that some of the themes include music. We'll talk about setting background audio later in this chapter.

▼ TASK

Task: Choosing a Theme

After you've started a new project:

1. Click the Customize button in the lower-left corner of the main iDVD window to display the Themes list. If the Themes list doesn't appear, you might need to click the Themes tab.
2. Click on a desired theme in the Themes list, and it automatically displays a theme in the main iDVD window.

▲

If you choose a theme that has background sound or motion (indicated by a small circular walking man symbol) or displays previews of the project clips as video buttons, you might want to temporarily disable the sound or motion if it becomes distracting or seems to slow your computer's reaction time.

You can do so by clicking the Motion button, displaying an icon of a walking person, at the bottom of the main iDVD window.

Working with Drop Zones

Earlier, you learned that some themes include Drop Zones, or areas that you can customize by adding slideshows, movies, and still images. To add a movie or image to themes containing a Drop Zone, select the media file and drag in on top of the Drop Zone, as shown in Figure 19.7.

19

FIGURE 19.7
The borders of the Drop Zone will change when you drag a file on top of it.

If you are using a Drop Zone theme and you want to add a movie as content to your project, drag it to an area of the screen that is not a Drop Zone. It will become a text button. If you'd like, you can change it to a picture button in the Settings pane of the Customize window. We'll talk more about customizing buttons shortly.

When your file is added, it will fit inside the Drop Zone, as shown in Figure 19.8.

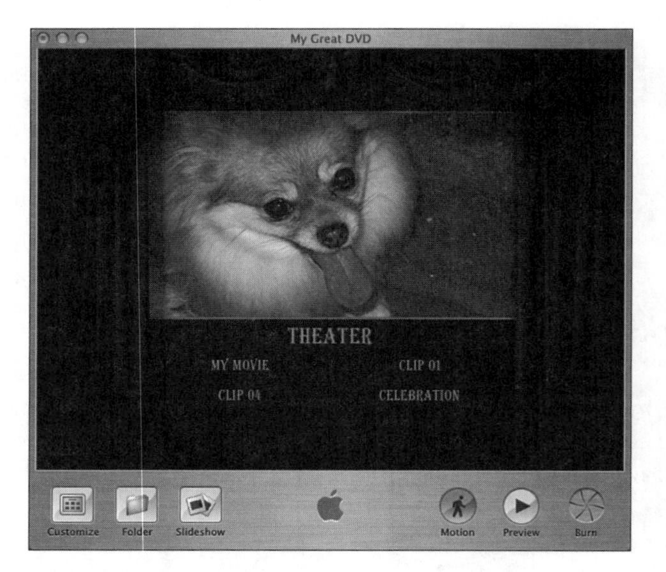

FIGURE 19.8
The Drop Zone now displays the file you added.

The aspect ratio of the image you insert will be preserved, with the image scaled to fit against either the top and bottom or left and right edges of the region. If the best part of the image doesn't fall in the center of the space, you can reposition it to choose which portion of the image is visible in the Drop Zone.

When you drag a movie to a Drop Zone in a DVD menu, the movie you added plays over and over again when the menu is onscreen. You can set the duration of the movies using the Motion Duration slider in the Settings pane of the Customize tray window. You can choose the number of seconds you want the movies to loop, up to 30 seconds.

To remove files from the Drop Zone, drag the image out of the Drop Zone and out of the iDVD window. Be sure you are dragging it outside the window, or else you will only move the image, not delete it!

Customizing Titles

The Title area of the Settings tab enables you to change various settings to customize the title text that appears on your DVD screens. iDVD automatically chooses a certain size for title text when you make your DVD, and the size is usually a good match for many DVD projects—large enough to read on the TV, but small enough so that you can type a reasonable number of letters. You'll probably want to change text at some point; the list below corresponds to the options in the Title section of the Settings Tab, shown in Figure 19.9.

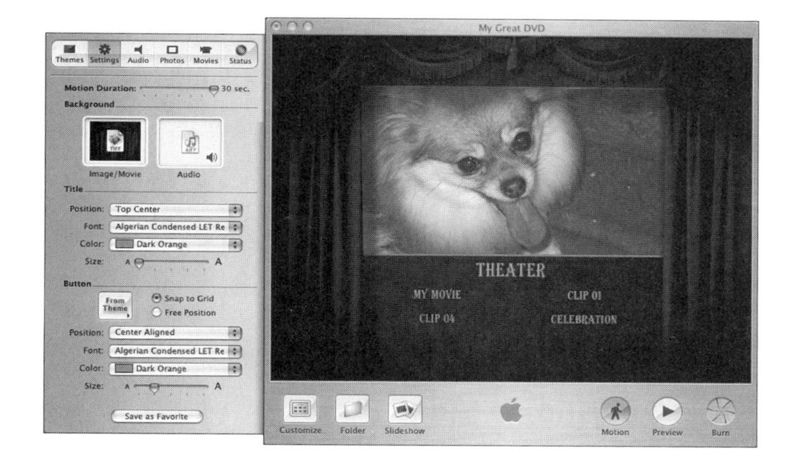

FIGURE 19.9
Options for changing the Title text in iDVD.

You can customize your title using the following settings:

- **Position**—Enables you to choose a preset position or Free Position
- **Font**—Enables you to choose a different style of text
- **Color**—Enables you to choose a color for your title text
- **Size**—Enables you to make the text bigger or smaller

DVD Buttons—Video and Text

In iDVD, you can have two different kinds of buttons, depending on the theme that you choose. In some themes, there are text buttons, which contain only letters (see Figure 19.8 above).

The process of making a text button is as simple as choosing a theme that supports text buttons, choosing a clip, and adding a video clip. The text button is automatically named according to the filename of the clip that's imported, but you can always click on the text in the button to change it if you want.

In other themes there are video buttons, which include letters and a preview of the video clip or slideshow you're linking to (see Figure 19.10).

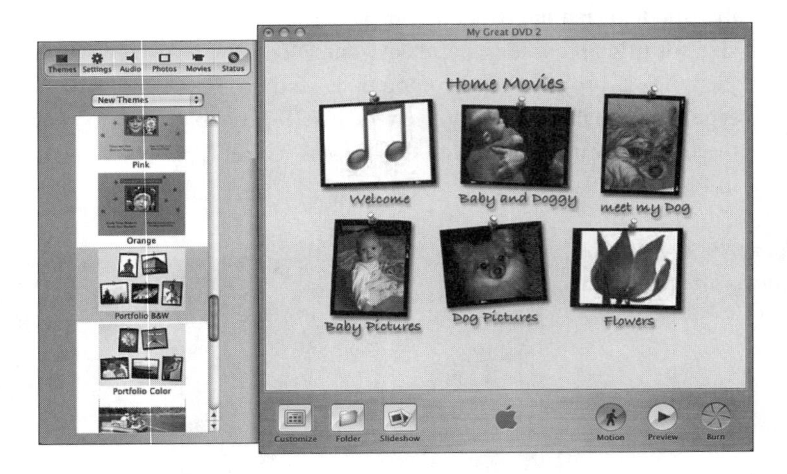

FIGURE 19.10
A video button with a preview of the clip.

Making a video button is as easy as making a text button. In fact, a video button is basically a text button that also includes video, except you must choose a theme that supports video buttons.

Task: Adjusting a Video Button

iDVD gives you a number of ways to make simple adjustments to a video button right in the main iDVD window. The automatic setting is for the button to start playing the movie from the beginning, but you can change where the video displayed on the button starts or simply have a picture appear instead of the video.

1. Click a video button to get the adjustment controls, as shown in Figure 19.11.
2. Click the slider and drag it to the desired position within the mini-movie to change where the mini-movie starts.
3. If you don't want the video button to be in motion, uncheck the Movie option and use the slider to choose the nonmoving image from the mini-movie.
4. When you're done adjusting, click on the video button again and you'll see the customized video button.

FIGURE 19.11
Clicking a video button gives you the button controls.

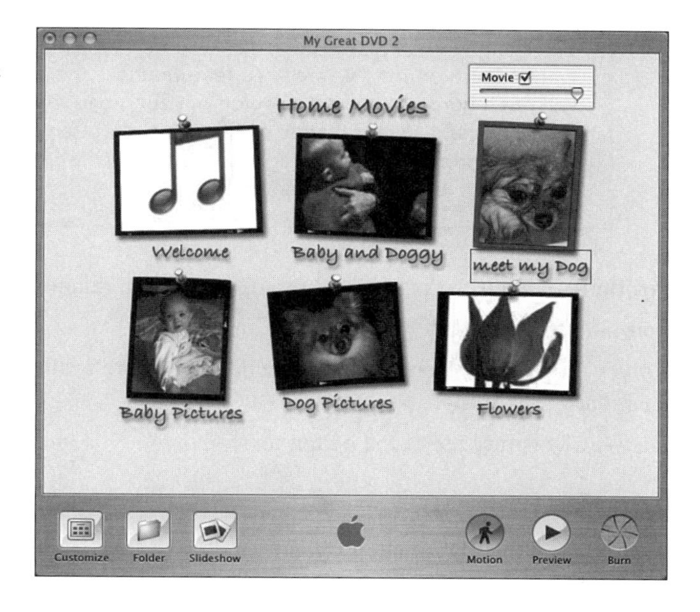

When working with video buttons, remember that they are in motion as you're working on them only if you have motion in iDVD turned on. If the Motion button at the bottom of the main iDVD window is green, motion is activated. Similarly, unless you specifically uncheck the Movie option as described earlier, your video buttons will move.

Customizing Buttons

The Button area of the Settings tab gives you the ability to choose from a variety of different options to add a nice touch to the way that buttons look in your DVD project. It also enables you to adjust things if the automatic settings don't suit your taste. Refer to Figure 19.9.

The adjustments you can make include the following:

- **From Theme**—Enables you to choose a different button shape and enables you to choose between text-only and video buttons.
- **Snap to Grid/Free Position**—Determines whether buttons on the screen start out being automatically aligned to each other (Snap to Grid) or not aligned (Free Position).

> If you choose to use Free Position for your buttons, be careful not to position them in ways that your viewers will find difficult to use! You may even want to turn on the TV Safe Area feature under the Advanced menu. This will put a border around the region of your menu that is most likely to be visible across different models of television. (In case you are wondering, the preset button positions that are used with Snap to Grid will already fall safely inside the TV Safe Area.)

- **Position**—Affects the position of the Button text in relation to the button.
- **Font**—Affects the style of text.
- **Color**—The same colors are available here that were available in the Title area mentioned previously.
- **Size**—Affects the size of the button text.

Adding Submenus

Earlier you learned that iDVD allows you to add up to 6 menu items per screen. But sooner or later, you'll probably want to add more than 6 items to your DVD. To do this, you'll need to add additional screens, or submenus, to your DVD project. Each submenu can contain an additional 6 items, up until you hit the limit of 99 movies or slideshows or 30 motion menus.

iDVD represents submenus with the metaphor of folders. Think of DVD folders just like you have folders on your hard drive. You can put multiple items in a folder, and to get to the contents, you click on the folder. Similarly, in iDVD, the folder provides the audience with a way to get to another screen.

When you add a DVD folder, you always add the first folder to the main menu, and then you can add additional folders to the main menu or within other folders.

> As you learned in Chapter 17, chapter markers can be set in iMovie for export to iDVD. When you import a movie with chapter markers, iDVD creates a button with the title of the movie, so the viewer can play the entire movie, and a Scene Selection button that links to a scene submenu, so the viewer can select which scenes to watch and in what order. If you'd like, however, you can set your iDVD preferences so that scene submenus are never created or so that iDVD asks what you'd like on each imported movie.

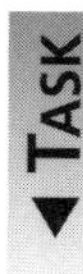

Task: Adding a DVD Folder

You can add a folder to a theme that includes text buttons or video buttons.

> You can change the type of buttons in any theme, so it doesn't matter whether the theme is preset to use text or video buttons.

Follow these steps to get a sense of how things work:

1. Import a video clip as you learned earlier in this chapter.
2. Click the Folder button in the main iDVD window to add a folder. If you are using a theme that supports video buttons, iDVD adds a button that displays an icon that looks like a folder (see Figure 19.12). (If your theme supports text buttons, your folder will be added as a button labeled "My Folder.")

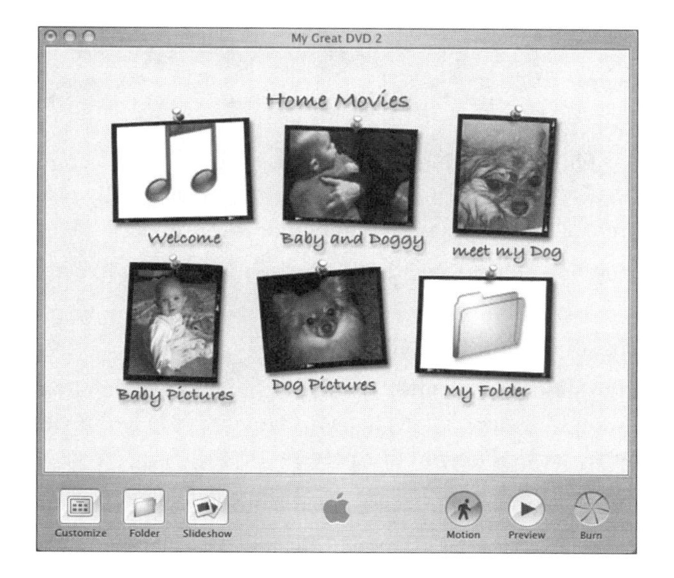

FIGURE 19.12
When added, a new folder appears with a generic icon like the one at lower right.

3. Double-click the new folder button in your menu to get to the new folder screen you have just added (see Figure 19.13).

> One thing that you might not realize is that if you want a different theme on different screens, you aren't limited to using one theme throughout your DVD. In other words, if you use the Portfolio B&W theme on one screen in a DVD, you could choose a different theme (such as Sky) for another screen on the DVD.

19

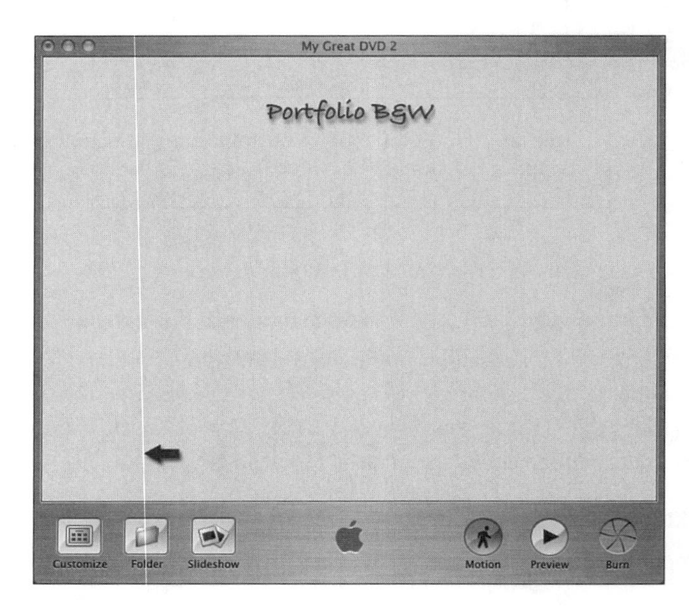

FIGURE 19.13
Double-clicking on the newly added button takes you to the new folder screen.

4. Drag additional files into the new screen. If desired, customize the buttons using the techniques you learned earlier. Then click on the small arrow in the lower-left corner of your folder screen, as seen in Figure 19.13, to get back to the main screen.
5. Single-click on the folder button in the main screen to active the button controls.
6. Drag the slider to the far right side to have the button display the background of the main menu for the folder.

   Use the slider in the button controls to choose which button from your submenu you want to feature. (The changes that you made to the video buttons on your sub-menu are carried over to this preview.)

When you're done, you will have a video button on your main menu that leads to a sub-menu.

Customizing Menus

While Drop Zones add a lot of opportunity to make a theme your own, customizing a menu by adding your own overall background or theme music is something you might want to do.

You can drag elements into two wells in the Background section of the Settings area in iDVD (see Figure 19.14).

FIGURE 19.14
The Image/Movie and Audio wells in the Background section of iDVD's Settings tab.

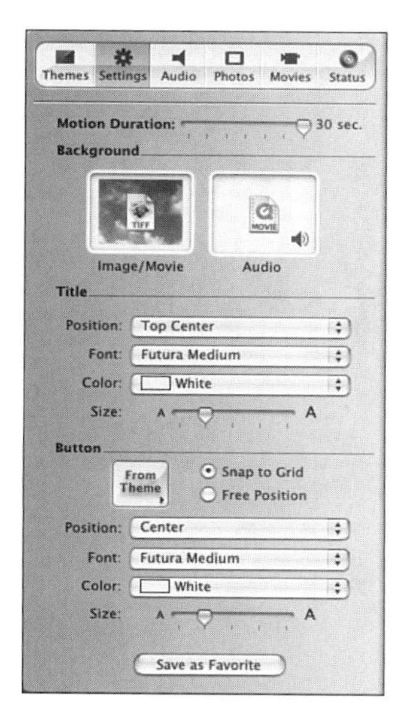

To add a new background image to a DVD project, you must have an image prepared that you want to drag in. It could be something like a digital picture you have taken, an image you have downloaded from the Web, or an image that you've prepared in a program such as Adobe Photoshop Elements (or its professional equivalent, Photoshop). Apple suggests you make sure your image is sized to 640×480 in order to fit the screen exactly.

To import a new background image:

1. Open a Finder window containing the file that you want to be the new background and position it next to iDVD.
2. Click and drag the file into the Image/Movie well in the Background section.

The new background file becomes the new image you see in your DVD screen (see Figure 19.15).

If you like the changes that you've made in customizing your DVD project, you can save this customized theme in the Favorites list of iDVD. Simply click the Save as Favorites button at the bottom of the Settings tab and give your creation a name in the dialog box that appears. When you want to choose your special theme, you can access it in the same Themes list where you normally choose a built-in theme by clicking the pop-up menu and selecting Favorites. The main value of this Favorites option is that it saves you from having to manually adjust things on every screen in a custom DVD project.

FIGURE 19.15
The new background image that was dragged into iDVD.

Task: Adding a Sound to a DVD Menu

If you want to add a sound to your DVD menu, you can drag it into the Audio well in the Background area of the Settings tab.

1. Open your iDVD project. In the main iDVD window, click the Customize button to see the tray window.
2. Click the Settings tab in the drawer.
3. Drag a sound file into the Audio well in the Background section of the Settings tab (see Figure 19.16).

FIGURE 19.16
Dragging a sound file into iDVD. You'll know where to drop the file because a "+" will appear next to your cursor.

The icon in the Audio well changes to reflect the type of file that you're dragging in. For example, compare the new icon in Figure 19.14 with the icon of the file that's being added in Figure 19.16.

Notice the Motion Duration slider near the top of Figure 19.16. The automatic setting is for 30 seconds, which is the time that the sound/music plays before repeating. This also holds true for the video portion of a motion menu.

If you decide that you no longer want the sound that you've added to a project, drag the sound file icon from the audio well to anywhere outside the iDVD window. When no audio file is set as the menu's background, the audio well will appear as in Figure 19.17.

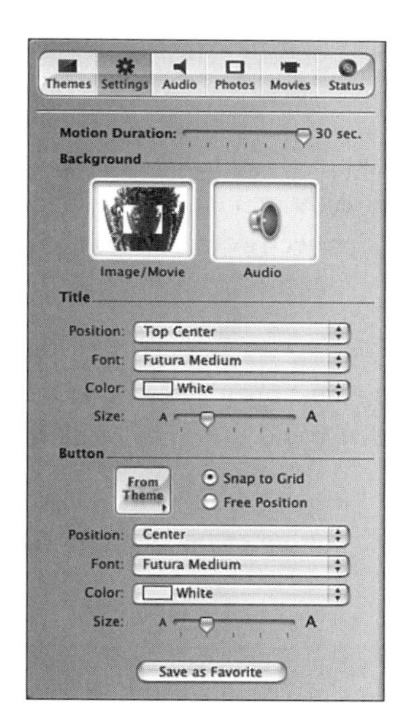

FIGURE 19.17
This menu is not accompanied by sound.

If you want to temporarily silence a menu to keep it from playing over and over again as you work, you can click the speaker icon in the lower right of the audio well to mute it. Remember to unmute it before you burn the final version to DVD, or no sound will be heard on the DVD.

DVD Slideshows

In this section, we examine how to work with DVD slideshows in iDVD. DVD slideshows are a nice way to enhance a DVD production; they enable you to add digital pictures to a DVD project that also has video in it. Or, you could make a DVD project that's nothing more than a slideshow.

You may recall from Chapter 12, "Using iPhoto," that you can export a slide show created in iPhoto directly to iDVD—including the slide duration and background music. However, slideshows exported from iPhoto need to be added to the top level of the DVD project, so if you want to add a slideshow to a submenu you may have to create the slideshow in iDVD. (But don't worry—that's not difficult!)

Using iDVD to create a slideshow is as simple as using other parts of the program; it's a simple matter of dragging your files directly into the iDVD window. After adding your pictures to the slideshow in your DVD project, you can make a number of adjustments if you like.

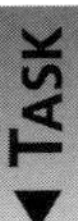

Task: Creating a Slideshow

Before you can create a slideshow, you must open a new iDVD project or reopen a DVD project that you've been working on that you'd like to add a slideshow to.

1. Open your DVD project.
2. Click the Slideshow button at the bottom of the main iDVD window to create a slideshow.

To customize the name of your slideshow, click the My Slideshow label. (We'll discuss how to customize the thumbnail image of the button and change it from the image of slides that appears a bit later on.)

3. To get into the slideshow editing window, double-click on the My Slideshow button that appears on your main DVD screen.

When you double-click the My Slideshow icon, the slideshow editing window opens. From there, you can add slides and make adjustments to your slideshow (see Figure 19.18).

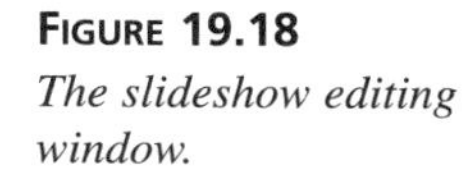

FIGURE 19.18
The slideshow editing window.

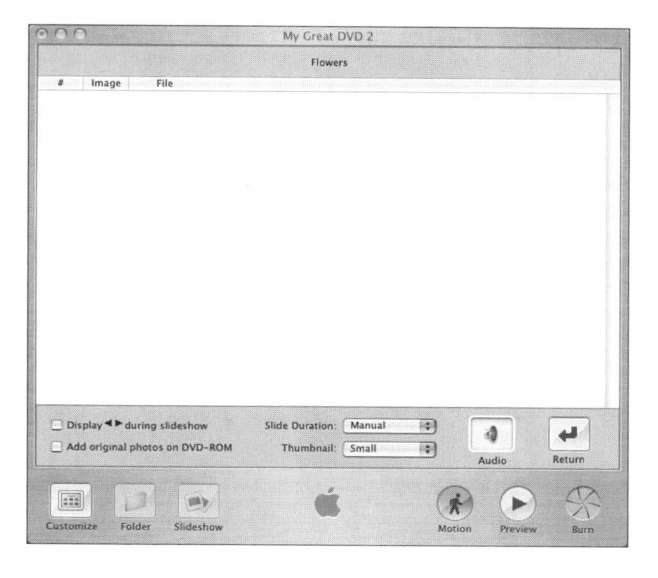

▼ TASK

Task: Adding Slides

Adding slides to an iDVD slideshow is as easy as dragging and dropping the files into the iDVD window. You can drag files in from the desktop, or you can drag images from your iPhoto library from the Photos tab. (Remember to open the Photos tab, you need to click the Customize button at the bottom of the iDVD main window.) You can also use the File, Import, Image option.

> In order for iPhoto and iDVD to integrate, you'll need to be using iPhoto version 2 or later. Also, you must have opened that version of iPhoto at least once for your photo library to be encoded in a format that iDVD can work with.

1. Open your iDVD project and click on the Slideshow button in the main iDVD window to reveal the Slideshow editing window shown above in Figure 19.18.
2. If you are importing photos from your iPhoto Library, open the iPhoto tab. If you are importing photos from somewhere else on your hard drive, position a Finder window with the picture files you want to import to the left of the iDVD window.
3. Click on one of the desired image files, and while holding the mouse button down, drag the file into the Slideshow window (see Figure 19.19).

▲

You can also drag multiple files at once into the Slideshow window. To accomplish this, place the mouse pointer near one of the file icons, click and hold the mouse button down, and drag upward and over all the icons you want to select. Then click directly on one of the selected icons and you can drag them all over at once.

FIGURE 19.19
Importing or dragging Slideshow picture files into iDVD.

The slides appear and can be repositioned and adjusted according to your taste, as we'll see in just a little while.

Slideshow Options

The Slideshow window has a variety of options that you can use to adjust both the order of slides and how the slides behave.

Display Arrows During Slideshow

The Display Arrows During Slideshow option causes arrows to be displayed on your slideshow screens, as shown in Figure 19.20, that are a reminder that there are previous or remaining slides.

FIGURE 19.20
Display arrows in a iDVD preview. They represent how a person can use the arrow keys on his DVD remote to go through slides.

Adding Picture Files to DVD-ROM

When you add a slideshow to you DVD project, the images are encoded as part of the DVD. If someone wanted to work with one of the images as a file to print or send in an email, she wouldn't be able to do this. However, the Add to DVD-ROM option enables you to add the individual slides to your DVD as graphics files—a nice option for enabling people to watch the slideshow on television, as well as being able to put the DVD in their computer to have the pictures files available.

When you burn your final DVD with this option checked, the slides in your slideshow are converted into a series of individual files. They're saved on the DVD disc along with the normal DVD project and are accessible by any computer with a DVD-ROM drive. We'll talk more about DVD-ROM content in Chapter 20, "Creating DVDs with iDVD."

Setting Slide Duration

The Slide Duration option enables you to set the time that a slide displays on a screen (see Figure 19.21).

FIGURE 19.21
The Slide Duration pop-up menu controls how long a slide appears.

The Manual setting basically means that the user presses the right or left arrow on her DVD remote control to advance to the next slide or go back to a previous slide. But if you want a slideshow to run on its own, you can adjust the duration. To adjust the duration of a slide, simply click the Slide Duration pop-up menu and choose a duration.

19

Thumbnail Size

The Thumbnail option determines the size that the mini-preview of each slide appears in the slideshow window in iDVD.

There are two options for thumbnail size. The Large setting works better to see a preview of the individual slides, whereas the Small setting works better when you need to see more slides in the window at a time, such as when you're adjusting the order of slides.

> The Thumbnail setting only affects the slideshow window that you see while you are working in iDVD—it has nothing to do with the slideshow on the finished DVD.

Audio

The Audio option enables you to add a sound file to a slideshow. It works the same as adding audio to a menu as we discussed earlier in the chapter—you simply drag a file into the well. To delete, drag the audio file from the Audio well out of the iDVD window.

> Under Slide Duration, the Fit to Audio option is available only after you've added background music to your slideshow, as we will discuss shortly. Also, once you've added an Audio file, the default setting becomes Fit to Audio and the Manual option is no longer available.

Working with Slides

One of the most common tasks you'll undertake when working with slideshows is rearranging slides so that they appear in a different order. It's really easy to do this and can be fun to play around with as you develop your slideshow. Remember, at any time, you can click on the Preview button at the bottom of the iDVD window to preview your slideshow. Just remember that to get back out of the preview mode, you have to either close the miniature remote control by clicking Enter or click the Preview button to return to editing mode.

Task: Rearranging Slides

▼ TASK

Rearranging slides is as simple as clicking and dragging:

1. Click on a slide, and while holding the mouse button down, begin to move the slide toward the position you want it to be in (see Figure 19.22). As you move the slide, its new position will be outlined in black.

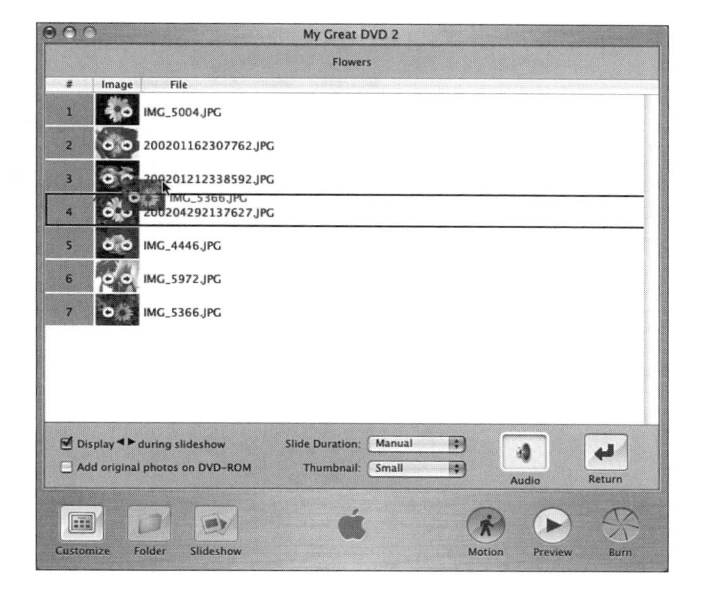

FIGURE 19.22
Moving the first slide to a new position in the slideshow window.

2. Put your slide into position and let go of the mouse button.

The slide snaps into position and you can continue to make adjustments to your slideshow or add new slides.

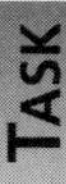

Task: Changing the Slideshow Icon Image

One of the nice things about the way that iDVD enables you to customize DVD menus is apparent when you're working with slideshows in a theme that supports video buttons. After you've added slides to your slideshow, the image on the button that leads to your slideshow can be changed to display one of the slides.

1. After adding slides to your slideshow, come back to the menu containing the button that leads to your slideshow and click it once (see Figure 19.23).

> To come back to the menu that leads to your slide show, click the button labeled Return, which displays a bent arrow, at the lower right of the slideshow editing window.

2. Move the slider to choose the picture you want to appear on the DVD button (see Figure 19.24).

FIGURE 19.23
Clicking on the button that leads to a slideshow gives you a slider that enables you to choose pictures.

FIGURE 19.24
No more boring generic icons: The DVD button for the slideshow with a new image in place. Great!

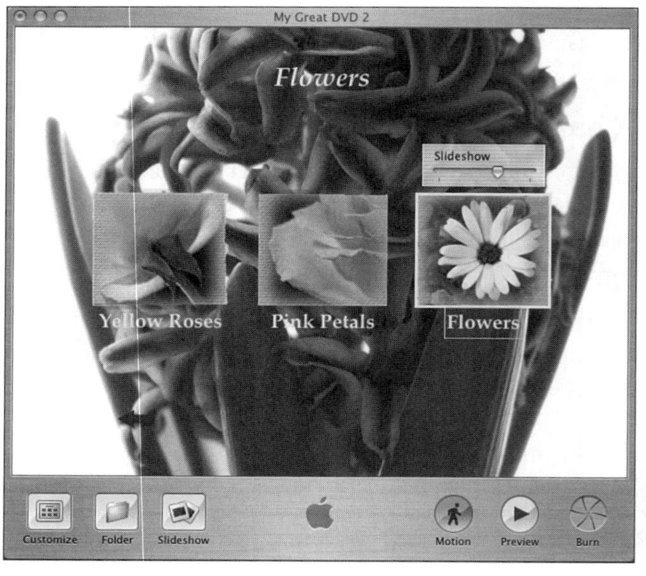

3. Click somewhere on the menu screen outside the button you have selected to deselect it.

Remember, iDVD also allows you to customize buttons representing folders, or submenus, in a similar way.

Summary

In this chapter, we learned how to design a DVD, including adding content and creating and customizing menus. We examined how DVD menus are put together, using a combination of backgrounds and buttons (and don't forget the movie clips and slideshows!). As you've seen, your projects can look just fine without adjusting any additional settings, but if you want to, there are ways to customize the way the DVD works and looks.

CHAPTER 20

Creating DVDs with iDVD

The ultimate outcome of most iDVD projects is, obviously, a DVD that you can play on your computer or your home theater system. This chapter will walk you through the final steps needed to "burn" your project onto a DVD, such as previewing the contents so you can catch any mistakes before they are permanently written to a DVD. We'll also learn how to add DVD-ROM content, which can be viewed by computers with DVD drives as a supplement to your video.

Burning Your DVD

Burning a DVD is really as simple as clicking a button and waiting for your masterpiece to be created. There are, however, several steps you should take to be sure that the DVD really is ready to go—Previewing the contents, Preparing your computer, and, finally, Burning the DVD. We'll cover these steps in detail now.

Task: Previewing Your Project

Before you burn your finished DVD to disc, you should preview it to make sure everything is exactly as you want it. While it's tempting to skip this step when your project is so close to being completed, you will have to burn the project all over again, and end up waiting twice as long to view it, if you made any mistakes.

1. To preview your project, click the Preview button.
2. In the remote control that appears on your screen, click the arrow buttons to select a menu button, as shown in Figure 20.1. When you press Enter, the content linked to the selected button will play.

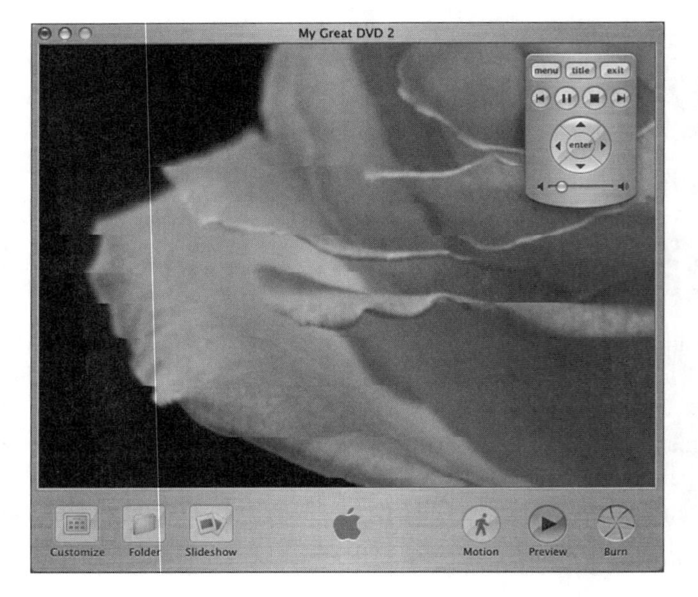

FIGURE 20.1
In Preview mode, iDVD displays a remote control so you can navigate through the menus of your project.

3. Repeat step 2 until you've tried all the elements in your project, even those in submenus, to make sure you finished all the portions of your project.
4. When you have tested everything, click the Preview button or click the Exit button on the remote control to return to edit mode.

> While previewing your project, make sure that you have motion activated so you can see any motion effects in the menus or menu buttons. You'll know motion is activated if the Motion button is green.

Preparing Your Computer

After you've tested your DVD project and are certain everything is as you want it in the final version, you're almost ready to burn your project to DVD disc. Before you do so, however, there are a couple of things you need to do to make the process go smoothly.

First, You should quit out of any other applications you have running, such as iMovie or an email program. Burning DVDs is a resource-intensive process, and it's best to let your computer focus all of its processing power on iDVD.

Next, you will want to make sure that your Mac doesn't go to sleep in the middle of burning. (This doesn't seem to affect all Macs, but it's better to be safe than to waste a DVD-R.) To do this, go to the Apple menu at the upper left, and open the System Preferences panel. Choose Energy Saver from the Hardware section, and set the slider that controls the length of inactivity before the computer sleeps to Never (see figure 20.2).

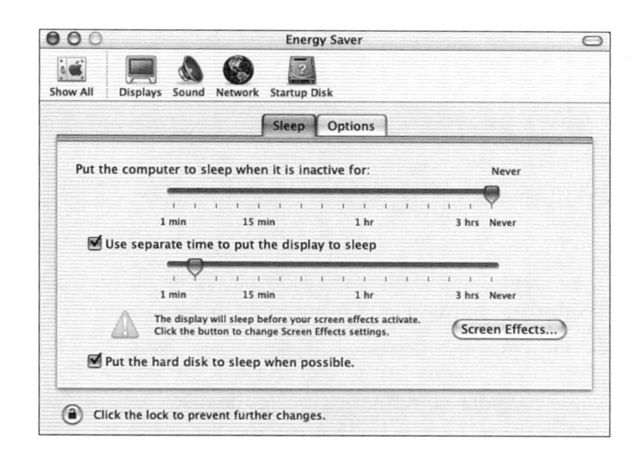

FIGURE 20.2
Open the Energy Saver pane of the System Preferences to ensure your computer doesn't sleep during disc burning.

TASK

Task: Burning Your DVD

After you've tested your project and prepared your computer, burning the actual disc is quite simple. Just make sure that there is nothing else you want to add to your project—remember, once you burn a DVD-R it can't be reused.

As you learned in Chapter 18, there are many kinds of DVD media. Make sure you are using 2.0 General DVD-R discs. Also, some brands of disc—even the right kind—don't seem to work in iDVD. For that reason, it's best to test a single disc before buying DVDs in bulk from one manufacturer.

1. Click the Burn button. When clicked, the gray button will retract to reveal a pulsing button in its place.
2. Click the pulsing button to confirm that you are ready to burn your project to DVD.

If you have forgotten to turn motion on, iDVD will ask if you wish to burn a DVD without motion menus. You can click Cancel to back out of the burning process you've initiated and turn motion on, or you can click Proceed to burn your disc with motion disabled.

3. You will be prompted to insert a blank DVD-R disc into the drive, as shown in Figure 20.3.

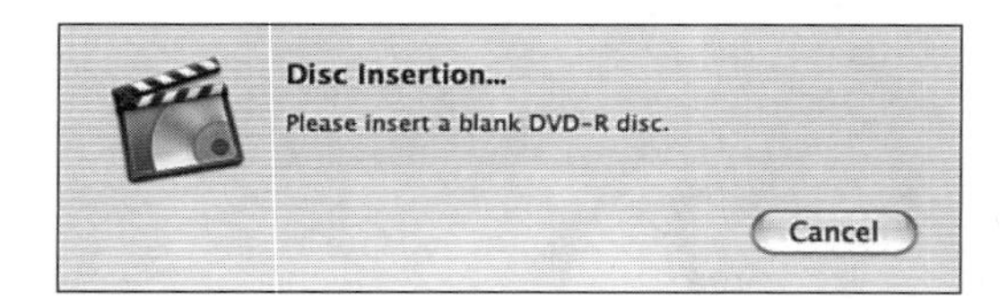

FIGURE 20.3
iDVD prompts you to insert a blank disc.

4. Insert your disc and wait for iDVD to do it's thing.

Be careful not to press the Eject key while burning is in progress. This may interrupt burning, and result in an unusable disc.

It will take a while for your computer to create the disc. Exactly how much time depends on your computer's processor and how much content is on the disc. Generally, it will take two to three times the length of the video on the disc for that video to be encoded and written.

TASK

Task: Testing Your DVD

After your DVD has been written, there's one step yet remaining--to make sure that the disc works! To find out if the disc has been created correctly, the best option is to try it in the computer that wrote it. If the DVD works in your computer, chances are good that it will play in most newer DVD players and DVD-drive equipped computers. (See `www.apple.com/dvd/compatibility/` for a list of compatible players.)

1. To test your DVD, insert it into your computer's drive.
2. The DVD Player application should open automatically with your DVD main menu visible.
3. Using the remote control that appears on your screen, click the arrows to select a button and click enter to watch that segment of your DVD.

Manufacturing Discs

More and more local video production-type companies are offering the service of duplicating DVDs, which basically means they can take your DVD and make copies of it, put labels on, and probably even have some options for packaging. This is basically another way of burning your own DVDs, it's just that someone else is burning them, onto the same discs you would, and is probably saving you a lot of time.

As there is still less than 100% compatibility for discs burned in iDVD, the only real way to ensure your project will play in all players is to send it off to be manufactured. Fortunately, DVD manufacturers will increasingly accept DVD-R discs as masters, and if you had the need, you can use a DVD you burned on your Mac and have small or large quantities reproduced.

Task: Having a DVD Commercially Manufactured

To get a DVD manufactured

1. Go online and investigate your options, see figure 20.4. Call a manufacturer or two and ask questions. One to try is EMVUSA, online at `www.emvusa.com`.

   Be sure to get enough information that you understand what you need to provide to them in terms of files, etc., and so you can get a sense of the options and prices.

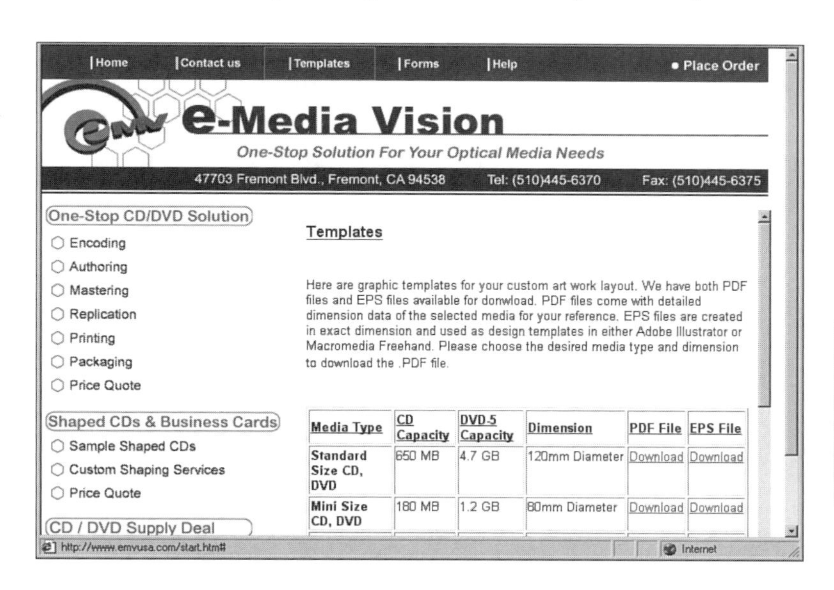

FIGURE 20.4
EMVUSA is an example of a DVD manufacturer that you can visit online and then work with to get a project done.

2. As your project is developing, think about the art that will appear on the disc. If you are not a designer, you may want to hire someone to make a nice looking design. Templates are usually available for download, such as the one shown below in Figure 20.5, which is for a small-sized 3" DVD that places like EMVUSA are capable of making.

Three-inch DVDs can play in anything except slot-loading drives found on some iMacs and PowerBooks, and they can hold a little over one gigabyte. These small discs are great attention-getters because they aren't that well-known yet.

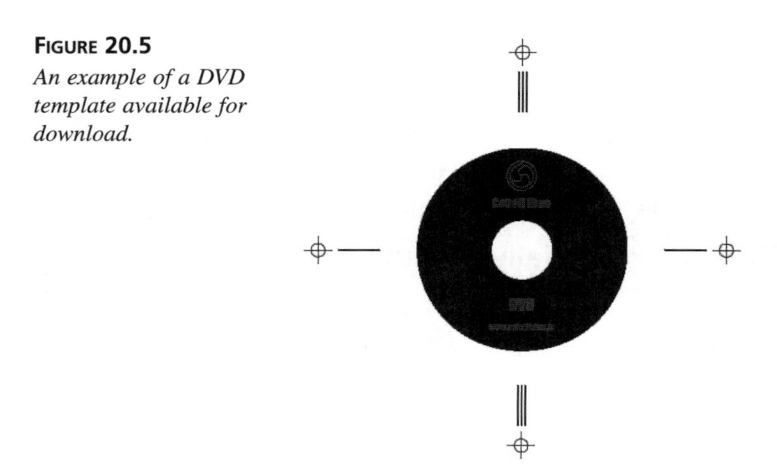

FIGURE 20.5
An example of a DVD template available for download.

3. After you've sent in your master disc, be patient as your DVD is being put together, and prepare for the pleasure of receiving the finished product.

DVD-ROM Content—Adding Computer Files on a DVD

DVD is a flexible medium for creating and sharing interactive presentations, but the possibilities aren't limited to what you can view on a television. Thanks to the nature of the DVD disc, you can also include files on a DVD that people can access using their computers. This feature is known as DVD-ROM.

DVD-ROM is essentially the equivalent of CD-ROM. ROM stands for *read-only memory*, which means that you can put data on the disc that can be read by a person with the appropriate drive in his computer. The most typical use for CD-ROM is the discs you use to install software on your computer. Software manufacturers haven't completely switched over to DVD-ROM discs yet, but DVD-ROM drives are becoming much more common in computers, so it's just a matter of time before DVD-ROM drives and discs become as popular as CD-ROMs.

Software that currently comes on several CDs could fit on a single DVD. If you installed iLife to run iDVD, that software is delivered on a DVD-ROM.

With Hollywood DVDs, the typical use of the DVD-ROM possibilities of DVD is WebDVD, which is sometimes referred to as *Web-connected DVD*. For example, you might have inserted a rented or purchased DVD in your computer and looked at special features of the DVD that are available only when looking at the disc through the computer. This could include things such as the opportunity to look at the screenplay of the movie, or games and other programs that aren't possible to view on a DVD player (see Figure 20.6).

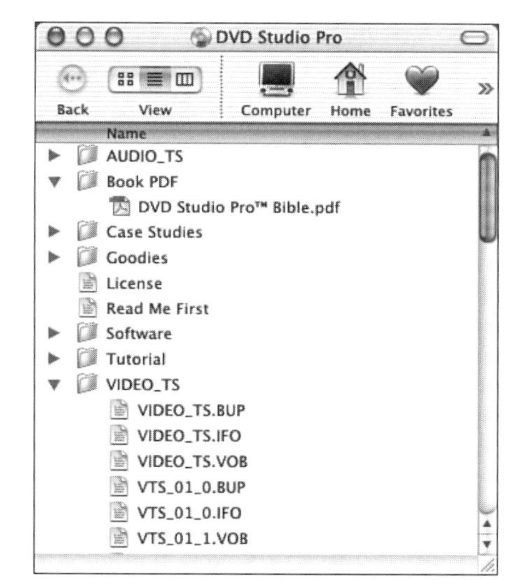

FIGURE 20.6
Example of DVD-ROM content, from the DVD that comes with the Macworld DVD Studio Pro Bible. The disc features the `VIDEO_TS` *folder that contains the standard encoded video for a DVD player, as well as the DVD-ROM content, a series of folders including tutorial files, a PDF version of the book, and so on.*

The great thing about DVD is that you can put your video on the DVD and someone can view it on his DVD player connected to a television, but you can also put data files that he can access on his computer. It could be that you want to include Web links, documentation, pictures, or any other kind of computer file.

For example, when you make your DVD, you start by creating an iMovie. Then, in iDVD, you can also use the slideshow feature to add pictures that can be viewed on the television. But let's say you want to pass a number of digital pictures along as files so that your colleagues can use the pictures on their Web pages. You might ask yourself, "Do I have to burn them on a CD?" With the DVD-ROM feature in iDVD, you can put the pictures right on the disc.

Or, let's say you have a number of stories or a screenplay that you've written in a word processing program such as AppleWorks or Microsoft Word. Now, if you want to, you could include the files on the DVD disc. So, you could make a DVD with the video that can be watched on the television, and if the recipient wants to, she could put the DVD in her computer and look at the original screenplay by opening the file as she would with any other kind of disc she inserts in her computer.

DVD-ROM content isn't anything that you have to do—it's just a great thing to have the flexibility to add computer files to your DVD.

- **Consideration Number One**—Does the person have a DVD-ROM drive? Many computers these days have DVD-ROM drives, but not all of them. If the person you want to share files with doesn't have a DVD-ROM drive, you might be better off using your SuperDrive to burn them a CD.

> The purpose of DVD-ROM feature in iDVD is to add extra material to video DVDs. It isn't recommended as a way to back up your data files. Instead, use the Burn Disc option available in the Finder's File menu to burn a data DVD.

- **Consideration Number Two**—Is the person on Mac or Windows? If you're burning files to a DVD and you want a person on Windows to be able to use them, be sure to include the appropriate file extensions on the end of your files.

> Microsoft Windows relies on the file extension in order to recognize which application will be needed to open a file. For example, JPEG files need a `.jpg` at the end in order for a Windows machine to launch a program capable of displaying JPEGs. These days many Mac programs automatically put on a file extension, but you'll want to be sure to use them if sending your DVD to Windows users.

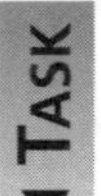

Task: Adding Computer Files to a DVD

You can easily add computer files to your DVD using iDVD.

1. Launch iDVD and open your project (see Figure 20.7).
2. Click the Customize button in the lower-left corner of the iDVD window.
3. Click the Status tab, which will initially give you a running report of how any background encoding is progressing. (This is the automatic encoding of video that's being done while you're working on your project) (see Figure 20.8).

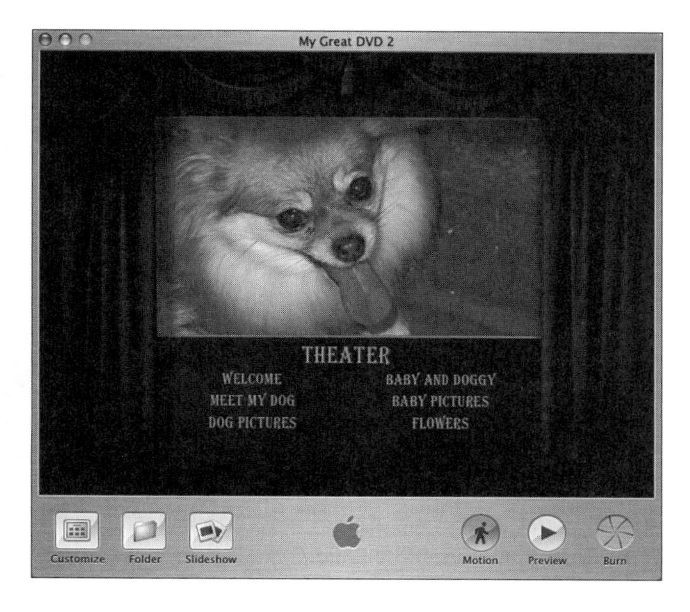

FIGURE 20.7
The main iDVD window.

FIGURE 20.8
The Status tab of the tray in iDVD.

4. Click the Status pop-up menu and switch from Encoder Status to DVD-ROM Contents as shown in Figure 20.9.

FIGURE 20.9
Add DVD-ROM files—and view what's been added—in the DVD-ROM Contents window.

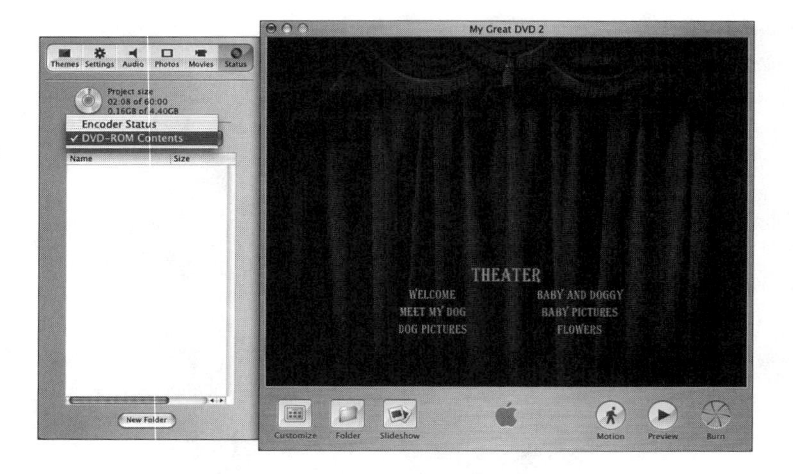

5. Drag files and folders into the DVD-ROM Contents area. In Figure 20.10, a number of digital pictures and a QuickTime movie have been added. iDVD also may add a file called `.DS_Store`, which you can ignore.

As you drag large media files in as DVD-ROM content, remember to keep an eye on the size of your project. (Conveniently, this information appears at the top of the Status tab.)

Technically speaking, the .DS Store file is created by the Finder. Per Apple: *"Each directory in the filesystem can contain a hidden object, ".DS_Store" containing data which includes a list of files stored there. This object is created when a local user views a given directory using the Finder."* The .DS_Store file isn't necessary for burning.

iDVD doesn't move the files you add as DVD-ROM content, or make duplicates of them. Instead, it creates a reference to the file on your system. If you delete a file or move a file after you've added it to the DVD-ROM list, its name will appear in red to tell you something's wrong. If you try to burn the disc anyway, a "File not found" error message will appear.

▼ To delete a file from the DVD-ROM Contents list, select it and press Delete.

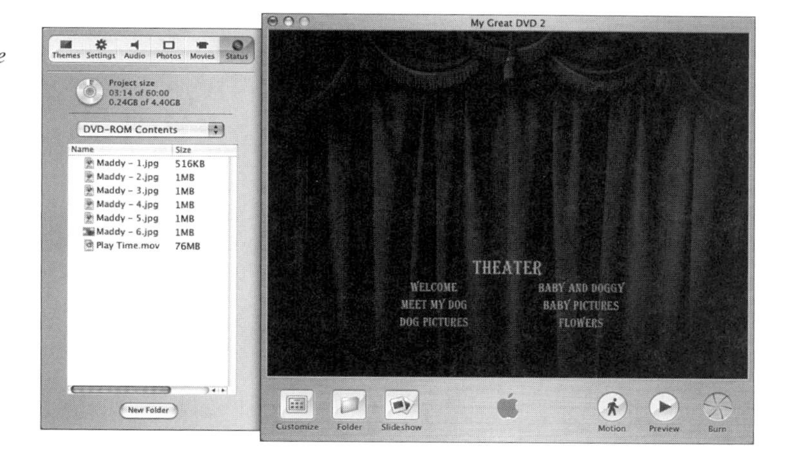

FIGURE 20.10
Dragging files from the hard drive into the DVD-ROM Contents area in iDVD adds them to the disc.

▲

Summary

In Chapter 20 you learned the steps you should follow when burning a DVD—Previewing the Contents, Preparing your computer, and burning the DVD. iDVD makes it simple to burn a DVD and it is often tempting to just click the Burn button as soon you've finished your creation. Unfortunately, this can sometimes lead to DVDs that don't burn properly, or aren't exactly what you expected. Following the steps presented here will make sure that your project turns out as close to perfect as possible on the first try. You also learned how to add additional, non-video files to you DVD using the DVD-ROM Content feature.

PART III

Photoshop Elements

Chapter

CHAPTER 21

Introducing Photoshop Elements

Adobe Photoshop Elements 2 is an amazing digital graphics program. Essentially, it is a program that juggles numbers. Changing the numbers in the computer memory changes what you see on the screen. If you're good enough at math to know which numbers change, and by how much, you could make all those screen changes by hand. Most people aren't. (Besides, it would be terribly inefficient to make all the changes manually.) That's where Elements steps in. Let's say you want to draw a red line about halfway down the page. You could figure out the positions of the pixels to change and change the color of each one from white to red. That's too much work. Let Elements do it. You just pick up a paintbrush, choose some red paint, and draw your line. There it is. The computer has taken all the math out of your hands and done the operation much faster than you could have on your own.

Now let's say you have a photo that's much too dark. If you were a photographer working in a darkroom, you would have to do some experimenting to find out how much lighter to print the photo. You'd probably find out that some parts need to be 15% lighter, some others 30% lighter, and some parts shouldn't change. You'd have to try to find a compromise and would probably waste several sheets of paper trying to get a good print. With Elements, you can look at the screen and lighten the image by moving a slider. More importantly, you can select and lighten specific parts of the picture without changing the rest. You've finally got control!

Photoshop Elements has two purposes: correction and creation. Use it to solve problems with pictures you've scanned or shot with a digital camera. Very few pictures are perfect right from the camera. You can recompose a picture by cropping away part of it. You can remove people or objects that shouldn't be there. You can make technical corrections for color, exposure, and even focus. Then you can get creative and have fun with it. Cure your kid's acne. Get rid of red eye. Change your lemons to limes, or your purple roses to sky blue ones. Liquify a clock face so it looks like one of Salvador Dali's dripping watches. Move your family group shot from the backyard to someplace more interesting. Add type to your pictures, remove backgrounds…. The only limit is your imagination.

Adobe Photoshop, despite being easy to understand, is a heavy-duty professional hunk of software. Each revision (version 7 is the most current) has added more tools and more bells and whistles for the pros. For its $600 price tag, you'll get a lot more features than most of us would ever use. Realizing that, the nice people at Adobe streamlined the software and created Photoshop Elements. They took out the more esoteric functions and added some nifty new ones, such as How To's: step-by-step recipes for all kinds of effects, tricks, and basic actions such as cleaning up a picture. They've given us almost the full power of Photoshop in a quick and easy-to-use program. Now there's no excuse for dusty scans, bad exposures, and other photographic sins. No more trees growing out of people's heads. No more faces too dark to see. Just picture after picture, better than you ever thought you could shoot.

Getting Help

The tools in Photoshop Elements are designed to make you feel as though you're dealing with the real thing, whenever possible. For instance, the paintbrush tools become pressure sensitive when you use a graphics tablet such as the Wacom Intuos2. *Dodging* and *burning*, which you might do in a real darkroom to lighten or darken parts of an image, are done in Photoshop Elements with tools that not only work the same way, but whose icons even look like their real-world counterparts. The Photoshop Elements desktop, which is far less cluttered than my own, has a toolbox, the usual menu bar, and a bar of shortcut buttons for actions, such as opening a new page, saving, and printing. The Shortcuts bar also has what Adobe calls a palette well.

When you first open Elements, you will probably notice several windows arranged along the right side of the screen. These are palettes. Each one has a particular function. Hints and How To are information palettes. The Layers and History palettes hold lists. History has a palette entry for each step you take in correcting your picture. It lets you choose an earlier step and revert to it, effectively giving you the ability to undo multiple changes. The Layers palette keeps track of whether each layer in a file contains type or an image, and in what order the layers should be displayed. The Color Swatches palette is a paint box. All of these are carefully designed to be user-friendly. You can generally guess what they do by looking at them, and if not, help is at hand.

Tool Tips

The most basic helper is one you should start to use immediately. (By the way, as I suggested in the Introduction, it's really a good idea to sit in front of the computer, with Elements active, while you read this book. You need to be able to try things out as they come along.) Figure 21.1 shows some tool tips. They are like little yellow sticky notes that pop up on the screen if you hold the cursor over any tool, icon, or dialog box caption. They are extremely helpful if you're not sure what something does. A tip gives you either the name of the tool, or if that's obvious, its function.

FIGURE 21.1
Tool tips pop up within a couple of seconds.

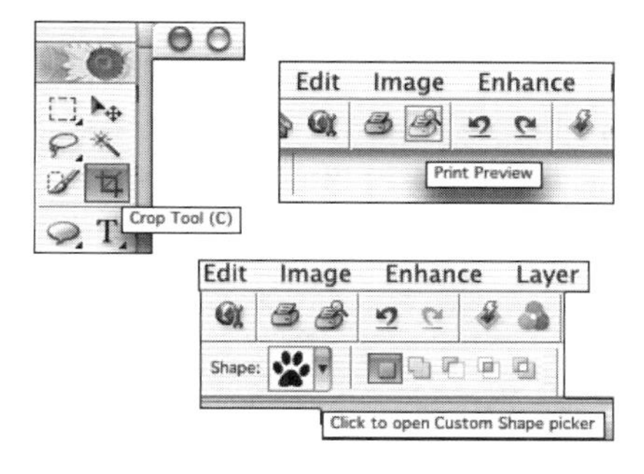

If you don't see the tool tips popping up, open the General Preferences window (select Edit, Preferences, General) and make sure that the Show Tool Tips option is checked.

Hints Palette

If the Hints palette is open, as soon as you hold the cursor over a new tool you'll see some suggestions on how to use that tool, effectively. (If the Hints palette isn't open, locate its tab in the palette well. Click and drag it away from the well, so it will stay open while you work.) When you're not a beginner anymore, you can put this palette away, but right now, keep it handy. It's a wonderful helper.

You'll notice a button labeled "More" on this and other palettes (see Figure 21.2). *Always* click it to see what's there. It will take you to other options, put the palette away, and possibly give you access to additional commands.

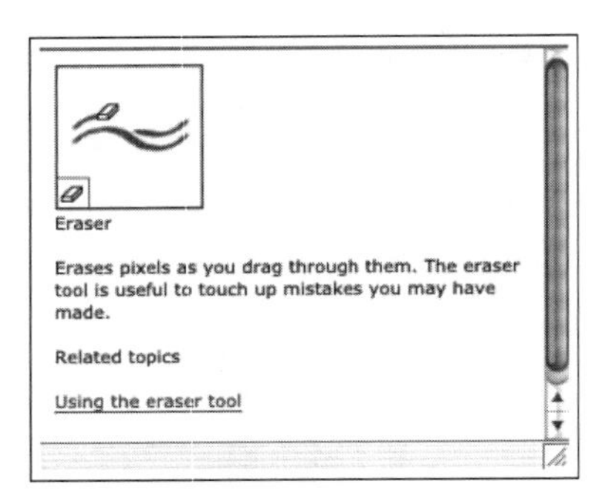

FIGURE 21.2
The menu pops up when you click the More button.

Figure 21.2 shows the Hints palette for the Eraser tool. Frequently, there are additional relevant topics to check on, as well. When you click any of the underlined topics, you will be taken instantly to the program's comprehensive Help system, which runs in your Web browser.

How To's

If Hints just doesn't tell you enough, or if you want some step-by-step directions, open the How To palette. Here you can find lists of "recipes" for common Photoshop functions such as "Change an Object's Color," or "Rotate an Object." Figure 21.3 shows an example of such a recipe.

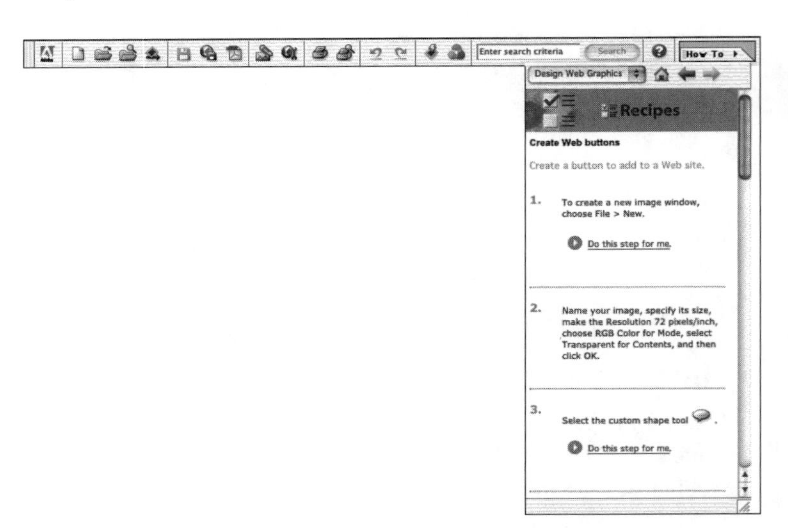

FIGURE 21.3
Recipes are reduced into simple steps.

As you can see, the recipe steps even have Do This Step for Me buttons, so you can make the task absolutely foolproof. If you're in a hurry or feeling lazy, just use the recipes that Elements provides.

If you don't see exactly what you're looking for, or if you just want to keep up to date, open the pull-down menu at the top of the palette and choose Download New Adobe How To Items. You'll be connected to Adobe's Web site, where you'll find a list of all the latest recipes and How To's.

The Help Button

When all else fails, and you don't even know what it is that you don't understand, click the big question mark icon on the Shortcuts bar. It will take you to the beginning of the program's excellent Help manual. Enter a topic if you know what you're looking for, or just scroll through until something looks relevant. Check out Elements-friendly Web sites, such as `www.PlanetPhotoshop.com` and `www.PhotoshopUser.com`.

A Tour of the Desktop

Luckily for us, the Elements working environment is a desktop, rather than a smelly, messy darkroom. It used to be that going into the darkroom was the only way you could do much of anything with a photo. That's why there are so many shoeboxes full of bad photos in so many attics, basements, and forgotten closets. Begin now to think about where they are. Pretty soon, you'll want to find them and fix them.

Let's start by looking at the Elements desktop shown in Figure 21.4. As with most other programs, there is a menu bar at the top. Next, there's a Shortcuts bar and beneath it, an Options bar. At the left is the toolbox and on the right end of the Shortcuts bar is the palette well. Rulers may or may not be displayed in the image area as shown here; their display is controlled by a command on the View menu, which is discussed later in this chapter.

There may or may not be palettes open on the right side of the screen. As you learned earlier in this chapter, a *palette* is a kind of window that gives you information about your project or lets you choose from a display of colors or styles. We'll look at the menus and tools in a moment. For now, let's jump ahead a step to the Shortcuts bar.

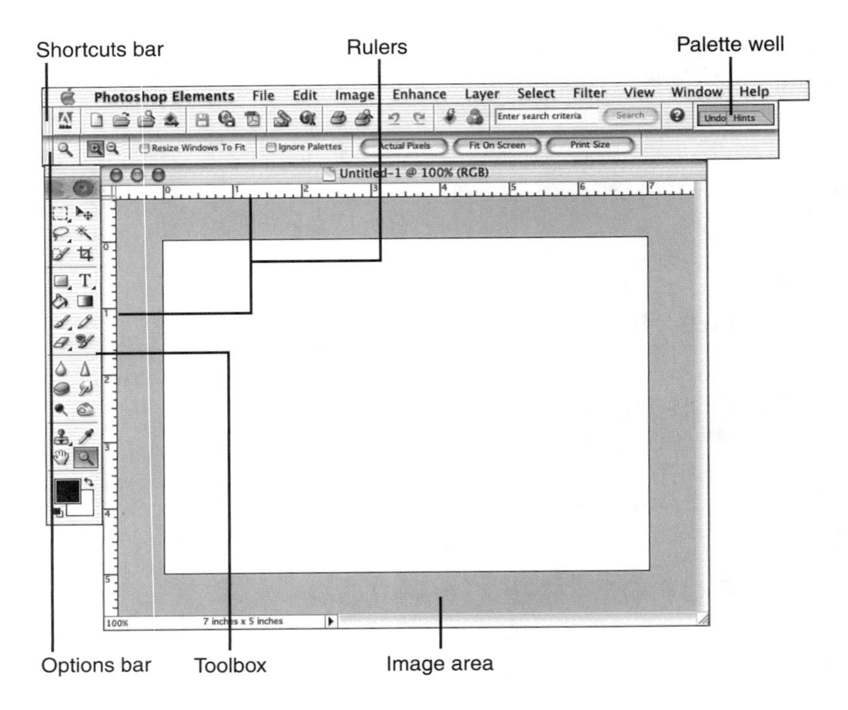

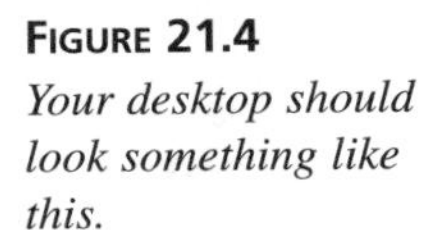

FIGURE 21.4
Your desktop should look something like this.

Understanding the Shortcuts Bar

The Shortcuts bar, shown in Figure 21.5, simplifies your workflow by providing buttons that correspond to the most common functions located on other menus. If you've used other software with similar button bars (Microsoft Word, PowerPoint, and Excel have them, to name just a few) then these buttons will be very familiar. The icons on the buttons should help you remember what's what. Starting with the first icon on the left and moving right, the Adobe logo opens your browser and takes you to www.adobe.com. The blank page icon, of course, means New image, and the partly open file folder icon stands for Open. The same folder icon plus a magnifying glass initiates a search by opening the File Browser. The last icon in this group, with a tilted image window and a right-pointing arrow, is used to import an image from a scanner, digital camera, or other source.

FIGURE 21.5
The Shortcuts bar, shortened to fit the page.

There are four different Save buttons, giving you several ways to handle your files. The floppy disk icon simply means Save. When you click it, a dialog box opens. You can choose to save the file in any location you like. The disk on top of the globe means Save for Web, and opens a rather unusual Save dialog that will optimize your pictures for display on the Web. The familiar Adobe PDF document icon enables you to convert your work to Portable Document Format (PDF), and to assemble multiple-image PDF files. PDF is rapidly becoming the only way to ensure file compatibility between platforms. If you want to email a photo album to your Windows-using relatives from your Mac, or show off the new kitten to a Mac-using friend, sending a PDF is the way to guarantee that everyone will be able to open it. Pressing the button with an envelope-and-paper clip icon enables you to send an image using your email program. It first prompts you to save the picture and then opens an email message so you can ship it off. This is very neat when you just can't wait to share the newest pix. The last icon in this group, a globe with a wrench, provides access to various online services, such as downloading program updates and new recipes, uploading files to an online image sharing service, uploading images to a printing service, and so on.

The next two icons are a printer and a printer with a magnifying glass, and they represent Print and Print Preview, respectively.

The Step Backward and Step Forward buttons are equivalent to the Undo and Redo buttons you may have used in other programs, such as Microsoft Word. With them, you can undo the last action, and then redo it if you don't like the result.

Clicking the Quick Fix button (with the lightning bolt) displays a dialog box that provides fast access to several image correcting tools. With the Color Variations icon (the three colored circles), you can access several color correcting tools instead. The next section of the toolbar contains the Search box and the Help button (labeled with a large question mark). Search finds specific help topics. Enter a word and click Search, and Elements will search through its entire Help file for it.

At the far right of the Shortcuts bar is what Adobe calls the palette well. (It looks like a set of file folder tabs.) It serves as a docking station for your palettes. You can decide how many palettes you want to keep there, how many you want open, and whether there are some you can just ignore. If palettes accidentally get lost, don't panic. You can restore them from the Windows menu.

Task: Starting a New Image

TASK

In a little while we are going to need a blank image file to try some of our tools on. Let's create one now, using the Shortcuts bar. We'll work with other kinds of images and other ways to create them in the following hours.

1. Point your cursor to the New button.
2. Click once to open the New dialog box shown in Figure 21.6.

▼

3. Click on the Preset Sizes drop-down list and choose Default Photoshop Size.
4. Check to see that the White option in the Contents area of the dialog box is selected.
5. Click OK or press Return and the new page will open.

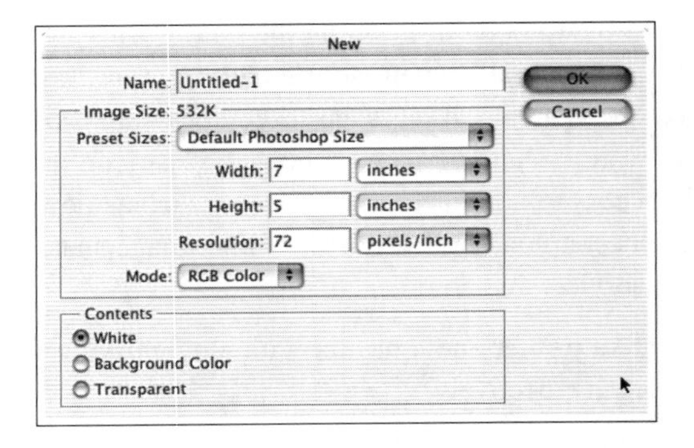

FIGURE 21.6
Your dialog box should look like this.

Now you have a blank image on your desktop, and we're about to look at the tools.… Go ahead and try them out. You can't break anything. Select something. Draw something. Paint a heart and move it around the screen. Try some colors. When the image gets too full, press Command-A (Mac) or Ctrl-A (Windows) to select everything. Then delete it by pressing Delete and start over again.

▲

Using the Tools in the Toolbox

Our next stop is the toolbox, at the left side of the screen. For reference, it is shown in Figure 21.7. It's like an artist's work table or paint box that holds all the tools you'll use to draw, paint, erase, and otherwise work on your picture. There are sets of tools to select, to draw and paint, to blur and sharpen, and to place type in the picture.

The toolbox has additional tools hidden wherever you see a black arrowhead. Click and hold on any tool with an arrowhead, and the additional tools associated with it will pop out on a short menu. Figure 21.8 shows the tools that are normally hidden in the Type tool menu.

The colorful icon at the top of the toolbox takes you, by way of the Web, to `www.adobe.com`. Once there, you can find and download program updates, advice, and excellent tutorials. Check this site frequently.

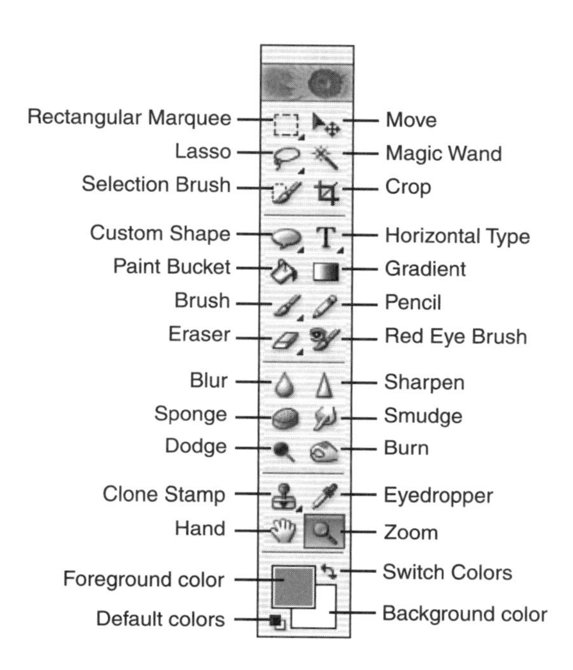

FIGURE 21.7
You must first click on a tool to select it.

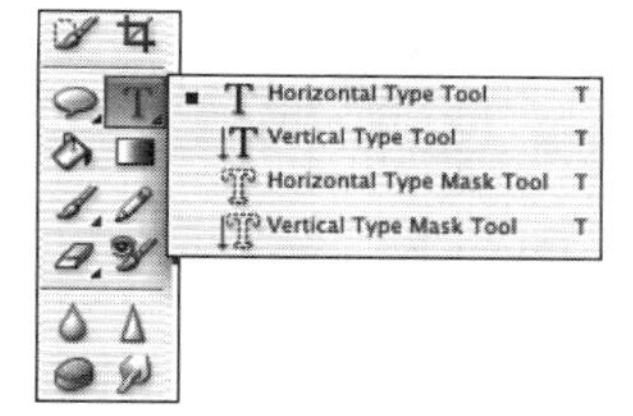

FIGURE 21.8
An example of additional tools normally hidden in the Type tool menu.

Selection Tools

The first section of the toolbox contains a group of tools called Selection tools. They are used to select all or part of a picture. There are four kinds: the Marquees, the Lassos, the Selection Brush, and the Magic Wand. When you select an area of the screen with the Marquee tools, a blinking selection border surrounds it. (The Marquee tools are named after the lights on movie theater marquees that flash on and off.) The Marquees make their selections as you click and drag the tool over the part of an image you want to select, drawing a box or circle.

The Lasso tools—three in all—draw a line as you click and drag the tip of the lasso across the page. Draw part of a free-form shape, and Elements will complete the shape automatically with a straight line from where you stopped back to the start. There are also Lassos to select by drawing straight path segments instead of a free-form line, and to select "magnetically" by separating an object from its background. Figure 21.9 shows the selections that result from using these tools.

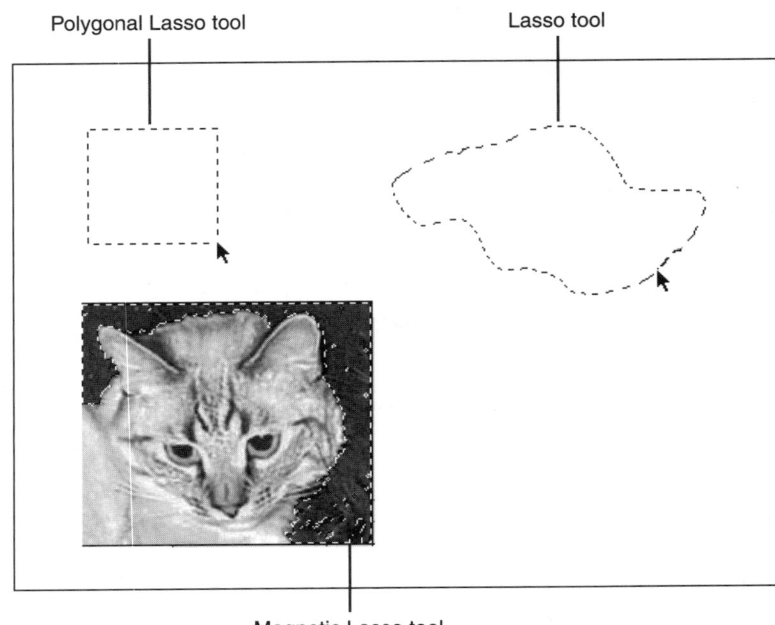

FIGURE 21.9
Each Lasso tool makes a different kind of selection.

The Selection Brush simply selects anything you paint over. Given that there are hundreds of standard paintbrushes, plus any you design yourself, this tool can be enormously flexible. Select it and drag your paintbrush over anything you want to turn into a selection. This tool doesn't exist in the "big" Photoshop program. I wish it did. You can use it to create masks over areas you want to protect when you're changing another part of the image. For instance, say you're working on a portrait of a lady, and you need to lighten her hair without bleaching out her face. Paint around the hair, or if it's easier, paint only the hair and then invert the selection so you've selected everything *but* the hair.

The Magic Wand tool selects by color. You can set the amount of similarity it demands, and just click to select all pixels of that color, or all adjacent pixels that match.

The final tools in this section of the toolbox are the Move tool and the Crop tool. After you have made a selection, use the Move tool to drag the selected area to another place on the image. The Crop tool works just like the rectangular Marquee tool, in that you drag a *bounding box* to surround the part of the picture you are keeping. When you do so, the area outside the box turns gray. You can drag a side to make the bounding box bigger or smaller. When you're done adjusting the box, double-clicking in the box removes everything outside it.

Painting Tools

Elements has an impressive set of Painting tools: Brushes, a Pencil, an Eraser, and Paint Bucket and Gradient tools. These all apply color to the screen in one way or another, just like the real tools they imitate. You can change the width and angle for the Pencil and Brush tools. The Brush tool and the Impressionist Brush share a space in the toolbox. The latter simulates different kinds of brushstrokes. Though there isn't a lot of use for it in photo correction or enhancement, it's fun to play with. The Red Eye Brush simply finds the odd color and replaces it with the correct eye color. Two clicks and your "devil eyes" photos can be pictures of saints. Many of these tools are covered throughout this section of the book, in chapters that discuss how to make specific types of repairs on photos and how to create an image from scratch. There are also various erasers that, as you might expect, take away part of the picture. You can use a block eraser, or erase with any of the paintbrush or airbrush shapes. There are two special-purpose erasers: the Background and Magic Erasers. Use them to automatically erase a selected part of the image. The Paint Bucket, also called the Fill tool by some people, pours paint (the Foreground color) into any contiguous area you select. (If no area is selected, it'll fill the whole image.) The Gradient tool lets you create backgrounds that shade from one color to another, or even all the way through the color spectrum.

Finally, there is a vector tool that draws shapes (the Custom Shape tool) and another that places type (Horizontal Type) as *vectors*—shapes defined by their outline rather than as bitmaps (tiny dots that form a shape). When you use these tools, you don't get the jagged effect you otherwise would when building an object from individual pixels because a vector image can be resized and its resolution adjusted without any effect on the clarity of the image. Figure 21.10 shows the difference between bitmapped and vector text and drawn lines. As you can see, the bitmapped text is ragged around the edges, especially when it's enlarged. Look closely at the curves of the *b*, *t*, *m*, *a*, *p*, *e*, and *d* to see this effect. The bitmapped line shares the same fate—it has bumps along its sides. The vector text and line, on the other hand, is quite smooth, regardless of the size at which you view it.

FIGURE 21.10
Vector type versus bitmapped type.

Toning Tools

Toning tools are tools that move, blur, and change the intensity of the image. The Blur, Sharpen, and Smudge tools change the level of focus and the Dodge, Burn, and Sponge tools change the degree of darkness or lightness of selected pixels. These tools will be covered in detail in Chapter 24, "Fixing Photo Flaws."

Viewing Tools

There are two Viewing tools: the Hand tool and the Zoom tool. The Zoom tool is shaped like an old-fashioned magnifying glass, and the Hand, not surprisingly, like a hand. The Zoom tool lets you zoom in by clicking the tool on the canvas to see a magnified view of your picture, or zoom out by pressing Option as you click the image. You can also click and drag the Zoom tool to enlarge a specific part of the image. When you zoom in, the picture is usually too big to see all at once. The hand moves it within the window and is helpful after you use the Zoom tool to enlarge the picture. Use the hand to slide the part of the picture you want to see or work on into a convenient spot.

Special Tools

There are two tools that don't quite fit into any category. The Clone Stamp tool copies a piece of the existing picture and pastes it somewhere else. The eyedropper picks up a sample of color, which you can make the active color or add to your Swatches palette. We'll talk more about these when we use them for photo correction in Chapter 24.

Colors

Finally, there are two large blocks of color displayed at the bottom of the toolbox. They are your foreground and background colors, and by default they are black and white, respectively. Change them by clicking once on the appropriate square to open the Color

Picker. There, you can click to select any color you like. The foreground color (logically, the one on top) is the color you'll apply when you paint a brushstroke, place type, or do anything that leaves a mark on the page.

Tool Shortcuts

You can select any of these tools by clicking its icon in the toolbox, but Elements gives you another, even easier way to access the tools. Instead of clicking the tools you want to use, you can type a single letter shortcut to select each tool. To toggle through the available tools where there are pop-up menus, press Shift plus the shortcut letter until you reach the tool you want. Table 21.1 lists the tools with their shortcuts. Dog-ear this page so you can refer to the table until you have memorized the shortcuts.

TABLE 21.1 Tools and Their Shortcuts

Tool	*Shortcut*	*Tool*	*Shortcut*
Marquee	M	Move	V
Lasso	L	Magic Wand	W
Selection Brush	A	Crop	C
Custom Shape	U	Type	T
Paint Bucket	K	Gradient	G
Brush	B	Pencil	N
Eraser	E	Red EyeBrush	Y
Blur	R	Sharpen	P
Sponge	Q	Smudge	F
Dodge	O	Burn	J
Clone Stamp	S	Eyedropper	I
Hand	H	Zoom	Z
Switch Colors	X	Return to Default Colors	D

Understanding the Options Bar

Every tool in the toolbox has many settings. For example, you're not stuck with a tiny little pencil and a big fat brush as your only drawing tools. You can make the exact tool you want by simply changing the way it behaves using the options bar. You can change a tool's degree of *opacity* (the degree to which the tool obscures the part of the image you use it on) and *blending mode* (the degree to which the tool's color blends with the existing colors in the image), and select from libraries of shapes and textures and styles. You can also save and store your own brushes and reach them via the Options bar. Note that the options bar changes with each different tool you select. For example, Figure 21.11 shows the Shape tool Options bar with a drop-down menu. This one displays the entire library of shapes included with Elements.

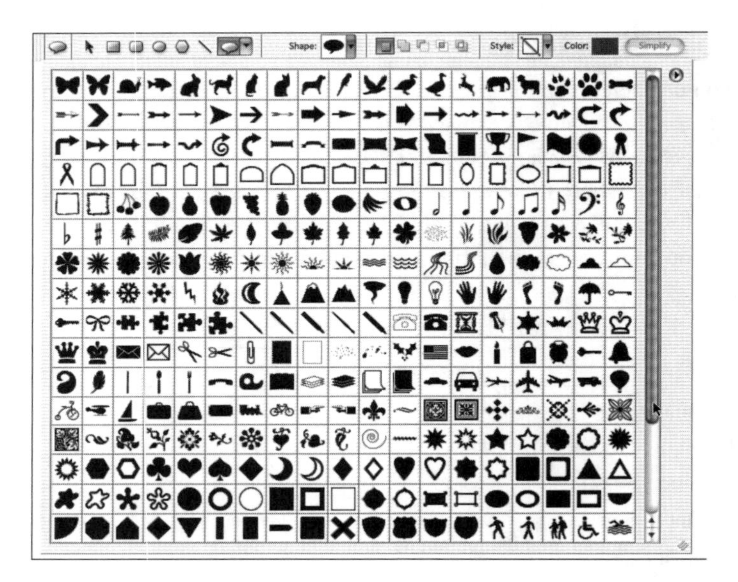

FIGURE 21.11
There are all sorts of pop-up menus and pull-out menus on each Options bar. Be sure to explore.

Typically, these drop-down menus will also have a submenu attached. To open it, click the right-pointing arrowhead at the top of the menu. As you explore Elements, try clicking arrows or buttons whenever you see them to find out what they do.

Using the Menus

If you have used *any* kind of computer software written in the past 20 years, you have used menus. The menus across the top of the Elements screen contain the commands that enable you to open and manipulate files. Access them by clicking the name of the menu to open it, and then selecting the desired command from the list. Whenever you see an arrow or an ellipsis (…) to the right of a menu command, it indicates that there is something more than just that command available. A right-pointing arrow indicates that there's a submenu. An ellipsis means that the menu item leads to a dialog box. Figure 21.12 shows the Elements File menu.

It's no coincidence that you'll find the same set of commands, more or less, on any File menu, and that the cut, copy, and paste commands on Macs and Windows computers are the same. One of the things that makes computers easy to use is the notion of a universal user interface. That's a fancy way to say that you do the same things the same way in most programs. Command/Ctrl-N always starts a new page. Command/Ctrl-Q always quits, and so on. This makes learning a new program simpler. Adobe's taken that even further, in that all Adobe graphics software uses the same tools and working methods. If you master using layers in Elements, as I am sure you will, you'll also know how to use layers in InDesign or Illustrator. As you work your way through this book, you will get a head start on learning the rest of the Adobe software. Similarly, if you already use Illustrator or PageMaker, or even Premiere, you'll find that you already know a lot about Elements. Of course, there's always something new to learn.

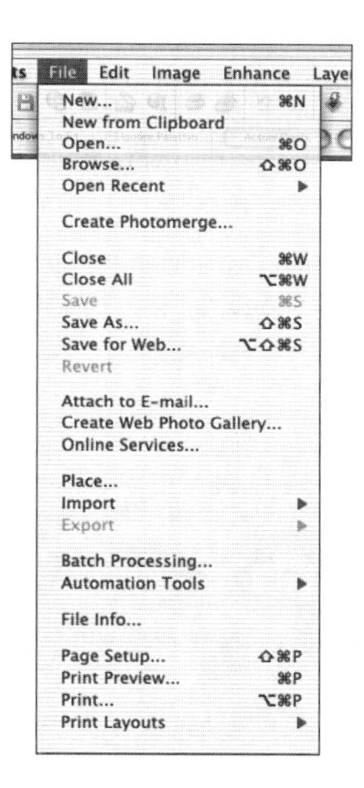

FIGURE 21.12
The Elements File menu. Note the arrows and ellipses.

Taking a Look at the File and Edit Menus

The first two Elements menus are File and Edit. The File menu lets you work with files: opening, closing, saving, importing, exporting, and printing them, and, of course, quitting the program. Here's where you can select several sequential shots to stitch together a panoramic photo. Here's where you can choose to email a picture to your friends.

The New option opens a blank screen on which you can paint or drag images from other open windows. Open will bring up a dialog box that lets you locate any specific graphics file and open it. Finding these files isn't always easy, however (especially if you're like me and forget what you called the shot the first time you saved it). That's why there's a browser.

Using the File Browser

You can open the File Browser by selecting Browse from the File menu or File Browser from the Window menu, by using its key shortcut (Shift-Command-O), or by clicking its tab in the palette well. You can also open the File Browser by clicking Browse for File in the Welcome Screen. Use it to locate and open your photos and other images. When you open the File Browser, you can search any of your graphics folders by selecting them. After you've selected a folder, thumbnail-sized views of all its pictures will appear as if they were slides on a sorting table. Figure 21.13 shows the setup. To open a picture, just double-click on it. If you select a picture and don't double-click, you'll also see all the information available about the picture, including its size, color mode, date and time it was shot, make and model of camera used, flash enabled or not, shutter speed, and a lot more than you'll ever need to know. Slide the partitions to make the information window smaller, and then you can see more thumbnails at once.

You can change the order in which the images are sorted by clicking the Sort By button and making a selection from its menu. To change the size of the thumbnails, click the View By button and make a selection. You'll learn more about the File Browser in Chapter 22, "Starting, Saving, and Printing Your Work."

FIGURE 21.13
You can find any photo you need with the File Browser.

Elements will also display disk icons, folders, applications, and whatever else it sees in the folder you select. Use the folder hierarchy to navigate down to the level where your picture is. The nice thing about the File Browser, as opposed to other image-indexing methods, is that when you find the image you need, you can just double-click, and you're ready to work.

Taking a Look at the Image Menu

The Image menu has the commands to do what I'd consider "physical" things to the picture. Turn it sideways, flip it, rotate a single layer or the whole image, distort it, make it bigger or smaller.... You get the idea.

Duplicate Image

The Duplicate Image command *does not* save a copy of the image. I want to be very clear about that. If you want to keep a copy of your picture, use Save As and check Save a Copy. Duplicate Image puts a temporary copy of the picture into RAM and in a window on the screen (see Figure 21.14). Use it to save a "before" version, so you can compare the updated image to the original as you retouch a badly damaged photo or experiment wildly. When you're done, you can save the copy or not, as you wish.

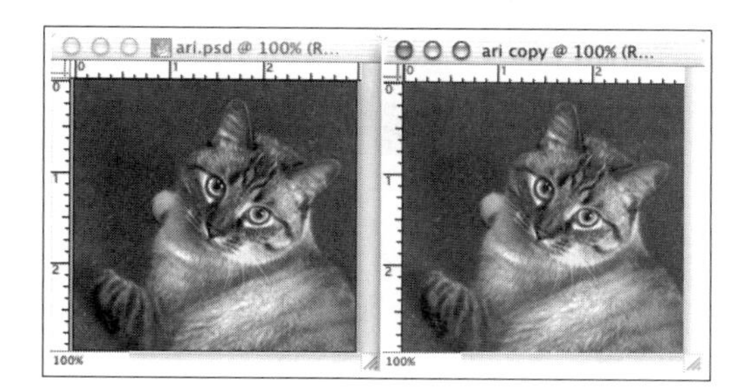

FIGURE 21.14
You can tell that the picture on the right is just a working copy. It has no file type attached, so it's not saved as a file.

Rotate

Cameras and monitors are designed to work with horizontal rectangular images, or pictures that are wider than they are tall. But not all pictures have that shape. Suppose you are visiting New York and want a shot of the Empire State Building. First, you find a spot where you can see the whole building. If you hold your camera normally, you'll have to step backwards all the way to New Jersey before you'll be able to see the top of the building, and of course, you will have several blocks worth of other stuff on either side. Instead, if you turn the camera sideways, you change the format to vertical, and you can see a lot more of the tall building with a lot less of the neighborhood. Of course, when you get the photo back home and open it up in Elements again, it's sideways. It's not very practical to rotate the monitor. For one thing, it weighs a lot more than a camera. That's why you'll use the Rotate commands shown in Figure 21.15.

As you can see, there are many Rotate options. For Custom, enter a number of degrees and choose left or right. You need to be aware of the difference between rotating and flipping. When you rotate, you move the picture around its center point. Flipping draws a midline axis and flips the image relative to it. The difference is depicted visually in Figure 21.16.

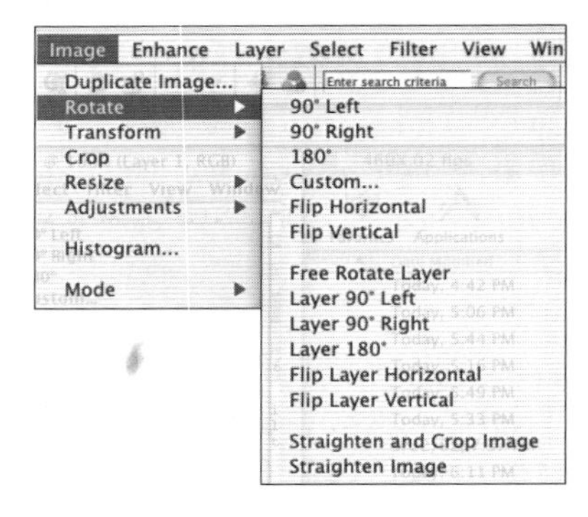

FIGURE 21.15
Rotate the entire image or rotate one layer at a time.

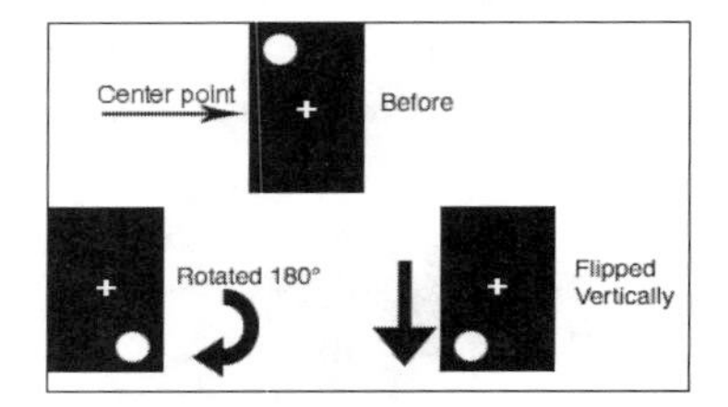

FIGURE 21.16
Flipping crosses an axis. Rotating travels around a center point.

Transformations

Transformations occur within the theoretical perspective of a bounding box and are used to warp an object or selection. A bounding box is very much like a marquee. It's a rectangular selection box placed over the object to be transformed. Each corner and the center point of each side of the box has a small square called a handle. When you drag a handle, only the lines connected or related to it will move.

The Transformation options available in Elements are

- **Free Transform**—Apply multiple transformation techniques at one time, including skew, distort, and perspective.
- **Skew**—Tilt the image horizontally or vertically.
- **Distort**—Pull the image in any direction.
- **Perspective**—Push the image backward or pull it forward along the third dimension.

Figure 21.17 shows some examples. You can see in the bounding box at the bottom left that we're using perspective. The two side lines are of equal length, and the two angles on each side are complementary (they add up to 180 degrees).

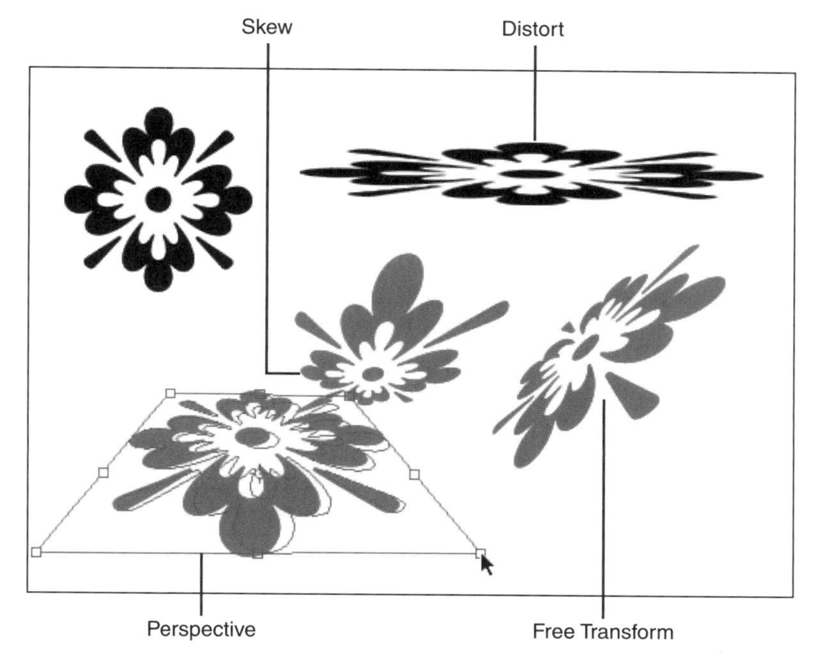

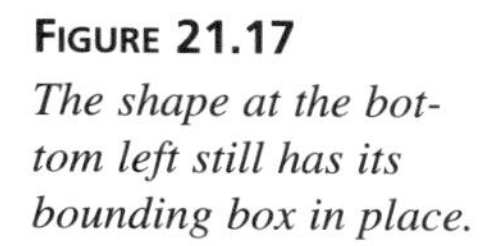
FIGURE 21.17
The shape at the bottom left still has its bounding box in place.

Crop/Resize

Cropping is usually the single most important thing I do to a photo. You can't always stand where you should when you take a picture, so you may not be able to compose your shots in the camera. Cropping gives you a chance to correct them. It also lets you reshape a picture to emphasize a different part. We'll talk more about the theory and uses of cropping in Chapter 23, "Using Basic Tools in Elements." Resizing is the process of changing the size of the image. There are many things you have to consider when you do this. Will your picture be seen in print or on the screen or both? Screen resolution becomes a factor here. There are right ways and wrong ways to resize. You can also keep the image the same size and in effect add more space around it by resizing the canvas. In Chapter 23, we'll deal with shrinking and stretching the canvas.

Adjust

The items on the Image Adjustments submenu are mainly used for special effects. Invert and Posterize are easily the most useful. Invert takes a positive image in black and white and coverts it to an artificial but correct negative. It also does strange and amazing things to color by rotating the color wheel 180°. Posterize reduces the image from full color to a given number of colors, based on the sum of the average number of colors being converted. All the fancy math can often result in a beautiful picture. Figure 21.18 shows 4 levels of posterization (four levels of brightness for each color channel, such as red, green, and blue). Reducing the levels of brightness for each color creates large areas of a single color, removing the subtleties of color from an image and making it appear flatter. Be sure to see this in the color section. You'll learn how to use posterization in Chapter 25, "Enhancing Your Photos with Filters."

FIGURE 21.18
The lower the number of levels, the more simplified the drawing becomes.

Histogram

Were you ever into math or statistics? If so, you can probably explain a histogram better than I can. Simply put, it's a graph. In Elements, it's a graph that shows the distribution of pixels throughout the color/tonal range of the image. You can look at a histogram like the one in Figure 21.19 and know whether there's detail in the highlights and shadows and how to make corrections to bring them out. Shadows (blacks) are graphed on the left, midtones in the middle, and highlights (whites) on the right. Quite simply, if there are only a few lines that are very short, you may not be able to raise the picture from the dead. If you do have a lot of data, even though you're not sure what it means, there's hope.

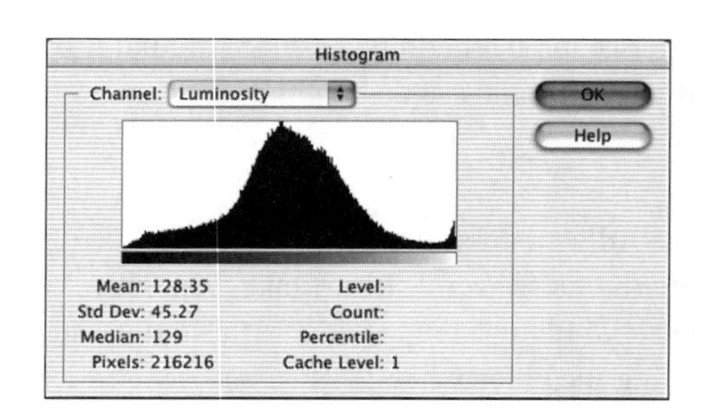

FIGURE 21.19
The picture from which this histogram was generated has few real whites (on the right), but a lot of light grays and beiges (middle), and few true blacks (on the left).

Modes

The four color modes available in Elements are Bitmap (which is 1-bit black and white), Grayscale (256 grays), RGB, and Indexed Color. When you work in color, as you will most of the time, stay with RGB. Indexed Color is for Web use, and since the adoption of JPEG compression (which you'll learn more about in the next chapter), it isn't often used except for line art (simple drawings of one or two colors) or spot color (a method of identifying the exact color desired in a section of a graphic image, typically by selecting a Pantone color from a chart) .

Taking a Look at the Enhance Menu

As the name of this menu suggests, these tools will improve your pictures. A little brightening here, a more intense shadow there.... But that's not all. You will find yourself doing a lot of your photo corrections from this menu, too. The kinds of problems solved here are mainly things that went wrong inside the camera or scanner—bad exposures, dull colors, the wrong colors—and these are all things that you can fix with a few clicks. Appropriately, the first item on the menu is Quick Fix.

Quick Fix

Quick Fix opens a window, shown in Figure 21.20, that suggests what problems exist in the picture, and tells you exactly how to fix them. The sliders are right there in the box, and you can watch Before and After images as you work. This is great for learning what the tools do and for making overall fixes.

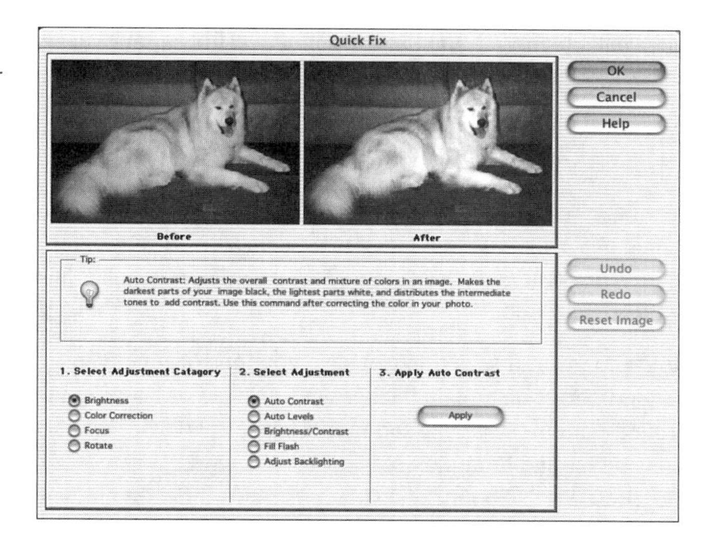

FIGURE 21.20
Click the other tool buttons to run through the entire list of repairs.

Also on this menu, you'll find a couple of "auto" settings for adjusting levels and contrast. If you're not too fussy, these are usually okay. Elements studies the picture, does some esoteric math, and tries to bring everything up or down to an ideal set of numbers. Well, sometimes ideal isn't what you want, and sometimes the program's idea of perfection isn't yours. Try these settings, but be prepared to undo them. You can make the same changes yourself to the degree that *you* think right.

Color adjustments and lighting adjustments can be a big help, both when you are trying to rescue a badly lit photo, and when you are trying to create a scene from several composite photos or from scratch.

Color Variations

We'll come back to this option a lot. The Color Variations command on the Adjust Color submenu is the best way to train your eye to really see color and to analyze what's wrong with it. It shows you the results of applying different color corrections to the same picture. Suppose you have a picture that has an orange cast. You know you want to add more of whatever color is the opposite of orange on the color wheel. But is that blue, green, or cyan? The Color Variations tool displays your picture with samples of each of the colors added to it. Choose the one you like best. It's that simple. You can vary the amount of color correction to apply. You can also look at samples of increased and decreased *saturation* (intensity of color).

Taking a Look at the Layer Menu

Layers are useful, so much so that they have a fairly large portion of Chapter 23 devoted to them. That's plenty. If you have burning questions, jump ahead to Chapter 23 now. You won't hurt my feelings.

Taking a Look at the Select Menu

You've already used the Selection tools. The Select menu (shown in Figure 21.21) has commands that will make them easier to work with. The Inverse command is especially useful, as it lets you make a selection and then invert it, selecting everything *but* the originally selected object.

The ability to invert a selection can save you tons of time when you need to select a complicated object on a plain background. Instead of lassoing the object, click on the background with the Magic Wand tool. That selects it. If you need to combine several selections, press and hold the Shift key as you work. When everything but the object is selected, press Shift-Command-I (Mac) or Shift-Ctrl-I (Windows).

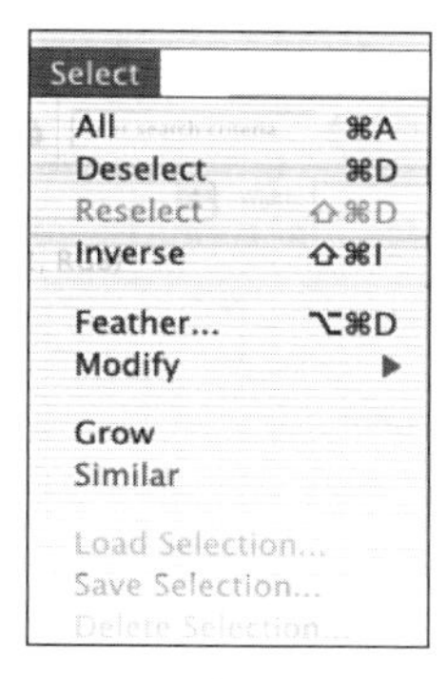

FIGURE 21.21
The Select menu allows you to select elements of an image in various ways.

Taking a Look at the Filter Menu

This is the fun menu. Expect to spend many hours of practice time trying out the Filter menu, especially if you also add on some third-party filters. If you count the different kinds of Liquify, there are over 100 filters on the Elements menu. You could learn one a week for the next two years and not run out of things to do, but we'll cover as many as we can in Chapter 25.

The Hints palette can display examples of each of the filters applied to a typical image. If you forget what a particular filter does, take a look here. You can also shop here for the filter look you want.

In addition to the Elements filters, there are hundreds more. Some are shareware or freeware. Others can be bought from a computer store or online software vendor. After you have installed them, they also show up at the bottom of this menu.

Taking a Look at the View Menu

You can't do much if you can't see what you're doing, especially in photo repair. Fortunately, you can zoom in and out on your pictures with a mouse click or a key combination. It's not an infinite zoom. Each mouse click enlarges or shrinks the image to a certain percentage of its original size. You can view at 25%, 50%, 66.7%, 75%, 100%, and so on up to 1600%. The menu also has a command to fit the picture to the screen, even though that may not be a precise percentage enlargement.

A Grid and Rulers are also included in the View menu. The Grid has a "snap-to" feature that you can toggle on and off from the menu. When it's on, if you try to align a line of type to a certain point, the grid will move it to the closest vertical and horizontal lines. Depending on where you want the type, that may or may not be helpful. Turn it off if it's a nuisance.

Taking a Look at the Window Menu

The Window menu, shown in Figure 21.22, actually tells you what all those windows and palettes and things on the screen are. Images, the topmost item, shows you a list of the images you have open. Selecting one brings it to the top of the pile.

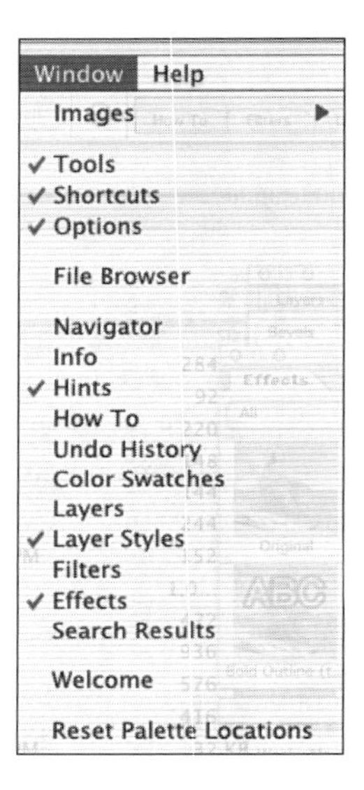

FIGURE 21.22
The Window menu allows you to display, hide, and arrange screen elements.

Next, you have the option of toggling the toolbox and the Shortcuts and Options bars on and off. I suggest leaving them on, unless you have a good reason for not wanting them to clutter up the scenery.

In the next section of the Window menu, there's a list of all the palettes available in Elements. Because they are also conveniently docked in the palette well, you needn't come here to open a palette. You can just drag the desired palette tab from the well onto the desktop and the palette will remain open as long as you need it.

Taking a closer look at the Swatches palette in Figure 21.23 (which you can display by choosing Window, Color Swatches), you can see that there's more to it than a child's box of watercolors. Open the Swatches menu to display a list of all the color libraries currently available to Elements.

Clicking the More button opens a menu that can name a particular swatch of color, or add one that's not part of the original set. If your company's logo has a particular shade of blue, for instance, you can scan the logo and then use the eyedropper to copy the color and add it into the swatch palette.

FIGURE 21.23
The Swatches palette displays the swatches of color in the current palette.

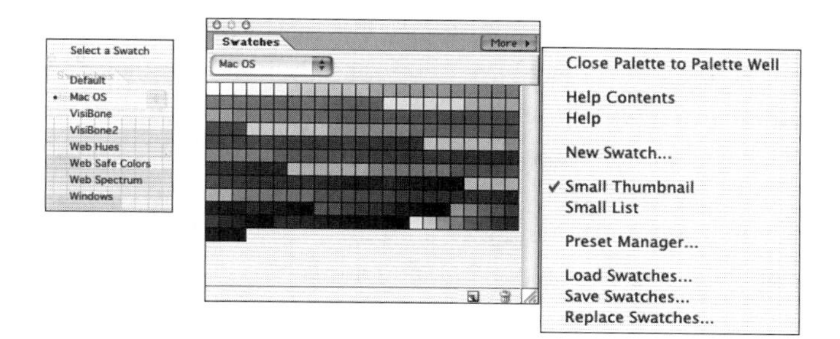

At the bottom right of the palette is a trash can, for deleting unwanted swatches, and a New Page icon. You can add the current foreground color as a new swatch by clicking this icon. Although each palette has its own menus and lists and icons, they all do roughly the same things in relation to the function of the palette. For instance, the New Page icon on the Layers palette makes a new layer.

To prevent desk clutter, only open the palettes you need. I like to keep Undo History, Layers, and Swatches available, and leave the rest docked. I recommend leaving Hints open when you're just beginning, but it's entirely up to you.

Setting Preferences

You can get to the Preferences dialog boxes either by selecting Preferences at the bottom of the Edit menu or by pressing Command-K (Mac). Once you're there you'll find eight different sets of options relating to everything from using smart quotes to changing the color of the grid lines. Figure 21.24 shows the first in the series: General.

FIGURE 21.24
Too many choices?

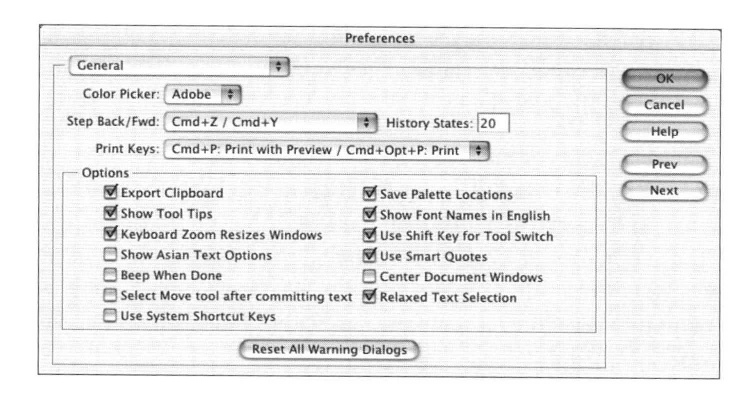

21

Some of these truly are common sense preferences. And as long as Show Tool Tips is checked, holding the cursor over any tool or button will display a short explanation. My suggestion is to look through the Preferences screens and take note of what's there. If you prefer to think metric rather than measuring in inches, that's an easy change. If you'd rather see your grid in a different color, go ahead and change it. But leave the options you don't understand on their default settings. As you learn more about working with Elements, you can come back and adjust the Preferences to suit your needs.

Undoing and Redoing

Before we wrap up this chapter, let's take a look at one last important function—Undo. Many Mac users know that Command-Z means Undo. To be able to undo with just a keystroke is a wonderful thing. It gives you the freedom to make mistakes, to experiment; and that is how you learn. (I often wish life came with an Undo key.) If the Shortcuts bar is displayed, you can also click the Step Backward button to undo the last action. To redo any change you've undone, click Step Forward or press Command-Y. To undo multiple changes, click Step Backward as many times as needed, or press Command-Z multiple times.

You can also find Undo at the top of the Edit menu, but the keystroke combination or the toolbar buttons are really easier to use.

Using the Undo History Palette

For those people who like to undo changes to their graphics, Adobe provides an Undo History palette, which makes it easy to back up step by step or jump back to an earlier state with just one click. (In regular Photoshop, and in the first version of this program, it was simply called History.)

In Figure 21.25, you can see a typical Undo History palette. To display the palette, choose Windows, Undo History, or click its tab in the palette well if it's displayed there. The Undo History palette lists all the tools I have used on the image so far. It reflects each use of a tool. If I select a brush and paint several lines, each line shows up as a history step because I have to press and release the mouse button in between lines. If I were to paint one very long continuous line without releasing the mouse button, there would be only one history step to show for it.

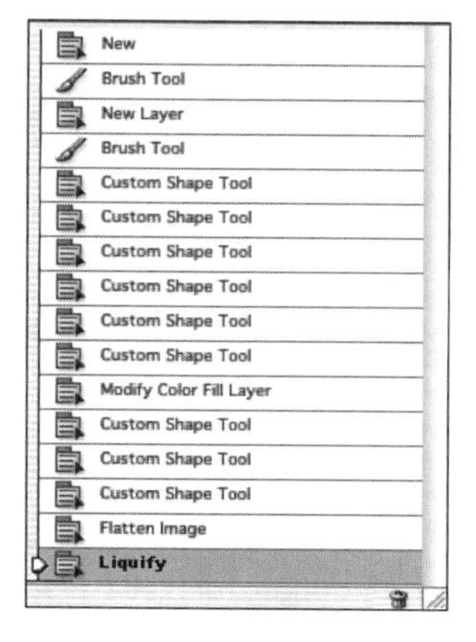

FIGURE 21.25
Changes I've made to an image are stored on the History palette.

If I select a step that's several steps back on the palette, all the subsequent steps will be undone. They'll appear dimmed on the palette and will be kept in memory until I do something different to the image. At that point, a new step will replace the ones I backed out of. Figure 21.26 displays a picture of the History palette before and after some changes are undone.

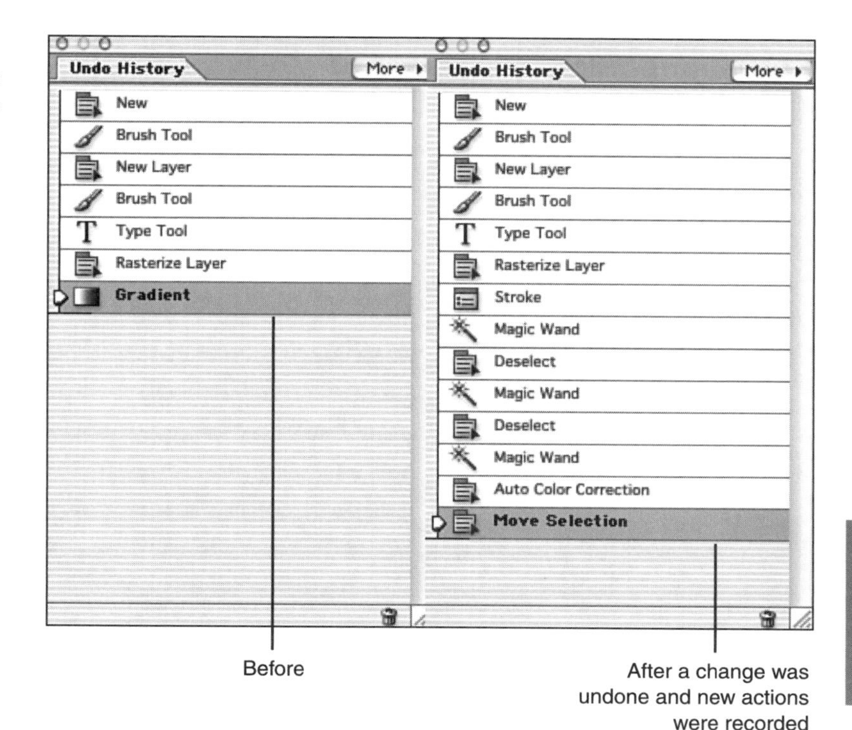

FIGURE 21.26
I was going to use the Gradient tool to make a change, and then changed my mind.

If you go to the General panel of the Preferences dialog box, you can enter a number of steps for the Undo History palette to remember. The default is 20 steps. Depending on your working style, you might find that 10 steps are enough or you may need as many as 50 if you like to draw with short pencil or brush strokes. The limit is 100. You can clear the history, if you are about to start a complicated revision to your picture and want to make sure you'll have enough space on the palette to keep track of the steps. Clear Undo History is on the pop-up menu that appears when you click the More button at the top of the palette.

Summary

You are starting to learn your way around the Photoshop Elements screen, and you have learned how to open a new page. You've looked at the toolbox and the palettes, at least a little bit. You know about the Shortcuts bar and the Options bar. Most important, you know where to look for help.

CHAPTER 22

Starting, Saving, and Printing Your Work

In the previous chapter, you learned a couple of ways to open a blank image file. (I sneaked it in ahead of this chapter so you could try out some tools.)

Starting a New Image File

Let's take another quick look at the New dialog box before we move on. Here it is again, in Figure 22.1, just to refresh your memory.

FIGURE 22.1
The New dialog box is used to create a new image file.

Starting at the top, you have the option of immediately naming your image, or leaving it untitled until you save it. Because I am almost always in a hurry, I skip that step and immediately consider page size. In this version of Elements and in the recent release of Photoshop 7, this dialog box has been modified to add a pop-up menu of possible page sizes, shown in Figure 22.2. The default is horizontal, 7×5 inches.

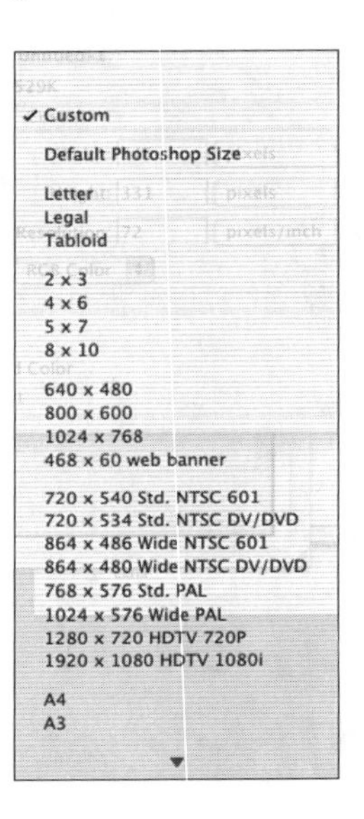

FIGURE 22.2
Most of the standard American and European page dimensions are included.

Choose a page size that's appropriate for what you want to do, remembering that screen formats are horizontal, while magazine covers and illustrations are more likely to be vertical. Landscapes and portraits dictate different orientations because of the shape of the subject.

If you have something on the clipboard that's waiting to be pasted into your new image, the dialog box will open with that item's dimensions in place of whatever other numbers might be there. You can still override it and choose a larger size, if you want.

Resolution is a tricky issue that we'll discuss in depth in the section, "Adjusting Resolution." Meanwhile, if your art project is to be viewed on the screen, perhaps as part of a PowerPoint slideshow or on the Web, or if you are just playing, as we are now, use 72 pixels/inch as the resolution. (By the way, we'll be taking a close look at options for online graphics toward the end of this chapter.)

You have only three choices for Mode in this dialog box. If you're working in color, you must choose RGB Color as the mode. Grayscale lacks color, and Bitmap means simply black or white pixels, with no grays at all. If you want to use Indexed Color mode, you'll need to select that option from the Image, Mode menu after creating the file using RGB Color or Grayscale.

The Contents options refer to what appears on the first layer of the image when it's created for you. White is the usual choice. Background applies whatever color is the current background color in the toolbox. (By default, it's white.) Transparent backgrounds are indicated by a sort of gray and white checkerboard effect. (You can change its color in the Preferences.) Transparent backgrounds are extremely useful when you are creating Web graphics.

When you're ready, click OK or just press Return to open the new image.

Browsing for a File

Most of the time, though, you won't be starting with a blank image. Instead, you'll have a photo that you want to work with. If you know where it is, you can press Command-O, click on the Open icon, double-click the file, or do whatever you generally do to open a file. If you don't know where on the hard drive your picture is, you'll turn to the File Browser. Open the File Browser by clicking its tab in the palette well, by choosing it from the File menu or the Windows menu, or by typing Shift-Command-O.

You can select the thumbnail size from the More menu or by clicking the View By button. The File Browser can also show you the file hierarchy and the creation data or camera file info, as well as a larger thumbnail of a selected image, as in Figure 22.3. Normally, all information about a file is displayed in the info window; to display only camera/scanner information, select EXIF from the menu on the lower right. As I mentioned the previous chapter, you can change the sort order using the options on the Sort By menu.

Use the top pop-up menu to locate the disk and folder you think the file is on, and just start scrolling through the folder list on the left until you find it. Drag it into an Elements window or double-click it, and it will open on its own.

To rotate the selected image 90 degrees to the right, click the Rotate button. To delete the file from your computer, click the Delete File button.

FIGURE 22.3
The info window includes creation date, camera used, and so on.

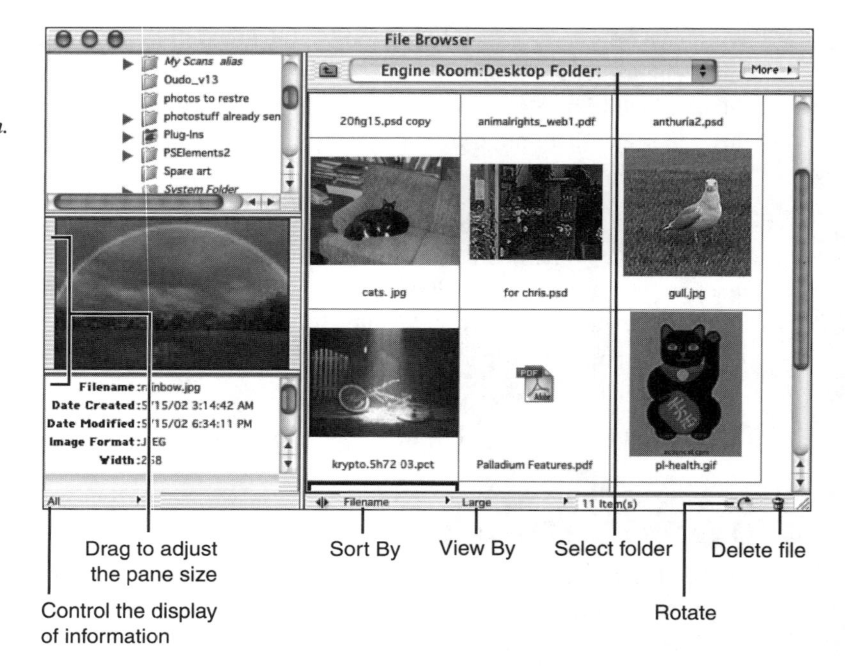

TASK

Task: Browsing and Opening an Image

Time for a little practice.... The following steps will walk you through the process of browsing for some picture files on your hard drive:

1. Go to the palette well and locate the File Browser tab. Click it once. If you don't see the File Browser in the palette well, choose Window, File Browser to open it.
2. After the window opens, use the scrollbar to review what's on the desktop.
3. Use the pop-up menu at the top of the browser to navigate to a different hard disk, disk partition, or other external storage device. Again, scroll through to see what's there.

Remember, you can customize iPhoto so that images in your photo library open directly in another photo editor, such as Photoshop Elements. Simply open the iPhoto preferences and change the Double-click setting to Open in Other. In the file browser that appears, navigate Photoshop Elements and choose it. Now, when you double-click an image in your iPhoto Library, Elements will start up and your image will be available for editing.

4. The top-left browser window shows the file hierarchy. Scroll down until you locate the folder where a photo you'd like to select lives. Then click the file when it appears in the list on the right. It should be highlighted.
5. Read through the image information in the bottom pane. If it is a digital photo that you've shot and saved to the computer, you can find out a lot about it. What was your shutter speed? Did you use a flash? If you scanned it in, when did you do so? What's the resolution?
6. Double-click the file to open it, or drag it into the Elements window.
7. Notice that the File Browser remains open. If you like, explore your hard drive(s) and locate more pictures you want to come back to and work on later. When you're done, close the File Browser.

Saving Your Work

Saving is the most important step in any project, but you probably don't realize how important it is unless you have had a computer crash while you're working. It happens to everyone, and eventually most of us learn to save our work often, work on a copy of the original, or learn other tactics that end up saving our sanity as well as our words and pictures.

Elements has a couple of different Save options. You can save the image in the format of your choice with the File, Save As command. (You can also save it optimized for the Web by choosing Save for Web from the File menu. We'll discuss this in depth later.) The first time you save any file, you'll be asked to give it a name (unless you already did so when you created the file or imported the image from a scanner, camera, or other application, such as iPhoto).

Figure 22.4 shows the Save As dialog box. It looks a lot like the Save dialog boxes in other applications, with a few minor differences.

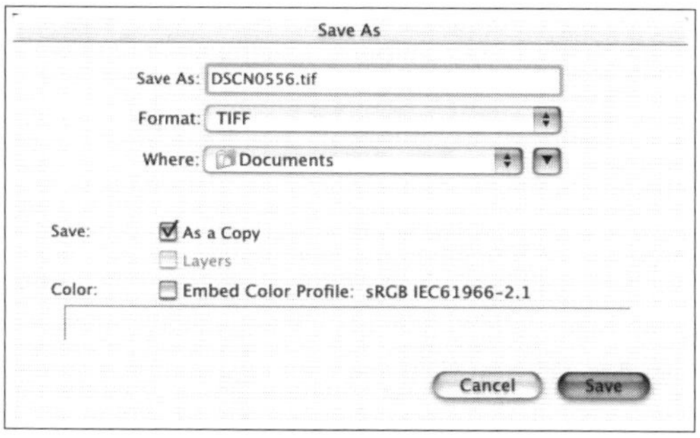

FIGURE 22.4
Be sure to use a name that will help you remember what the picture is. Raw camera filenames, like the ones shown here, don't tell you much.

Choosing a File Format

The Format pop-up menu, which will indicate the current file format, lists about 17 different file formats you can use. How do you choose? That will depend on the kind of image you are working on, and what you intend to do with it. Web browsers can only display images in three formats: GIF, PNG, and JPEG. You must choose one of the three if your picture is for Web use. If you are going to place the picture into a page of text, such as a newsletter, advertisement, or brochure, you will need to save it in a format compatible with the word processing or desktop publishing program you plan to use. It must also be compatible with the printing system you'll be using. Finally, you must consider whether your image will be printed in black and white, in full color, or using "spot color."

Spot color refers to individual accent colors applied by an artist, as opposed to *full color*, as in a photograph. Spot color is often used by graphic designers in places where a specific color must appear, such as on an official logo. Full color, also called process color or CMYK color, is printed with overlapping dots of cyan, magenta, yellow, and black inks.

The file format determines how the information in a file is compressed (if in fact it is compressed) and whether it contains data for multiple layers of the image as well as the color management system used and other important details. Elements can work with files in any of the types shown on its menu, but there are some you will probably never use.

Let's take a quick look at the formats available and what they actually do (the three-letter combination in parentheses after each format name is the file extension for that format):

- **Photoshop (.psd)**—This is the native format for both Photoshop and Elements documents. It saves all possible data about the picture, and is compatible with Adobe Illustrator and Acrobat as well as Photoshop itself. This is the best format to use while you are working, or if you intend to return to this image at some other time.
- **Bitmap (.bmp)**—Bitmap is a standard graphics file format for Windows. Because it must describe each pixel on the screen, a bitmap file can be quite large.
- **CompuServe GIF (.gif)**—GIF stands for Graphical Interchange Format. It was first used (prior to the Internet) by the CompuServe online network to enable members to view each other's graphics. It is still in use as one of the three common graphics formats for Web publishing. It compresses file size by limiting the number of colors. Because it is a compressed format, files are smaller and take less time to transfer. (We'll discuss GIF format options in greater detail later in the chapter when we discuss saving images for the web.)

- **Photoshop EPS (.eps)**—EPS stands for Encapsulated PostScript, a format developed by Adobe to go transparently cross-platform to many graphic, page layout, and illustration programs. For best results, use it when your work will be printed on PostScript-enabled printers.
- **JPEG (.jpg)**—JPEG stands for Joint Photographic Experts Group, the group that developed this format, which relies on 8-bit color (RGB only) and a "lossy" compression system (a system that selectively removes data from the file). It is a popular format for Web publishing because it can produce small files, but each save results in further compression and files will deteriorate quickly. Use JPEG as a Web format, but never as a working format. (We'll discuss JPEG format options in greater detail later in the chapter when we discuss saving images for the web.)
- **PCX (.pcx)**—PCX is a common graphics format for IBM-compatible PCs.
- **Photoshop PDF (.pdf)**—Adobe's Portable Document Format is a system for creating documents that can be read cross-platform. (You'll learn more about saving your files as PDFs later in this chapter.)
- **Photoshop 2.0 (.psd)**—This is an early Photoshop format for the Macintosh that doesn't support layers and flattens your image. Use this format only if your files must be opened by a very early version of Photoshop.
- **PICT file (.pct)**—This is mainly a Macintosh format, and is equivalent to PCX.
- **PICT resource (.rsr)**—This format is used by Macintosh for icons, sprites, and other graphic resources.
- **Pixar (.pxr)**—Pixar is the proprietary format used by high-end Pixar graphics workstations.
- **PNG (.png)**—PNG stands for Portable Network Graphic. It's a newer and arguably better format for Web graphics than GIF or JPEG. It combines GIF's good compression with JPEG's unlimited color palette. However, older browsers don't support it. (We'll revisit PNGs in our discussion of saving images for the web.)
- **Raw (.raw)**—This format saves image information in the most flexible format for transferring files between applications and computer platforms.
- **Scitex CT (.sct)**—This is another proprietary format for a brand of graphics workstation.
- **Targa (.tga)**—Another proprietary format, this one works with a specific kind of Truevision video board used by MS-DOS machines.
- **TIFF (.tif)**—TIFF stands for Tagged Image File Format. Files in this format can be saved for use on either Macintosh or Windows machines. This is often the preferred format for desktop publishing applications, such as PageMaker and QuarkXPress. Enhanced TIFF is a similar format that supports saving layers.

Photoshop format (.psd) is the default format in Elements, and is the best choice for saving a file that you intend to keep working on. As noted, it saves layers, layer style information, and color management information.

If you are opening a file in Elements that was created in Photoshop, you will not have access to unsupported features such as clipping paths or layer sets, but the data will remain with the file if you later reopen it in Photoshop.

Choosing Other Save Options

If you select the Save: As a Copy option in the Save As dialog box, Elements will save a (closed) copy of the current image and allow you to continue working on the open one. Save: As a Copy is especially useful for making a backup copy before you try a drastic change or for saving the file in a different format. Suppose that you create a logo for your business and want to use it in print and on the Web. You should save it as a TIFF or EPS file to print from, and save a copy as a JPEG, GIF, or PNG file for your Web page. The word *copy* is automatically added to the filename.

If you select the Save: Layers check box, your file format options are limited to the file types that can save layers separately. The Embed Color Profile option will save a color profile with the image file if you choose particular formats that use them. Use Image Previews Options to save a thumbnail of the image in the file. Choose Extension Options to save the file with a lowercase extension, which makes it compatible with Web/network servers that use Unix.

Saving Images for the Web

The full-blown version of Photoshop ships with a second program called ImageReady, which is used to optimize images for the Web. It helps you find the best combination of file format, image size, and image quality to place the image on a Web page so it will load quickly and look as good as possible. Elements has a feature, which is simply called Save for Web. In a related vein, Elements allows you to optimize images before sending them in email. We'll look at these options now.

To optimize a graphic is to adjust the image size and number of colors to get the best quality possible with the smallest file size.

22

Optimizing Images for the Web

Elements makes optimizing a photo or a graphic easy and almost automatic. Instead of saving your work in the usual way, choose File, Save for Web or click the Save for Web button. You'll open a dialog box like the one in Figure 22.5.

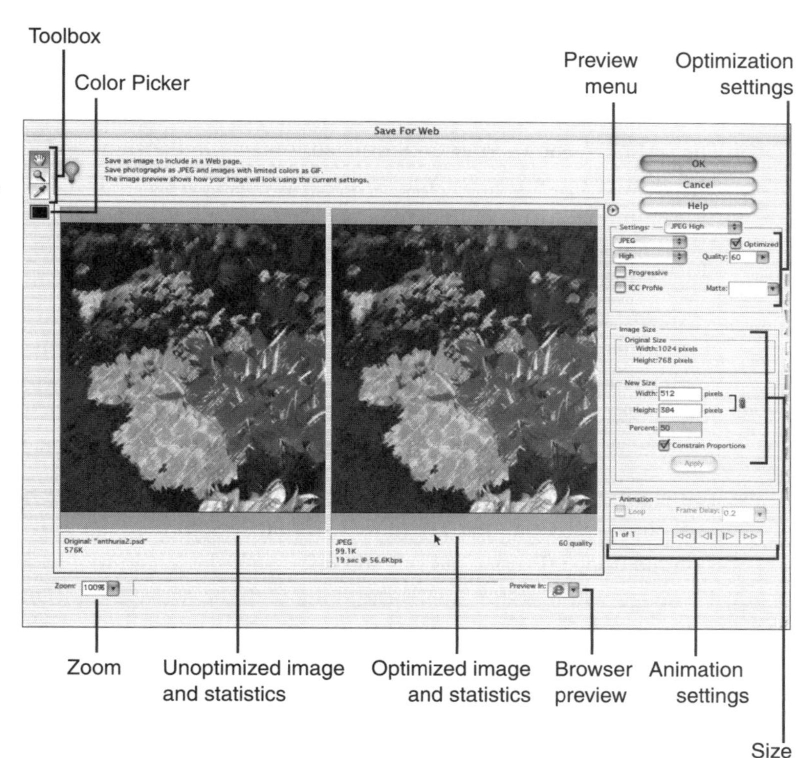

FIGURE 22.5
You can see how your changes affect the quality of the art, and decide what's acceptable.

Here you can try out different ways of saving your picture, and see which method gives you the smallest file with the least degradation to the image. Yes, degradation—every time you save a picture as a file smaller than it was originally, you lose some data. If you save the same picture several times in the compressed format, you can end up with so much loss—and so little data remaining—that your photo starts to look like a seventh generation photocopy, barely visible. This is *not* a good thing to do. Always save the original in a noncompressed format like PSD. When you convert it for the Web, compress it and save it only once.

There are three formats that all Web browsers can open automatically: JPEG, GIF, and PNG. If your browser has a QuickTime plug-in installed, it can also open TIFFs, but there's no guarantee that everyone with whom you want to share your pictures has QuickTime available.

After displaying your image in the Save for Web dialog box, Elements suggests a suitable image format compatible to the Web. You can change to a different format if you don't like the displayed results. I'll get to those formats shortly, but first let me explain a bit more about the dialog box.

The left pane shows your unoptimized image. On the right is your image as it might appear after optimization. Your considerations don't stop there, however. By clicking the right-pointing arrow and opening the Preview menu, you can change to various modes that simulate how your graphic will look when optimized and then displayed on a generic Windows monitor, a Mac monitor, or with its color profile. (You might select this if you are using a profile and you want to see how the image will look when printed.) Notice that the file size for both the original and optimized images is displayed underneath each pane. From this same menu, you can adjust the download time to match what you think most of your visitors will be using. By default, 28.8Kbps modem speed is used to calculate the download times shown below the optimized image.

You can zoom in or out of the image using the Zoom list at the bottom left. You can also zoom in by selecting the Zoom tool from the toolbox in the upper left and clicking with it on the image. Press Cmd/Alt and click with the Zoom tool to zoom out. You can move the image within the frame by dragging with the Move tool, to view hidden sections of it. If you have more than one Web browser installed (which you might, if you are seriously testing graphics for the Web), you can switch from one to another using the list on the lower right.

Finally, after adjusting the view, you're ready to change from one optimization type to another. Select the type you want, such as JPEG Medium, from the Settings list. The options displayed in the Optimization Settings area have been set to values that typically provide the best quality image for that setting. However, you can still adjust the individual options as needed. In the following sections, I'll explain each of these options.

JPEG (Joint Photographic Experts Group)

As you may recall from our discussion for file formats earlier in this chapter, JPEG is the most commonly used Web file format. Depending on your needs, JPEG is probably the best file format for you, too. It is great for photographs and other *continuous tone* (full-color) images, primarily because it lets you use 16 million different colors. (Of course, some Web browser programs, and some older monitors, can't handle that color depth.

Instead, they display a reasonable approximation of your artwork.) JPEG maintains color information, but does however employ a *lossy* compression scheme, which means that you can adjust and reduce the file size—at the expense of the image quality. It does this by examining adjacent pixels and averaging them against those closest.

When you select JPEG High, JPEG Medium, or JPEG Low format from the Settings list, the options appear. The differences between high, medium, and low relate to the quality of the result, and thus, the amount of lossy compression. With Low, you'll get a smaller file, but with a greater loss of clarity. If your image will only be seen in a very small format, that may not be a big deal, and with some graphics, even Low compression results in a nice-looking image.

After selecting the JPEG format you want from the Settings list, you can change other options as desired. You can choose Optimize to compress the file as much as possible in that format; however, you should be aware that some older browsers do not support this extra-optimized JPEG format. Adjust the quality level (compression level) by opening the list and dragging the slider. Choose Progressive to display the image in a browser, first at low quality, then gradually improving until the image is displayed in its saved format. Select ICC Profile to save the color profile (assuming you're using one) with the image; some browsers can use the profile to do simple color corrections for the user's monitor on the fly. If your image includes areas that are transparent, they must be filled with some color because the JPEG format doesn't support transparency. Open the Matte list and select a color that closely matches your Web page background.

GIF (Graphics Interchange Format)

If you save an image as a GIF file, you lose color information. The millions of colors present in a photograph are reduced to a palette of only 256 colors. That's how GIFs shrink files. If your picture happens to have relatively few colors—for instance, if it's a drawing rather than a photo—you won't lose any quality. In fact, if you know that there are only six colors, you don't even need to save the other 250. Obviously, GIF is not as good as JPEG for continuous tone art, but it's great for line art, logos, and anything with limited color. GIF also lets you save files with transparent backgrounds, which is extremely useful when you are creating Web buttons or other round graphics and you want the background of the Web page to appear around their edge. Furthermore, you can animate a GIF.

Even though GIF supposedly uses 256 colors, the reality is that there are only 216 of them that Mac and Windows computers have in common. These are said to be "Web-safe" colors, because they'll look the same on both kinds of machines. So in the process of converting to GIF, a color table of the most common 256 colors in the image is generated. When a color exists in the image but not on the table, a close color is chosen.

When selecting GIF from the Settings list, your first consideration is whether or not to use dithering. In Elements, and in other graphics programs, dithering mixes colors so that when you convert an image to a GIF or to an 8-bit PNG, you don't notice the missing colors. When you select a GIF that uses dithering (or PNG, as you'll see in the next section), you can select the dithering method and the dither amount. A higher amount dithers more colors, but might increase file size. After selecting a GIF dithering option from the Settings list, you can select the following dither options from the drop-down list in the Optimization Settings area:

- **None**—Does not dither, but instead uses a color from the color table that comes as close as possible to the missing color.
- **Diffusion**—Uses a method that produces a more random dither than the Pattern option. To protect colors in the image that match those in the color table from being changed, select Preserve Exact Colors. You'll want to use this option if your image contains text or fine lines, which you quite naturally wouldn't want "fuzzified."
- **Pattern**—Uses a variation of a halftone pattern to simulate colors not found in the color table. Halftone is a process of dithering that uses circles of various sizes to simulate the intensity of a color—the more intense the color, the larger its dot. The Pattern option uses squares rather than dots, but the principle is the same: The more intense the color, the larger the square.
- **Noise**—Uses a random pattern to dither, like the Diffusion option, but without dithering adjacent pixels. Instead, it dithers pixels in the "neighborhood." This dithering method reduces the "seams" that sometimes appear in the Diffusion method, especially along the edges of adjacent images with similar backgrounds.

After selecting a GIF with or without dithering, adjust the individual options if desired. Select Interlaced to display a lower-resolution version of the image quickly, while the higher-resolution version is downloading. Choose a method for generating the list of colors for the color table from the second drop-down list. You have these choices:

- **Selective**—This is the default. This option adds Web colors (the 216 colors shared by Windows and Mac operating systems) to the table over other colors that may be present. Colors that appear in large patches are added to the table over other colors as well.
- **Perceptual**—Chooses colors for the table that the eye normally sees with the greatest accuracy.
- **Adaptive**—Looks for the most commonly occurring hues, then adds a proportionate sampling of those colors to the table.
- **Web**—Uses the 216-color palette common to Windows and Mac operating systems.
- **Custom**—Saves the current palette of colors, and doesn't update it even if you change colors within the image.

In the Colors box, you can enter a number lower than 256 and reduce the number of colors in the color table, and thus, the file size. The Web and Custom color table methods allow you to select Auto from this list, in order to have Elements tell you the optimal number of colors that provides the best quality in a small file size. To preserve transparency in your image, you must turn on the Transparency option; otherwise, transparent and semitransparent pixels are filled with the Matte color you select. Turning on Transparency creates jagged edges on round objects, so you might consider leaving it off, and instead selecting a Matte color that closely matches your Web background color. For animated graphics, make sure the Animate option is selected.

PNG (Portable Network Graphics)

There are two kinds of PNG: 8-bit and 24-bit. The PNG-8 format uses 8-bit color, which means that each image can contain only 256 different colors. Like GIF, PNG-8 compresses solid areas of color very well while preserving sharp detail, such as that in line art, logos, or illustrations with type. Because PNG-8 is not supported by older browsers (although it is supported by the not-so-old versions of those same browsers), it might be a good idea to avoid this format for situations in which your image must be accessible to as much of the Web-viewing audience as possible. The PNG-8 format uses a *lossless* compression method, with no data discarded during compression. However, because PNG-8 files are 8-bit color, optimizing an original 24-bit image—which can contain millions of colors—as a PNG-8 will degrade image quality. PNG-8 files use more advanced compression schemes than GIF, and can be 10%–30% smaller than GIF files of the same image, depending on the image's color patterns.

The PNG-24 file format uses 24-bit color and is suitable for continuous tone images. PNG-24 also uses a lossless compression scheme. However, PNG-24 files can be much larger than JPEG files of the same image. The PNG-24 format is recommended only when working with a continuous tone image that includes multilevel or variable transparency, such as you'd have in an antialiased image on a transparent layer—an image whose edges are blurred with varying levels of transparency so that the edges are smoother and less jagged. You might also use varying levels of transparency to blend the edge of an object with its background, again smoothing out the transition. (Multilevel transparency is supported by the PNG-24 format, but not the JPEG format.)

If you'd consider GIF for an image, consider PNG-8 as well. It might give you a smaller file, and can do the job well. If you're thinking about JPEG, consider PNG-24 if your picture has multilevel transparency. If it's a straight image, JPEG will probably give you a smaller, more efficient file.

If you select PNG-8 from the Settings list, you'll be presented with options similar to those described in the GIF section. If you select PNG-24 instead, you'll see only some of those options listed. Choose Interlaced to display a lower-resolution version of your image as the higher-resolution one is downloading. Select the Transparency option to preserve transparency in your image, or select a Matte color with which to fill them.

If you're concerned about color accuracy, check your picture on both Mac and Windows platforms, if possible.

Making Transparent GIFs

One trick of Web graphics, to make them appear something other than rectangular, is to focus on a subject inside the image space and try to make the edges disappear. In this case, the last thing you want is to paste down a graphic and have it show up in a white or colored square instead of on your page background. Figure 22.6 shows what this looks like.

FIGURE 22.6
This is one of biggest problems beginners face, and it's also one of the easiest to solve.

To make a transparent GIF, follow these steps:

1. Place the object on a transparent background by selecting and deleting the current background, using an eraser to remove the background, or selecting the object and copying it to a new image file or a new layer that you have set up with a transparent background. (If you copy the object by itself to a layer that has a transparent background, you can remove the other layers in the file.) You'll know it's transparent when you see the gray checkerboard pattern (see Figure 22.7).

FIGURE 22.7
I copied this image to a new page with a transparent background.

2. Save the transparent version of the image as a GIF or PNG file using the File, Save for Web command, and then apply whatever tool your page assembly program uses to locate and place the image. In Netscape Composer, it's simply Insert, Image.

Creating a Web Gallery

Elements, like iPhoto, has an easy and elegant method of converting your stacks of photos into a Web-ready gallery that will display thumbnails of your pictures. Visitors clicking on a thumbnail will open up a full-page view of the image to appreciate it more fully. There are 14 different styles you can choose from, ranging from simple to elaborate. Bears is great for kid pictures, while Office is more businesslike, and Antique Paper is ideal for scanning in the old family album. Figure 22.8 shows a typical gallery page, as viewed from my Web browser. I chose the Horizontal Frame style, and selected pink for the background to best suit these little princesses.

To access this feature, choose File, Create Web Photo Gallery. You'll see the dialog box shown in Figure 22.9. First, though, make sure your pictures are all in one folder. Because they will be listed in alphabetical order by default, if you'd prefer some different arrangement, add numbers to the front of their filenames. Choose a gallery style from the Styles list and then click Browse and select your folder. Choose whether or not to include subfolders as well. Click Destination, and tell Elements where to place the completed gallery.

FIGURE 22.8
These old photos and etchings are displayed in the Antique Paper format.

FIGURE 22.9
Select the gallery style and set other options from this dialog box.

Web Photo Gallery
Site
Styles: Lace
Email:
Extension: .htm
Folders
Choose... Engine Room:Desktop Fold...dding:wedding web:images:
Include All Subfolders
Destination... Firewire X:Users:carla:Desktop:Valentine:
Background
Options: Banner
Site Name: Josh and Melissa's Wedding
Photographer:
Contact Info:
Date: 9/1/01
Font: Helvetica
Font Size: 3
OK
Cancel
Help
Some of the options may not apply to this style.

Some gallery styles have options; others do not. Here's a list of the options you may be able to set by selecting their category from the Options list:

- **Banner**—Enter information that will appear in the text banner at the top or bottom of the gallery. The site name appears in the browser's title bar.
- **Large Images**—Set the size of the images when they are selected from the home page, which displays the images as thumbnails. You can establish a size used for all images, or select a height or width, and allow the other dimension to be set proportionate to the image's original size. You can also select the JPEG quality used in the large displays. Add a border around the large version of each image by entering a value in the Border Size box. Select what you want to display as the title of the large image pages from the Title Use list.
- **Thumbnails**—Set the options for the home page, where images are displayed as thumbnails. Select a size for the thumbnails, add a border around each thumbnail with the Border Size box, and select a title for the thumbnail page(s) from the Title Use list. If you select the Simple, Table, or Web gallery style, choose the number of columns and rows for each thumbnail page.
- **Custom Colors**—Select the colors you want to use for each element of the gallery by clicking the appropriate color swatch and choosing a color from the Color Picker.
- **Security**—Protect your images from unauthorized use by selecting an option from the Content list. If you choose Custom, enter the text you want to use.

If you select the Table gallery style, you can choose your own graphic to use as the background if you like, by clicking the Background button. Click OK after choosing all your options to create the gallery. The home page opens in your browser so you can try out your creation. The destination folder you select will contain folders with the thumbnails and larger pictures, plus the HTML code to go into your Web page editor. Follow the usual procedures for adding pages to your Web site.

Emailing a Picture

You might not want to share a ton of pictures with everyone on the planet. You just have one that you'd like to send to one special person, attached to an email. Elements can do this for you, without even making you open up your mail program yourself. Just open the picture you want to send, and then choose File, Attach to E-mail, or click the Attach to E-mail button. If the file isn't currently saved as a JPEG, you'll be asked whether you want it converted. You probably do, unless you're quite sure the recipient has the software to see it in whatever format you are sending.

Next your usual message window will open. The file is already attached, so all you need to add is the address, subject, and a message. Then click the Send button to send it off.

Exporting a PDF

If you have ever read Douglas Adams's *Hitchhiker's Guide to the Galaxy*, you already know about babelfish. As the story goes, if you stick one in your ear, it acts as an automatic translation system, so you can understand what's being said in any given language from Abyssinian to Vogon. Too bad babelfish don't actually exist; software file formats could use such a device. Adobe's PDF format comes close. PDF files can be passed back and forth from PC to Mac to SGI workstation to Palm and Pocket PC devices.

There are generic PDFs and Photoshop PDFs. Photoshop creates single-image PDF files. Generic PDFs (which can contain multiple pages, pictures, and text) come from Adobe Acrobat, or from Illustrator, or from other programs that make use of the Acrobat Distiller. You can save a single-image PDF file using the regular Save As box. As an alternative to creating a single-image PDF file, you can create a PDF slideshow. The slideshow will run on any computer system that has Adobe Acrobat or a similar PDF reader. The slideshow starts automatically when opened and displays the images you selected when you created the file, one at a time. To start, assemble a group of images in a folder, and then choose File, Automation Tools, PDF Slideshow. The PDF Slideshow dialog box is shown in Figure 22.10.

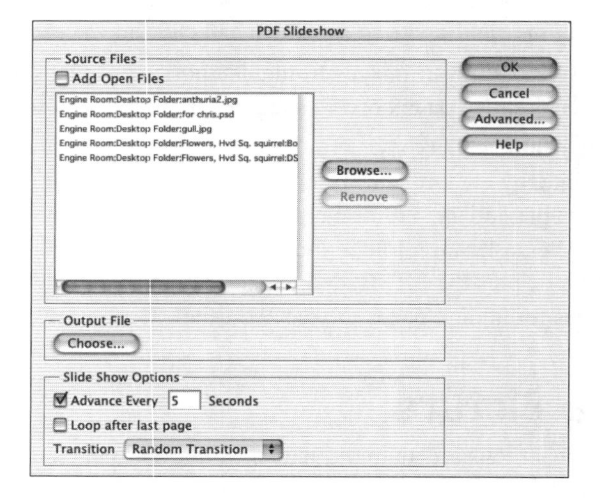

FIGURE 22.10
Be sure to check out the Transition pop-up menu. There are 18 possibilities, ranging from Blinds and Wipes to Glitter Down.

Click Browse and navigate to the folder you assembled. Select the files you want to use in the slideshow, and click Open to add them. Click Choose and type a name for the slideshow file, and then click OK. Choose the length of time that you'd like each slide to stay on the screen, and decide whether you want the show to run once and stop or to loop and run continuously. Finally, choose a transition. If you like surprises, choose Random Transition. When you're ready to create the file, click OK. Anyone with a PDF reader on any platform can open and enjoy your show.

Adjusting Resolution

As you learned in the chapters about iMovie and iDVD, resolution is an important concept to understand in digital imaging and can be just a little bit complicated because it means different things in different situations. To refresh your memory, resolution is what determines the quality of what you see on the screen—and what you see in print. You already know that your Elements images are bitmaps. A bit, in this case, is a pixel, an individual picture element. You can enlarge a piece of your image enough to take a good look at individual pixels. Figure 22.11 shows an image of flowers in various stages of enlargement up to 1600%. At that size, you can see that the image consists of little squares in different colors or shades of gray.

FIGURE 22.11
A pixel is a pixel, however large or small it is.

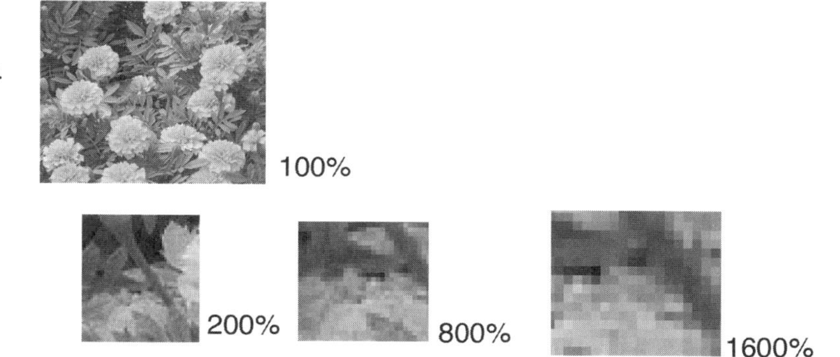

When you shrink the squares down to a smaller size, let's say 1/72 of an inch, they are too small to be seen individually. What you do see at that resolution is the picture as it appears on your monitor. Typical monitor resolution is either 72 or 96 dpi (dots per inch). (72 dpi is the traditional resolution of older Mac screens. New monitors are more likely to use 96 dpi resolution for a clearer picture. However, most people still think in terms of 72 dpi screen resolution. So will we.) In the case of 72 dpi, a square inch of a picture has 72 pixels, squared, or a total of 5,184 pixels per square inch.

When you go to print a picture, you'll see that your printer most likely has a much higher resolution than your screen. So an image displayed in a 1:1 ratio on your monitor will appear smaller when printed because the dots of ink per square inch are more numerous and therefore smaller than screen pixels.

Of course, if you have a higher resolution image, you have a lot more data and a much sharper, clearer picture to work with. That also means a bigger file to store and work on. So, the problem lies in deciding whether you want to work slowly on a large file with high resolution that will print well, or quickly on a smaller file that will look fine on the Web. If you already have plans for the picture, your choice is simple. If it's only going to be seen on the screen, you might as well work at 72 dpi. If you are placing the photo into another document at something close to or smaller than snapshot size, or printing small copies at home on your inkjet printer, you can get away with using 150 dpi as a working resolution. For more flexibility or larger prints, keep the resolution at 300 while you are cleaning it up, cropping, retouching, and so on. You can always save a low-res (lower resolution) copy later. For instance, if you're saving a copy of the picture for a Web page, you can reduce the resolution when you convert it to a JPEG, and end up with a clear *and* very small file.

Most printers do a fine job of adjusting resolution, particularly if the printer's resolution is a close or exact multiple of the file it's printing. Typically, a home/office inkjet printer will have a resolution of 300, 600, or even as much as 1,200 dpi. If you send a picture that's an exact multiple (for instance, 200, 300, or even 150 dpi), the printed result should have nice even tones with smooth transitions from one color to another. You shouldn't see jagged edges or obvious blocks.

There are times when you have to change the image resolution, even though it may mean losing some image quality. If you have access to a high-end digital camera or scanner, it will present you with very large files at a very high resolution. You may find that you have to reduce the resolution of the image before you can work on it, especially if your computer is an older, slower one or doesn't have enough RAM to work on a large file.

Photoshop Elements does a pretty good job of changing resolution by *resampling* the image. When you *downsample* (decrease the number of pixels in an image and thus decrease the image's size), you can reduce the size of the image, or the resolution, or both. Suppose you have a picture that's six inches square. You want it to be three inches square. You open the Image Size dialog box by choosing Image, Resize, Image Size, shown in Figure 22.12, and change the numbers to make the image size 3"×3" instead of 6"×6". You don't change the resolution. When you click OK, the image shrinks to half the size it was on the screen. Because you haven't changed the resolution, the file size shrinks to a quarter of what it was.

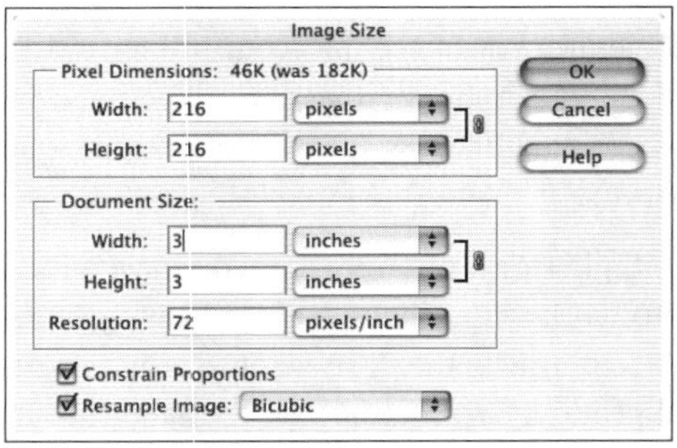

FIGURE 22.12
You can change the size and/or the resolution in this dialog box.

If you change the resolution while keeping the image the same size, the screen display will double, because you are now looking at an "inch" that's twice as long (144 pixels instead of 72).

Downsampling condenses the file information into a smaller spread of pixels, so you won't lose detail in the image as you might when upsampling. When you increase the resolution, Elements has to invent new values for the pixels you're adding. There are three different ways it can do this, and you can choose which of the three to apply by selecting it from the Resample Image pop-up menu at the bottom of the dialog box. Your choices are

- **Nearest Neighbor**—This is the quickest method, because it essentially copies what's there, assigning a value to the next pixel based on the average of the ones on either side of it. It works best on edges that are not *antialiased*. (Antialiasing is a technique that's applied to artificially produced edges such as the curve of a letter or a drawn line. It adds bits of gray along the edge to smooth it out and make it less jagged in appearance.) It will also produce a smaller file. It may, however, result in lines that appear jagged because of the lack of antialiasing.
- **Bilinear**—This method, considered better than the nearest neighbor method, is based on averaging the four pixels above, below, and to the sides of a target pixel and assigning it the resulting value.
- **Bicubic**—Instead of taking an average of four pixels, the bicubic method takes an average of eight, surrounding the target pixel on all sides and corners. This method produces the best results but takes a longer time to complete.

Figure 22.13 shows the differences between these three methods.

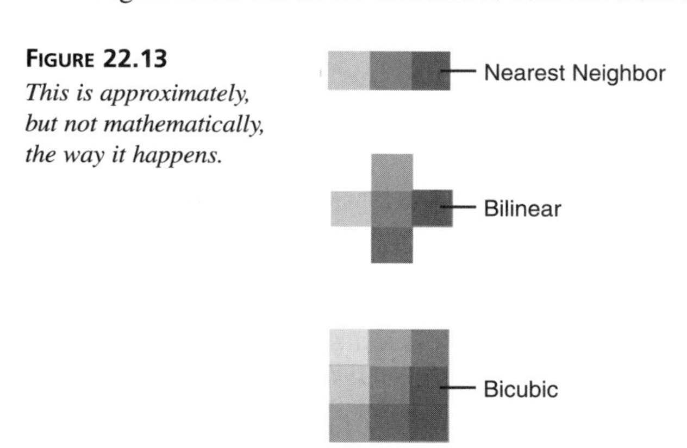

FIGURE 22.13
This is approximately, but not mathematically, the way it happens.

Remember, too, that the program goes through the entire set of calculations for each pixel in the image. When one is changed, all the ones around it must also change slightly.

Importing Source Images

You've learned how to start blank images in Elements, and it's something you'll find yourself doing whenever you need a quickie Web graphic, like a button or a logo. But the real reason that Elements exists, just like Photoshop, is to clean up, retouch, edit, color correct, and work with photographs and scanned images in general. (That's why it's bundled with many of the better cameras and scanners.)

Making a Scan

The first step in scanning a picture is to put it into the scanner face down. Until you've actually made a scan, you may not know what end of the scanner is the "top." Quite often, you can't tell by looking, or with logic. Of course, if your picture doesn't fill the scanner screen, you may choose to place it sideways to shorten the scanning time, as I have in Figure 22.14. Turning the image 90 degrees on the screen is probably quicker than scanning a correctly oriented portrait. However, you'll do yourself a favor and save a ton of time if you learn to place pictures in the scanner straight against an edge. You can always rotate it back, a half degree at a time, but why should you, when you can be a little careful and get it scanned right to begin with?

FIGURE 22.14
The picture as shown on the left will take about 1/3 longer to scan.

Okay, now what? Do you push the button on the scanner, or do something else? Because we're scanning into Elements, it makes sense to start from Elements. In the File menu, select Import and choose your scanner, as in Figure 22.15. You can also click Connect to Camera or Scanner from the Welcome window, and then choose your scanner from the Import list and click OK. You will probably see TWAIN as one of your choices. The TWAIN interface handles images from scanners, digital cameras, and frame-grabbers (it takes a single frame from a video camera). If you can identify the scanner's own plug-in, use it. Otherwise, TWAIN is generic and will work with most scanners. Oh, and be prepared to jump out of your skin when the scanner starts up. Most of them make a strange series of chirps and beeps and burps as they're starting up.

Selecting the scanner opens a window, which may or may not look like the one in Figure 22.16. There are, of course, dozens of different brands and models of scanner on the market, and each uses its own drivers. Unless you use the same model of Microtek scanner that I do, your screen will look different because your software is different, but that's okay. The elements in each are similar. At the very least, you'll see the scanner window, and the buttons for preview and scan. Preview gives you a quick, low-resolution version of the scan, mainly for positioning. Scan is the real thing.

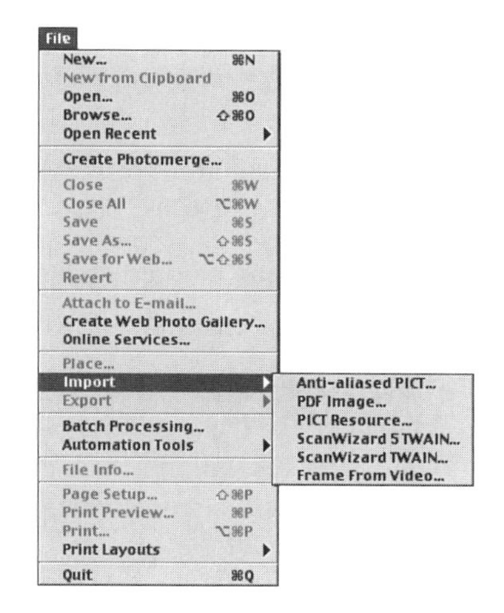

FIGURE 22.15
Scanning is done through the Import submenu in the File menu.

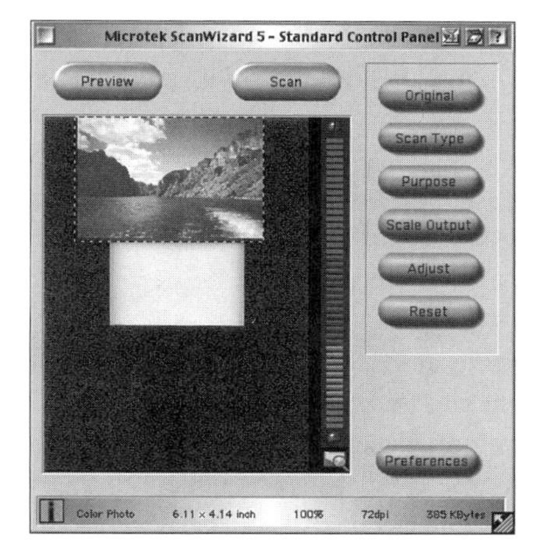

FIGURE 22.16
Your scanner window may look different. See if you can identify the Preview screen and button, and the Scan button.

You probably also have a set of buttons or a drop-down list with choices similar to the ones at the right of the Microtek window. These help you set up the scanner by having you identify what you are scanning and what you want to do with it. I'll review the choices I have available on my Microtek scanner, with the hope that our choices are similar. The Original option seeks to determine the probable resolution of what you are scanning and gives you these choices:

- **Photo**—Any size black-and-white or color photograph
- **Text Document**—A page to which you will apply OCR

- **Illustration**—Drawn or painted art, regardless of the number of colors used
- **Printed Material**

  Magazine—Any standard-quality printed magazine such as *Newsweek*, *People*, or *Good Housekeeping*, or a laser-printed newsletter or pamphlet

  Art Magazine—A very high quality printed magazine such as *Art News* or *Architectural Digest*

  Newspaper—Lower quality (low resolution) printing
- **Film**

  Positive—Kodachrome or other 35mm colored slides, any size film positives.

  Negative—Either black and white or color

This covers most of the items that you're scanning, but what if you're copying your coin collection or other small objects? Think about it. If you classify them as illustrations, you'll get the best combination of quality and resolution possible. If you don't much care what you get, call them newspapers. The scan will be much faster and still legible.

Scan Type refers to the number of colors to be scanned. Your choices are True Color, Web Color, Gray or Black and White. True Color allows all the millions of colors available. Web Color limits the scan to the 216 "Web-safe" colors. Gray gives you 256 shades of gray, and black and white is just that: one-bit b/w "color."

> If you are scanning type for OCR, always choose b/w. It doesn't try to interpret smudges or spilled coffee on the page.

Purpose affects the output resolution. (Remember the discussion of resolution earlier in this chapter?) If the picture's only going to the Web or for onscreen viewing, there's no point to giving it high resolution. Therefore, Onscreen Viewing outputs at 72 dpi. Inkjet printing, in search of a reasonable compromise for all kinds of inkjet printers, outputs at 200 dpi. Laser Print, Standard and Fine give you respectively, 100 and 150 dpi. Faxes are sent off at 200 dpi. OCR, which requires the most accurate scan of any, will output at 300 dpi. Finally, you can elect Custom and set any number between 10 and 9600 dpi. Remember that you don't need to go to the highest possible resolution. As long as your printer can print to a *factor* of the resolution supplied, you should end up with a nice clear picture.

The reason for this is easy to understand. Let's say you have an inkjet printer that outputs at 9600 dpi. You can scan and save the file at 9600 dpi. The scanner can handle that, but the resulting file is so big you'll probably choke the computer in the process. Whether you have enough RAM to handle all that, you'll still be limited by the speed. Handling that amount of data, as you learned last chapter, takes a long time even with a fast computer. However, you can divide the 9,600 dpi by any *factor*, which is to say, any number that divides in evenly with no remainder, and have a guaranteed good result. 200 pixels goes into 9,600 pixels 48 times. You can also use 300 because 9,600/300 = 32, and so on. The computer and printer agree on this very simple math and make the interpolation from 200 up with no trouble at all.

Scale Output or Adjust Output Size enables you to shrink or enlarge the output of the file by a percentage, maintaining the same aspect ratio. Increase to 150 or 200%, or decrease size to 75 or 50% of the original, precisely and with no loss of resolution.

The Adjust button gives you access to a panel of sliders, shown in Figure 22.17, which can correct obvious color and or exposure problems while scanning the image. It's good for fixing major flaws, like a photo that's turned purple from sitting in the sun. Because you can't really see what you're doing close up, it's not good for subtle adjustments.

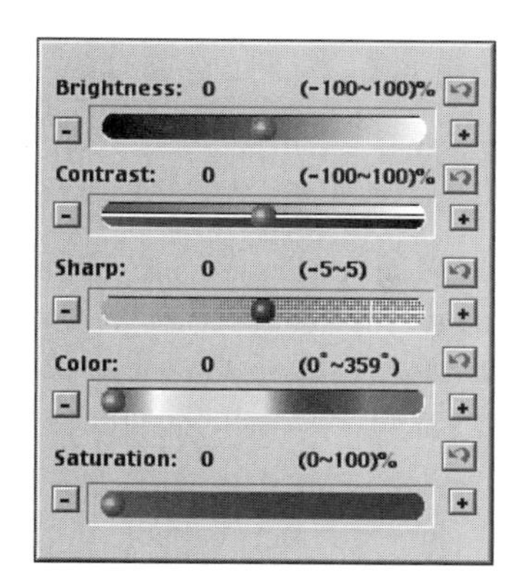

FIGURE 22.17
Your scanner may do this differently, but the same kinds of sliders are somewhere in the interface. Look on the menus for them, too.

The last button (almost), Reset, puts every setting back to where it was originally. Use it if you're starting a new scanning job unlike the last one, for instance going from scanning a photo of Great Uncle Hector to copying his typewritten love letters to Great Aunt Sue.

Finally, you're ready to click the Scan button or a similar one. Because you've initiated the scan from Elements, you don't need to deal with other options. The scanned image will appear as any other image in the Elements window. Be sure to save it before you start working because it is only a temporary file at the moment.

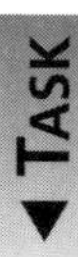

Task: Scanning

If you don't have a scanner, please consider buying one. It will be very useful as you continue in computer graphics. Assuming you have a scanner available, try this:

1. Make sure the scanner is connected to the computer and that you can find it under the Import submenu of the File menu.

2. Find an old family photo in grayscale.
3. Place it in the scanner and choose File, Import to begin the import process from Elements.
4. Elements initiates the scan. Drag the sides of the selection box so it just fits the image. This will prevent scanning more area than necessary.
5. Check the settings. You should scan at 200 dpi, in 256 grays.
6. When you're ready, press the Scan button to send the image back to Elements.
7. Be sure to save your scanned picture with a filename such as Old Family Photo.psd. We'll use it later on.

Importing Images from a Digital Camera

Digital cameras and scanners have a lot more in common than digital cameras and film cameras. Film cameras rely on light and chemistry to produce an image. Digital cameras use a device that collects image data much like the scanner does. Scanners send the data directly to the computer. They don't have any storage media. Cameras have memory. They may have an internal memory and/or a removable memory card, stick, or floppy disk. When you fill up a card and need more memory, you remove the full card and pop in an empty one. Memory cards (and for our purposes, Sony's Memory Sticks are also considered "cards") are intended to be reused. They're not for data storage. So, at some point, you need to get the data off the card or out of the camera and into the computer. There are several ways to do this, depending on the make and model of camera you use.

The easiest method for importing digital pictures from a camera is to connect the camera to the computer with a USB cable. If your camera is capable of this, it will have come with the appropriate cable and, perhaps, a driver on a CD-ROM. If your camera is compatible with iPhoto, you may not need to install any special driver. (Visit `www.apple.com/iphoto/compatibility/camera.html` for a list of supported cameras.) Refer to Chapter 12 for more information about importing photos into iPhoto.

When you start to really use your digital camera or to scan and store lots of regular photos on your computer, using a good photo organizer like iPhoto can make life much easier.

If you do choose to use the software that came with your camera, install the driver. When you connect the camera to your Mac, you'll probably see your camera as an icon sitting on the computer desktop, as it is in Figure 22.18. If you don't see a desktop icon, connect the camera via USB and start the camera's software if it doesn't start up on its own. Be sure you have set the camera to play or transfer mode as directed by your camera's manufacturer.

FIGURE 22.18
Other brands of camera have their own icons. Some cameras do not display an icon on the desktop.

The connectors on the USB/camera cables are very delicate. Be sure you are inserting them right side up, and don't use force. You can replace a damaged cable, but getting either the camera's or computer's USB port replaced is expensive and time-consuming.

With the camera mounted this way, you can use it like any other hard drive. The Nikon software creates a page of thumbnails you can view and a folder with all the raw pictures (see Figure 22.19). The first thing I always do with my pictures is to copy them into a folder in the computer labeled with date and subject. Then I immediately back this folder up onto a CD-ROM and check it to be sure everything transferred correctly.

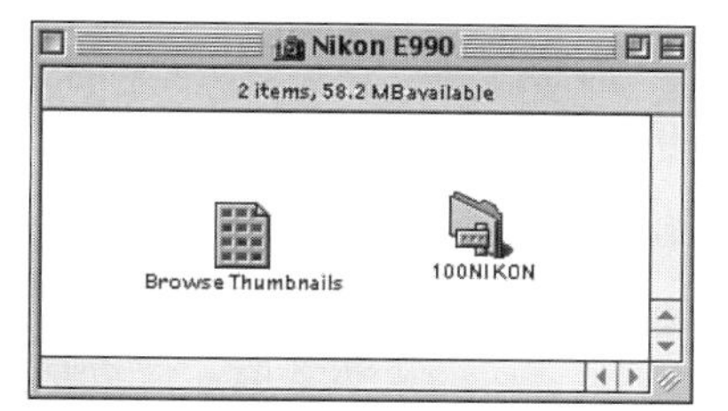

FIGURE 22.19
My Nikon lets me browse through thumbnails or open the folder containing the images.

That's the easiest way to import batches of pictures at the same time. If you simply need to locate and open a single photo, let your camera pretend to be a hard drive. Use the Open command in Elements to locate and open the picture you want. Then save it to the hard drive. Be sure you turn the camera off when you're done copying pictures. Leaving the camera on, even if it's "asleep," will eventually drain the batteries.

For some cameras with removable storage disks, it's easier to download stored images using a card reader. The card reader is a small box that plugs into a SCSI or USB port. When you place a memory card into it, it acts like an external drive. Older digital cameras may use regular floppy disks, which can be inserted into any computer or external drive that read floppies. Plugging the card into the reader, just like attaching the camera to the computer, places it on the desktop so you can copy the pictures onto your hard drive, store a copy, and work on them as much as you like.

When you're done transferring photos from removable storage media in this way, it's always a good idea to put the card back into the camera and reformat it, rather than simply erasing it by dragging the pictures to the trash. Reformatting clears the entire disk, not just the directory. Also, if you use the disk in more than one camera, whenever you switch cameras, reformat the disk for the camera with which you will be using it.

Importing Still Frame Captures

If you have a digital video camera, you can work with single frames from your favorite video. Save your video in a compatible format such as AVI, WMV, MPEG, or QuickTime, and choose File, Import, Frame from Video, as I've done in Figure 22.20. Click Browse to locate your video. It will open in the window in the dialog box. Use the video controls to steer to the frame you want to use, and click Grab Frame as it goes by. It will be copied into an Elements window, ready to work with and already labeled with a name similar to the video file. Continue grabbing as many frames as you like, and then click Done to close the window.

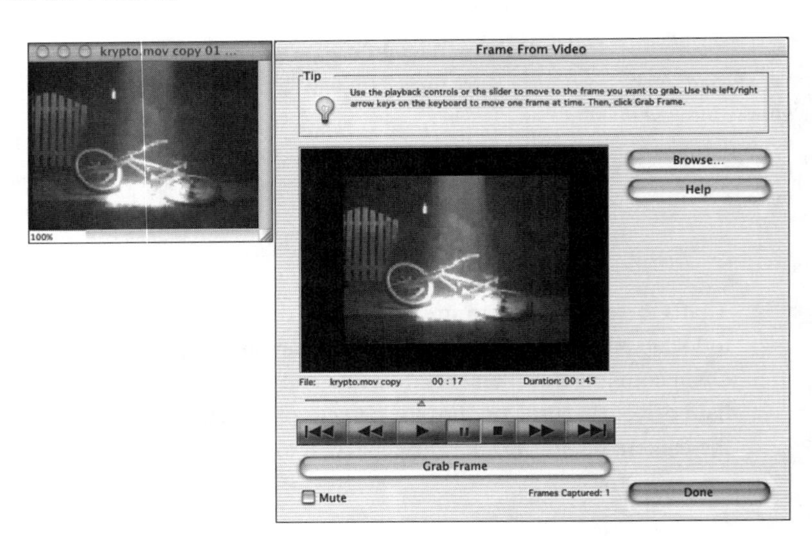

FIGURE 22.20
This is a frame from a TV commercial my husband worked on. (Used by permission.)

You should be aware that the quality of a single digital frame won't be very good, but you can still use it as a basis for filters and other tricks.

Changing Image and Canvas Sizes

The size of the image you import from your digital camera or digital video system is directly dependent on the file resolution. My favorite camera, a Nikon CoolPix 990, gives me the same number of pixels per image, regardless of the resolution I use. It just makes the picture correspondingly larger or smaller. If I shoot an image at my usual 1,260×980 resolution, when I open it in Elements, it can be 17.7×13.3 inches at 72 dpi, or it can be 4.2×3.2 at 300 dpi, depending on how I have chosen to save it. Because I hardly ever need a picture as big as 17 inches, I can reduce the size of the original to something more reasonable and increase the resolution as needed with no loss of quality.

Remember that the amount of detail you see in an image depends on its pixel dimensions, whereas image resolution controls the amount of space the pixels are printed over. The difference between a 72 dpi image and a 300 dpi image that are both the same printed size is that the latter has smaller dots and more of them, hence greater detail.

If you change the resolution of the picture, without changing anything else, you will change the printed size. Increasing the resolution makes the picture smaller. If you want to keep the picture the same size as before, and still increase the resolution, you need to resample the image. You learned about resampling methods in the last chapter. It simply means that Elements re-computes the data for each pixel based on adding or subtracting some of them. If you increase the resolution from 200 to 300 dpi, Elements has to add 100 extra pixels per inch, jamming them in between the existing ones. What color they will be depends on the color of the pixel they are next to.

Image Size

Changing the image size happens in the Image Size dialog box, shown in Figure 22.21. To display this box, choose Image, Resize, Image Size. As you can see, you can learn a lot from this dialog box. First, it tells you how large the current file is. (The file size will change as you add layers to the picture.)

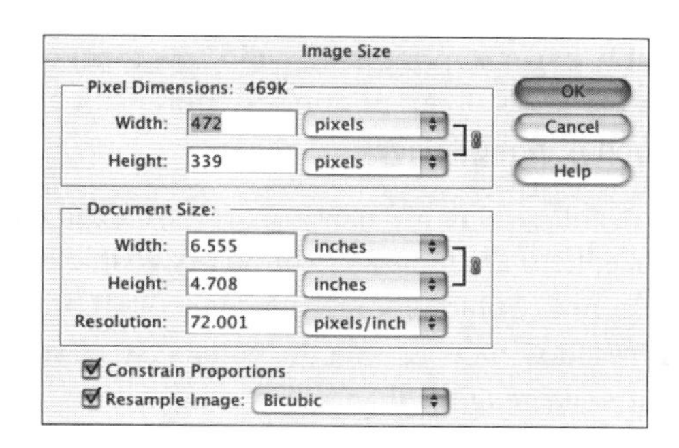

FIGURE 22.21
This dialog box is located under the Resize submenu of the Image menu.

You can change the width and height by typing new numbers into the boxes. To be sure that you keep the proportions as they were, and to avoid doing all the math yourself, check Constrain Proportions and only enter one dimension. Elements will take it from there. Remember to use `Bicubic`, if you need to resample the image. It's the most accurate method.

Canvas Size

Sometimes you don't need to make the image bigger, you just need to add blank space around it. That's when you use the Canvas Size dialog box shown in Figure 22.22. To display it, choose Image, Resize, Canvas Size. Use the grid to indicate where to "anchor" the current image inside the larger one. Leave the anchor square in the middle if you are adding space all the way around the image or move it to the appropriate side or corner to add space at the opposite sides.

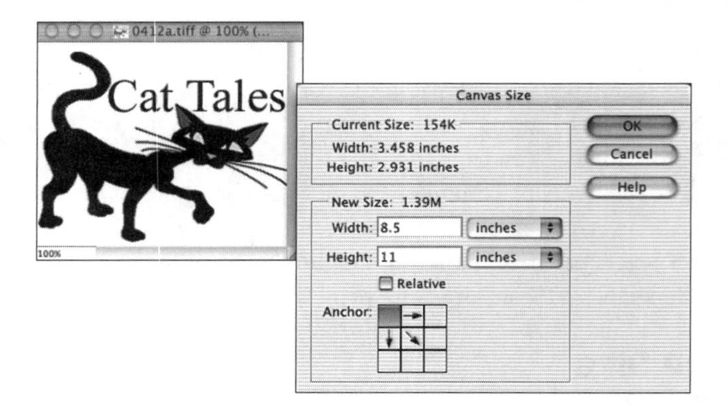

FIGURE 22.22
The old image is anchored in the corner so I can print the page as letterhead.

Understanding Color Systems

You've learned how to open files, and although we haven't talked much about how to improve your photos yet, you know how to import them into Elements and make a few changes, so you're probably eager to print them and show them off. In this section, you'll learn everything you need to know about printing, starting with color systems and how they relate to preparing and printing images.

When it comes to printing color, there are many models you can use to specify the colors to print. Naturally, because there are thousands of colors visible to the human eye, it's difficult for any color system to accurately reproduce them all. If printing a color photograph is your goal, your result will depend on the color system you choose to display, save, and ultimately print your image with.

RGB

RGB (short for Red, Green, Blue) uses a system that defines a particular color by the amount of red, green, and blue it has in it. If you mix all three colors in equal amounts, you get white. If you don't add any of them, you get black. Computer monitors, television sets, and Photoshop Elements use the RGB system to define and display the colors you see onscreen.

Typically, a scale from 0 to 255 is used to specify the amount of each color (red, green, and blue) that exists in a particular color you're looking at. You may have noticed that when you open the Color Picker, instead of clicking on the color you want, you can define it by typing in the appropriate formula—the amounts of red, green, and blue in the color.

Closely related to the RGB color system is CMYK, short for Cyan, Magenta, Yellow, Black. When you mix cyan, magenta, and yellow in equal amounts, you get black. If you don't add any of them, you get white. CMYK is also known as the four-color process, and it's used by many computer printers and professional four-color printers. Unfortunately, Elements does not support this system—but that shouldn't matter too much, because if you want to print in four colors (which is expensive) it's probably because you want to produce a nice-looking color brochure, sales catalog, or similar project, and the program you use to create such a project will certainly support CMYK.

HSB

The Hue, Saturation, Brightness (HSB) model is mathematically similar to the RGB model—it produces the same number of colors, but in a different way. The hue value specifies the color, such as red. The saturation value specifies the purity of the color—a lower saturation value gives you a more grayed-out version of your hue—in this example, a more grayed-out red. The final value, brightness, specifies the amount of whiteness in the color; in other words, how light or dark the red is. Brightness is sometimes also called luminance, value, or intensity. You might have noticed the Hue, Saturation, and Brightness boxes in the dialog box for the Color Picker. You can use these values rather than the RGB values to specify the exact color you want.

Pantone Color Matching System

With the Pantone Color Matching System, values are not needed. Instead, the system uses a series of color charts and accompanying print formulas to assure a designer that the color he chooses from a chart will be reproduced exactly. This system is often used to recreate colors critical to a printout—typically, a signature or logo color. All a designer has to do is select a color from a Pantone Color chart, and then specify the number of that color on the order form, or within the software program generating the image (assuming the program supports the Pantone system). If needed, you can use this system as well—Elements provides a place in the Color Picker dialog box for entering the Pantone color desired.

Preparing the Image

Professionals know the value of having color-compensated monitors and color-printing profiles (you may remember color profiles from Chapter 8, "Monitors and ColorSync"), which guarantee that what you see on the screen is as close as possible to what you will see on paper. Because the process of mixing colors for a screen is inherently different from the process of mixing colors for print, what seems to be just the right color for an object when you chose it onscreen may appear altogether wrong on paper. Likewise, if you're designing graphics for use on the Web, the proper colors for one brand of monitor or even one resolution may appear completely wrong when seen on another monitor or at another resolution.

Elements solves this problem by giving you the power to invoke a background process called *color management*. This process translates the color you see when you're creating your image into a color that's as close to the original as possible for the finished product. For color management to work, you first have to turn it on. Doing so is a one-time process that is very simple and applies to all your work in Elements from that point on—or at least until you turn color management off. Here's how to turn it on:

1. Choose Edit, Color Settings.
2. In the Color Settings dialog box, select a color management option:

   Limited Color Management enables Elements to translate the colors you see for Web users with high-class monitors. This option slows down the program somewhat.

   Full Color Management is your best choice. This gives Elements the clearance it needs to optimize the colors you use for the printer that will render your image. This option slows down the program even more.
3. Click OK.

With that done, you can set up any image you edit for optimal printing or display on a wide variety of media, including your own printer. But first, let's talk about some other issues such as choosing the right paper, selecting your page setup options, and previewing an image.

Selecting Page Setup Options

You can make minor changes to your printed output from the Page Setup dialog box. Choose File, Page Setup to display it. Figure 22.23 shows a typical Page Setup dialog box.

FIGURE 22.23
Your dialog box will look different unless you use the same printer I use.

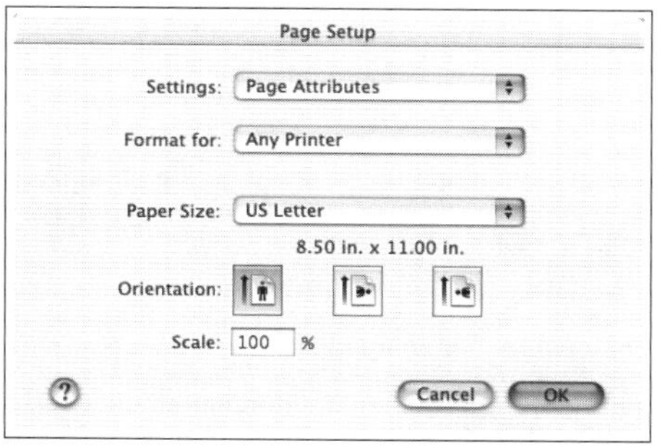

Each printer's Page Setup dialog box looks a little different, but they all provide the same basic functions. Here's a list of some of the more typical options:

- **Printer**—The name of the printer may appear at the top of this dialog box. If it's wrong, or if you don't see it listed, select the printer you want from the Printer list, or click the Printer button.
- **Properties**—Click this button (located near the Printer list) to access a dialog box that enables you to change things such as paper size, layout, printer resolution, and halftone settings. You can also make these changes here or in the Print dialog box.
- **Paper Size**—Choose the size of the paper on which you're printing.
- **Source**—If your printer has two paper trays or gives you a choice of tray or single-sheet feed, you can choose the paper source that you want the printer to use.
- **Orientation**—Choose how you want the printed image to be placed on the page: portrait (the narrow edge of the page at the top) or landscape (the wide edge at the top).
- **Reduce or Enlarge**—If you see these options, use them to adjust the size of the image by a percentage.
- **Margins**—Use these settings if they're available to adjust the space between the image and the edge of the page.

When you actually print the image (we'll get there soon, I promise), you might run into a problem with files that are especially large. If the image dimensions are larger than the dimensions of the paper you're printing on, Elements will warn you. You can then choose to print anyway, resulting in only part of the image being printed, or you can cancel and adjust the Reduce or Enlarge value so that the whole image fits on the page.

Previewing an Image

After making page setup adjustments, if any, it's time to preview your image as it might look when printed. Take a look at the Print Preview dialog box in Figure 22.24. To display a similar box on your screen, choose File, Print Preview or click the Print Preview button.

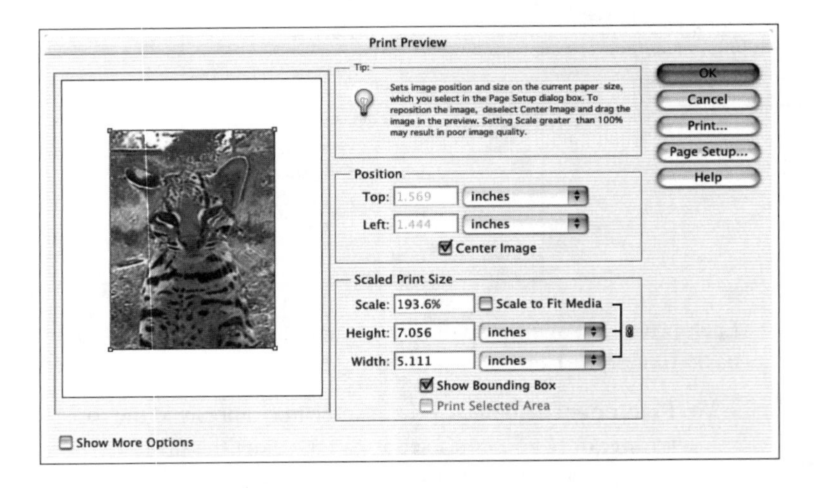

FIGURE 22.24
Notice the options in my Print Preview dialog box.

The first option here is Position. If you uncheck Center Image, which is checked by default, the image will print wherever it appears on the page in the preview window. If you then turn on the Show Bounding Box option, you can slide the picture around on the page, placing it wherever you want. If you drag a corner of the image, you can rescale it. The Scaled Print Size values will change accordingly. You can also scale the image by typing a percentage into the Scale field. Scaling is done relative to the original image size. If you have a photo that's 6 inches wide and you want it to print 9 inches wide, scale it to 150%. You might also be able to change this setting through the Page Setup box. To scale the image to fit the size of your page, select the Scale to Media option.

If the Print Selected Area box is checked and you have a rectangular area currently selected in your Photoshop image, you can print just that area. This works only with rectangular selections created with the Marquee tool, and it doesn't work for feathered selections.

When you click Show More Options, you can choose between Output options and Color Management options. In Figure 22.25, I've added crop marks and a caption line to my photo. By default, the caption is the file title. Here's a list of the Output options:

- **Background**—If you want to print a background color around your image, click the Background button and you'll be greeted by the standard Color Picker. Whichever color you pick is used only for printing and does not alter your actual image file. Be careful about using this feature. It eats up a lot of ink!

- **Border**—Similarly, if you'd like a border around your printed image, click the Border button. In the resulting dialog box, you can set the width of the printed border in inches, millimeters, or points. The border is always black; you can't change the color. (As with Background, using this feature doesn't affect the actual image file.)
- **Caption**—Check this box, and on the printed page you'll see the text that appears in the Caption area of the File Info dialog box for that file. (To get to this dialog box, choose File, File Info and make sure that Caption is selected in the top pull-down menu.) This can be helpful for providing contact info or details next to your image. If there's nothing entered here, the filename will be the default caption.
- **Corner Crop Marks**—Corner crop marks appear around each corner of your image, defining where it should be trimmed. They're simply horizontal and vertical lines.

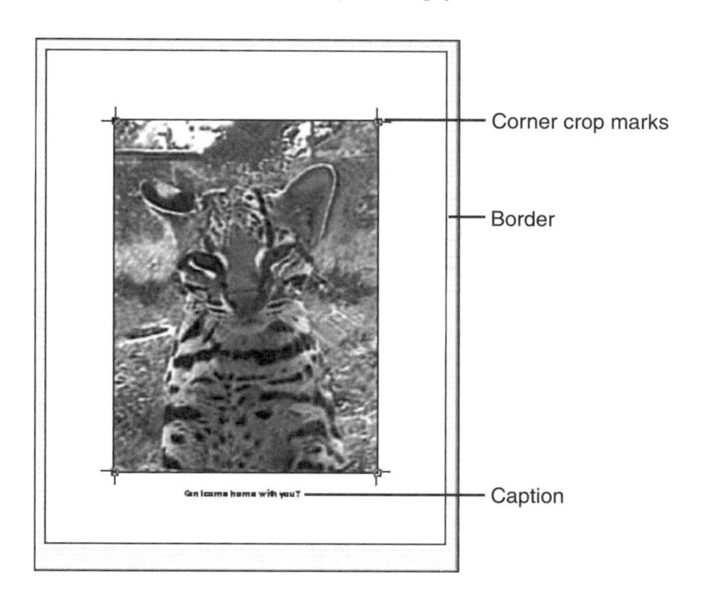

FIGURE 22.25
A picture ready to print, showing various crop marks, a border, and a caption.

Earlier, I explained how to turn on color management within Elements. But to get it to work with the current image, you must select a *profile* for your image. The profile instructs Elements with regard to how it should translate colors for output on its intended medium. To display the Color Management options, click Show More Options in the Print Preview dialog box; then choose Color Management from the drop-down list.

The area marked Source Space lists the native color management profile in use by the current image. Generally, there is none, so it will most frequently show something like "Untagged RGB." From the Profile list, choose the profile that best suits your printer, or the device you intend to use to render the image. Toward the bottom of this list, you'll see dozens of printers and monitors—some branded, some generic. You may very well find your printer in this list. In any event, here's generally what you should choose, and why:

- Choose your printer model (if available) when you intend to print your image on your own printer.
- Choose your monitor model if you intend for your graphics to be used over the Web and seen on your monitor.
- Choose a generic monitor for everyday Web graphics, or a high-end monitor (such as a Trinitron) for highest-quality Web graphics.
- Choose Printer Color Management (second in the list) to have your own printer driver handle the job of color management. Most major brands of color inkjet printers sold today include their own color management options, which are accessible through their drivers' Print dialog boxes.

  Leave this option set to Same As Source if your image is saved using a newer format that includes its own print profiles. You can find out whether your image uses such a format by checking the Source Space area for the name of this profile.

After selecting your options and previewing your image, you're ready to print.

Printing the Page

Okay, now we're finally ready to print the image. I told you there were a lot of variables involved in printing, didn't I? One more thing before you print—consider making your image file smaller before sending it to your printer. This not only speeds up printing, but also reduces the chances that the printer will quit halfway through the print job. To reduce a file's size, flatten all the layers into one by choosing Layers, Flatten Image. You can also reduce the resolution and the image size by choosing Image, Resize Image. When you're ready to print, choose File, Print or click the Print button.

The Print dialog box for my Epson printer is shown in Figure 22.26. This dialog box's appearance varies depending on the printer you have, the platform you're running on, and the mode of the image. Select the number of copies to print, set other options as available, and click OK to print the image.

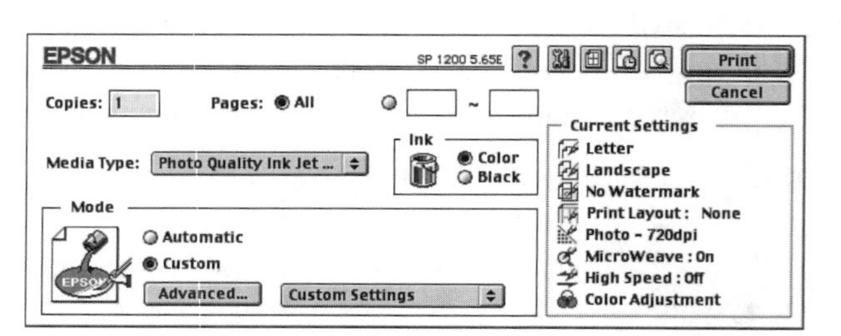

FIGURE 22.26
The ultimate dialog box: Print.

Making Contact Sheets and Picture Packages

In this automated world, it's only fair that our computers should provide ways to automate some of the more mundane tasks that we must occasionally do, such as making contact sheets and picture packages.

Contact Sheets

If you have a background in darkroom photography, as I do, you're already used to making contact sheets of every roll of film you process. Fortunately, Elements enables you to print pages of thumbnails. All you need to do is save the images for the contact sheet into a folder or, if you use iPhoto, locate the folder for the roll you want to work with.

To refresh your memory, iPhoto stores your images in the Pictures folder of your home account in a subfolder called iPhoto Library. Each roll is placed in it's own folder labeled with a number for the day of the month, which is inside a folder numbered for the month of the year, which is inside a folder labeled with the year. I wish my tax papers were that well organized.

You can even place several subfolders inside one main folder. Then select File, Print Layouts, Contact Sheet to open the dialog box shown in Figure 22.27 and select the folder you want to make contacts of.

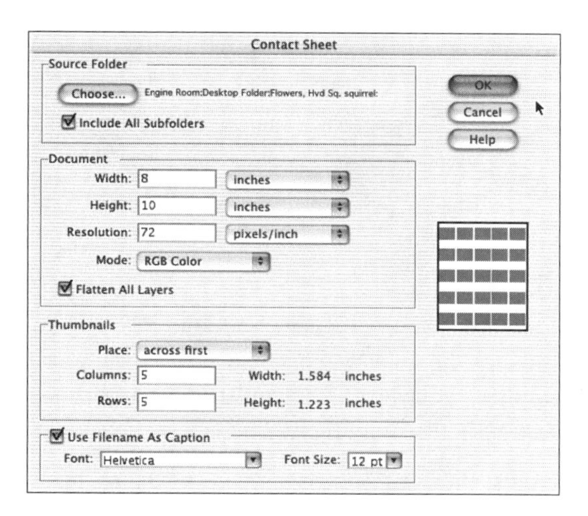

FIGURE 22.27
Click Include All Subfolders if you want their contents to be included in the contact sheet.

If you're going to print your contact sheets, be sure that the document size is no larger than the paper in your printer. Low resolution (72 dpi) is usually good enough to see what's going on, and saves time and space. The Flatten All Images option has to do with the finished thumbnail file, not your images. It's typically best to select this option, unless you plan to manipulate the individual thumbnails for some reason.

Decide how many thumbnails you want per page, and arrange them across or down as you prefer. Finally, if you want their filenames to appear on the contact sheet (which I strongly recommend), click the Use Filename As Caption check box and select a font and size for the caption. When you click OK, Photoshop will automatically open your files one at a time, create thumbnails, and paste them into a new document. You can then save and print this contact sheet just like any other page. Figure 22.28 shows a typical contact sheet. Note that the pictures are in alphabetical order. Filenames, if too long, will be truncated.

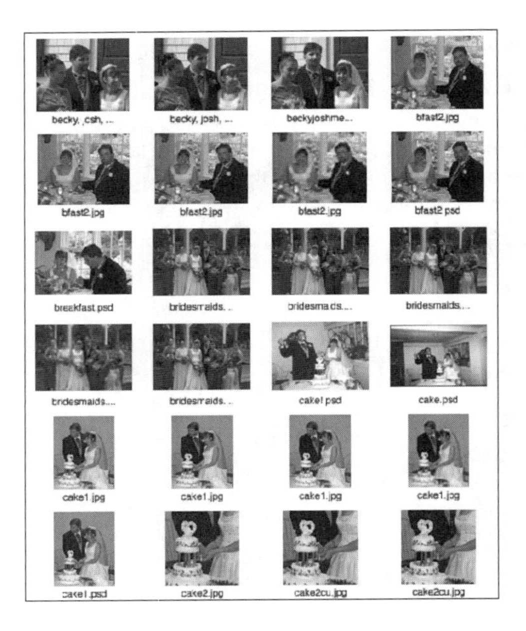

FIGURE 22.28
Each little photo has its filename as its title.

Picture Packages

Remember school pictures? You got a page with one 5×7 print, a couple of "stick-on-the-fridge"-sized pictures for the grandparents, and several wallet-size photos for mom and dad. Around the holidays, your local discount store or department store offers similar deals. You don't need to bother with them. You can do your own and save a bundle.

Use File, Print Layouts, Picture Package to open the dialog box. There's a menu in the Source area that lets you locate the photo you want to package, or you can use whatever's already open. Choose a paper size based on what your printer can handle. In Photoshop Elements 2, you have options for 10×16 and 11×17 paper as well as 8×10. Figure 22.29 shows the dialog box with a layout selected.

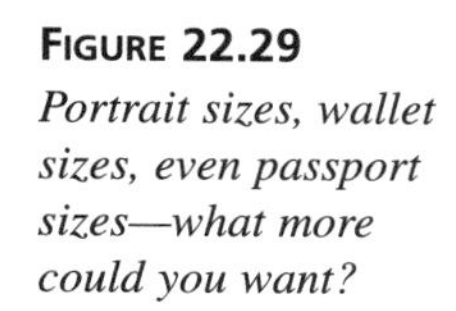

FIGURE 22.29
Portrait sizes, wallet sizes, even passport sizes—what more could you want?

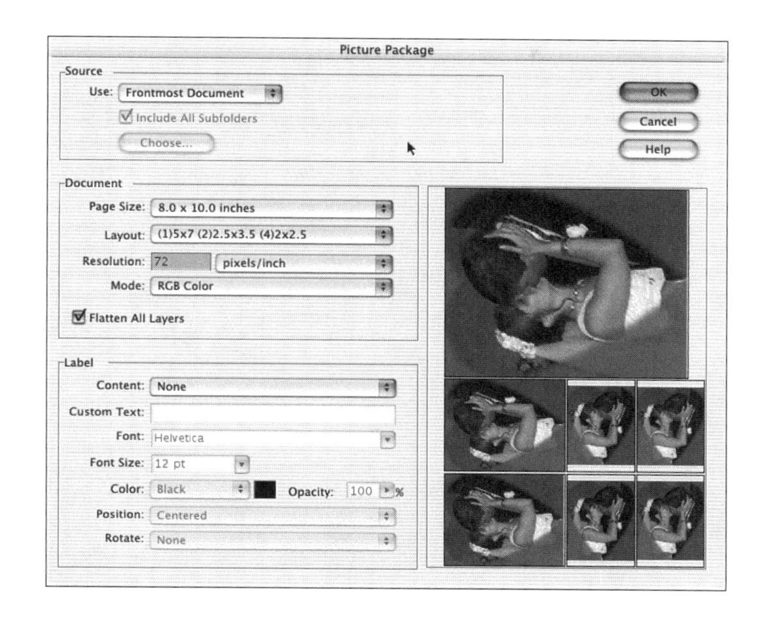

Label your photos, if you want to, with the name of the subject, your studio name and copyright notice, date, proof warning, or whatever else you want. Choose a font, size, color, and opacity for this type, and decide where on the page it should go. Unfortunately, you are limited to only a few fonts, most of which are more suitable for copyrighting or captioning than for adding an elegant title.

Set the resolution as appropriate for your printer, and click OK. Elements will assemble the package for you in a new file, just as it does with the contact sheets. When you're ready, save and/or print it.

Summary

In this chapter, we covered a lot of territory. You learned to use the File Browser to find your images and about saving your work. We listed the file formats and color systems Photoshop supports, and covered file resolution and canvas size and how they can be changed. (You also found that Web images are saved differently from print images and learned how to find the most efficient way to save a Web graphic.) On top of all that, you learned how to import images using scanners and digital cameras, as well as several formats in which to print them.

CHAPTER 23

Using Basic Tools in Elements

Now we're getting into the real nitty-gritty business of working with Photoshop Elements. The ability to make selections and add extra layers to your page gives you some very powerful tools. Instead of making a change to the entire picture, you can work on pieces of it, segregating them, so that the rest is preserved as it was. There are also easy solutions for making the subject of the picture bigger, changing its orientation, getting rid of the junk at the edges, and generally improving the composition. Finally, there are some text tools that allow you to place text horizontally or vertically as well as stretch and distort it. You can even fill the letters with a picture, or cut them out of a picture, using the Type Mask tool. Let's start with the Selection tools.

Using the Selection Tools

The selection tools are conveniently located in the top section of the toolbox. You have four kinds of selection tools:

- Marquees—rectangular and elliptical
- Lassos—regular, polygonal, and magnetic
- The Magic Wand
- The Selection Brush

The Crop and Move tools are also in the same section. From a philosophical point of view, these last two tools really do belong there. After all, you need the Move tool to move selections, and cropping is the ultimate selection. By the way, you may have noticed that you can only see one Lasso and one Marquee. The others are on a pop-up menu that will appear when you click the small black triangle, as in Figure 23.1.

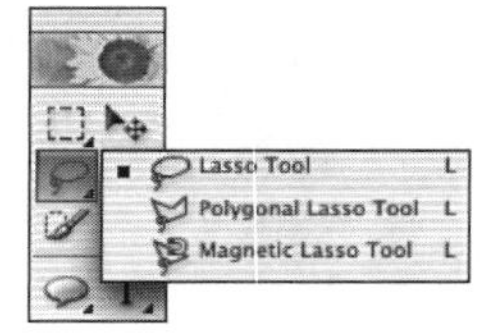

FIGURE 23.1
I wish that I could find the hidden tools on my real desktop this easily.

Making Selections with Marquees

Using the Marquees is quite simple. Select the proper tool for the job—either the rectangle or the circle—and position it at the start of the selection. Press the mouse button and drag until your selection is complete. By adding selections to an existing selection, you can build quite elaborate shapes, as I have in Figure 23.2.

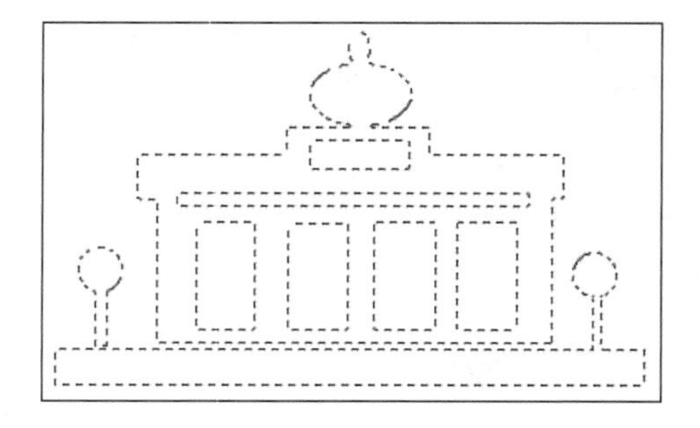

FIGURE 23.2
It's not the Taj Mahal.

To constrain the shape to a perfect square or circle, press the mouse button and as you start dragging, press and hold the Shift key. This gets tricky, because pressing the Shift key *after* you have made a selection allows you to continue to add more pieces to the selection. If you have trouble with these, don't worry, you can accomplish the same thing by using the buttons on the tool Options bar, shown in Figure 23.3.

FIGURE 23.3
Use the key commands or these buttons; it's your choice.

From the left, choose either the square or circle as the Marquee shape. Then choose from the set of four small icons according to what you need to do: New Selection, Add to Selection, Subtract from Selection, or Intersect with Selection. Or, press the Shift key to add, and the Option key to delete part of a selection.

Instead of pressing the Shift key as you drag to constrain proportions, you can choose a Style, such as Fixed Aspect Ratio and enter 1:1 for a square or circle or any other pair of numbers for constrained rectangles and ovals. To drag a marquee from its center out, press and hold Alt (Windows) or Option (Mac OS) after you begin dragging.

Task: Drawing a Donut with the Marquee Tool

Start a new image.

1. Select the Elliptical Marquee tool. Starting near the top left of the image, drag the crosshairs down and to the right, pressing the Shift key as you drag. This will give you a perfect circle. Make this circle whatever size you wish.
2. Holding down the Option/Alt key, draw a smaller circle inside the first. You can also click the Subtract from Selection button and draw the inner circle if you like.
3. Select the paint bucket tool, and pour paint into the area between the two circles.
4. Press Command/Ctrl-D to deselect and chase away the marching ants. Enjoy your donut.

Selecting with the Lasso Tools

Marquees are great when you have to select something with nice neat edges, or if you want to draw and fill a shape. For selecting small bits of a picture or pulling one flower out of a bunch, they're not the best tools for the job. That's when you need a Lasso. Use the Lasso to draw a selection line that is a single pixel wide around any object. As long as you're dragging the mouse while holding down its button, the Lasso tool will draw a line where you want it. As soon as you release the mouse button, the two ends of the line automatically connect, giving you a selection box in the shape you've drawn.

In addition to the "regular" lasso, you have two others, the Polygonal Lasso and the Magnetic Lasso. The Polygonal Lasso tool Options bar is shown in Figure 23.4.

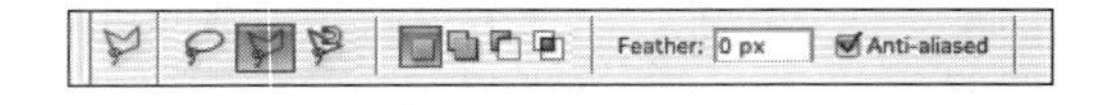

FIGURE 23.4
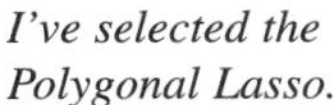
I've selected the Polygonal Lasso.

The Polygonal Lasso is useful both for selecting objects and for drawing shapes to be filled or stroked. To use it, first select it from the tool Options bar. Place the cursor where you want to start drawing, and click once. Move it and click again. You've drawn a straight line between the two points where you clicked. Each time you move and click you add another line to the shape. When you're ready to place the last point to join the ends of the shape, the cursor changes to the one shown in Figure 23.5, adding a small circle to the right of the lasso. You can close the shape yourself, or double-click to draw a line between the point where you double-click and the beginning of the shape.

FIGURE 23.5
The next click will join the ends of the selection together.

The Magnetic Lasso is one of the tools I use most often. It's very useful when you need to make a specific or detailed selection of something that's not all one color. The tool detects the edge of an image near the spot where you click or drag, based on the degree of sensitivity you select. If the area you're trying to select contrasts well with its surroundings, you can set a large Width (click/drag area) and a high Edge Contrast value and drag quickly and quite roughly around the image, and Elements will select it. If the area does not contrast well with its surroundings, set a smaller Width and a lower Edge Contrast value, and click or drag more carefully around the selection. In Figure 23.6, I'm using the Magnetic Lasso to trace around the seagull. Each time I click, Elements places a square box to anchor the line in place. After the entire object is selected, the line will change to the familiar marching ant marquee.

FIGURE 23.6
This tool works by looking for differences in pixels. Contrasting objects are easiest to select.

Making Selections with the Magic Wand

The Magic Wand is, in many ways, the easiest of the selection tools to use. It selects by color, and can be set to select all pixels of a particular color or range of colors in the entire image, or only those pixels that qualify and are adjacent to each other. It's the perfect tool for tasks such as selecting the sky, prior to turning it from gray to blue, and for what I'm attempting in Figure 23.7, which is to select the big red tulip, without selecting the smaller one tucked in back, or any of the yellow ones.

FIGURE 23.7
Selecting the red tulip took about eight clicks, because there were many shades of pink included. Here, I'm almost done.

The Magic Wand's tool Options bar has check boxes for Antialiased and Contiguous selections, and for selecting through all layers or just the top one. These are obviously going to be useful, but the truly important option is to set a degree of tolerance for the wand. With zero tolerance, you'll select only the few pixels that are identical to the one you clicked the wand on. (If Contiguous is checked, the selected pixels must also be touching each other.) If you set a very generous tolerance, perhaps as much as 100, you will find yourself selecting much of the image with just one click. That's probably not what you wanted to do. Try a tolerance between 10 and 35 for tasks such as picking up the red tulip. After setting the options you want, simply click on a pixel of the color you wish to select. Don't forget that you need to keep the Shift key pressed to add to your wand selections, just as you do when drawing multiple marquees. When you accidentally select more than you wanted, Undo or Command/Ctrl-Z will immediately subtract the last pixels you selected.

You can combine selection methods, too, with the help of the Shift key. If you use the Magic Wand and get most of your red flower, but not the black seed pod in the center, you can circle that part with the Lasso while keeping the Shift key pressed, and add it right in.

Using the Selection Brush Tool

If you have a steady hand, and possibly a drawing tablet and pen instead of a mouse, you might find the easiest selection method, at least for some things, is to paint over them with the Selection Brush tool. It looks like a paintbrush, and in some circumstances works like one. To understand what it does, you need to think of making a selection as a way of isolating the part of the picture you're working on, from the parts you don't want to change. With the Selection Brush, you can either select the area you want to work with, or select the area you don't want to use by covering it with a mask.

Using the Selection Brush is like using any other brush. You have a choice, however, as to whether you are painting to mask the area around an object, or to select the object itself. The Options bar for the Selection Brush is shown in Figure 23.8. If you choose Selection from the Mode list, the area you drag over adds to the selection. If you choose Mask instead, the area you drag is subtracted from any existing selection (adding to the mask, or the area you don't wish to affect). What this actually means is that, when you choose the add icon, with your first brush click the image completely covers it with a layer of mask. Each subsequent brush stroke adds to the selection by erasing some of the mask. Select the brush type, size, and hardness of the edge from the lists on the Options bar. Then drag to select or mask part of the image.

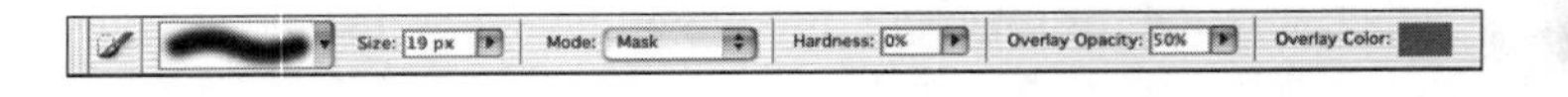

FIGURE 23.8
Select the options you want to use with the Selection Brush.

Red isn't always the best choice for a mask, especially if you're working on a picture that has a lot of red or pink in it. Change the mask to a different color or opacity by clicking the swatch on the tool Options bar, and use the Color Picker to find a more effective color. Change the opacity by entering a different percentage. Higher numbers are more opaque.

In Figure 23.9, I have changed the mask color to blue for better contrast with the red flower, and I'm in the process of selecting it with the paintbrush. It's very easy to make an accurate selection this way, especially if you enlarge the image and work with a small brush.

FIGURE 23.9
In Photoshop, this feature is called Quick Masking.

Selecting and Deselecting All

In addition to the selection tools, there's another quick and easy way to make a selection. To select the entire image, rather than dragging a marquee around it, or clicking the Magic Wand repeatedly, just type Command/Ctrl-A to select all. To deselect whatever is selected, use Command/Ctrl-D. If you want to clear the image and start over, select all and press Delete. To erase part of the image, draw a marquee the size and shape you want to erase, and press Delete. Memorize these commands. They will save you tons of time.

If you reach a point at which Elements seems to freeze or doesn't do what you want it to, try pressing the deselect keys. You may have accidentally selected a single pixel, and not noticed it.

Modifying Selections

After making a selection, you may want to modify it somewhat, expanding or shrinking it, or softening its edge. You'll learn how to do all this and more in this section.

Inverting a Selection

There are many ways in which you can modify your selections. Take a look at the Select menu in Figure 23.10. You've already learned to select all and deselect. Adding the Shift key to the deselect combination (Shift + Command/Ctrl-D) will reselect your last selection in case you accidentally dropped it.

Inverse is an incredibly useful command. Suppose you have something with very complicated edges on a simple background; perhaps a baby lying on a blanket, or a sunflower on a table. You can use one of your Lassos and trace around it. You can use the Selection Brush and paint neatly around the edges. Or, you can use the Magic Wand once or twice to pick up the entire, plain background, and then select Inverse, or press Shift-Command-I. Rather than selecting the background, you've inverted the selection and gotten the baby or flower, or whatever it is instead.

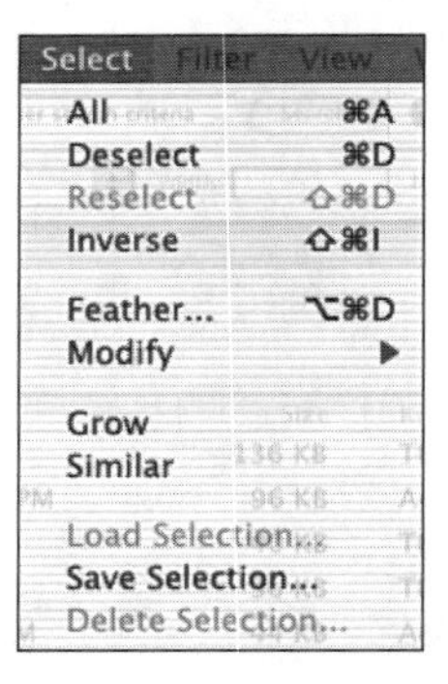

FIGURE 23.10
There are many choices on the Select menu.

Feathering a Selection

Feathering a selection makes it have a fuzzy edge. This isn't something you will want every time you drag a marquee, but under the right circumstances, it's very useful. The right circumstances can be anything from making a portrait vignette, so that it fades into the background, to copying some grass to paste over the trash in a park picture. Figure 23.11 shows the vignette effect, one of the more obvious uses for feathering. In this case, I drew the oval selection marquee where I wanted it, and then feathered it by 20 pixels. (The original photo is quite large.) How much you should feather a selection is going to be something to experiment with. It depends on the size of the image, and on what you're planning to do with the result. Just a couple of pixels of soft edge may be all you need to make something fit into its new background.

FIGURE 23.11
Feathering the edges of a portrait is called vignetting. Photo courtesy of D. Maynard.

Apply feathering after you have made the selection. Choose Select, Feather and type an appropriate number into the dialog box shown in Figure 23.12.

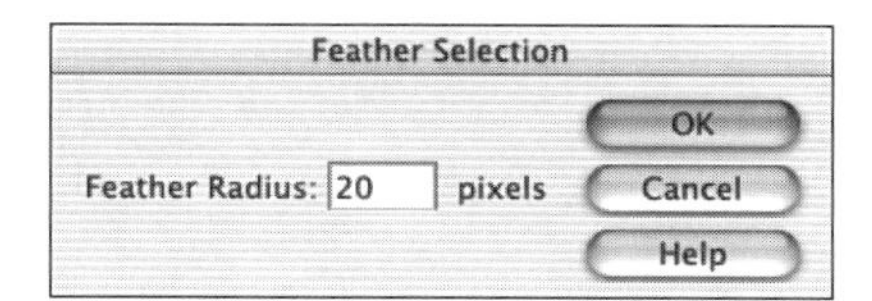

FIGURE 23.12
There's no right or wrong number of pixels to choose for feathering.

Changing Your Selection with Modify, Grow, Similar

Selecting Modify from the Select menu gives you four ways to modify your selection. Each requires entering a pixel value in the dialog box. Your choices include the following:

- **Border**—Places a second selection line outside of the first, at a distance you specify, making the selection into a border or frame.
- **Smooth**—Evens out lumpy lasso and brush selections.
- **Expand**—Adds as many pixels outward from the selection as you specify, enlarging it.
- **Contract**—Subtracts the pixels you specify, shrinking the selection.

Choosing Grow from the Select menu expands the selection outward to pixels of similar color. Similar locates and selects pixels located anywhere in the image that are similar to the ones already selected. Prior to choosing these commands from the Select menu, set the tolerance level for matching similar pixels by clicking the Magic Wand tool first and changing its Tolerance value.

Saving and Loading Selections

After you've gone to the trouble of making a complex selection, it seems a shame to lose it, especially if it's something you might want to work on again later. If you stroke the selection outline or fill it with color as explained in the next section, that information is saved as well. Fortunately, you can save your selection with the file, and use it whenever you want it. At the bottom of the Select menu are two commands called Save Selection and Load Selection. Selections are only saved with images stored in Photoshop (.psd) format.

To save a selection, select Save Selection to open the Save Selection dialog box. Give the selection a name, and click OK. To open and reuse it, use the Load Selection box, shown in Figure 23.13, to locate and activate your selection. To display this dialog box, choose Select, Load Selection. Remember, you can also start a new image with just the selection if it's something you expect to use often.

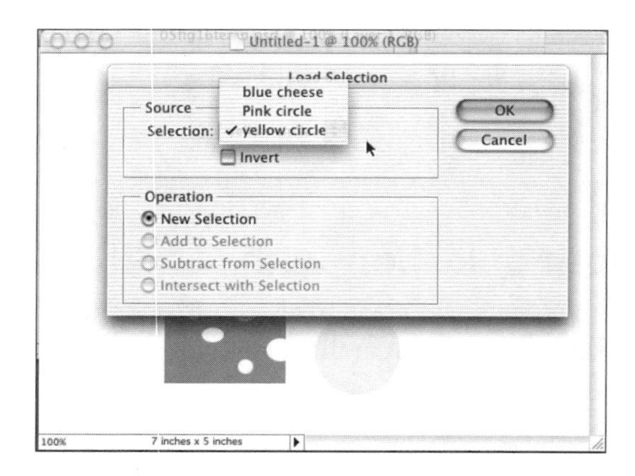

FIGURE 23.13
Save unique selections so you can reuse them.

Stroking and Filling Selections

No matter how you've made your selections, you have the option of filling or stroking them to make them objects in their own right. Let's say I need to draw some abstract shapes to use as part of a logo. I can use any of the selection tools to select a shape, and then Elements can turn the selection into an object by filling it with color or a pattern, or stroking it with a colored line.

The Stroke and Fill commands are both found under the Edit menu. Filling places your choice of color, gray, or a pattern into the selected shape. Stroking places a line, of whatever color and thickness you determine, over the selection marquee. In Figure 23.14, I'm preparing to fill a complex shape with gray. Create a selection using your tools of choice. If you want to fill the selection with a particular color, click the Foreground or Background icon at the bottom of the toolbox, and select a color from the Color Picker. Then choose Edit, Fill.

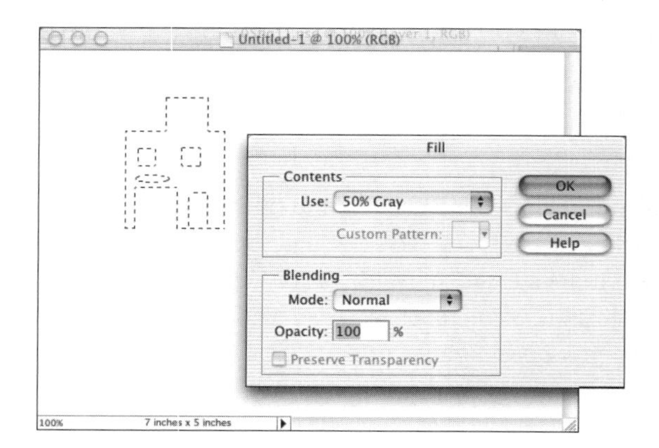

FIGURE 23.14
Create a shape with a selection tool, and fill it with a color or pattern.

Select the color (foreground, background, white, black, or 50% gray) or pattern you want from the Use list. If you choose Pattern, you can select the exact pattern you want from the Custom Pattern palette. When you open this palette, it displays a small selection of patterns. To display a different selection, click the right arrow and choose a set of patterns from the list. Choose a blending mode and a level of opacity if you like. Because blending is a pretty advanced concept, I'll spend more time on it in Chapter 26, "Creating Digital Art from Scratch." As for opacity, it's pretty easy to grasp. Basically, it's the strength of the fill—with a low percentage of opacity, the color or pattern already within the selection (if any) will show through the fill color or pattern you're applying. A higher percentage of opacity creates a more solid fill, with less of the original color/pattern within the selection still apparent. If you choose 100% opacity, you'll completely replace any color/pattern in the selection with your new choice. You can use the Paint Bucket instead of the Edit, Fill command to fill a selection—I'll discuss this tool in a moment.

To stroke the outline of your selection, choose Edit, Stroke instead. Select the width of the border you want. To choose a color, click the Color box and select one from the Color Picker. Next, choose the location for the line—on the inside, outside, or centered over the selection marquee. Once again, you can change the blending mode and opacity.

Stroking a line isn't necessarily a one-time event. You can build some very interesting designs by using different colored strokes, and placing narrow ones over wider ones. Figure 23.15 shows a few of the possibilities. These were all drawn with the selection tools, and then stroked and filled. To create the first object, I used the Rectangular and Elliptical Marquee selection tools, and filled and stroked the resulting compound selection. To create the second object, I used the Polygonal Lasso selection tool to create a star, then filled it with a pattern and stroked it several times with lines of varying widths, positions, and colors. To create the third object, I used the Selection Brush tool with the Dry Brush pattern, then filled and stroked the resulting compound selection. For the fourth object, I created a rectangle with the Rectangular Marquee selection tool and filled it with a dark color. Then I created a series of stars with the Selection Brush tool, star pattern, and stroked them with a medium color. I created more stars and stroked them with a lighter color. How many of these can you re-create?

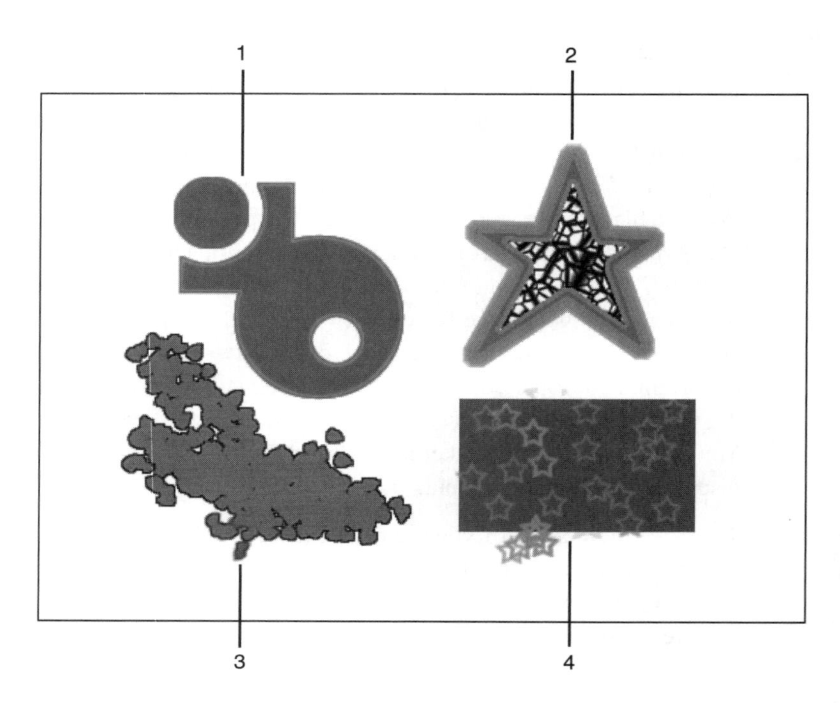

FIGURE 23.15
It's easy to get carried away.

Using the Paint Bucket Tool to Fill a Selection

Earlier, I mentioned that you could fill a selection with the Paint Bucket tool. Using the tool is fairly simple: First select the tool; then from the Fill list on the Options bar, choose either Foreground or Pattern. If you select Foreground, the current foreground color will be used. If you don't like the current foreground color, you can change it. If you choose Pattern, you can select the pattern you want from the pattern list. As before, you can display additional patterns by clicking the right arrow and selecting the set of patterns you want to view. Select the blending option from the Mode menu (to learn about blending, see Chapter 26), and set the opacity level you want.

The rest of the options are the same as those described earlier for the Magic Wand tool. The Tolerance option defines the type of pixel to be filled—a low tolerance tells Elements to fill only pixels within the selection that are very close in color to the one you click with the tool. A high tolerance is not as picky. The Antialiased option softens the edge between the filled selection and its background. The Contiguous option has no effect unless you have made at least two non-contiguous selections. Then, if you choose Contiguous, only the applicable pixels within the selection you click will be changed. Turn this option off to fill pixels in all selections. The All Layers option allows you to fill the selection within all layers; we'll get to layering in the next section.

After setting options for the Paint Bucket tool, click on a pixel within the selection. The pixel you click may or may not affect the outcome, depending on the selections you've made.

Working with Layers

Layers sound complicated, but they're not. They're really quite simple, if you've ever seen an animated cartoon. Animators work with two kinds of materials, sheets of white Bristol board, or something similar as backgrounds, and sheets of heavy transparent cellophane, called cells. The background holds the things that don't change: trees, grass, Marge's kitchen walls, Homer's couch. There are up to four or five cell layers for each character. Hands and feet move more than heads and trunks, so that the bodies are dismembered and placed on different layers. If Homer is to wave, for example, three or four drawings will be done of just his arm in different positions, from down to up. Then the sequence will be photographed with a different arm in each frame of film. It's layers that make it possible to see this movement.

Working with layers enables you to build up multipart collages of many images, paint over an original photo without destroying it, make color corrections that you can apply selectively to parts of the picture, stack picture elements behind others, and…I can go on and on.

When you open a new image in Elements, it has a background layer. No others. If you then paste something in what you've copied to the Clipboard, you'll automatically make a new layer. You can use the Layers palette to keep track of your layers. Think of it as a sort of command center for layer management. You can add and remove layers from the palette itself and manage them with its menu.

In Figure 23.16, I've assembled a page with a bunch of different layers. Type goes on a separate layer. Adjustment layers enable you to correct color and exposure, with the advantage of letting you also control how much of the correction you want to apply. A layer can change both opacity and blending mode as needed.

You can start a new layer in any of several ways. Whether you're pasting something in, or dragging it from another open file, the new part of the image will automatically be placed on a new layer. As soon as you position the Type tool on the picture and start entering letters, you've created a type layer to set them on. Because they are on their own layer, you can move the words around, correct spelling, even erase them and try different words or a different font, without risking the rest of the image. However, if you want to paint on a new layer over your image, create a new layer manually by selecting New from the Layer menu, or by clicking on the small New Layer icon at the bottom of the Layers palette.

FIGURE 23.16
A variety of layers.

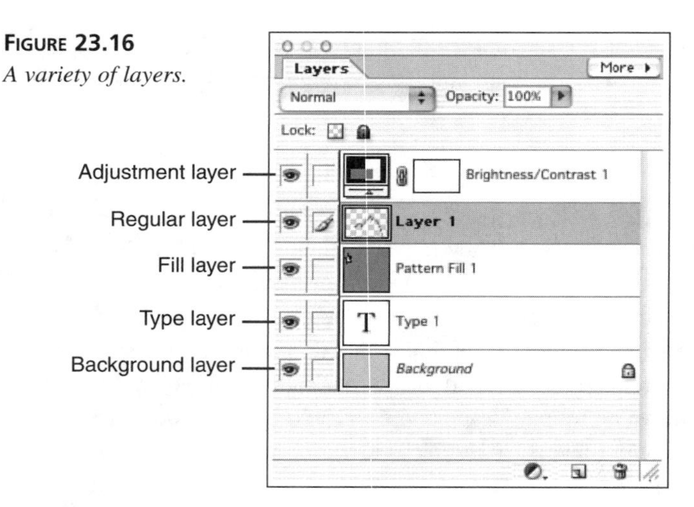

As you add more and more layers to your document, you'll probably need to give them more descriptive names, so that you can easily identify their content. To change the name of a layer, double-click the layer to open the Layer Properties dialog box. Type the name of the layer in the text box, and click OK. You can also simply double-click the name in the Layers palette, and type the new name right there. Press Enter when you're done.

Task: Experimenting with Layers

TASK

1. Start a new image (default size is fine). Open the Layers palette and drag it away from the palette well, so that it stays open on the screen.
2. Click the New Layer icon at the bottom of the palette. Now, you have Layer 1 on top of the background.
3. Go back to the background for a moment by clicking on the word "Background" on the Layers palette, and pour a color into it. To do this, set the foreground color to something light by first clicking its swatch and then choosing a color from the Color Picker. Select the Paint Bucket and click on the background. (Yes, you can use the Paint Bucket to fill a layer with color just as you can use it to fill a selection marquee or drawn object. You can also use the Edit, Fill command to fill a layer.)
4. Notice that, on the far left, the palette shows a brush on the active layer, and each layer has an open eye, indicating that both layers are visible. Click Layer 1 again, and see the brush move up to it.
5. Draw a large star with the Polygonal Lasso tool and fill it with a color that is darker than your background. To do this, click the arrow on the Lasso tool and select the Polygonal Lasso tool. Click once in the layer to establish the first star

point. Click to draw each side of the star and double-click to complete the last side. To fill it with color, select a darker foreground color, click the Paint Bucket, and then click inside the star. At this point, your screen and Layers palette will look something like Figure 23.17.

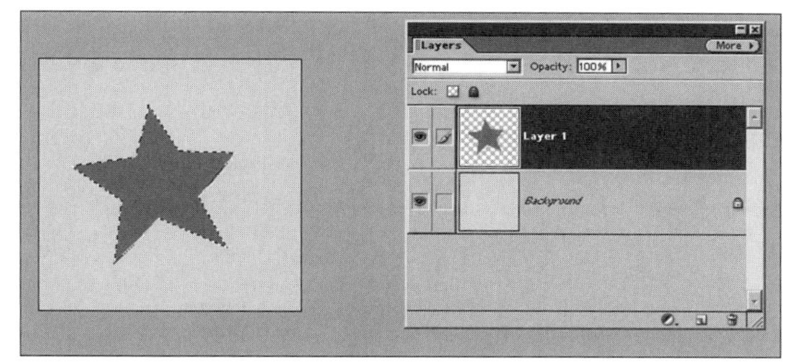

FIGURE 23.17
Layer 1 is active, because that's where the brush is.

6. Click the eye next to the Background thumbnail. The background disappears, being replaced by a gray checkerboard indicating transparency. That happens because Layer 1 is transparent until you put something on it. If you look closely at the thumbnail, you will see the star you painted. Click the eye again to bring back the background. Save and close your star image.

Managing Layers

The Layers palette has a very helpful menu (you can access it by clicking the palette's More button), shown in Figure 23.18. Use it or the Layer menu, also shown, to add and delete layers, rename them, group and ungroup them, and eventually merge them and flatten the image.

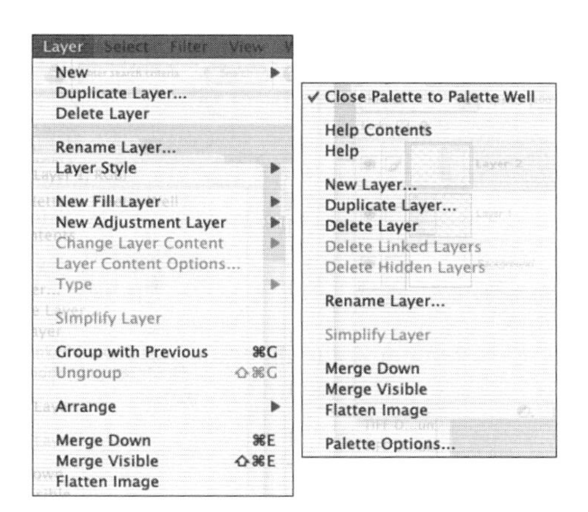

FIGURE 23.18
The Layer menu on the left has much in common with the Layers palette menu, shown on the right.

Although the Layer menu and the Layers palette menu provide access to all the commands you need to manage layers, you can perform most of the more common tasks by simply clicking buttons and manipulating items in the Layer palette, shown in Figure 23.19. If your image has multiple layers, you can see and manipulate them here. As I mentioned earlier, the eye icon on the far left means that the layer is visible, and the brush icon tells you which layer is active. You can have all of your layers visible—or invisible, if you want—but only one layer can be active at a time.

FIGURE 23.19
The Layer Palette with the More menu shown on the right.

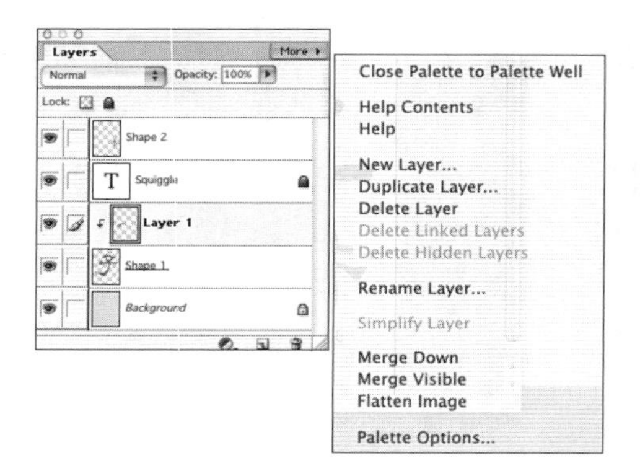

Adding a New Layer

There are, of course, several different ways to create a new layer. Whenever you copy and paste an object into your picture, it comes in on a new layer. If you add text using one of the type tools (which we'll cover later in this chapter) or add a shape with a shape tool (which you'll do in Chapter 26), a new layer is created automatically.

You can also add layers manually when needed. When you click the New Layer button at the bottom of the palette, you create a new layer above the current layer. Objects placed on the new layer can obscure objects placed on lower layers. If you click the black-and-white circle icon at the bottom of the palette, you have the choice of opening a fill layer (solid, gradient, or pattern) or an adjustment layer (a layer in which adjustments such as brightness or color changes reside, without permanently affecting the image itself—you'll learn more about adjustment layers in Chapter 24, "Fixing Photo Flaws"). When you choose Layer, New, Layer, or select New Layer from the palette menu, or type Command/Ctrl-Shift-N, you open a dialog box that gives you access to some extra settings for the new layer. This box is shown in Figure 23.20.

If you use the dialog box, you can name the layer, adjust its opacity and blending mode, and group it with the previous layers as you're creating it. We'll discuss grouping in a moment.

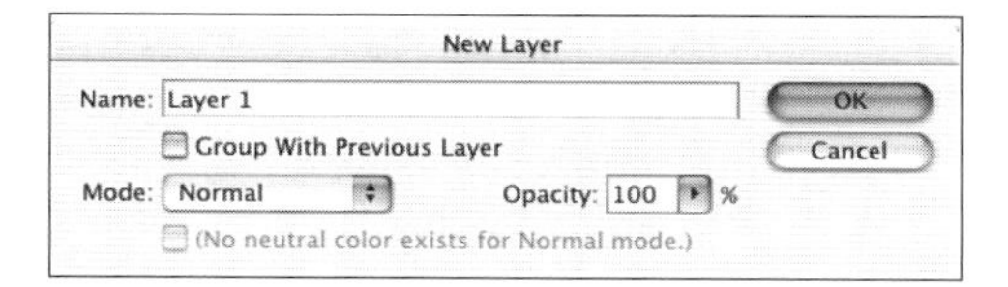

FIGURE 23.20
The New Layer dialog box.

If you don't display the New Layer dialog box when creating a new layer, you can access most of those functions from the palette. You already know how to rename a selected layer. You can make changes to its opacity or its blending mode at the top of the Layer palette.

Moving or Removing a Layer

Layers play an important role in the final image, because objects on one layer can obscure all or part of an object on a lower layer. If needed, move layers up or down in the stack. The easiest way to move a layer on top of another is to grab it on the Layers palette and drag it to its new location.

In a perfect world, file size wouldn't matter because we'd all have fast computers with unlimited memory. Well, we're not quite there yet. Layers add to the size of the file, and with a lot of layers you can end up with a file big enough to choke computers with modest resources. So you need to use layers wisely. Good layer management means discarding layers you aren't going to use, and merging the rest when you are done using them. This will happen automatically and unexpectedly unless you're careful; not all file formats can handle layers. As of now the only formats that do are TIFF and the native Photoshop format. If you save your image for the Web, it will be flattened as part of the process. To remove a layer manually, drag it to the trash or click the Delete Layer icon after selecting the layer you no longer want.

Grouping Layers Together

When you group two or more layers together, they work in concert with each other. If you place an object such as a star on the bottom layer, then place a photo such as a flower on a higher layer and then group them, the flower image will appear to be star-shaped. In other words, the flower will show only within the star outline.

Grouped layers must be in succession. You can group a new layer with the previous one, or ungroup them, using either key commands or the Layers menu. To group a layer with the one directly below it, select the top layer and press Command/Ctrl-G or select Layer, Group with Previous. To ungroup, press Command/Ctrl-Shift-G or select Layer, Ungroup. You can also press Command/Alt and click on the line separating the two layers in the Layers palette to group them.

The base layer (lowest layer) is preceded by a bent, downward-pointing arrow. Its name is also underlined. The base layer defines the boundaries for what's displayed from the upper layer(s). Upper layers in the group are indented above this base layer in the list. If you look back at Figure 23.19, you can see that Layer 1 is grouped with the Shape 1 layer; the Shape 1 layer is acting as the base layer. This base layer controls the opacity and mode settings for the group.

You can also link layers together in order to treat them as a group for purposes of moving, copying, pasting, and applying transformations in a single step. To link layers, select a layer; then click in the first column to the left of the layer you want to link to this active layer. A link icon (a chain) appears in front of the layers you select. Later, if you select a layer that's linked to others, the other layers will be highlighted by this link icon, reminding you that they are linked. To unlink a layer, click any other layer in the linked group, and click its link icon to turn if off.

Changing Layer Opacity

Being able to control the opacity of individual layers gives you enormous flexibility, especially as you start to get into multilayer, multi-image composites, as we will in later chapters. Opacity adjustments are also useful for making minor color changes. Suppose you have a landscape with a pale blue sky that you'd like to be a little more intense. Select the sky and copy it to a new layer. Then choose Layer, Fill Layer, Solid Color. (If you instead click the icon at the bottom of the layer palette, you won't have the option of linking the fill layer to the sky copy layer, and this is something you need to be sure to do. If you don't, the color correction will apply to the whole picture.) Type a name for the layer, and select the Group with Previous Layer option. You can guess at the opacity level now, but it's best to adjust it later when you can see the result. Click OK to open the Color Picker, so you can select an appropriate sky color. Click OK. In the Layer palette, use the Opacity slider to bring in just enough of the additional color that it looks right. Figure 23.21 shows the Layers palette with a color fill applied only to the sky.

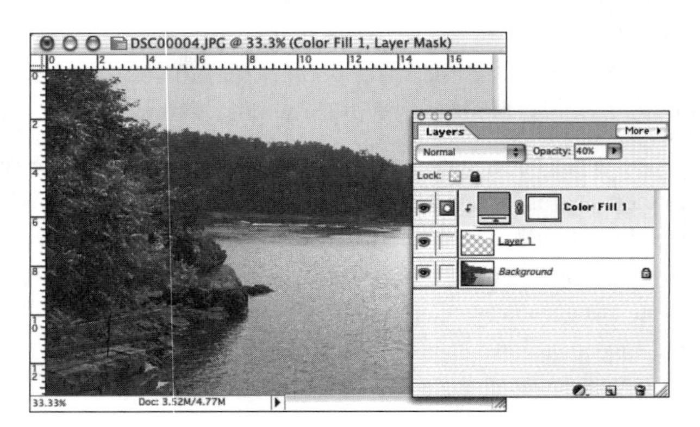

FIGURE 23.21
You can also use this technique to apply gradients and pattern fills.

In the figure, the photograph is located on the Background layer. I selected the sky and copied it to Layer 1. You can see its white outline at the top of the thumbnail. The solid color fill layer, which is linked to Layer 1, is just above it. I could have used a pattern or gradient fill instead to create a strange sky effect.

Cropping and Resizing Your Pictures

It would be pretty unusual to have your pictures come out of the camera perfectly composed, showing nothing more than the subject as you visualized it. Even the fanciest cameras, with the biggest and best zoom lenses can't always give you what you want. Maybe you're standing on a cliff, about to slide into the Grand Canyon, as I was in one of the examples that follow. Maybe there's something in the way of where you needed to stand to get that perfect shot. Maybe you just can't get close enough. (Those darned security guards…) Maybe you shot the picture as a landscape, and then found out you could sell the middle part as a magazine cover.

Cropping

Cropping is the artistic term for trimming away unwanted parts of a picture. You can think of it as a specialized kind of selection, which is probably why the people who created Elements put the Crop tool in the same toolbox section as the Selection Marquees (see Figure 23.22).

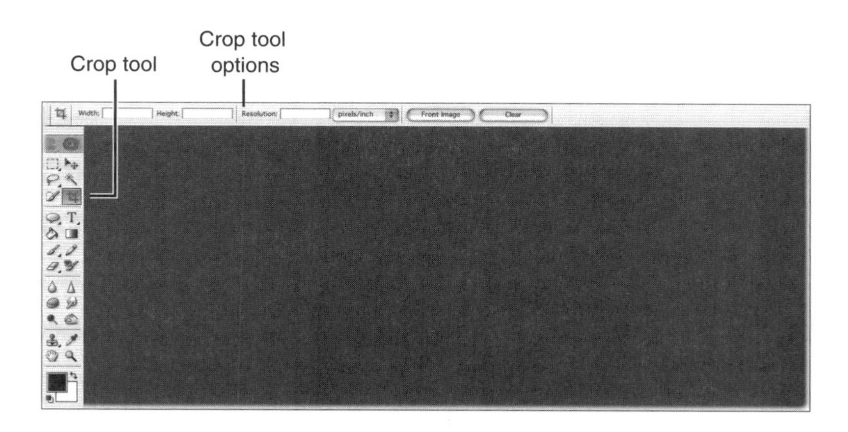

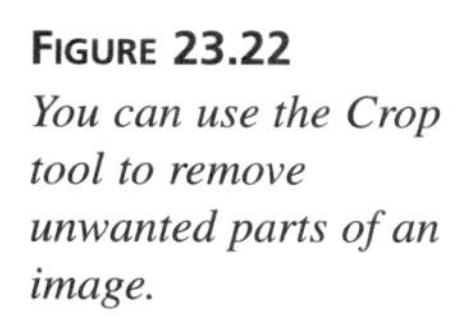

FIGURE 23.22
You can use the Crop tool to remove unwanted parts of an image.

To crop part of an image, click the Crop tool. You can specify the width and/or height of the final image and its resolution by entering those values in the Options bar. To enter the values of the current image so that the final cropped image will use the same dimensions, click Front Image. Then click in the image and drag downward and to the right to select the area you want to crop. When you've selected the part of the image you want to keep, the Options bar changes, as you can see in Figure 23.23.

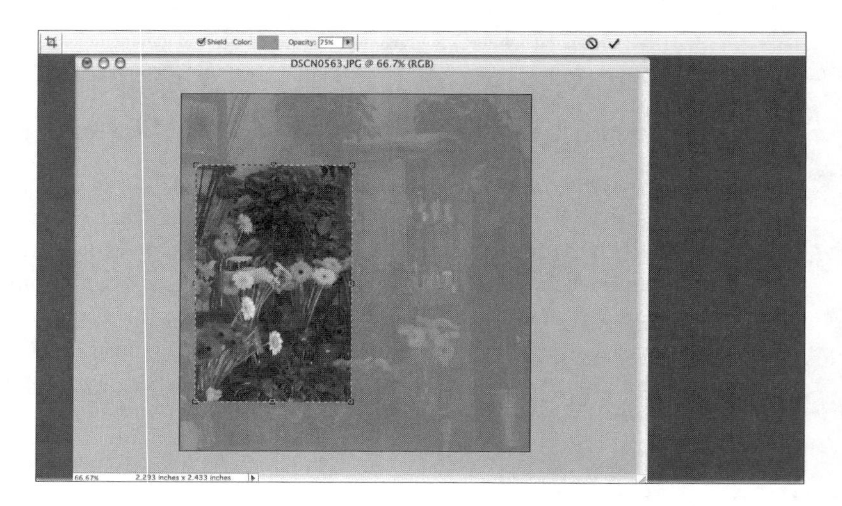

FIGURE 23.23
After cropping, the Option bar changes.

If needed, click Shield on the tool Options bar to make the uncropped area go dark, so that it's easier to see what will remain. You can adjust the color and opacity of the shield using the Options bar. Drag any of the boxes (handles) located around the edges of the selection to adjust the size of the cropped area. Rotate the selection by moving the mouse pointer outside the selection and dragging. You can also click in the middle of the selection to adjust its position on the image. To crop the image, click the button labeled with a check mark.

> You can also crop by making a selection with the Rectangular Marquee and then choosing Image, Crop to trim the picture.

Task: Crop a Picture

To crop a picture, open any image and follow these steps:

1. Select the Crop tool from the toolbox or press `c` on the keyboard. (It looks like two overlapped pieces of L-shaped matboard—the same tool artists use to help compose paintings.)
2. Starting at the top-left corner of the selection, drag your mouse down and to the right, across the picture, while holding the mouse button down.

3. Notice the small boxes at the corners and midpoints of each side. These are *handles*. Drag the handles on the cropping box to make the box smaller or larger and fine-tune the selection. Click in the middle of the selection and move it around on the image. Rotate the bounding box. The area outside the box will be dimmed.
4. After you have the cropping box placed where you want it, double-click inside it to delete the area outside the box.

Remember, if you crop too much of the picture, you can undo what you have just done. If it's too late to undo because you have already done something else, just go back to the Undo History palette and click the uncropped picture. You can also choose File, Revert to go back to the last saved version of your picture. As long as you don't close the file, you can keep cropping and undoing it as much as you want.

Resizing

Elements make it easy to change the size of the picture, or of anything in it. This is often necessary. For instance, say you import pictures from a digital camera and accidentally set them to import at 72 dpi. If you have one of the current multi-megapixel cameras, your picture can easily be 14×17 inches or more.

You have two options: resizing the image or resizing the canvas. Resizing the image makes the picture bigger or smaller. Resizing the canvas makes the picture *area* bigger, while leaving the image floating within it. You'd do this if you need more space around an object without shrinking the actual image.

Resizing an Image

In Chapter 22, "Starting, Saving, and Printing Your Work," I talked about changing resolution. The resolution of an image is measured by the number of pixels it contains per inch. Obviously, the more pixels per inch, the more data, and the clearer the image. Resolution and size are tied together. If you increase the resolution of an image, shrinking the pixels so that there are more of them per inch, the image's size is shrunk as well. If you want to have your cake and eat it too (that is, increase the resolution of an image [the number of pixels per inch] while maintaining its size), Elements has to come up with more pixels per inch than actually exist. It does so through a process called *sampling*—educated guesswork, as it were.

To resize an image, open the Image Size dialog box (shown in Figure 23.24) by choosing Image, Resize, Image Size. Here's where you decide whether or not you want to resample—that is, add more pixels to an image based on the colors of the neighboring pixels. Resampling typically results in a loss of clarity, or general fuzziness, but you have to weigh that against your intentions. If you want a higher resolution in order to get a better printout, but the printout will be no good to you if the image is two inches by two inches, you'll have to resample. But if you don't care about the final dimensions of an image and you just want good quality, don't resample.

After opening the Image Size dialog box, turn on or off the Resample Image option as desired. Resampling, by the way, will either enlarge or reduce a file's size, depending on whether the image size increases or decreases. If you turn on Resample Image, select the type of resampling you want Elements to use—see Chapter 22 for a complete description of each option.

In this dialog box, you can see the pixel dimensions in pixels (logically) or percentages, by choosing the appropriate option from the pop-up menu. If you turn off the Resample Image option, however, the Pixel Dimensions area becomes grayed, because you won't be changing the total number of pixels. Regardless of whether you're resampling or not, you can still enter the desired image print size (in the Document Size section of the dialog box) in inches, centimeters, points, picas, or columns; you can also set percentages by selecting that option from the pop-up menus. As I mentioned earlier, if your desire is to change the resolution and not bother with the resulting image size, you can adjust the Resolution value instead. Of course, if the Resample Image option is turned on, changing either the image size or its resolution will result in a change in the total number of pixels (and the file size).

The easiest way to enlarge or reduce the image is to make sure that the Constrain Proportions option is checked at the bottom of the dialog box, and then simply enter a value in any one of the fields and click OK. As if by magic, the other numbers will change to give you the correct matching values. Changing the percentage to 200% doubles the size of the picture, for example. Unfortunately, if you choose to also resample in order to maintain the current resolution, it more than triples the file size.

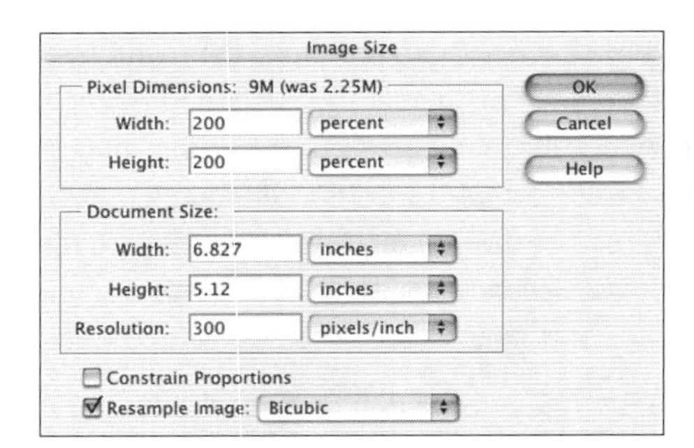

FIGURE 23.24
The Image Size dialog box allows you to resize your image.

As you make changes in the Image Size dialog box, Elements will automatically update the file size at the top of the dialog box so you'll know before you commit to a change how that change will affect your file's size.

If you resample an image and it looks fuzzy, try using the Unsharp Mask filter (described in Chapter 25, "Enhancing Your Photos with Filters") to bring it into better focus.

Resizing a Canvas

Resizing the canvas to a larger size gives you extra workspace around the image; it does not change the size of the image. Because resizing uses the current background color to fill in the added space, be sure that it's a color you want. I always resize with white as the background color. Resizing the canvas to a smaller size is another way of cropping the picture by decreasing the canvas area. It's not recommended because you can accidentally lose part of the picture and not be able to recover it.

To resize the canvas, open the Canvas Size dialog box by choosing Image, Resize, Canvas Size and specify the height and width you want the canvas to be (see Figure 23.25). You can specify any of the measurement systems you prefer on the pop-up menu, as you saw in the Image Size dialog box earlier. Photoshop calculates and displays the new file size as soon as you enter the numbers. If you turn on the Relative option, you can enter the size of the border you want. For example, if you enter 2 inches in the Width box, the edge of the canvas is set 1 inch from the sides of the image (for a total of 2 inches). Enter the same value in the Height box, and you have a nice, even border around the image that you can fill with color or a pattern to create a frame.

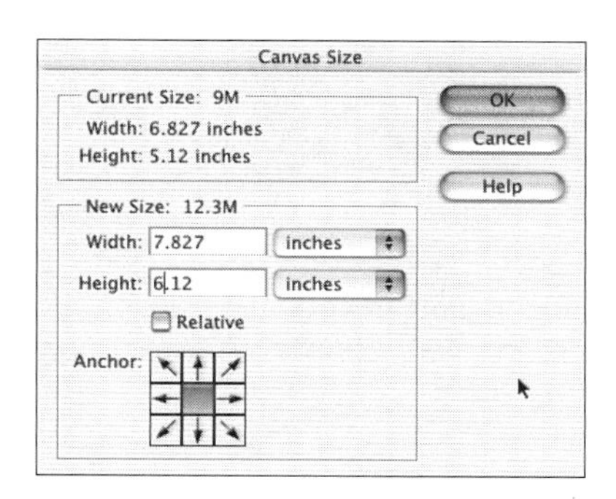

FIGURE 23.25
By adding an inch to the size of the canvas, I've given it a 1/2 inch border all around.

Use the anchor proxy to determine where the image will be placed within the canvas. Click in the middle to center the image on the enlarged canvas, or in any of the other boxes to place it relative to the increased canvas area. When you're ready, click OK to change the canvas size.

Resizing a Portion of an Image

You can also resize a portion of any image. To do so, first select the object or a piece of an image to be resized, using the most convenient Selection tool. With the selection marquee active, choose Image, Resize, Scale. This places a bounding box that looks like the cropping box around your selected object (see Figure 23.26). Drag any of the corner handles on the box to change the size of the object/image within the selected area while holding down the Shift key to maintain its proportions. If you drag the side handles of the box, you'll stretch the selection's height or width accordingly. If you don't like having to hold down the Shift key as you drag, you can click the Maintain Aspect Ratio button on the Options bar to maintain the proportions of the image/object within the selection. You can also enter a percentage in the Width and/or Height boxes on the Options bar to resize the selection without dragging.

FIGURE 23.26
Remember to keep the Shift key pressed to retain the proportions.

> You can resize everything on an entire layer if you choose Select, Deselect to deselect everything first; then activate the layer you want to resize, and choose Image, Resize, Scale.

Rotating an Image

Under the Image, Rotate menu shown in Figure 23.27, you've got more ways to turn things around than you're likely to ever need. However, if you have a scanned picture or a digital camera image that should be vertical but opens as a horizontally oriented picture, you'll need these rotation options to straighten things out. Actually, this is a common occurrence when you use a scanner because it's usually quicker to scan with the picture horizontal, regardless of its normal orientation.

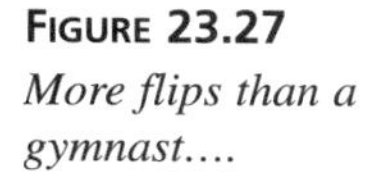

FIGURE 23.27
More flips than a gymnast....

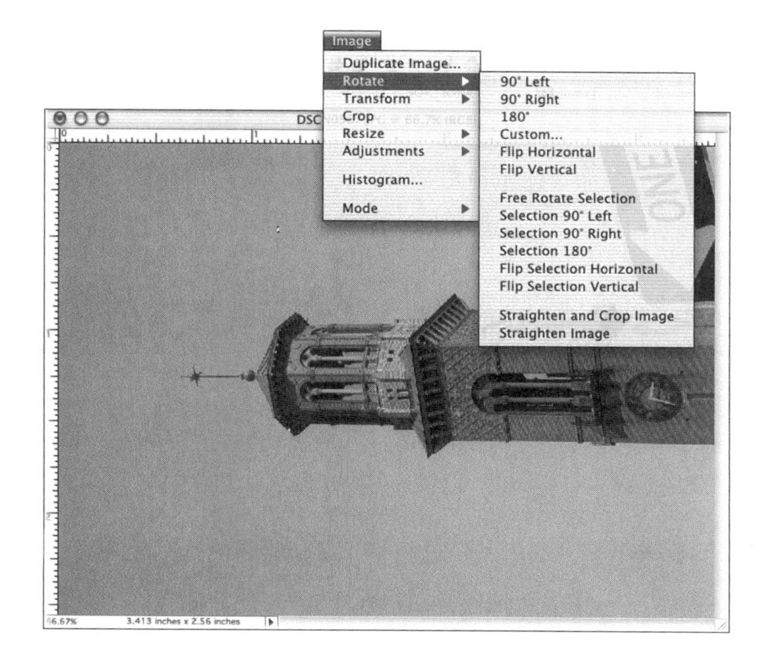

Choose 90 degrees clockwise (right) or counterclockwise (left) to straighten up a sideways image, or 180 degrees if you somehow brought in a picture upside down. Until I realized that my new scanner worked backwards from the old one, I did that a lot.

Flipping Images

Flipping is not just for pancakes. The Flip options on the Rotate menu allow you to flip an image vertically or horizontally, as if it were a piece of paper. If you have a picture of a girl facing left, for example, and you flip it horizontally, she'll face right. This might come in handy if you need her to look at some text or something on a page that's located to the right of her image. If you flip the image vertically instead, she'll stand on her head!

Sometimes you need to flip an image before you print it, so it will read correctly. For instance, suppose you're making a sign printed on acetate, which is transparent. If you simply print it as is, the ink can come off when anyone touches the sign. If you flip the text horizontally first, then print it on the back of the acetate so that the text is read through the acetate, the ink is protected by whatever you have mounted the sign on. You can even sponge off the fingerprints left by those wise guys who try to scratch it and fail.

If you want to print to a T-shirt iron-on, as shown in Figure 23.28, the image actually gets flipped twice, once in Elements before you print it and again as it is ironed face down on the shirt. When you are finished, it reads correctly.

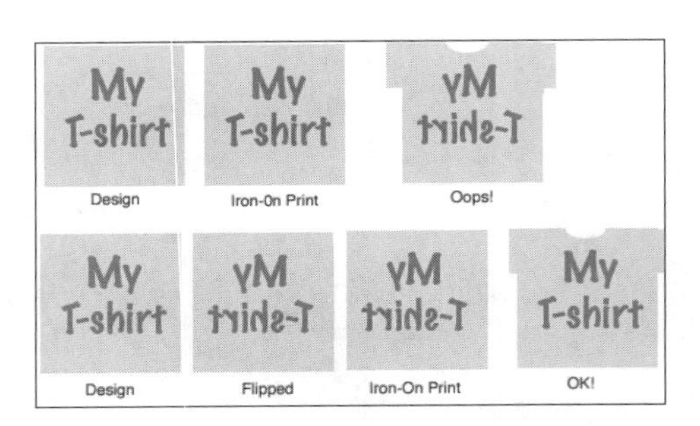

FIGURE 23.28
Sometimes you have to flip images.

You can rotate and flip a selection or layer instead of an entire image if you want. Just select the area/layer you want to flip or rotate; then choose one of the flip/rotate selection commands from the Image, Rotate menu. Remember this feature. It will come in very handy when you start making composites of elements from several different pictures. For instance, you can make a quick reflection of an object by copying it onto a second layer and then flipping the copy (the layer) vertically. You can create a cool reflection effect by using a combination of flipping and skewing type.

Rotating by Degrees

To rotate the image by something other than a right angle, choose Image, Rotate, Custom to open a dialog box such as the one shown in Figure 23.29. Enter the number of degrees to rotate. If you're not sure, guess. You can always undo or reopen the box and rotate more, or even change the direction if needed. Click the radio button to indicate the rotational direction: right or left. Then click OK to perform the rotation.

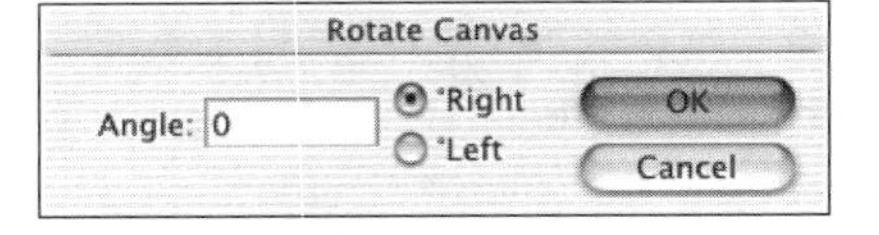

FIGURE 23.29
You can even rotate by fractions of a degree.

Straightening Images

The last two items on the Rotate menu are the Straighten and Crop Image command and the Straighten Image command. You might use one of these commands to straighten an image that was scanned in rather crookedly, but you should be careful when using them. I don't know what criteria Adobe's creative department used to determine whether an image is straight. These two commands are "automatic" and just happen while you wait. However, they don't seem to work very effectively. If repeated often enough, or if your horizon's just a tiny bit tilted, the Straighten Image command might eventually get you flattened out, but it works in very small increments. One trick that helps is to increase the canvas size first, so that Elements has a better idea where the edges of the image are.

Still, it's much quicker and easier to do the job yourself. In the next section, you'll learn how.

Straightening the Horizon

The crooked horizon line is one of the most common problems, and one of the easiest to fix.

Open an image that needs straightening. Figure 23.30, my example, can be downloaded from this book's page on the Sams Publishing Web site.

FIGURE 23.30
The horizon should not run downhill.

1. With an image that's right up against the edges of the window like this one, it's typically easier to change the zoom level (and thus the size of the image in the window) to give you room to work. To do this, change the zoom percentage to a smaller number, drag the window border outwards, or simply maximize the window.
2. Choose Image, Rotate, Free Rotate Layer. You'll be asked if you want to change the layer from a background layer to an ordinary one; click OK. Click OK again to finish the job.
3. Now you're ready to straighten the image. Move the pointer off the image and onto the canvas, and it will change to the rotation pointer, which is curved almost in a circle. Drag in the direction you want the image to move, until the part that should be horizontal (in this case, the horizon) is parallel to the top of the screen.
4. When you're happy with the results, click the check mark button on the Options bar to commit your change.
5. With the Crop tool, crop away any revealed edges or other leftovers, as in Figure 23.31. You should now have a nice photo in which the ocean doesn't look as if it's falling off the Earth.

Figure 23.31
When we're done with this, you won't get seasick looking at it.

If you try this with an image of your own, you'll need to get the photo off the background layer just as we did in the example, because Elements can't straighten a background. Sometimes, you can simply choose Image, Rotate, Free Rotate Layer, and Elements will ask if you want to move the image from the background to a layer (as it did in our example), but if that doesn't happen to you and the Free Rotate command is unavailable, simply drag the image from the layer palette into a new file, which causes Elements to place the image on its own layer (and not a background layer). If your image has multiple layers and you want to straighten them in one step, link them by clicking the bottommost layer in the palette, and clicking the icon immediately to the left of each layer you want to link.

> Remember that you can always attempt to straighten an image (even if it's on the background layer) with the Image, Rotate, Straighten Image command. It works in a lot of cases, but as I mentioned earlier in this chapter, sometimes it makes things worse.

Use this same procedure any time you have to fix something that's out of kilter, vertically or horizontally. The same trick was applied to a steeple in Figure 23.32. If you have trouble telling when it's straight, add a layer to the picture and draw a line across or down as needed. Use a brush about three pixels wide and a nice, bright color; hold down the Shift key as you draw the line so it stays straight. When you're finished, just drag the layer with the line onto the Trash button at the bottom of the Layers palette. Don't flatten the image until you have gotten rid of the line.

FIGURE 23.32
The green line gives me something to line it up against.

Straightening an Image

Frequently, you need to straighten just part of the picture. It might be a perspective problem, or perhaps the furniture really *is* crooked. Antiques frequently lean a little. In the example below, I love the effect of the wide-angle lens on the car, but not on those brass posts holding up the rope around it. My choices are to get rid of the posts and the rope, which would be a lot of work, or to straighten the posts. Being lazy, my course is clear. I'll just fix the posts. Figure 23.33 shows the basic car.

FIGURE 23.33
The brass posts don't look right.

The posts lean in different directions, so I'll have to fix them separately. First, select one. The magnetic lasso is ideal for this job. After tracing carefully around the post, I can use the Image, Rotate, Free Rotate Selection command to make it vertical. Figure 23.34 shows this step.

FIGURE 23.34
Just a little kick to the left and it's straight again.

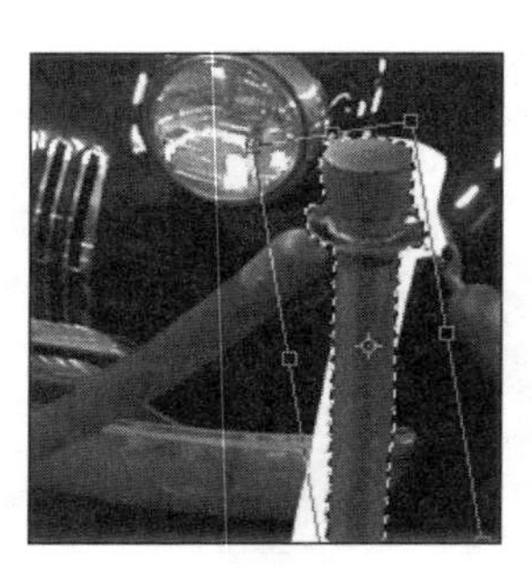

Now all I need to do is fill in where it was. The Clone Stamp tool is a good choice for this job. I cover it in more detail in Chapter 24, so here I'll just gloss over the details so you can get the idea of how I used it to fix my photo. Two preparations will help you use the Clone Stamp tool. First, zoom in close enough to see what you are doing. This sounds obvious, but many people forget about the magnifying glass and just squint or leave nose prints on the monitor. Press Z to select the zoom tool and click the part you want to see close up.

When you need to work in close quarters replacing a background, as you often do when using the Clone Stamp, a second trick for making your work easier is to select the area you need to work on. Use the Magic Wand and click in the open area to select. Once the area is selected, it's as if you'd masked everything around it: You can stamp like crazy and only the selected area will pick up the color. Figure 23.35 shows the selection trick applied to a zoomed-in section of the car.

FIGURE 23.35
Working only on the selection is much easier.

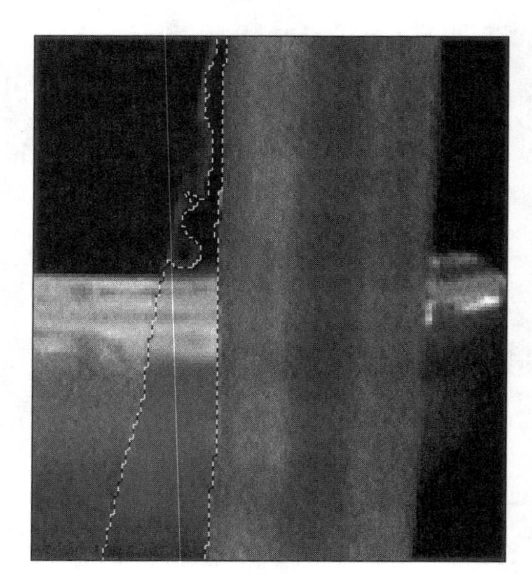

On the car image, if I crop off the tilting signs and the other post on the far left, I can forget about the red velvet rope and leave the rest of the photo as is, at least for now. Figure 23.36 and the color section both show the final picture.

FIGURE 23.36
The picture is all done and much less distorted.

Skewing Images

A certain amount of confusion surrounds skewing, distorting, and changing perspective. Which is which? Skewing allows you to tilt any side of an object, selection, or entire layer. For example, you can use skew to tilt a building to the left, and create your own Tower of Pisa. Distortion allows you to pull at the corners of a shape, selection, or layer, and stretch it in that direction. Use distortion to really twist a shape. If you use distortion on the bottom of our building, you can make the bottom seem really wide or really skinny. If you use distortion on a person's face, you can create the kind of effect you typically see in carnival mirrors. When you change an object's perspective, you change where it appears in three-dimensional space. With perspective, you can make a building seem to fall toward you or away from you. You can make a building that was shot straight on seem as if you're viewing it from a corner across the street.

Figure 23.37 compares these three techniques on a simple rectangle. You can apply the skew technique to text as well. To distort or change the perspective of type, you must simplify the layer it is on, which of course makes the type uneditable. To do this, select the type layer and choose Layer, Simplify Layer. You'll learn tips on how to warp text within a shape later in the chapter.

FIGURE 23.37
Skewing, distorting, and changing perspective are very similar, yet different.

Select what you want to skew: shape, selection, or layer. Then choose Image, Transform, Skew. A bounding box appears, with small handles along its sides. *Do not touch any of the corner handles, because that will distort the image instead of skewing it.* To skew, drag any one of the middle handles along the side. If you select a building, for example, you can click the handle in the middle of its top side, drag it to the left, and tilt the building toward its left side. To apply the setting, click the check mark button, double-click inside the selection, or press Enter/Return.

Using the Type Tools

The Type tool is actually four tools in one. As you can see in Figure 23.38, the toolbox holds both horizontal and vertical Type tools in both letter and mask modes. The masks allow you to do some very cool tricks with type and photos.

FIGURE 23.38
There are four Type tools.

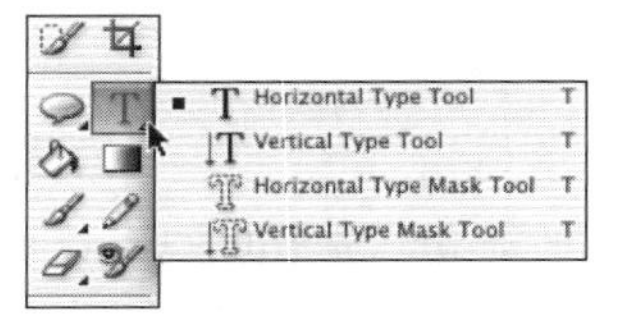

To use the Type tool, simply select it and click on the page where you want the type to begin. Before you do, however, you'll probably need to adjust the settings on the Options bar (see Figure 23.39).

FIGURE 23.39
Set your type options before you begin typing.

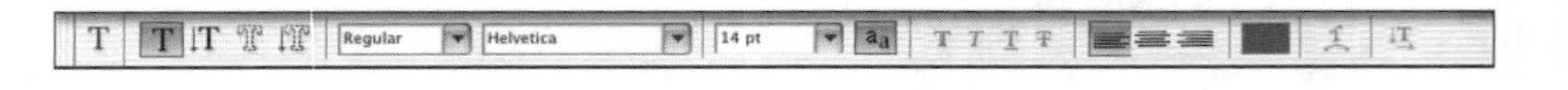

The first choice on the bar, which kind of type to set, is the same as in the toolbox: horizontal or vertical, masked or not. Next, a drop-down menu offers type styles. This will change according to the font you have selected, but generally you can choose from regular and italic, and often light, bold, or demibold, as well. The next drop-down menu displays a list of fonts installed, and the one after that offers a selection of point sizes. If you don't see the size you want, enter numbers into the window.

The next button, which looks like two *a*'s, is important. It determines whether to antialias the type. Antialiasing smoothes out jagged type. It's important to apply antialiasing if your work will be seen onscreen. Few things look worse, or less professional, than jagged type. Figure 23.40 shows the difference.

If your type is to be printed, however, turn off antialiasing. The same process that makes it look better onscreen adds a blur when the page is printed.

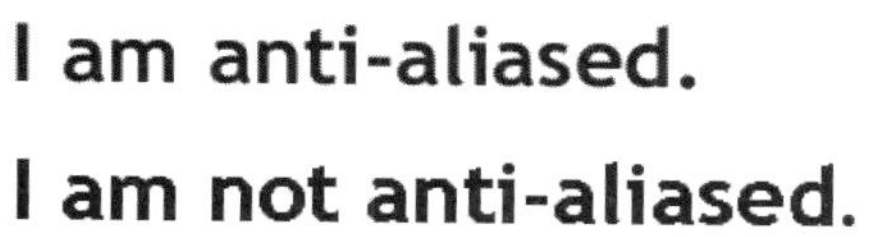

FIGURE 23.40
Notice the curves in the nonantialiased type. They appear lumpy, as if made of bricks.

I am anti-aliased.

I am not anti-aliased.

The next four choices give you false (or *faux*) bold, italic, underlined, and strikethrough type. The bold and italic options can be used to enhance a plain font or to increase the boldness and/or slant of already bold or italic faces. Strikethrough and underline have very limited uses, as far as I can see. Underlining was a way of indicating emphasis, back in the days of the typewriter, but it was always understood to be read as italic. Since you now have lots of options for italics, underlining isn't typographically correct. Nor is strikethrough, since the invention of the Delete key. Use them if you think you must, but don't tell me about it.

The little stacks of lines indicate alignment: flush left, centered, or flush right. Justified type, set flush left *and* right, is unfortunately not an option in Elements. Elements isn't a word processing program, after all. Its type functions are mainly intended to add a few words to a picture, not to typeset a newsletter or advertisement.

The color swatch, black by default, lets you choose a type color independent of the foreground and background colors. Just click it to open the usual Color Picker.

The sort of twisted letter with the curved line under it takes you to one of the more interesting aspects of setting type in Elements: warped type. I'll come back to it later on. But first, let's finish off the Options bar. The final button lets you change horizontally set type to vertical type, or vice versa. It's most useful if you tend to use type as a design element rather than a means of communication. Simply click it to change a selected string of letters or symbols from reading left-right to up-down.

Adding Horizontal and Vertical Type

Horizontal type is what we're used to seeing in the English-speaking world. Other cultures use different alphabets and different typographic styles. Outside of short words on neon signs, we rarely see English, French, or similar horizontal languages intended to be read vertically. It's unnecessarily difficult, which doesn't mean you can't do it—just that you might want to think before you do.

To set type vertically, follow these steps.

1. Choose a legible font. Decide on a size and color, and make the settings on the Options bar. Be sure to click on the vertical type option.
2. Position the cursor where you want the first letter.
3. Start typing. If your word(s) runs off the image, try a smaller font.

To set type horizontally, do the following:

1. Make the appropriate settings as you did when placing type vertically, choosing the horizontal type option.
2. If you've chosen flush left justification, position the cursor where the type starts. If you've chosen flush right, position it where the type ends. Position it at the midpoint if you want the type centered.
3. Start typing.

Type is always set on its own layer. Each time you position the cursor and start typing, you create a new type layer. You can edit the type and apply layer commands to it. You can change the orientation of the type, apply or remove antialiasing, and warp the type into a variety of shapes. You can move, copy, and change the position or layer options of a type layer just as you would with a normal layer. To change the type's font size or color, or to edit the message, activate the type layer and click within the type to edit, or select all the type by dragging over it, and then make your changes. You can also select all the text in the text layer by clicking on the layer in the Layers palette, and double-clicking the T thumbnail icon. After editing text, be sure to click the check mark button on the Options bar to let Elements know you're done.

Edits involving distortion or perspective (found on the Image, Transform menu) can't happen until the type is *simplified*, or rendered in bitmap form. In addition, you can't apply filters to text until that text has been simplified. To simplify text, click the type layer in the Layers palette, and choose Layer, Simplify Layer. Once simplified, text is no longer editable.

Choosing Fonts

Literally hundreds of thousands, if not millions, of fonts are available. And, that's before we start adding styles and special effects to them. But when you install Elements, the only fonts you'll see are the ones you've already installed. You can find fonts all over the Internet, as well as in your local computer store, catalogs, and so on. Some you can get for free; others cost money. I've found several CDs full of useful fonts advertised in the back pages of computer magazines, at very reasonable prices. And of course, there's Adobe, with everything from the classics to fonts made of bones or kids on skateboards. Figure 23.41 shows a few of the stranger examples.

FIGURE 23.41
Not all of these are right for all occasions.

How many fonts do you need? That depends on what you intend to use them for. Certainly, you already have some useful ones, including classic serif fonts such as Palatino or Times New Roman. (*Serifs* are short lines that finish the ends of letters, like this: T. They make it easier to read small type.) You probably have one or two sans serif faces such as Helvetica or Arial. (*Sans serif* means *without serifs*, and looks like this: T.) You have something like Courier, which imitates a typewriter, and you probably have one or two script fonts, such as Chancery or Dom Casual. Beyond that, why not wait and see what you need? Adding dozens of fonts can actually make your computer run more slowly.

Using the Type Mask Tools

Photoshop's Type Mask tools are fun to use and can create some really cool effects. Unlike the horizontal and vertical Type tools, which create type that you can fill with color, the Type Mask tools create a selection in the shape of the type, which you can fill with an image or pattern. You can also use the Type Mask tools to punch type out of a picture (leaving a blank area in the shape of the type) or to mask the rest of the picture (leaving nothing but letters filled with the picture). Half the battle is finding a picture to work with. The other half is finding a nice fat typeface that leaves plenty of room for your picture to show through. Let's try filling some type.

To use the Type Mask tool, first select it. Set your font, size, and any other options you like. Faux Bold is often useful here, as big bold letters work best as cutouts. When you position the cursor and start to place the letters, something surprising happens. The screen goes into Mask mode and turns pink. As you enter the letters, they appear to be in a contrasting color, but when you finish typing and deselect the Type Mask tool, they turn into paths and the temporary mask goes away. Figure 23.42 shows how this looks onscreen. Don't forget that this is essentially another selection tool, rather than a Type tool, so you won't be working on a type layer. Your letters appear on whatever layer is selected.

FIGURE 23.42
Now you have the letters as selection outlines.

What you do with your text selection from this point on is up to you. You can fill it with a pattern or stroke it just like any other selection. You can use the selection to cut the letters out of the image on which it was typed, essentially "punching out" the letters. You can invert the selection and cut the image away from the text, leaving the text filled with a portion of the image (assuming that you typed the text onto an image layer). Regardless of how you fill the selection, you can add some layer effects as I have in Figure 23.43. I applied the Wow Chrome, Shiny Edge layer effect and the Drop Shadow, Hard Edge layer effect to the top text, the Drop Shadow, High and Complex, Molten Gold effects to the middle text, and Bevel, Simple Pillow Emboss and Drop Shadow, Soft Edge to the bottom text. Be sure to check these out in the color plate section, too. (You can also add layer effects to horizontal or vertical type, by the way.)

You can group two layers (one with the type mask, the other with an image) and cut out letters to reveal a picture that's actually on the layer behind them, as I have in Figure 23.44. I placed the image on one layer, and the text or a text selection on another, and then grouped them as described in earlier in this chapter. By using two layers instead of typing the text directly on the image with a Type Mask tool and cutting it out, I gave myself a bit more room in which to grab the exact portion of the image I wanted to cut into letters. After cutting out the text, I applied an Outer Glow, Simple layer style to them. Again, please see this in color. If you're thinking, "Wow! I want to try that!" don't worry—you'll get your chance in an upcoming task.

FIGURE 23.43
Don't be afraid to experiment.

FIGURE 23.44
I added a glow to help define the letters.

Working with Layer Styles and Text

Layer styles might not have been exclusively meant for working with type, but they do it so well that I nearly always use at least one, and sometimes more. That's why, although I intend to come back to using layer styles in Chapter 26, I want to tell you a bit about them here.

A layer style is a special effect such as a shadow or glow that affects all the objects on a layer. You can combine layer styles, such as an outer glow and chrome, to create a complex effect. If you want to use a layer style to format just the type in an image, that type must be on its own layer. With the horizontal and vertical Type tools, that's not a problem, since Elements creates a new layer whenever you use the tool. But if you use the Type Mask tools to create a type selection, make sure you first create a new layer to put it on.

Once you have some type or a type mask on a layer, to apply a layer style, open the Layer Styles palette. If it's not in the palette well, you can display it by choosing Window, Layer Style. Open the drop-down list and select a category such as Drop Shadow. The palette displays a list of layer styles for that category. Click a style to apply it to the text on that layer.

When you apply a style, it shows up in the Layers palette as a cursive letter *f* to the right of the layer name, as shown in Figure 23.45. Because the Undo History palette only tells you that you've applied a style, and not which one, you'll need to pay attention to what you are doing. Also, if you select another layer style, it's added to the first style. Thus, it's easy to get confused about which styles you've added. To remove all styles from a layer, click the Clear Style button at the top of the Layer Styles palette. (It looks sort of like an aspirin tablet.)

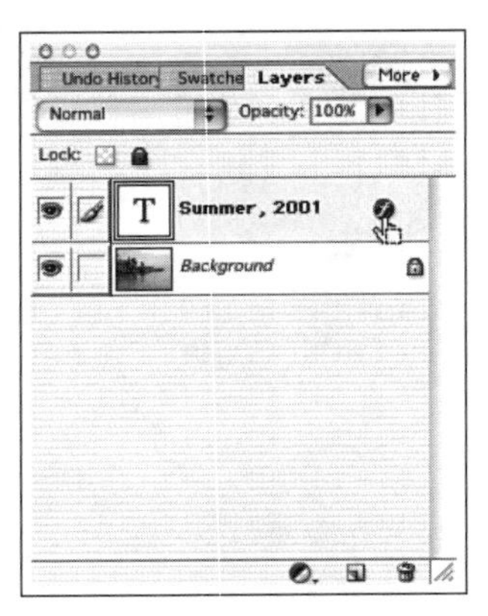

FIGURE 23.45
I suppose it's meant to be a "stylish" f.

The most effective layer styles to use with text include Drop Shadows, Bevel (which provides bevel and emboss styles), Wow Chrome, and Wow Neon, to name a few. For example, you can improve the appearance of most type with a drop shadow, which adds dimension. Just don't overdo it. In Figure 23.46, you can see what a difference a simple shadow makes.

The Shadow Knows...

The Shadow Knows...

FIGURE 23.46
This is the preset shadow, called Low.

You can vary the effect of these layer styles by changing the blending modes and varying the opacity. As always, the best way to see what they do is to experiment with different settings.

Editing Layer Styles

If a layer style gives you almost, but not quite what you want, you can go back and edit the settings. You can reach the Style Settings dialog box either by choosing Layer, Layer Style, Style Settings, or by double-clicking on the style symbol (the cursive *f*) on the Layer palette. The Style Settings box is shown in Figure 23.47. You can change the position of the light, which determines the direction in which shadows are dropped, glows are cast, textures are lit, and so on.

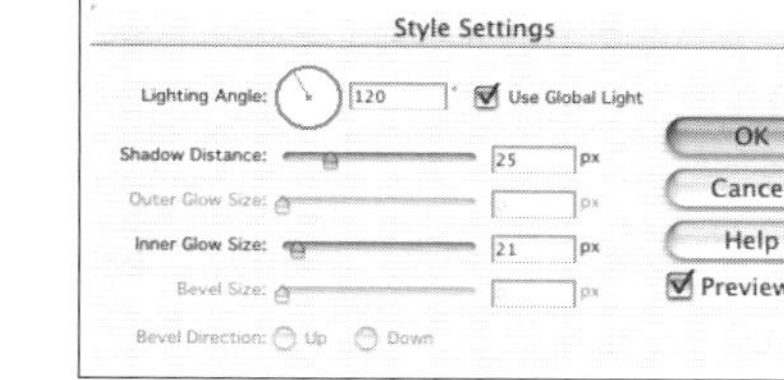

FIGURE 23.47
Items that don't relate to a particular setting are grayed out and can't be changed.

You can also apply global light, which is a very clever way of keeping your shadows in line. Global light dictates that the light setting (in degrees) that you make here, or in any of the other dialog boxes that deal with light or shadow direction, will remain constant. If you put type with a drop shadow on another layer, the new shadow will match the old one. If you add a shape with a reflected glow, it will be lit from the same source. This is more important than it sounds at first. We live on a planet that has a single sun as its main light source. One light source produces one shadow, and that's what we are used to seeing. When you come inside and turn on a couple of lamps plus maybe the overhead fluorescent bulb, you've complicated things. Now there are several possible directions in which the shadow can go. The strength of the brightest light determines what you actually see. Designating a global light in your composition forces all the shadows you apply to fall in line. With the Style Settings dialog box, you can also change the height and size of a bevel, glow, or shadow.

▼ TASK

Task: Applying Layer Styles to Text

1. Start with a new image. Use the default size, with a white background and RGB color.
2. Click the Horizontal Text tool. Using the Options bar, select a serif font and set the point size to 128. Set the font color to blue by clicking the color swatch at the end of the Options bar and choosing blue from the Color Picker.
3. Click along the left side of the image and type your name. Click the check mark button to indicate when you have finished typing. (If your name is too long to fit, change the text size using the Options bar.)
4. Open the Layers palette. Notice that Elements creates a new text layer for you, as indicated by the T thumbnail on the left.
5. Make sure that the text layer is active, and then open the Layer Styles palette. Select Drop Shadow from the list. Click the Soft Edge icon to apply a soft shadow.
6. Select Glass Buttons from the list, and click the Yellow Glass icon. Notice how the text changes to green when the yellow color is placed on top of blue. Some layer styles completely override the text color, while others add to it.
7. Click the Clear Style button to remove all layer styles.
8. Select Outer Glows, and click the Heavy icon. Hmmm. Nothing seems to have happened.
9. Open the Layers palette, and change to the background layer. Use the Paint Bucket tool to fill the layer with red paint. Ahhh. Now we can see the glow. It just needed something to contrast with.
10. Open the Layers palette and change back to the text layer. Choose Layer, Layer Style, Style Settings. Reduce the Outer Glow Size to 10.
11. Save the image with the filename Glowing Name.psd and close it. ▲

Warping Text

One of the major complaints about Photoshop used to be that you couldn't set type on a path within the program. If you wanted, say, a wavy line of text, you could either position the letters one by one or set the type in Illustrator or something similar and import it into Photoshop. It was a nuisance, at best. Photoshop, and now Elements, have finally added a feature called warped type. You can find it on the type Options bar.

It's not totally flexible. Rather than drawing your own path, the Warp Text dialog box allows you to select from 15 preset paths. You can also warp and distort the paths as necessary. Figure 23.48 shows a list of the presets. The Arch, Wave, Flag, and Rise presets are typically the best ones to choose when you have multiple lines of text, although any of the presets will work.

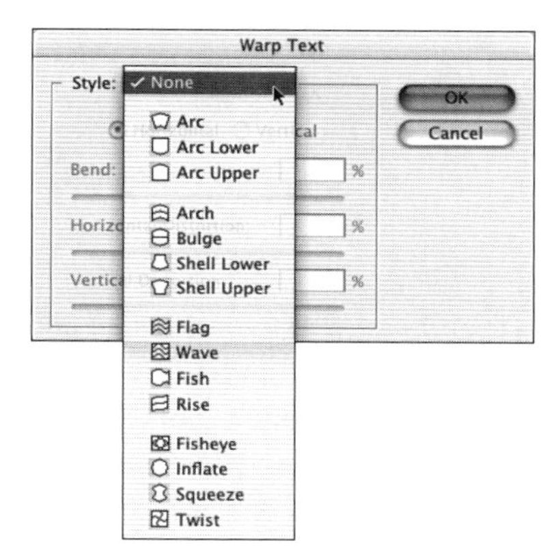

FIGURE 23.48
Select a warp path.

The dialog box settings, shown in Figure 23.49, are a bit tricky at first. Use the sliders to increase the amount of Bend applied to the path. Moving to the right bends words up; to the left (negative numbers), bends them down. Distortion makes the line of type appear to flare out on one end (Horizontal Distortion), or from top to bottom (Vertical Distortion).

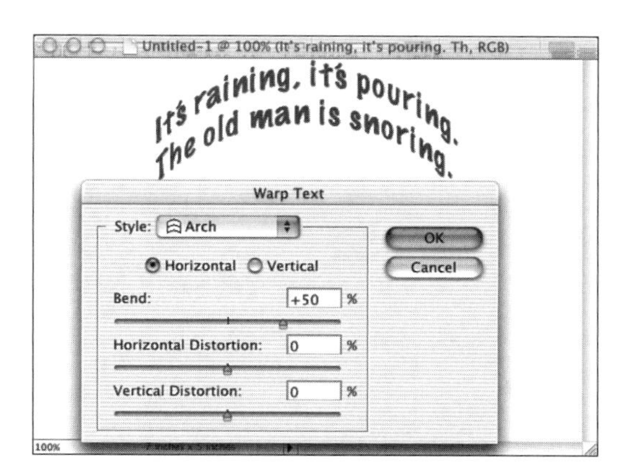

FIGURE 23.49
Move the sliders left or right to change the settings.

In Figure 23.50, I've applied some of the warp styles to various bits of type. The best way to master this tool is to play with it. Set a line or two of type and try the different kinds of warp on it. Try it with and without layer styles added. Move the settings sliders around. You can't break anything.

FIGURE 23.50
The only thing to watch out for is that the type stays legible.

Summary

It has been a long chapter, and a useful one. First you learned about the selection tools (Marquees, Lassos, the Magic Wand, and Selection Brush), and how to use them not only to select an object, but as drawing and mask making tools as well. Then, you learned about the importance of layers and how to create, delete, copy, link, and group layers as needed. You also learned how to adjust a layer's opacity, and how to use a fill layer to control the color of an object in another layer. We then moved on to cropping, resizing, and rotating your images. You also learned to straighten horizons, roofs, poles, or anything that should be horizontal or vertical and isn't. You learned about the Skew feature. Finally, we covered Elements' type capabilities.

CHAPTER 24

Fixing Photo Flaws

Good photos can suffer from a host of problems, some of which are easy to fix. Others require more patience. Dust and scratches are most common on old pictures, and particularly on scans of them. Red eye is seen mainly on pictures taken with a flash camera, but it can happen at any time, if the subject's eye catches the sun or an indoor light. And nearly every picture needs a little bit of cleanup, especially outdoor shots that can be spoiled by litter on the ground, dead leaves, or whatever is there that shouldn't be. Old black and white or color photographs may need some overall sprucing up as they fade, discolor, or begin to disintegrate over time. In this chapter we'll look at many techniques for fixing photo flaws ranging from minor to drastic.

Making Basic Cleanups

The basic cleanup should be your first step when working on any picture. Study the picture. Ask yourself some questions:

- Would cropping help improve the composition? If so, see Chapter 23, "Using Basic Tools in Elements," for help.
- Is it crooked? Do you need to straighten the whole picture or just a piece of something? See Chapter 23.

- Is there something in there that doesn't belong? If so, you'll learn how to remove small elements with the Clone Stamp and larger ones with other techniques later in the chapter.
- If it's a scanned photo, was the glass in the scanner clean? You can pick up dust, pet or human hair, and all sorts of scuzz in your pictures if you don't keep the scanning surface clean. Find out how to remove dust, hairs, and similar small items in this chapter.

Here's a photo I just scanned for these examples (see Figure 24.1). It was shot about eight or nine years ago when the Tall Ships came to Boston. This is the training ship Esmeralda, a four-masted schooner from Chile.

FIGURE 24.1
At close to 370 feet long, I barely got her in the frame.

As you can see, this is definitely in need of some cleaning up. First, I'll crop out the black edges from the scanner. It looks pretty straight, so we won't mess with rotating it. However, if you look carefully, you'll see that the black speck between the two middle masts is a helicopter. It's not big enough to see clearly, so we'll take it out with the Clone Stamp.

Removing Small Objects with the Clone Stamp Tool

When small objects wander into your photographs uninvited, use the Clone Stamp to get rid of them. The Clone Stamp works by copying the color of nearby pixels onto the pixels you drag over with the tool. So to fix my photo, I used the tool to copy the colors of the sky nearby, and to paint with those colors over the image of the helicopter, thereby removing it.

To use the Clone Stamp tool, zoom in on the area you're trying to fix, and then select the tool from the toolbox. Choose a brush from the drop-down list. Typically, a soft-edged brush is best, because it will soften the effect and make it less obvious. Next, select a brush size. Choose a brush that's large enough to cover the telephone wire, tree branch, or stray dog you want to remove, but not too big. Select a blending mode and opacity. For this kind of repair, I usually leave these set to Normal, 100%. Turn on the Aligned option if you want to copy colors from nearby pixels. Turn it off if you want to copy the colors in one area of the image to several different places. If you want to "mix your paint" using colors from all layers, turn on the Use All Layers option.

After setting options, press Command-Alt and click in the image to take a sample of the colors there. Then click and drag to begin painting. Short strokes are best. If the Aligned option is turned on, you'll paint with colors taken from a spot that's roughly the same distance from the mouse pointer as the original spot and the place where you first began painting. The spot where your colors are coming from is marked with a big *X*. If the Aligned option is not on, your paint color will come from the place where you first clicked to take a sample.

To get rid of the offending helicopter, I zoomed in, clicked the Clone Stamp tool, selected a relatively small soft brush, sampled some sky, and used one short stroke to remove the helicopter from the sky.

Removing Small Objects with Copy and Paste

The cluster of little boats just at the stern of the ship, under her flag, is a distraction. Fortunately, it looks like there's enough water at the bottom-left edge to cover them up. For this, I'll start by copying some water and pasting it into a new layer over the boats.

When you want to cover something in an area of your image that should look like another area of the image, why not simply copy the good section and paste it over the bad? You can fix large areas with a single click using this method. Of course, you'll have to soften the edges of the pasted area, but that's not a problem.

To remove those distracting boats from the left side of my photo, I copied a small piece of water from below them, then pasted it back into my image. Elements automatically creates a new layer for the pasted data, which is placed exactly above the spot on the image where I copied it. This makes the pasted area a bit tough to see, so I temporarily hid the image layer by clicking its eye icon in the Layers palette. Then I used the Move tool to position the patch as carefully as I could. I repeated this process a few times, because I needed several different patches of water to cover the boats. When I was done, I merged all the layers by selecting Layer, Merge Visible. Then I used the Clone Stamp to sample the correct water color nearby, and paint it over the edges of my patches, hiding them. Follow the horizon when you drag with the Clone Stamp, in order to imitate the ripples in the water (see Figure 24.2).

FIGURE 24.2
Zoom in so you can see what you're doing.

With my careful copying and pasting, and some help from the Clone Stamp, the little boats are gone in no time. Now I'm ready to go on to color corrections, lighting changes, and any other major changes. I might try applying a watercolor filter (which makes the photo appear as if it were painted with watercolors), Chalk & Charcoal (which simulates that artistic effect), or Spatter (which spreads out the colors in a spattered pattern). On the other hand, I might just leave it as it is, which isn't bad. See this in color in the color section.

Fixing Red Eye

You've seen it a thousand times—that "devil eye" look that spoils pictures of everyone from grandma to the new baby, puppy, or cat. Usually the eerie glow is red, but it can be green, blue, or even yellow. It's caused by light reflecting back to the camera lens from the inside of the eye, which can only happen if the pupil of the eye is open—as it would be in a dimly lit room, or outside in full shade. Red eye appears red in humans because of the network of blood vessels back there. Our four-footed friends are more likely to display green or yellow eye, although normally blue-eyed Siamese cats eyes will also glow fiery red. Figure 24.3 shows an especially awful example, with both eyes affected.

FIGURE 24.3
He's really a very gentle cat.

Elements has an "automatic" red eye repair tool called the Red Eye Brush tool. It's in the toolbox, shown in Figure 24.4 along with its Options bar.

FIGURE 24.4
Pay attention to the Options bar settings.

The brush isn't exactly automatic, but the accompanying directions will walk you step-by-step through the process of using it. To find them, look in the palette well on the Shortcuts bar, or under the Windows menu for How To and locate Remove Redeye (see Figure 24.5).

FIGURE 24.5
It's simple when you have the recipe in front of you.

Whenever you are using a palette, drag it down the screen to disconnect it from the toolbar. Otherwise, it will automatically close whenever you click somewhere else on the screen.

From there, you simply follow the directions, which tell you to do the following:

1. Select the Red Eye Brush and choose a brush tip from the drop-down list. By default, it's a soft-edged brush, and I typically don't change it.
2. Next, set your brush to roughly the size of the pupil. (If the area is small, zoom in to see clearly.) Don't worry if the pupil you need to fix is partially covered by an eyelid; you'll only be changing the bad color (called the Current color) to a good color (known as the Replacement color).

3. Set the Sampling option to First Click. This tells Elements to sample the color you want to replace from the area under the brush when you first click on the image. Alternately, you can choose Current Color from the Sampling list, which tells Elements to use the color shown on the Current swatch. To set this color to the default (dark red), click the Default Colors button. This also sets the Replacement color to black, which is the other default. You can click the Current swatch and use the Color Picker to select a unique color of your choice.
4. Change the Replacement color if needed by clicking the swatch and choosing a color from the Color Picker. It's unlikely that you'll need to do this, though, because the color is set to black by default, and that's what most pupils should be.
5. Adjust the Tolerance level as desired. A lower value tells Elements to replace pixels that are really close to the Current color (If you selected First Click in step 3, the Current color will be set to the color of the pixel you first click on.)
6. Center the brush crosshairs over the red part of the eye, and click, as in Figure 24.6.

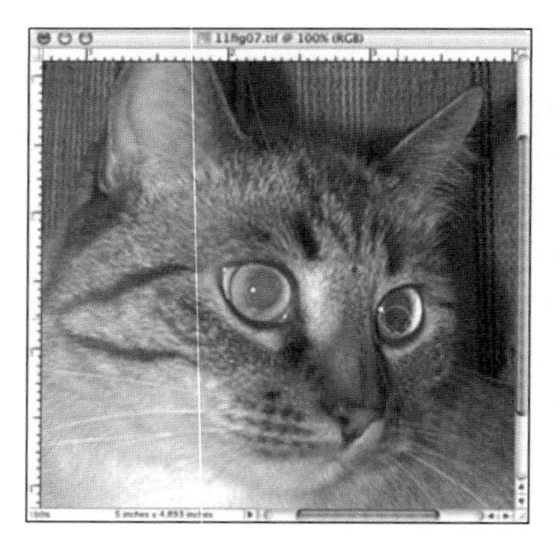

FIGURE 24.6
One click just about does it.

7. Drag the brush as needed over the red areas to remove them. Because you selected a brush size that matches the size of the pupil, you won't have to drag much. Don't worry about "coloring outside the lines." The color will only change where it should, unless you drag across something else the same color, like the cat's nose in this case.

That's the official Elements way to do it. It's quick, easy, and somewhat effective. Figure 24.7 shows the final result, as does the corresponding color figure in the color section. It works fairly well in grayscale, but I'm not very happy with the color result. It's unnaturally gray, as if the poor cat has cataracts. After selecting the "wrong" gray part of the eye, I can add a Hue/Saturation adjustment layer and darken it by moving the Lightness slider to the left, or I can start over and do the job differently. (An adjustment layer lets you isolate part of an image and make changes to just that part. Adjustment layers also let you try out effects on an entire image without committing to them. You'll learn how to use them later in this chapter. You'll also learn about adjusting Hue/Saturation for an entire image.)

FIGURE 24.7
The recipe didn't do enough.

TASK

Task: Fixing Red Eye From Scratch

When the official Elements method doesn't do it, here's another way that's almost as easy, and generally more effective. Just follow these steps:

1. Zoom in to make the eyes as large as possible. (You can work on one eye at a time.) Use the Magic Wand to select the off-color parts of the pupil. Usually, they are the same color or close to it. (Adjust the Tolerance value as needed to select as much as you can.) Leave the small white circles in the middle of the eyes. Those are "catchlights" from the flash (see Figure 24.8).

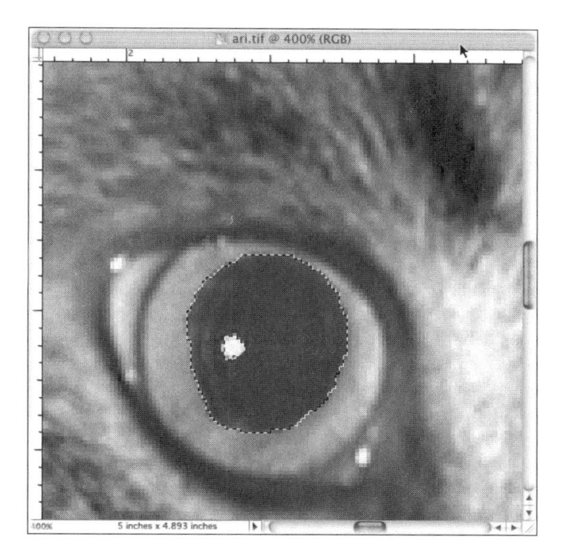

FIGURE 24.8
Select as much of the red as you can.

2. Press Ctrl-Shift-U (or select Remove Color from the Enhance, Adjust Color menu) to desaturate the selection. Now the incorrect color is gray. Saturation, as you may recall, is the intensity of a color. By removing it, you take out the color hue, and reduce the selection to gray tones similar to what you might see in a grayscale image. The lightness and darkness are still there, just not the color. You'll learn other ways to play with saturation in an image later in this chapter.

3. Make sure the foreground color is set to black or very dark gray. Switch to the Brush tool (located in the toolbox), select a large soft brush from the drop-down list, and click the Airbrush icon on the Options bar (it's on the far right). Set the blending mode to Darken and the opacity to no higher than 20%. Although we'll cover blending modes in Chapter 26, "Creating Digital Art from Scratch," I can tell you now that the Darken mode will darken only the pixels that are lighter than the foreground color. Pixels darker than that color are not touched. Brush in layers of black, letting the color build up naturally. Because you turned on the Airbrush function, you'll be spraying only bits of color each time you drag over the eye. Continue until it looks right, zooming out to see it in context. If you make a mistake, you can use the Undo History palette as shown in Figure 24.9.

FIGURE 24.9
Use the Undo History palette to step backward if you go too far.

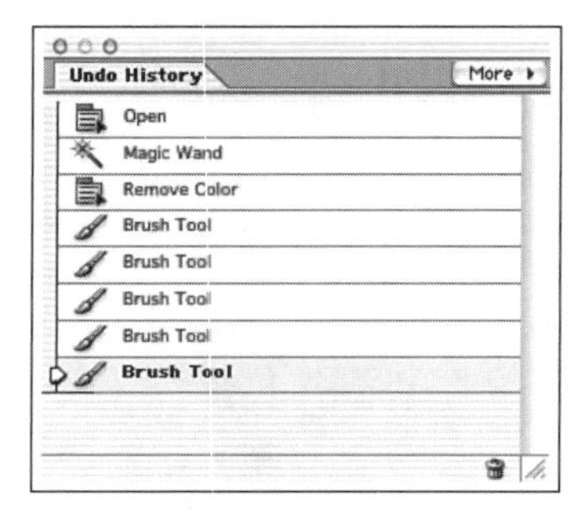

4. Repeat with the other eye. Figure 24.10 and the corresponding color plate show the final result.

FIGURE 24.10
Now he looks quite normal. Pity he doesn't act it.

Removing Dust and Scratches

The Dust & Scratches filter can be a tremendous time-saver when you're doing basic cleanup on a photo, particularly an old scanned one. If you're not careful, though, it can ruin the picture by overcompensating for the spots and losing detail. The filter works by adding a slight blur, which you can carefully adjust to produce a good compromise between spots and sharpness. To use it, choose Filter, Noise, Dust & Scratches.

Figure 24.11 shows the filter's interface, applied to a very detailed scan of an old photo. As you can see, there are large chunks of dirt, as well as smaller bits of dust and at least one hair running through the picture. But it's a good, clear scan, and worth the time it will take to clean it.

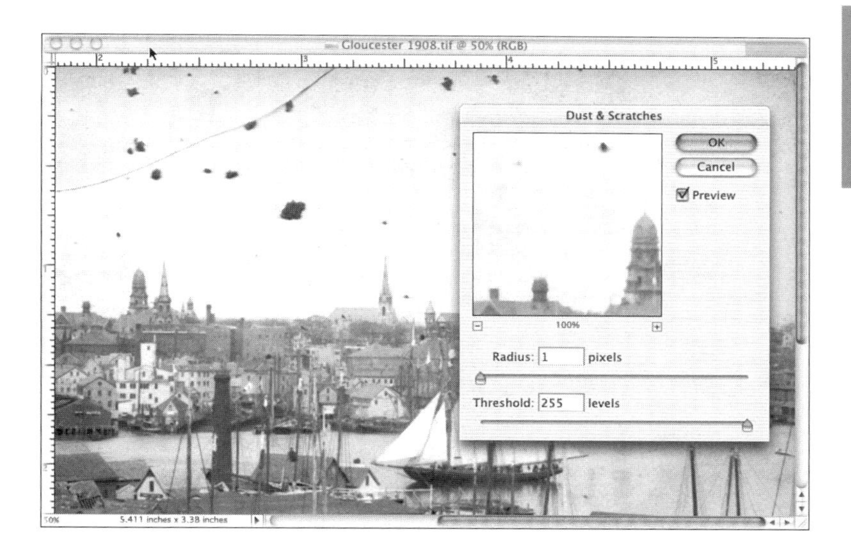

FIGURE 24.11
Gloucester Harbor, circa 1908.

The filter has two sliders, one for the radius of the area it examines for differences, and one for how much different in color or value the pixels in that area must be in order to be noticed and removed. You want to keep the radius value fairly low, to avoid over-blurring your image. Also, keep in mind that the Threshold range of 0–128 seems to work best for the majority of photos. You can set the Threshold to 100 and select a small radius, and then lower the Threshold value gradually until you achieve a balance between removal and sharpness.

Using this filter to remove the large pieces of dirt in this particular image would require such a degree of blur that you wouldn't be able to see the details of the picture. In Figure 24.12, I've raised the radius of the particles slightly (increasing the individual areas to be examined for differences) and lowered the threshold a good deal so that more pixels will qualify for removal, and now, just as we begin to see some differences in the spottiness, the detail is rapidly disappearing. One way to compensate for this is to isolate the area you want to change. Because most of the scratches, dust spots, and so on are in the sky, I could select the entire sky and use the filter on it. Or I could try a completely different method—applying the Despeckle and Unmask filters.

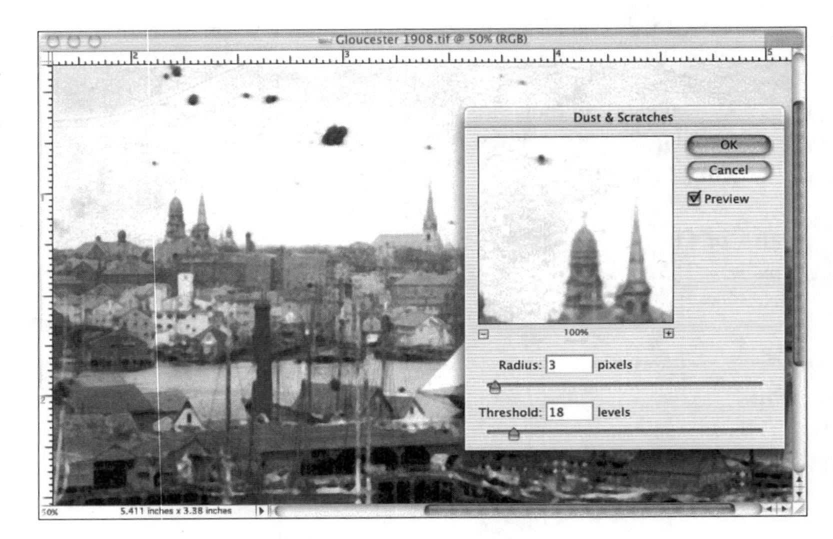

FIGURE 24.12
Compare the large picture with the previous one. A lot of sharpness is gone.

Using the Despeckle and Unsharp Mask Filters

So, perhaps the Dust & Scratches filter is not the right tool for this job. Unfortunately, most of the time the only way to tell is to try it. Still, the picture certainly needs cleaning up. What other options might we have? Despeckle? It's just above Dust & Scratches on the Filter, Noise submenu. The Despeckle filter looks for areas in the image where sharp color changes occur, such as the areas you might find in our sky dotted with dust. Then it blurs the area, but not its edges. This helps to preserve the sharpness in a photo, while removing dust and dirt. The filter is also helpful in photos that have banding—visible bands of contrast that often appear in digital captures and scans of magazine photos and other slightly reflective material. To try the filter, choose Filter, Noise, Despeckle. There are no options, so Elements applies the filter right away. If you don't like the effect, click Undo to remove it. Applied several times to our photo, it had no visible effect, so let's try something else.

The Unsharp Mask filter (Filter, Sharpen, Unsharp Mask) definitely did some good, as shown in Figure 12.13. Not only did it remove some of the smaller dust spots, it added contrast and sharpness to the photo, making it even more worthwhile to take the time to remove the dirt by hand.

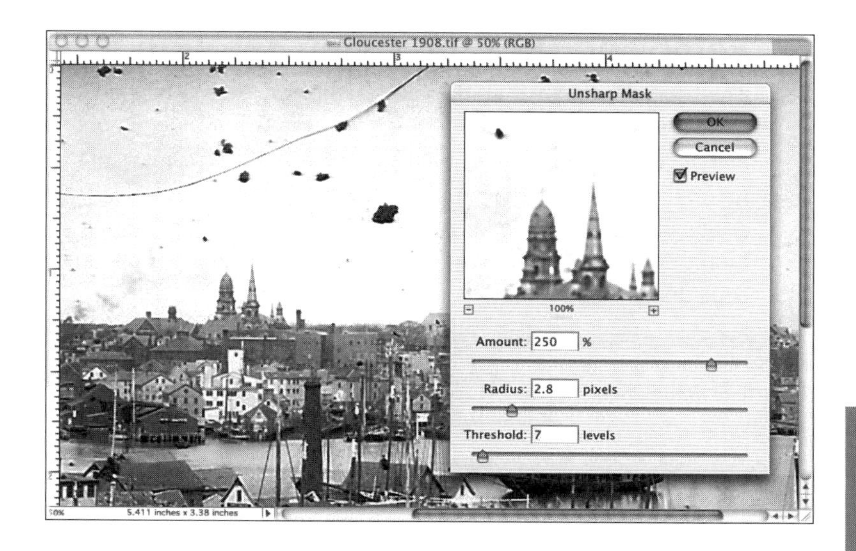

FIGURE 12.13
Unsharp masking is going to help a lot.

The Unsharp Mask filter is one of the most useful, and most misunderstood, filters in the bunch. Unsharp masking is a traditional technique that has been used in the printing industry for many years. It corrects blurring (sharpens the edges) in an original image or scan, as well as any blurring that occurs during the resampling and printing process. The Unsharp Mask filter works by locating every two adjacent pixels with a difference in brightness values that you have specified, and increasing their contrast by an amount that you specify. Because it perceives the dust spots as slightly darker blurs, you can manipulate the settings so that it removes the smallest spots. At the same time, it does tend to accentuate the larger ones, sometimes even placing a white band around a particularly large black spot. That's actually not a problem, because we'll be using the Clone Stamp tool to cover the big ones—and their "halos." (You can learn more about the Unsharp Mask filter as well as related filters in Chapter 25, "Enhancing Your Photos with Filters.")

Start by setting the Amount value, which tells Elements how much to increase the contrast of the pixels that qualify. Typically, a number between 150 and 200 is about right (One and a half to two times their original brightness).

The Radius control sets the number of surrounding pixels to which the sharpening effect is applied. I suggest that you keep the radius fairly low—around 2–3. The Threshold setting controls how different the pixels must be to be sharpened. The lower the setting, the more similar the pixels can be and still be affected by the filter. The higher the setting, the greater Photoshop's tolerance of difference will be. A value less than 20 usually works best. Of course, as always, feel free to go wild and try all the settings. That is the best way to learn. Be sure that you check the Preview box so that you can see the effect of your changes. When you like it, click OK.

Removing Dust and Scratches with the Clone Stamp

The best way to cover all the spots, tedious though it may be, is to stamp them out. Switch to the Clone Stamp tool, select a large, soft-edged brush, and be sure to press Alt and click in the sky as close to the spot as possible, because sky tones can vary quite a lot, and you want to copy a good one (see Figure 24.14). Be sure you have not checked Aligned. Though it's helpful when you need to copy something, it's not right for this kind of cover-up job. Figure 24.15 shows the final photo, looking pretty darn good for something nearly a century old.

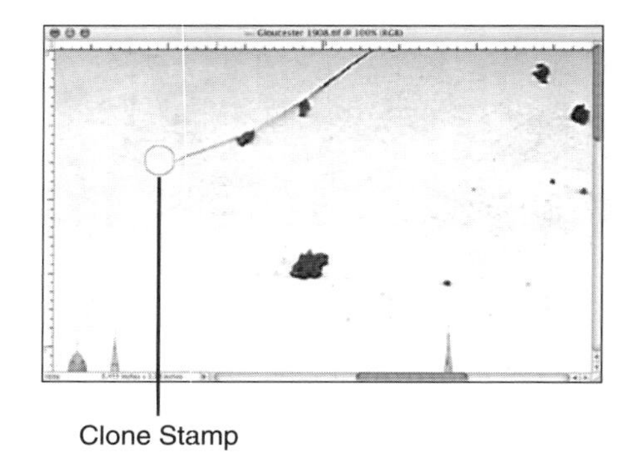

FIGURE 24.14
The Clone Stamp tool at work.

FIGURE 24.15
Don't try to catch every little spot. If it's too perfect, it doesn't look authentic.

Too Light/Too Dark: Adjusting Brightness, Contrast, and Color

Digital cameras generally give you good, accurate color, but a lot depends on the amount of light available. Pictures shot outdoors toward the end of the day often take on an orange tone, as the sun goes down. Rainy day pictures might be drab as the weather itself. Indoor photos can pick up all kinds of color casts depending on the lighting in the room. Scanning photos can add color shifts caused by the scanner. Or maybe you've scanned old, faded prints in hopes of saving them in Elements. You'll be amazed at what you can do by just making some small adjustments to an image's brightness, contrast, and color.

Being somewhat lazy, I always start to fix a problem image by trying anything that says Auto. Elements offers three: Auto Levels, Auto Contrast, and Auto Color Correction. All are on the Enhance menu, along with the other color correction tools we'll be looking at later in this chapter. Remember that all these corrections can be applied to the entire image, to a selection, or to one or more layers.

Auto Levels

It's certainly worth a click. Auto Levels automatically adjusts the tonal range and color balance in your photo, to make sure that there is a range of values (shadows, midtones, and highlights). It defines the lightest and darkest pixels in an image, and then redistributes the intermediate pixel values proportionately. If Elements doesn't think the levels need adjusting, it won't change anything. If it does, the screen will blink and your image will reappear, looking better (hopefully). If you don't like the changes, click Undo.

If you don't like the result of Auto Levels, but you agree that the picture could use some tweaking, choose Enhance, Adjust Brightness, Contrast, Levels to open the Levels dialog box, shown in Figure 24.16, and do it yourself. What you're looking at is called a *histogram*, and it's essentially a graph of the number of pixels at each level of brightness from 0 to 255. (Stop and read the upcoming sidebar to learn more about histograms.) The image in Figure 24.16 has a good spread all the way across the spectrum—just enough light and dark spots, and not too many boring middle tones.

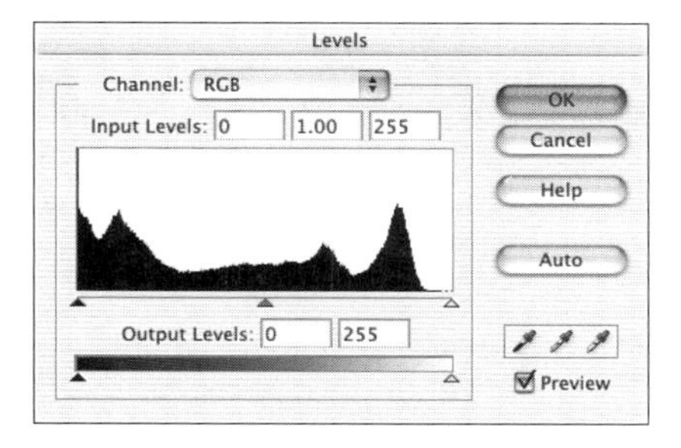

FIGURE 24.16
Levels aren't hard to adjust.

There are several ways to use the Levels dialog box. The easiest is to move the Input Level sliders (up arrows) just under the histogram until you like the result. Just be sure that you have checked the Preview box, so you can see the effect of your changes on the picture.

More scientifically, you can drag the sliders to the points at either end of the scale where the histogram begins to rise steeply. Typically, these will have numerical input values somewhere between 0–30 and 225–255. Then, move the middle slider, which represents the midtones, to about halfway between the two. This remaps the values; narrowing the range increases the contrast while widening the range decreases it.

Drag the Output Level sliders at the bottom of the dialog box to adjust the range of shadows and highlights. This increases or decreases the amount of contrast and brightness in an image.

You can also use the eyedroppers to adjust the levels. Click the Set White Point eyedropper (on the right) and click the lightest part of your image. Then click the dark-tipped eyedropper (Set Black Point, on the left) to select it and click the darkest point on the image. If you have an area in the image that seems to be right in the middle, click it with the midrange (Set Gray Point) eyedropper (in the middle).

There's a menu command in the Image menu called Histogram. It doesn't actually *do* anything, but if you learn how to use it, you can save yourself lots of time.

If you've ever taken a course in statistics, you already know that a histogram is a kind of graph. In Photoshop Elements, it's a graph of the image reduced to grayscale, with lines to indicate the number of pixels at each step in the grayscale from 0 to 255.

You might wonder why this is important. The main reason is that you can tell by looking at the histogram whether there's enough detail in the image, so that you can apply corrections successfully. If you have an apparently bad photo or a bad scan, studying the histogram will tell you whether it's worth working on or whether you should throw away the image and start over. If all the lines are bunched up tight at one end of the graph, you probably can't save the picture by adjusting it. If, on the other hand, you have a reasonably well spread-out histogram, there's a wide enough range of values to suggest that the picture can be saved.

The Histogram command has another use, which is to give you a sense of the tonal range of the image. This is sometimes referred to as the *key type*. An image is said to be *low key*, *average key*, or *high key*, depending on whether it has a preponderance of dark, middle, or light tones, respectively. A picture that is all middle gray would have only one line in its histogram, and it would fall right in the middle.

All you really need to know is that, when you look at the histogram, you should see a fairly even distribution across the graph, if the image is intended to be an average key picture. If the picture is high key, most of the lines in the histogram are concentrated on the right side with a few on the left. If it is low key, most of the values will be to the left with a few to the right.

You can also adjust levels by color. The Channel pop-up menu at the top of the dialog box gives you access to the three color channels—red, green, and blue. You can use this feature to adjust the amount of a single color in the image, and to keep shadows and highlights from getting muddy or developing a color cast.

Auto Contrast

Auto Contrast works in a similar manner, but doesn't attempt to adjust color channels separately, so it often gives a different (and in my experience, more satisfactory) result (no color cast). It also doesn't seem to over-correct, as Auto Levels can. But, of course, a lot depends on the image to which you're applying it. Some images need more careful tweaking than any "auto" adjustment can make. To try out Auto Contrast, choose Enhance, Auto Contrast. Again, if you don't like the result, click Undo.

You can also adjust brightness and contrast in an image by using the Brightness/Contrast dialog box shown in Figure 24.17. Choose Enhance, Adjust Brightness/Contrast, Brightness/Contrast. Just move the sliders to the right to increase the amount of brightness and/or contrast, or to the left to decrease them. Experiment until you like the result. Remember that you can apply any of the corrections discussed in this section to a selected area of your image. To lighten or darken areas of an image, you can also use the Dodge and Burn tools described later in this chapter when we discuss repairing black-and-white photographs.

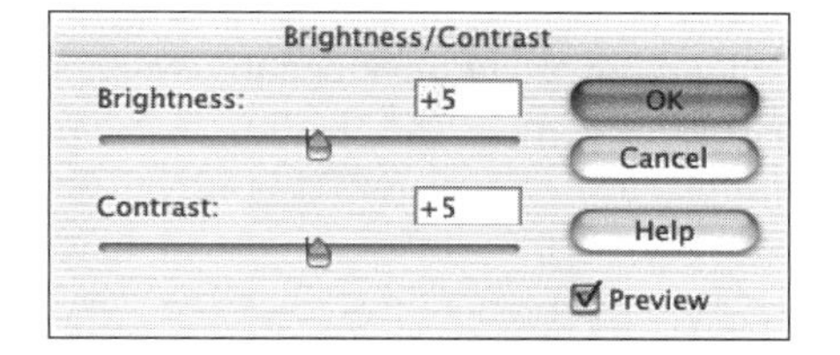

FIGURE 24.17
Be sure the Preview box is checked.

Auto Color Correction

I like really bright, saturated color. The person who wrote the algorithm for Auto Color Correction apparently prefers a more subdued palette. I'm seldom really happy with the results of Auto Color Correction, but—as they say—your mileage may vary. It might be just right for the image you're working on, so don't hesitate to try it by choosing Enhance, Auto Color Correction. Next, we'll cover various ways you can adjust color levels yourself.

Adjusting by Eye with Color Variations

Sometimes if you want something done right, you have to do it yourself. This applies to color correction as much as to any other endeavor. Figure 24.18 shows the Color Variations dialog box. You can find it in the Enhance, Adjust Color submenu. Use the Color Variations command to add or remove red, blue, or green to or from the shadows, midtones, or highlights in an image; lighten or darken the shadows, midtones, or highlights; and increase or decrease the intensity (saturation) of color.

FIGURE 24.18
See this in color in the color plate section.

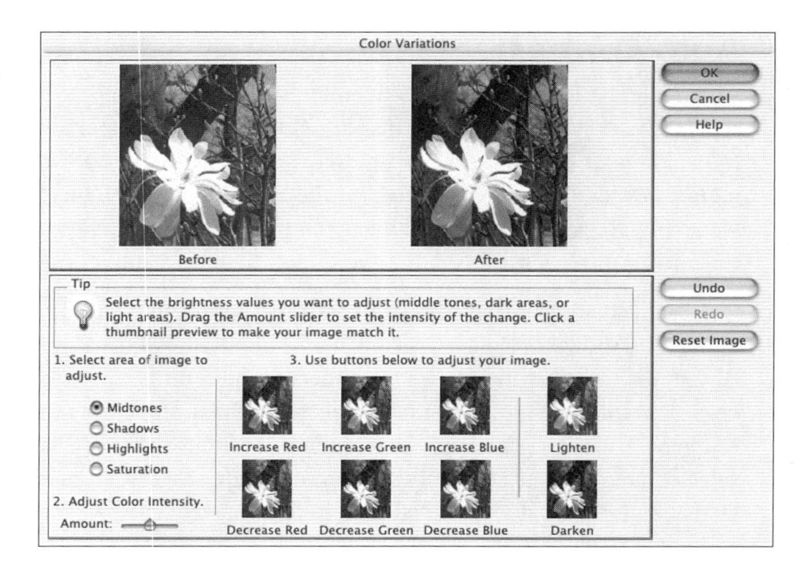

To use it, first decide whether you need to correct the shadows, midtones, or highlights, or the color saturation, which will affect all three equally. Move the intensity slider if you think you need more or less correction, and finally, choose the small image that looks most like the kind of adjustment you want. (You might want to use a magnifying glass. Because the previews are so small, subtle changes are hard to see.) If you like the direction it's going, but need more correction, just click the same image again. You can undo as many changes as you like by clicking the Undo button more than once. The Reset Image button removes all changes.

Adjusting Color with Color Cast

Color cast is the term experts use when an image has too much of one color in it. Sometimes an image will get a cast from poor lighting, bad scanning, or as an after effect from some other adjustment such as Auto Levels. The Color Cast Correction dialog box, shown in Figure 24.19, removes color casts by having you locate a point in the picture that should be pure white, middle gray, or black, and then adjusting the color so that it actually is white, gray, or black. To adjust the target color (and thus, the other colors in your image), Color Cast adds the color opposite the target color on the optical color wheel to cancel out or neutralize whatever color is too strong in the black or white or gray. For example, if the target color is magenta and it should be black, Color Cast adds green (magenta's opposite on the color wheel).

To use Color Cast, choose Enhance, Adjust Color, Color Cast. Then use the eyedropper to click a point in your image that should be pure white, pure black, or medium gray.

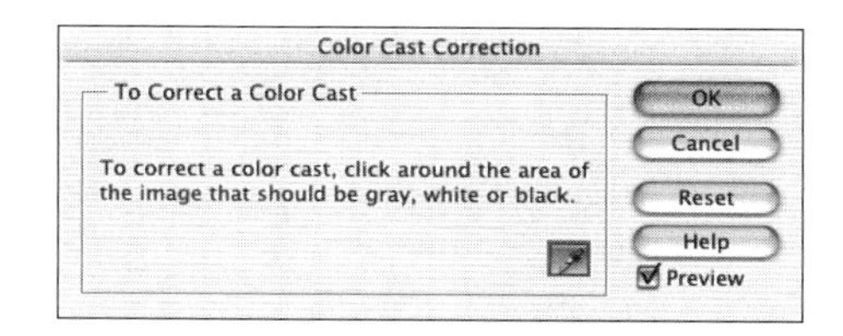

FIGURE 24.19
Just click on something in the picture that should be white, black, or neutral gray. Elements will do the math and change the colors.

If you don't like the result the first time, try a different black or white spot, with or without clicking Reset first. The results will vary according to the color strength of the pixel you select.

24

Adjusting Color with Hue/Saturation

The Hue/Saturation dialog box is the most complicated of the lot, mainly because it has three sliders instead of two. Display it by choosing Enhance, Color, Hue/Saturation. As you can see in Figure 24.20, it also has a pop-up menu that lets you adjust a single color rather than all of them at once. (This is also the only place in Elements where you can do anything at all with cyan, magenta, and yellow, the key components of the CMYK color model.) However, I'd suggest sticking with Master until you start to understand how the algorithm works.

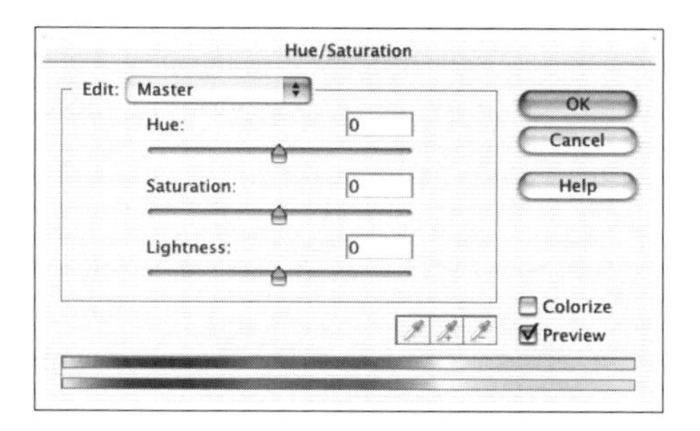

FIGURE 24.20
The Hue/Saturation dialog box.

As always, check Preview so that you can see the effects of your changes in the picture you're working on.

There are three sliders: Hue, Saturation, and Lightness. The Hue slider moves around the color wheel from color to color. With Master selected, you can move all the way from red (in the middle of the slider), left through purple to blue or blue-green, or right through orange to yellow and green.

The Saturation slider takes you from 0% in the center, to 100% saturated (pure colors) on the right, or 100% unsaturated (no color, or essentially a grayscale image) on the left.

When you move the slider from right to left, the colors opposite the image colors on the optical color wheel are added, so the image colors move toward gray.

The Lightness slider lets you increase or decrease the brightness of the image, from zero in the center, to +100 on the right (pure white), or –100 (pure black) on the left.

As you move these sliders, watch the two spectrum strips at the bottom of the window, as well as the image itself. The upper strip represents the current status of the image, and the lower one changes according to the slider(s) you move. If you move the Hue slider to +60, for example, you can see that the reds in the picture turn quite yellow, and the blues turn purple. Also, the reds in the upper spectrum line up with the yellows in the lower spectrum. In effect, what you are doing is skewing the color spectrum by that amount. If you move the Saturation slider to the left, you'll see the lower spectrum strip become less saturated. If you move the Lightness slider, you'll see its effects reflected in the lower spectrum strip as well.

If you select a color instead of selecting Master from the pop-up menu, the dialog box changes slightly, as you can see in Figure 24.21. The eyedroppers are now active, enabling you to select colors from the image, and the adjustable range sliders are centered on the color you have chosen to adjust. You can move these sliders back and forth to focus on as broad or narrow a range within that color as you want. This might not seem like a big deal, but it's really very powerful. For example, I was trying to adjust a picture of a girl wearing a dark magenta shirt. Her skin seemed too pink to me, but the shirt seemed almost right. So I selected Reds from the Edit list, and moved the sliders to narrow my definition of "red" so that it fit her skin tone but not her purplish-red shirt. Then I adjusted the saturation level to remove red from her skin, leaving it a more natural color.

I could have used the eyedroppers to be more precise in selecting my range, by taking samples of color from various points on her skin. To do this, you start with the first eye-dropper on the left. Click on a point on her skin that's a middle-tone color, not too light and not too dark. Then use the middle eyedropper to add other samples to the range, lighter and darker. Use the eyedropper on the right to remove colors from the range, such as the red in her shirt.

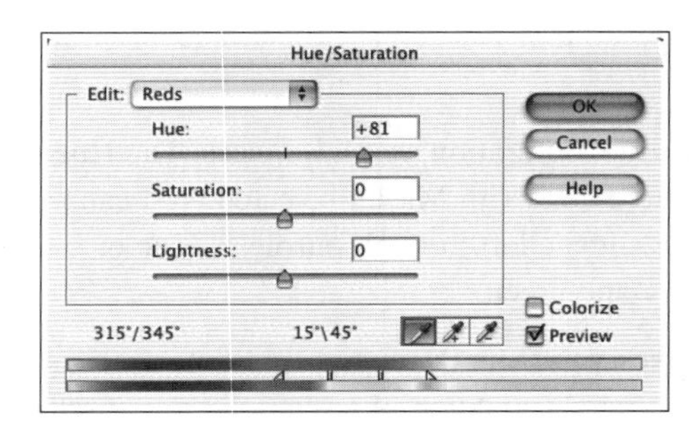

FIGURE 24.21
This tool could make your brown eyes blue.

Suppose I want to change a single color within a picture. Let's say I want to convert some of the yellow flowers in Figure 24.22 to some other color. All I need to do is select the two flowers I want to change, open the dialog box, and choose Yellows from the pop-up menu at the top. Then I can move the Hue slider around until I find a color I like, maybe a nice turquoise. Because I'm working on a selection, only the selected flowers will change color. However, these flowers have a brownish center that is included in the Yellow range, so when I change the Hue to turquoise, the brown centers take on a bluish cast. Since that's not what I want, I set the sliders back to the center and start over. This time I subtract the brown centers from the range by first dragging the left slider to the right, eliminating oranges, and clicking on various spots within the brown centers using the third dropper.

FIGURE 24.22
Why not blue daisies?

You can create a neat effect by using the Hue/Saturation dialog box to colorize a photo, essentially turning it into various shades of the same color such as red or blue. You can use this technique on a grayscale image as well, if you first convert it to RGB by choosing Image, Mode, RGB.

In the Hue/Saturation dialog box, select the Colorize option. The colors in the image are changed to variations of the current foreground color. To select a different color as your base, move the Hue slider. You can adjust the Saturation and Lightness levels as well, if you like. This is a nice technique to "dull down" an image to make it suitable for use in Web backgrounds, stationery, business cards, and so on. Try it sometime!

Removing and Replacing Color

Remove Color is easy to understand and easy to use. When you select it from the Enhance, Adjust Color submenu, it simply removes all the color from your picture, converting it to grayscale, but without changing the color mode to grayscale, too. Why is that important? Because, having turned the picture to grays, you might want to paint back some colors, perhaps different ones, or paste things in color on layers over it, or…who knows? It's your picture. By the way, you can use the Remove Color command on a selection, removing color from just an area of an image. You might select the background and remove the color from behind a person, for example, to make her stand out in an interesting way. This technique is used in advertising all the time to draw attention to products.

Replace Color, on the other hand, is in my opinion the least comprehendable dialog box in any form or version of Photoshop. You can use Replace Color to replace one color in an image with some other color. For example, you can change all the yellow roses in a photo into red ones, or try out a new paint color on your house. Still, the dialog box is a bit intimidating. I've taught you an easier way to do it, but in case you really want to try out Replace Color, the following task will show you how.

Compensating for Lighting Mistakes

When light comes from behind a subject, it can make the subject a bit dark. But it can also make for a strong contrast between your subject and its background. If you adjust the exposure so that the subject is properly lit, you risk making the background overexposed. To compensate for washed-out skies, sun-kissed lakes, and other light backgrounds in your images, use the Adjust Backlighting tool. It adjusts the midtones in the image, darkening the background without lightening the subject too much.

You can select an area if you want your changes to affect only that portion of the image; then choose Enhance, Adjust Lighting, Adjust Backlighting. Drag the Darken slider to the right until the background is no longer washed out; then click OK.

The Fill Flash tool has almost the opposite effect; it adds light to the subject, just as a camera flash would. Again, in backlit situations, a subject can become too dark and lose detail. This tool helps to compensate for that. Select an area to affect if desired; then choose Enhance, Adjust Lighting, Fill Flash. Drag the Lighter slider to the right until you can see some detail in the subject. Because this effect might wash out the subject too much, bring up the colors by adjusting the Saturation levels. When you're satisfied, click OK.

Using the Quick Fix Dialog Box

The Quick Fix dialog box gives you access to the most-used correction tools with one or two clicks. With it, you can adjust the brightness, color, sharpness, and alignment (straightness) of your image. If you're going to do your own corrections from scratch, this is a good place to start.

To use Quick Fix, choose Enhance, Quick Fix. Select the type of adjustment you want to make: Brightness, Color Correction, Focus, or Rotate. In the second column, select the specific adjustment you want to make. A set of controls relating to that adjustment type appears in the third column; use these controls to make the actual adjustment. If the adjustment is an automatic one, click Apply to let Elements apply the adjustment.

If you like what you see but need to make other changes, change any option in the first two columns; new changes will build on the first one. If you don't like a change, click Undo to remove it. You can click Undo more than once to remove multiple levels of adjustments. If you click Reset Image, you'll remove all the changes you've made in the Quick Fix dialog box. When you're through making changes, click OK.

Remember that with automatic adjustments, you can click the Apply button as many times as you want. Each time you do, the selected correction will be applied again. For example, if your photo improves with Auto Levels, but not quite enough, try it again by clicking Apply a second time. Also, remember that you can affect just a selected portion of your image if you like, by making a selection before you open the dialog box.

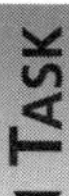

Task: Fix a Badly Overexposed, Very Blue Photo

The photo shown in Figure 24.23 has a lot of things wrong with it. It actually looks as if the flash didn't go off, or someone tried to shoot in the dark without one. It's too dark and its colors are too washed out. It needs more saturation to bring out the colors, and it needs more light. It's also too blue. Let's try fixing it.

FIGURE 24.23
You can't put it in the wedding album looking like this. (Photo courtesy of Judy Blair.)

1. Open up the Quick Fix dialog box by selecting Enhance, Quick Fix.
2. The first step is to lighten this a little. Let's see what Auto Contrast can do for us. Choose Brightness from the first list, Auto Contrast from the second, and click Apply. It certainly increased the contrast, but I was looking for something more.
3. Choose Auto Levels from the second list, and click Apply. This makes a big—and helpful—difference, as you can see in Figure 24.24.

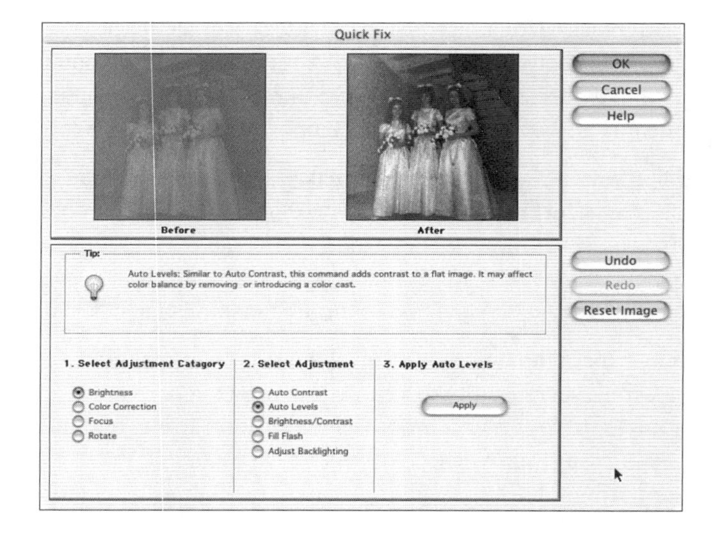

FIGURE 24.24
That was a good first step.

4. Because increasing the contrast seemed to help a little, we'll move down to the Brightness/Contrast Adjustment and do some more tweaking there. Select the Brightness/Contrast option from the second list. In the third column, set the Brightness to +38 and the Contrast to +8. That perks it up some more.
5. Now that the contrast and brightness seem to be about right, let's start working on the color. Select Color Correction as the Adjustment Category. We'll do this ourselves, so choose Hue/Saturation from the second column. I shifted the hue just a tiny bit to warm up the skin tones, and added a tiny bit more saturation and some lightness. To duplicate this effect, set Hue to –1, Saturation to +1, and Lightness to +12. The changes, shown in Figure 24.25, seem to help.
6. What about focus? Because the picture has ended up looking grainy, adding a little blur will smooth it out. The Blur filter applies the opposite effect of the Unsharp Mask and the other Sharp filters—instead of increasing the crispness within an image, this filter softens it. Select Focus from the first column, and Blur from the second column; then click Apply. This is the equivalent of applying the Blur filter once.

FIGURE 24.25
When all you need are subtle changes, alter the settings by one number at a time.

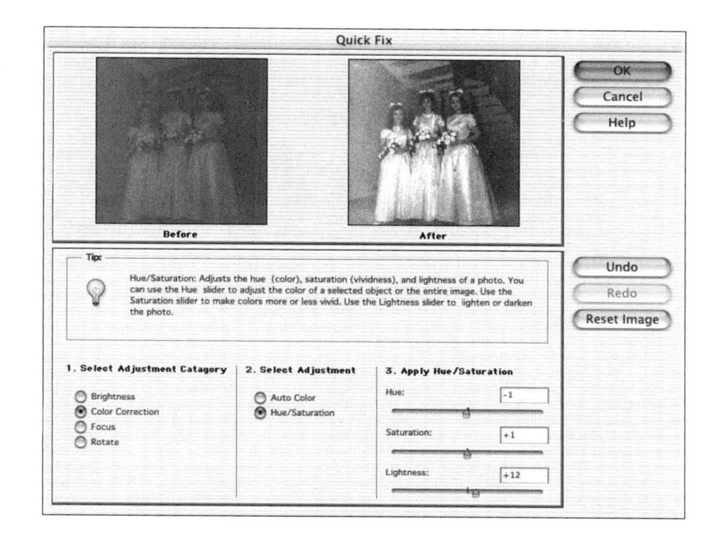

7. We're done. It's not a great photo, but compare the final version in Figure 24.26 to the original in Figure 24.23. Be sure to look at these in the color section, too.

FIGURE 24.26
This looks much better than before.

As you are making any of the adjustments that require dragging sliders on the Quick Fix dialog box, make sure you stop and release the mouse button before you attempt to judge the result of your change. For some reason, Elements doesn't make those changes while the mouse button is down. This is not a problem in the individual tool windows, only in Quick Fix.

Using Repair Recipes and Tutorials

Adobe has made many of the complicated photo rescue and enhancement procedures much easier for you by supplying easy-to-follow "recipes" for them. If you follow a recipe, your results are pretty well guaranteed to be good.

The only hurdle to overcome in using recipes is finding them. For reasons known only to Adobe, they live on a palette called, not Recipes, but How To. When you first start Elements, the How To palette presents itself and opens in the work window. If for some reason it doesn't, or if you've already closed it to make room to work, you can open it by selecting How To from the Windows menu, or by clicking its tab in the palette well on the Shortcuts bar, if that's active. (By the way, you can also activate the Shortcuts bar, or shut it off, from the Windows menu.) The How To palette is shown in Figure 24.27.

FIGURE 24.27
You'll find the recipes in the How To palette.

After you open the How To palette, use the drop-down menu to locate the kind of recipe you want, and then click on the recipe to open it (see Figure 24.28).

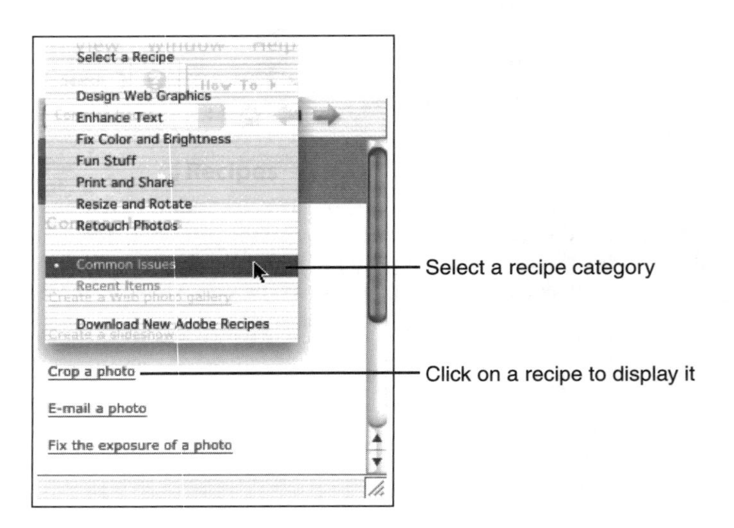

FIGURE 24.28
The Recipes pop-up menu.

There are several different recipe categories, and more will undoubtedly be added as they are written. Here's a list of the recipe categories you might find:

- **Design Web Graphics**—In this category, you'll find recipes for creating Web buttons and adding polish with bevels, shadows, or glows. You'll find out how to create Web animations and banners for the top of your pages.
- **Enhance Text**—This category is filled with recipes that enable you to do neat things to type, such as adding a bevel, filling it with a gradient or image, and adding a shadow.
- **Fix Color and Brightness**—Look here for quick ways to fix problems with color and light in a photo.
- **Fun Stuff**—When you feel confident with Elements, explore this category and learn some neat techniques, such as colorizing a black and white photo, creating a coloring book page from an image, and creating a collage of photos.
- **Print and Share**—This category is full of recipes for printing and sharing your images in a Web gallery, attached to an email message, or with a slideshow.
- **Resize and Rotate**—Learn how to crop, resize, and straighten a photo using the recipes in this category.
- **Retouch Photos**—Use these recipes to repair torn photos, remove red eye, clean up scratches and dust spots, and repair other common problems.
- **Common Issues**—If you have a question or problem, chances are good that someone else has had it too. Adobe has assembled recipes that solve the most common problems, and placed them in this category.

Once you have opened the recipe that you want, be sure to drag the palette down the screen a little, away from the Shortcuts bar. As long as it remains docked, it will disappear as soon as you do something else. This is true, incidentally, of all Elements palettes. You must cut them loose from the bar by dragging them if you want to keep them visible.

Read the recipe. Make sure it sounds as if it will do what you want. Prepare the image to which you want to apply it or, if it's something that will stand alone, start a new page in Elements.

With some of the steps in a recipe, you may find a Do It for Me link. Clicking here tells Elements to complete the step for you. This is good to use when a step is confusing to you, and you want to see how it's done before trying it yourself.

At the bottom of some recipes, you'll find links to related recipes. Click one if you wish to view that recipe. Go back to the previous recipe and eventually to the category list—the list of recipes for that category—by clicking the left arrow. Go forward to recipes you've viewed in that category by clicking the right arrow. The Home icon takes you back to the category list.

Looking for New Recipes

At the bottom of the Recipe pop-up menu in the How To palette is the Download New Adobe Recipes option. If you have an active Internet connection, clicking this will do one of two things, depending on your operating system. If you're using a Mac, you'll see the dialog box shown in Figure 24.29. A list of product updates, along with new recipes, will be displayed. The View menu lets you decide whether to display just new updates, or all updates, even if you've already downloaded them. Select the ones you want and click Choose to select the location to which you want to download them. You don't need to click the Tell Me More button, but if you do click it, you'll see a page on Adobe's Web site that gives a general explanation of what updates are. Finally, click Download to download the updates and new recipes to your computer. You'll need to restart Elements to view them.

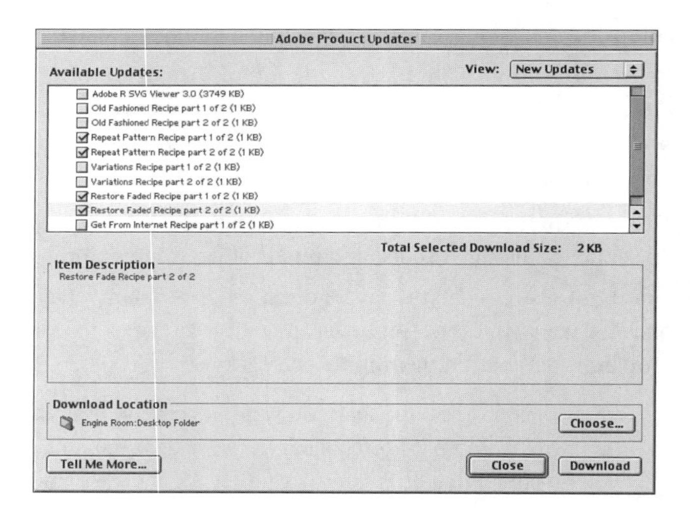

FIGURE 24.29
Check Adobe often to see what's cooking.

Following a Tutorial

Sometimes you'll need to create an effect for which there's no recipe and no shortcut. The best way to master the techniques that will eventually make you a great photographer or digital graphics artist is to go through the Elements tutorials, which you probably installed along with the program. Assuming you did an Easy Install, they'll be in a folder called Tutorials, inside the main Elements folder. To open a tutorial, go to the Help menu and choose Photoshop Elements Tutorials.

When you select the Photoshop Elements Tutorials option, a browser window like the one in Figure 24.30 will open with a list of what's available. Choose an interesting topic from the pane on the right, and click to open it.

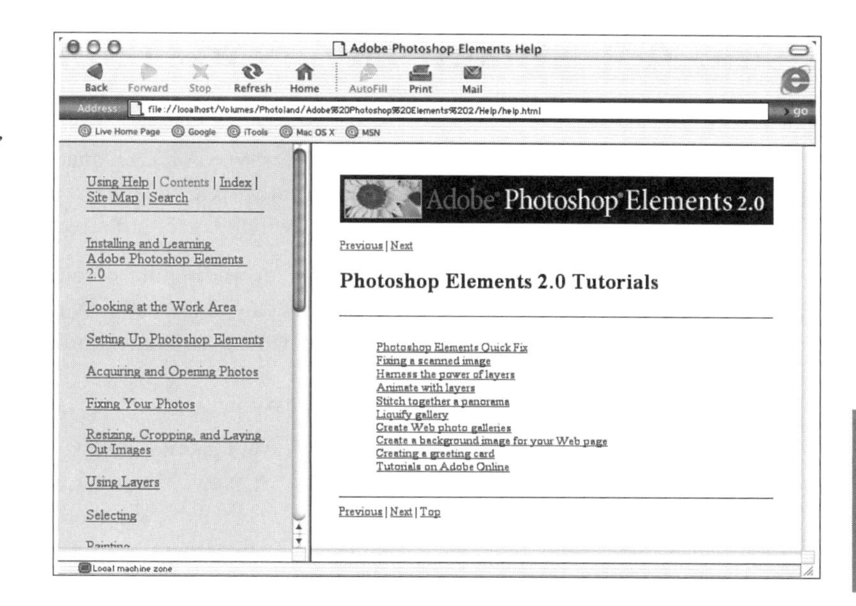

FIGURE 24.30
These tutorials, and the entire Photoshop Elements help system, actually run in your browser.

Tutorials are longer and more conversationally written than recipes, and come with the image files you'll need to follow along. There are no Do It for Me links, so you'll have to read carefully and follow the directions closely. Figure 24.31 shows a typical page from a tutorial. This one, called "Harness the Power of Layers," happens to be all about layers, and if you're still having trouble using them, I recommend it.

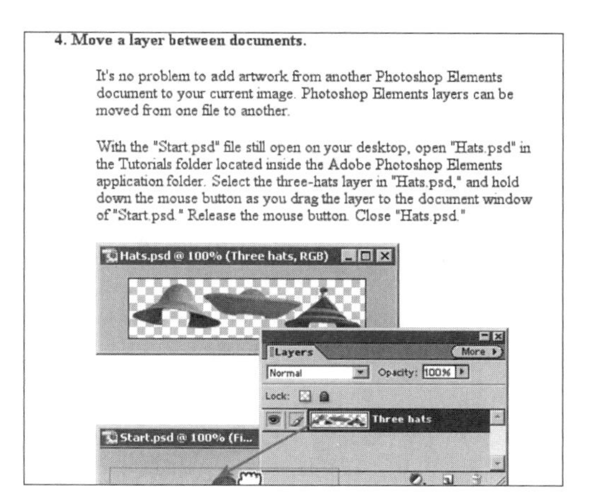

FIGURE 24.31
Tutorials take you through specific exercises, unlike recipes, which work with your own pictures.

There are more tutorials at Adobe Online, along with many other useful things. This is also where you'll go—automatically, if you choose—to look for updates, bug fixes, and enhancements to make Elements run better. The quickest way to get to Adobe Online is to click on the yellow flower at the top of the toolbox.

Using Adjustment Layers to Fix Image Problems

Adjustment layers are used to make particular types of adjustments to the layers below the adjustment layer, or to the layers grouped with it. After I list the types of adjustments you can make, we'll talk about controlling which layers are affected.

With an adjustment layer, you can adjust the levels, brightness/contrast, and hue/saturation. These adjustments correspond to the commands you learned how to use on an entire image in the discussion on adjusting Brightness, Contrast, and Color earlier in the chapter.

Adding an Adjustment Layer

To create an adjustment layer, click in the Layers palette, below where you want the adjustment layer to appear. Then choose Layer, New Adjustment Layer and choose the adjustment type from the submenu that appears. The New Layer dialog box will appear; type a Name for the layer and click OK. The adjustment layer will be placed above the current layer and will affect that layer and all layers below it unless you choose the Group with Previous Layer option. The dialog box corresponding to the type of adjustment you selected then appears. (For example, if you're creating a hue/saturation adjustment layer, the Hue/Saturation dialog box appears.) Make the adjustment you want and click OK.

If you click the Create New Adjustment or Fill Layer button in the Layers palette, you won't be able to name your layer or group it with the previous layer.

After you add an adjustment layer, you'll see it appear in the Layers palette, just above the layer you clicked before you inserted the adjustment layer. The adjustment layer looks like the one shown in Figure 24.32. The first icon on the left tells you that this layer is visible, or in this case, active—the adjustment is being applied. If you click this icon to hide it, the adjustment layer will no longer be in effect. The next icon, the mask icon, tells you that a mask is being used to partially obscure the effects of the adjustment to the layers below. A mask is simply a selection. If you have selected something on the current layer or the layers below the adjustment layer (assuming that you're not limiting the adjustment to a single layer), only the selected area on that layer will be affected by the adjustment. You can actually edit this mask, refining the area you want to affect—more on that later.

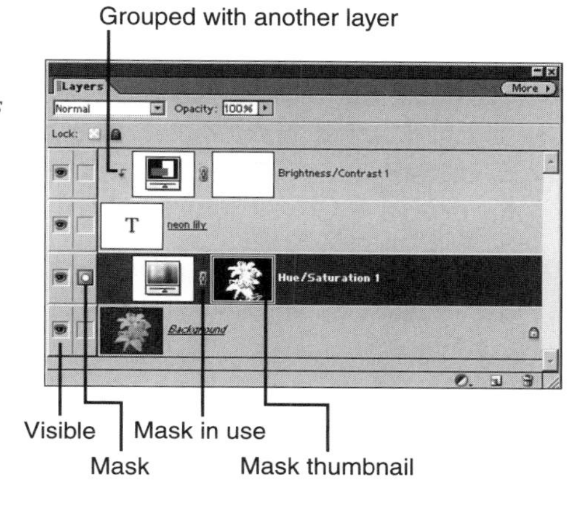

FIGURE 24.32
The adjustment layer is listed separately in the Layers palette.

Masks are also used on fill layers, to hide or partially obscure some of the fill.

The next icon, a bent arrow, will only appear if you chose the Group with Previous option. It tells you that this adjustment layer is grouped with the layer below it. Next is the adjustment thumbnail, which depicts an icon that shows you what kind of adjustment has been made. Here, a Hue/Saturation adjustment layer (selected) and a Brightness/Contrast adjustment layer were used. If you want to change the adjustment settings, double-click this icon and the dialog box you originally saw (in this case, the Hue/Saturation dialog box) will be redisplayed. Make your changes and click OK. The next icon, the link, tells you that a layer mask is linked to its underlying layer. The final thumbnail, the mask thumbnail, shows you the shape of the mask that's in place.

If you selected the Group with Previous Layer option in the New Layer dialog box, the adjustment layer is grouped with the layer just below it, and the adjustments affect only that layer. To add the layer immediately below the bottommost grouped layer to the group, press Option-Alt and click the line that separates the two layers in the Layers palette.

Editing the Adjustment Layer Mask

Unless you made a selection prior to inserting an adjustment layer, the adjustments will apply to all objects on the affected layers. In such a case, the mask thumbnail on the Layers palette will be completely white, which indicates that the mask is not blocking any part of the adjustment.

To mask part of the adjustment's effects or to adjust a mask that's already in place, click on the adjustment layer in the Layers palette to select it. Then display the mask on the image so you can see it. To display the mask in grayscale, press Option-Alt and click the mask thumbnail. To display the mask in red, press Shift-Option-Alt and click the mask thumbnail. If you started with no mask and you're adding one, the mask will not be displayed because there isn't one to show.

Initially, a mask is white. White areas indicate where adjustments are in effect. Black areas block the adjustment effects, and gray areas block the adjustments only partially, based on how dark the gray is. To add or change a mask, you simply paint with white to expand the area of the adjustment's effects, or with black to mask it. Paint with any tone of gray to partially obscure the adjustment.

When you select the adjustment layer in the Layers palette, Elements automatically changes the foreground and background colors to get ready for any changes to the mask you might want to make. Click the Brush or Pencil tool, choose a brush tip, size, blending mode, and opacity, and paint to create or change the mask, as shown in Figure 24.33. You can also use a shape tool to fill an area with white or black. In addition, you can select an area to work on with any of the selection marquee tools, and then when you paint, you'll only affect that area—this is a nice way of making sure you don't erase parts of the mask you want to keep. When you're done making adjustments, press Option-Alt and click the mask thumbnail to reveal the image again. Elements will update the display and show you the outline of the current mask.

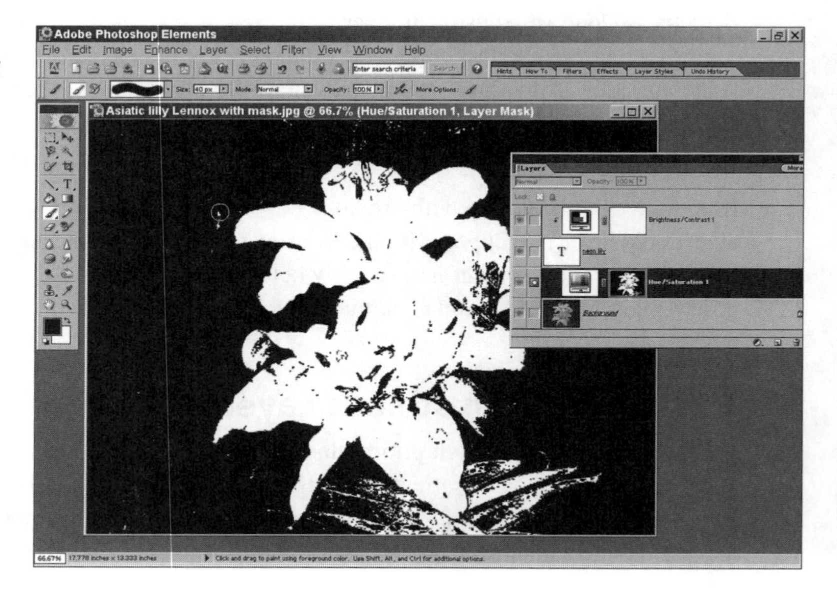

FIGURE 24.33
Paint with white to add to the mask, and with black to subtract.

You can use a gradient fill in black and white to create the mask; see Chapter 26 for tips on creating a gradient. You can also partially obscure the entire adjustment layer by changing its opacity and/or blending modes (which you'll learn about in Chapter 26 as well). To turn off the mask, press Shift and click the mask thumbnail. Repeat this step to turn the mask back on so that the effects of the adjustment are once again partially obscured.

Repairing Black-and-White Pictures

> Why is it that the pictures you care about most are the ones that inevitably fade, get wrinkled, get chewed up by the dog, or fall prey to so many other disasters? It probably has some relation to Murphy's Law—whatever can go wrong, will.
>
> The good news, though, is that you're not totally stuck when your kid smears peanut butter on the only decent picture of Great-Grandma, or the cat thinks your parents wedding photo is a new cat toy. First, as soon as you discover the damage, wipe off any residual cat slobber or other foreign substances, if you can do it without damaging the photo any more. The second thing is to scan it into your computer.
>
> Depending on the size of the photo, scan it same size. If it's a tiny snapshot, size it larger—you might as well be able to see what you're doing. 300 dpi is plenty for most uses, especially if it's an old photo. The film grain will be about that size, too.

Some pictures need a little help; others need a lot. Let's start with things that can be easily fixed. The little girl shown in Figure 24.34 is badly exposed, and it appears as if this picture, and two others that were sent with it and shot the same day, were taken with a camera that leaked light. That explains the dark streak in the same place on all three. Still, there's a lot of hope for this one. It just needs some contrast.

The first step, as always, is to straighten and crop. She looks as if she's about to tip over backward, and whether the camera was crooked or she was, it's an easy fix that might as well be made. Cropping will not only improve the photo, but will take away some of the stuff we'd otherwise have to retouch, saving us some time and effort. Look for tips on how to crop and straighten your old photos or scans in Chapter 23.

Now that the girl's standing straight up, let's examine another obvious problem—lack of brightness and contrast. To do this, choose Image, Histogram. Looking at the histogram (see Figure 24.35) tells us that there's plenty of detail (lots of pixels) in the middle darks, and that's what we need to work on, so we're good to go. I'll use Levels (Enhance, Adjust Brightness/Contrast, Levels) to remap the gray scale. As you can see in Figure 24.36, I've moved the black and white points (the triangles at either end, just below the histogram) in toward the center of the scale, to the points at which the graph indicates more activity. Then, I've moved the middle gray point to the place where there's the steep rise in darks. This spreads the lighter grays over a greater area of the graph and compresses the darks, giving the photo more light grays and increased contrast. For help in making this type of adjustment, see the section earlier in this chapter on adjusting Brightness, Contrast, and Color.

Figure 24.34
Little girl, circa 1950? (Photo courtesy of Judy Blair.)

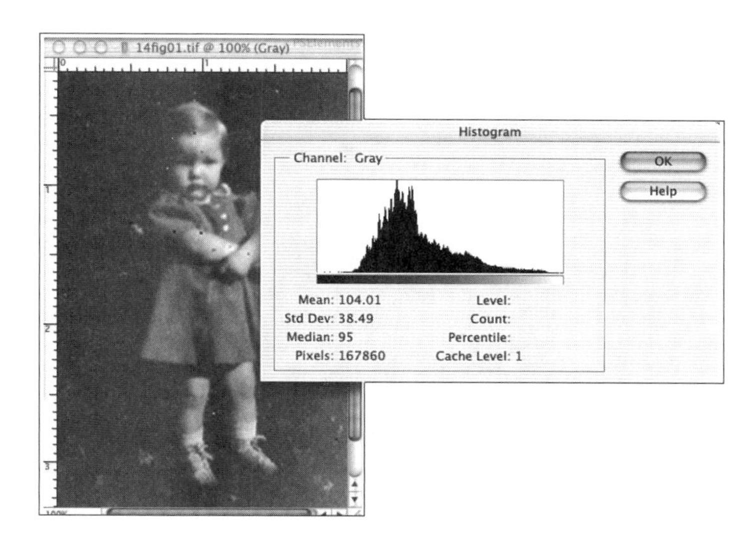

FIGURE 24.35
The histogram shows good detail in the darks.

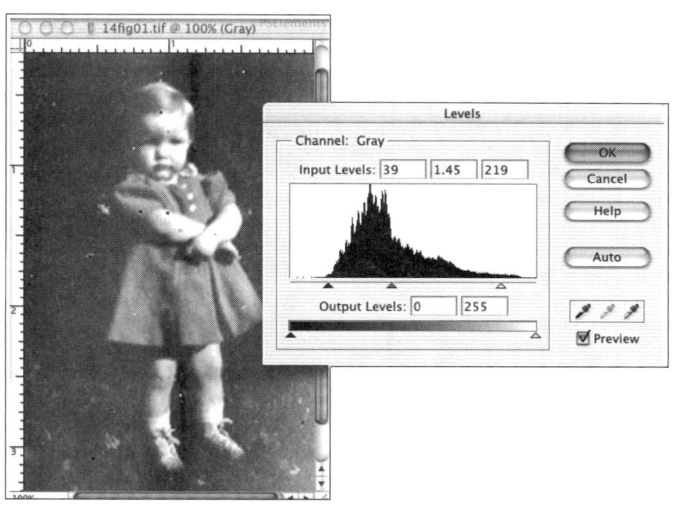

FIGURE 24.36
Use Levels to improve the contrast.

As a last step, I'll get rid of the dust with the Clone Stamp tool, choosing a brush just big enough to cover the spots, and setting the blending mode to Darken for the light spots and to Lighten for the dark ones. That way, the surrounding areas aren't changed. And there she is, in Figure 24.37, nearly as good as new. If you need help using the Clone Stamp, that tool was covered in more detail earlier in the chapter.

FIGURE 24.37
The little girl, looking much better.

Lack of Contrast

As you saw in the picture of the little girl, lack of contrast is one of the most common problems with older photos. They fade over time, of course, but many didn't have much contrast to start with. That's obviously the case with Figure 24.38, shot in bright sun and looking very washed out. This, by the way, is part of the same set as the previous example. Again, notice the black streaks down the middle, probably caused by light leaking into the camera. We'll have to try to lighten them or hide them, too.

FIGURE 24.38
This photo is too light to see details.

As before, first we'll crop, and then look at the histogram to see what we've got to work with. This histogram, shown in Figure 24.39, is unusual in that it's shifted so far toward the light shades. There are very few darks, but there seems to be plenty of detail in what's there, so we should be able to improve this photo.

FIGURE 24.39
This histogram shows that we still have something to work with.

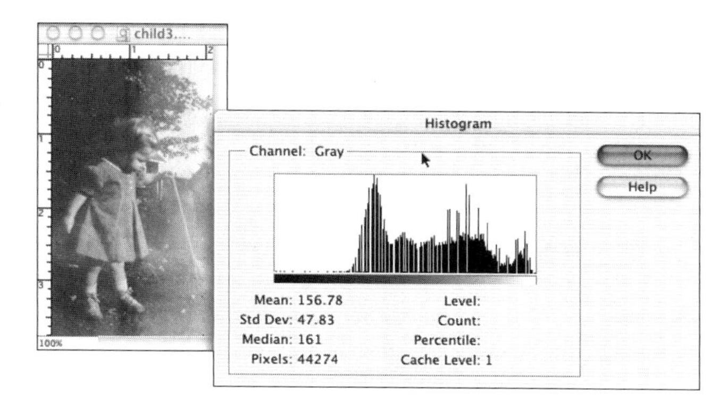

We'll start with Levels (Enhance, Brightness/Contrast, Levels) again, and shift the black and white points to where the action begins on the histogram. This time, though, I'll use the eyedroppers to set the black and white points. First, I click the white eyedropper up in the sky (a part of our photo that should be white) to set the white point. I chose the upper-right corner of the picture for this because it seems to be the lightest area. Then, I click the black eyedropper on the darkest spot, which is behind the child, in her shadow. That sets the dark point. Now, I can slide the midpoint back and forth until I find a middle gray point that looks right to me, and reveals as much detail on the child's face as possible. After all, she's the subject, and although it's nice to have detail everywhere, it's most important there. Figure 24.40 shows my settings, and the result.

FIGURE 24.40
Better, but not there yet....

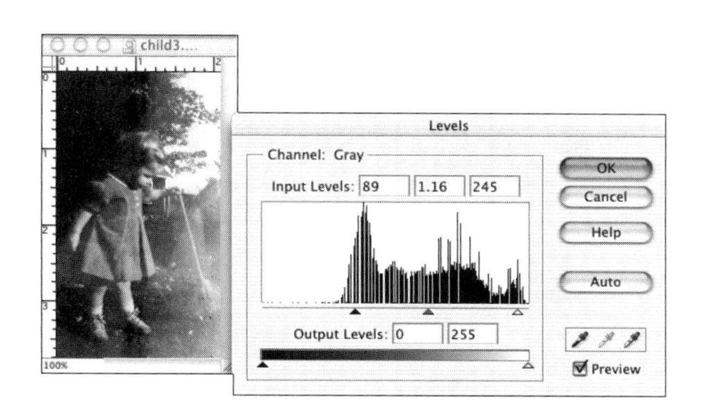

Dodging and Burning

There are still a few more tricks we can use. The Dodge and Burn tools are based on dark room photography techniques that have been used for more than 100 years. Dodging means putting your hand, or some sort of dodging tool, in between the enlarger light and the printing paper while you're making the exposure. This blocks the light from hitting the paper and leaves that area of the print less exposed, and therefore lighter. You have to keep the dodging tool in motion, so you only block some of the light and not all of it. Otherwise, you'd simply have a white spot. The usual dodging tool is a cardboard circle on a flexible wire handle, which looks like a lollipop. Not surprisingly, it's also the Elements icon for the tool. The burning tool has the opposite effect. You can use a sheet of cardboard with a small hole in the middle, or simply hold your hand so a small beam of light gets through, while the rest is blocked—again, this is just like the tool icon. Burning is done after the initial exposure of the paper, and means turning the enlarger lamp back on and giving additional light to a part of the picture, darkening the area you re-exposed.

To use the Dodge tool to lighten or the Burn tool to darken, select the one you want to use from the toolbox. Both tools have the same options. Select a brush size that's appropriate for the area you want to affect—you can change the brush style too, but I find that the soft round brush, which is the default, typically works well. Next, select the tonal Range you want to affect: highlights, midtones, or shadows. Then select the amount of exposure you want. For the most subtle changes, I typically use a large soft brush that I can sweep through my photo in a quick motion. I also set the exposure to a low level, and select a tonal range opposite of what I'm trying to add. For example, if I want to darken an area, I choose the Burn tool and select the highlight or midtone range. I choose the shadow range to have the quickest effect. When using the Dodge tool, I choose the shadow range for the most subtle changes.

I can use the Dodge and Burn tools to even out the exposure on this photo. I'll dodge behind her to lighten the trees, and burn around her face to darken that area and increase the detail. Figure 24.41 shows the final version of the photo.

FIGURE 24.41
Still not perfect, but much better. Compare it to the original.

TASK

Task: Using the Dodge and Burn Tools

Before we go on, let's practice with the Dodge and Burn tools.

1. Open a new page in Elements. Make sure it has a white background. The default size is fine.
2. Click the Brush tool. Choose a medium large paintbrush from the drop-down list, and set Mode to Normal and Opacity to 100%. Select a paint color by clicking the Foreground swatch on the toolbar. Use middle gray or a medium value of any color you want. Click on the image and drag to make a squiggle of paint across the page.
3. Select the Dodge tool. Because it uses brush shapes, choose a large soft brush and set the Range to Midtones and the Exposure to 50%, as shown in Figure 24.42.

FIGURE 24.42
Setting the dodge tool options.

4. Hold down the mouse button as you move the tool a few times up and down across the line. Each time you go over an area it lightens more. In Figure 24.43, I've nearly erased a piece of the line.

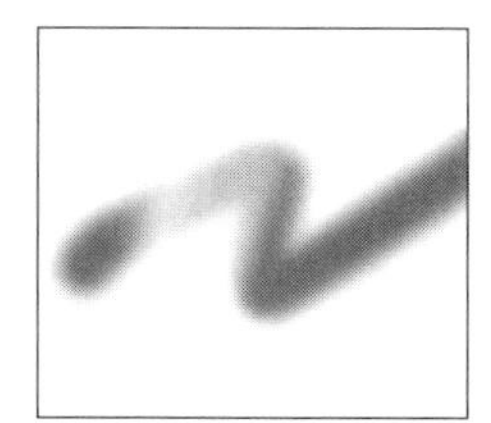

FIGURE 24.43
The tool only works when it's moving.

5. Now switch to the Burn tool, keeping the same options. Drag it over a different piece of the line. See how each pass darkens the line? (It's actually increasing the saturation of color, which has the effect of making the line look darker.) Figure 24.44 shows what this looks like.

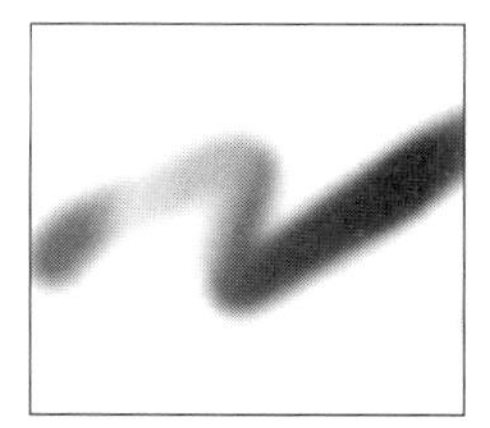

FIGURE 24.44
The rule to remember: Burning darkens, dodging lightens.

6. Practice with both the Dodge and Burn tools. See if you can put back the area you dodged out, and lighten the burned area to match the rest.

Painting Over Small Blotches

Some pictures need touching up with a brush. The girl shown in Figure 24.41 looks very good, but there are a few distracting dots around her feet. There are several ways to fix such problems—you can use the Clone Stamp to paint nearby colors over a rip or a large splotch, as we will on a badly damaged photograph later, but you can simply paint over small dots or blemishes.

Using the Brush tool, which you'll learn more about in Chapter 26, is not terribly difficult. Select a brush style, size, and color; then drag over the area you want to paint. When trying to brush color onto a photo to cover a small blotch, the hard part is picking a color that matches the one that is missing. Do you know how to select the right color to do the touch-up? You probably can't do it from the Color Picker. Perhaps 1 person in a 100,000 is good enough at color recognition to select a perfect match for a given color. And even then, it would be as much luck as knowledge, because every pixel on the Color Picker is slightly different from its closest neighbors. Instead, select an exact match with the Eyedropper. Look at the picture and find an area with the exact shade you need. (Usually, it will be immediately adjacent to the damage you're going to repair.) Then, just click it with the Eyedropper to make it the foreground (active) color. If you press Option-Alt as you click, it will instead become the new background color. You can then use the brush to touch up spots of uneven or missing color.

Preparing an Old Photo for Repair by Removing Sepia

One of the characteristics that really distinguishes old photos is the brownish tone they have. It's called sepia, and it comes from dipping the finished print in a bath of squid ink and water. Sepia toning was done to give the print a rich, warm quality rather than the original drab gray. This process also had the effect of stabilizing the print, making it last longer.

I find it harder to work on sepia-colored pictures, so I always remove the color before I start editing them. It's easy to replace it afterward. You'll learn how later when we talk about duotones.

There are several ways to remove color. Probably the easiest is to use the Remove Color command that we discussed earlier in the chapter: Enhance, Adjust Color, Remove Color, or Command/Ctrl-Shift-U. You could also convert the picture to grayscale, which would have the same effect, but doing so would require you to convert back to RGB mode if you wanted to add back the sepia when you were finished. Another option is to open the Hue/Saturation dialog box, and move the saturation slider all the way to the left to completely desaturate the picture, again removing all color. All three methods produce the same results; I typically use the Remove Color command if I plan to restore the sepia later, change to grayscale if I don't intend to use the sepia again, and use the Hue/Saturation command to put the sepia back (although you can use this command to remove the sepia as well).

Removing color also can get rid of coffee and tea stains, colored ink smudges, and many of the other things that get spilled on a photo. Even if it leaves a gray blob; that will be easier to cover.

Repairing Serious Damage

So far, all the pictures we've looked at have been easy to fix. Let's try one that is more difficult. Take a critical look at Figure 24.45. This one's much too dark, and the sepia is turning sort of greenish. It's also scratched and torn, and needs some spotting.

FIGURE 24.45
This one's been seriously beaten up and damaged. (Photo courtesy of K. Rudden.)

First Steps

This will actually be easier than it looks. First, I'll remove the color by choosing Enhance, Adjust Color, Remove Color. Then, I'll crop away as much of the damage as I can. Then, I'll reset the levels using the Enhance, Adjust Brightness/Contrast, Levels command. Just these small adjustments improve it a lot, as you can see in Figure 24.46, but we still have corners missing, and cracks and scratches to cover. The perfect tool for this job is the Clone Stamp tool.

Figure 24.46
We're already at least half done.

Repairing Tears

You learned how to use the Clone Stamp tool earlier, but let me remind you of a couple of things. First of all, make sure you are using the right size brush. One that's too big will cover too much of an area, possibly leaving a smooth spot or color that doesn't quite match. Using one that's too small will make you go over and over the same spot, building up dark bits wherever the stamps overlap. When repairing a small tear, set the brush size to just cover it. With larger tears, you'll want to go more slowly, with a smaller brush. Also, make sure that it's a soft-edged brush for most general purposes.

For this repair, do not check the Aligned option. If you use that option here, you might accidentally copy the folds of her dress or the edge of her sleeve to someplace where they don't belong. Better to copy the colors you want, and paint them onto the places where they belong.

When you're using any of the brush-related tools, go to Preferences, Display & Cursors and make sure that the Painting cursor is set to show brush size. It will help a lot in placing the stamp if you can see where its edges are.

Remember that you can zoom in on small areas to make them easier to see. In Figure 24.47, I have come in close on the lady's sleeve to show you a trick. Here, there's a crack running through a seam. I can go above it, to where there's an untouched piece of seam, and copy it as a source. Then, when I move the stamp tool down over the damage, I'm replacing it with a good piece of the same seam. As long as I am careful to stay centered on the seam as I move the stamp, the original and the repair will stay aligned and the seam will look right, as it does in the After view.

Figure 24.47
Before and after stamping.

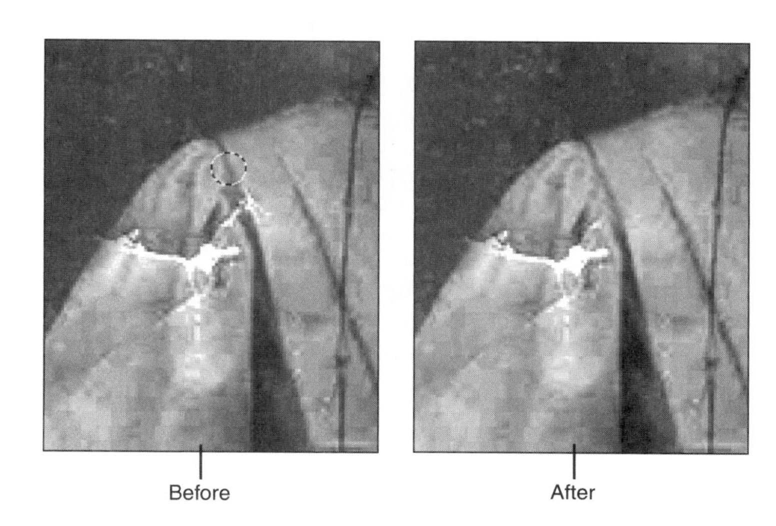

After cleaning the picture up with the Clone Stamp tool, we can use the Dodge tool with a very light pressure, to lighten the woman's face. If you look back at Figure 24.46, you'll see that her face is too dark, but the man's face isn't. With the Dodge tool, I can lighten just the area of her face. I've also applied the Despeckle filter (Filter, Noise, Despeckle) at its lowest settings, to suppress some of the dust. A filter applies a series of changes in a single step—]for instance, the Unmask filter sharpens all the edges. As you learned in the beginning of this chapter, the Despeckle filter (Filter, Noise, Despeckle) is a handy tool for removing dust and dirt from an image. It works by looking for areas of sharp contrast (such as dark spots on a light background), and then blurring such areas into their surroundings, without blurring edges.

Figure 24.48 shows the final, much-improved version. But I might not stop there; I might use the Burn tool to darken the bottom of her dress and the top of the man's forehead, which both seem unnaturally light to me. And I might work a bit more on her sleeve, but I don't want to do too much, or I'll remove the charm of this old photograph.

FIGURE 24.48
This photo is close to 100 years old.

Applying Vignetting

Vignetting was a technique frequently used in the early days of photography to make up for deficiencies in both the camera lens and the glass plates used for negatives. Not much was understood about the art and science of lens grinding, except that the lens tended to be sharpest in the middle and the focus would fall off rapidly as you moved from the center to the edges of the resulting photo. Photo plates were prepared by brushing plain glass with a solution of gum Arabic or some other colloidal (sticky stuff) and silver nitrate. (Chemists, don't come after me. I'm sure there was more in the mix, but those were the important elements.) The gunk seldom went on evenly, especially near the edges of the plate, so the edges of the photo would be correspondingly messy. Today, that messy edge look is considered a special effect, and is frequently seen in black-and-white digital photography.

Anyway, both of these factors resulted in pictures that were okay in the middle and both fuzzy and messy at the edges. Soon, the better photographers figured out a way to disguise the bad parts, while making it look like an extra fancy effect. They invented the vignette. It's simply a mask that fades from the edges of the picture toward the middle, so that the photo appears to be fading out at the edges.

I have an old photo of a friend's grandmother that's a perfect candidate for a vignette. Grandma Fish appears in Figure 24.49.

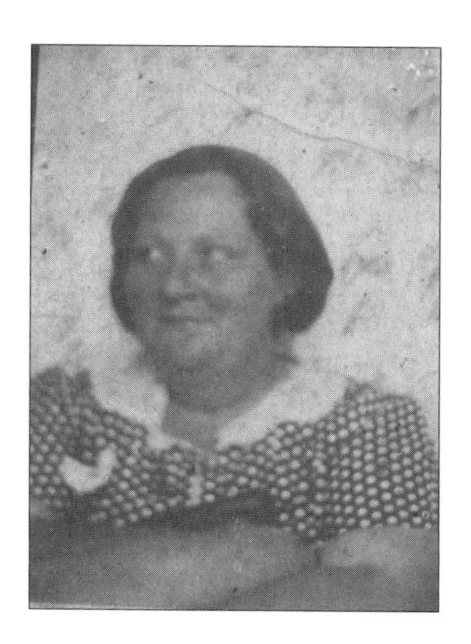

FIGURE 24.49
This picture needs some help. (Photo courtesy of Peggy Ogan.)

Old vignettes were typically oval, so that's what we'll apply here. But with Elements, you can use this technique with any shape.

Ordinarily, we'd start by cropping, but we'll be vignetting this one and we'll want the extra space for the vignette mask. Thus, we'll ignore that step, and just remove the yellow color (with the Replace Color command) and the dust and spots (with the Clone Stamp). Correcting the levels and adding some contrast (Enhance, Adjust Brightness/Contrast, Levels) helps, too. In Figure 24.50, I've started the vignette process by placing an oval marquee where I want the frame to start. To make marquee placement easier, click the Elliptical Marquee tool, select Fixed Aspect Ratio in the Style pop-up menu on the tool Options bar, and designate a ratio. I prefer W = 2, H = 3 for a tall oval frame. To make a vignette marquee, I find that it's often easier to drag outward from the middle, rather than from the edges in. So, press Command/Ctrl and click on the center of her face (the location of the cross in Figure 24.50) and drag the oval outwards until you've selected the area you wish to feature with the vignette. Then, invert the selection (Select, Inverse, or Command/Ctrl-Shift-I). That means that the edges are selected instead of the area in the middle.

We also need to feather the selection by about 25 pixels. (I could have done this when I dragged the marquee, but I wasn't sure at the time how much edge I would need.) We want a soft edge on the vignette, but not too soft. To create such an edge, choose Select, Feather, type **25** as the amount, and click OK. Next simply double-check to make sure that the background color is set to white; then press the Delete key and the background disappears. Figure 24.51 shows the finished portrait.

FIGURE 24.50
It's easier to drag the marquee from the center outward.

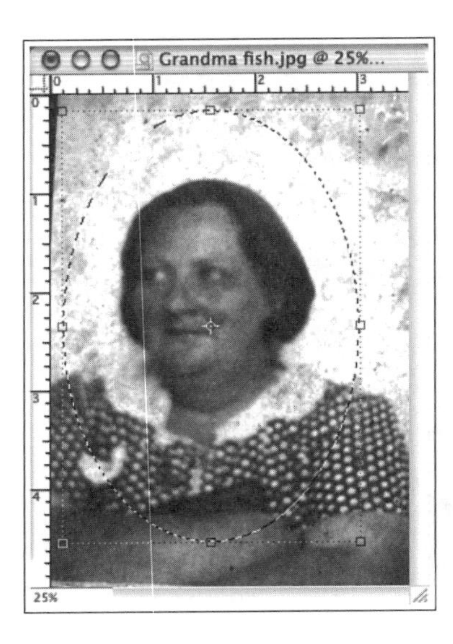

FIGURE 24.51
Here it is, a less cluttered, more interesting portrait.

Applying Tints

Working with strictly black-and-white images can get boring. Sometimes it's fun to turn the black into a different color, especially if the image is a drawing, map, or other line art. Here's a quick trick I often use on grayscale images, using the Color

Variations dialog box we discussed near the beginning of this chapter. First, change the color mode from grayscale to RGB (Image, Mode, RGB). Then, choose Enhance, Adjust Color, Color Variations, as I have in Figure 24.52. (Be sure you look at this in the color section.)

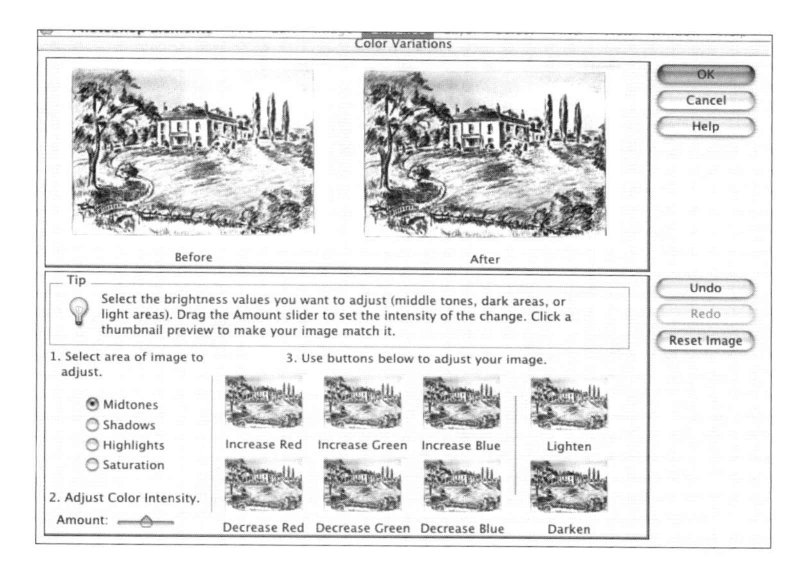

FIGURE 24.52
Even though there's no color in the picture, Variations tries to add some.

With the Midtones option selected, choose any one of the thumbnails that you like. I chose Decrease Green, which gave me a sort of purple-toned image. You can also lighten or darken the picture if necessary. Click OK to save the change. The result is a line drawing with a "color look."

The capability to create duotones isn't included in Elements, although it is in Photoshop. A duotone adds a color to black, or combines any two colors, giving you a much richer-looking image. It's commonly used to replace sepia in a corrected black-and-white photo. Several pages back, I showed you one way to re-create that sepia look using the Colorize option in the Hue/Saturation dialog box. Here's a way to get a duotone effect in Elements:

1. Open the black-and-white photo and convert it from Grayscale mode to RGB color mode. Select the entire image (Select, All or Command/Ctrl-A). Then, use Edit, Copy or Command/Ctrl-C to copy it, and immediately choose Edit, Paste or Command/Ctrl-V to paste. The copy of the image will appear on a new layer. Rename this "color layer" by double-clicking its name in the Layers palette and typing a new name, if you think you'll forget which is which.

2. With the color layer active, go to the Layer menu and choose New Adjustment Layer, Hue/Saturation. Be sure to check Group with Previous Layer. Click OK to open the Hue/Saturation dialog box. This step adds a new layer for adjusting the hue and saturation levels of the grouped layer, which in this case is the "color layer" we added. Our adjustments will not affect the original layer.
3. Use the Hue/Saturation dialog box to add color to the image. Check both Colorize and Preview, so you can see what you're doing (see Figure 24.53). The Hue slider will change the basic color, and the Saturation slider will make it more or less intense. Be careful about using the Lightness slider because decreasing lightness will turn the background "paper" dark, along with the image. A small increase (less than 6) in lightness, however, will make your "paper" look whiter without substantially affecting the image. When you like what you see, click OK.

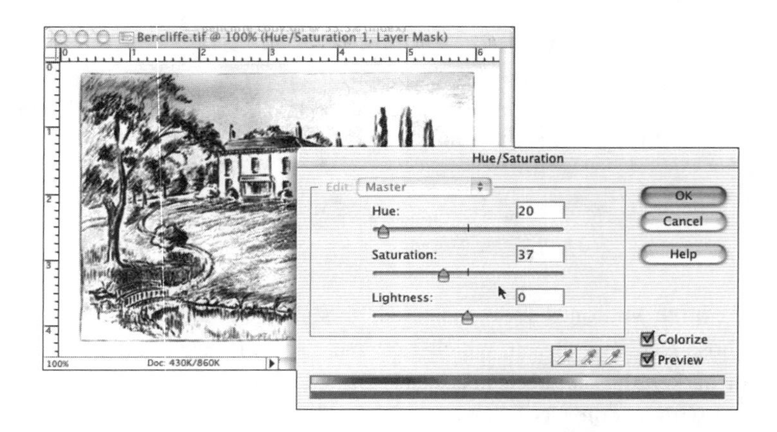

FIGURE 24.53
When you check Colorize, Elements automatically adjusts the saturation to 25%.

4. Go back to the color layer, and adjust the opacity of the layer using the slider at the top of the Layers dialog box to somewhere between 50% and 75%. This allows the black to show through and combine visually with the color to give the effect of the duotone. Be sure to see the final image in the color section.

Making Color Repairs

Color repairs are apt to be easier than black-and-white repairs, for several reasons. First, the pictures aren't as old, so they are somewhat less likely to be physically damaged. The paper tends to be heavier, and with its glossy coating, is sturdier and less prone to tearing. Very old sepia-tinted photos get brittle with age in a way that pictures printed after about 1950 never do.

The single biggest problem I've seen with color photos from the late '40s and '50s is color cast, or in its more severe form, color shift. When this happens, the entire photo can take on what looks like an overdose of a single color (often pink or purple, but any color can be affected). It's generally blamed on heat or exposure to sunlight, but having seen it happen to pictures that were tucked away in an album or used as a bookmark, I don't think that's necessarily the case. The dyes used back then just weren't stable. Bad processing or letting the film sit in the camera outdoors on a warm day were enough to throw off the color, perhaps not immediately, but as the photos aged.

Of course, bad things can happen to recent pictures too. The sun ducks behind a cloud just as you shoot, and the colors look washed out. The flash doesn't go off as expected. Nothing is immune to spilled drinks, dog/cat/kid damage, and all the other perils of daily life.

You can't save them all. Some are just too far gone, or the data (color, detail) was never there in the first place. But with Elements, you can pull off some pretty amazing rescues.

Elements makes color cast correction nearly automatic. Figure 24.54 shows an old photo that's so badly yellowed, it's almost brown.

FIGURE 24.54
Can this one be saved?

I typically start by straightening and cropping an image. The ground seems to be higher on the right than on the left, and we can greatly improve the photo by cropping around the central image of mother and child, and getting rid of the border and that big chimney on the right. After using the Image, Rotate, Free Rotate Layer command to level the ground and the Crop tool to crop the image down a bit, we're ready to begin color correcting.

To correct this kind of color cast, choose Enhance, Adjust Color, Color Cast. You probably remember this command from our discussion in adjusting Brightness, Contrast, and Color earlier in the chapter. Figure 24.55 shows the very simple Color Cast Correction dialog box. This tool evaluates the amount of color in what ought to be a black or white pixel. It then applies the same amount of the opposite color on the color wheel to cancel out the overdone one. In this case, the color cast is yellow, so Elements adds an equal amount of blue. If the color cast turned the picture red, it would add cyan. If the cast were green, it would add magenta, and so on.

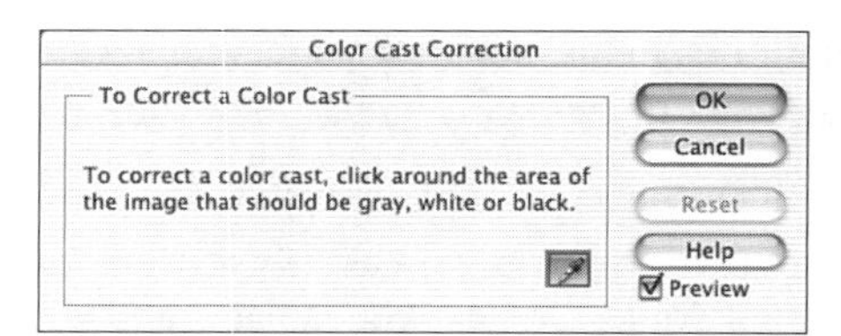

FIGURE 24.55
Try to find the darkest black or the whitest white.

As I mentioned earlier in the chapter, this command doesn't always do the best job of correcting color cast. To help Elements judge the "correctness" of its first correction, click on any part of the picture that should be either pure white, pure black, or medium gray. To judge whether the correction has worked or not, find part of the picture that's critical, color-wise. Flesh tones are always a good benchmark. I didn't think that the flesh tones looked very good, so I clicked on several areas that I thought should be white, and most seemed to make things worse instead of better. When I tried the baby's dress, though, the flesh tones looked right, even though the picture still needed a lot of work. So I guess the rule for using this dialog box is to keep clicking until you find the right benchmark for Elements to base its corrections on. Of course, if nothing works, click Cancel to undo its attempts to remove the color cast. You learned about alternatives you can use to remove the color cast manually in the previous section on Color. The command worked for me, however, as you can see in Figure 24.56.

FIGURE 24.56
This is better, but not there yet.

Using Fill Flash

Even though the picture was shot in bright sun, there are shadows on both faces because the sun was coming from the side. We'll use Fill Flash to correct this before we finish color correcting. After all, it's the faces that are the most important part of the photo. To open the dialog box shown in Figure 24.57, select Enhance, Adjust Lighting, Fill Flash. As you can see, I have just moved the sliders up a little, to lighten the picture and increase the overall color saturation a small amount.

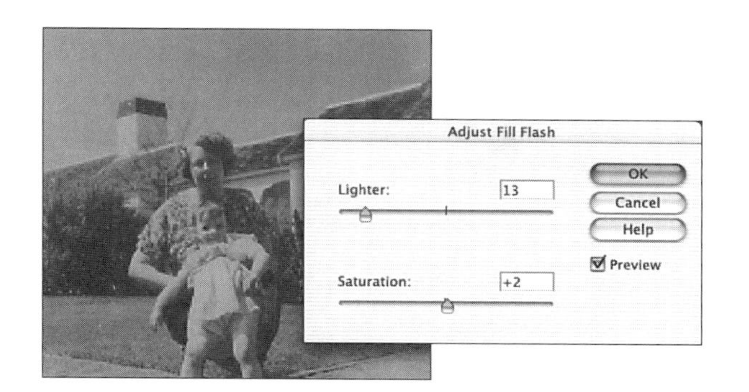

FIGURE 24.57
If the photographer had used a fill flash, we wouldn't need this step.

Making Selective Color Adjustments

Nothing we've done so far has had an effect on the sky. It's still brown, and the only way we are going to turn it blue is to select it and force the change. So that's what we'll do. We can select the sky with either the Magic Wand or the Lasso tool, or a combination of both. Because the sky is mostly one color, the Magic Wand is the best tool for selecting it. Using the Lasso tool might prove more difficult because of the irregular edges of the sky area. So I clicked with the Magic Wand tool on a representative part of the sky. Just adjust the Tolerance value so that when you click, most of the sky is selected. Then hold the Shift key down or select the Add to Selection button and continue to click on unselected spots to keep on adding to your selection. If you select a piece that you don't want, immediately Undo (just once) and the rest of the selection will remain selected. You can also click the Subtract from Selection button and click the area you don't want. With the entire sky selected, I can open the Hue/Saturation dialog box (see Figure 24.58) by choosing Enhance, Adjust Color, Hue/Saturation, and make the sky as blue as I want it. In this case, because the rest of the colors are quite subtle, I'll resist the urge to improve the weather and go with a pale blue.

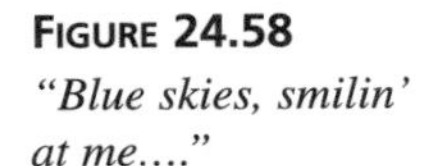

FIGURE 24.58
"Blue skies, smilin' at me...."

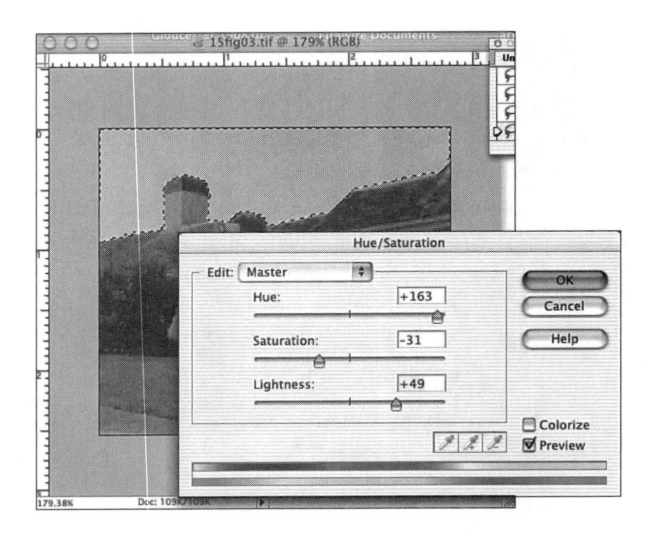

That worked so well, and looks so good, I'll do the same thing with the grass, turning it green instead of blue, of course.

Image Correction Tools

The Elements toolbox has several image correction tools, grouped together on the toolbar. If you look at the third section of the toolbox, you'll see a pair of focus tools: Blur and Sharpen. Blur looks like a drop of water. Sharpen looks like the tip of a pencil or some other sharp instrument. Below them are the Sponge tool, which looks like a natural sponge, and the Smudge tool, a hand with an extended index finger. (Considering the millions of smudged fingerprints I've wiped up over the years, this is a very appropriate icon.) The last two tools in the group, Dodge and Burn, were discussed in detail in a previous section.

Blur and Sharpen

The Blur tool blurs individual pixels by lowering the contrast between them and their adjacent neighbors. Using brush shapes, sizes, and blending modes, you can design a blur to hide a background, to remove graffiti from a fence, or to make faces in a crowd less obvious. When you're trying to pretend your subject is out in the forest, you can blur the cell phone tower and power lines showing though the trees. You can blur the gum wrappers and soda cans in an otherwise pristine landscape.

To use the Blur tool, select it in the toolbox. Choose your brush tip from the drop-down list, and set the brush Size. Choose an Effect Mode (essentially the blending mode—the various types are described in Chapter 26), and then set the strength of the blur. You can drag the Blur tool over a hard edge to soften it or over an image area to eliminate detail.

The Sharpen tool is theoretically and literally the opposite of the Blur tool. Instead of decreasing the contrast between adjacent pixels, it increases it. The additional contrast has the effect of making the image appear sharper. To use the Sharpen tool, follow the same steps as before: Select the tool, choose a hard or soft brush tip, adjust the brush size, select an Effects mode (see the discussion of blending modes in Chapter 26), and adjust the strength of the sharpening effect. Then simply drag over the part of your image you want to sharpen.

Figure 24.59 shows a nice but rather ordinary picture of some flowers. I think that if one of the bundles of flowers were better defined, the picture might be more interesting. This is definitely a case for the Sharpen tool, with a fairly small brush and medium strength.

FIGURE 24.59
Right now, there's no real center of interest. Sharper flowers would create one.

The one thing to watch out for when you use this tool is that you don't overdo it. Figure 24.60 has two examples: first, the flowers correctly sharpened, and second, the flowers oversharpened. As you can see, when you oversharpen, the image eventually breaks down to a random pattern of black and white, as the tool keeps on increasing the contrast until nothing else is left.

The fun doesn't stop here; there are other ways to blur and sharpen an image, as you'll learn in Chapter 25.

FIGURE 24.60
Here's proof that you can *have too much of a good thing.*

The Sponge Tool

The sponge represents a piece of photographic history. Darkroom photographers often kept a clean sponge next to the jug of developer. When the picture in the developing tray wasn't "coming up" fast enough, they'd grab the sponge and the jug, and slosh some fresh chemical on the paper. The combination of fresh developer and the friction from the sponge rubbing it in were generally enough to darken the image and save the print. In your digital darkroom, the Sponge tool does much the same thing. Because this sponge works in color, rather than merely darkening whatever it touches, it changes color saturation. Unlike the sponge in the darkroom, though, it can desaturate as well as saturate, making colors either less intense or more intense. If the image is grayscale, the Sponge tool will increase or decrease the contrast as it raises or lowers the intensity of the gray pixels.

To use the Sponge tool, select it and choose a brush tip and sponge size. To increase color/gray value intensity (saturation), choose Saturate from the Mode list. To tone down colors/gray values, choose Desaturate instead. To control how much the tool adjusts saturation, change the Flow value. To smudge all visible parts of the image rather than just the current layer, turn on Use All Layers.

By the way, if you're looking for a way to make an image look as if it had been painted with a sponge, try the Sponge filter. You'll learn more about it and the other Artistic filters in Chapter 25.

The Smudge Tool

It's easy to get the Blur tool and the Smudge tool mixed up. They sound as if they might do the same thing, but they don't. The Smudge tool picks up the pixel(s) where you click, and moves them where you drag. If you imagine dragging your finger through wet paint, you'll get an idea of the effect that the Smudge tool reproduces. In Figure 24.61, I have drawn a line with some sharp up *V*'s and down *V*'s using a hard-edged brush. On the left, I've blurred the two *V*'s at 50% strength using the Blur tool. On the right, I've smudged the two other *V*'s at the same strength using the Smudge tool. There's quite a difference.

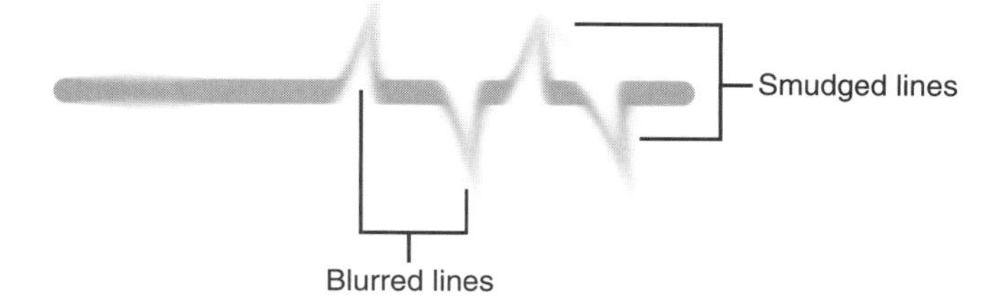

FIGURE 24.61
There's a big difference between using the Blur tool and using the Smudge tool.

To use the Smudge tool, select it and then choose a brush tip and size. Choose a blending mode (again, these will be discussed in Chapter 26.) Adjust the Strength to control the effect—a lower value creates less smudging. To smudge all visible parts of the image rather than just the current layer, turn on Use All Layers.

The Smudge tool also has a setting called Finger Painting. It places a brush full of paint (the foreground color) on the screen, and then smudges it as you drag. The effect you get when using the Smudge tool is a combination of brush size and softness, and the Strength setting. Higher Strength numbers drag a longer tail behind the brush. Figure 24.62 shows the effects of using the Smudge tool on a photo.

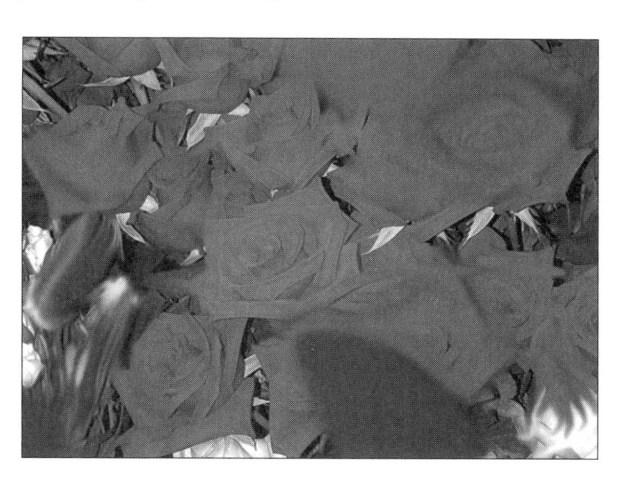

FIGURE 24.62
Smudging can give you interesting effects.

Hand Coloring a Black-and-White Photo

The art of hand-coloring or hand-tinting photographs dates back to the 1920s, or perhaps even earlier. A black-and-white or sepia-toned print would be painstakingly hand-colored with a very thinned out wash of either oil paint or watercolor. Oils were preferred for their longer working time. Watercolors would dry on the paper before they could be properly spread, but they were used nonetheless.

The main characteristic of a hand-colored photo is that the colors are very transparent. There is little or no attempt to paint in detail, as that comes through from the underlying photo. You can achieve this effect in Elements. Start with any black-and-white photo that lends itself to this technique. Though this technique is generally used on portraits, a hand-colored landscape might be interesting.

You'll paint with the Brush tool, which is explained in full detail in Chapter 26. Choose light colors for the effect (change brush colors by changing the foreground color) and set the brush opacity to 20% or less. Always paint on a new layer (Layer, New Layer), not on the background. That way, if you go outside the lines, you can simply erase your mistake and continue. I like to keep each color on its own layer so I can adjust the opacities individually, using the Opacity slider on the Layers palette. For instance, if I have chosen a shade of pink for a lady's blouse and then find it's too pink, I can set the opacity to 12% instead of 20%, making it paler, and not have to redo the color. Figure 24.63 shows a colorful couple. I haven't collapsed the layers yet, but I have added about all the color I'm going to use. If it's not subtle, it doesn't look right. Be sure to flip to the color plate section to see this one.

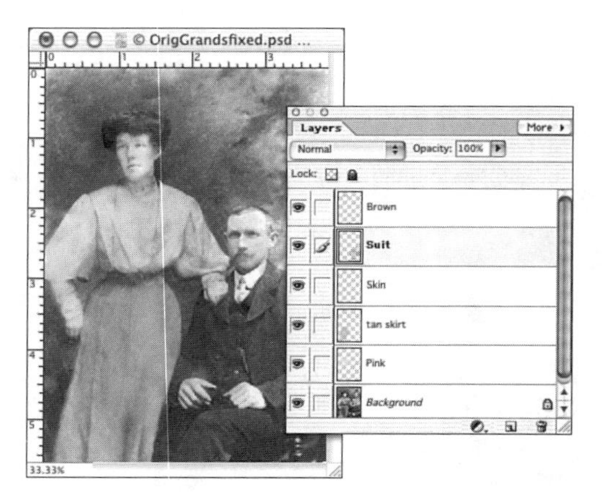

FIGURE 24.63
Don't get bogged down in details. In a picture of this size, you wouldn't see eye color or small details such as the man's suit buttons.

Removing and Replacing Objects

It's easy enough to use the Clone Stamp to hide small objects in a picture, but what happens when the object is a large one? You can't use the same tools and techniques on something big. Fortunately, there are other ways to get rid of unwanted parts of the picture and replace them with something else, even when they're right in the middle of it.

The simplest way to hide something is to cover it up. The trick I'm about to show you is an easier method of hiding something than the one we used to hide the small boats earlier in this chapter. I call this trick drag-and-drop copying. You simply select something that has the right color and shape to cover up what you want to hide. Then, you select the

Move tool and press the Option-Alt key. This tells Elements that you want to copy and move the original selection instead of simply moving it. Thus, when you drag the selection with the Move tool you're actually dragging a copy of it, so the original stays where it was, and the copy fits nicely over the object, person, or whatever you wanted to hide. Figure 24.64 shows a simple example. If the edges of your copy are obvious, undo the dragging, and feather the edges of the selection (Selection, Feather) by a few pixels before you move it, to help hide them.

FIGURE 24.64
I lassoed some grass and dragged it over the sleepy student.

Maybe it's me, but I don't like the sloppy kids in Figure 24.65 either. Removing them will be a lot more difficult because there's a lot going on behind them that we'll have to patch up.

FIGURE 24.65
The baggy shorts look may be "in" this year, but by next year it will be laughable.

I'll start with the feet. Dragging a sort of boot-shaped piece of brick sidewalk and concrete background, I align it using the line between brick and concrete near the kid's leg, and get rid of one leg very quickly. Figure 24.66 shows a close-up of this move.

FIGURE 24.66
A little more work, and he won't have a leg to stand on.

Using pieces of the sidewalk and the next granite post, I can hide his other leg, and rebuild the post. Note the tiny shadow at the bottom right of the post in Figure 24.67. I copied that with a small Clone Stamp. I then copied some of the concrete pavement to cover his upper leg, as shown in the figure.

FIGURE 24.67
The body is trickier. I don't know where the bench ends or what's on the sign.

Now I'm going to have to improvise. I have one end of the bench behind our guy. This time I'll have to do something different, though. Instead of dragging a selection, I'll copy and paste it, and then flip the copy. Remember that when you copy and paste, the pasted object will appear on a new layer, directly over the old one. This sometimes causes confusion because it looks as if nothing has happened. Take the Move tool and drag it over the copied and pasted area. You should be able to drag the copy off the original. If not, check the Layers palette to make sure it actually copied. After flipping the bench and putting it back, so the sign legs line up with the right side of the sign, I can do a little Clone Stamping to cover some more of the student. Figure 24.68 shows the end of this step.

FIGURE 24.68
I still have work to do.

I can use the same copy-and-flip technique to replace most of the sign. Figure 24.69 shows a close-up of the photo.

FIGURE 24.69
Not much more to go with this guy.

Some final rubber stamping, and he's completely gone. Figure 24.70 shows the final version of this one. To remove the other figure from the photo, you would apply the same techniques.

FIGURE 24.70
All gone, and good riddance.

Replacing a Face

There are times when you wish a certain person weren't in a certain photograph. While you can use the techniques above to remove an entire person, sometimes that's a bit more work than we'd like to do or there isn't enough to work with to fill the remaining gap. When it's not possible to cut somebody out, you might consider replacing him or her. Instead of your ex-husband, maybe you could sit next to Tom Cruise or Matt Damon or even your current husband, in all those old family photos. You could turn your ex-wife into Julia Roberts or Granny from the Beverly Hillbillies, if you can find a photo to work with.

The difficult part of replacing a face is finding the right one to put in its place. You need to find another head shot with more or less the same lighting conditions (shadows falling in the same direction) and at the same angle, though the angle is not as critical. You can always do a 180-degree flip, if you need to, and then rotate the head so it's straighter or more tipped, as necessary. Figure 24.71 is a photo of Josh and Melissa. What if Melissa had married Tom Cruise instead of Josh?

I got lucky and found an Internet fan page with a picture that works. It's facing the wrong way, and is not quite the right size, but those are easy problems to solve. The more difficult problem will be matching skin tones, but even that can be managed with the Color Variations dialog box (Enhance, Adjust Color, Color Variations) and some patience. In Figure 24.72, I've enlarged Tom, flipped him, removed some of the background, and pasted him into the original photo. I still need to rotate him so his nose lines up with Josh's, and then blend him in.

FIGURE 24.71
The happy couple....

FIGURE 24.72
Don't try to position the replacement perfectly until you've made sure that major features line up. In this case, Tom has to rotate several degrees.

In Figure 24.73, I've moved Tom's face, used the Sponge to desaturate the redness from it, and used Image, Transform, Skew to make his face fit over Josh's face a little better. Next, I will continue with the task of blending him in using the Clone Stamp and the Smudge tools. (I used Smudge to fix his hair so that it looked right after I rotated and skewed his face.)

FIGURE 24.73
From here on, it mainly takes patience and the Clone Stamp.

Because Tom's face is on a separate layer, I can add adjustment layers over him to make the color corrections more believable. It's really just a question of removing enough red. California summer sun has little in common with September sun in New England. Adding a Levels adjustment layer and setting the Channel so the adjustment only affects the red parts enabled me to take more from the darker areas (which are very red) and less from the lighter areas, which was just what the picture needed. To do that, I moved the left triangle in, didn't adjust the right one, and shifted the middle triangle toward the right a little. In Figure 24.74, you can see the final result. It's worthy of the *National Enquirer*.

FIGURE 24.74
I don't think I'll show this to either one of them.

How Far Can You Go?

You can take people out of the places they've been, or put them into places or situations they haven't been in. You can turn that can of beer in the politician's hand into a harmless can of soda, or vice-versa, depending on your party affiliation. The question at hand is not "can you?" but "should you?"

Editing a picture to improve the composition seems entirely reasonable if it's a picture for your own use, but this is precisely what got the esteemed *National Geographic* magazine in trouble some years ago. They were doing a piece on Egypt and sent a photographer to get pictures of the pyramids. The art director studied the pictures and decided the composition would be better if he moved one of the pyramids closer to the one next to it. As soon as the issue was published, astute readers began calling and writing to the magazine to complain. An apology appeared in the following issue, but simply knowing that the manipulation was possible raised a red flag for many people both inside and outside the publishing industry. The question has been debated ever since. How much change is okay? How much is too much?

To me, it depends on what's being done and its effect on communication. If it changes the meaning of the photo, particularly in a way that could get you sued, don't do it. Could anyone's reputation be harmed by it? Don't do it. If it's just for fun and not for public display, go ahead, but be careful that the photos don't end up in the wrong hands or displayed on the Web.

Putting Back What Was Never There

Sometimes you need to hide a large part of a picture, and simply don't have enough material to do so. Maybe the photo got torn too much at the edge, or it has a hole. If you use the Clone Stamp to stamp the same piece of grass, tree, or brick wall over and over, it will quickly take on a repeating pattern that you probably didn't even see in the original. The presence of the pattern sends a clear signal that you're hiding something, but not very well.

So what can you do to avoid this? In Figure 24.75, I have a pair of seagulls. The one showing us his backside really doesn't look very good. Suppose I want to stamp it out?

FIGURE 24.75
He just wouldn't turn around.

Even if I choose the most generic piece of grass I can find, there's the pattern, showing clearly in Figure 24.76. What you have to do to avoid this is to clone a little bit at a time and keep changing the stamp source. I did this on the second try, with much better results.

FIGURE 24.76
Sometimes you'll want to keep a pattern, like a brick sidewalk. Mostly, you'll want to avoid them.

If necessary—if there's not enough grass or whatever you need to cover—you can start a new document, stamping a couple of times. Then, select the stamped area, flip it upside down, copy and paste (using the Paste command will place the copy on a new layer). Select it again, and flip sideways, and paste that. When you have a good-sized patch of covering material, flatten the layers, and copy the whole thing or as much as you need back into the original picture.

The real trick in making any of these "photo saves" work for you is to be creative. Think about what could be removed to make the picture better, and what could be put in. If you start by realizing that nothing is impossible, you have a lot of possibilities to try.

Using the Magic Eraser

Magicians have lots of ways to make things disappear. There is an Elements tool that can do a similar kind of magic. It is called, appropriately, the Magic Eraser. It can remove a simple background with just a few clicks, leaving a transparent background for Web use or for layering in a composite. If the layer is locked for transparency, however, the Magic Eraser will replace the pixels with the background color.

To reach the Magic Eraser, click and hold on the regular Eraser to open the menu. The Magic Eraser is the one that has the sparkly part of the Magic Wand tool attached to it (see Figure 24.77).

FIGURE 24.77
The Magic Eraser and the picture we'll use it on.

The background in this photo is fairly plain, with two distinct areas: shadow and plain wall. To remove it, first set a reasonable amount of tolerance on the tool Options bar. Tolerance here works just as it does with the Magic Wand. The higher the setting you give it, the greater the range of pixels it will select with each click. If you overdo the tolerance, you may find yourself erasing part of your subject as well. You may need to experiment with several settings to find the best one.

To erase, simply click *once* on the part of the picture you want to erase. The Magic Eraser erases pixels similar in color (within the Tolerance you set) to the one you clicked. If you turned on the Contiguous option, only matching pixels surrounding the pixel you click will be erased; otherwise, matching pixels throughout the layer will be erased. To leave a few pixels at the edges of the background you're erasing (and smooth the edges there), turn on the Anti-Aliasing option. Adjust the strength of the eraser by changing the Opacity. Figure 24.78 shows the result of one click with a tolerance of 5.

FIGURE 24.78
Just one click!

That removed a good-sized piece of wall. Figure 24.79 shows the result after a dozen more clicks. It's not perfect, but a couple of strokes with the regular Eraser will finish the job quite nicely.

FIGURE 24.79
I never liked that wall color.

By the way, when you make part of a Background layer transparent, as I've done here, the name of the layer automatically changes to Layer 0 and it loses its background status, so you can paste it over another background. (If you don't want the background layer converted to a regular layer, use the Eraser tool instead of the Magic or Background Erasers.) Figure 24.80 shows my subject, out of the studio and into the mountains.

FIGURE 24.80
A nicer setting for a portrait.

If you have a photo with a complicated background, Elements has another eraser that will do the job for you. It's called the Background Eraser, and appears on the same menu as the Magic Eraser. Its icon is an eraser coupled with a pair of scissors. Unlike the Magic Eraser, which only requires clicking, the Background Eraser makes you do the erasing by dragging the mouse pointer. However, because the tool samples and removes a range of background colors (instead of pixels that closely match the color of a single pixel), it's practically mistake-proof.

Figure 24.81 shows a cute little teddy bear that I'd like to take out of his box.

First, I'll choose a fairly large brush, just to make the work go quickly. The tool allows me to get in close without erasing my subject, which means that I don't have to be so careful with my often-shaky hand. I'll set the tool options to a fairly low tolerance (about 5). Setting the Background Eraser to Contiguous means that it will only erase matching pixels adjacent to the point that's being sampled. (The sample point is represented by the crosshairs in the center of the brush.) Again, you don't have to be too precise here, just make sure that the crosshairs never move onto your subject, or you'll erase part of it. By choosing a large brush size, you can easily prevent that catastrophe.

FIGURE 24.81
No place for a bear.

Figure 24.82 shows teddy, his box mostly erased in less than a minute. Notice that I can bring the eraser right up to the edge of the bear without losing any of his fur. That's because the contrast in color between the bear and the box is sufficient to fall outside the 5% tolerance.

FIGURE 24.82
Now to find someplace more suitable.

However, because the tolerance setting is low, the eraser has left the darker lines of the box. I can go back over these with the regular eraser and remove them before I relocate teddy to a new setting (see Figure 24.83).

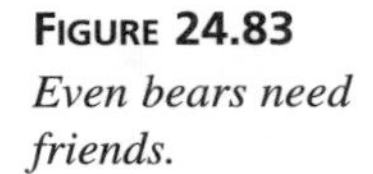

FIGURE 24.83
Even bears need friends.

Putting Together Stitched Panoramas

People have been sticking photos together to create panoramic images for close to a hundred years, with varying degrees of success. The scissors and glue method rarely succeeds. Shooting a panorama all in one photo with a wide-angle lens seems to work, until you notice that the ends of the Grand Canyon are very fuzzy, or the two outermost bridesmaids in the wedding lineup appear fifty pounds heavier than they actually are. Distortion is the main problem. Wide-angle lenses aren't good choices in situations where you want to avoid distortion. The more curve you apply to the front of the lens, the more glass the image has to pass through. Glass adds distortion. The more logical way to shoot a panorama that stays in focus from one end to the other is to take a series of pictures and splice them together. Prior to computers, that was exceptionally difficult, though it certainly was done. Now, thanks to clever software, it's easier than ever to get good results with panoramic photography.

Working with Photomerge

Photomerge is a plug-in that automates the process of assembling a panorama. After you've gone out and taken the photos, you plug your camera or memory stick into the computer and download the pictures. Then you open Elements and Photomerge (File, Photomerge), and tell it where to find the pictures you want to use. The dialog box is shown in Figure 24.84. Click Browse and navigate to the folder in which your separate images are contained, select the pictures you want to use, and then click OK.

When you click OK, the magic begins. First, Elements opens all the photos you specified, and opens a new image file. Then it arranges them in order, matching the edges where images overlap. It opens a window similar to the one shown in Figure 24.85, so you can watch its progress.

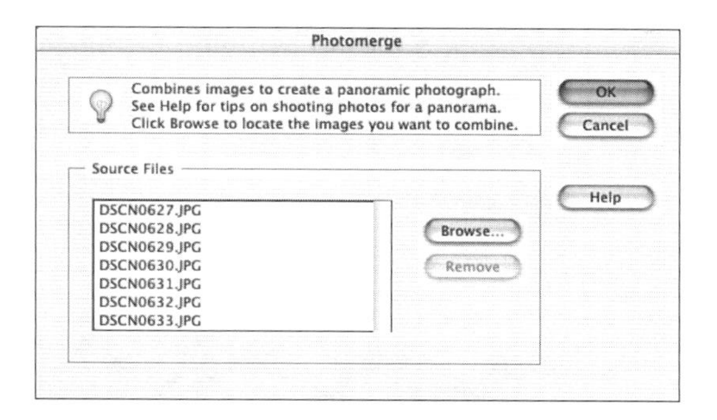

FIGURE 24.84
It's easiest if you download your pictures to a single folder. That way you don't have to go hunting for them.

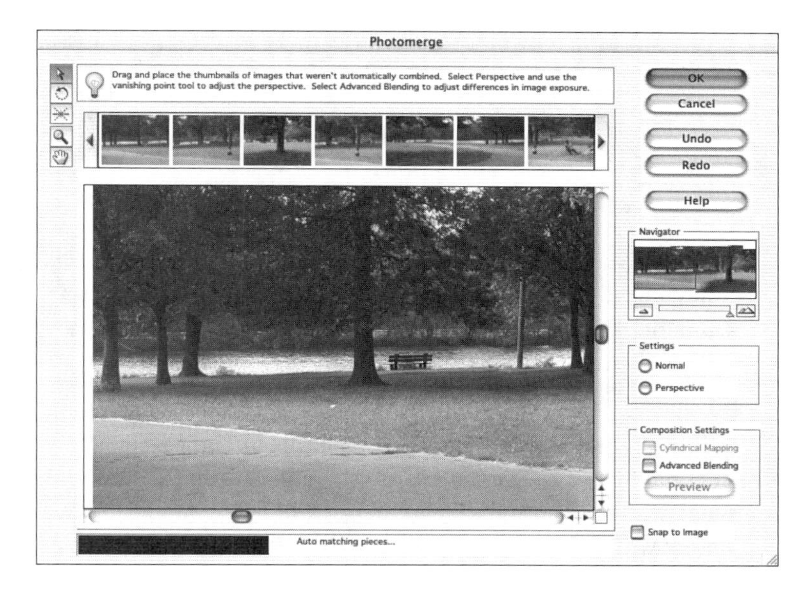

FIGURE 24.85
A panorama in progress.

24

The pictures appear to come in at 50% opacity, so the computer can easily line up areas of major contrast. In this series of pictures, tree trunks seem to be the major point of reference for matching. Pictures that Photomerge can't match are left at the top of the strip, so you can drag them from the box at the top of the window into the work area at the bottom of the window and match them later. When all the pictures have been merged in (see Figure 24.86), Photomerge continues the process by adjusting the brightness and contrast of each pair of pictures so you have a consistent exposure from one end to the other. If the sun has gone behind a cloud and emerged again, as it did for me, you'll have to do some extra tweaking. Apparently, it can only cope with *logical* changes.

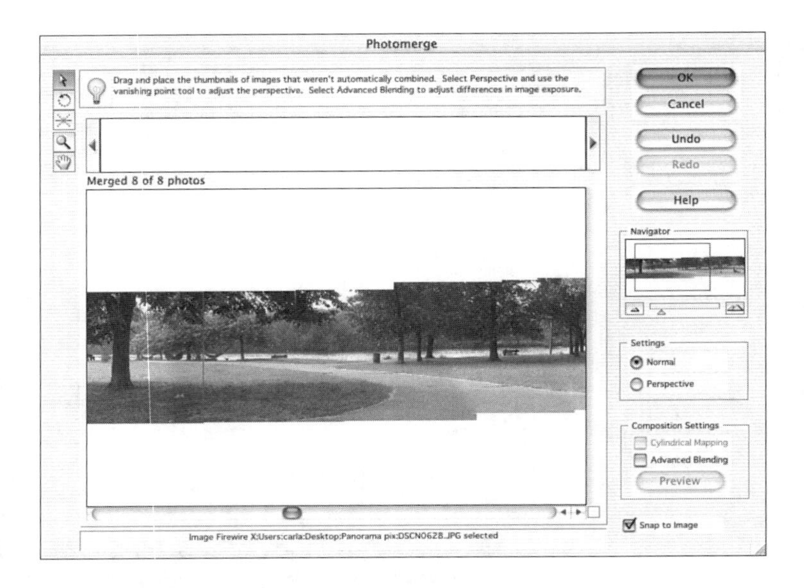

FIGURE 24.86
Processing the exposures.

You can do some tweaking using the tools in the Photomerge dialog box. Drag a corner of any image in the work area with the Rotate Image tool to rotate it. Move the panorama within the work area by scrolling or by dragging it with the Move View tool. Zoom in with the Zoom tool.

By clicking Perspective in the Settings pane, you can make some other adjustments. To establish which image contains the vanishing point (which image contains the highest point on the horizon, and therefore should be treated as the "middle" image), click that image with the Vanishing Point tool. It will be highlighted with a blue border. The other images will be adjusted in relation to this new vanishing point. If needed, make your own adjustments as well by clicking the Select Image tool and scooting the non-vanishing point images up or down.

There are other options you can choose as well. The Cylindrical Mapping option transforms the panorama as if it were on a cylinder, reducing the bow-tie effect shown in Figure 24.86. This brings the viewer closer and into the panorama a bit, but you'll gain a lot of extra image space for cropping, so it's worth a look to see which view you prefer.

If your panorama has some inconsistencies with brightness and contrast, try the Advanced Blending option. It blends together areas of color, while retaining detail. The effect is a softening of these differences, making the panorama seem more like a whole image rather than a collection of images.

After choosing Cylindrical Mapping, Advanced Blending, or both, click Preview to view the results. Click Exit Preview to return to Normal view. When you're through making adjustments in the Photomerge window, click OK.

The finished product is an untitled file (Figure 24.87) with all the pictures assembled and matched as well as possible. Unfortunately, when you get it, the image has already been flattened, making it difficult to adjust the exposure of one frame that's a little "off."

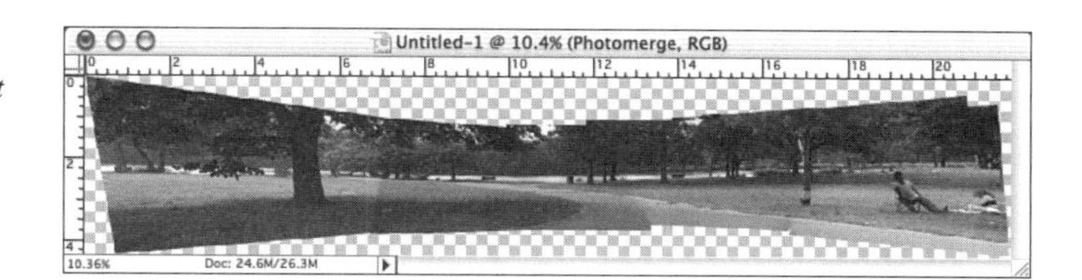

FIGURE 24.87
The edges suggest that this is more than one photo.

It's still up to you to crop the picture, if you want to. Some photographers argue that the slanting edges and unevenness of the "raw" panorama somehow add to the experience. Others, myself included, prefer to crop. A lot depends on whether, and how, you intend to print the picture. The eight images I assembled for this test of Photomerge produced a strip 4 inches high by 36 inches long. At 300 dpi resolution, that's a 37MB file. I can print it myself if I want to do so; one of my inkjet printers takes banner paper. But I'd prefer to go to a service bureau and come home with a strip 8 inches high by 6 feet long on a nice shiny, heavy poster paper.

Considerations When You Shoot a Panorama

Obviously, the main thing to consider when you shoot pictures for a panorama is that you should hold the camera steady at one height. Don't take it away from your eye while you're shooting. If you get interrupted mid-sequence, start again. Better yet, if possible, use a tripod to keep the camera steady. Remember, digital photos don't waste film. Stay away from the focus and zoom buttons. Autofocus the first picture and let that one dictate the focus for the rest.

Practice the "panorama shuffle." Start shooting with your body aimed at one end of the scene. Take small steps circling to your right as you shoot your pictures from left to right.

Don't use a flash. Particularly, don't use auto-flash, as it will throw varying amounts of light as it sees a need. This makes the exposure all but impossible to correct.

Use a normal lens for best results. Set your zoom lens about halfway between zoom and telephoto, and leave it there. Don't use a wide-angle or fish-eye lens. Such lenses defeat the purpose of the panorama, which is to have everything in the same focus and not distorted. Nothing distorts more than a fish eye.

Make sure you have enough overlap between pictures, but not too much. Somewhere around 20% is good. As you pan across the scene, remember what was on the right side of each picture you take, and just cover it again on the left of the next shot.

Take a picture of something clearly different between shooting panorama sequences. That way you won't try to assemble pictures that don't go together. Keep each set of pictures in a separate file as you download from the camera.

Have fun creating your panorama!

Summary

This has been a very busy chapter. You learned the steps for basic photo cleanup, something you should do with every image you open, before you get fancy by applying filters, changing colors, or using any of the hundreds of tricks Elements can do. We explored several methods for removing objects, both large and small, that might distract from the subject of your photo—and how to add objects that were never there! You learned how to remove red eye, dust, and scratches and how to adjust color, brightness, and contrast. You also learned how to create adjustment layers and layer masks to control how particular adjustments affect your image. We also demonstrated the potential of these techniques with several examples of black-and-white and color photo retouching.

CHAPTER 25

Enhancing Your Photos with Filters

I'm not sure whether Adobe actually invented the concept of filters, or just took the ball and ran with it. (A *filter*, by the way, is a series of commands that, when applied to a layer or selection, change its appearance in some manner.) It really doesn't matter. Filters are my favorite Photoshop/Elements tools. Elements has all the Photoshop filters on board, and you can also load third-party filter sets to do everything from framing your pictures in your choice of materials to changing the weather in the scene to creating strange abstractions based on fractal geometry.

Working with Filters

The filters that we're going to be working with first are all "corrective" filters. They are used to change focus or to add or remove noise and speckles.

All the filters in this chapter will be applied to the current layer, or a selection within the current layer. When using a selection, it's usually best to feather the edge to create a better transition between the affected area and the rest of the image. If your image has multiple layers, you can apply the filter to each layer and blend the effects by adjusting each layer's opacity.

In most cases, if you want to apply a filter, your image must be using RGB mode. (Some filters may be applied to images using Grayscale mode as well.) Filters are found on the submenus of the Filter menu. Some filters are applied without making any selections at all, while others let you make adjustments before applying them. The last filter you used, with the exact settings you selected, will be listed at the top of the Filter menu. To reapply it with those settings, simply choose the filter from there rather than from the submenu.

You can compare filters visually using the Filters palette, shown in Figure 25.1. Change from one category to another using the drop-down list. The filters in each category are displayed in sample thumbnails so you can compare them. To compare the sample original image with the selected filter style, click the List View button at the bottom of the palette. To display thumbnails again, click the Thumbnails button, also located at the bottom of the palette. Double-clicking the thumbnail will open the filter's dialog box, if there is one. If this is one of the filters with no options to set, such as the Blur or Blur More filters that you'll learn about later in this chapter, Elements will simply go ahead and apply it.

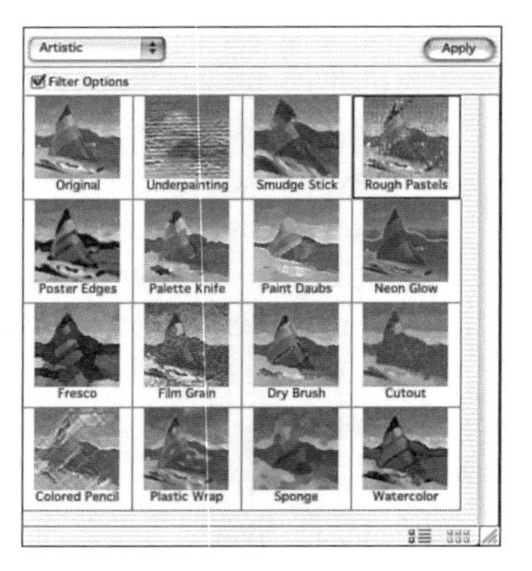

FIGURE 25.1
Browse through the many filters using the Filters palette.

Using the Sharpen Filters

There are four filters in this set: Sharpen, Sharpen More, Sharpen Edges, and Unsharp Mask. You'll find them all on the Filters, Sharpen menu. The first three are very straightforward—there are no options to set. You select them from the Filter menu, and your picture changes accordingly. Sharpen More gives twice as much sharpening as Sharpen, and Sharpen Edges only sharpens areas where there is a lot of contrast between adjacent pixels—such as the edges of the flower next to the dark background, the shadow in the center, and the light-colored stamen. The Sharpen Edges filter treats these contrasting pixels as edges, and increases the contrast between them. It does not increase the contrast everywhere, as Sharpen and Sharpen More do. Figure 25.2 shows some examples.

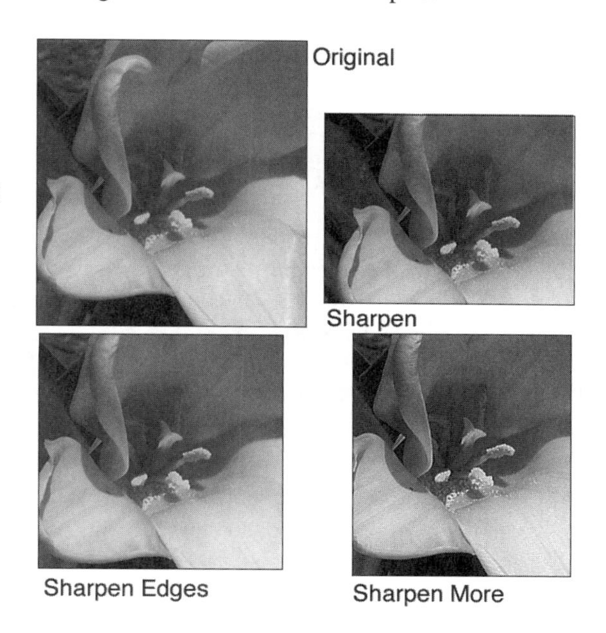

FIGURE 25.2
You can try applying any of these filters a second time if the first application doesn't do enough. Just be careful not to oversharpen.

The Unsharp Mask filter is a lot more complicated. It also visually sharpens the photo by seeking out edges and adding contrast to them, like Sharpen Edges, but with the variables involved, it can do a much more selective and therefore better job. Choosing Filters, Sharpen, Unsharp Mask opens the dialog box shown in Figure 25.3.

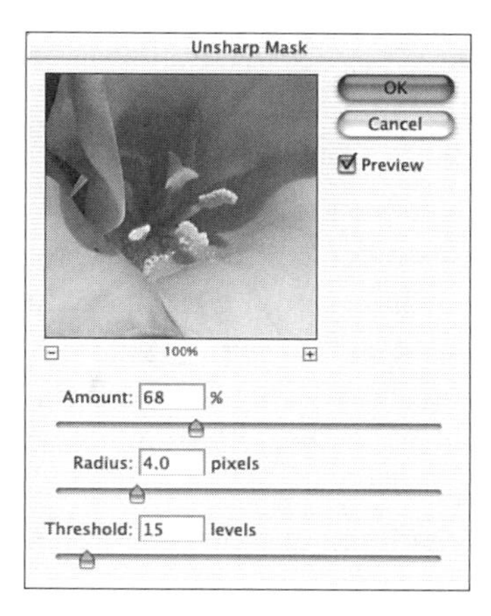

FIGURE 25.3
The Unsharp Mask dialog box.

As you can see, there are three settings you must deal with: Amount, Radius, and Threshold. Amount refers to the degree of contrast (sharpness) you'll be adding to the edges of objects in the picture. Radius determines the size of the area that will be sharpened. A large radius sharpens a large area around each perceived edge. A small one sharpens a smaller area. Threshold lets you determine how much of a difference there should be between adjacent pixels before Elements treats them as an edge and enhances them. When you have areas with only minor differences in color, such as sky or skin tones, a very low Threshold setting can make them look blotchy. Still, you want to keep the Threshold as low as you can without letting it add unwanted noise or spottiness to the picture.

Sharpening with any of the filters, and particularly with the Unsharp Mask, should always be the very last thing you do to your picture before saving it. If you were to sharpen an image first, and then make additional changes, you would probably make the sharpness that Elements put in stick out like a sore thumb.

Task: Applying the Unsharp Mask Filter

1. Open an image in Elements and make whatever corrections or alterations it needs. Zoom in or out so the picture is at its full size on the screen. (This will let you see the effects of sharpening, without exaggerating them.) When you're satisfied with everything except the sharpness, open the Unsharp Mask dialog box (Filter, Sharpen, Unsharp Mask).
2. Set the Amount to 500% to start with. This is the maximum, and starting here will help you see and understand what the other two variables are doing.
3. Set the Radius to 1 pixel, and the Threshold to 0. The picture won't look right—it will probably look very grainy, but this is our jumping-off point.
4. If there is obvious grain or noise, increase the Threshold. Start with 2, and then try 5, 8, 12, and so on until the noise disappears.
5. Now, we'll work with the Radius. Increase the Radius until the picture just starts to lose detail, and then back it off a bit. Figure 25.4 shows my image at this stage. (Don't worry about the white halos around edges. We'll lose them next.)
6. Now, reduce the Amount until the picture looks good. You want to get rid of the white edges, but still keep the sharpening effect. You'll probably find that the correct setting for Amount is somewhere between 100 and 250. Of course, it also depends on the amount of contrast and fuzziness in the picture you're working on. If you're not going to use the image onscreen (on the Web, for example) and you're just trying to get the sharpest image you can for printing, you may want to oversharpen the image just a bit.
7. Finally, save the picture and print it or put it on your Web page, or do whatever you'd planned. It's as sharp as it's ever going to be.

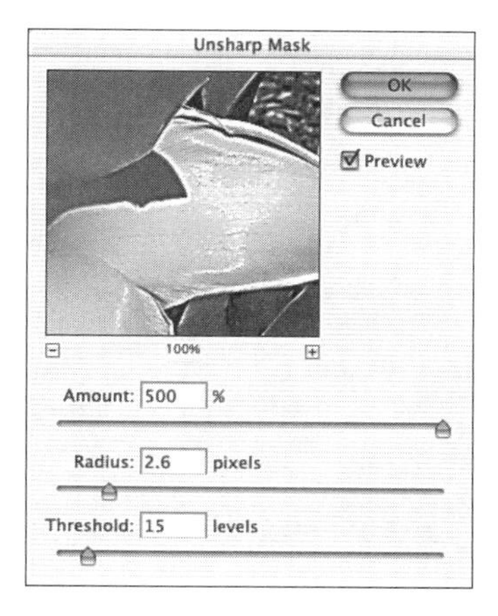

FIGURE 25.4
We'll lose the halos in the next step.

Using the Blur Filters

The Blur filters logically ought to be the direct opposite of the Sharpen filters. Some are. Blur and Blur More have the same global, one amount fits all, method of application. Choose either one of these two filters from the Filter, Blur menu, and the filter is applied automatically, without options. I actually tried a sequence of Blur, Sharpen, Blur More, and Sharpen More on a picture, and aside from some obvious quality loss, I got back to about where I started. However, I don't recommend this as a technique. The image loses some detail at each step.

Blurring, generally, is *not* something you want to do to the entire image. If you are applying a combination of filters for a special effect, Blur could certainly be one of them, but most of the time we want our pictures sharp. Blurring *part* of the image, though, is a very useful technique. When you blur an object against a sharp background, you create the illusion that it's in motion. When you blur a background, you create the illusion of depth of field, where the subject is in focus, but the background is so far away that you can't see all the details. Blur and Blur More are best applied to selections.

Smart Blur

In Figure 25.5, I'm going to use one of the Blur tools to clean up the beach. The heavy shadows on the sand from too many footprints create a texture that nearly hides the seagull. I've selected the sand and everything on it except the gull.

Now I'll open the Smart Blur dialog box (Filter, Blur, Smart Blur). Smart Blur has the most flexibility of any of the Blur tools. In its dialog box, which is shown in Figure 25.6, you can set Radius and Threshold, just as you can for Unsharp Masking. You have a choice of Quality settings: High, Medium, or Low. High creates more blur than Low. You also have a choice of effects modes: Normal (which applies the effect to the entire layer or selection), Edge Only (which applies the effect to the edges), or Overlay Edge (which also applies the effect at the edges). The difference between Edge Only and Overlay Edge is the effect—Edge Only makes the image or selection black and the edges white, while Overlay Edge doesn't change the colors in the image, but makes the edges white.

FIGURE 25.5
Before blurring the sand.

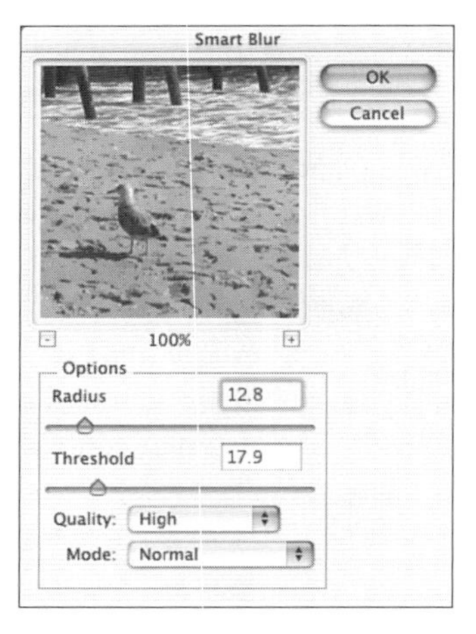

FIGURE 25.6
The Smart Blur dialog box.

Setting the Radius and Threshold here are the same in theory as setting them for Unsharp Masking. The Radius determines how much of the area around the perceived edge is blurred. The Threshold determines how much difference there needs to be between adjacent pixels before Elements will interpret them as an edge, and will apply the blur to the area.

Figure 25.7 shows the final version of this picture.

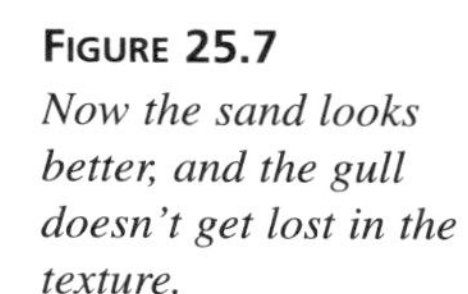

FIGURE 25.7
Now the sand looks better, and the gull doesn't get lost in the texture.

Gaussian Blur

The Gaussian Blur filter is less adjustable than Smart Blur. Its only adjustment is for Radius. What makes it so useful, though, is that it has a built-in randomness factor that varies the amount of blur applied. This gives it a much more natural look, so you can actually use quite a lot of blur without it being obvious. Gaussian Blur is a wonderful tool for portraits. It evens out skin tones, removes fine lines and wrinkles, and takes years off with a single click. Keep in mind, however, that too much blur tends to make skin look as if it were made from plastic.

Radial Blur

The Radial Blur filter is just plain fun, especially when you apply it to a round object. The only drawback to using it is that there's no way to preview, so you have to be prepared to do and undo your changes several times until you find the right setting. Figure 25.8 shows the Radial Blur dialog box. There are two different kinds of blur available: Spin and Zoom. Spin simply rotates the pixels around the center point (which you can move). Zoom blurs them outward from the center (again, you can move this spot). Both effects are interesting, if not particularly useful. Figure 25.9 shows examples of both. The Spin amount was only 10, but the Zoom amount was 50. Zooming requires much more "travel distance" within the image to see the full effect.

To use Radial Blur, select the type of blur—Spin or Zoom—and the Amount of blur you desire. To adjust the center point of the blur effect, click in the Blur Center box and drag the center point.

Note the quality settings in the window, too. They determine how quickly, and how carefully, the blur is applied. The Draft setting works very fast, and leaves some rough edges. Good is sort of a compromise between speed and smoothness, and Best, which is noticeably smoother, can take several minutes to apply on an older, slower computer.

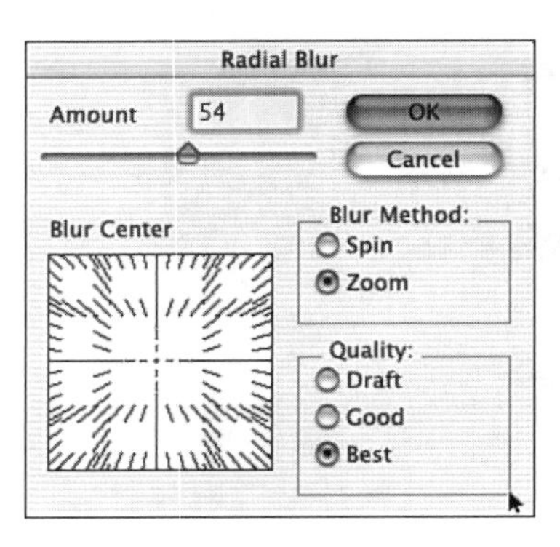

FIGURE 25.8
The Radial Blur dialog box.

FIGURE 25.9
Three flavors of flower: Original, Spin, and Zoom.

Motion Blur

When we see lines drawn behind a car, a cat, or a comic strip character, we instinctively know that the subject is supposed to be in motion. Those lines represent *motion blur*, which is actually a photographic mistake caused by using a slow shutter speed on a fast subject. The Motion Blur filter (Filter, Blur, Motion Blur) can add the appearance of motion to a stationary object by placing a directional blur for a predetermined distance. In the Motion Blur dialog box, shown in Figure 25.10, you can set both the distance and direction of the blur according to how fast and in what direction you want the object to appear to be traveling. The Distance sets how much of a blur is applied—or how far the original image is "moved." The Angle sets the direction of the blur. To adjust, drag the directional bar in the circle, or enter precise values into the Angle box next to it. The trick is to select the right area to which to apply Motion Blur. To get a convincing blur, you need to blur the space where the object theoretically was, as well as the space to which it has theoretically moved. You don't want to blur the entire image, so you might want to select the area to blur before using the Motion filter.

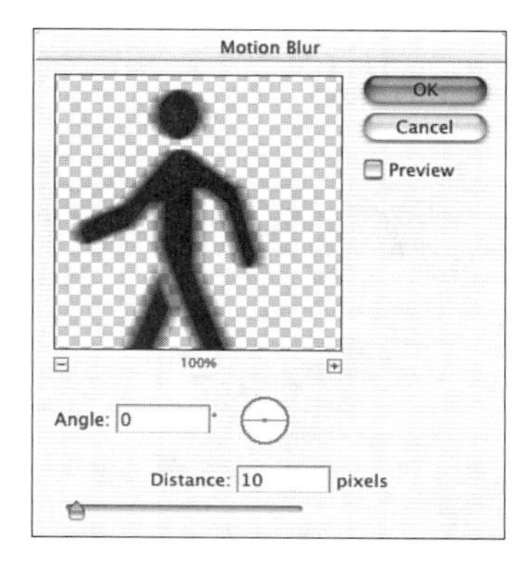

FIGURE 25.10
Using the Motion Blur filter is tricky at best.

Adding or Removing Noise

The Noise filters have nothing to do with sound. The kind of noise we're dealing with here is electronic noise. It's displayed on a TV screen or computer monitor as a pattern of random dots, usually in color. It's also called snow, and before we all got cable TV, it was common whenever you tried to tune in a TV station that was too far away.

Noise doesn't sound like a useful tool, but rather something you'd like to get rid of. Three of the four Noise filters are, in fact, designed to remove noise. It's fairly obvious from the names what Despeckle and Dust & Scratches are trying to remove, but what about Median? Median reduces noise by looking for individual pixels that are too bright or too dark, and changing them to the median brightness value of the pixels around them. Sometimes you don't want to remove noise, but add it, and of course, that's what the Add Noise filter is for.

Despeckle

Despeckle is the easiest of the filters to use. All you have to do is select it from the menu. It automatically looks for areas that have sharply contrasting pixels, and blurs the "misfits" to blend into the pixels around them. If you have a scan from a magazine that's showing visual banding or other noise, this filter will usually remove it. But be careful about using it on photos with fine detail. The Despeckle filter is likely to blur the detail.

Dust & Scratches

The Dust & Scratches filter, unlike Despeckle, has a dialog box with Threshold and Radius settings. This makes it much more useful, in that you can set the Threshold to the amount of blur you're willing to tolerate, and still get rid of dust, cat hair, and whatever else is messing up the picture. The Radius setting controls the size of the area that's examined for dissimilarities. In Figure 25.11, I have scanned an old photo with many scratches and cracks in the paper.

FIGURE 25.11
Can we lose the scratches without losing the face?

Finding the right combination of Threshold and Radius settings simply requires patience and a willingness to experiment, but as you can see in Figure 25.12, it is possible to get rid of all but the heaviest scratch without losing too much sharpness. The remaining one can then be easily Clone Stamped out of the picture. Typically, it's best to try keeping the Threshold at the lowest value possible (to avoid losing too much detail) while gradually increasing the area to examine (the Radius). If you can't seem to find a proper balance, try selecting the area that contains the largest amount of dust and dirt, and applying the filter just to that area.

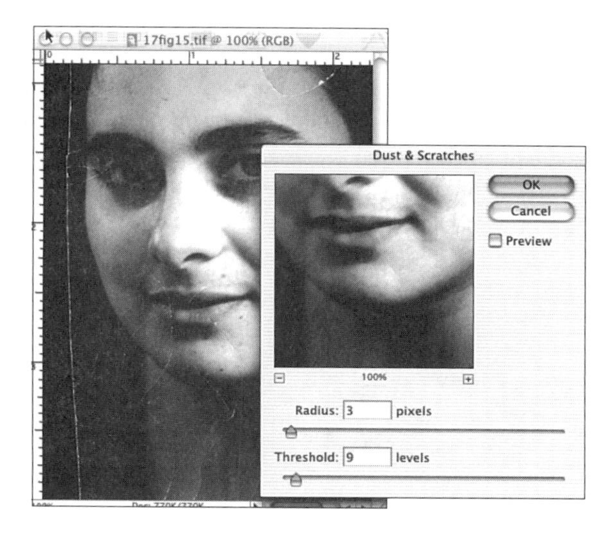

FIGURE 25.12
This sure beats stamping out every line.

Median

As I mentioned earlier, the Median filter removes noise caused by neighboring pixels that vary too much in lightness or darkness. This filter blurs details even at very low levels, so be careful when using it. I use it sometimes to even out skin tone, reduce freckles, and the like. It seems to work better than applying any of the blur filters, at least when I select a small area, as shown in Figure 25.13.

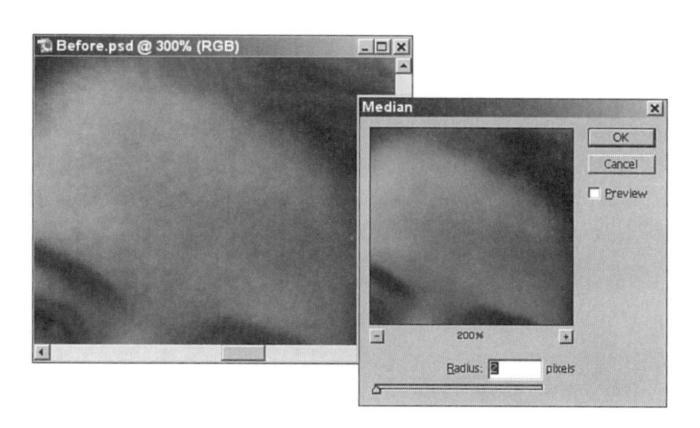

FIGURE 25.13
Median is useful when removing unevenness in tone from small areas.

To use Median, select the area you want to affect, then choose Filters, Noise, Median. There's only one option to set—the Radius of the area that's examined for discrepancies. You'll want to leave this set very low, to avoid losing detail. Of course, if you lose some detail, you may be able to put it back in using the Unsharp Mask.

Add Noise

Given that Elements offers you so many tools to *remove* noise, why would you want to *add* any? Actually, noise can be very helpful. I use it a lot when I am creating backgrounds from scratch, as part of the process of turning photos into paintings, or to cover up areas I've retouched a lot. You can apply noise to a picture, as I've done in Figure 25.14. In this case, I want the finished product to look like a hand-colored steel engraving. Adding monochromatic (black) noise and then using the Find Edges filter will give me the look I want, with very little work.

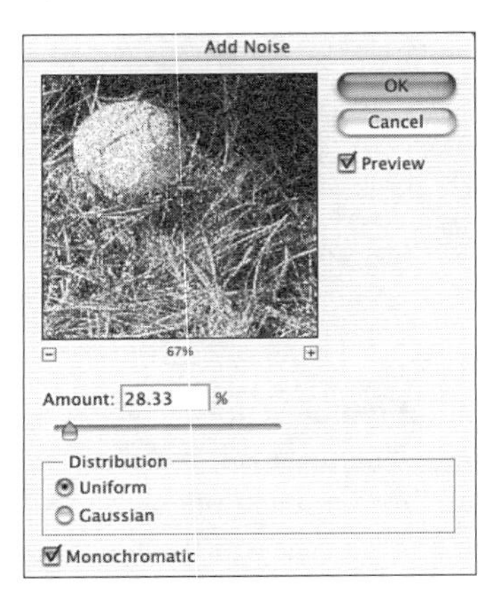

FIGURE 25.14
Choose colored or monochrome noise, and an even or Gaussian distribution.

If you apply noise to a blank canvas, and then apply another filter (or two or three), you can create some beautiful textured backgrounds for Web pages or anything else you might think of using them for. In Figure 25.15, I've used Gaussian colored (non-Monochromatic) noise to put down a layer of confetti (shown here in the upper left), and I've added some other filters to change the original. See if you can identify the Stained Glass, Colored Pencil, Sumi-e, Mosaic Tiles, and Crystallize filters. You'll get to play with these filters yourself later in this chapter.

FIGURE 25.15
By changing the amount of noise, you could change each of these to something quite different.

Adjusting the Effect of Filters

In Photoshop, you have the ability to apply a filter and then fade it out by a percentage. Unfortunately, Elements lacks this feature. (For now—the next edition will probably have it.) But you can create a fairly good imitation of the effect by copying the image to a new layer before you apply the filter. Filter the top layer, and then adjust the opacity of that layer until you have just enough of the effect, with the unfiltered background layer showing through and putting back as much of the original image as you want it to. In Figure 25.16, I've applied the Dust & Scratches filter too generously to a copy of the picture.

FIGURE 25.16
Oops, that's too much blur.

By reducing the opacity of that layer to about 50%, I can get what I wanted—enough blur to wipe out the spottiness of the leaves, but not enough so they're out of focus. Figure 25.17 shows close-ups without the filter, with the filter applied at 100% opacity, and finally, with it reduced to 50% opacity.

FIGURE 25.17
From left to right: the original trees, the filter applied at 100% opacity, the filter opacity reduced to 50%.

Using the Artistic Filters

One of my favorite activities in Photoshop, and now in Elements, is to turn some of my less spectacular photos into fine art. I am constantly surprised at the effects I can get by combining several filters, or by changing the order in which I apply them. The Artistic filters will enable you to mimic most of the available art media, from oil painting to neon tube sculpture. You can rescue a "bad" picture, or create a real masterpiece from a good one. More to the point, it's fun. Under the general heading of Artistic filters, I've chosen to also include the Brush Strokes, Pixelate, Sketch, and Stylize filters. Each category includes filters that mimic a specific art style or medium.

Watercolor

Elements includes a filter (Filter, Artistic, Watercolor) that gives you one style of watercolor, which is kind of dark and blotchy. There are ways to make this filter work better, and there are other filters that also create watercolors in other styles, but we'll start with the official one. First of all, let's look at the photo that will eventually be a watercolor (see Figure 25.18). As a photo, it's not very exciting. The composition and focus are okay, and it's well exposed, neither too dark nor too light.

FIGURE 25.18
Hampton Beach, NH.

The Watercolor filter, like most filters, has a dialog box with several options, which are shown in Figure 25.19. You can set the Brush Detail, Shadow Intensity, and Texture. Brush Detail ranges from 1 to 14, with greater detail at the high end of the scale. Shadow Intensity can be set from 1 to 10, again with much deeper shadows as the numbers get bigger. Texture ranges from 1 to 3, but there's not a lot of difference between the settings.

In 25.20, I lightened the original photo by about half using Enhance, Adjust Brightness/Contrast, Brightness/Contrast, and then applied the filter. It still came out darker than I wanted, so I went to the Levels dialog box (Enhance, Adjust Brightness/Contrast, Levels) and brightened it there. It's looking much better now, but I think that what I really need is a different kind of watercolor.

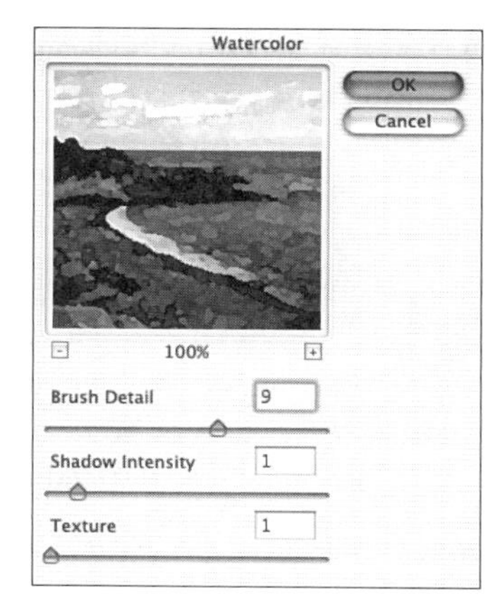

FIGURE 25.19
The Watercolor filter dialog box.

FIGURE 25.20
To make some filters work properly, you often must make changes in the original that you wouldn't accept otherwise.

Dry Brush

The Dry Brush filter (Filter, Artistic, Dry Brush) simulates a watercolor technique that, as the name suggests, uses less water, and more pure pigment. It's good for detail and doesn't darken the picture the way the Watercolor filter does. With this filter, you can set the Brush Size, Brush Detail, and Texture. Brush Size controls the level of detail—with a larger brush, you'll get bigger splotches of color and you'll lose the parts of the image with small areas of color. Brush Detail increases the number of tones, softening the edges. Texture again ranges from 1 to 3, and it controls the level of contrast. The highest setting, 3, makes the areas of individual color more apparent.

Spatter

Spatter is an interesting filter, which can be used for a different watercolor style or perhaps to simulate a gouache painting. (Gouache is a thicker, water-soluble paint, more opaque than typical watercolors.) It is located on the Filter menu under Brushstrokes. The Spatter dialog box has only two settings: Spray Radius and Smoothness. If you imagine that you're using an airbrush, you'll soon get the idea: Spray Radius adjusts the range of the spray, while Smoothness adjusts the density or coverage of the spray, and hence, its smoothness.

Underpainting

There are as many styles of oil painting as there are people who paint; all the way from ultrarealistic, tight little brush drawings to big, splashy, abstract swipes of color. Traditional painters begin a new canvas by creating an underpainting, which lays out the scene with a big brush in blocks of color showing little or no detail. When they have the basic underpainting done, they go back with smaller brushes and add detail.

To use the Underpainting filter yourself, choose Filter, Artistic, Underpainting. Select a brush size—a big fat brush for larger splotches of color and less detail, or a smaller, finer brush for more detailed work. The Texture Coverage setting adjusts the thickness of the paint and its coverage of the texture you select.

You can also choose a textured surface; the defaults are Burlap, Brick, Canvas, and Sandstone, but you can also load in any texture file (in .psd format) and use it instead. You can size the textures by adjusting the Scaling percentage, and also by setting the Relief or "lumpiness" (higher numbers will make the texture more intense). In addition, you can decide from which direction to have the light strike the texture by changing the Light Dir setting. To reverse the direction of the light quickly, without changing the Light Dir setting, click Invert.

Palette Knife

Other oil techniques include painting with a palette knife, with thick brushes, and using strongly directional strokes. When painting with a palette knife, you spread paint over the canvas with the flat side of the knife. The result is a painting with thick, flat strokes. To start, choose Filters, Artistic, Palette Knife. Adjust the Stroke Size—a larger stoke gives you large, flat areas of color, and you'll lose the areas of the image with smaller patches of color. Next, select the Stroke Detail. This controls the number of tones used in areas of similar color, thus reducing or increasing the detail. Finally, select the Softness you want. This adjusts the "edge softness" of the stroke, or the level of contrast at the edge of the stroke. You won't see a lot of difference here between the high and low settings.

In Figure 25.21, I have used the Palette Knife filter, with Stroke Size and Detail of 9 and 3, respectively, and a Softness of 10.

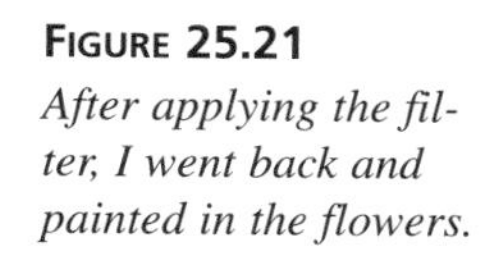

FIGURE 25.21
After applying the filter, I went back and painted in the flowers.

Paint Daubs

The Paint Daubs filter (Filters, Artistic, Paint Daubs), which simulates the look of a painting, either works well with your picture or not at all. It breaks up the image into blobs of color. Its dialog box has a pop-up menu for Brush Type as well as sliders for Brush Size and Sharpness. If you are willing to spend some time experimenting, you can discover combinations that do amazing things to a still life or landscape. However, this is one filter I do not recommend for portraits.

A larger brush size will give you larger daubs of paint, and less detail. Next, adjust the Sharpness (level of contrast). Finally, select the Brush Type—your choices include a regular Simple brush, a Light Rough brush (which emphasizes the light values in an image), a Dark Rough brush (which emphasizes dark values), a Wide Rough or Blurry brush (which uses wide strokes), or a Sparkle brush (which produces a twirly effect).

Working with Pastels, Chalk, Charcoal, and Pen

The next category of art media that we'll consider are pastels, chalks, and charcoals. (It would be convenient if these tools were at least lumped into the same category. Because they aren't, you will have to go hunting for them.) These are all drawing or sketching materials rather than painting materials, so the look is completely different. The image is created from lines rather than blocks of color. Thus, these media lend themselves to pictures with delicate detail rather than areas of flat color. They are good for portraits, because the level of abstraction they provide disguises small flaws and makes anybody look good.

Rough Pastels

Rough Pastels simulates the look of chalky pastels on a rough surface, such as canvas. With this filter, you'll see more texture in the dark areas than you will in the light. It's on the Filter, Artistic menu. You can adjust the Stroke Length. Pastels are brushed on the surface using the edge of the pastel stick and long, smooth strokes. You can also adjust the contrast as well, and make the strokes more apparent by adjusting the Stroke Detail. Like the Underpainting filter we looked at earlier, the Rough Pastels filter allows you to change the texture of the surface on which the pastels are applied.

Smudge Stick

Smudge Stick is smoother than the Rough Pastels and makes the image look as if it has been carefully rendered in soft crayon or pastel, and then the dark areas carefully smudged with a soft cloth or fingertip in a suede glove. See a close-up in Figure 25.22.

Choose Filters, Artistic, Smudge Stick. A smudge stick is used in a manner similar to a hard pastel, in long stokes whose length you can adjust using the Stroke Length slider. Adjust the range of values to be lightened with the Highlight Area slider. The higher the value, the broader this range of values. To brighten the values defined by the Highlight Area value, drag the Intensity slider.

FIGURE 25.22
Smudge Stick is a nice soft look that reveals textures and details.

Chalk & Charcoal, Charcoal

Chalk & Charcoal (Filters, Sketch, Chalk & Charcoal) works with whatever colors you have set as the foreground and background colors. Chalk, the background color, is used to render the light areas of your image. Charcoal, the foreground color, is used to render the dark areas. The medium tones in the image are not rendered, but are displayed as a simulated medium gray paper. Being somewhat traditionally oriented, I usually choose to use a combination of black and white, though you could just as well use pink and green or any other colors you want.

After displaying the Chalk & Charcoal dialog box, widen the range of dark values rendered with charcoal (the foreground color) by raising the Charcoal value. Lowering this value narrows the dark range. Adjust the range of light values rendered with chalk (the background color) by dragging the Chalk slider. Adjust the Stroke Pressure as desired. More pressure leaves more of the foreground/background color on the paper, increasing or decreasing the contrast.

The Charcoal filter (Artistic, Sketch, Charcoal) is not as effective as the Chalk & Charcoal filter unless you're looking for lots of contrast. When rendering your image in charcoal, Elements draws the edges of high contrast with a strong, bold stroke. Areas filled with midtones are drawn with a lighter, diagonal stroke. The color of the charcoal is the same as the foreground color. The paper used with this filter is not a medium gray; instead, it's the same as the background color.

In the Charcoal dialog box, adjust the thickness of the stroke using the Charcoal Thickness slider. The Detail slider controls the range of values rendered in charcoal. By default, only the dark tones in an image are rendered; with a high Detail value, more of the midtones will be rendered as well. Light values are left unrendered, and are filled with the background color. The Light/Dark Balance slider controls how strong a stroke is used—a strong, dark stroke or a light, medium stroke.

Figure 25.23 shows examples of the same image, rendered with both filters.

FIGURE 25.23
On the left, the Chalk & Charcoal filter. On the right, plain Charcoal.

Conté Crayon

Conté Crayon (Filters, Sketch, Conté Crayon) is a soft, compressed chalk-and-graphite crayon, typically used on medium gray or brown paper in earthy colors. Like the Chalk & Charcoal filter described previously, the Conté Crayon filter uses the foreground color to render the dark tones in an image, and the background color to render the light ones. For an authentic look, use a dark iron oxide (blood red), black, or sienna brown crayon for your foreground color. As your background color, use white, another earthy color, or a light-toned version of the foreground color.

After displaying the Conté Crayon dialog box, adjust the range of dark values rendered with the foreground color using the Foreground Level slider. Lowering this value narrows the dark range. Adjust the range of Background Level values rendered with the background color by dragging the Chalk slider. You can also change the texture of the background from canvas to something else, in a manner similar to the Rough Pastels dialog box: Choose the texture to use from the Texture list, or select a texture file you've created. Adjust the size of the texture with the Scaling box. Change the roughness of the texture by adjusting the Relief value. Change the direction of the light source with the Light Dir setting. To reverse the direction of the light, click Invert.

Graphic Pen and Halftone Pattern

These two filters (both located on the Filter, Sketch submenu) do very similar things. Both reduce the image using whatever foreground and background colors you set. Graphic Pen then renders the image in slanting lines, whereas Halftone Pattern renders it in overlapping dots. On the proper subject, the Graphic Pen filter can be very effective, though I can't decide whether it looks more like an etching or a pen-and-ink drawing. Take a look at Figure 25.24 and see what you think. Halftone Pattern, shown in Figure 25.25, looks like a bad newspaper photo.

FIGURE 25.24
It's a drawing. No, it's an etching.

FIGURE 25.25
Create the "high-quality" look of real newspaper!

To use the Graphic Pen filter, set the foreground color to the color of the ink you want to use; set the background color to the color of the paper you want to draw on. Next, choose Filters, Sketch, Graphic Pen. Adjust the Stroke Length as desired. Adjust the range of tones that the pen renders by dragging the Light/Dark Balance slider. If you drag it left toward the light side, the pen will render more light tones; drag it to the right to narrow the range. Finally, select a direction for the pen strokes—choose a direction in which your eye seems to move through the picture.

To use the Halftone Pattern filter, choose it from the Filters, Sketch submenu. The pattern is rendered in newspaper photo style, using dots of various shades of gray. Change the pattern to concentric circles or horizontal lines by selecting that option from the Pattern Type list. Adjust the size of the dots, circles, or lines using the Size slider. Adjust the range of tones rendered by the pattern using the Contrast slider.

When you're working in Grayscale mode, you notice that many of the filters are grayed out. To get access to these filters again, just change your image back to RGB mode (Image, Mode, RGB Color) and apply your filter. Then, switch back to Grayscale mode and click OK when asked to discard color information.

Sumi-e

Sumi-e is the very old Japanese art of brush painting. As few strokes as possible are used to convey the subject, which is typically rendered in black ink on white rice paper. A carefully chosen photo should be an ideal medium for sumi-e. You want something that has textures, but is not too complicated (not too much detail, not too many edges) and not too dark. Because a lot of sumi-e art is black and white or uses only muted colors, you might want to adjust the hues in your image (the filter will not replace them). The filter will blur areas of similar colors together, while adding dark strokes along edges of different colors, and within dark areas.

Many of the Elements filters, including this one, tend to darken a picture. If I know I'm going to continue working on an image after I've done the basic corrections, I'll often create a light version or one with extra contrast just for the filtering process.

I shot these clownfish (see Figure 25.26) at an aquarium. As shown in Figure 25.27, the filter softened the shapes, as if a big, wet brush had painted them. It intensified the colors and turned the shapes just abstract enough to make them interesting.

FIGURE 25.26
Send in a couple more clowns....

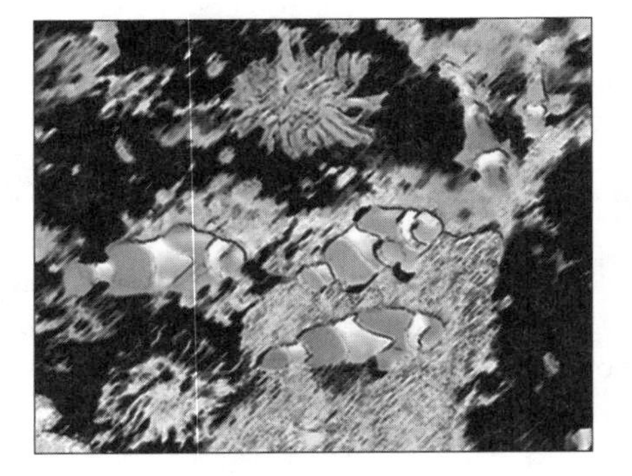

FIGURE 25.27
Adding the Sumi-e filter produced exactly what I wanted.

To use the Sumi-e filter yourself, choose Filters, Brush Strokes, Sumi-e. Select the width of the brush strokes with the Stroke Width slider. Adjust the Stroke Pressure as well; a greater pressure will increase the darkness of the brush strokes. The Contrast slider adjusts the level of contrast in the image. Typically, you'll want to lower the contrast to achieve the soft look found in sumi-e paintings.

Sponge

Before closing this discussion of artistic filters, I'd like to mention the Sponge filter (Filter, Artistic, Sponge). With it, you can create a kind of watercolor effect that looks as if it were done with a sponge rather than a paintbrush. This filter blends areas of color, but retains the edges to give some detail to the image. Adjusting the Brush Size slider changes the size of the individual areas of color used to render the image. The Definition slider adjusts the darkness of the paint used on the sponge—from light gray to dark gray. With the Smoothness slider, you can change the amount of blending between the areas of color that make up the image, and the gray spots left by the sponge.

Going Wild with Filters

You've seen what filters can do to improve your images and add some standard artistic styles. In addition to its many useful filters and effects, Elements also has a few that I haven't yet found a use for, and some others that are strange but interesting. Let's take a brief look at some of the stranger ones. I won't go into all of the remaining filters and possible settings, but surprise outcomes are part of the fun of filters so don't be afraid to play. (And, remember, you can always use the History panel to undo something if you don't like it.)

Liquify an Image

Liquify (Filter, Liquify) lets you distort things, not geometrically, but pixel by pixel, exactly as if you were dragging your finger through wet paint. And it has a few other tricks up its sleeves as well. Let's look at Figure 25.28.

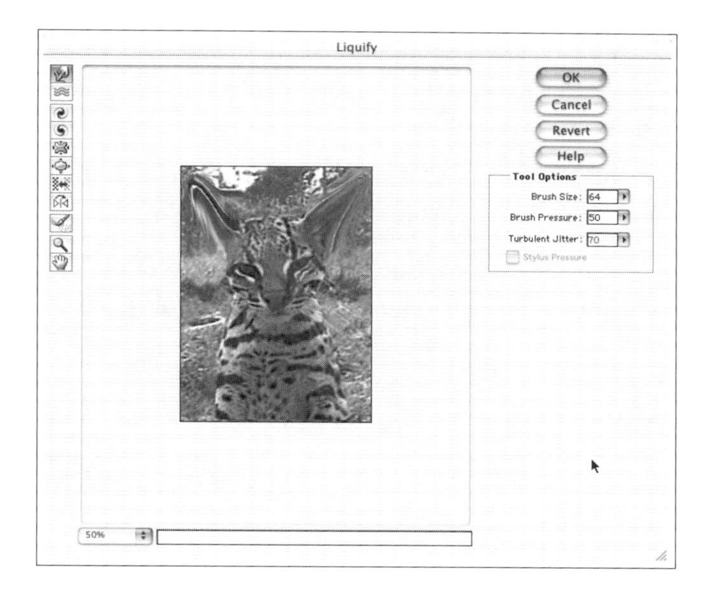

FIGURE 25.28
Liquifying can put your image through a blender, or just scrunch it a little. It's up to you.

To start, select the layer or area you want to liquify. (To liquify a text layer, you must simplify it first using the Layer, Simplify command.) Then choose Filter, Distort, Liquify. The Liquify interface, shown in Figure 25.28, takes over your screen for the duration. Liquify has its own toolbox with shortcuts that are the same letters used for different tools on the Elements toolbox, which might be confusing. For example, *W* opens the Magic Wand tool in Elements, but it gets you the Warp tool in Liquify. Figure 25.29 shows the Liquify toolbox with its tool names and shortcuts. Note that tool options for changing brush diameter, pressure, and turbulence jitter are also present.

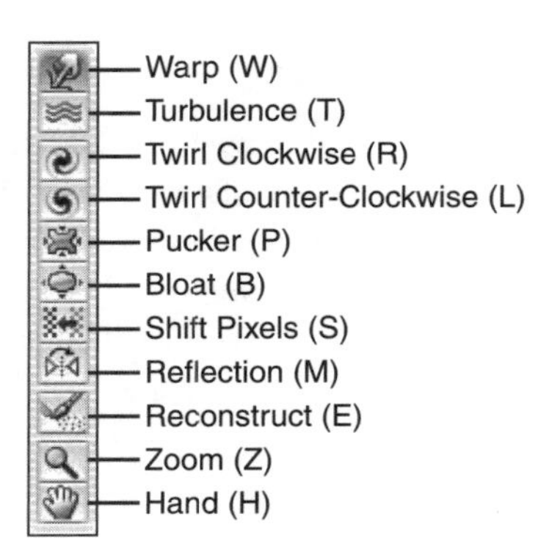

FIGURE 25.29
Be careful with the shortcuts or just click the individual tools to select them.

The Warp tool is the easiest to master. It works by pushing pixels forward as you move the mouse. Its effect depends not only on brush size and pressure, but on how quickly you move your mouse or tablet stylus. To set the brush size and brush pressure for any of the tools, adjust the appropriate value in the Tool Options section, located on the right. Larger numbers get you a bigger brush/more pressure. Don't be afraid to try out the other tools to see what they do—Liquify has a Revert button that will take you right back to the beginning of your adventure.

To remove an effect from only part of your image (either partially or totally), use the Reconstruct tool. Simply drag over the area you want to affect—drag slowly to remove an effect more completely. To completely remove all effects in a direct line between two points, click at the beginning and then Shift+click at the end. On the other hand, if you like what you've done, click OK to close the Liquify dialog box and apply your changes.

The Render Filters

The Render filters can create some awesome special effects. You can add lens flare, lighting effects, clouds, and textures, and even map your art onto three-dimensional objects. You'll find these amazing filters on the Filters, Render menu. Try them out and see what interesting effects you can create.

Adding Texture

All the Texture filters (Craquelure, Grain, Mosaic Tiles, Patchwork, and Stained Glass) allow you to adjust the size of the texture and its effects so you can achieve a look that is either subtle or not-so-subtle.

To use them, select the layer or area you want to affect, then choose your filter from the Filters, Texture submenu. Adjust the size, spacing, intensity, depth, brightness, and other options as desired, using the preview window as your guide. Then click OK to apply the effect.

Neon Glow

The Neon Glow filter (Filter, Artistic, Neon Glow) is guaranteed to turn your landscapes into post-Apocalypse and your in-laws into space aliens. The dialog box, shown in Figure 25.30, gives you options to choose a glow color, size, and brightness. When you choose a color such as lime green, hot pink, or purple, the picture can get very strange indeed.

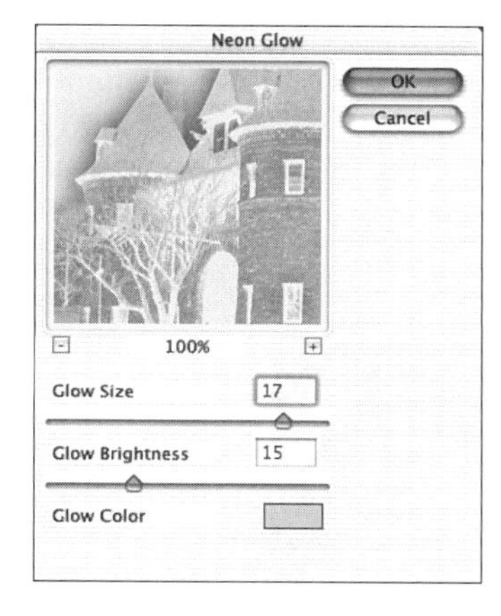

FIGURE 25.30
Why is this building glowing?

Plastic Wrap

Another unusual filter, Plastic Wrap (Filter, Artistic, Plastic Wrap), pours a layer of plastic over your picture. The effect on the building photo in Figure 25.31 is to turn it into something resembling bas-relief. The plastic wrap is actually quite thick, and forms puddles as it goes down, but accents definite edges such as the roof line.

FIGURE 25.31
Wrapped in plastic, or drowning in it?

The interface is fairly simple. Smoothness determines the degree of shine on the plastic, and Detail determines how closely the plastic follows the contours of the image. Highlight Strength controls the intensity of the light shining down on the plastic, and therefore, the lightness of the highlights.

Diffuse Glow

This filter (Filters, Distort, Diffuse Glow) uses the background color and dumps what looks like powder onto the highlights of the image. If it's a light color, it'll look like powdered sugar. If it's dark, it will come closer to mildew. In Figure 25.32, I tried for snow, but got baby powder instead. It's still interesting, just not what I wanted. You'll find as you work with this program that this happens a lot. What you get is not what you wanted, but it's kind of cool anyway.

FIGURE 25.32
A powdered daisy.

Use the Graininess slider to adjust the smoothness of the "powder," from a smooth hazy glow to a noisy rough surface. Use the Glow Amount to control the range of tones that are considered highlights, and thus are replaced with the background color. Higher values widen the range. Control how much the non-highlighted areas are covered with the background colored powder. Higher values narrow the range.

Ocean Ripple and Wave

The Ocean filter (Filters, Distort, Ocean Ripple) makes a definite rippling, even bubbly, effect. In Figure 25.33, I'm trying it on a duck, and it's much like viewing the duck through a sheet of pebbled glass.

You have two settings with this filter. The Ripple Size value controls the number of ripples—with the highest value, you'll get fewer ripples, but of larger size. Ripple Magnitude controls the height (amplitude) of the ripples. The higher the value, the taller the ripples become.

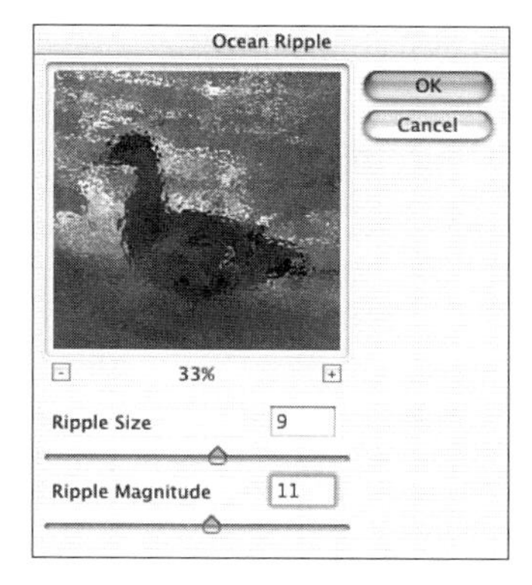

FIGURE 25.33
A bubbling duck.

The Wave filter (Filters, Distort, Wave) is really strange. First of all, you need to be an engineer to understand the interface, shown in Figure 25.34. Its purpose is to create an undulating wave pattern on a layer, making it appear as if the image is underwater. The Sine option gives you the most even undulation, with smooth upside-down U-shaped waves. The Square options create vertical or horizontal rectangular waves of color, like sharp-edged tubes into which the picture has been poured, and the Triangle option creates M-shaped waves with sharp corners.

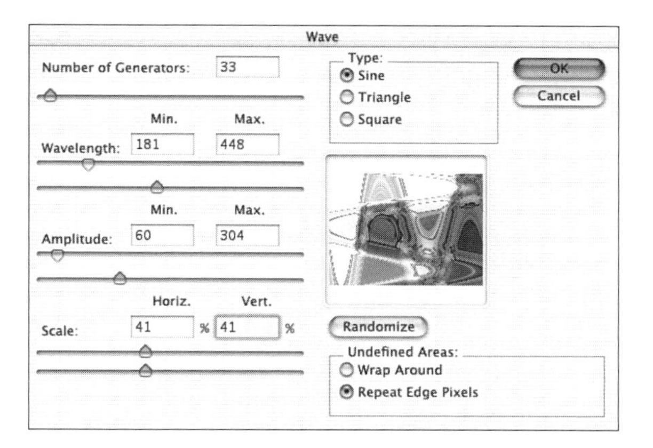

FIGURE 25.34
A thoroughly confusing dialog box.

To set the number of waves, use the Number of Generators slider. You can have as many as 999, but lower numbers are less destructive to the image. The minimum and maximum Wavelength values determine their length. Keep the numbers the same or close to each other for symmetry. The Amplitude sliders dictate the wave height. The horizontal and vertical Scale sliders adjust the distortion. If you click Randomize, you will see various wave patterns generated with the same settings.

The Wrap Around option wraps pixels pushed off the canvas by the waves onto the opposite side of the layer/selection. The Repeat Edge Pixels option cuts off the pixels pushed off by the waves, and fills the holes with a color close to the pixels on the edge.

Solarize

The Solarize filter (Filters, Stylize, Solarize) uses a darkroom trick, imported from the film world to the digital world. Solarizing a photo means exposing it to light in the middle of the developing process. The results are usually unpredictable, and often worthless, as the entire picture turns black. But if it's done at the right second, with the right amount of light, you'll partially invert the colors in the picture, with interesting results. With Solarize, the values in the image are changed: the highlights become shadows, and light midtones become dark midtones. The values of shadows and dark midtones are left unchanged. Then colors are swapped for their opposites on the color wheel, producing an interesting effect.

There are no options with this filter. But because solarized pictures can turn dark, you may need to readjust brightness and contrast levels after you solarize.

Using Third-Party Filters

In addition to the filters native to Photoshop Elements, many third-party plug-ins are available. Some are strange, some are just utilitarian, and some are wonderful! Because of the way Elements is designed, almost all Photoshop filters work with it. Let me show you some of my favorites.

Elements is compatible with all the third-party Photoshop filters, and with most plug-ins that work with other graphics programs such as Painter. You can install them very simply, by copying them into the Filters folder. If you already have filters installed in another Photoshop-compatible graphics program, you don't need to reload them. You can designate a second plug-ins folder by going to the Preferences dialog boxes (Edit, Preferences), displaying the Plug-Ins & Scratch Disks options, clicking Choose, and locating the folder containing the additional plug-ins you want to use. When you restart Elements you'll see the new ones listed at the bottom of the Filters menu.

Alien Skin: Eye Candy 4000 and Splat!

Eye Candy 4000 is a compilation of Photoshop filters. As the name of the publisher (Alien Skin Software—`www.alienskin.com`) suggests, some of these filters are a little out of the ordinary. There are 23 in all, ranging from anti-matter to wood. Fire, Fur, and Water Drops are some of my favorites. Fire adds very realistic flames to areas you have selected. Some of these, particularly marble and wood, can be used to create very realistic backgrounds or textures. Eye Candy's interface, though it seems complicated at first glance, is really quite simple. Move the sliders to see what each one does. Be forewarned: Some of Eye Candy's filters may take a while to render. Try to be patient, especially if you are using an older, slower computer.

Remember that you can use these third-party filters in combination with Photoshop's own filters, and you can use the same filter several times for a stronger effect.

Alien Skin's latest filter set is called Splat! Splat! Filters include Border Stamps, Edges, Fill Stamps, Frames, Patchwork, and Resurface. Surround your girlfriend with white roses, or the baby with jelly beans. A lot of the contents are silly, but some are quite beautiful. As a final example, Figure 25.35 shows one of Splat's Resurface filters, Canvas, with a picture I'd already converted to an oil painting. Notice how much realism this adds.

Figure 25.35
The cat photo looks kind of like a painting, but the canvas in Splat! works better than the one provided in Elements.

Before

After

Andromeda Software Filters

Andromeda Software (`www.andromeda.com`) has several sets of cool filters with a user-friendly interface. There's Prism, which makes your subject appear as it might if you were looking at it through a real glass prism. Funky, huh? And there are a number of photographic filters, plus excellent focus correction. These are well worth checking out.

Summary

This chapter covered some of the plug-in filters available in Elements. These filters can be applied to an entire image or to selected parts of it. First, you learned about the Sharpen filters, including Unsharp Masking, to take the blur out of digital photos and scanned pictures. Then, we looked at the Blur filters. We also explored an array of artistic and, well, interesting filters with the potential to transform a regular photograph into something truly unique, and maybe even beautiful.

CHAPTER 26

Creating Digital Art from Scratch

Up to now, we've mostly talked about how to correct existing images such as photographs. Sometimes, you need to create your own images, such as logos and Web buttons. Using the painting and drawing tools in Elements, it's easy to create art. And by adding some special touches, such as layering and effects, you can develop some pretty impressive images. Let's begin by setting color.

Choosing Colors

The tools in Elements use the foreground color, the background color, or a combination of both. So before you use most tools, you should set these colors. Some tools give you the option of selecting a color for use with just that tool, as you'll see shortly.

The simplest way to select a color for the foreground or background, or for exclusive use with a particular tool, is to click the appropriate color swatch, and then choose a color from the Color Picker (more on this in a moment).

You'll find the swatches for the foreground and background colors at the bottom of the toolbox; a separate swatch may appear on a tool's Options bar, and if so, click it to display the Color Picker so you can change the color used with that tool.

Using Color Pickers

You actually have a choice of Color Pickers. Which one you use (Adobe Apple, or Windows) depends on which one you selected in the Preferences dialog box. You can always open the General preferences to see which is selected, if you forget. Adobe's Color Picker, shown in Figure 26.1, is probably your best bet. It gives you the most options.

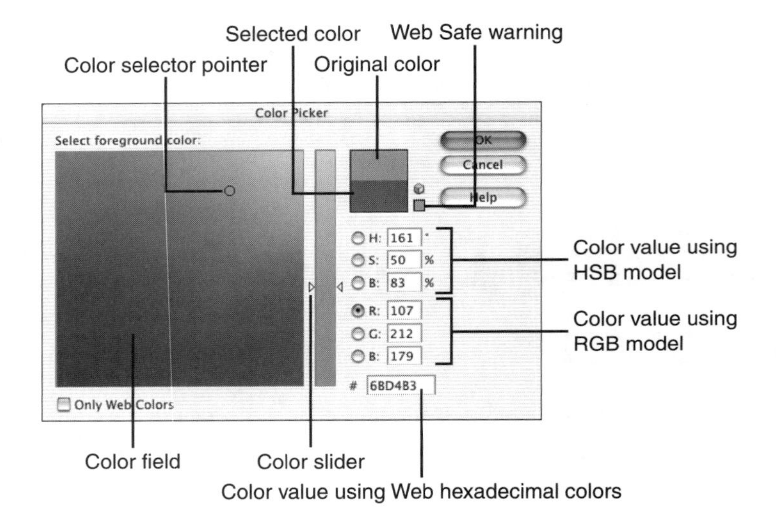

FIGURE 26.1
Select a color with the Adobe Color Picker.

The original color appears in the top swatch on the right; the color you're about to change it to appears beneath. To select a new color, you've got lots of options. To select a color visually, adjust the color slider so that the range of colors from which you want to select appears in the color field. Then just click the color you want, or drag the Color Selector pointer around until the exact color you're looking for appears in the Selected color swatch.

If you'd rather not select a color visually, you can choose a color by entering values into either the HSB or the RGB box, to the right of the color slider. You can also enter the hexadecimal value for the number if you prefer—this is the same number you would enter within your HTML code to specify a particular color. If you're one of those people who can think of colors in terms of numbers, one of these methods is probably for you. If you want a refresher course on the various color models used by Elements, jump back to Chapter 22, "Starting, Saving, and Printing Your Work."

Notice the warning cube just to the right of the Selected color swatch. It's telling me that the color I've just selected is not one of the Web-safe colors—the 216 colors shared by the Windows and Mac operating systems. If I'm not going to display this image on the Web, I can safely ignore this warning. However, if I want to limit my choices to only Web-safe colors, I can select the Only Web Colors option. This prevents non–Web-safe colors from appearing in the color field.

After choosing the color you want to use, click OK.

Using the Swatches Palette

Another method for selecting the color you want to use is to click it within the Swatches palette, shown in Figure 26.2. The palette, as you can see, looks like a sort of paint box. The Swatches palette helps you build and store a consistent set of colors for use in refining an image. To display the Swatches palette yourself, click its tab in the palette well, or if it isn't there, choose Color Swatches from the Window menu.

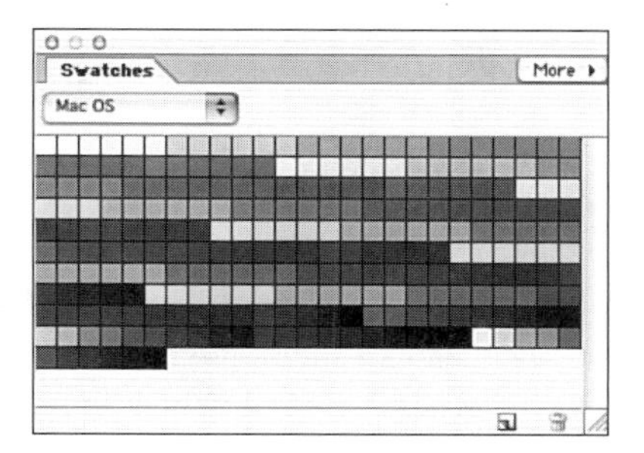

FIGURE 26.2
The Swatches palette has several different sets of colors, including Web-safe colors and Windows OS colors.

Elements comes with eight different sets of swatches, which you can select from the pop-up menu at the top of the palette. The Default swatch set contains a sample of the most often used colors, but you can add colors to this set or any of the other swatch sets if you'd like. To add the current foreground color as a new swatch to the displayed swatch set, just click in the empty area of the Swatches palette. You'll be asked whether you want to give the new color a name, and then it will be saved for you at the bottom of the palette. If you want to replace a swatch with the current foreground color, press Shift as you click it. To remove a swatch from a set, drag it to the trash can icon at the bottom of the palette.

After opening the Swatches palette and choosing a swatch set to display, you can select a color for use as the foreground color by simply clicking it. To select a color as the background color, press Option/Alt as you click it.

Other Tips for Selecting Colors

If the image itself contains the color you want, there's a simple method for choosing it. Simply click with the Eyedropper tool on the color in the image, and the foreground color will immediately be changed to match. You can click with the Eyedropper in any open image, even if it's not the one you're working on. To change the background color using the Eyedropper, press Option/Alt and click within the image.

If the colors you want to use as the foreground color and the background color are reversed, switch them by clicking the Switch Colors icon, as shown in Figure 26.3, or by pressing X. To set the foreground color and background color to the default colors (black and white), click the Default Colors icon or press D instead.

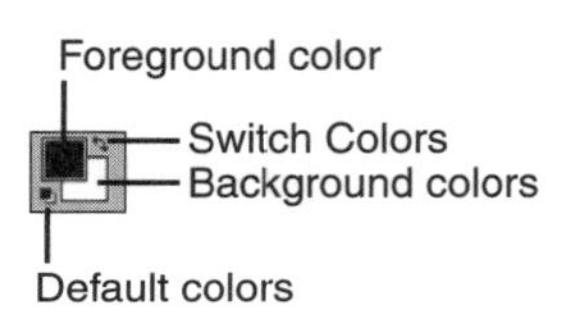

FIGURE 26.3
The current foreground and background colors appear at the bottom of the toolbox.

Using the Shape Tools

Using the various shape tools, you can create rectangles, ellipses (circles and ovals), lines, polygons (shapes with flat sides such as diamonds), and even custom shapes such as musical notes, dog paw prints, and word balloons. When you create a new shape, it's placed on a new layer by default. You can override this setting whenever you want to place more than one shape on a layer. You might want to group shapes this way to make them easier to format and place within an image.

You can also combine shapes on one layer to create a single shape. Or you can choose to display only the area where the shapes intersect, or to exclude this overlapping area. For example, if you draw a square and then add a second square that overlaps it partially, using the option to display only the area where the two shapes intersect, that intersecting area will be the only portion of the two squares that is retained. If you draw the second square using the exclude option, the only portions retained will be the areas where the shapes *do not* overlap.

To draw a shape, follow these general steps:

1. Click the Shape tool button (the fourth one down on the left; it looks like a blue pillow) and select the specific shape you want to draw, such as Rounded Rectangle, from the left end of the tool's Options bar. You can also select the shape you want to draw by clicking and holding down the Shape tool button and choosing a shape from the menu that appears.

2. Set your options on the Options bar. We'll discuss each of these options in a moment.
3. Drag in the image to create the shape. Typically, I click at the upper left and drag down and to the right to create a shape.

Changing the Style

The preceding steps describe how to draw a single shape using the current settings, which will typically draw the shape without a border, and filled with the color shown in the tool color swatch (which initially matches the foreground color).

But as you can see on the Shape tool's option bar (shown in Figure 26.4), there are many settings you can adjust. Some settings you can change after the fact, as you will see later in this section. But first, let's take a look at the settings you might change before you draw your shape.

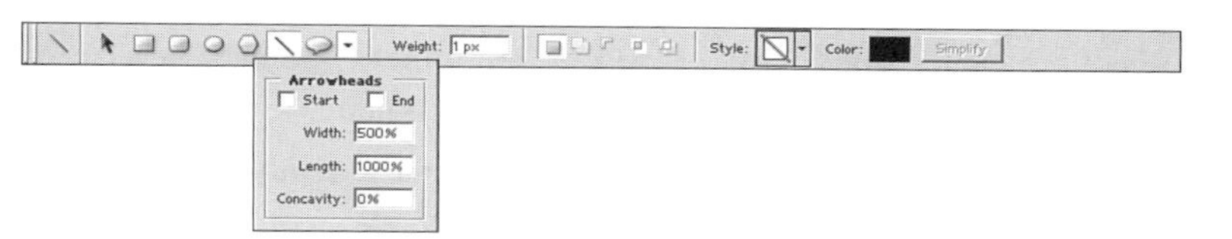

FIGURE 26.4
Set your options before drawing your shape.

The simplest option to change is whether or not the shape has a different style, such as a border of some sort, a shadow, or a textured fill. You select a style from the Style list (before or after drawing a shape—the Style setting affects the current selected shape, but if none is selected, it affects the shape you're about to draw), which is located toward the right end of the Options bar, as shown in Figure 26.4. Initially, the style is set to None, which means you'll get a shape filled with the tool color, and with no border. Click the down arrow on the Style list to reveal a group of styles, such as the Bevel styles, which add a bevel edge to a shape. You can display a different group of styles by clicking the right arrow at the top of the palette and choosing another set from the menu that appears. To return to drawing shapes without a style, select Remove Style from the menu.

You cannot use the Edit, Stroke command to add a border to a shape, as you can a selection or a layer. That's because the shape is editable. If you first simplify the layer on which you've drawn shapes (Layer, Simplify Layer), you can use one of the selection marquees to select the shape's outline and stroke it. But first try out some of the many style options explained here; you may find exactly what you're looking for, and with less trouble.

Setting the Geometry Options

You might also want to change the Geometry Options before (but not after) drawing a shape. These options control how a shape is drawn, and can help you draw a shape with more precision. The Geometry Options vary with the type of shape you've chosen from the left side of the Options menu. To display them, click the Geometry Options down arrow at the end of the shapes group, as shown in Figure 26.4.

The only way to explain the Geometry Options is to take them one shape at a time. The Rectangle, Rounded Rectangle, and Ellipse tools share similar Geometry Options:

- When you select Unconstrained, your dragging motion determines the shape.
- If you select Square or Circle, you can determine the size by dragging, but the shape will be drawn as a perfect square or circle.
- Select the From Center option to draw the shape from the center out, rather than from the upper-left corner to the lower-right corner.
- Select the Snap to Pixels option to help you draw a rectangle/rounded rectangle with borders that sit on the pixels' boundaries.
- To constrain the shape to a particular height/width, select Fixed Size and enter one or both values.
- To retain a particular proportion to the shape as you drag, select the Proportional option and enter the proportions in either or both boxes. The resulting shape will be proportionate to the size of the shape you drag to create. For example, if you enter a 2 in the W box and a 1 in the H box, your shape will be twice as wide as it is high.

The Rounded Rectangle tool has one other option on the Options bar itself, and that's Radius. The value you enter here determines the curve at the corners of the rectangle you draw.

The Polygon tool has its own set of Geometry options. The Radius value sets the exact distance from the center of the polygon to its corners; by changing this value, you can draw a polygon of an exact size. The Smooth Corners option renders a polygon with rounded corners rather than sharp angles. To draw a star, select the Star option. Then set related options: Indent Sides By sets the angle of the points by forcing the sides to fit the proportion you enter, and Smooth Indents adjusts the angle of the points even further, to lessen the inside angles. The Polygon tool has one other option, displayed on the Options bar but not on the Geometry Options palette: the Sides value. As you may have guessed, this tells Elements how many sides of equal length you want your polygon to have.

As you can see from the Geometry Options for the Line shape shown in Figure 26.4, you can add an arrowhead at the beginning or end of the line by choosing Start or End, or both. After turning on either arrowhead, set the arrowhead's width and length, which are proportionate to the width and length of the line itself. Curve the sides of the arrowhead by entering a Concavity value other than zero. The Line tool has one other option as well that is not shown on the Geometry Options palette, but appears on the Options bar: the Weight option, which controls the thickness of the line. Fat lines, by the way, are filled with the tool color.

Now that you know a bit about drawing each type of shape, let's discuss the other settings on the Options bar.

Drawing Additional Shapes

After drawing one shape, you may want to draw another. After all, most shapes are actually made up of many ellipses, rectangles, lines, polygons, and so on. To change to a different shape tool so you can draw a different shape, click the shape's button (located at the left end of the Options bar). Then change any Geometry Options you want, and change any additional settings we've already talked about. You're now ready to click in the image and drag to draw the new shape. Before you do, however, you might want to consider how that shape will affect the other shapes in your image.

The shape area buttons on the far right of the Options bar (see Figure 26.5) require a bit of explanation before you use them. The first button on the left is Create New Shape Layer. If this is selected (which it normally is by default), a new layer will be created automatically when you draw the shape. If you choose any other option, you'll draw the new shape on the current shape layer. The next button, Add to Shape Area, dictates not only that the shape you draw will appear on the current shape layer, but that the two shapes will be treated as one shape for the purposes of formatting, resizing, moving, and so on. If you select Subtract from Shape Area, the second shape will not be filled and the area where the two shapes overlap will be removed from the original shape. Think of this option as cutting away part of the original shape with a shape tool.

If you select Intersect Shape Areas, only the intersection of the two shapes is filled. If the second shape doesn't intersect the first, neither shape is filled. The last button, Exclude Overlapping Shape Areas, is the exact opposite; the area where the two shapes intersect is left unfilled, and other non-overlapping areas are filled.

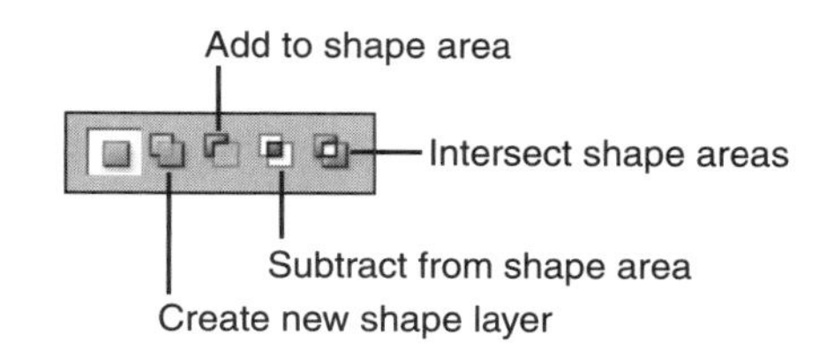

FIGURE 26.5
Use these buttons to control how a new shape affects other shapes.

There's one last thing you need to consider before you draw additional shapes: the fill color. When you draw your first shape, it's filled with the tool color shown in the color swatch at the right end of the Options bar. Initially, this color is set to the foreground color, but you can change it before you draw the shape in any of the ways discussed earlier.

When you're ready to draw additional shapes, *do not change the tool color or the style.* If you do, you'll change the fill color or style of the shape you just drew. Instead, draw the shape, and then, while it's still selected, change the color and/or style as desired.

Creating a Custom Shape

To create a custom shape, such as a rabbit, choose the Custom Shape tool from the Shape tools list. On the Options bar, open the Shapes list, and a palette of default shapes appears. If the shape you want to draw is not shown, click the right-pointing arrow to open a menu of other shape groups. To draw a rabbit, for example, click the arrow and select Animals. Then click the rabbit shape in the palette.

After selecting the custom shape you want to draw, set other options as desired, such as the color and shape area options. Then drag in the image to create a shape.

Selecting a Shape

Use the Shape Selection tool (the arrowhead pointer located to the left of the shape buttons on the Options bar) to select a shape so you can move, copy, delete, rotate, or resize it. Just click the tool and then click on the shape you want to select. Handles (small squares) appear around the selected shape, as shown in Figure 26.6. Drag the handles outward or inward to resize the shape. Dragging a corner handle maintains the *aspect ratio* (the width in relationship to the height). To change only the horizontal or vertical width, drag a side handle. To resize a shape by a certain amount (that is, to *scale* it), enter the appropriate values in the boxes on the Options bar. You can enter a value in the Set Horizontal Scale box, and click the Maintain Aspect Ratio button to automatically adjust the Vertical value by a proportionate amount. When you're done, set the check mark to commit the change.

Click the center handle (which looks like a cross) to move the shape. If you want to move all the shapes on a layer together, use the Move tool instead. Click the Move tool, then click anywhere on the shape layer. Drag the selection to move the shapes as a group.

You can also rotate a selected shape using the techniques you learned in Chapter 23, "Using Basic Tools in Elements."

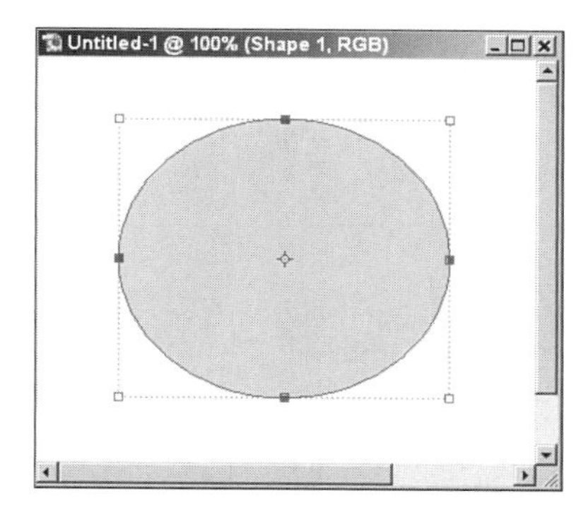

FIGURE 26.6
Handles appear around the selected shape(s).

Task: Create an Umbrella

TASK

We'll use the Shape tools to create a small object: an umbrella. Start a new image using default size, RGB color, and a white background.

1. Select the Ellipse shape tool. Select a bright color for your umbrella, such as blue or yellow. Make sure that the Create New Shape Layer option is selected.
2. Click in the image and drag to create an oval umbrella shape.
3. Click the Subtract from Shape Area option. Then click the Rectangle tool, and use it to cut out the bottom of the oval, flattening it.
4. With Subtract from Shape Area option still selected, select the Ellipse shape again. Draw small circles with the Ellipse tool that cut out portions of the flattened bottom of the umbrella shape, creating its scalloped edge. Your shape should look roughly like the one shown in Figure 26.7.

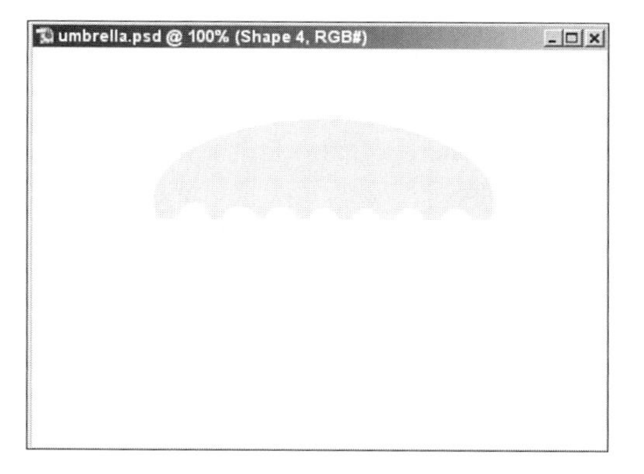

FIGURE 26.7
Our umbrella is taking shape.

5. Select the Rectangle tool and the Create New Shape Layer option.
6. Draw a small rectangle at the top of the umbrella. Draw a long, thin rectangle at the bottom of the umbrella for the handle.

Remember that you can move a selected shape by dragging it. This will help you get all the pieces of your umbrella in line. To select a shape, click on it with the Shape Selection tool.

7. Select the Ellipse tool, and draw a small circle at the base of the thin rectangle, creating the bottom of the curved handle.
8. Select the Subtract from Shape Area option, and draw a smaller circle slightly above the first circle, creating the upper part of the curved handle. At this point, your image has several layers; that's okay. Your umbrella should look roughly like the one shown in Figure 26.8.
9. Name your file umbrella.psd and save it. You will be refining it shortly.

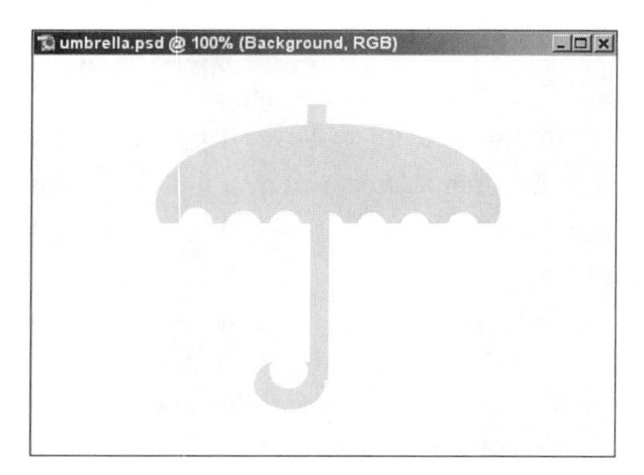

FIGURE 26.8
Let a smile be your umbrella.

Using the Brush Tool

With the Brush tool, you can paint color on an image with hard or soft brushes of various widths and degrees of opacity. There are also brushes with special tips, for painting with stars, grass, leaves, and other shapes. You can even imitate chalk, charcoal, hard pastels, oil pastels, dry brush, watercolor, oils, and other artistic techniques.

When you paint with the Brush tool, the paint is applied to the current layer, so make sure you change to the layer you want to use before painting.

Also, if you paint on a layer containing text or a shape, that layer will need to be simplified first, which means that the text/shape will no longer be editable. In such a situation, Elements will typically ask you if you want to simplify the layer, and all you'll need to do is click Yes to proceed. If you want to simplify a layer yourself, select it from the Layers palette and choose Layer, Simplify Layer.

Setting Brush Options

To use the Brush tool, click it and then choose the color you want to paint with (the foreground color). Set your options from the Options bar, shown in Figure 26.9. First, choose the brush tip you want from the drop-down list. Adjust the size as needed.

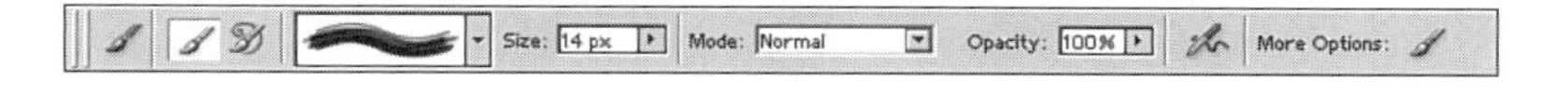

FIGURE 26.9
Set the brush options before you start.

Choose a blending mode and a level of opacity if you like. Blending is explained in detail later in the chapter. Opacity, as explained in Chapter 23, adjusts the strength of your paint—with a low opacity, the paint color will not cover any color or image beneath it. A higher opacity creates a more solid paint that covers any color or pattern you paint over.

If you click the Airbrush button, you'll be able to control the flow of paint by varying the amount of time you press the mouse button down and remain in one spot.

After making selections, paint with the brush by clicking on the image and holding the mouse button down as you drag. Release the mouse button to stop painting.

Painting with the Impressionist Brush

The Impressionist Brush doesn't paint, so you won't use it to create art. Instead, you use this brush to change the texture of an image to simulate the look of an impressionist painting or a pastel drawing. The effect is that the brush creates a wet paint–like pattern by borrowing the colors that are already present in the image. This makes the image look as if it were painted using a freestyle, pointillist technique, as shown in Figure 26.10.

26

FIGURE 26.10
Give your images the look of a classic painting with the Impressionist Brush.

To begin, click the arrow on the Brush tool and choose Impressionist Brush. Select a brush tip and size. A small brush tip works best for me, but feel free to experiment. Set the blending mode and opacity. The blending mode controls how the pixels painted by the brush are blended with the original pixels—again, you'll learn more about blending soon. If you want more definition in the finished image, set a low opacity value so the brush doesn't completely obscure the sharp edges in the image underneath.

Before you begin painting, click the More Options button to set these options: the Style menu controls the style of the brush stroke, from tight, short strokes to loose and curly strokes. The Area value controls the area of pixels painted by the brush. If you enter a large number, a large number of pixels surrounding the brush tip will be changed. A smaller area provides more control, but requires you to paint more strokes to change a large portion of an image. Finally, set the Tolerance level: With a low tolerance, you'll change only pixels that are very close in color to the ones you brush over. A higher Tolerance value allows more pixels in the designated area to be changed, as long as they are sufficiently similar to the pixels you paint over.

After setting options, drag over the image to change pixels of similar color within the designated area.

TASK

Task: Create Rain for Your Umbrella

There are many ways in which you might create a rain effect for an image. We'll use the Brush tool to create a simple effect.

1. If it's not already open, open the umbrella.psd file you created earlier.
2. Open the Layers palette and make the Background layer active.
3. Select the Brush tool. Choose a 14-pixel Spatter brush tip (You'll find Spatter near the middle of the brush tip list—just rest the mouse pointer on a brush tip style in the list, and its name appears). Use Normal blending mode, 100% opacity. Set the foreground color to a light grayish blue.
4. Draw diagonal lines close together, in the manner of wind-swept rain. Make sure you don't draw rain under your umbrella!
5. Click the Impressionist Brush button on the Options bar. Click the More Options button, and set the Style to Loose Medium, the Area to 20 pixels, and the Tolerance to 0.
6. Drag back and forth over your rain streaks, softening them. Your image will look something like the one shown in Figure 26.11.
7. Save the image and leave it open.

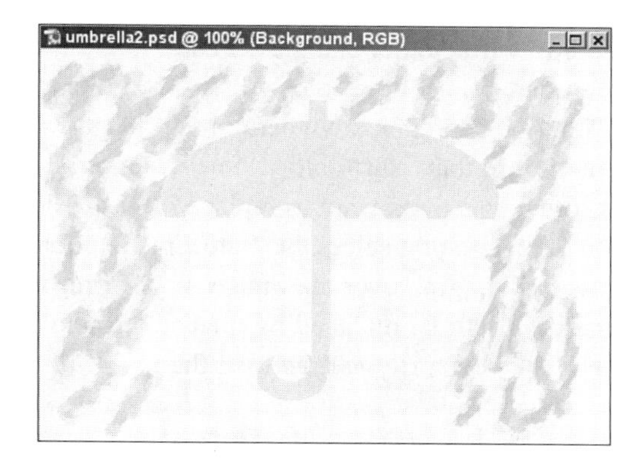

FIGURE 26.11
A little rain never hurt anybody.

Using the Pencil Tool

Using the Pencil tool is remarkably like using the Brush tool. With the Pencil tool, you can draw hard-edged lines on an image in your choice of color.

Setting Pencil Options

Simply click the Pencil tool and select a color by changing the foreground color. Select a pencil tip, adjust the width of the drawn line, set the blending mode, and change the opacity as desired. Then click on the image, hold the mouse button down, and drag to draw a line.

Selecting the same tip with the Brush tool and the Pencil tool produces different results, as you can see in Figure 26.12.

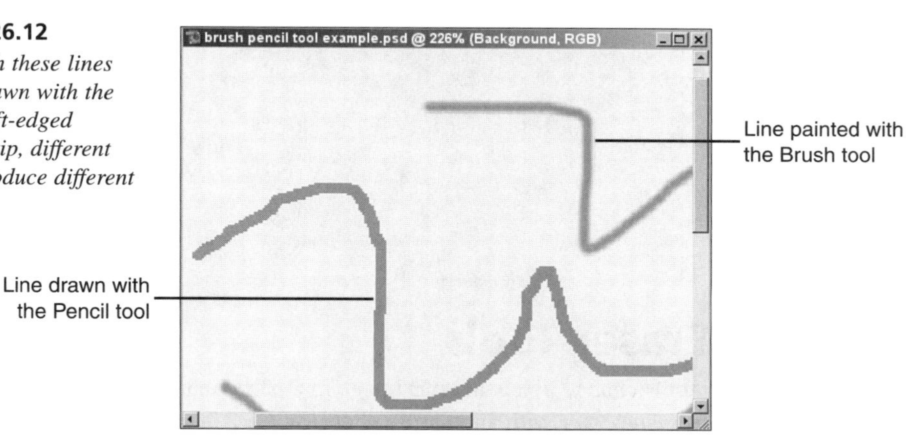

FIGURE 26.12
Although these lines were drawn with the same soft-edged 5-point tip, different tools produce different results.

Replacing One Color with Another

You can replace one color with another using the Pencil tool and the Auto Erase option. First, change the foreground color to the color you want to replace. Remember that, after opening the color picker, you can click anywhere in the image with the eyedropper pointer to "pick up" or choose that exact color. After selecting the color to replace, set the background color to the color you want to replace it with. Then choose your pencil tip and set your options. Be sure you select the Auto Erase option at the right end of the Options bar. Then draw by dragging over the image. If you drag over an area that contains the foreground color, it will be replaced by the background color. Other parts of the image will remain unaffected even if you drag over them.

Task: Adding Ribs to Your Umbrella

With the Pencil tool, it's easy to add ribs to your umbrella.

1. With the umbrella.psd file open, click the Pencil tool.
2. Create a new layer above the others.
3. Set the foreground color to one that's slightly lighter than the umbrella color, such as a light yellow or light blue.
4. Select the Hard Round brush tip style from the list, set the tip size to 3 pixels, and draw ribs from the top of the umbrella to each of its points. The result is a rather whimsical rendition of an umbrella in the rain, shown in Figure 26.13.
5. Save and close the image file.

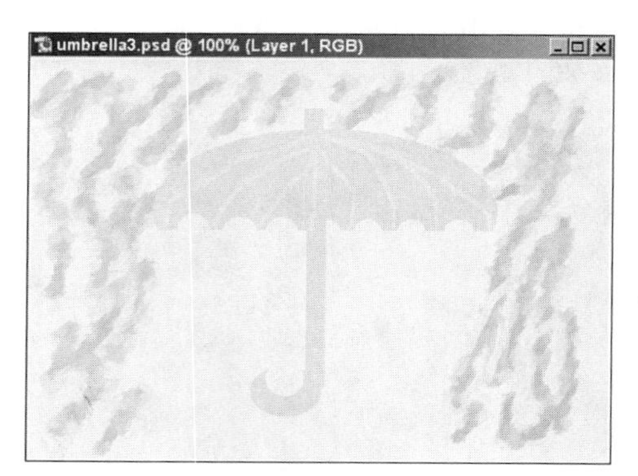

FIGURE 26.13
The final version of our umbrella.

Using the Eraser Tools

All of the Eraser tools change pixels in your image in a particular way. You've learned that you can replace one color with another by choosing the Auto Erase option and drawing with the Pencil tool. In this section, you'll learn about two of the other tools Elements provides for erasing parts of an image: the Eraser tool and the Background Eraser tool.

Erasing with the Eraser Tool

When you drag over pixels with the Eraser tool, the pixels are removed and made transparent, so lower layers can show through. If you use the Eraser tool on the Background layer or any other layer with locked transparency, the result is different. Instead of erasing pixels and making them transparent, the tool replaces the pixels you drag over with the background color.

To use the Eraser, activate the layer you want to erase a portion of, and click the Eraser tool. Select from one of three Modes: Brush (which provides a soft-edged brush tip), Pencil (which provides the harder-edged pencil tip), or Block (which provides a square blocky tip). If you choose Brush or Pencil, select the exact tip to use from the drop-down list and adjust the size. With the brush or pencil tips, you can also adjust the opacity to limit the strength of the eraser—a lower opacity level causes the brush to erase to only partial transparency or to the background color, depending on which level you are erasing on.

After setting options, click and drag on the image to erase pixels, as shown in Figure 26.14.

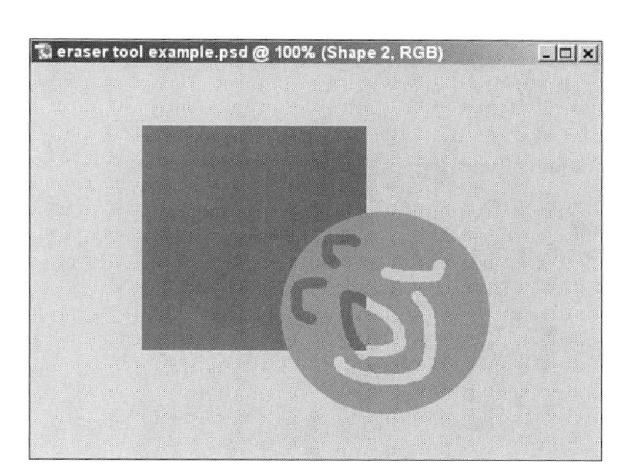

FIGURE 26.14
Erase on a layer and let the background shine through.

Erasing with the Background Eraser Tool

You use the Background Eraser to erase or remove the background from around an object without erasing part of that object in the process. The theory behind its operation is that an object's color generally differs greatly from the color of the background that surrounds it. As you click and drag the brush over the image, the Background Eraser continually samples the color under the *hotspot* (the small cross in the center of the tool's pointer), and sets that color as the background color. It then erases only colors that closely approximate this background color, over the entire area of the eraser.

You can safely set the eraser to a large size (the pointer will then look like a wide, transparent circle). The large size is safe to use, because the Background Eraser does not erase all the pixels in that circle (under the eraser); instead, it erases only the pixels within the circle that match or nearly match the one under the hotspot. To erase all the background pixels surrounding any object—for instance, a car on a street, or a single flower in a garden—you carefully drag the eraser with its hotspot *near*, but not *inside*, that object. If the circle area of the eraser should fall within the object's border, the object remains safe, so long as the hotspot rests over a color that's substantially different. So if you drag this eraser entirely around an object whose color stands out from its background, you'll erase only the background and leave the object intact.

To use the Background Eraser, click the arrow on the Eraser tool button and select it. Adjust the size of the eraser as desired, and then select one of the two options from the Limits menu. Contiguous erases pixels under the eraser that match the sampled color, and which are touching, or contiguous to, the hotspot itself. If you select Discontiguous instead, any pixel under the eraser whose color closely matches the sampled hue will be erased. You can control how closely pixels must match the sampled pixel by adjusting the Tolerance value. A lower value limits the number of pixels that will match the sampled pixel. A higher value allows you to erase a greater variety of pixels. After setting the options you want, click on the background to sample its color, then drag with the Background Eraser on the image to erase the background, as shown in Figure 26.15.

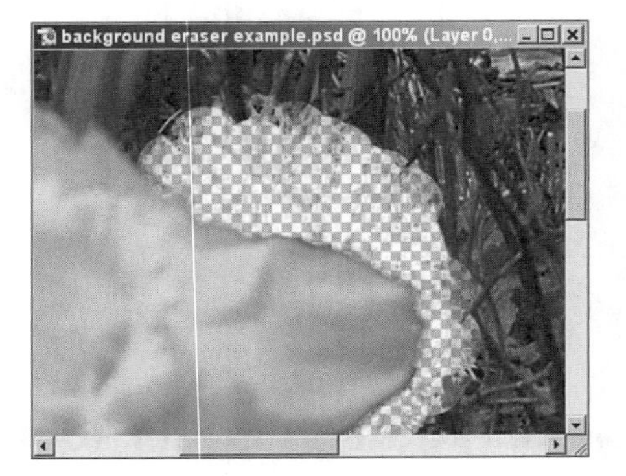

FIGURE 26.15
Use the Background Eraser to separate an image from its background.

Creating Backgrounds with the Gradient Tool

Gradients can be exceptionally useful tools when you're trying to suggest depth or shading or to make a smooth blend between two or more colors. Elements comes with a default set of 15 gradients, plus 8 more sets that you can load from the Presets folder. Of course, unless you are amazingly lucky, none of these gradients will do exactly what you need. That's why you may need to create your own, based on one of the existing gradients.

First, let's take a look at the existing gradients for use with the Gradient tool. Unlike the Gradient Map, which exchanges the colors in an image for the colors in the gradient, the Gradient tool fills a layer or a selection with the gradient you choose.

Select the Gradient tool—it's next to the Paint Bucket. You'll want to set your options on the Options bar before using the tool to create a gradient fill. When you click the down arrow next to the currently selected gradient, you'll open the Gradient palette, shown in Figure 26.16. Click the right-pointing arrow at the top-right corner of the palette to display a different category of gradients. If you can't find one that has exactly the right color combination and spacing, don't despair. At the very least you should be able to find one with the right number of colors.

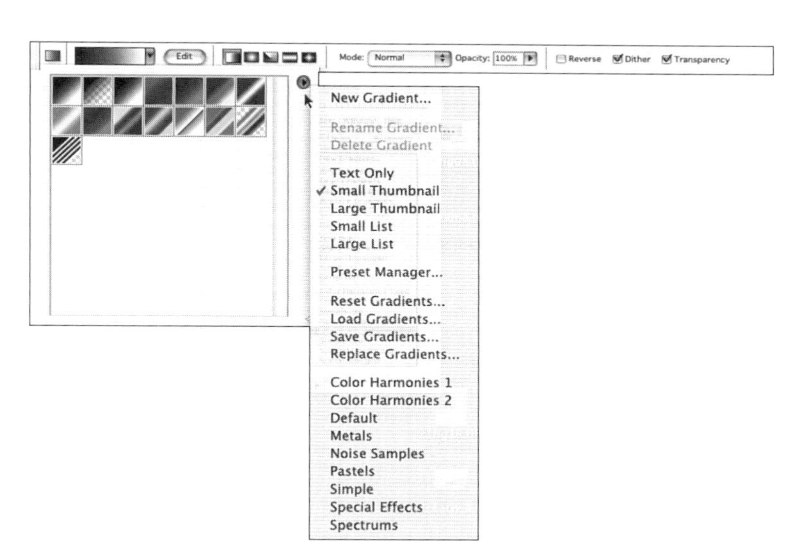

FIGURE 26.16
Choosing a gradient with the Gradient tool.

Suppose you want a three-color gradient that looks like a sunset. There's nothing quite right, but you can edit one. First, you need to select the gradient you want to work with from the palette. This gradient will replace whatever was previously on the Options bar. Now, click that gradient swatch or click the Edit button to open the Gradient Editor, shown in Figure 26.17.

Click the New button to add your gradient at the end of the palette and give it a name. Choose the gradient type from the pop-up menu. Solid makes the three colors change smoothly from one to the next. Noise gives you a random mixture of the three colors. It's an interesting effect, but not at all what you want for a sunset. See both in Figure 26.18.

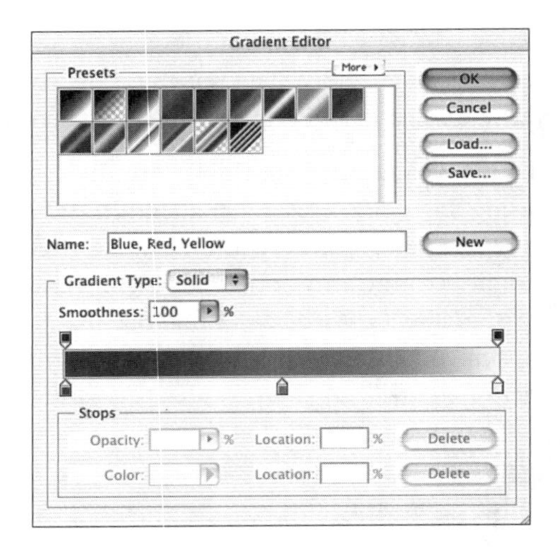

FIGURE 26.17
The Gradient Editor dialog box.

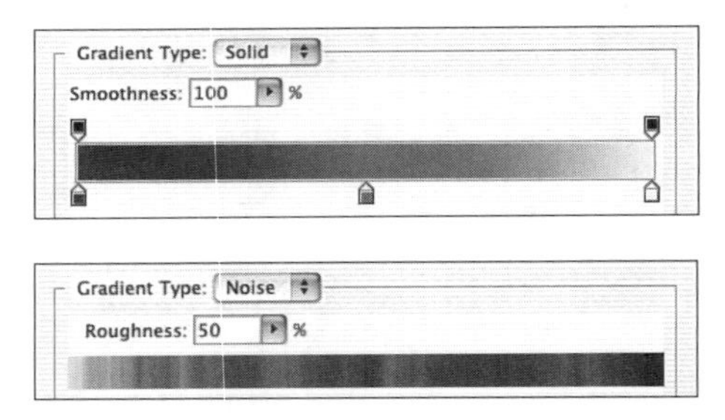

FIGURE 26.18
Solid and noisy gradients.

With the gradient type set to Solid, you'll notice tiny swatches with arrows that point to the gradient. They're called stops, and are rather like the stops on a church organ. Just as each stop on an organ adds another dimension to the sound, the stops on the gradient add color or change the opacity. The color stops are on the bottom and the opacity stops are on the top. Their purpose is to let you set the spot where one color changes to the next or where a gradient starts to go from completely opaque to some degree of transparency.

By changing opacity, you can build a gradient that totally covers whatever's under it at one end and is partially or completely transparent at the other end. It's useful for such tricks as adding a metallic highlight to make a shape appear round. You can go back to partial or complete opacity by adding more stops. To add a stop, click the point where you want the opacity to change at the top of the color strip.

To change the amount of opacity, either type a percentage into the Opacity field, or drag the slider. You'll see the swatch inside the stop change from black to gray to white as you turn that section of the gradient from opaque to transparent. In Figure 26.19, I've added a stop (shown above the gradient bar) that reduces the opacity to 25%. I've placed it at 60% of the distance between the two ends of the gradient. You'll notice that the swatch on that stop is now light gray, rather than black. There are also two diamonds, one on either side of the stop. These indicate the midpoint of the gradient change. You can move them by dragging, or by clicking one to select it and changing the percentage in the Location window. Remember that when you select a midpoint, the location indicates the position of the midpoint relative to the two stops on either side, not the beginning and end of the entire gradient.

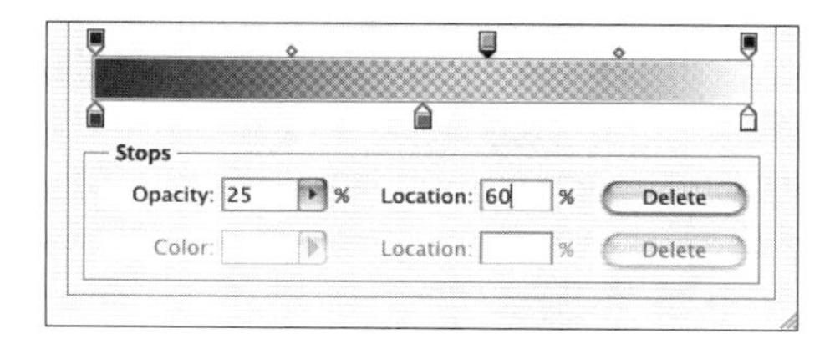

FIGURE 26.19
You can place as many stops as you need.

To get rid of a stop, simply click and drag it off the color bar. You can't remove the end stops, but you can move them in, if you want a shorter gradient. (That's why distances are measured in percentages, rather than in inches or centimeters.)

Changing and adding color stops works in much the same way. Click on a color stop (located below the gradient bar) to select it. The swatch color will appear below, in the Stops section of the dialog box, as in Figure 26.20. When you click the arrow on the swatch, a menu that allows you to select the current foreground or background color as a component of your gradient appears. The menu also has an option called User Color. Double-click on either the tiny swatch under the color bar or the larger one in the Stops area to open the Color Picker. Choose your color(s) by clicking on the color picker. If there's a shade somewhere in the gradient that you want to use as one of the gradient's base colors, first click on the stop you want to change to select it. Place the cursor on the color within the gradient that you want to use. The cursor then becomes an eyedropper. When you click the color, the stop changes to that color. You can also click with this eyedropper in the image to pick up a color from there.

26

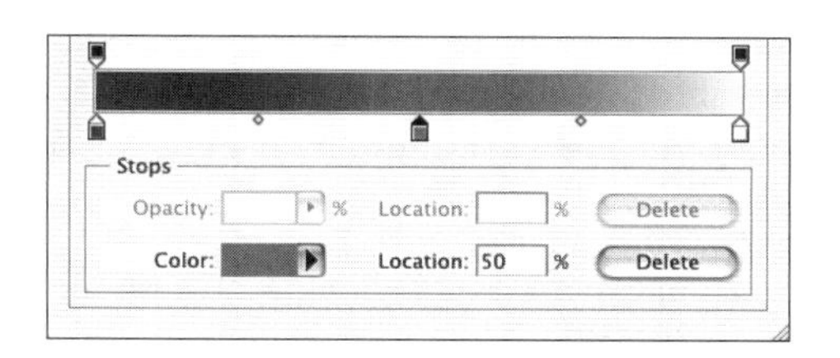

FIGURE 26.20
Changing a color stop.

Add more colors to your gradient by clicking below the bar to place additional color stops. If you have selected the foreground or background color from the menu, the new stop will be in that color. If you have selected User Color, the new stop will appear in the color closest to the spot where you have clicked.

Now that you've got precisely the gradient you want, you can save it permanently to the Gradient palette by clicking Save. You can reload the gradient file for use in a later session with Elements by clicking the right arrow on the Gradient palette and choosing Load Gradients. If you just want to use it once, click OK.

To apply the gradient, first select the gradient type you want, as shown in Figure 26.21 (enlarged and rotated so there's room for the labels). The Linear style is your standard blend from the start color to the end color. Although it shows the blend going from the top to the bottom of the layer/selection, you can actually blend from side to side or corner to corner as well. The direction of any gradient (regardless of the style you choose) is determined by a line you draw across the layer/selection—more on that in a moment.

FIGURE 26.21
Choosing a gradient.

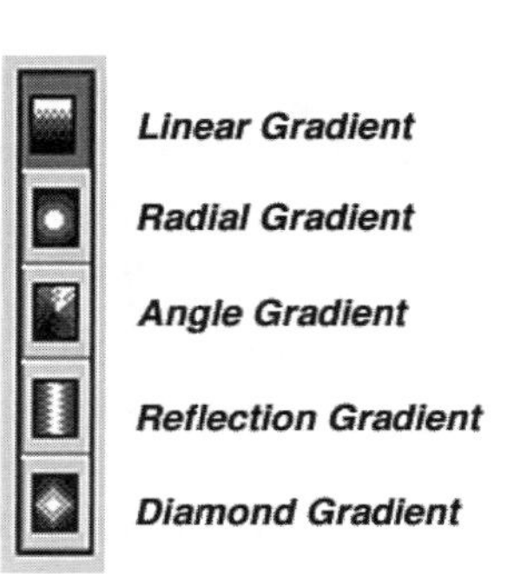

The next style, Radial, blends from the center out, in a circular pattern. If you draw the line from one corner or edge to another, you'll get a half-circle pattern, like a sunset. The Angle style divides the colors in the gradient in half, and then fans them out on both sides of the line you draw on the image to create the gradient. The Reflection style blends from the beginning of the line you draw to the end, and then repeats the blend in the other direction. So with this style, you should draw your line from some point near the center of the layer/selection out to an edge. The Diamond style is similar to the Reflection style, but it reflects the blend four times, creating a diamond in the center. Again, with this style, you should draw your line from the center of the layer/selection to a side or corner. Select the style you want to use by clicking on it, and you're ready to draw the gradient line.

Make sure the gradient that appears in the gradient swatch on the Options bar is the one you want to use, then draw a horizontal line from right to left or from left to right to create the blend, or draw a vertical or diagonal line to make it go in a different direction (see Figure 26.22). As noted earlier, with the Reflection or Diamond styles, you should start at a point somewhere within the layer or selection and draw to an edge. You might want to use this technique with the Radial style as well, so that the circle pattern will be in the middle of the layer/selection. Keep in mind that the start color is placed at the point where you begin to draw the line, and the end color appears at the line's end. For example, you might want to draw from a corner or an edge inward, to lay down the colors in the order you want. You can also reverse the start and end colors by selecting the Reverse option before drawing the line.

FIGURE 26.22
The gradient blends colors in the direction in which you draw.

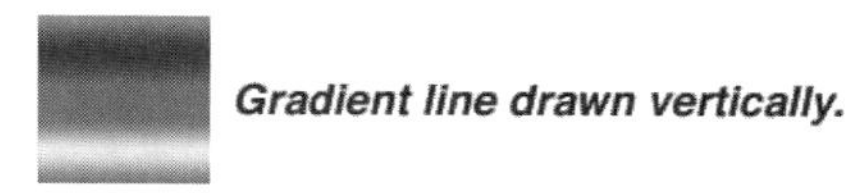

Note that when you draw a gradient line on a page, the gradient will fill the entire layer. If that's not your intention, use the selection tools to draw the shape you want, and then place the gradient within it.

You can fill type with a gradient if you use a type mask to create it or if you simplify the text layer and select the text. You can fill a shape or any other selection with a gradient as well. As with other aspects of Elements, the best way to learn how to handle gradients is to practice. You'll soon have gradients that make the grade.

TASK

Making Composite Images

Whenever you combine elements from more than one source, you're said to be making a composite. The process of creating a composite can include something as simple as adding a gradient, or as complex as making a montage of half a dozen pictures or images, plus type and effects. How you want to use the technique is up to you. Some people create wonderfully surrealistic photos. Others simply improve the composition by throwing extra sheep in the meadow or fish in the aquarium. Still others use it simply to put a drop shadow behind the type on a title page.

Using Layer Styles to Create Composites

Layer styles apply a style such as a shadow, bevel, or metallic fill to all the objects on a layer. There are 14 different kinds of layer styles, ranging from Bevels, Glows, and Drop Shadows to Glass Buttons, Patterns, and Wow Chrome. You can apply layer styles to any kind of object.

Before I tell you some of the ways you can use layer styles with objects to create composite pictures, let's review what we know about layer styles. A layer style is a special effect, and when you add it to a layer, it's applied to all the objects on that layer—text, shapes, or the outer edge of an image. So be sure to move objects you don't want affected to other layers before you proceed, and if working with an image, make sure you resize it so you can see the edge effect (if any) for the layer style you select. For example, you won't see a drop shadow on your image if that image takes up the entire layer.

Adding a layer style is fairly simple: First, change to the layer you want to affect by clicking its name in the Layers palette. Then, open the Layer Styles palette (Window, Layer Styles), choose a category from the list (such as Drop Shadow, Bevel, or Wow Chrome), and when the palette opens to display a list of the styles in that category, click on the thumbnail of the particular style you want to apply. The cursive *f* appears after the layer name on the Layers palette to remind you that the layer is using a layer style.

You can combine styles if you want. Some styles, you'll find, completely overlay any layer styles you have already applied, leaving few if any remnants of them. Others combine well to create interesting effects. The only way to know which layer styles work well together is to play around with various combinations and make note of the ones you like. To remove all styles from the current layer, click the Clear Style button at the top of the Layer Styles palette. There is no way, unfortunately, to remove one style without removing the rest, unless you want to remove the last style you applied, in which case you can simply click Undo.

Here's a quick summary of the various layer styles you can use. Most of them are probably best used with text, unless your idea is to create a rather surreal-looking image. However, you never know what layer style might prove useful, given a particular situation:

- **Bevels**—Puts a sharp or soft edge on the sides of an object. This edge appears to raise or lower the object above or below the surface of the layer. The emboss styles produce a softer effect than the bevel styles.
- **Drop Shadows**—Adds a soft- or sharp-edged shadow behind objects.
- **Inner Glows**—Adds a soft glow to the inner edges of objects, so they seem to glow inside.
- **Inner Shadows**—Adds a shadow to the inner edges of objects, so they seem to fall below the surface of the layer.
- **Outer Glows**—Adds a soft glow to the outside edges of objects.
- **Visibility**—Softens the fill color of objects, or hides them entirely. Click Show to redisplay the fill color at full saturation.
- **Complex**—Combines several layer styles to create a unique effect. There are too many styles here to list them all, but some of the more notable ones are Chrome—Fat, Molten Gold, Rivet, Star Glow, Diamond Plate, and Paint Brush Strokes.

- **Glass Buttons**—Fills an object with the color you choose, and makes it appear slightly opaque like glass and raised like a button.
- **Image Effects**—These layer styles are probably most useful for working with objects rather than text, although they can be applied to either. Here you'll find such things as Fog, Rain, Snow, Water Reflection, Night Vision, and Circular Vignette, which is similar to the vignette technique we used in Chapter 24, "Fixing Photo Flaws."
- **Patterns**—A collection of interesting textures you can apply, including fabric textures such as Batik, Satin Overlay, Tie-Dyed Silk, Blanket, and Denim; surface textures such as Painted Wallboard, Brushed Metal, Ancient Stone, Asphalt, Stucco, Marble, Brick Walk, Dry Mud, and Wood; and unique effects such as Nebula, Abstract Fire, and Smoke. There are too many to mention them all, so be sure to check out this category.
- **Photographic Effects**—From their name, you can probably guess that these layer styles are especially well suited for working with images. Here you'll find such styles as Negative, Sepia Tone, and Teal Tone.
- **Wow Chrome**—Applies various chrome textures to objects. I like the Wow Chrome—Shiny Edge the best, especially when combined with Wow Chrome—Reflecting.
- **Wow Neon**—Adds a neon-like glow in your choice of colors. The neon tubing can appear to be either on or off, depending on your selection. When you apply these styles, the fill color is removed from any objects.
- **Wow Plastic**—Replaces the fill color with plastic in your choice of colors. This layer style is similar to, but not the same as, the Glass Buttons style.

In the example in Figure 26.23, I've applied various layer styles to a simple rectangle shape. I simply created the rectangle on one layer, and then used Layer, Duplicate Layer to copy it several times. After each copy, I used the Move tool to move each rectangle into a unique position within the image so I could see them all. Then I applied one Drop Shadow layer style plus a layer style of some other category to each rectangle so I could compare the effects. How many can you identify? The rectangle I drew was bright yellow. Notice how some of the styles completely replaced the fill color, while other styles look as if they are laid on top of the color.

You can add a layer style to text if that text is on its own layer; otherwise, all objects on the layer will be affected. You can add layer styles to shapes as well. You can also create the effect of painting or drawing with a texture layer style if you do the following: First, fill a layer with a textured layer style such as one of the Patterns (Bumpy, Stucco, or Manhole, for instance). Create a new layer above this patterned layer. Select the Brush or

Pencil tool, and choose the Clear blending mode. Then paint or draw as usual. You'll notice that instead of painting with the foreground color, you're actually erasing pixels, allowing the texture on the layer below to show through. If you later remove the layer style from the bottom layer, the paint or drawn line will appear in the foreground color you used originally, instead of the pattern.

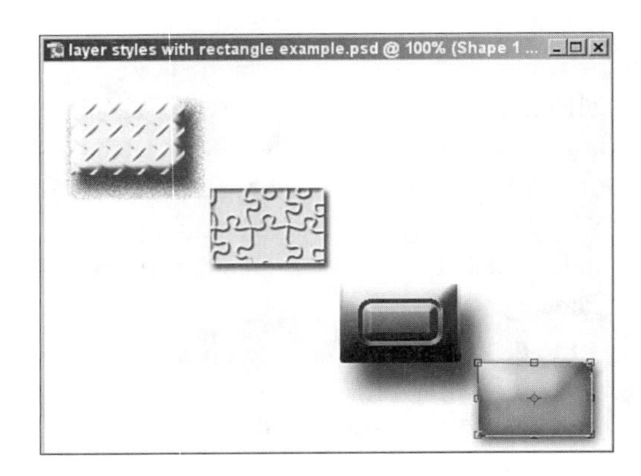

FIGURE 26.23
Which style do you like best?

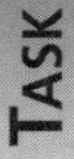

Task: Add Layer Styles and Adjustment Layers to Our Umbrella

To practice what we know about layer styles and refresh our memory of adjustment layers (see Chapter 24 for information), let's edit the image of the umbrella in the rain.

1. Open the umbrella.psd file you created earlier.
2. Change to the background layer. Select a rainy-day medium bluish gray as the foreground color, and use the Paint Bucket tool to fill the background with paint. This will cover over the rain we created earlier, but we'll add it back with a layer style.
3. Open the Layer Styles palette (Window, Layer Styles). Select the Image Effects category, and click the Rain thumbnail. You'll be asked whether you want to make the background a regular layer; click OK to proceed. Type Rain in the Name box and click OK. The image should look like Figure 26.24.
4. Well, not bad. But I'd like to darken the sky a bit without darkening the umbrella. If I use the Enhance, Adjust Brightness/Contrast, Brightness/Contrast command right now, it will only darken the rain layer, and not the umbrella. However, I'd like to prevent the sky *under* the umbrella from getting darkened as well, so let's use an adjustment layer instead. First, select the area under the umbrella using the Rectangular Marquee tool. We don't have to worry if we select any part of the umbrella, because it won't be affected by the adjustment layer anyway.

FIGURE 26.24
Rain, rain, go away.

5. Because any part we don't select will be masked when we create the adjustment layer, choose Select, Inverse to invert the selection and place the marquee around the entire sky except for the area under the umbrella.
6. Choose Layer, New Adjustment Layer, Brightness/Contrast. You can change the name of the new layer if you want, but I think I'll just leave it. We don't need to turn on the Group with Previous Layer option because the rain layer is the only layer below this one, so just click OK.
7. Drag the Brightness slider to the left, darkening the sky so that it's almost night, but not quite. I set my Brightness at –22. Click OK. The result is shown in Figure 26.25.

FIGURE 26.25
Well, at least I'm staying dry.

Understanding Blending Modes

In the real world, when you place a second brush full of paint over paint that's already there, the effect depends on the color of the paint you're applying, how opaque it is, whether the first layer is wet or dry, and so on. In Elements, you can control all these factors by using what are called *blending modes*. Blending modes apply to layers (controlling a layer's effect on the layers below it) as well as to all tools that can draw or paint, including the Brush, Pencil, Clone Stamp, and Paint Bucket, just to name a few. You'll find the tool blending modes on the Mode menu on the Tool Options bar, and the Layer blending modes on a similar menu on the Layer palette, as shown in Figure 26.26. As you can see, there are quite a few different modes. Not all are available with all the tools. Let's take a quick look at the blending modes and what they do.

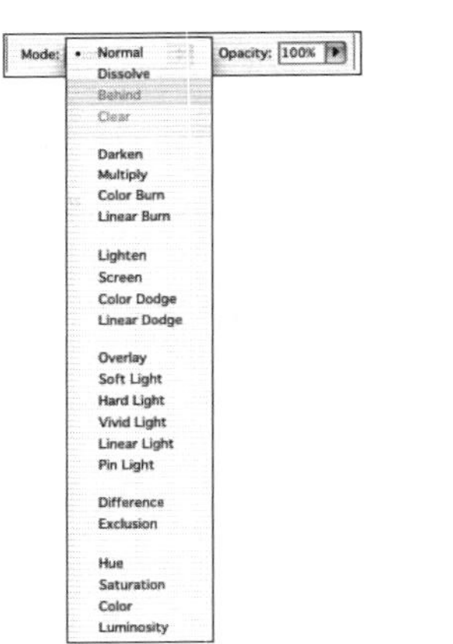

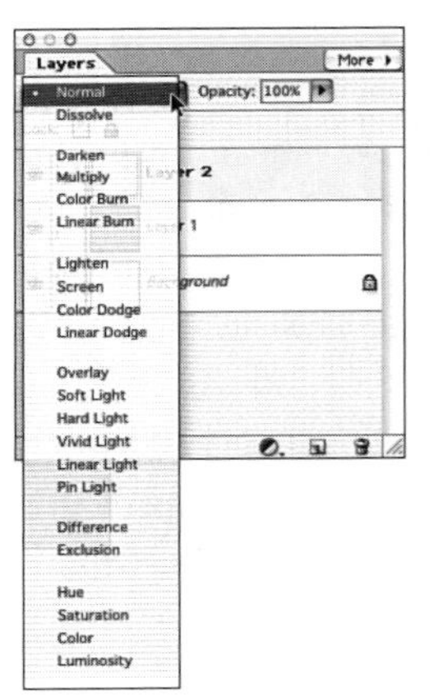

FIGURE 26.26
The Tool Options list here shows the Brush blending modes.

Suppose that you're working with only two colors. One is the *base* color—the one that's already in place. The second is the *blend* color—the color that you're applying with your tool, or the color on the layer(s) below the one whose blending mode you're adjusting. Depending on the blending mode you choose, you get a third color, a *result* that varies according to how you blend the first two.

Figures 26.27–26.49 show what happens when you choose each of the blending mode options. (The examples were painted with a firm brush in hot pink on a lime green background.) In most cases, the blending mode was applied to the pink brush on a single layer. Where the results of applying the blend to a separate layer are different, I have shown both. Please be sure to see these in color, as it's difficult in some cases to see what's happening in black and white.

FIGURE 26.27
Normal—*This is the default mode. The blend color replaces the base color.*

FIGURE 26.28
Dissolve—*A random number of pixels are converted to the blend color. This option gives a splattered or "dry brush" effect.*

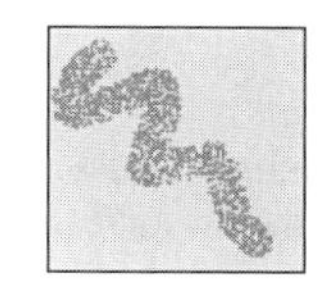

FIGURE 26.29
Dissolve—*Applied with a normal brush to a second layer at 50% opacity.*

FIGURE 26.30
Darken—*Evaluates the color information in each channel and assigns either the base color or the blend color, whichever is darker, as the result color. Lighter pixels are replaced, but darker ones don't change.*

FIGURE 26.31
Multiply—*Multiplies the base color by the blend color, giving you a darker result color. The effect is like drawing over the picture with a Magic Marker. Where the background is light, you see the original blend color.*

FIGURE 26.32
Color Burn—*Darkens the base color to match the value of the blend color. This effect is very subtle.*

FIGURE 26.33
Linear Burn— *Darkens the base color to reflect the blend color by decreasing the brightness. Blending with white produces no change.*

FIGURE 26.34
Lighten—*Evaluates the color information in each channel and assigns either the base color or the blend color, whichever is lighter, as the result color. Darker pixels are replaced, but lighter ones don't change. This is the exact opposite of Darken.*

FIGURE 26.35
Screen—*Multiplies the base color by the inverse of the blend color, giving you a lighter result color. The effect is like painting with bleach. I drew the hearts with the brush set to Wet Edges.*

FIGURE 26.36
Color Dodge—*Brightens the base color to match the value of the blend color.*

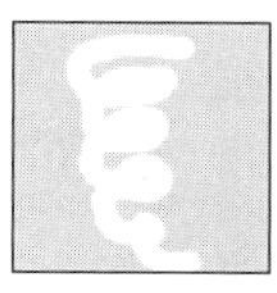

FIGURE 26.37
Linear Dodge—*Brightens the base color to reflect the blend color by increasing the brightness. Blending with black produces no change.*

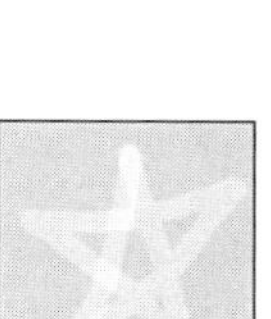

FIGURE 26.38
Overlay—*Evaluates the color information in each channel and assigns either the base color or the blend color, whichever is darker, as the result color. Lighter pixels are replaced, but darker ones don't change.*

FIGURE 26.39
Soft Light—*Darkens or lightens depending on the blend color. The effect is said to be similar to shining a diffused spotlight on the image. With a light blend color, it has very little effect.*

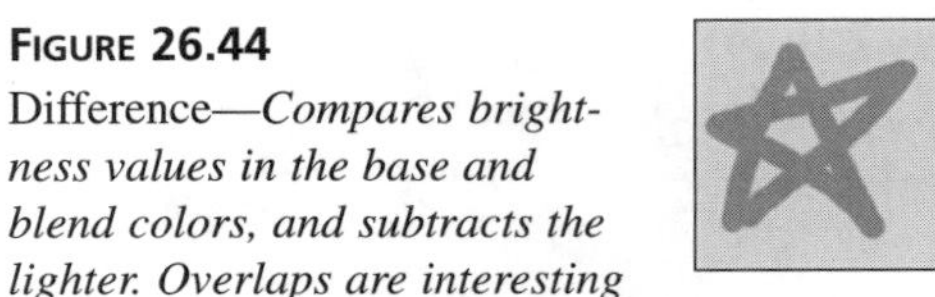

FIGURE 26.40
Hard Light—*Multiplies or screens the colors, depending on the blend color. The effect is similar to shining a harsh spotlight on the image.*

FIGURE 26.41
Vivid Light—*Burns or dodges the colors by increasing or decreasing the contrast, depending on the blend color. If the blend color (light source) is lighter than 50% gray, you can lighten the image by decreasing the contrast. If the blend color is darker than 50% gray, you can darken the image by increasing the contrast.*

FIGURE 26.42
Linear Light—*Burns or dodges the colors by decreasing or increasing the brightness, depending on the blend color. If the blend color (light source) is lighter than 50% gray, you can lighten the image by increasing the brightness. If the blend color is darker than 50% gray, you can darken the image by decreasing the brightness.*

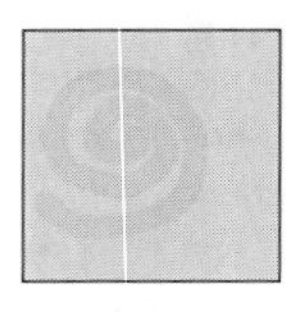

FIGURE 26.43
Pin Light—*Replaces the colors, depending on the blend color. If the blend color (light source) is lighter than 50% gray, pixels darker than the blend color are replaced and pixels lighter than the blend color do not change. If the blend color is darker than 50% gray, pixels lighter than the blend color are replaced and pixels darker than the blend color do not change. This is useful for adding special effects to an image.*

FIGURE 26.44
Difference—*Compares brightness values in the base and blend colors, and subtracts the lighter. Overlaps are interesting in this mode. They cancel the previous action.*

FIGURE 26.45
Exclusion—*This is similar to the Difference mode, but has a softer effect.*

FIGURE 26.46
Hue—*Gives you a result combining the luminance and saturation of the base color and the hue of the blend color.*

FIGURE 26.47
Saturation—*Gives you a color with the luminance and hue of the base color and the saturation of the blend color. Unless you reduce the saturation of the blend color significantly, nothing shows.*

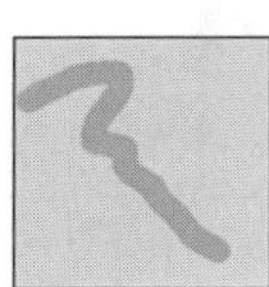

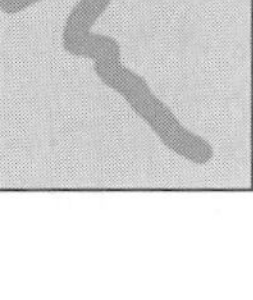

FIGURE 26.48
Color—*Combines the luminance of the base color with the hue and saturation of the blend color. This option is useful for coloring monochrome images because the Color mode retains the gray levels.*

FIGURE 26.49
Luminosity—*Gives a result color with the hue and saturation of the base color and the luminance of the blend color. This mode and the Color Blend mode produce opposite effects.*

Spend some time playing with the effects of darken, lighten, and dissolve. These seem to be the ones I use the most.

Applying Effects

Effects are a time-saver. There's really nothing included in the Elements effects package that you couldn't do yourself from scratch, but why bother, when applying an effect is so simple? In all, there are 51 effects on the palette. Figure 26.50 shows some of them.

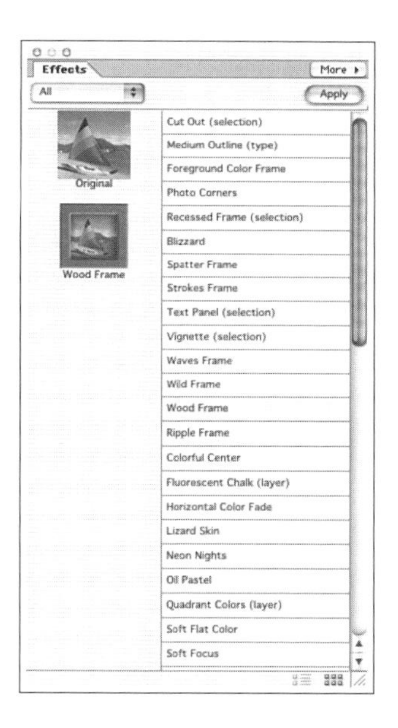

FIGURE 26.50
A piece of the Effects palette.

In the palette, you can view each effect's result, as it is applied to the sample image marked "Original." To apply an effect, double-click it, or click the thumbnail and then click Apply.

As you browse through the effects list, you'll notice that some of the effects are labeled "(Text)." These effects can be applied to text on a text layer, but not to text created using a text mask. Some effects are labeled "(Selection)," and can only be applied to a selected area. Some are labeled "(Layer)," and can only be applied to an entire layer. Finally, some effects can only be applied to a flattened image. When you choose them, you'll be asked whether you want to flatten your image. Click OK to proceed.

To limit the display of effects in the palette, select a category from the drop-down list. Here's a description of the various categories:

- **Frames**—Adds a frame around the edge of the current layer or a selection (if the effect is marked with the "(Selection)" label).
- **Textures**—A collection of various textures. The effect is applied to a new layer above the current layer, but it can be partially masked by a selection first.
- **Text Effects**—Effects suitable only for use on a text layer.
- **Image Effects**—Effects applied to a copy of the current layer. If you combine several image effects, you may be prompted to flatten the image before proceeding.

Some effects create extra layers; some don't. Adding the Rusted Metal effect to an image makes it look as if it's covered in reddish-orange rust. Actually, Rusted Metal and some of the other image effects simply add a layer filled with color and pattern. If you really want to see your image through the rust, you must go to the Layers menu and change the layer opacity so the image under the effects layer shows through. This is also a really good time to play with layer blending modes. In Figure 26.51, I've applied rust to a picture of rocks on the beach, changed the opacity so we could actually see the rocks, and chosen Overlay as a blending mode. The results are a lot more interesting than either the original or the effect as it was first applied.

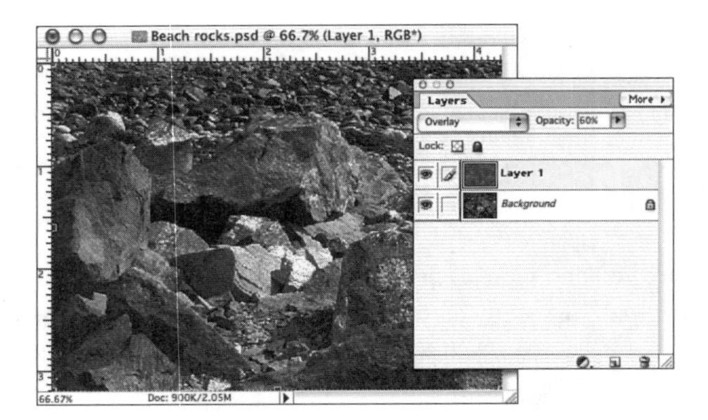

FIGURE 26.51
Effects don't turn into art until you work with them.

The biggest drawback to using effects is that, with the exception of layer opacity and blend modes, there is no way to customize them. The wood grain in the frame always runs in the same direction and is always the same sort of light oak. The Glass effect is only available in one color combination, and you can't even preview it. However, because a lot of the effects are simply filters or combinations of filters, you may be able to achieve a similar effect with customized results by applying the filters manually. As an effect is applied, you can see the various steps involved, including the names of any filters. So just as you wouldn't buy a "one size fits all" bathing suit, don't feel that you have to be stuck with an all-purpose effect.

Creating Drop Shadows from Scratch

According to my friend Scott Kelby, editor of *Photoshop User Magazine*, type *always* needs a drop shadow applied. Personally, I always try to steer clear of words such as *always* and *never*, but you can certainly improve most type with a little shadow. Here's a quick way to apply a shadow without using a Drop Shadow layer style. (You might not be able to use a layer style in some cases, but this method always works.)

First, set your type. Make a copy on a new layer (Layer, Duplicate Layer). Slide the duplicate under the original until it's in a good position for a shadow. Reduce the layer opacity to about 20% or whatever looks right to you. Add some blur (Filter, Blur, Gaussian Blur) and you have a drop shadow (see Figure 26.52).

FIGURE 26.52
A simple but effective drop shadow.

Just a shadow,
in an alley...

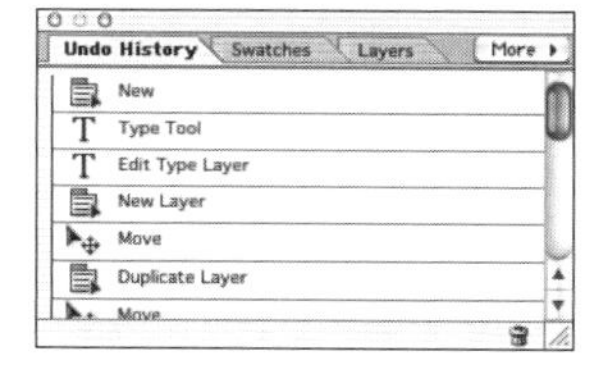

Adding shadows to type is easy. How about adding shadows to objects? That's really not much more difficult. In Figure 26.53, I have selected an object and set my foreground color to gray so I can create a light shadow.

FIGURE 26.53
Select your object first.

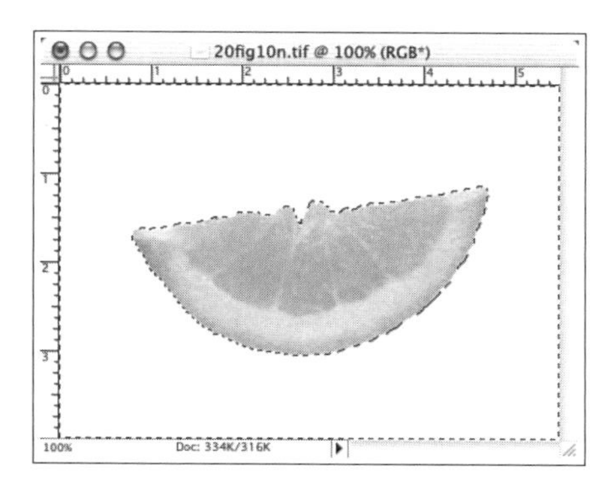

I duplicate the layer, then select the background using the Magic Wand and invert the selection so the lemon slice is highlighted. Then I feather the selection by 10 pixels. The next part is a tiny bit tricky. Select the Paint Bucket tool, and make sure your preferred shadow color is the foreground color. Position the tool just outside the edge of the lemon

26

and click once. Figure 26.54 shows the resulting shadow. For a larger one, set the feather distance to a larger number. Although you can add a shadow to an object using one of the Drop Shadow layer styles, you can't get the light directly above an object with the shadows on all sides, as shown here, and you can't change the shadow color. Learning how to create these effects yourself will come in handy some day, believe me.

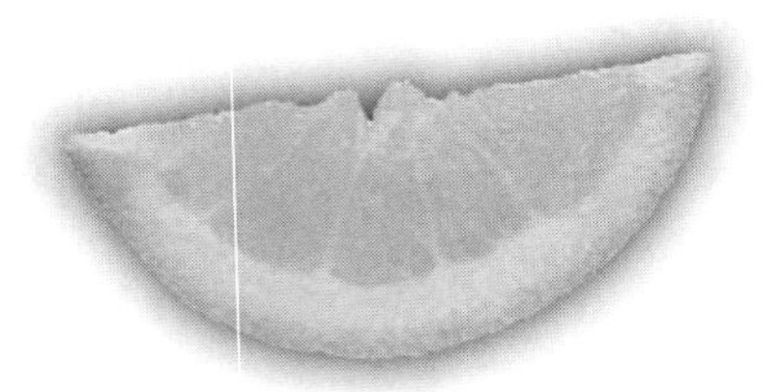

FIGURE 26.54
This time I left the shadow centered on the lemon.

Glows are basically colored shadows, and they usually extend on all sides of an object like the shadow shown in Figure 26.54. To create a glow from scratch, follow the steps you'd use to make a shadow, but choose a light or bright glow color.

Making Reflections

Let's stop and reflect for a moment. Adding a reflection to an object can make it seem more three-dimensional, because, like a shadow, a reflection interacts with the space around the object.

Figure 26.55 shows a very basic reflection. All I did was duplicate the type on another layer and flip it 180 degrees. This makes it look as though the word is sitting on a floor that has a reflective surface. I blurred the reflection a little because my floors are never really clean.

FIGURE 26.55
This kind of reflection is used for water, shiny floors and tabletops, and sheets of ice.

Reflections can face forward or backward, depending on the position of the reflective surface. Sometimes they can do both. The simplest reflections are created by flipping a layer 90 or 180 degrees. More complicated reflections, such as the ones shown in Figures 26.56 and 26.57, are a matter of applying transform, skew, and perspective until you get what you need. See Chapter 23 for help in making these transformations.

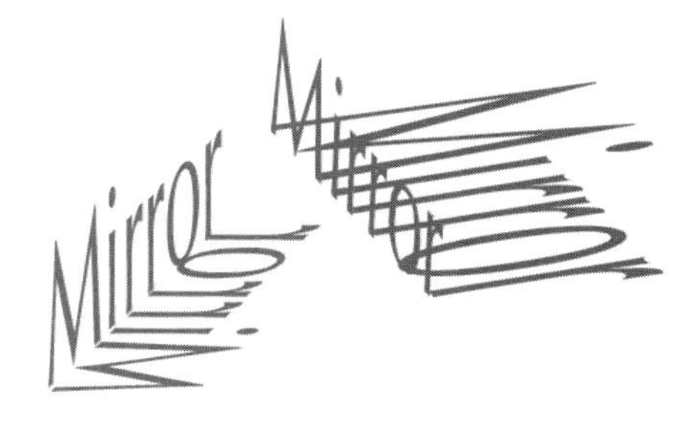

FIGURE 26.56
One reflection in each direction.

FIGURE 26.57
And one in both directions at once.

Using Distortions to Blend Composite Images

Distortions are mainly used when you need to wrap something around something else. You can stretch type around a can of soup or show how a design will look on a mug. This kind of composite is more practical than artistic. If you're wrapping type, you may be able to use the Warp Text button. Otherwise, if you're trying to wrap an image or shape around an object, Distort (or possibly Skew) is what you need. Let's try warping some type around a can.

In Figure 26.58, I've drawn a can and set some type to go on it.

FIGURE 26.58
A basic can of beans.

After looking at the available Type Warp styles on the Horizontal Type tool's Options menu shown in Figure 26.59, I realize that I need to choose Arch, rather than Arc, so all three lines will be set on the same curve. (Arc sets them in a fan shape with the bottom line smallest and everything fanning outward.)

FIGURE 26.59
There are lots of warp choices.

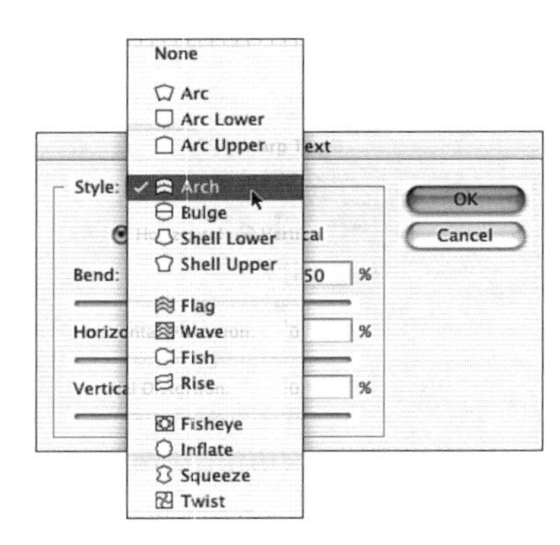

When I slide the words into place, the default bend amount is obviously too much. The can has less than a 50% bend. By gradually reducing the bend of the text using the Bend slider in the Warp Text setting dialog box, and comparing the angle of the top word with the angle of the top of the can, I can get a fairly accurate curve for the letters. Figure 26.60 shows the curved letters.

FIGURE 26.60
Align the letters with the top of the can.

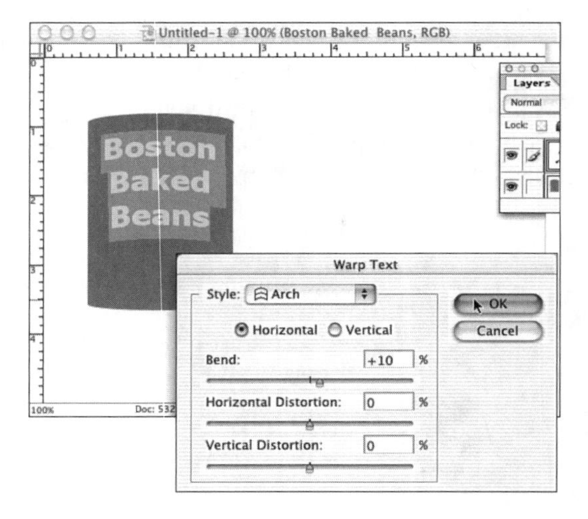

Now, all we need to finish up the job is a little glow around the letters to emphasize them, the company logo (also with a glow), and a gradient on the can to add some more roundness. In Figure 26.61, we've put it all together.

FIGURE 26.61
The finished can. It looks good enough to eat.

Putting type on a box is also easy to do by eye. Draw the box. Set the type in two pieces so you can maneuver each piece separately. Align the first piece of type to the lower-left edge of the box using the Skew command. Move it around until it looks correct. Then do the same for the rest of the type. My effort appears in Figure 26.62.

FIGURE 26.62
Remember that the type needs to remain vertical and should be skewed in one direction only.

Next, I'll try a can with an image on it. I could use Distort to twist the image to fit, but because my shape is a can (essentially a cylinder), I can use the 3-D Transform filter (Filters, Render, 3D Transform). The result appears in Figure 26.63.

FIGURE 26.63
Add an image to a can if you can.

Summary

With the drawing tools in Elements, it's easy to create simple images such as logos and clip art, or to edit an existing graphic so that it suits your needs more exactly. The options for each tool give you control, while allowing you the freedom to experiment as you wish. And, through the use of gradients, layer styles, effects, blending and distortions, you can create complex images without the use or photographs.

PART IV

Advanced System Management

Chapter

CHAPTER 27

Sharing (and Securing) Your Computer

Now that you've learned how to use multimedia applications, including the iLife suite and Photoshop Elements, it's time to return focus to your operating system and some topics dealing with advanced system management. The chapters in this section are more challenging than in the previous ones, but with powerful tools such as your Macintosh often come complex features and their related upsides and downsides.

In this chapter, our attention will be on sharing your system and files with others and the flip side of that, protection from unwelcome visitors. First, we'll delve into how to set up your computer so other users can have their own space. We'll then look at the ways that you can share files from your Mac. (You'll also learn how to connect to other computers that are sharing their files.) Our last topic will be security, both local and online, where you will learn some ways to protect your computer from unauthorized users.

Sharing Your Computer with Multiple Users

As you've heard in previous chapters, Mac OS X is a true multiuser operating system because everyone who works on the computer has a separate, private area in which to store personal files. While you don't have to make use of the multiuser capabilities of your Mac, they affect the system's structure which may require special attention, in terms of both their benefits and problems.

Understanding User Accounts

In a multiuser system, everyone who works on the computer can have a separate account. In practice, that means when one user saves a document to the desktop, it does not appear on the desktop that the other users see when they sit down to use the same computer. Also, each person can set system preferences that show up only when he or she is logged in. Users can customize the Dock and the desktop appearance and expect them to remain that way.

An interesting feature of multiuser operating systems has to do with remote access. Because the operating system assigns a separate desktop to each account, multiple people can use files on a single computer at the same time. Although this requires connecting to the machine from another computer and enabling remote login, the OS is designed to cope with different simultaneous processes so that users can work as though they were alone on the system. We'll take a look at remote login later in this chapter.

The home folders for user accounts are located in the Users folder of the Mac OS X hard drive, as shown in Figure 27.1. A house icon is used in the Finder window toolbar to represent the current user's home folder. Inside the home folder are several different folders, which were discussed briefly in our look at the Finder's file system during Chapter 2, "Exploring the Desktop."

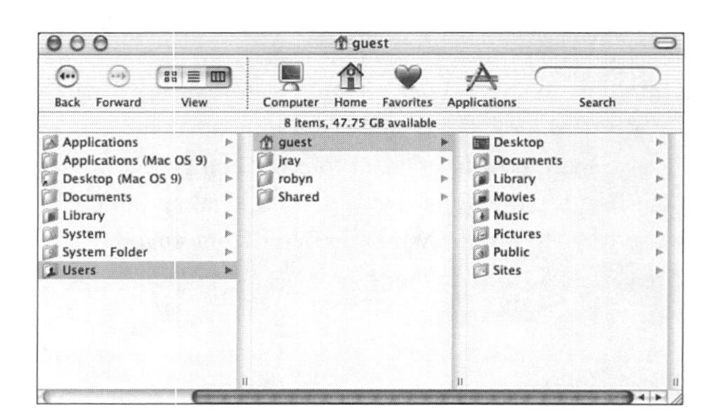

FIGURE 27.1
Every user has a home folder in which to store his or her files.

Although individual users can see the contents of most files on the hard drive, they might not be able to see each other's files. That's because users in a multiuser system can set permissions on their files that restrict access to keep their work private. They can specify whether a file can be read or altered by everyone, by a limited number of other people, or only from within the account in which the files were created.

For example, Figure 27.2 shows what the home folder of the user `robyn` looks like to another user. Most of the folders have an icon with a red circle containing a minus sign. That means these folders are not accessible from user accounts which did not create, or own, them.

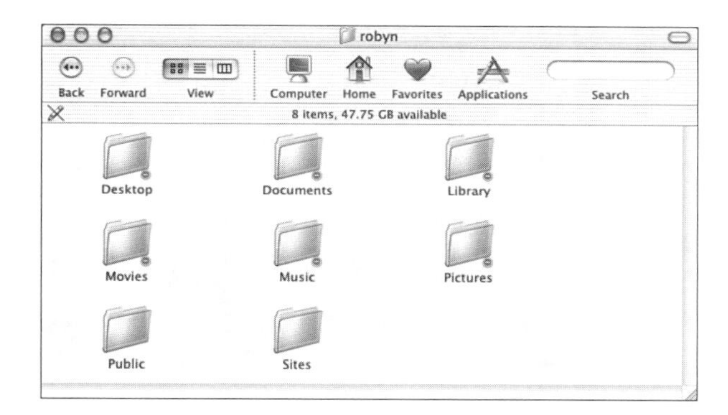

FIGURE 27.2
By default, other users are restricted from accessing all but the Public and Sites folders.

You can change the permissions on a file or folder that you own under the Users and Permissions section of the Get Info panel (Commmand-I). We discuss how later in this chapter.

Adding and Removing Users

When you first installed Mac OS X, an account was created using the name you supplied. The system uses the short name you gave as your account name, but you can use either your full or short name to log in to the system at the console. Because this account can access system settings and install new software, it's referred to as an *administrator account*.

When logged in with an administrator account, you're granted the privilege of adding other users and you can choose to give them administrative privileges as well. Remember, that means other people can add new accounts and modify the system, so you should be cautious about creating other administrative accounts. Be sure that you trust your users not to delete important files or disrupt the system in other ways before you give them administrator privileges.

New user accounts are added from the Users pane of the Accounts Preferences panel, shown in Figure 27.3.

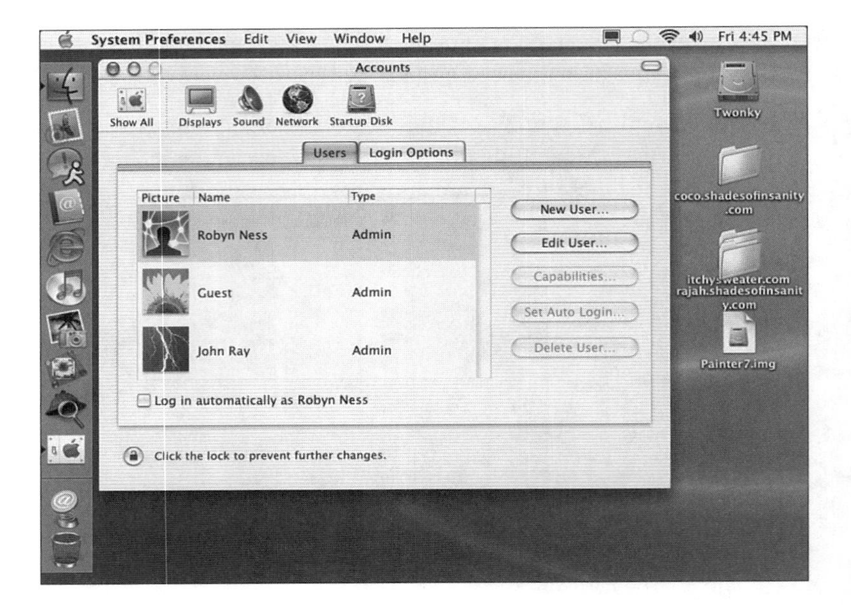

FIGURE 27.3
The Users pane of the Accounts Preferences panel lists current users and enables you to edit them or add new ones.

To create a new user account, follow these steps:

1. Click the New User button to open the sheet shown in Figure 27.4.

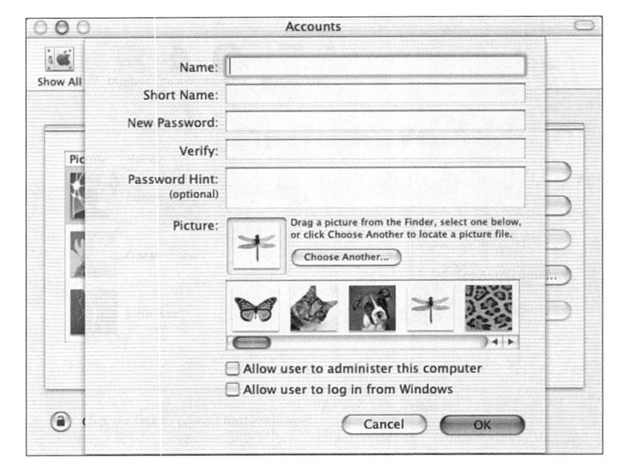

FIGURE 27.4
Enter a username and password and select an image for the new user.

2. Type the name of the person using the account as well as a short name to be displayed for logging in.

3. Type the password once, and then type it again to verify it. The Password Hint box is for a short description or question to remind the user of his password when he forgets it.
4. Choose the picture that shows up next to the user's name in the login screen.
5. If you want your new user to have administrative powers, as discussed previously, check the box labeled Allow User to Administer This Computer.
6. If you want Windows users to be able to connect to the new user's home folder, check the box for Allow User to Log In from Windows.
7. When you're done, click OK.

The Users Preferences panel now lists your new user, who has a folder in the Users folder.

If you want to further control the access of users who aren't allowed to administer the computer, you can click the Capabilities button to choose which applications are visible to them, whether they can access System Preferences, and burn CDs or DVDs. You can also enable a setting called Simple Finder, which simplifies system navigation by opening all Finder elements in a single window.

Through a similar process, you can edit an existing user account, including changing the password. Simply select the user account to be edited and click the Edit User button. Note that although you can change many things about a user account, you can't alter the short name used to log in. Choose wisely the first time.

To alter the settings for the currently active administrative account, you must enter your current password to provide authorization.

Now that you know how to add a user, you should learn how to remove a user. This again requires you to open the Users tab of the Accounts Preferences panel. To delete a user account, simply select the account to be deleted and click the Delete User button. In this way, you can delete any user account *except* the original administrator account. A sheet appears to confirm your choice and to inform you that the deleted user's files are stored as a disk image (`.dmg` file) in the Deleted Users folders. If you don't want the contents of the deleted account, you can open that folder and delete the `.dmg` file.

When an account is deleted for the first time, the Deleted Users folder is created. Even though you can delete the `.dmg` files inside it, there is *no* way to delete the folder itself from within the Mac OS X interface. If you attempt this, you will be denied permission.

Logging In

One aspect of maintaining a multiuser system is controlling who can use the computer, which files they have access to, and where their work is stored. These objectives are met by requiring people to sign in before using the machine. This process of identifying yourself to the system, which involves presenting a username and password, is known as a *login*.

If you're logged in on a Mac that's used by other people with their own accounts, you must log off when finished. This allows the computer to return to a state that enables others to log in. If someone forgets to log off, that person's account and files could be accessed by anyone because the system does not know that the owning user is no longer at the controls.

By default, Mac OS X sets the system to login automatically to the account of the first-created user every time the computer starts up. In this mode, your computer won't require you to enter your username and password. If you don't see a need to force a login each time your computer turns on, you can keep this setting.

However, if other people have access to your computer, you might want to create separate accounts for them and require them to log in. Many people dislike the idea of requiring a login to use their computers, but it is a good idea to disable automatic login if your computer has more than one user. Why? Without required logins, your documents and system settings can be modified by whoever uses the machine. Besides, giving each user his or her own desktop can cut down on clutter, prevent accidental deletion of files, and enable everyone to customize his or her settings.

To change your system so that it requires each user to log in, go to the System section of the System Preferences panel, and click the Accounts button. In the Accounts panel, uncheck the box in front of Log In Automatically as [Username]. We look at the options for customizing the login screen in the next section.

Customizing the Login Window

The screen in which users supply their names and passwords is referred to as the *login screen*. An example is shown in Figure 27.5.

FIGURE 27.5
Mac OS X gives the option to choose an icon for each user.

Although the login screen looks quite simple, several of its characteristics can be altered in the Login Options tab of the Accounts Preferences panel. You can indicate what you would like the login window to look like: either a list of usernames with an associated picture or two blank fields for username and password. When a login picture format is used, clicking on a user reveals a space to type the user's password.

> To disable the login screen from an administrator account, return to the Users tab of the Accounts Preferences panel and click the button for Set Auto Login. You are prompted for your password to authorize the change. Then, the next time you login, your computer automatically opens to the account of the first-created user.

Another option in the Login Options tab is whether to display the password hint onscreen after three tries. A *password hint* is a clue that users specify when creating their accounts. It serves to remind forgetful users of what they chose for their secret password. However, hints should be used with caution. Providing hints after several failed login attempts might help users, but it can also aid unauthorized users who are trying to guess passwords and gain access to your system.

You can also choose whether to allow users to access the Shut Down and Restart buttons on the login screen.

Adding Login Items

There's another benefit of having individuals log in, even if they are friends or family members. That is the option to have applications boot automatically on startup.

When you log in to your Mac OS X computer, you can choose to have it start applications for you automatically. However, if all users had their favorite applications start at once, regardless of who was using the machine, it would take a long time for the system to be ready. With separate accounts, only the applications of the logged-in user are started.

Figure 27.6 shows the Login Items Preferences panel where you can add applications to start automatically when you log in. To do this, just drag the application icon in the system Applications folder to the Login Items pane.

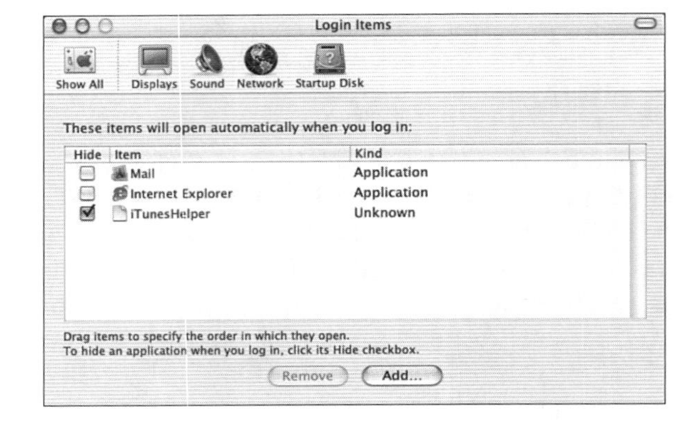

FIGURE 27.6
By using the Login Items pane, your favorite application can be ready and waiting every time you log in.

Controlling File Permissions

In addition to letting you decide who can log in to your computer, Mac OS X enables you to control who can interact with your files. If you create a file while you're logged in to your account, you own that file. Without your password, other users can be prevented from accessing your folders and files in any way; they can neither read nor alter your files and folders. For example, the folders in the home folder created for each user have some of these restrictions set by default.

Changing privileges in a file or folder is done though the Info panel of the Finder. These are the steps to use this panel:

1. Highlight the icon of the file or folder whose access you want to change. Users who are administrators can change the permissions on almost any file, but those who are normal users can change the permissions only on files they themselves own.
2. To open the Info panel, choose Get Info from the File menu. Alternately, you can use the key command Command-I.
3. Open the Ownership & Permissions section of the panel. If the lock button shows a closed lock, click it to unlock the settings.

4. Access can now be set so that different users have different privileges. The main options for levels of access are Read & Write, Read Only, and None. For folders, there is also the Write Only option, which enables a drop-box feature so that users can copy files into the folder, but only the owner can view it.
5. When you've set the permissions you need, close the panel.

When changing access options for a folder, you also have to Apply to Enclosed Items button to apply the access rights you've selected to all files and folders within the original folder. Remember, just because a folder doesn't have read permissions doesn't mean that the files inside it can't be read or modified.

Understanding Groups

You might have noticed that the Ownership & Permissions section of the Info panel enables you to specify permissions for the owner of the file, the group to which that user belongs, and others. But what is a group? Let's look at that concept briefly now.

In Mac OS X, users can be classified into many different groups so that they can access, or be excluded from accessing, certain information. There are many possible groups to choose from in the Owner and Group pop-up menus of the Ownership & Permissions section. Among them are the names for each of the user accounts on your computer, which are used to assign a file to those users. Other than those, the only groups you should be concerned with are admin and staff, which grant access to only administrative users and everyone with an account on the computer, respectively. (The other options are specialized groups that you won't need as an average user.)

During the discussion on Mac OS X's file structure in Chapter 3, "Working with Windows, Folders, Files, and Applications" you learned that the folders at the top level of the hard drive can't be modified, which has been done to preserve system order and stability. The technical reason that even administrative users can't make these changes is that those folders are owned by another account called the root, or superuser, account. This account exists on a completely different level, one that most users of Mac OS X never need to see. Although the administrator account works for most Mac OS X system administration, the root account is much more powerful. For this reason, Apple has tried to ensure that only users who understand its power will use the root account. Mac OS X comes with the root account shut off. Because the power, and consequences of the root account are beyond the scope of this book, you may want to read "*Mac OS X Unleashed*," or another in-depth book about OS X, to learn more.

Using Network Sharing

In addition to sharing your computer with other users, the Mac makes it easy to share files with other computers on the same network and over the Internet. At the same time, some limitations are placed on what you can share that might require changes in the way your Macintosh network is set up.

Sharing Services

A *service* is something that your computer provides to other computers on a network, such as running a Web server or sharing files. In Mac OS X 10.2, you can enable or disable all the standard information-sharing services from the Services tab of the Sharing panel in System Preferences, as shown in Figure 27.7.

Be aware that turning on or off any service in the Sharing panel activates that service for everyone on the machine. If sharing is on for one user, it's on for everyone. If it's off, it's off for everyone!

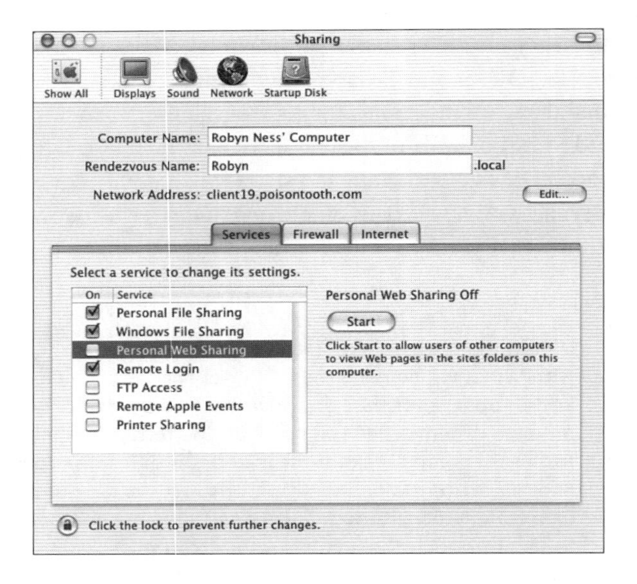

FIGURE 27.7
The Services tab of Sharing Preferences enables you to choose which sharing services you want run running on your computer.

You can enable or disable the following services:

- **Personal File Sharing**—Share your files with other Mac users across a local network. We'll discuss activating AppleTalk, if needed, in just a moment.
- **Windows File Sharing**—Share your files with Windows users on your local network.

- **Personal Web Sharing**—Serve Web pages from your own computer using the built-in Apache Web server. You'll learn more later in this chapter.
- **Remote Login**—Allow Secure Shell (SSH) command-line access to your machine from remote machines. You'll learn more later in this chapter.
- **FTP Access**—Allow access to your machine via FTP, (File Transfer Protocol). You'll learn more later.
- **Remote Apple Events**—Allow software running on other machines to send events to applications on your computer using the AppleScript scripting language. As this requires some specialized programming, we don't delve into this option.
- **Printer Sharing**—Grant other computers access to the printers connected to your computer. With this service enabled, your printers appear in the Print Center's printer list for other users on your local network.

The Firewall tab of the Sharing control pane contains a list of the same options as the Services tab. A *firewall* is something that sits between the outside network and network services on your computer to protect your computer from network-based attacks. The Firewall tab enables you to activate Mac OS X's built-in firewall software to prevent access to your computer through those services you don't want to run. We'll discuss this further later in this chapter.

Now, let's take at look at sharing and using these services.

Activating Personal File Sharing and AppleTalk

Personal File Sharing is Apple's method of sharing files with other Mac users over a network, either via TCP/IP or AppleTalk. AppleTalk is a legacy protocol for browsing and accessing remote workstations that share files or services, such as printers. Apple is transitioning to using the TCP/IP-based Service Locator Protocol (SLP) and Rendezvous to provide this functionality on modern Mac networks. Unfortunately, until everyone is running Mac OS X, you might still need to enable AppleTalk to access older devices.

Follow these steps to share your files with another Mac user:

1. Determine whether you need to use AppleTalk to access computers and printers on your network. If all the other computers are Mac OS X machines and your printer is USB-based, you probably don't need AppleTalk support—skip ahead to step 8. If you're not sure, go to step 2.
2. Open the Network Preferences panel, found in the Internet & Network section of System Preferences.

3. Use the Show pop-up menu to choose the device you're using to access your network (such as AirPort or Ethernet).
4. Click the AppleTalk tab.
5. Check the box for Make AppleTalk Active, as shown in Figure 27.8. (To make the change, you might first have to click the small lock button at the bottom of the window and type an administrator's username and password.)

Remember that the first-created user account is an administrative account. Other accounts may or may not be administrative, depending how they were set up.

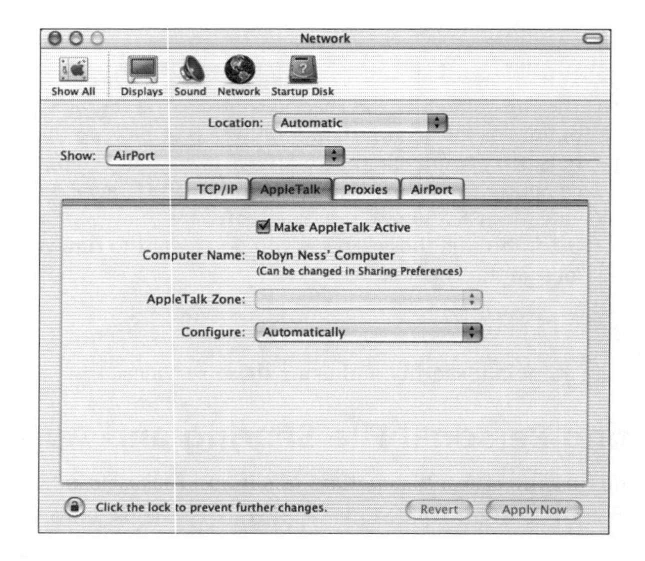

FIGURE 27.8
Make sure that AppleTalk is active before trying to share files on a Mac OS network composed of both OS X users and users of older operating systems.

6. If necessary, choose an AppleTalk Zone to use. You might want to speak to your network administrator if you aren't sure what to choose.
7. Click Apply Now.
8. Open the Sharing Preferences pane, as shown in Figure 27.7, and check the box for Personal File Sharing, or highlight it and click the Start button.
9. Close the System Preferences window.

Your Mac OS X computer should now be able to share files with other Macs on your network. We'll talk about how to actually connect to other users' files later in this chapter.

Activating Windows Sharing (Samba)

Windows computers use a system called SMB (Simple Message Block) for file and print sharing. To share files with Windows computers, your Mac uses the same protocol through a piece of software called Samba.

> The latest version of SMB is known as CIFS (Common Internet File System), which is an open version of SMB with some Internet-specific modifications. For the sake of remaining reasonably sane, you can assume that CIFS and SMB are synonymous.

To turn on Windows Sharing (Samba), open the Sharing System Preferences panel to the Services tab, and then either click the check box in front of the Windows File Serving line, or highlight it and click the Start button. The Sharing panel updates and shows the path that can be used to map (mount) the drive of your Mac on a Windows-based computer, as demonstrated in Figure 27.9.

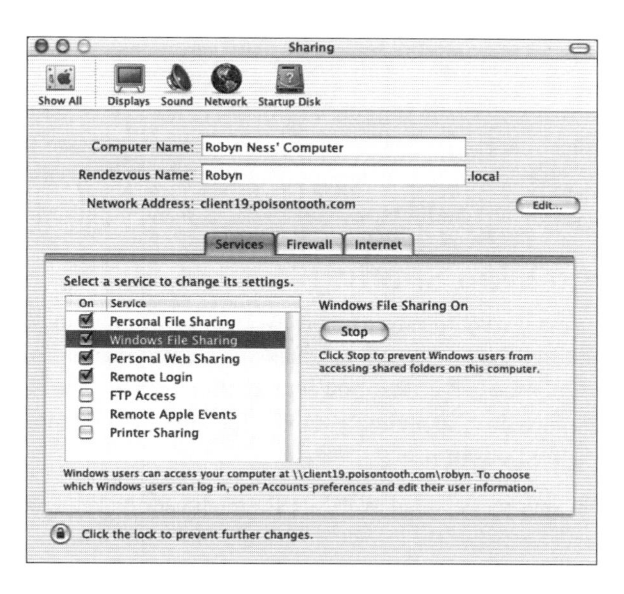

FIGURE 27.9
Activate Samba for file sharing with Windows computers by using the Sharing preference panel.

Like AppleShare file sharing in Mac OS X, the built-in Samba configuration is limited to sharing each user's home directory. By default, none of the user accounts are enabled for login. Enable login from Windows by opening the Accounts System Preferences panel, selecting the user to have Samba access, and then clicking the Edit User button. Your screen will look similar to Figure 27.10.

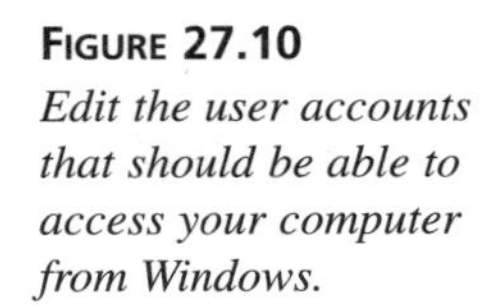

FIGURE 27.10
Edit the user accounts that should be able to access your computer from Windows.

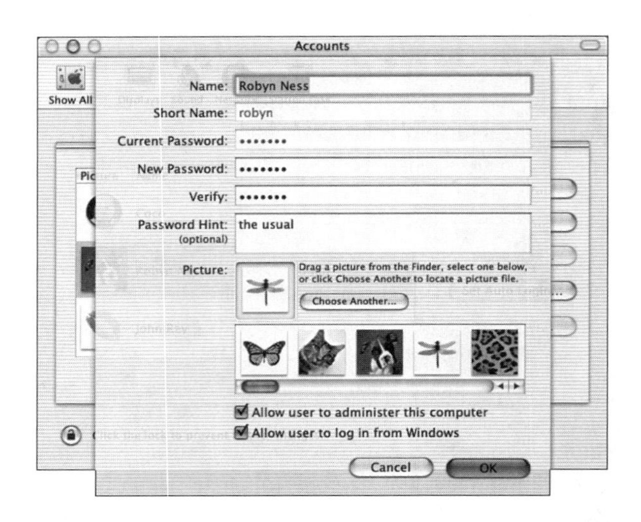

If necessary, enter the current user password, press the Return key, and then click the Allow User to Log In from Windows check box. The home directory of the user can now be accessed through a path following the format:

```
\\<hostname or IP address>\<username>
```

Keep in mind that the person logging in from Windows must be identified as the same user the Mac account recognizes, meaning it is necessary to log in to Windows using the username and password of the account on Mac OS X. Be sure to enter your username in all lowercase characters and the password just as you entered it in Mac OS X.

Activating Web Sharing

Mac OS X makes it easy to run a simple Web server from your own personal computer, using popular server software called Apache. What makes this so astounding is that Apache is actually the server that powers most Internet Web sites. It's built to run extremely complex sites, including e-commerce and other interactive applications—and it's running on your desktop.

Mac OS X can share a personal Web site for each user on the computer. In addition, it can run a master Web site for the whole computer entirely independent of the personal Web sites.

To turn on Web sharing, open the Sharing System Preferences panel (shown in Figure 27.7), and check the box for Personal Web Sharing or highlight it and click the Start button. The Apache server starts running, making your Web site immediately available. Make a note of the URL shown at the bottom of the window, and then start Internet Explorer to verify that your personal site is online.

To test this, launch a web browser, such as Internet Explorer, and enter your personal Web site URL, which should look like the following:

```
http://<server ip or hostname>/~<username>
```

The tilde (~) is extremely critical. It tells the server that it should load the Web pages from the Sites folder located inside the user's home directory. Note that after you activate Web sharing for one user, it's active for all users, so be sure that all users are ready to have their Web sites shared with the rest of the world.

Assuming that you entered your URL correctly, you should see the default Mac OS X home page, as demonstrated in Figure 27.11.

FIGURE 27.11
Apple includes a default personal home page.

To edit your Web site, just look inside the Sites folder in your user account. The default page is generated from the file `index.html` and the Images folder.

> Under Mac OS X's user interface, it isn't possible to change the filename of your home page. When you start creating files, be certain that the first page you want to be loaded is named `index.html`; otherwise, your site might not behave as you hope.

If you're the adventurous sort, you've probably tried typing in the URL of your machine without including the *~<username>* portion. If you haven't, try it now. What you should see is that a different Web page loads. This is the system Web site and it can be used for anything you want, but you must do a bit of digging to reach the directory that holds it.

The system-level site is located in `/Library/WebServer/Documents`. Any administrator can make changes to this directory, so be sure that the other admin users on the system understand its purpose and that they don't assume that it's related to their personal Web sites.

Activating Remote Login and FTP

Two additional methods of file sharing available are FTP and SSH. File Transfer Protocol provides cross-platform file-transfer services so others can connect to your computer and download files. The second type of sharing, SSH (secure shell), enables a remote user to send commands to a Mac OS X computer from anywhere in the world.

As you might expect, both of these protocols can be turned on using the Sharing System Preferences panel. SSH is turned on through the Remote Login check box, as you saw in Figure 27.7. Activate FTP by simply clicking the Allow FTP Access check box. Alternatively, you can highlight the option you want to activate and click the Start button.

Now that you know how to turn these services on, let's see what they can do for you!

Remote Login (SSH)

SSH, or as Apple calls it in the Sharing panel: Remote Login, is an entirely new concept for most Mac users. If you've seen a Windows or a Linux computer before, you've probably occasionally seen someone open a command prompt and start typing. Contrary to the sentiment many Mac users have, the command line is not evil! In Mac OS X, it's a very powerful and entirely optional tool. As you start to explore the command line later in this book, you'll understand that it can be used to manage your files, monitor your system, and even control server processes.

SSH isn't the command line itself, but it provides a secure means of accessing the command line from a remote location. In an SSH connection, the entire session is encrypted. As such, administrators can log in to their systems using SSH and edit user accounts, change passwords, and so on, without the fear of giving away potentially damaging information.

If you're not interested in the command line, don't worry—there's absolutely no reason why you have to use SSH.

If you're planning to serve FTP and SSH only occasionally, shut off the services in the Sharing panel until you're ready to use them. This closes some open doors that unwelcome "visitors" may use to access your computer. With SSH and FTP shut off, you can still use the Mac OS X clients and command line to access other SSH/FTP servers, but remote users can't connect to your machine. We'll talk more about security issues at the end of this chapter.

FTP

With FTP enabled, someone in another place can reach files on your machine by typing the following into an FTP application:

```
ftp://<mac os username>:<mac os password>@<ip address or hostname>
```

This tells the Web browser to contact the Mac OS X computer running the FTP server, login with the given username and password, and display the files in that user's home directory.

If you have the need to transfer large files between computers over the Internet, here are several FTP clients that can be used to access remote FTP servers:

- **Fetch**—`http://fetchsoftworks.com/`
- **Interarchy**—`http://www.interarchy.com/`
- **NetFinder**—`http://members.ozemail.com.au/~pli/netfinder/sw_and_updts.html`
- **Transmit**—`http://www.panic.com/transmit/download.html`

If you need to share files over the Internet, FTP is one of the best ways to do so. It's fast, effective, and a very efficient protocol. Unfortunately, it's also not easy to work with behind firewalls, and it transmits its passwords unencrypted. If you set up a nonadmin user account, perhaps called Transfers, for the sole purpose of moving files around, the password issue shouldn't be much of a problem. Firewalls, on the other hand, are something you might need to discuss with your network administrator before you activate FTP.

You will learn how to use FTP from the Finder in the next section.

Connecting to Shared Folders

Your computer can connect to a number of types of network resources from the Finder, specifically:

- **Macintosh Systems**—Other Mac computers that are sharing files via AppleTalk or AppleShare IP.
- **Windows/Linux Computers**—If Windows or Linux computers are using SMB or CIFS file sharing (the standard for most Windows networks), your Mac can access the files easily.
- **WebDAV Shares**—WebDAV is a cross-platform file sharing solution that uses the standard Web protocols. Your iDisk uses WebDAV.
- **FTP Servers**—File Transfer Protocol servers are popular means of distributing software on the Internet. Your Mac OS X machine can connect (read-only) to FTP servers.
- **Linux/BSD NFS Servers**—NFS is the Unix standard for file sharing. Your Mac (being Unix!) can obviously talk to them as well!

Connecting to Macintosh and Windows servers is the easiest of the bunch. In Mac OS X, you use the Go menu in the Finder to choose Connect to Server (Command-K). This opens a new dialog box, shown in Figure 27.12, that enables you to connect to remote computers.

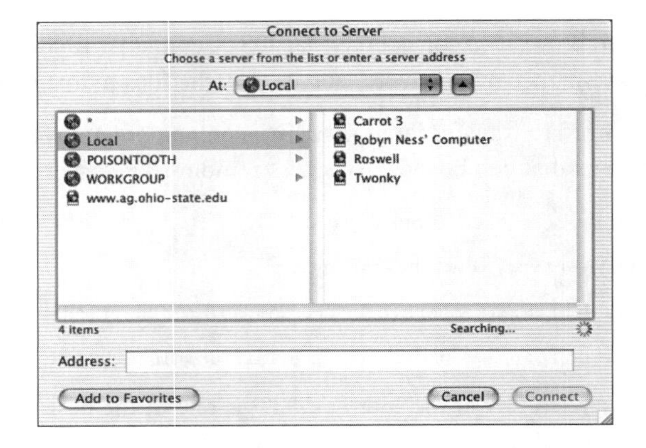

FIGURE 27.12
The Finder has the power to connect you to remote volumes directly.

Depending on your network, you'll see several selections, including AppleTalk zones and Windows workgroups. Clicking the Network option displays servers and groups of servers located on your local network.

You can navigate through the AppleTalk zones or server groups the same way you navigate through the Finder in column mode. To make the connection, choose the server you want to use from the list and then click Connect. After a few seconds, you're prompted for a username and a password, as shown in Figure 27.13.

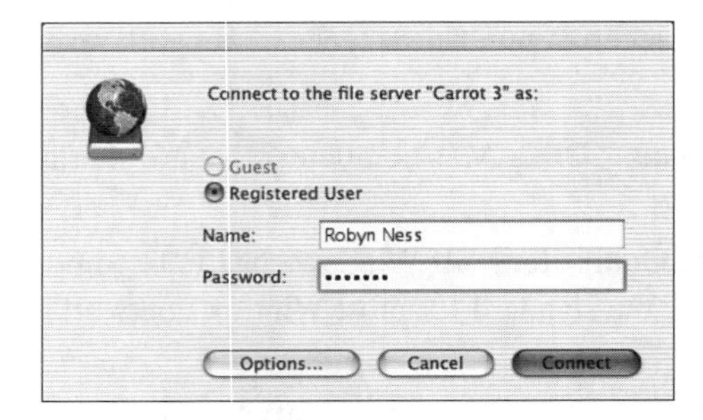

FIGURE 27.13
Enter your username and password, and then click Connect.

Click Connect, and after few seconds, the volume is mounted on your desktop.

If you're connecting to another Mac OS X computer, you can use either your full name or your username to connect.

Connecting to WebDAV and NFS shared volumes is only slightly more difficult. You can't browse these resources on your network unless the administrator has registered them with a Service Locator Protocol server. Instead, you must type in a URL for the object you want to use into the Address field of the Connection window.

Your network administrator should be able to give you the exact information you need, but for the most part, the URLs follow a format like this:

FTP shares: `ftp://<server name>/<path>`

For example, I have an FTP server named Xanadu on my network (poisontooth.com) containing a folder called waternet at the root level of the server. To access it, I would type **`ftp://xanadu.poisontooth.com/waternet`** and then click Connect.

WebDAV is even simpler. WebDAV shares are actually just Web resources, so they use the same URLs that you would type into your Web browser. For example, to access the iDisk storage of your Mac.com account, you would type **`http://idisk.mac.com/<your Mac.com username>`**.

NFS follows the same pattern. If the remote server is configured to allow connections, an NFS connection URL looks like this `nfs://<server name>/<shared volume>`.

Security Considerations

Your computer running Mac OS X is a powerful operating system, and with that power comes a new set of security risks. If you're connecting your computer to the Internet, it's necessary that you pay attention to your system as well as take preventive measures to guard against unwanted connections. (While this may sound paranoid, my personal computer, which is connected to the world via cable modem, is attacked dozens of times a day by people who simply search for unprotected computers online.)

Local Security

27

As we talked about at the beginning of the chapter, Mac OS X is a true multiuser operating system. In Mac OS X, you have complete control over who can do what.

Much of local system security is common sense coupled with a reasonable amount of watchfulness. Because implementing a local security policy is easier than maintaining network security, that's where we'll start.

Let's take a look at a series of steps you can take to minimize the risks to your system.

Create Only "Normal" Users

As we discussed earlier, two types of user accounts can be created in the User Control panel: normal users and admin users. The only difference when setting up accounts is the presence of a check box that reads Allow User to Administer This Computer.

Many systems that I've visited have had all the users set to be administrators. When asked why, the owners replied that they wanted everyone to be able to use the computer to its fullest. An understandable sentiment, but the implications of using this setting are enormous. A user who has this check box set can

- Add or delete users and their files
- Remove software installed in the systemwide Applications folder
- Change or completely remove network settings
- Activate or disable the Web service, FTP service, or SSH (secure shell)

Although it's unlikely that administrators could completely destroy the system (they aren't able to delete the System folder and files), they can make life difficult for others even if they don't mean to.

To add or remove administrative access from an existing user, follow these steps:

1. Open the System Preferences panel.
2. Click the Accounts item under the System section.
3. Double-click the name of the user to edit, or select the name and click Edit User.
4. A sheet showing the administrative check box you're looking for appears. It's shown in Figure 27.14.

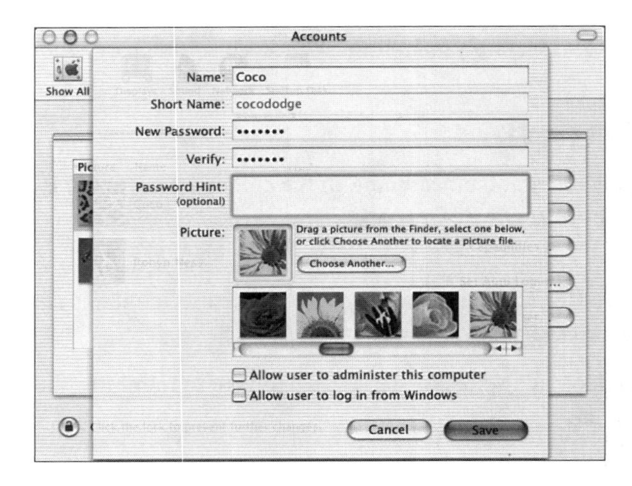

FIGURE 27.14
Create as few administrative users as possible.

5. Uncheck Allow User to Administer This Computer to remove administrative access.
6. Click Save to save to apply the changes.

If your computer has only a few accounts for people you know, this security precaution is probably the only one you need. However, if you want your system to be a bit more impenetrable, keep reading.

Disable Hints and Names

It's obvious that Apple wanted to create a system that would be friendly and accessible for any level of user. In doing so, it made it easier for uninvited users to try to log in by guessing your password.

There are two options to consider if you plan to place your computer in a public area without strict monitoring:

- **Password Hints**—By default, Mac OS X displays a hint for a password if the user fails to correctly enter it three times in a row. It's easy enough to just not enter password hints, but it's safer to disable the feature globally.
- **Login Window Names**—Another default setting—the capability to display icons for each user account on the machine and require only a click to start the login process—is nice, but it also gives away part of the system's security. Attackers usually need both a username *and* a password to log in to a machine. If the usernames are prominently displayed, attackers are already halfway to their goal.

Both of these risky features are disabled from the Login Preferences panel. To shut off both features, follow these steps:

1. Open System Preferences.
2. Click the Accounts button in the System section.
3. Choose the Login Options tab.
4. Click the Display Login Window as Name and Password radio button to select it.
5. Uncheck the Show Password Hint After 3 Attempts to Enter a Password check box.
6. When you're finished, the Login panel should resemble Figure 27.15. Close the panel to save the settings.

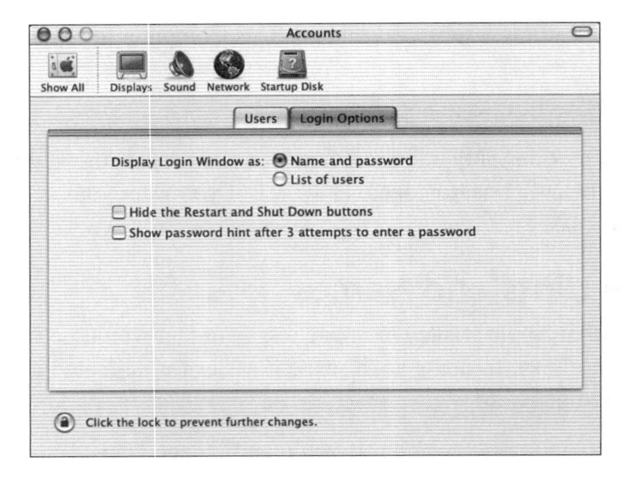

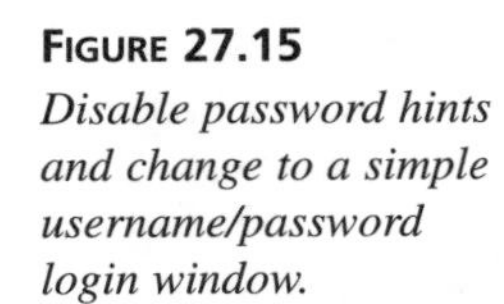

FIGURE 27.15
Disable password hints and change to a simple username/password login window.

Maintaining Security Online

When your computer is connected to the Internet via a direct connection to a cable modem or DSL line, it can be a direct target for attack from outside.

Earlier in the chapter, you learned how to use network sharing and services. Now let's find out what security issues are related to their use. (To put it bluntly, the more network services that are running, the greater the chance that a potential intruder can discover and access your system.)

Network Sharing Services

Although it's tempting to go through your system and activate every feature in the Sharing panel, doing so isn't always a good idea. If you turn on *everything* in the Sharing Preferences panel, someone else could scan your system over the Internet and find the following services active and available for use:

- **FTP Access** (port 20 or 21)—FTP is a quick and easy way to send and retrieve files from a computer. FTP Sharing starts an FTP server on your computer. Unfortunately, it provides no password encryption and is often targeted by attackers. If you don't have to use FTP, don't enable it.
- **Remote Login—ssh** (port 22)—The secure shell enables remote users to connect to your computer and control it from the command line. It's a useful tool for servers, but only presents a security risk to home users.
- **Personal Web Sharing** (port 80)—Your personal Web server is really an enterprise-class Apache server. Apache is a very stable program and should be considered the least of your concerns, unless you've manually customized its configuration files.

- **Windows File Sharing** (port 139)— Enables Windows users to access the shared folders on your computers.
- **svrloc** (port 427)—The Service Locator Protocol allows remote computers to detect what services are available on your computer over the Internet.
- **afpovertcp** (port 548)—The Apple File Protocol is used to share your disks and folders over a network. If you have Personal File Sharing turned on, be aware that potentially anyone on the Internet can connect to your computer.
- **Printer Sharing** (port 631)—Enables other users on the network to use printers connected to your computer.
- **ppc** (port 3031)—Program-to-program communication enables remote applications to connect to your computer and send it commands. It's unlikely that you would need this feature in day-to-day use. PPC is controlled by the Remote Apple Events setting in the Sharing Preferences panel.

To disable any of these built-in network services, follow these steps:

1. Open the System Preferences panel.
2. Click the Sharing item under the Internet & Network section.
3. In the Services tab, uncheck the boxes for the listed services to toggle them on and off, as shown in Figure 27.16.

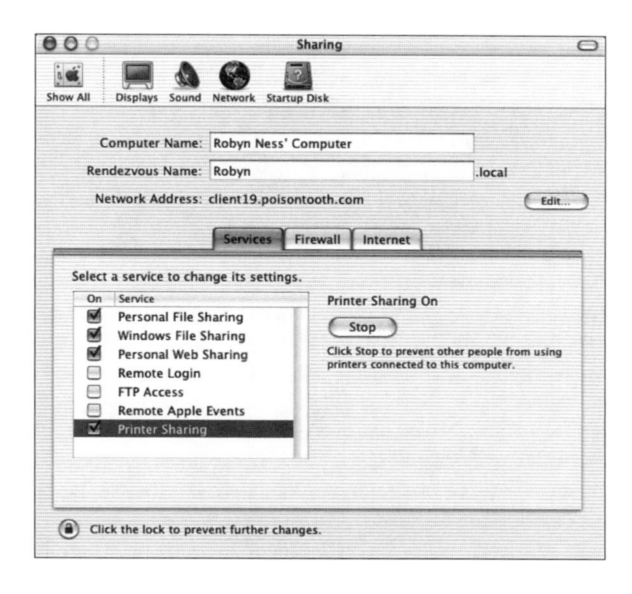

FIGURE 27.16
The Sharing Preferences panel controls the built-in network services.

4. Close the Sharing Preferences panel to save your settings.

Firewalls

The "ultimate" solution to network security is the use of a *firewall*, a piece of hardware or software that sits between your computer and the Internet. As network traffic comes into the computer, the firewall looks at each piece of information, determines whether it's acceptable, and, if necessary, keeps the data from getting to your machine. (Examples of data it would block are attempts by unauthorized users to contact the services listed earlier.)

> You might be asking yourself, "If a firewall can be a piece of software that runs on my computer, how can it both look at network traffic *and* keep it from reaching my machine?" After all, to look at the information and determine whether it's trouble, the data obviously must have reached my computer!
>
> That's true, but firewall software operates at a very low level, intercepting network traffic before your computer has a chance to process it and make it available to components such as your Web server or FTP server.

Though both hardware and software-based firewalls are available, a software firewall is the quickest way to get unwanted traffic blocked from your machine.

Mac OS X 10.2 includes a built-in personal firewall, accessible from the Firewall tab of the System Preferences Sharing panel shown in Figure 27.17.

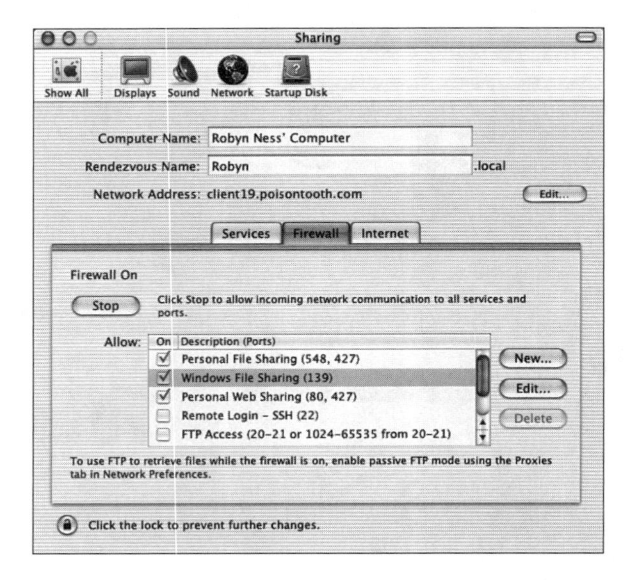

FIGURE 27.17
The Mac OS X personal firewall can be enabled to secure the services/port you don't want to operate.

To activate the firewall, click the Start button. Checked boxes appear next to those services/ports that you've turned on under the Services pane of the Sharing Preferences panel.

Other than starting or stopping your personal firewall, there are no other settings to configure in the Firewall panel. Because disabling a port disables its service and unenabled ports require no securing, you must go to the Services panel to change the active/inactive status of the services in the Firewall panel.

If you need more flexibility, there are several other firewall builder packages that make it easy to point-and-click your way through setting up a firewall on your computer. You may want to consult another source, such as Maximum OS X Security, for deeper coverage of security issues.

Summary

This chapter contains the most advanced topics we addressed so far in this book. We began with a discussion of multiuser systems and how to set up new user accounts. From there, we talked about ways you can share files from your Mac and connect to other computers that are sharing their files. Finally, you learned about some of the dangers of sharing your computer—or even connecting it to the Internet. We talked about shutting off file sharing and turning on the built-in firewall to help keep your computer from being accessed by uninvited users.

CHAPTER 28

Managing Your System

In the chapter, you learn some maintenance tips that will help keep your computer running smoothly and keep your files safe. As Apple frequently releases critical security updates and patches that should be installed quickly, we'll talk first about automating system software updates. Then, we'll discuss the importance of backing up your files so you won't loose all of your hard work and important data in the event of system disruption. We'll also touch on use of commercial software to optimize your hard drive. Finally, we'll check out a built-in tool for monitoring the effort expended by your system.

Automating Software Updates

One great feature of Mac OS X is the capability to automatically receive software updates from Apple. All you need to set this up is an Internet connection and maybe a minute of your time.

Mac OS X automates the process of upgrading software through the Software Update Preferences panel.

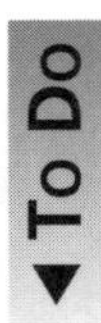

Running Software Updates

1. Launch the System Preferences application from the Dock, the Apple menu, or the Applications folder.
2. Click the Software Update panel, which opens the screen shown in Figure 28.1.

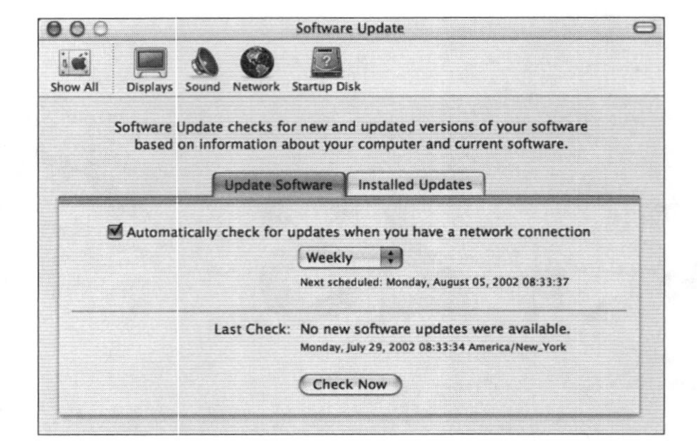

FIGURE 28.1
Apple enables you to download the latest updates for your computer automatically from its Web site.

3. If you want to simply check for updates, click the Update Now button. Your Internet service will be dialed up, and Apple's support Web site checked for possible updates.
4. If updates are available for your computer, you'll see a screen listing what's available. From there you can click the check boxes for the items you want, and accept the download process.
5. When the downloads are complete, the software installers will launch and your computer will be updated with the new software. Then there will usually be an "optimizing" process, which allows the update to function with full efficiency. All you have to do is click the Restart button to finish the process (sometimes a Restart won't even be necessary).
6. If you want to have your computer check for Apple software updates automatically, click the Automatically check box, and then click the Check for Updates pop-up menu to set the interval. You can choose Daily, Weekly, or Monthly (Weekly is best, considering the unpredictable nature of the software update process).

If you want to keep abreast of software updates from Apple and other companies, point your Web browser to VersionTracker.com (`http://www.versiontracker.com/macosx`). If you see information on a new Apple update, you can go right to the Software Update preference panel and click Update Now to retrieve it (though it sometimes takes a day or two for the update files to be available after an announcement).

7. After you've set the schedule choose Quit from the application menu to close System Preferences. If you selected Automatically, Software Update will check Apple's Web site at the specified intervals as soon as you login to the Internet.

It goes without saying that if your computer isn't on when the scheduled update scan is set to take place, it just won't happen. The check will be skipped until the next scheduled run.

Sometimes the list of updates includes features you don't need or want, such as printer drivers for foreign languages. Although not checking the box for those items prevents them from being installed, they continue to show up in your Software Updates window unless you choose Make Inactive from the Update menu. If you ever change your mind, you can choose Show Inactive Updates and Make Active from the Update menu to allow the system to perform the update.

Backing Up Your Data

Although keeping a secure and updated operating system is important, that's not as important as maintaining an archive of your important data.

Even if you keep close tabs on your data, don't get overconfident about the safety of your files. One thing is certain (other than death and taxes, of course)—your Mac will crash on occasion, just as any personal computer. When a program or computer crashes, it's possible one or more files on your computer's drive can be affected (especially if you're working on a file when the computer locks up). Even though Mac OS X offers strong resistance to system ills, the world is unpredictable, and the potential for events ranging from simple human error to theft, make backups an important consideration.

Backup Strategies

Computers drive our daily lives. Nearly every business has a computer system of some sort, whether a personal computer or a large mainframe with huge boxes of electronics and disk drives. The systems aren't perfect, no matter how well you prepare for problems.

I don't want to be an alarmist, but it's very true that nothing is foolproof. If you want to create documents on your computer that you need to keep safe (from a newsletter to your personal financial information), you should take steps to make sure that you'll always be protected in case of trouble.

You can follow different types of backup techniques, depending on the kind of documents you're creating and how many of them there are. Here's a brief look at the sort of things you can do without having to buy extra software:

- **Back up only document files**—You already have copies of your programs on a CD. A complete packet of CDs came with your computer, containing all the software Apple installed on your computer. In addition, any new software you buy will also come on an installation disk of some sort. So the fastest backup method is just to concentrate on the documents you make with those programs.
- **Back up everything**—Even though you already have a separate copy of the software, it can be very time-consuming to restore all your software and redo special program settings. If you back up everything, however, it's easier to restore a program with your settings intact without fuss or bother. In addition, having a complete backup of your computer's drive is extra protection in case something happens to both the computer and software disks.
- **Incremental backups**—This technique requires special software (such as Retrospect or FWB's BackUp ToolKit, both of which are described later), but it is designed to make a backup strictly of the files that have changed since your last backup. A thorough backup plan might include a full backup at regular intervals, say once a week, and then a daily incremental backup. This method also takes a lot less time, and you won't need as much disk space to store it all.

Data Storage Options

Another part of your backup plan is deciding where and how to store the data you will be copying from your hard drive. The best method is to get a separate drive with media (disks) that you can remove. That way you can store the backups in a separate location for the ultimate in safekeeping. That's the method the big companies use.

Here are some storage options you should consider:

> It's just not a good idea to back up your files to the same drive they were made on (such as your Mac's hard drive). If something should happen to that drive, or the entire computer, your backup would be gone.

- **Data CDs**—Many Macs come equipped with an optical drive that can make CDs. You can use this drive to copy your files to a CD/R or CD/RW disc (the latter is the one that's rewritable). This is a convenient and inexpensive way to copy your valuable data on a medium that will last for years. If you don't have a built-in CD burner on your Mac, no problem. There are plenty of low-cost external drives that can work from your computer's FireWire or USB ports (but of course the first will run much faster).

Does your Mac have Apple's SuperDrive? If so, you can also burn data DVDs in the same way you make a CD. The advantage is that you can store much more data on the DVD—4.7GB compared to 650MB or 700MB for a CD. Though DVDs are more expensive than CDs, if you have a well-populated hard drive this might be a good option.

- **External backup drive**—Iomega Jaz, Peerless, or Zip drives are convenient, and the drives and disks aren't too expensive (well, the Jaz and Peerless media aren't exactly cheap). There are also several varieties of tape drives that will work with backup software as a fairly stable backup medium.
- **Networked disks**—If your computer is on a network, a drive on another Mac (or actually even a Windows-based PC that's set up to handle Mac files) can be used for your regular backups. Before you set up a networked drive for this purpose, you'll want to set up a strategy with the folks who run the network. Some companies plan on having all files backed up to one drive or drives, and then they do their own special backup routine on those files.

Notice, I'm not saying anything about floppy disks here. Unless you only make a few small files, floppy disks aren't practical, even though such drives are readily available at low cost. You'd need dozens of them at the minimum, and they just aren't as robust as the larger disk techniques. I cannot begin to tell you how many of my floppies have gone bad over time. No wonder Apple doesn't include standard floppy drives on its computers any more.

- **Internet backups**—If you have a good Internet connection and you don't want to back up a large number of files, you can use backup via the Internet. An easy way to get storage space is to sign up with Apple's .Mac program. As part of the package, you get 100MB of iDisk storage space at Apple's Web servers and you can buy extra space if you need it. Visit `www.mac.com` to sign up. However, unless you have really fast Internet access, the process of copying files to your iDisk can get mighty slow.

After you've set up a .Mac account, you can access your iDisk. Simply click the iDisk icon on the Finder's toolbar to connect to your disk. If you aren't connected to the Internet, the service will be dialed up first.

Here are some additional considerations related to storing backups of your data:

- **Careful labeling**—Make sure that your backup disks are carefully labeled according to date and content. If the label isn't large enough, you might want to prepare a short listing of contents in your word processor and then pack it with the disk. Often something such as "Backup for February 28, 2002" is sufficient.

CDs and DVD media are write-once media, which means that when you burn one of these discs that's it unless, of course, you opt for CD/RW media, where you can rewrite data up to 1,000 times.

- **Reuse of media**—If you need to keep an older version of a file, you'll want to keep the backup in a safe place. When you no longer need a disk, however, there's no problem in putting it back into service for newer backups. Otherwise, you'll end up with a huge number of disks.
- **Rotation of media**—Although Jaz and Zip media are pretty solid, you'll want to reduce wear and tear by having several disks around. And, in case one backup file goes bad, having another recent one never hurts.
- **Making multiple backups**—If your files contain important data on them (financial or otherwise), make a second backup and store it in a secure location (such as a bank vault). In the unlikely event something happens to your home or office, you'll be protected.

There's one more important element in a backup plan—setting a consistent schedule. It's a good idea to set aside a time to do your backup at regular intervals—perhaps at the end of your work day before leaving your office (or shutting down your computer if you're at home). Remember, it does no good to *intend to* backup your files if you never actually do it, so try to work out a system and a schedule that you can maintain over time.

▼ To Do

Making Backup CDs

Mac OS X Finder makes writing a CD very similar to moving files to any other storage device. To make the process as simple as possible, Mac OS X stores applications, files, and folders in a special folder until you tell the system to burn the CD. Files are actually transferred to the CD media only after the burn starts.

To burn a CD using an external burner, you must have your CD writer connected and powered on. Check Apple's Web site for supported writers.

Of all the methods mentioned above for storing backup copies of your data, the simplest is burning a data CD. Here's how:

To choose Burn Disc from the File menu, the active Finder window must be the CD's window. If the CD is not the active window, the menu item will be disabled.

These are the steps to write your own data CD using the Finder:

1. Insert a blank CD into the CD writer. The Mac OS X Finder prompts you to prepare the CD. This doesn't actually write anything to the CD yet, but it tells the computer what your intentions are for the disc in order to ensure that you use the appropriate kind of CD.
2. Choose the Open Finder option from the Action pop-up menu. (We talked about burning from iTunes in Chapter 11, and we will look at burning CDs from a utility called Disk Copy later in this chapter.)
3. Enter a name for the CD you're writing. The disc appears with this name on the desktop.
4. Click the OK button to start using the CD on your system. An icon representing the CD appears on your desktop. At this point, you can interact with this virtual volume as you would any other under Mac OS X. You can copy files to it, delete files, and so on.
5. When you create the CD layout you like, you can start the burn process by choosing Burn Disc from the File menu or by clicking the Burn toolbar shortcut. In addition, dragging the CD to the Trash also prompts burning to begin. This process takes a few minutes, and is tracked by the Finder much like a normal Copy operation.

If you decide against writing the CD, you can click the Eject button in the CD burning dialog box to remove the media and erase the CD layout you created. If you want to insert a CD in the drive but don't want to prepare it (for use in another CD-burning application, such as iTunes), click Ignore rather than OK in the window that appears when you first insert a CD.

6. Eject the backup media when you're done and put the disks in a safe place.

When the disc is done, eject it from the drive and put it a safe place. It's not a good idea to subject backup media to hot sunlight, high humidity, moisture, or extreme cold. If you live or work in a climate with temperature extremes, try to locate a cool, dark place (such as a metal closet) to put the backup disks.

Disk Copy

In addition to the methods previously mentioned for storing your data, your Mac comes equipped with a piece of software that turns files into *disk images* that are read by computers as if they were CDs. This software, called Disk Copy, is located in the Utilities folder within the Applications folder of your hard drive. Disk Copy is a slick tool that is useful for creating an exact duplicate of software or large files you don't want to lose, or for making a master image to distribute files or applications over a network. It even has built-in CD-burning capabilities to make turning a disk image into a real CD a matter of a few clicks.

To launch the Disk Copy application, double-click its application icon. The icon for Disk Copy appears in the Dock, but no windows open.

Disk Copy is used to open disk images as well as create them. You can launch Disk Copy by double-clicking an image file (usually named with a .dmg extension); the image will be automatically mounted. The application checks the image's validity and the image appears as a white drive icon on your desktop or at the Computer level of the Finder.

From this point, you can copy files from the disk to wherever you want, or use them directly from the mounted image.

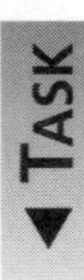

Task: Creating Disk Images

For each image you create, you must have enough free space on your hard drive. For example, to create a CD image, you need approximately 650MB free. Currently shipping Apple computers come with at least 10GB drives, so this really shouldn't be an issue.

1. There are two ways to generate an image: by copying an existing item, or by creating an empty image file, mounting it, and then copying files to it. To create an empty image file, choose Blank Image (Command-N) from the File menu's New submenu. The dialog box shown in Figure 28.2 appears.

FIGURE 28.2
Make a new image, and then copy to it.

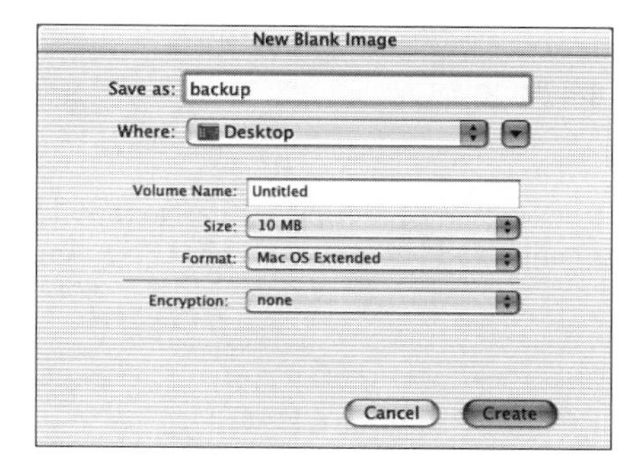

2. Fill in the Save As field as you normally would—this is the name of the image file, not the volume that's going to be created. Set the name of the volume in the Volume Name field. Choose a size for the image from the Size pop-up menu. There are a variety of preset sizes for common media, such as Zip disks, CDs, DVDs, and a Custom setting for arbitrary sizes.
3. Next, choose a volume format in the Format pop-up menu. In addition to the Mac OS Standard (HFS), Mac OS Extended (HFS+), and Unix File System (UFS) options supported as native Mac OS X file systems, you can also choose MS-DOS File System to create a Windows-compatible image.
4. Finally, if you want to encrypt the disk image, choose AES-128 in the Encryption pop-up menu and click Create. The new disk image is created and can be used immediately.

Creating an image from an existing folder or drive is even easier and is a great way to make quick backups that retain all the attributes of the originals.

1. Choose Image from Folder or Volume (Command-I), or Image from Device (Option-Command-I) [to work with the entire hard drive]) from the New submenu of the File menu. Disk Copy opens the standard Open File window from which you can surf to the item you want to make an image of.

   If you choose New Image from Device, Disk Copy displays a list of all active devices. Click the disclosure triangle in front of each device to display the individual partitions.
2. Select the item to image, and then click the Image button. You are prompted for the location to save the image. Using the Format pop-up menu, choose the type of image to create: read-only, read-write, compressed, or CD/DVD master. Apply encryption to the image file by choosing AES-128 in the Encryption pop-up menu.
3. Finally, click Save to copy an image to your hard drive.

▼ Once you have a disk image of your data, you can move it over the internet or network to a safe storage place or burn an actual CD of it.

To burn a CD from Disk Copy, follow these steps:

To burn a CD from within Disk Copy with an external burner, you must have your CD writer connected and powered on. Check Apple's Web site for supported writers.

1. Place a blank CD-R or CD-RW in your CD writer.
2. Select Burn Image from the File menu, and choose a disk image file when prompted. If the image is suitable for CD burning, Disk Copy prepares to burn a CD-R or CD-RW.
3. Expand the Burn Disk dialog box by clicking the disclosure button. You see settings for the speed you want to use during the burn process, along with whether you want to verify and eject the disk after it finishes. (A check box for Allow Additional Burns also appears because some burners enable you to continue adding data to a CD containing data until the disk is full.)
4. When you're satisfied with your settings, click the Burn button, and Disk Copy begins writing the CD. ▲

Using Backup Software

If you have a large number of files, or files need to be backed up from more than one Mac OS computer on a network, you'll do better with some backup software.

Such software can

- **Perform scheduled backups**—You can set the software to perform the backups at a regular time (daily, every other day, weekly, whatever). At the appointed time, you need to only have the backup media in place and the computers turned on for the process to go.

Although automatic backups are great, a backup can stop dead in its tracks if the media runs out of space, isn't ready, or the computer was shut down by mistake. If you have a large number of files, check to make sure that your disks have enough space, or be prepared to check the backup process every so often in case of trouble.

- **Perform networked backups**—With the right software, backups can be done from all computers on a network to one or more backup drives.

Each computer on the network will need its own licensed copy of the backup software for backups to be done across a network. A number of Mac applications, such as Microsoft Office v. X, are designed with network prevention schemes. That means, the program will not run if there's another copy with the same serial number on a network. Fortunately, networked backup software comes in relatively inexpensive multiuser packs.

- **Back up the entire drive or selected files or folders**—When you set up your backup, you can instruct the software to limit the backup to the items you want. By default they do the entire drive, and then incremental backups for each disk, unless you pick a full backup.

Choosing Backup Software

When you've decided on the backup software route, you'll want to know what to choose. Fortunately, there are several good Mac OS software packages that will give you great automatic backups. They vary in features, and you'll want to pick one based on what you need.

Regardless of the software you choose, make sure it is compatible with Mac OS X. The file structures of Mac OS X files are often different from the ones used in the Classic Mac OS. This means that non-native applications won't recognize those files, hence your backup won't be complete. If you only intend to back up document files, of course, this doesn't matter, but if you want to back up your applications and operating systems (or the whole drive), it's very important.

Here's a brief description of backup programs:

- **Personal Backup** (`http://www.intego.com`)—This simple program, now published by Intego, enables you to do simple automatic backups with a number of options. There's also a feature for on-demand backups, where you do them when you want. For added protection, Personal Backup gives you a keystroke recorder feature that makes a text backup of the files you write. In case something goes wrong with the original file, at least you'll have a way to recover the words (but not the artwork or layout).
- **Retrospect**—From Dantz (`http://www.dantz.com`), this is a heavy-duty backup program that does just about everything you can imagine in backup planning with little fuss or bother (see Figure 28.3). You can use its EasyScript feature to create a complete backup plan simply by answering some basic questions. Backups are compressed (to save space) and saved in a special format for efficient retrieval. Unlike other backup programs, Retrospect can work with tape drives, which can

store many megabytes of files on little cartridges. Retrospect can also work with Internet-based backup services. For large networks, there's the Retrospect Network Backup Kit and even a Windows version with similar features.

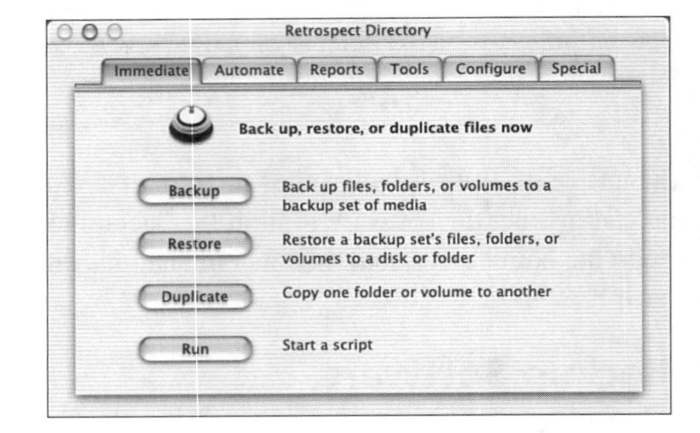

FIGURE 28.3
Though brimming with powerful features, Retrospect is remarkably easy to use.

- **Retrospect Express**—This program distills the most important features of Retrospect and puts them in a smaller, less-expensive package. Express doesn't work with tape drives, and there's no networked version.
- **FWB Backup ToolKit**—The publisher of Hard Disk ToolKit (`http://www.fwb.com`), a disk formatter used by professionals, has released this simple personal backup utility that might be all you need (see Figure 28.4). As with Retrospect, it can handle incremental backups (just the files you've changed). Backup ToolKit also sports a simple drag-and-drop user interface, and the capability to handle file synchronization chores. The latter feature is very useful if you work on more than one computer because it enables you make sure that both computers have only the latest files.

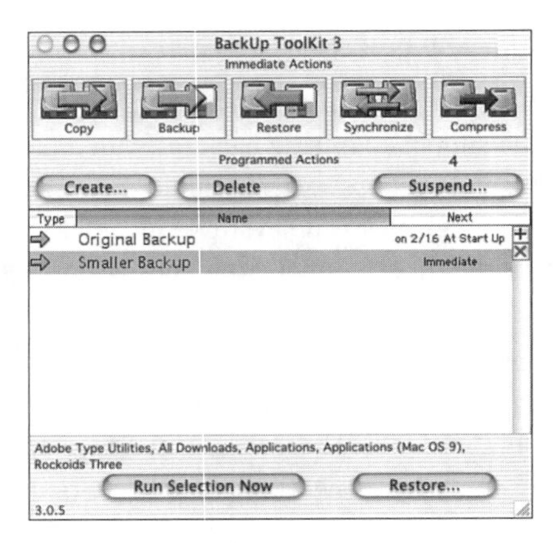

FIGURE 28.4
FWB's BackUp ToolKit combines simple setup and a powerful range of features to ensure robust backups.

Optimizing Your Hard Drive

Whether you're working with the built-in hard drive on your Mac or using an external hard drive to store your files, it can improve the performance of your system if you regularly defragment your hard drive.

In the course of normal use of your Mac, the computer is constantly writing various files, deleting others, and fitting them in to various leftover spots on the hard drive. Like a cluttered room, the hard drive can end up becoming *fragmented*, where part of a file is on one spot on the hard drive and another part of the same file is stored on a different spot.

This isn't because you've done anything wrong, it's simply the way that hard drives store data. But because of the demands that digital video places on the hard drive, this fragmentation can have a significant impact. *Defragmenting* basically takes the various bits of each file from various spots on the hard drive and reassembles them into contiguous, nonfragmented files. That means the computer can read the file without having to jump around the hard drive.

To defragment and optimize your hard drive, you must purchase a tool such as SpeedDisk, which is part of Norton Utilities. This suite contains a number of useful tools for maintaining your system (`www.symantec.com`).

CPU Monitor

After looking at software updates and backing up data, we'll round out our system management discussion with a discussion of system resources. With the multitasking capabilities of Mac OS X, you find it interesting to check just how much of your computer's processor time is being used. In Mac OS X, each program has a small slice of time it can use to complete its task. As more and more programs use the system, there are fewer slices to give out.

CPU Monitor, found in the Utilities folder of the Application folder on your hard drive, can illustrate how busy your system is on a simple graph, showing a range from 0% to 100%. (If you have a computer with multiple processors, a graph is displayed for each CPU in your machine.) Three types of graphs can be displayed in a number of different ways (configurable through the Preferences panel and Processes menu). Figure 28.5 shows several available graph styles.

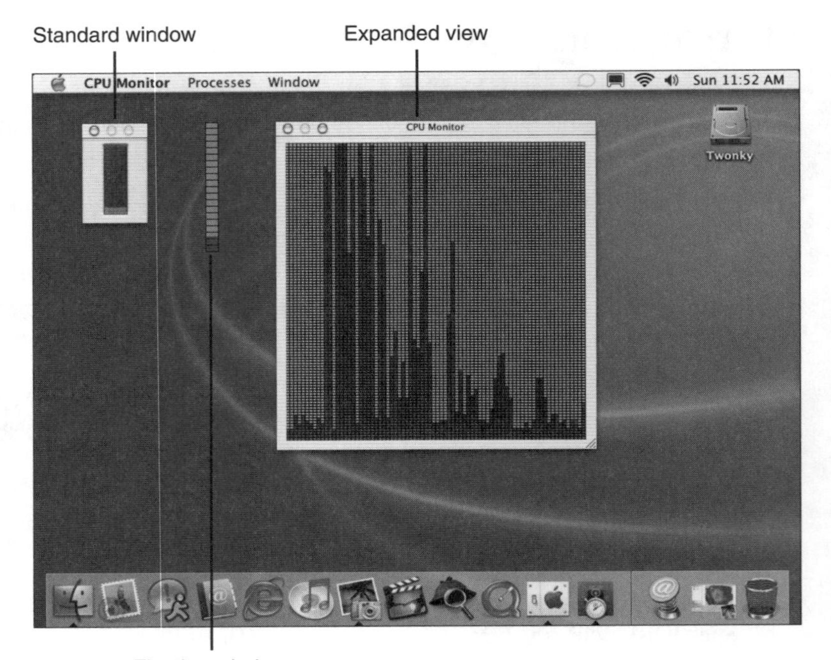

FIGURE 28.5
The CPU Monitor has a number of ways to display how busy your computer is.

Most users are comfortable with the Standard view. In this mode, the CPU monitor displays a window with a vertical graph of the CPU activity. If you prefer to keep the monitor visible at all times, choose the Floating Window view, which creates just the graph itself as a floating image that can be positioned anywhere on the screen—including the menu bar. An alternative to the Floating Window view is the Icon view of either the standard or expanded view, which can be set in the application Preferences panel. These views take advantage of the Dock's ability to display dynamic information in its icons. The CPU activity is graphed within CPU Monitor's Dock icon instead of taking up additional screen space.

The Standard and Floating Window views show an average of all the activity on your computer. The Expanded Window view differentiates between three types of processes:

- **System**—Processor usage by the system functions, such as drawing windows and making the beautiful Aqua interface.
- **User**—CPU time used by your (and other users') processes and applications.
- **Nice**—CPU time used by processes running with an altered scheduling priority. These processes have been changed at the command line by using the `nice` or `renice` commands, so it's unlikely you'll see anything here.

You can control the windows displayed, their orientation, and their appearance through a combination of Preferences settings and the use of the Processes menu.

TASK

Task: Adding the CPU Monitor to Your Menu Bar

I prefer putting a horizontal processor graph in my menu bar. To configure your system similarly, follow these steps:

1. Open the CPU Monitor application.
2. Choose Toggle Floating Window (Command-F) from the Processes menu to display the floating CPU usage window.
3. Open the application Preferences panel, and click the Floating View tab.
4. In the Display the View section, click the Horizontally radio button.
5. Close the Preferences panel.
6. Click and drag the floating processor graph onto your menu bar.

You can set the CPU Monitor to launch automatically upon login using the Login Items Preferences panel to set the CPU Monitor application to automatically launch when you log in.

By using the CPU Monitor Preferences panel, you can change the CPU graph's colors, its level of transparency, its position, and whether it's displayed as part of the Dock icon. The monitor helps keep track of your system's resources, and if you're using it as a server or to run software in the background, it lets you know whether you should consider upgrading your system's capacity.

Summary

Mac OS X gives you a great deal of flexibility, but it also requires more responsibility to run. To successfully keep your computer running smoothly and safely, you must stay current with system patches, create backups, optimize your hard drive and understand the effort your computer is expending to do the tasks you ask of it. We began the chapter with a look at Apple's automated software updates. Next, we looked at several options for backing up your data, including burning data CDs and creating disk images to transfer over the Internet or network to a safe storage place. Then, we talked about software available to defrag your hard drive. To finish up, you learned about the CPU Monitor Utility, which allows you to observe the processor function of your computer.

CHAPTER 29

Recovering from Crashes and Other Problems

In this chapter, you'll learn ways to react to application and system crashes and ways to be proactive about virus protection. You'll also learn to use your OS X install CD to reset your password and, in times of wide spread system failure, to reinstall your operating system.

Application Unexpectedly Quits

One of the more common problems you'll face is an application quitting. Suddenly, without warning, the document window disappears from the screen and you'll see a message similar to the one shown in Figure 29.1.

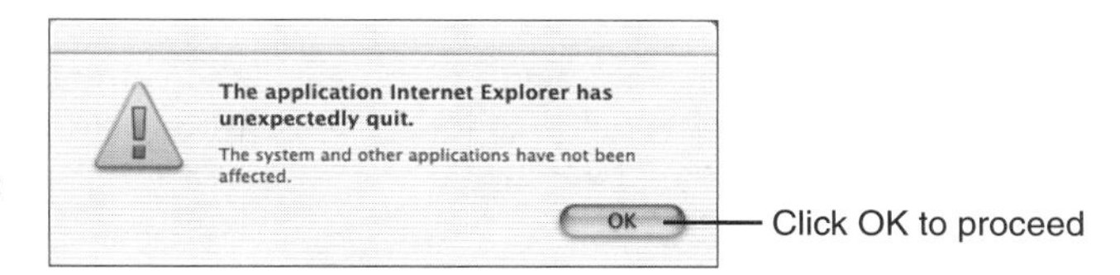

FIGURE 29.1
This unfriendly message might sometimes appear when you're working on a document (yes, I actually had to force my iMac to crash to get this picture).

Unfortunately, when a program quits while you're working on a document all the work you've done since the last time it was saved will be gone—unless the application has a recovery feature that auto-saves, such as Microsoft Word. That's why I always recommend that you save your documents often, so you won't lose much if something goes wrong.

Mac OS X is designed to be stable despite localized problems with applications because of its protected memory feature. So if an application unexpectedly quits, you can continue to compute in safety without needing to restart.

But when there's a rule, there's always an exception: If the application happens to be running in the Classic environment (see the section on running Classic applications in Chapter 2, "Exploring the Desktop"), the net effect is that Classic itself becomes unstable, so it's time to take the safe way out and follow these steps:

▼ To Do

Restarting Classic

1. Quit all your open Classic programs if you can.
2. Launch the System Preferences application from the Dock, the Apple menu, or the Applications folder.

Even if Classic seems to run satisfactorily after a program quits, don't just sit there and continue working (and definitely don't consider trying to launch the program that quit again). It's the nature of the Classic Mac Operating System to be unstable after a crash, even though it won't affect your regular Mac OS X system. To avoid an even worse crash (and possibly lose information in your files), you should restart the Classic immediately.

3. Click the Classic icon (see Figure 29.2).
4. Click the Restart button. If it fails to work, click Force Quit (see section below) and OK the choice, and then try Restart again.

If you don't plan on using a Classic application after using the Force Quit function you don't have to restart that environment. Whenever you do launch a Classic application, Classic will be restarted as part of the package.

▼

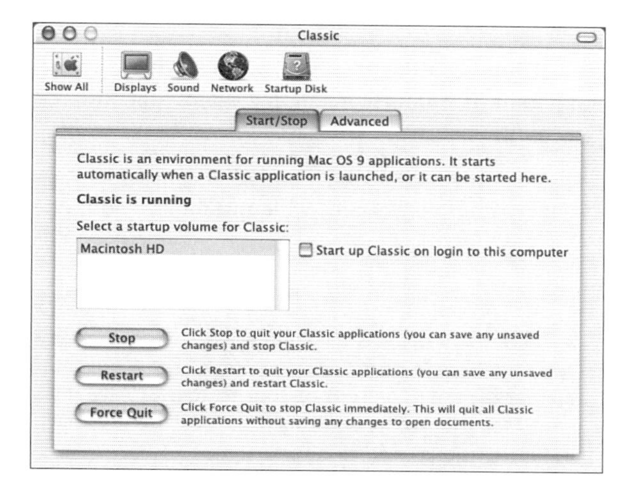

FIGURE 29.2
You can restart or configure Classic from this preference panel.

Other System Crashes

Not all crashes cause an application to quit. Sometimes the application will just stop running. The mouse might freeze, or it might move around but it won't do anything.

If this happens, follow these steps:

To Do

Using Force Quit

1. Force quit the program. Hold down the Cmd-Option-Esc keys, or choose Force Quit from the Apple menu. You will see a Force Quit Applications window (see Figure 29.3 for the Mac OS X version).

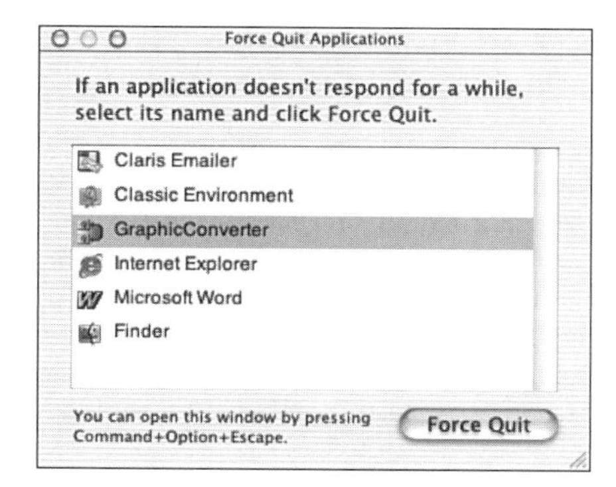

FIGURE 29.3
Choose the application to Force Quit from this window.

2. Normally, the application you were just running will be selected. If not, select the application.
3. Click Force Quit. Over the next few seconds, Mac OS X should be able to make the program quit. If it fails to occur, try again. Sometimes it takes two tries for the system to get the message.
4. If the program really doesn't quit, go to the Apple menu and choose Restart. At this point, there might be system-wide instability and it doesn't hurt to start from scratch.

An occasional Mac OS X system error is what's called a *kernel panic*. The symptoms are jarring, but don't freak out! A block of white on black text appears at the upper left of your screen. Usually, if you just press the r key, your Mac will restart and everything will be A-Okay. If not, use the following instructions to force a restart.

Forcing a Restart

If your computer refuses to restart in the normal fashion, you'll have to force the process by using the reset function. Resetting is done in different ways on different models of Macs. On flat-panel iMacs and other newer models, you must press and hold the power button for five seconds. After the computer shuts down, turn your computer on as you normally would.

On older Macs, you may have to search for a tiny button labeled with a triangle-shaped icon and then press it. (On some models you may need to use the point of a pencil or a straightened paperclip to press the button.) As soon as you press and release the reset button, your Mac should restart normally.

Consider this action only if the previous process won't work because it's much more drastic. If attempting to reset your Mac fails, your only remaining option is to pull the plug, literally. Now wait 30 seconds, plug in your Mac again and turn it on. At this point, you should be able to start normally, except you might find the startup processes pauses for some extra seconds at the Checking Disks prompt on the Mac OS X startup screen. This is because a forced shutdown could cause minor disk directory damage, which is being fixed during the startup process. This should not be any cause for concern.

Don't push the start button or reset button too hard.

What's Causing Those Crashes?

A rare system crash, maybe once every few days or so, is normal behavior for a Mac OS computer or even one of those computers from the *other* side. Don't get me wrong—Mac OS X is a resilient system; you could go for days or weeks before a crash occurs, but it can still happen. It's just the nature of the beast. If you encounter crashes several times a day, however, then something is definitely wrong. You might be seeing a conflict with some new software or hardware you've installed.

Fortunately, there are ways to check for the cause of such problems. Consider the following:

- **Recent software installations**—What did you do just before your computer began to crash? If you just installed some new software that only runs in the Classic environment and puts files in the Classic System Folder, maybe one of those files is causing a conflict. You'll want to check the program's documentation (or Read Me, if there is one) to see if the publisher is aware of any problems. As a test, with a Classic application open, you can open Extensions Manager (from the Control Panels folder) and disable any system programs that are used with the new software, by running a Mac OS 9.x Base set (or the set that applies to the system you have). This restricts it to the bare bones stuff you need to boot your computer. Then restart and see if the problems continue. Of course, you might be disabling something that is needed to make the program run, but at least you'll be able to see what might have caused your problem. If the problem goes away, go back to Extensions Manager and restore the other extensions a few at a time. After a few restarts, you're apt to come to a probable solution.
- **Recent hardware upgrades**—If you just installed a RAM upgrade on your computer and it is now crashing away, maybe the RAM module you installed is defective. It's always possible and not easy to test for. You might want to consider removing the RAM upgrade, strictly as a test. Then work with your Mac to see if the crashes go away. If they do, contact the dealer for a replacement module. If you've installed an extra drive, scanner, or other device, disconnect it (and turn off its software) and see if the problem disappears.
- **Hardware defects**—As with any electronic product, there's always the very slight chance one or more of the components in your computer might fail. In the vast majority of cases, however, a software conflict (or defective RAM) causes constant crashes. If you've tested everything and your Mac still won't work reliably, don't hesitate to contact Apple Computer or your dealer and arrange for service.

Viruses

Without getting overly technical, a computer virus is simply a chunk of code that attaches itself to a document or program. After the program is run, the virus begins to do its thing. Some viruses are downright destructive and will destroy your files and possibly damage your hard drive.

Few, if any, viruses affect Mac OS X. Unfortunately, this doesn't mean that viruses that affect it can't, or won't, be created—it's better to be safe than sorry.

Protecting Your Computer

There are things you can do to protect yourself against computer viruses that enable you to continue to work in safety:

- **Don't accept unsolicited files from strangers!** Sometimes you see them on an online service. You get a message saying "Here's that file I promised to send," or something similar. But you've never heard of the person and never expected to receive a file. Fortunately, most of those files are PC-based (with .SHS, .EXE, and .ZIP attached to the filenames). Even if there's potential damage from a file, if you don't download and try to run that file, you're safe.
- **Don't accept files from people you know unless you really expected the file!** Now this can get mighty confusing, but email viruses exist that can grab someone's address book and spread by sending attachments to everyone on the list. So if you receive a file from a friend or business contact that you didn't expect to receive, contact that person just to make sure. It can happen to you.

America Online will put up a warning message whenever you attempt to download a file of the type mentioned previously. Again the danger is primarily to the users of the *other* platform, but there's no telling when some vicious prankster will develop equivalent Mac viruses.

- **Download software *only* from major online services and known commercial sites!** The folks who run the software repositories on AOL, AT&T WorldNet, CompuServe, EarthLink, Prodigy Internet, and other services, as well as regular software publishers, will check their files for problems before they make them available. That helps ensure the safety of those files (although there's always the slight possibility of a problem with an undiscovered virus).
- **Get virus protection software!** This is the best way to ensure that your computer will be kept safe from virus infections. I'll cover this subject in more detail in the next part of this lesson.

If you happen to receive a virus-infected disk from a friend or colleague, don't be shy about telling him. It's no insult to inform folks of such a problem; in fact, it might save their valuable files before it's too late.

A Look at Virus Protection Software

Virus protection software isn't expensive. The popular products I'm describing here usually go for less than 60 bucks at most computer dealers. When you compare that to the potential devastation as a result of getting a virus infection, it's a small price for safety and peace of mind.

As with any software product a specific set of features might be more appealing to you, but any of the programs I'm describing will do the job.

- **Norton AntiVirus**—This program, published by Symantec, at `http://www.symantec.com` (see Figure 29.4) is designed to check for viruses every time you insert a disk into a drive, mount a networked disk on your computer's desktop, or download a file from the Internet; the latter courtesy of its Safe Zone feature. So-called suspicious activities are also monitored. You can perform scheduled scans, where the program will launch automatically at a predetermined hour and scan your drives. One intriguing feature is called Live Update, where the program will log on to the publisher's site every month and check for updates to protect against newly discovered viruses.

Such features as Live Update, which retrieve minor program updates and new virus definitions, don't mean you'll never have to pay for a new version of the software. From time to time, usually every year or two, a publisher will release an upgrade that you actually have to purchase. That's how they stay in business.

To benefit from all the features described previously, you need Norton Utilities version 8.0 or later. An earlier Mac OS X native version, 7.0.2, was not capable of automatic background protection and had to be run manually. The same holds true for Virex, which did not incorporate an auto-protection feature in its first Mac OS X release.

FIGURE 29.4
Norton AntiVirus can be set to update itself automatically with new detection modules.

- **Virex**—This is published by Network Associates, at `http://www.nai.com` (see Figure 29.5). Many of the features offered by Norton AntiVirus are also available with Virex. The program will scan files from a networked drive or the ones you download, and it will do scheduled scans. A special technology called heuristics is designed to check for virus-like activity to help protect you against unknown viruses. Updates to the program are usually offered on a monthly basis and are available via its Auto Update feature.

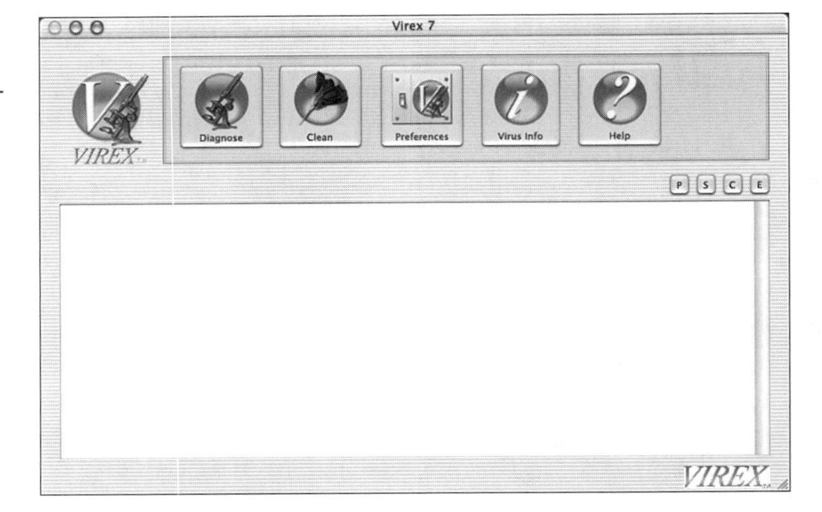

FIGURE 29.5
Virex offers drag-and-drop detection and regular updates.

- **VirusBarrier**—A third contender, VirusBarrier, comes from Intego (`http://www.intego.com`), a fairly new software publisher in the Mac marketplace, but one that's attracting a lot of attention for its product line, which also includes Internet protection and security software. Similar to the virus protection applications, there's an automatic update feature so your virus protection remains current.

The Right Way to Use Virus Software

Buying and installing virus software isn't necessarily a guarantee that you'll be protected. Here are some further issues you should be aware of:

- **New viruses are discovered all the time!** The publishers of virus software share information, so everyone can be protected in case a new virus strain crops up. You'll want to check a publisher's Web site at least once a month for virus detection updates. The information on how to keep updated is usually included with the publisher's documentation. Using a program's capability to do automatic scheduled updates is a real plus.
- **Virus software might slow things down!** Every time you insert a removable disk into a drive, the virus program will spend a few moments checking it out (assuming you've configured the program for the automatic scanning routine). You can defeat this protection and save a few seconds, but I wouldn't recommend it. Virus infections might come from unexpected sources, too.

Restoring the Administrator Password

If the Mac OS X administrator password is forgotten or misplaced, Apple provides a facility for restoring a password. Boot your computer from the Mac OS X install CD (hold down the C key while turning your computer on with the CD in the CD-ROM drive). When the Installer application starts, choose Reset Password from the Installer application menu. Figure 29.6 shows the interface to the Password Reset facility.

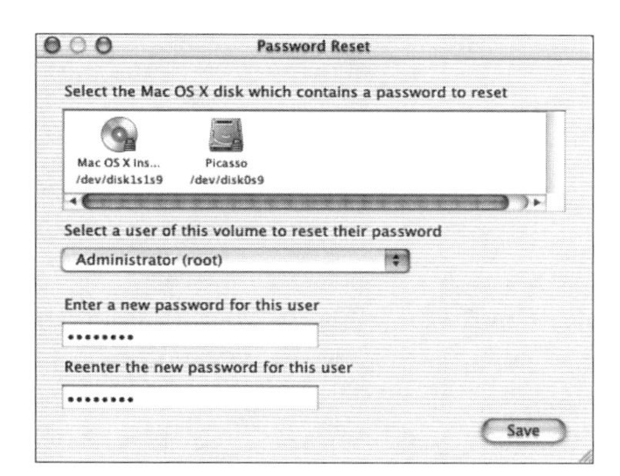

FIGURE 29.6
Use the boot CD and Password Reset application to ease your forgetful head.

Detected Mac OS X volumes are listed along the top of the window. To reset a password, follow these steps:

1. Click the main boot drive to load the password database for that volume.
2. Next, use the pop-up menu to choose the user account that you want to reset.
3. Fill in the new password in both of the password fields.
4. Finally, click Save to store the new password.

After rebooting your system, you can immediately log in with the new password.

Fixing Hard Drive Problems

Your computer comes with a handy tool that can check for and repair a hard drive problem. The program is called Disk Utility and you'll find a copy in your Utilities folder.

You can run the First Aid component of Disk Utility at any time, simply double-click the program's icon, and then click the First Aid tab. Finally, select the drive or drives you want to repair (see Figure 29.7).

FIGURE 29.7
The First Aid component of Mac OS X's Disk Utility can check your drive for basic directory problems and fix them.

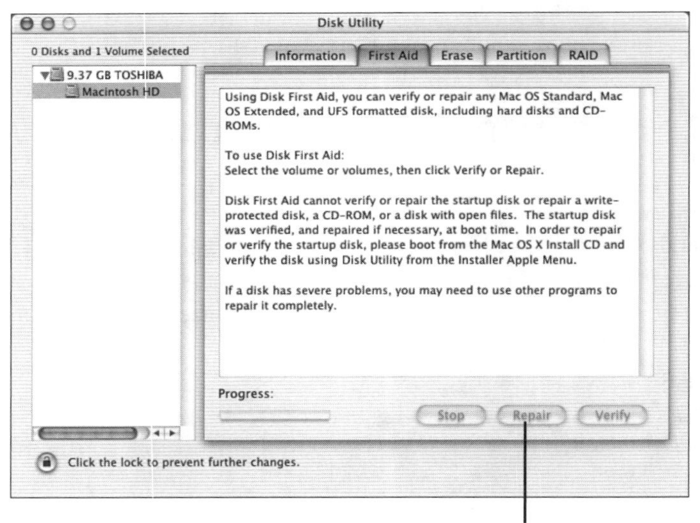

Choose Repair to check and fix your drive

The nice thing about Disk Utility is that it's free, but it's not a 100% solution. Several popular commercial programs offer to go beyond Disk First Aid in checking your drive and repairing catalog damage.

Unfortunately, you cannot repair directory problems on a startup drive. Fortunately, as an added ounce of protection, your computer and all drives connected to it are checked during the Mac OS X startup process. But if you keep your Mac running for long periods of time without a shut down or restart, running First Aid from time to time to see if there's a problem is a good ounce of protection.

Here's a brief description of the better-known hard drive diagnostic programs and what they do:

- **DiskWarrior**—This single-purpose program is from Alsoft (`http://www.alsoft.com`), a publisher of several Mac utility products. Its stock in trade is the capability to rebuild, rather than repair, a corrupted hard drive directory file. The original catalog is checked to locate the files on your drive, and then that information is used to make a new directory to replace the damaged one.
- **Norton Utilities**—From Symantec, this is the oldest available hard drive maintenance and repair package. The centerpiece is Disk Doctor, which will check your hard drive and fix problems. Additional components of the package can optimize your drive (see the following list) to speed up file retrieval and to recover your drive in the event a crash makes it inaccessible. The program can also help you recover the files you trash by mistake.

Older versions of Norton Utilities cannot work with the file system on your computer, which is known as HFS+ (or Mac OS Extended). At the very least, they might even make catalog damage worse, and the end result is that your computer's drive contents will become unavailable. In addition, you cannot scan disks running Mac OS X unless you use version 6.0 or later of this program. Version 7.0, which shipped when this book was written, is the first Mac OS X native release.

- **TechTool Pro**—In addition to hard drive repairs, TechTool Pro (`http://www.micromat.com`) can optimize the drive and even run a wide range of diagnostic checks on all your computer's hardware and attached devices. One great feature is the capability to perform an extended test of your computer's RAM. This might be helpful if you suddenly face lots of crashes after doing a RAM upgrade. To add to its bag of tricks, TechTool Pro can also do virus checks. Unfortunately, you can only check a Mac OS X drive by restarting from your TechTool Pro CD.

- **Drive 10**—As the name implies, this is a special purpose utility from the publisher of TechTool Pro that's designed to diagnose hard drives running Mac OS X (see Figure 29.8). Although it can run a pretty hefty suite of tests, you need to restart your Mac from the supplied CD to fix problems. Running a scan first is a real time saver; you only have to restart if a problem is reported.

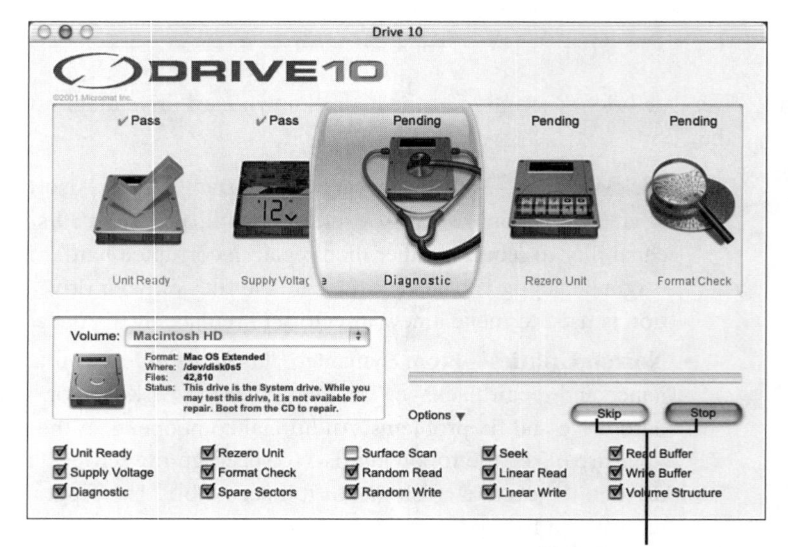

Click a button to start or stop scan of your drive

FIGURE 29.8
Drive 10 is a Mac OS X-only utility for hard drive diagnostics and repairs.

Using Disk Repair Software

The best way to benefit from a repair program is to install it. Either Norton Utilities or TechTool Pro will work best if you install the package as instructed in the program's documentation.

Although the application can be run directly from the CD without installing anything on your computer's drive, the regular installation will provide the following:

- **A catalog directory record**—During the installation process, both Norton Utilities and TechTool Pro create special (invisible) files on your hard drive to track information about the drive's catalog. This information is used so the files can be recovered in case your hard drive crashes. The file is updated whenever you copy or change files on your computer's drive.
- **Deleted file record**—The system extensions from Norton Utilities and TechTool Pro track the files you trash. Although there are no guarantees, this information can be used to help recover a file if you dump it by mistake.

- **Automatic scanning**—Both Norton Utilities and TechTool Pro can automatically scan your drive at regular intervals (and before each restart and shut down) to check for problems. If your computer is forced to restart because of a crash, these programs will run a directory scan of your hard drive automatically after startup. These features, by the way, can be switched off if you don't want them.

Reinstalling System Software

Why do you want to reinstall system software? Perhaps your Mac is unstable, no matter what you do. At this point, all your efforts to clean things up have gone for naught.

There is a drastic method to fix everything, but it's not something you would do normally, and that's to run your Mac Restore CD (or CDs, because some models come with several). When you do that, however, you might lose all your custom program settings, and (if you opt for the erase disk option), all the files you created on your Mac. What's more, if you have updated your Mac Operating System, all that will be lost as well. So I mention it here as an option, but only as a last resort.

Reinstalling Mac OS X *does not* necessarily replace your system accounts, information, or configuration. There are, however, a few drawbacks—most notably, the system updates are replaced by the original version of the operating system. After running the Mac OS X Installer to recover a damaged system, you must force an update on your computer by going to Software Update and clicking the Check Now button.

Here are the steps needed to reinstall OS X:

▼ To Do

Using Your System Installer CD

1. Get out your system Install CD, press the CD button, and insert the CD in your CD drive.
2. Restart your Mac. If need be, force a restart as described previously.
3. As soon as you hear the computer's startup sound, hold down the C key. This will enable your computer to start from your system CD.
4. The installer will launch automatically.
5. After your system installation is done, go ahead and restart and check that everything is working properly.

▲

Summary

System crashes and application quits can be downright annoying, but you learned in this chapter that you are not helpless against them. You learned to force quit unresponsive applications and to restart unresponsive computers. You discovered the secret of resetting your password with your system install CD. You also learned how to set up a preventive regime to defend against computer viruses. Finally, you learned how to reinstall your operating system in case your computer begins to experience wide-spread failures.

INDEX

Numbers & Symbols

A

B

C

D

E

F

G

H

I

J-K

L

M

N

O

Q

R

S

T

U

W

X-Z